Critical Thinking

Sixth Edition

Critical Thinking

BROOKE NOEL MOORE ▲ RICHARD PARKER
California State University, Chico

CHAPTER 13
by Nina Rosenstand and Anita Silvers

Boston   Burr Ridge, IL   Dubuque, IA   Madison, WI   New York
San Francisco   St. Louis   Bangkok   Bogotá   Caracas   Kuala Lumpur
Lisbon   London   Madrid   Mexico City   Milan   Montreal   New Delhi
Santiago   Seoul   Singapore   Sydney   Taipei   Toronto

McGraw-Hill Higher Education

A Division of The **McGraw-Hill** *Companies*

CRITICAL THINKING, SIXTH EDITION

Published by McGraw-Hill, a business unit of The McGraw-Hill Companies, Inc., 1221 Avenue of the Americas, New York, NY, 10020. Copyright © 2001, 1998, 1995, 1992, 1989, 1986 by The McGraw-Hill Companies, Inc. All rights reserved. No part of this publication may be reproduced or distributed in any form or by any means, or stored in a database or retrieval system, without the prior written consent of The McGraw-Hill Companies, Inc., including, but not limited to, in any network or other electronic storage or transmission, or broadcast for distance learning.

Some ancillaries, including electronic and print components, may not be available to customers outside the United States.

This book is printed on acid-free paper.

4 5 6 7 8 9 0 DOC/DOC 0 9 8 7 6 5 4 3 2 1

ISBN 0-7674-1067-X

Library of Congress Cataloging in Publication Data

Moore, Brooke Noel.
    Critical thinking / Brooke Noel Moore, Richard Parker.—6th ed.
        p.   cm.
    Includes index.
    ISBN 0-7674-1067-X
    1. Critical thinking.   I. Parker, Richard.   II. Title.
B105.T54M66   2000
160—dc21   99-086473

Sponsoring editor, Kenneth King; production editor, Julianna Scott Fein; manuscript editor, Joan Pendleton; design manager and cover designer, Glenda King; text designer, Terri Wright; cover illustration, © Terry Hoff, courtesy Freda Scott; art editor, Rennie Evans; illustrators, Mitch Rigie and Jim Dandy; photo researcher, Emily Smith; manufacturing manager, Randy Hurst. The text was set in 10/12 Trump Mediaeval by Thompson Type and printed on acid-free 45# Somerset Matte, PMS 286, by R. R. Donnelley & Sons Company.

Text and illustration credits appear at the back of the book on pages C-1–C-2, which constitute an extension of the copyright page.

www.mhhe.com

To Alexander, Bill, and Sherry,
and now to Sydney and Darby

Preface

Last spring we administered a ten-question critical thinking diagnostic quiz to several groups of people—select faculty, deans, our provost, plus a couple hundred students enrolled in critical thinking, calculus, statistics, history, and upper division English classes.

Faculty did well; you'd expect that. Who did the worst? Nope. Sorry. As a matter of fact, the provost didn't miss a question. The deans, however, did poorly—but we think they didn't take the quiz seriously.

Among the students who hadn't already taken a course in critical thinking, the math students did better than others, and the English students did better than general education students (mostly lower division) who had just signed up for a course in critical thinking or history. If anyone thinks beginning university students don't need to improve their skills in critical thinking, they ought to have a look at our test results.

This doesn't mean taking a course in critical thinking will improve student critical thinking skills; but our students, at least, do better on this particular test after they complete our class in critical thinking. We can't claim the new approaches we have been experimenting with in our course produced this result, but we'd like to think they had something to do with it. We incorporated several of them into this edition of this text, along with other changes. Here's what's new this time.

Changes in the Sixth Edition

Why adopt a new edition of this book? First of all, we've freshened things up culturally so that the book might speak better to today's incoming university students. We've updated examples, illustrations, boxes, and sidebars to reflect current social and political issues. Bill Clinton is by no means completely gone from our pages, but his predecessors mostly are. Even more important, however, are the following changes.

■ *Rhetoric, Nonargumentative Persuasion, and Pseudoreasoning*

Reviewers (as well as our own students) have noticed that the line between what we have always called pseudoreasoning (mostly just informal fallacies) and what we have called "nonargumentative persuasion" is pretty subtle; maybe it is too subtle. In this edition, we use the term "rhetoric" to denote the broad category of linguistic techniques people use when their primary objective is just to influence beliefs and attitudes, and when strength of argument is a concern only to the extent it contributes to that objective. (This usage of "rhetoric" is consistent with the currently popular and slightly pejorative meaning of the term.) So rhetoric (as we use the concept) includes slanting devices like innuendo and euphemism, as well as ridicule, emotional appeals, bogus dichotomies, red herrings, and the rest of what traditionally are called informal fallacies. With this new schematic, instructors won't be called on to define the difference between "nonargumentative persuasion" and "pseudoreasoning." We still use the word "pseudoreasoning" in this edition as loosely denoting a type of rhetorical ploy that gives an appearance of reasonable argument; but instructors can now apply themselves more directly to what is surely the principal task at hand, teaching students to recognize when and how and in what way somebody may be trying to manipulate their beliefs and attitudes through rhetorical gimmickry. As always, we are at pains to emphasize that the presence of what we call rhetoric doesn't weaken an argument; it just doesn't strength it, either.

■ *Collaborative Exercises*

In our own courses, and in this edition, we have been doing our darnedest to involve students more actively in the learning process. In this edition, you'll find more collaborative exercises. Yes, not everyone likes such things. If a collaborative exercise isn't done right, better students feel cheated, the party crowd loafs, and hard learning is diluted with socializing. Students may think to themselves, "Hey, if we already know it, what do we need this teacher for?" Nevertheless, the collaborative exercises we've included in this edition work well; we've used them with pleasing results, and we hope you give them a try. We often use these exercises *before* explaining the material in the chapter in which they occur or assigning the chapter as homework. (If you do this, you'll have to modify the instructions to the exercises in the obvious ways.)

By the way, research described in the December 3, 1999, issue of *Hispanic Outlook* suggests that group work, if done right, helps break down social stereotypes and reduce prejudices. If true, that would be a nice side benefit of using this teaching strategy wherever possible.

■ *Other New Exercises*

The new exercises aren't all group exercises. In fact, we've included numerous fun new exercises of all sorts, while trying to expunge the ones from previous editions that don't work so well. You'll find quite a few new items in Chapter 6, which covers informal fallacies; instructors tell us you just can't have too many exercises of this type.

■ *Inductive Generalizations and Analogical Arguments*

In this edition, we have attempted to integrate the criteria used to evaluate analogical arguments with those used to evaluate inductive generalizations. (This pertains to Chapter 11.) The result, we hope, is an overall simplification of the principles used to evaluate these two types of argument. In the past our students have wondered why, despite the obvious similarities between analogical arguments and inductive generalizations, the criteria used to evaluate the two types of argument seem somewhat different. This shouldn't be a problem any longer. As you will see, we effect this simplification by treating the inductive generalization as the basic argument form, with the analogical argument as a version of an inductive generalization.

We have also fine-tuned the discussion of fallacies of generalization in Chapter 11, to alleviate some of the questions of overlapping categories that always seemed to bother students.

■ *Causal Arguments*

In this edition, we aligned Chapter 12 with Chapter 11 pedagogically. (Chapter 12 deals with causal arguments; Chapter 11 with inductive generalizations and analogical arguments.) In both chapters, in this edition, evaluative criteria are presented in the form of key questions that critical thinkers should ask about an argument. Why we haven't used parallel evaluative procedures for the two chapters before this is a mystery to us.

In addition, we've substantially rewritten the sections on Relevant Difference reasoning and Common Thread reasoning in Chapter 12, to remedy various sources of confusion that cropped up in our own classes when covering this material. We've also revised the material on weak causal arguments to conform to our own evolving classroom coverage. We suggest you read these chapters through to get the feel of them before you work through them in class; revisions have been substantial.

■ *Identifying Unstated Premises and Finding Categorical Syllogisms in Real Life*

In Chapter 9 (Categorical Logic) we've added new material and exercises on identifying unstated premises in categorical syllogisms and finding categorical syllogisms in real life, additions which several reviewers will welcome. Also, if you have worked with our text before, you know that at the end of the book are several essays which can be used in various ways: for analysis, to provide topics for written work or in-class discussion, or as a source of additional exercises of your own devising. In this edition we've noted where several of these essays contain passages that can be treated as real-life categorical syllogisms or truth-functional argument patterns. It's hard to get students to see the disguised arguments at first, but once they get the hang of things, they perceive that a whole lot of real-life reasoning consists in categorical syllogisms and truth-functional arguments.

■ *New Essays*

Also, concerning the essays at the end of the book, we included three new specimens, provided better instructions for all the essays, and integrated all of them better with the rest of the book. In general, they should be even more useable.

■ *Internet Coverage*

We've expanded coverage of the Internet in this edition, including material on evaluating Web sources. You'll also find a paragraph (in Chapter 3) that offers some advice on buying through online auction houses, an increasingly popular way to purchase goods.

■ *Organizational Changes*

In this edition, we moved material on the news media from Chapter 4 (which deals with rhetorical devices) to Chapter 3 (which discusses evaluating informative claims). Also, we've moved the material on ridicule from its old location in Chapter 5 (which dealt with "pseudoreasoning") to Chapter 4 (Rhetorical Devices). These moves were probably overdue.

■ *At Long Last, a Chart of Rules of Deduction*

You'll now find the rules of truth-functional deduction all gathered together on one page in the form of a handy chart. This should make life easier for both teachers and students.

■ *Persuasive Writing*

A reviewer thought the section in the last edition on persuasive writing might encourage students to short-change logic in favor of other desiderata such as persuading a reader no matter what. We've changed the section to avoid creating that impression.

■ *Essay Grading Rubric*

In our classes we've been experimenting with a rubric for grading essays. Rubrics are widely used in K-12, and are found increasingly on the college scene as well, for good reason. A grading rubric is really just a grid: Across the top appear broad categories of evaluation such as "Issue Selection," "Organization," and the like. Down the columns under each category are descriptions of superior work, average work, and poor work. (Ideally an instructor provides examples of superior, average, and poor work to illustrate what these descriptions mean to him or her.)

Students like rubric-based grading. They like having grading criteria clearly stated (so do administrators), and a good rubric does this. Students also think rubric-based grading reduces the subjectivity involved in evaluating essays. Our rubric is tucked into the Instructor's Manual, which we will be saying more about later. We don't have the space to give you student examples for the rubric categories, but you can illustrate your own standards for essays by showing how this or that essay from the essay section, or from your own class' work, measures up, in your opinion, on the rubric.

Distinguishing Features of This Text

We would like to explain why you might like this text if you haven't used it before. Among the features you may well find useful are these.

■ Focus

Critical thinking includes a variety of deliberative processes aimed at making wise decisions about what to believe and do, processes that center on evaluation of arguments but include much more. We believe the best way to teach critical thinking is to integrate logic, both formal and informal, with a variety of skills and topics useful in making sound decisions about claims, actions, and practices—and to make it all palatable by presenting it in real-life contexts. This book is informal in tone—an author of another text griped about this. But it does not duck important issues. The illustrations, examples, and exercises are taken from or designed to resemble material undergraduates will find familiar. First- and second-year university students generally enjoy this text.

■ Organization

Some real-life claims are supported by attached arguments and some are not. One part of the book deals mainly with unsupported claims and the various nonarguments and quasi-arguments that are urged upon us; another part deals mainly with genuine arguments.

■ Alternative Teaching Strategies

If you want to teach a traditional course in logic, you can do so. We advise covering Chapters 1 and 8, then working your way through Chapters 9–12.

In whatever time remains, take advantage of some of the material in Part 1—for instance, Chapter 4, which covers rhetorical devices of various sorts. Such devices play a big role in the attempts people make to persuade each other. Adding this material to a traditional class in logic adds a powerful practical dimension to the course.

On the other hand, if you do not want to teach elementary logic from the foundations up, skip Chapters 9 and 10, which give pretty complete treatment of categorical and truth-functional logic.

■ Writing

If you teach critical thinking with a basic writing course or teach basic writing within a critical-thinking course, you can adapt this book to your needs. Chapter 2 in particular is devoted to subjects related to argumentative essays. At the end of the book is a collection of essays that you can use for a variety of assignments as well as for exercises in critical thinking. As already mentioned, you'll also find some new writing exercises that are fun to do.

■ Rhetoric

Chapters 4, 5, and 6 deal with rhetorical devices—a large and diversified inventory of persuasive devices, emotional appeals, and irrelevancies that all too often induce people to accept or reject a claim when they haven't a decent reason for doing so. These chapters help students distinguish weak reasons from irrelevant considerations, a subtle but important distinction. The various types of pseudoreasoning can be treated as informal fallacies if you prefer.

■ Exercises

The exercises in this book do heavy lifting. There are more than one thousand in the text and many more in the accompanying Instructor's Manual, *The Logical Accessory.* Questions marked with a triangle in the book are answered in the answer section in the back of the book (easy to find, with colored page edges), and sometimes discussions that extend material in the text proper are also found there—we've had very good response to the "goodies" that turn up back there. Instructors may find the answer section useful as a direct teaching aid or as a foil for their own comments.

■ Interactive Student Support Material

A fine student Study Guide, by Nickolas Pappas of the City College of New York, is available to students (and to instructors). It contains answers to the questions asked most frequently about each chapter, as well as answers to certain exercises. Professor Pappas has provided excellent new exercises as well.

Your students also have access to *www.mayfieldpub.com/CT,* a new Web site designed specifically to accompany and supplement this text. The Web site, developed by Eric R. Salahub of Front Range Community College, has the following features:

▲ A list of *Learning Objectives* for each chapter.

▲ *Review Quizzes* aligned with the Learning Objectives.

▲ *Exercises* and *Quizzes* aligned with each problem type for each chapter. These quizzes, and the review quizzes, are autograded and may be sent to the student's instructor by e-mail. There will be a total of 8–12 quizzes per chapter.

▲ A *Glossary* including all the important terms and concepts from each chapter that includes links to relevant Web sites for each. These links often provide further explanation, examples, or practical or topical applications.

▲ *Tutorials* that walk students step-by-step through the process of solving problems from each chapter. Each tutorial includes multiple examples of varying difficulty.

▲ A *Critical Thinking Diagnostic Test* that is designed to assess a student's mastery of various critical thinking skills. This may be used to measure improvement in these skills.

■ *The Logical Accessory: Instructor's Resource*

While in the past we've mainly left well enough alone in *The Logical Accessory,* the instructor's manual for this text, we've done more revising and made more additions to it this time around. It now contains over 1,700 test questions and exercises. We refer you to the *Accessory* itself for details of the changes.

Additional Features

No, the book isn't short, in part because of the following features which (we might add) are easy to miss:

▲ Discussion of the importance of writing in ways that don't reinforce dubious assumptions and attitudes about ethnicity and gender— with appropriate exercises.

▲ A glossary at the end of the book that provides definitions of key terms.

▲ A treatment of statistical studies designed for individuals more likely to encounter media reports of such studies than to read the studies themselves.

▲ Critical thinking across the disciplines: discussions of moral, legal, and aesthetic reasoning.

▲ A serious treatment of causal arguments that avoids tedious discussion of Mill's methods and recasts key concepts in accessible language.

▲ An account of analogies used as explanations and in arguments.

▲ A treatment of credibility, authority, and expertise.

Not everyone will wish to cover all the topics presented in the book—it's very difficult to do in most circumstances. Parker has never tried; Moore has never succeeded. Topics can be selected to accommodate each instructor. There are as many ways to combine topics as there are creative instructors of critical thinking.

Acknowledgments

Moore disclaims responsibility for any errors in the book; Parker does, too. Since any errors certainly aren't the fault of the many people we are about to acknowledge, we infer that they must be the fault of our editor, Ken King. Nah. Ken is a good fellow, and we thank him for his splendid commentary and other help.

We also feel great gratitude toward our other friends at Mayfield, who have lavished us with help, especially in the persons of Julianna Scott Fein, Marty Granahan, Susan Shook Malloy, Glenda King, Rennie Evans, Emily Smith, and our copyeditor for this edition, Joan "Redpencil" Pendleton.

Those who have advised us, given us material, and otherwise assisted us, and to whom we are especially grateful, include: Marcel Daguerre, Anne Morrissey, Marco Del Seta, and our other colleagues at Cal State Chico, Dan Barnett of Butte College, Linda Bomstad at Cal Poly-San Luis Obispo, Rhonda Shipley and the other folk at IUPUI, Dan Fawkes of Fayetteville State University, and Bangs L. Tapscott of the University of Utah. We are also grateful for the insight and advice of those who reviewed the previous edition for us: Julia J. Bartkowiak, Clarion University; Jay Campbell, Kirkwood Community College; Jeffrey Coombs, University of Nevada, Las Vegas; Michael Finkenbinder, Pasadena City College; Jay Gallagher, California State University, Chico; Keith Allen Korcz, University of Southwestern Louisiana; Rick McKita, Colorado State University; William C. Pamerleau, University of Pittsburgh at Greensburg; Harold Ravitch, Los Angeles Valley College; Kenneth Stern, State University of New York at Albany; Bruce B. Suttle, Parkland College; and W. E. Tinsley, Foothill College.

Finally, we add special thanks to Patricia Edelmann Parker and Marianne Larson.

Contents

Glossary   *G-1*

Answers, Suggestions, and Tips for Triangle Exercises   *A-1*

Essays for Analysis   *E-1*

Chapter 1

What Is Critical Thinking?

We are a very smart bunch, we humans. We've figured out how to send spacecraft through the solar system and beyond. We've learned to identify, select, transform, and combine tiny bits of genetic material so as to alter the varieties of life on our planet. We've built computers that can solve problems and complete tasks in ways that were almost unimaginable just a few years ago.

On the other hand, we constantly come face to face with examples of human error, ignorance, oversight, and misjudgment. There's the person in Chicago, for example, who tied knots in the cords of her lamps and electric appliances in the belief that it would cut down on the amount of electricity she used and thus help her save on her utility bill. Surveys indicate that almost half of all adult Americans believe that the sun revolves around the earth rather than vice versa. It's probably a safe bet that a very large proportion of our fellow citizens—possibly including many of your own friends, relatives, and classmates—do not understand the multitude of important issues that shape our lives. But failing to understand those issues does not prevent people from adopting opinions on them—opinions that are uninformed, poorly thought out, biased, or simpleminded—and even acting on those opinions, sometimes with disastrous results.

One of the advantages of living in a free society is the opportunity to think for oneself. But having the *opportunity* to do it is one thing, and having the *ability* to do it is quite another. Thinking—especially clear, reasoned thinking—is not easy work, and it doesn't always come naturally. But we can get better at it if we're willing to work a bit and accept some guidance here and there. Surely a species capable of the triumphs mentioned in the first paragraph has the potential to do better in other areas of daily and social life. Our hope is that this textbook, in conjunction with whatever course you may be using it in, will help you develop some of the skills required to form

Logic Breakdown

"You don't need money to get beautiful women," Donald Trump, the billionaire developer, assured the (male) readers of *New York Times* columnist Maureen Dowd.

"All of my life," he continued, "I've had friends who were successful and can't get a date, let alone a date with a beautiful woman. I have watched men worth hundreds of millions who have all the trappings—a G-5 [Gulfstream jet], the Fifth Avenue apartment, the Palm Beach estate—and they can't get a date. They're sitting at home watching TV."

Mr. Trump thinks he is providing evidence that a man's being wealthy is not a necessary condition of getting a date. In fact, he is providing evidence that a man's being wealthy is not a sufficient condition of getting a date.

By the time you finish this book, you'll be able to spot bad logic like this a mile away.

---

intelligent opinions, make good decisions, and determine the best courses of action—as well as recognize when someone else's reasoning is faulty or manipulative. In short, we hope this book will help you become a more critical thinker.

It is important to understand at the outset that thinking critically is not about attacking other people. If you are reading this book for a course, chances are you will be expected to critique others' ideas, and they will be asked to critique yours. Doing this, however, doesn't mean putting people down. Every single one of us makes mistakes, and it can be quite useful to have others help us see them. We appreciate it when someone points out that we have a low tire or that we aren't gripping the golf club properly. Likewise, we can appreciate it if someone points out that our position, theory, or idea is incomplete or unclear, insufficiently supported, or in some other way unconvincing. And when we're on the other side, we can help others see the holes in their arguments. We don't do our friends a favor by pretending their ideas are wise or profound when they are actually half-baked. So critical thinking is more about helping others than attacking them, and to the extent we are able to think critically about our own ideas, it is about helping ourselves. Our goal, remember, is knowledge and understanding, not "winning" or "coming out on top."

The pride and presence of a professional football team is far more important than 30 libraries.

—ART MODELL, Baltimore Ravens owner (reported by Larry Engelmann)

Claims and Critical Thinking

We humans are extraordinarily versatile in the use of words. We can sing songs, yell in surprise, warn others, lie to them, make promises, and do lots of other things. *One* of the things we can do with words is make claims. A **claim** is a statement that is either true or false. Now, many of the things we say are neither true nor false, as when we ask a question ("What time is it?"), greet a friend ("Hello, Theresa!"), or give an order ("Shut the door"). Such questions, greetings, and orders, as well as many other things we say and write, may be appropriate or inappropriate, clever or stupid, but we do not ordinarily think of them as true or false. Thus, none of these remarks counts as a claim in our sense of the word. A claim must always have a truth value— that is, it must be true or false (although we do not have to *know* whether it is true or false). Here are some examples of claims:

> It is 5 P.M.
>
> It ought to be easier to register for classes at this university.
>
> You won't believe it's winter when these fragrant daffodils bloom during the holidays!
>
> 2 + 2 = 4.
>
> There is ice on the moon.
>
> There isn't ice on the moon.
>
> If I tie knots in this lamp cord, my utility bills will go down.
>
> Bill Clinton certainly looked a lot younger when he took office than he did at the end of his presidency.

The official job of claims is to communicate information. But in fact we use claims to accomplish a variety of goals. Oftentimes we communicate a fact to others when our main interest is not simply to make them aware of the fact but rather to persuade them, warn them, amuse them, comfort them, or annoy them. We'll keep this in mind, especially in Part 2 of the book, because there will often be times when a person's motivation for making a claim is more important than the information contained in the claim itself.

When we are confronted with a claim, we can respond in lots of ways. We can ignore the claim, or we can consider it. We can question or challenge it. We can criticize, defend, or make fun of it. Usually, though, what we want to do is determine whether to accept it (that is, believe it), reject it (believe that it is false), or suspend judgment about it (possibly because we don't have enough information at the time to accept or reject it). When we accept or reject claims, we do so with varying degrees of confidence: We may have full confidence in the truth (or falsity) of one claim but only modest confidence

What Do Americans Believe?

The following item from the Reuters news service wire claims to tell us a lot—maybe more than we want to know—about what the American people find believable.

DATELINE: NEW YORK—Three-quarters of Americans believe the U.S. government is involved in conspiracies, . . . according to a survey released Tuesday.

The random survey of 800 people, summarized in the December issue of *George* magazine, also showed that more than half of Americans believe there is life on other planets.

Asked about their other beliefs, 78 percent of the survey's respondents said they believed in angels, 29 percent in witchcraft, and 30 percent in reincarnation.

Asked if the U.S. government was currently involved in cover-ups and conspiracies, 74 percent said yes and 19 percent said no.

Forty-one percent said they believed the government was covering up the truth about TWA Flight 800, which exploded and crashed near New York July 17, killing all 230 people on board. No cause [for the crash] has been determined, and conspiracy theories have abounded.

Ten percent believed Elvis Presley was still alive.

in the truth or falsity of another. The degree of confidence in our acceptance or rejection of a claim should depend on the amount of evidence we have for or against the claim.

Critical thinking is the careful, deliberate determination of whether we should accept, reject, or suspend judgment about a claim—and of the degree of confidence with which we accept or reject it. The ability to think critically is vitally important; in fact, our lives depend on it. The way we conduct our lives depends on what we believe to be true—on what claims we accept. The more carefully we evaluate a claim and the more fully we separate issues that are relevant to it from those that are not, the more critical is our thinking.

We do not do our critical thinking in a vacuum, of course. When we are confronted with a claim, usually we already have a certain amount of information relevant to the topic, and we can generally figure out where to find more if we need it. Having both the desire and the ability to bring such information to bear on our decisions is part of the critical-thinking process. Critical thinking involves a lot of skills, including the abilities to listen and read carefully, to evaluate arguments, to look for and find hidden assumptions, and to trace the consequences of a claim.

If you are beginning to sense that there is no simple way of deciding when to accept a claim, you are on the right track. We could say, of course, that we should accept a claim only when we have a good reason for doing so.

Who Is William Rehnquist?

According to a national survey released by the mayor of Philadelphia testifying at a U.S. Senate appropriations subcommittee:

- About 25 percent of American teenagers knew the Constitution was written in Philadelphia. About 75 percent knew that 90210 is the zip code of Beverly Hills.

- About 75 percent knew that the vice president (at the time) was Al Gore. About 90 percent knew that the male star of the movie *Titanic* was Leonardo DiCaprio.

- About 75 percent knew Bart Simpson lives in "Springfield." About 10 percent knew that Abraham Lincoln came from Springfield, Illinois.

- About 2 percent knew that William Rehnquist is chief justice of the United States. Nearly 95 percent knew that Will Smith played the Fresh Prince of Bel-Air on TV.

- About 20 percent knew there are 100 U.S. senators. More than 80 percent knew there are three brothers in the Hansons musical group.

- More teenagers could name all Three Stooges than could name the three branches of government.

Later on, we'll explain how important background information is to critical thinking. These findings (if true) suggest that American teenagers may have information shortcomings in some areas.

—Survey reported by the Cox News Service.

This wouldn't help much, though, because there is no shortcut to determining what constitutes a good reason for accepting a claim. People learn to recognize a good reason through example, illustration, and informed guidance. And that's where this book comes in. In these pages we'll give you examples of good reasons, and bad ones too, and help you to see the difference. We'll explain many of the principles that distinguish good reasoning from bad, and, most important, we'll try to guide you to an understanding of good reasoning and allow you to practice and develop your own skills as a critical thinker.

If you are to improve these skills, you will have to practice. Like playing baseball or the piano, critical thinking requires constant practice if you are going to become skilled in it. Fortunately, you'll have plenty of opportunity for practice. We have supplied lots of exercises throughout the book, and you'll find that examples of the material we cover will turn up regularly in your everyday life. Put what you learn into practice—critical thinking is not just a classroom activity.

On the Purpose of Claims

People make claims to communicate information but often have other objectives as well:

Once you do this, you'll never be the same.

—*CHALERISRI KIATBUSABA, sister of Thailand's premier kickboxer Pirinya Kiatbusaba, before his sex-change surgery. [Purpose: To discourage]*

I'm not going to have some reporters pawing through our papers. We are the president.

—*HILLARY CLINTON [Purpose: to serve notice]*

We're going to turn this team around 360 degrees.

—*JASON KIDD, when drafted to the Dallas Mavericks [Purpose: to express resolve]*

Whenever I watch TV and see those poor starving kids all over the world, I can't help but cry. I mean, I'd love to be skinny like that but not with all those flies and death and stuff.

—*Popular singer Mariah Carey [Purpose: to express compassion]*

Things are more like they are now than they ever were before.

—*DWIGHT D. EISENHOWER [Purpose: beats us]*

If you don't go to other men's funerals, they won't go to yours.

—*CLARENCE DAY [Purpose: to amuse]*

Other times, they just want to communicate information:

Outside of the killings, Washington has one of the lowest crime rates in the country.

—*Former Washington, D.C., mayor Marion Barry*

I've never had major knee surgery on any other part of my body.

—*WINSTON BENNETT, University of Kentucky basketball forward*

Issues and Arguments

Whenever we have to think critically, the first item of business is to make sure we are focusing on the correct claim. It does us no good to come to a correct decision about whether to accept a claim if that claim is not the one we should have been concerned about in the first place. "Issue" is the word most frequently used to identify the focus of a debate, discussion, or dispute, and we'll adopt it here.

In the broadest sense, an **issue** is any matter of controversy or uncertainty; it may be in dispute, in doubt, or simply "up for review." If Moore

Gov. Ventura does not recommend reading this book.

▲   *(He doesn't recommend against reading it, either.)*

believes there will be a recession and Parker believes there won't, then we say they are divided (that is, take opposite sides) on the issue. In most cases, we can state the issue neutrally by using the word "whether" in front of the claim that one party accepts and the other rejects. In this case, what's "at issue" is "whether there will be a recession."

We don't need a dispute between parties to have an issue; an issue can be a matter of "internal dispute" for a single individual. "Whether I should buy a new car" might state an issue that is important for me but that nobody disagrees with. *My* uncertainty is what makes it an issue for me.

Issues can be posed in a number of ways. We might wonder how many miles per gallon this car will get, when the train arrived, or who fired the fatal shot. We can rephrase these questions as "whether this car will get more than thirty miles per gallon," "whether the train arrived on time," or "whether Colonel Mustard fired the fatal shot," making it easier to recognize them as issues.

■ Identifying the Issue

Note that an issue is different from a topic of conversation. Pet care can be a topic of conversation, but it is not an issue. Whether wild animals such as ferrets and skunks should be pets *is* an issue, because it is a matter of controversy. Again, notice that the word "whether" helps to show that an issue is involved.

Note as well that an issue is not a psychological problem, at least not in the sense that we are using the term here. These days it is common to say of someone who has an unusual concern or fear or worry that he or she "has an issue"; there is indeed a popular song ("She's Got Issues") that uses the word this way. But for our purposes, an issue is not something a person *has* (or has *got*); it is something a person raises or addresses or tries to resolve.

In everyday conversation, it is often difficult to figure out exactly what the issue is. Most of us have been part of heated discussions with friends or family members. Grandpa yells that taxes are too high under the new administration, Aunt Daisy laments that the Republicans are out to destroy education in America, Uncle Ernie clamors that corporations do not pay their fair share, and Dad shouts that the government funds too many social programs and allows too many immigrants into the country. Such discussions are hopelessly unsatisfying because they are not focused on one clear and precise question at issue. A worthwhile discussion focuses on a single topic and then on a particular question at issue.

For example, the topic of abortion raises many different questions: Should abortion be legal? Should the government pay for abortions? Is it the Supreme Court's job to decide whether fetuses have the rights of persons or should it be left to the states? Should teenagers be allowed to have abortions without parental consent? Unless the parties to this discussion focus on one question at issue, the ensuing argument will be disorganized and incoherent.

Sometimes we get issues confused or out of order even when we're not discussing them with someone else. This is one way *uncritical* thinking can lead to unnecessary disputes, unwarranted conclusions, and wasted time. For example, let's say that Johnson is considering helping his son buy a car. Things such as price, reliability, safety, and so on, are all factors in the decision. Now, let's say that Johnson spends a lot of time and effort worrying about whether a Python GTZ roadster is a safe enough car for his son, because an overall evaluation of a car's safety must take many factors into account. What should we think about his worries if, in fact, the cost of the Python roadster is well beyond the limits of what the Johnsons can afford? We'd say that Johnson is considering the issues in the wrong order, for if they can't afford the Python—a matter that is pretty easy to settle—the issue of its safety is irrelevant. It would be possible, of course, for them to identify all the cars that are safe enough first, and then eliminate all those they cannot afford. But considering the issues that way would be much less efficient.

Keeping issues straight often involves more than just efficiency. Disputes often occur when two parties will not address the same issue. Listen to these two, just leaving an outdoor café:

FELICIA: You were pretty rude to those young women who asked for the ashtray from our table. You didn't have to say we wouldn't be needing it because smoking is a filthy, disgusting habit.

▲ *Calvin does have a pretty good idea of how issues and arguments are related. He could stand a little improvement in the open-mindedness department, however.*

> FELIX: But it *is* a filthy, disgusting habit. I hate to see young people smoking!

Felix is addressing the issue of whether people should smoke, but Felicia's point is that one does not always have to say exactly what one thinks about others' behavior. Here's another example:

> THERESA: That nuclear power plant is too dangerous to have been built so close to the city.

> DANIEL: If it weren't for that nuclear power plant, Theresa, you wouldn't have enough light to read your newspaper.

Theresa and Daniel are addressing *related* issues, but they are not discussing the *same* issue. If Daniel thinks he has given a response to Theresa's remarks, he is mistaken. He may be correct, but his being correct on his point does not do the least to help us decide whether Theresa is correct on hers: The nuclear power plant may be the only power source nearby yet *still* have been built too close to the city.

Sometimes people purposely confuse issues in order to draw attention away from a claim they don't want to deal with or to make it look as though they've proved a point when in fact they haven't. We'll see examples of such attempted trickery later.

■ *Settling an Issue Through Argument*

When we attempt to *settle* an issue—that is, when we attempt to determine which side is correct—one of our most important tools is argument. (The others are observation and consulting reliable sources, both discussed in Chapter 3.) Generally speaking, an argument can be thought of as an attempt to support a claim by giving reasons for believing it. The claim one attempts to support is known as the **conclusion** of the argument; the claims that serve as reasons for believing the conclusion are known as **premises.** We must be careful here, because not everything that looks like an argument is properly classified as one. For example, if Moore wants to convince Parker that he has some money with him, he might reach into his pocket and pull out a roll of bills. This display of cash is indeed excellent evidence that he has money with him: the best evidence he could offer. But evidence is a set of circumstances or facts that we can observe and that is relevant to the issue; only when we put our observation of this evidence into verbal form do we actually have an argument.

Let us define **argument,** then, as an attempt to support a claim (the conclusion) by providing a reason or reasons for believing it (the premises). In other words, in an argument, premises are designed to provide support for a conclusion. Here's an example. Suppose Moore says to Parker:

> Senator Leghorn will support gun control legislation. After all, she's a liberal, and nearly all liberals are in favor of gun control.

The conclusion, the claim Moore is trying to convince Parker to accept, is that Leghorn will support gun control. The issue is *whether* Leghorn will support gun control. (Generally, the issue an argument addresses can be stated by inserting the word "whether" in front of the argument's conclusion.) Moore states his reasons for the conclusion in the rest of the passage—that Leghorn is a liberal and that nearly all liberals are in favor of gun control.

Sometimes when you're reading, the point that is at issue in a passage is not made very clear. (Good writers try to be clear about what the issue under discussion is as well as what their position on that issue is.) Because of the connection between issues and the conclusions of arguments, one way to pin down the issue in a passage is to look for the conclusions of arguments contained in it. For a variety of reasons, conclusions are not always easy to spot. But they and their accompanying premises can *often* be identified because of some verbal clues that are used to introduce them. For example, the words "therefore," "consequently," and "hence" are generally used to introduce conclusions.* "Since" and "because" are two words used to introduce premises.

A couple of pages back we mentioned that we often accept or reject claims without having full confidence that we are correct. That is because oftentimes the arguments on one side of an issue are stronger than those on the other side, but they are still not strong enough to be absolutely convincing; there may still be some lingering doubt about which side is correct.

---

*They can be used to do other things as well, unfortunately, but we'll get to that later. (See Chapter 7 on the differences between arguments and explanations.)

This Flat Earth

A few years ago the assistant to the governor of Arizona told a panel of educators that the issue of whether Earth is round is "just a matter of opinion."

"Any student who believes the Earth is flat," he said, "is entitled to his opinion, and his teachers shouldn't try to tell him otherwise."

If all opinions are equally reasonable, as this official appears to think, then there doesn't seem much point in a teacher's trying to teach anybody anything.

Unfortunately, we frequently do not have the luxury of waiting until we are absolutely certain about an issue before we must act on our decision. If we waited until we were absolutely certain which automobile was the best for our purposes before buying one, we'd probably spend the rest of our lives on foot. The point is, if we act on the basis of the best evidence and the strongest arguments we have available to us, we'll have done the most reasonable thing, even if later, after more evidence is available, we discover another alternative would have been better.

The construction, evaluation, and, where necessary, criticism of arguments is really at the heart of critical thinking, and Part 3 of this book is devoted exclusively to such matters. However, when dealing with issues in our everyday lives, we are not always given good arguments, or even any argument at all! Part 2 of the book is designed to help us learn to deal with those situations.

Facts and Opinions

The word "fact" is often used to indicate or emphasize that a claim is *true*. "It's a fact that Mars is smaller than Earth" means the same as "It's true that Mars is smaller than Earth" or, more simply, "Mars is smaller than Earth." The word "opinion," on the other hand, is used to indicate that a claim is *believed*, or judged to be true, by someone, often after a certain amount of thought. For example, "It's Moore's opinion that Mars is smaller than Earth" says that Moore believes Mars is smaller than Earth. Similarly, "It's Parker's opinion that Mars is made of mozzarella cheese" says that Parker believes this peculiar claim about Mars. Now, the first of these opinions is true; the claim is not *just* Moore's opinion, it is *also* a fact. The second opinion is false; it is not a fact that Mars is made of cheese. So, some opinions are factual (true), and some are not. One of the goals of critical thinking is to help us form opinions of the former sort and avoid those of the latter.

We can also make a distinction between issues that are factual matters and those that are not. We can say that an issue is about a **factual matter** (or a **matter of fact**) when there are established methods for settling it—that is, when there are generally accepted criteria or standards on which the issue can be judged—or when we can at least describe what kinds of methods and criteria would apply even though it may be impractical or impossible to actually apply them.

Let's say that Parker thinks Mars is made of cheese and Moore does not. This is a disagreement about a factual matter, for there are accepted means for settling the issue. Indeed, we know that Moore's opinion about Mars is true and Parker's is not. But we can determine that an issue is about a factual matter even if we are not able to tell which side—if any of them—is correct. That is, we can say that an issue is about a factual matter even if we cannot determine what the actual facts are. (Notice that saying something is a *factual matter* in this sense is different from saying that it is *a fact*.) Consider the question of whether leukemia in humans is caused by a virus. As we write these words, it isn't known whether human leukemia is caused by a virus or not. But even though we do not know whether it is *a fact* that a virus causes leukemia, it is a *factual matter* because there are accepted methods and criteria by means of which the question can be answered: the methods of laboratory science. Remember, claims about factual matters don't have to be true. "Mars is made of cheese" is *about* a factual matter, although of course it's false.

Here's another example: whether Julius Caesar took a bath on the day he was murdered on the steps of the Roman Senate. There is of course no way we can determine for sure whether Caesar took a bath that day, although we might poke around a bit in history books to see if anybody mentions such a thing. But the issue is still a factual matter, because it's very easy to describe methods and criteria that, *if* we could apply them, would settle it. For example, following Caesar around would enable the observer to determine if Caesar took a bath on the day he was murdered.

Compare the preceding issue with this one: Suppose Moore thinks dogs make better pets than cats, and Parker thinks cats are better. After some discussion, it might be that either Moore or Parker could convince the other to change his mind, but it's at least as likely that both will stick with their original opinions. There is no set of facts we could determine and no generally accepted method or standard we might employ that would enable us to decide the issue definitively one way or the other. We think of issues like this as **matters of pure opinion.** Here's a way to test whether you have before you a factual matter or a matter of pure opinion: When two people disagree about a factual matter, it is certain that at least one of them is wrong; that is, two conflicting opinions about a matter of fact cannot both be correct. But we allow two people to hold conflicting opinions about matters of pure opinion, and we don't say that either of them is wrong.

■ *Objective and Subjective Claims*

Claims about factual matters are also known as **objective claims;** claims about matters of pure opinion are known as **subjective claims.** Objective claims are statements that are true or false regardless of our personal preferences, tastes, biases, and so on. Subjective claims are expressions of those preferences, tastes, biases, and so on, although they may appear at first to be about something else. "Vanilla tastes better than chocolate" can be another way of saying "I like the taste of vanilla better than I like the taste of chocolate." So, if Moore says that dogs make better pets than cats and Parker says cats make better pets than dogs, they can both be correct because each is really expressing his own tastes.

Many students assume that a claim is subjective—a matter of pure opinion—simply because it's controversial. That is a bad mistake. Whether raising taxes last year would have caused a recession, whether the death penalty lowers crime rates, whether human beings evolved from more primitive primates—these are all controversial issues, but all of them are factual matters. That is, we can imagine procedures by which they can be tested to determine whether they are true.

There are legitimate disputes about the objective or subjective nature of some claims. Many place claims about moral issues in this category. "Stealing is morally wrong" is said by some to be an objective claim, a statement of fact; others take it to be a subjective claim, an expression of pure opinion. There are some sophisticated arguments about how such claims should be classified. The same is true for claims like "Mozart's music is better than Madonna's." Something similar applies to claims like "God exists." Some say this is a straightforward objective claim; others say it isn't a claim at all. However one sorts out these kinds of claims, they do have one thing in common with objective claims about factual matters: Whether or not we can finally determine the truth about them, it is still the case that *some opinions are better reasoned—indeed, more intelligent—than others.*

You can fool all the people all the time if the advertising budget is big enough.

—ED ROLLINS, presidential campaign adviser

Not if they've read this book, Ed.

Because some of these issues are very important to how we lead our lives, it is important to bring one's critical-thinking skills to bear on them.

Problems occur when we fail to understand the differences between matters of fact and matters of pure opinion and between the objective and subjective claims with which we state them. We can waste time by trying to convince someone to change his or her mind on a matter of pure opinion, since, in the long run, there is no way to finally settle the matter. On the other hand, we make a more serious mistake if we treat a matter of fact as if it were one of pure opinion. Calling it pure opinion can be an excuse for failing to pursue the issue; it can be a way of avoiding a difficult problem or abandoning it before we've tried our best to settle it one way or another.

Let's take stock: That a claim "states a fact" just means that it's true; that it "states an opinion" means only that somebody believes it to be true. Some opinions are helpful, important, and true; others are false, silly, or dangerous. Some claims are objective—they are about matters of fact; others are subjective—they are about matters of pure opinion: personal preferences, tastes, and so on. These distinctions should help you organize your thoughts about facts and opinions and keep you from making some elementary mistakes.

■ *"Everyone's Entitled . . ."*

Speaking of mistakes, there is another mistake that is so egregious it deserves special consideration. You can usually spot this mistake because it almost always takes the same form, even the same words: "Everyone is entitled to his or her own opinion."

Now, it's true that, in some sense, everyone *is* entitled to his or her own opinion on anything. The reason for this is that, in anything except a completely authoritarian dictatorship, people are not forced to hold a given set of opinions. (And they probably couldn't be made to agree completely even in a totally authoritarian society.) But—and this is the mistake—the fact that we do not *force* people to have this or that opinion on a subject does not mean that one opinion may not be much more intelligent, much more practical, much more humane than some other opinion. Indeed, some opinions are so bad, so stupid, or so dangerous that it may be hazardous or even immoral to hold them. Remember the woman from the beginning of this chapter who tied knots in her lamp cords? Would you say she is "entitled" to her opinions about electricity? It makes more sense to say she's entitled to an explanation of why those opinions are wrong. Other opinions are even worse: How could one be "entitled" to the opinion that people should be allowed to abuse their children whenever they want to or that human slavery is a justifiable form of labor?

Although it is vital to argue against such defective opinions, the real danger of the "entitlement" error is that it keeps people from talking and reasoning with one another. We shouldn't confuse the equal value of people with the equal value of people's opinions. All too often someone says, "Well, you're entitled to your opinion" as a way of giving up, a way of saying that he or she doesn't want to argue about the issue anymore. Certainly, there are times when further discussion is useless, but that does *not* mean that every opinion is as good—as "entitled"—as every other. Remember, just because our value system gives equal worth to *people,* it does not give equal worth to people's *opinions.*

■ Beliefs, Opinions, Views, Convictions, Prejudices

Some people make distinctions among beliefs, opinions, views, and convictions, but for our purposes these are essentially all the same thing: something you believe. Even a prejudice is just a belief, one that is based on insufficient knowledge or held in the face of evidence that it is mistaken. Just remember that when you express something you believe, you make a claim, which is an expression that is either true or false. If the claim is true, it states a fact.

Before wrapping up this chapter, it may help to add a few remarks about truth. Truth, after all, is our "bottom line" concept; the primary job of critical thinking is getting at the truth—that is, discovering which claims are true and which are false. We want to impress upon you that the truth of a claim is an objective fact about the world, something that does not depend on our feelings or beliefs (unless, of course, the claim is *about* our feelings or beliefs). "There is a book on the table" is true if and only if there is in fact a book on the table, regardless of whether we know there is such a book or how we feel or believe about its being there.

There are those who would say that for us to *know* there is a book on the table we would have to be able to prove it with mathematical certainty, in the way we can prove that two and two are four. But this standard for facts about the world is too high. For our purposes, we'll say we know such and such is true if we believe it is true and have evidence that shows it to be true beyond any reasonable doubt. So, if we see and touch a book on the table, and others agree there's a book on the table, and there's no reason to think any of us might be mistaken or suffering from hallucinations or other problems, then it is perfectly proper for us to say we *know* that there is a book on the table—to say that we know the claim "There is a book on the table" is true.

A Note About Feelings

Our goal in this book is to encourage and aid you in the application of reason to your decisions. This doesn't mean, though, that critical thinking rules out feelings. A person with no feelings would hardly be human at all. Our feelings and emotions can supply powerful (and often perfectly safe) motivations for making a decision, believing a claim, or performing an action. But it's important that we also employ our ability to reason—to consider relevant facts and cogent arguments—if we are to live up to our potential as reasonable creatures.

Discreet Nit Nabbing?

What does critical thinking tell you about their "we are discreet" claim? Hint—check out that truck.

Recap

Claims are statements that we may accept as either true or false. Critical thinking is the careful, deliberate determination of whether we should accept, reject, or suspend judgment about a claim. Critical thinking also involves deciding what level of confidence we can have in our acceptance or rejection of a claim. When we consider a claim's truth or falsity, we are facing an issue, which can be defined as any matter of controversy or uncertainty. It is very important to identify exactly what issue we're discussing before we try to deal with it. One way to deal with and settle an issue is through argument. An argument is a combination of a conclusion and one or more premises, the latter designed to give support to—reasons for believing—the former.

When someone believes a claim, that claim is said to state the person's opinion. If the claim is true, we say it states a fact. Subjective claims—those that express a person's tastes or preferences—are said to be about matters of pure opinion. If there are generally agreed upon ways of determining whether a claim is true or false, then we say the claim is objective and is about a factual matter.

Although we value every person equally, we should not do the same for every opinion a person might hold. Some opinions are carefully reasoned and are worth our consideration; others are dubious, misleading, or downright dangerous. A critical thinker is one who has the motivation and skills to tell the difference.

Having read this chapter and the chapter recap, you should begin to be able to

▲ Define critical thinking and explain why it is an important skill

▲ Define the terms "claim," "issue," "argument," "premise," and "conclusion" and explain their significance in critical thinking

▲ Distinguish between factual matters (or objective claims) and matters of opinion (or subjective claims)

▲ Explain why some opinions are better than others

Exercises

The exercises in this book are designed to provide practice in critical thinking. Some can be answered directly from the pages of the text, but some will require your careful consideration. For many exercises in this book, there is no such thing as *the* correct answer, just as there is no such thing as *the* correct way to serve a tennis ball or to make lasagna. But some answers, like some tennis serves and some lasagnas, are better than others. So in many exercises, answers you give that differ from your instructor's are not necessarily incorrect. Still, your instructor's answers most likely will be rational, sound, and worth your attention. In general, his or her judgment will be very reliable. We recommend you take advantage of your instructor's experience to improve your ability to think critically.

Exercise 1-1 _____

Answers to the exercises marked with a triangle, as well as occasional comments, tips, and suggestions, are found in the answer section (the one with the colored edges) at the back of the book.

   Answer the questions based on your reading of the text.

▲ 1. What is a claim?

   2. What are the alternatives to accepting a claim?

   3. Are there situations when the wisest move is to accept a claim even though we are not entirely certain that it is true?

▲ 4. According to the text, what is critical thinking?

   5. If a claim might be false, should it automatically be rejected?

   6. If a claim might be true, should it automatically be accepted?

▲ 7. What is an argument? What are the parts of an argument called?

   8. True or false: An issue is designed to settle an argument.

   9. How can the word "whether" be used to connect an issue and an argument?

▲ 10. For what reason might a person *purposely* confuse two issues?

   11. The issue is whether sixteen-year-olds should be allowed to drink alcoholic beverages. Construct an argument on one side of the issue or the other.

   12. LINDA: Arnold says that the new highway overpass is a waste of money.

   JAVIER: So that's Arnold's opinion. Opinions are a dime a dozen.

Has Javier given a reason for believing that the overpass is *not* a waste of money?

▲ 13. In the previous dialogue, has Linda given a reason for believing that the overpass *is* a waste of money?

14. True or false: Because we are all entitled to our own opinions, any two opinions are equally reasonable.

15. What does it mean to say that an issue is about a matter of fact?

▲ 16. Complete this sentence: We say that a claim is subjective when . . .

17. Give an example of two opinions from two different sources on the same issue, one opinion that is worth considering and one that is not worth considering.

18. Some claims are difficult to classify as either objective or subjective; indeed, some examples can be quite controversial. Give an example.

▲ 19. True or false: If it is not obvious whether an issue is about a factual matter or a matter of pure opinion, then it doesn't matter what opinion you hold on that issue. Explain your answer.

20. Discuss: No matter what the issue, every person is entitled to his or her own opinion.

21. True or false: If an issue is a controversial one, then it cannot be a factual matter.

▲ 22. If it is not possible for us to actually ascertain the truth or falsity of a claim, then that claim must not state a factual matter—that is, it is not an objective claim.

23. Under what circumstances would it be appropriate to say that we *believe* that the paper in this book is flammable?

24. Describe a situation in which it would be appropriate to accept the claim that the paper is flammable but in which we would not know that it is.

▲ 25. Under what circumstances would it be appropriate to say that we *know* that the paper in this book is flammable?

Exercise 1-2

For each passage in this exercise, identify which of the items that follow best states the primary issue discussed in the passage. Be prepared to say why you think your choice is the correct one.

▲ 1. Let me tell you why Hank ought not to take that math course. First, it's too hard, and he'll probably flunk it. Second, he's going to spend the whole term in a state of frustration. Third, he'll probably get depressed and do poorly in all the rest of his courses.
   a. Whether Hank ought to take the math course
   b. Whether Hank would flunk the math course
   c. Whether Hank will spend the whole term in a state of frustration

    d. Whether Hank will get depressed and do poorly in all the rest of his courses

2. The county has cut the library budget for salaried library workers, and there will not be enough volunteers to make up for the lack of paid workers. Therefore, the library will have to be open fewer hours next year.
   a. Whether the library will have to be open fewer hours next year
   b. Whether there will be enough volunteers to make up for the lack of paid workers

▲ 3. Pollution of the waters of the Everglades and of Florida Bay is due to multiple causes. These include cattle farming, dairy farming, industry, tourism, and urban development. So it is simply not so that the sugar industry is completely responsible for the pollution of these waters.
   a. Whether pollution of the waters of the Everglades and Florida Bay is due to multiple causes
   b. Whether pollution is caused by cattle farming, dairy farming, industry, tourism, and urban development
   c. Whether the sugar industry is partly responsible for the pollution of these waters
   d. Whether the sugar industry is completely responsible for the pollution of these waters

▲ 4. It's clear that the mainstream media have lost interest in classical music. For example, the NBC network used to have its own classical orchestra conducted by Arturo Toscanini, but no such orchestra exists now. One newspaper, the no-longer-existent *Washington Star,* used to have thirteen classical music reviewers—that's more than twice as many as the *New York Times* has now. H. L. Mencken and other columnists used to devote considerable space to classical music; nowadays, you almost never see it mentioned in a major column.
   a. Whether popular taste has turned away from classical music
   b. Whether newspapers are employing fewer writers on classical music
   c. Whether the mainstream media have lost interest in classical music

5. This year's National Football League draft lists a large number of quarterbacks among its highest-ranking candidates. Furthermore, quite a number of teams do not have a first-class quarterback. It's therefore likely that there will be an unusually large number of quarterbacks drafted early in this year's draft.
   a. Whether teams without first-class quarterbacks will choose quarterbacks in the draft
   b. Whether there is a large number of quarterbacks in this year's NFL draft
   c. Whether an unusually large number of quarterbacks will be drafted early in this year's draft

6. An animal that will walk out into a rainstorm and stare up at the clouds until water runs into its nostrils and it drowns—well, that's what I call the world's dumbest animal. And that's exactly what young domestic turkeys do.

a. Whether young domestic turkeys will drown themselves in the rain
b. Whether any animal is dumb enough to drown itself in the rain
c. Whether young domestic turkeys are the world's dumbest animal

7. The defeat of the school voucher initiative was a bad thing for the country because now there won't be any incentive for public schools to clean up their act. Furthermore, the status quo perpetuates the private-school-for-the-rich, public-school-for-the-poor syndrome.
   a. Whether there is now any incentive for public schools to clean up their act
   b. Whether the defeat of the school voucher initiative was bad for the country
   c. Two issues are equally stressed in the passage: whether there is now any incentive for public schools to clean up their act and whether the private-school-for-the-rich, public-school-for-the-poor syndrome will be perpetuated

8. From an editorial in a newspaper outside southern California: "The people in southern California who lost a fortune in the wildfires last year could have bought insurance that would have covered their houses and practically everything in them. And anybody with any foresight would have made sure there were no brush and no trees near the houses so that there would be a buffer zone between the house and any fire, as the Forest Service recommends. Finally, anybody living in a fire danger zone ought to know enough to have a fireproof or fire-resistant roof on the house. So, you see, most of the losses those people suffered were simply their own fault."
   a. Whether there were things the fire victims could have done to prevent their losses
   b. Whether insurance, fire buffer zones, and fire-resistant roofs could have prevented much of the loss
   c. Whether the losses suffered by people in the fires were their own fault

9. "Whatever we believe, we think agreeable to reason, and, on that account, yield our assent to it. Whatever we disbelieve, we think contrary to reason, and, on that account, dissent from it. Reason, therefore, is allowed to be the principle by which our belief and opinions ought to be regulated."

   Thomas Reid, Essays on the Active Powers of Man
   a. Whether reason is the principle by which our beliefs and opinions ought to be regulated
   b. Whether what we believe is agreeable to reason
   c. Whether what we disbelieve is contrary to reason
   d. Both b and c

10. Most people you find on university faculties are people who are interested in ideas. And the most interesting ideas are usually new ideas. So most people you find on university faculties are interested in new ideas. Therefore, you are not going to find many conservatives on university faculties, because conservatives are not usually interested in new ideas.
    a. Whether conservatives are interested in new ideas

   b. Whether you'll find many conservatives on university faculties

   c. Whether people on university faculties are interested more in new ideas than in other ideas

   d. Whether most people are correct

11. In pre–civil war Spain, the influence of the Catholic Church must have been much stronger on women than on men. You can determine this by looking at the number of religious communities, such as monasteries, nunneries, and so forth. A total of about 5,000 such communities existed in 1931; 4,000 of them were female, whereas only 1,000 of them were male. Seems to me that proves my point about the Church's influence on the sexes.

   a. Whether the Catholic Church's influence was greater on women than on men in pre–civil war Spain

   b. Whether the speaker's statistics really prove his point about the Church's influence

   c. Whether the figures about religious communities really have anything to do with the overall influence of the Catholic Church in Spain

12. The movie *Singleton* might have been a pretty good movie without the profanity that occurred all the way through it. But without the profanity, it would not have been a believable movie. The people this movie was about just talk that way, you see. If you have them speaking Shakespearean English or middle-class suburban English, then nobody is going to pay any attention to the message of the movie because nobody will see it as realistic. It's true, of course, that, like many other movies with some offensive feature—whether it's bad language, sex, or whatever—it will never appeal to a mass audience.

   a. Whether movies with offensive features can appeal to a mass audience

   b. Whether *Singleton* would have been a good movie without the bad language

   c. Whether *Singleton* would have been a believable movie without the bad language

   d. Whether believable movies must always have an offensive feature of one kind or another

▲ 13. "From information gathered in the last three years, it has become clear that the single biggest environmental problem in the former Soviet Union—many times bigger than anything we have to contend with in the United States—is radioactive pollution from nuclear energy plants and nuclear weapons testing and production. Soviet communist leaders seemed to believe they could do anything to hasten the industrialization process and compete with Western countries, and that the land and natural resources they controlled were vast enough to suffer any abuse without serious consequence. The arrogance of the communist leaders produced a burden of misery and death that fell on the people of the region, and the scale of that burden has only recently become clear. Nuclear waste was dumped into rivers from which downstream villages drew their drinking water; the landscape is dotted with nuclear dumps which now threaten to leak into the environment; and the seas around Russia are littered with decaying hulks of nuclear submarines and rusting metal containers with tens of millions of tons of nuclear waste. The result has been radiation poisoning and its awful effects on a grand scale.

"A science advisor to Russian President Boris Yeltsin said, 'The way we have dealt with the whole issue of nuclear power, and particularly the problem of nuclear waste, was irresponsible and immoral.'"

Adapted from the Washington Post

a. Whether communism failed to protect people from nuclear contamination as well as capitalism did
b. Whether nuclear waste problems in the former Soviet Union are much worse than had been realized until just recently
c. Whether former leaders of the Soviet Union made large-scale sacrifice of the lives and health of their people in their nuclear competition with the West
d. Whether communism, in the long run, is a much worse system than capitalism when it comes to protecting the population from harm

▲ 14. "The United States puts a greater percentage of its population in prison than any other developed country in the world. We persist in locking more and more people up despite the obvious fact that it doesn't work. Even as we build more prisons and stuff them ever more tightly, the crime rate goes up and up. But we respond: 'Since it isn't working, let's do more of it'!

"It's about time we learned that fighting criminals is not the same thing as fighting crime."

Richard Parker, radio commentary on CalNet, California Public Radio

a. Whether we build more prisons than any other country
b. Whether we imprison more people than do other countries
c. Whether reliance on imprisonment is an effective method of reducing crime
d. Whether attacking the sources of crime (poverty, lack of education, and so on) will reduce crime more than just imprisoning people who commit crimes

▲ 15. [As the administration planned to raise the fees charged for grazing animals on public land, several members of the Senate argued against the proposal.] "Senator Alan K. Simpson of Wyoming said higher prices would 'do those old cowboys in.'

"But a review of the top 500 holders of grazing permits on federal land shows that many of those 'old cowboys' are more likely to wear wingtips than boots. They include the Metropolitan Life Insurance Company, with 800,000 acres under its control, the Mormon Church, a Japanese conglomerate, the Nature Conservancy and some of the wealthiest families in the nation.

"The largest permit holders, the top 10 percent, control about half of the nation's public grazing land, according to Interior Department figures.

Only 12 percent of the permit holders are listed by the Government as small operators."

New York Times

  a. Whether Senator Simpson understands who holds grazing permits on federal land

  b. Whether permits to graze on most public land are held by corporations or by individuals and families

  c. Whether permits to graze on most public land are held by small operators or by large, wealthy operators

  d. Whether the administration's plan to raise grazing fees is a reasonable idea

Exercise 1-3

This exercise is designed to be done as an in-class group assignment. Your instructor will indicate how he or she wants it done. On the basis of a distinction covered in this chapter, divide these items into two groups of five items each such that all the items in one group have a feature that none of the items in the second group have. Describe the feature upon which you based your classifications. Compare your results with those of a neighboring group.

1. You shouldn't buy that car because it is ugly.
2. That car is ugly, and it's expensive too.
3. Rainbows have seven different colors in them, although it's not always easy to see them all.
4. Walking is the best exercise. After all, it is less stressful on the joints than other aerobic exercises.
5. The ocean on the central coast is the most beautiful shade of sky blue. It's more green as you go north.
6. Her favorite color is yellow because it is the color of the sun.
7. Pooh is my favorite cartoon character because he has lots of personality.
8. You must turn off the lights when you leave the room. They cost a lot of money to run and you don't need them on during the day.
9. Television programs have too much violence and immoral behavior. Hundreds of killings are portrayed every month.
10. You'll be able to find a calendar on sale after the first of the year, so it is a good idea to wait until then to buy one.

Exercise 1-4

This exercise is designed to be done as an in-class group assignment. Your instructor will indicate how he or she wants it done. On the basis of a distinction covered in this chapter, divide these items into two groups such that all the items in one group have a feature that none of the items in the second group have. Describe the feature upon which you based your classifications. Compare your results with those of a neighboring group.

1. Sampras is unlikely to win the U.S. Open again this year. He has a nagging leg injury, plus he just doesn't seem to have the drive he once had.

2. Hey there, Marco!—don't go giving that cat top sirloin. What's the matter with you, you got no brains at all?

3. If you've ever met a pet bird, then you know that they are very busy creatures.

4. "'Water resistant to 100 feet,' says the front of this package for an Aqualite watch, but the fine-print warranty on the back doesn't cover 'any failure to function properly due to misuse such as water immersion.'"

   Consumer Reports

5. Everybody is saying the president has made us the laughingstock of the world. What a stupid idea! He hasn't made us a laughingstock at all. There's not a bit of truth in that notion.

6. "Is the author really entitled to assert that there is a degree of unity among these essays which makes this a book rather than a congeries? I am inclined to say that he is justified in this claim, but articulating this justification is a somewhat complex task."

   From a book review by Stanley Bates

7. As a long-time customer, you're already taking advantage of our money management expertise and variety of investment choices. That's a good reason for consolidating your other eligible assets into an IRA with us.

8. MOORE: Well, I see where the new chancellor wants to increase class sizes.
   PARKER: Yeah, another of his bright ideas.
   MOORE: Actually, I don't think it hurts to have one or two extra people in class.
   PARKER: What? Of course it hurts. What are you thinking, anyway?
   MOORE: Well, I just think there is good reason for increasing the class size a bit.

9. John Montgomery has been the Eastern Baseball League's best closer this season. Unfortunately, when a closer fails, as Montgomery did last night, there's usually not much chance to recover.

10. Yes, I charge a little more than other dentists. But I feel I give better service. So I think my billing practices are justified.

11. If you want to purchase the house, you must exercise your option before June 30, 2003. Otherwise, you will forfeit the option price.

Exercise 1-5 _____

This exercise is designed to be done as an in-class group assignment. Your instructor will indicate how he or she wants it done. On the basis of a distinction covered in this chapter, divide these items into two groups such that all the items in one group have a feature that none of the items in the second group have. Describe the feature upon which you based your classifications. Compare results with those of a neighboring group.

1. The governor is not as old as Nelson Rockefeller was when Rockefeller was nearing the end of his second term as New York governor.
2. Mark McGwire hit home runs more often than Sammy Sosa did.
3. There is a dragon living at the bottom of Lake Superior.
4. Leno tells better jokes than Letterman.
5. Learning calculus is about a billion times more difficult than learning French.
6. The president ought to resign.
7. Believe me, golf is much more challenging than tennis.
8. Believe me, golf costs more to play than tennis.
9. Laboratory mice who have been placed on a starvation diet live about 30 percent longer than mice who are fed normal amounts.
10. I admit it. I was scared out of my mind.

Exercise 1-6

Decide for each of these whether the issue is about a factual matter. If some of the items are difficult to decide on, say why you think that is so.

▲ 1. Manuel weighs more than 150 pounds.
▲ 2. Diet soda tastes bland compared with regular soda.
   3. Diet soda contains less sugar than regular soda contains.
▲ 4. Diet soda will help you lose weight better than regular soda will.
   5. It's more fun to sail on a cruise ship than to lie on the beach at Hilton Head.
   6. It's expensive to sail on a cruise ship.
▲ 7. It's more expensive to sail on a cruise ship than it is to lie on the beach at Hilton Head.
   8. There is life on some other planet somewhere in the universe.
   9. Most people would find this bath water uncomfortably hot.
▲ 10. The lake is too cold for swimming.
   11. Tom Brokaw is better looking than Dan Rather.
   12. Tiger Woods is a better golfer than Jack Nicklaus was.
▲ 13. Dwight Eisenhower was smarter than Richard Nixon.
   14. Abortion is immoral.
   15. Elvis is alive and living in Pittsburgh.

Exercise 1-7 _____

For each of the following passages, select the option that most accurately states the primary issue in the passage.

▲ 1. Letting your children surf the Net is like dropping them off downtown to spend the day doing whatever they want. They'll get in trouble.
   a. Whether letting your children off downtown to spend the day doing whatever they want will lead them into trouble
   b. Whether letting your children surf the Net will lead them into trouble
   c. Whether restrictions should be placed on children's activities

2. When Rep. Paul McHale became the first Democrat to call for Clinton's resignation, the press pointed out that McHale wasn't running for reelection. But when Barbara Boxer, who was in a pitched battle for her Senate seat, lashed out at the president from the Senate floor, it became clear that attacking the president was politically safe.
   a. Whether Barbara Boxer was fighting for her political life in California
   b. Whether it was politically necessary for Barbara Boxer to attack the president
   c. Whether attacking the president was politically safe
   d. Whether Paul McHale's call for Clinton's resignation was sincere

▲ 3. "My nomination for best overall automotive design? Buick Riviera. This large, near-luxury coupe, which debuted in the mid-90's, is easily the most creative, most interesting automotive design of the decade. The Riviera is one of those love-hate designs you get when you push the envelope of acceptable styling. Some people really love it; others really hate it. I'm a big fan. What's particularly wonderful about this sleek and beautifully proportioned design is the way it changes when viewed from different angles. In effect, it keeps reinventing itself as you walk around it."

   Al Haas

   a. Whether Buick Riviera has the best overall automotive design of the decade
   b. Whether Buick Riviera's design changes when viewed from different angles
   c. Whether designers of Buick Riviera "pushed the envelope" in designing it
   d. None of the above

4. Illinois state employees, both uniformed and non-uniformed, have been loyally, faithfully, honorably and patiently serving the state without a contract or cost-of-living pay increase for years, despite the fact that legislators and governor have accepted hefty pay increases. All public employee unions should launch a signature-gathering initiative to place on the ballot a proposition that the Illinois constitution be amended to provide for compulsory binding arbitration for all uniformed and non-uniformed public employees, under the supervision of the state supreme court.
   a. Whether Illinois state employees have been loyally, faithfully, honorably

and patiently serving the state without a contract or cost-of-living pay increase for years

    b. Whether public employee unions should launch a signature-gathering initiative to place on the ballot a proposition that the Illinois constitution be amended to provide for compulsory binding arbitration for all uniformed and non-uniformed public employees, under the supervision of the Illinois Supreme Court

    c. Neither of the above

5. That Japan needs reform of its political institutions is hardly in doubt. The country is experiencing the worst recession since the Second World War, with forecasts of up to minus 3 percent growth this year. Japan is not only the world's largest economy, but it also dominates the East Asian economic zone, so recovery through that region depends directly on Japan. Reforms are urgently needed to ensure this recovery will happen.

    a. Whether Japan needs reforms of its political institutions

    b. Whether Japan is experiencing its worst recession since the Second World War

    c. Whether Japan is the world's second largest economy

    d. Whether reforms will ensure that recovery will happen

▲ 6. MOORE: So, what do you think of the governor?

    PARKER: Not much, actually.

    MOORE: What do you mean? Don't you think she's been pretty good?

    PARKER: Are you serious?

    MOORE: Well, yes. I think she's been doing a fine job.

    PARKER: Oh, come on. Weren't you complaining about her just a few days ago?

    a. Whether Parker thinks the governor has been a good governor.

    b. Whether Moore thinks the governor has been a good governor.

    c. Whether the governor has been a good governor

    d. Whether Moore has a good argument for thinking the governor has been a good governor

Exercise 1-8

Each of the following items contains a remark followed by four other remarks. Pick the option among the four that would serve the same general purpose as the original remark. Note: Some of these items are quite difficult.

Example

    Be careful! This plate is very hot.

    a. Around here, the trees don't lose their leaves in the winter.

    b. If you feel like going, I can get tickets for you at a discount.

    c. I wonder why there is no graffiti in this town?

    d. Watch it. There is ice on the road tonight.

Analysis

The purpose of the given utterance is to warn someone. Thus (d), which is also used to warn someone, is the correct answer.

▲ 1. GE's profits during the first quarter were short of GE's projections. Therefore, we can expect GE stock to fall sharply in the next day or so.
  a. Over the long haul GE will outperform other companies in the same sector.
  b. The president apparently thinks what he does in private is nobody's business but his own.
  c. The dog is very hot. Probably he would appreciate a drink of water.
  d. The dog's coat is extremely thick. That explains why he is hot.

2. Your battery can be recharged, sir, and then it will be almost as good as new.
  a. Adobe Photoshop is software for producing images, animations, and other Web graphics.
  b. Purchasing one CD at the regular price would entitle you to buy an unlimited number of CDs at only $4.99.
  c. So that we might all be more comfortable, please turn the air conditioning down.
  d. I shall now serve dinner, after which you can play if you want.

3. Given those two missing teeth, I'd expect that zipper to last about a week.
  a. All the wrinkles on that dog make me think of an old man.
  b. The south wind certainly helps to clear out the air.
  c. Given the state of their bull pen, I'm not surprised they collapsed in the ninth.
  d. Adolphus won't stick with Sydney very long, once he gets a load of her spending habits.

▲ 4. To put out a really creative newsletter, I suggest you get in touch with our technology people.
  a. Do unto others as you would have them do unto you.
  b. To put an end to this discussion, I'll concede your point.
  c. Rodney said he was so ugly as a child, his cat tried to cover him with sand.
  d. You'd better cut down on your smoking, if you want to live longer.

5. Most of the students around here live in the dorm. Therefore, chances are Daphne lives in the dorm, too.
  a. The reason Daphne lives in the dorm? Her parents want her to.
  b. Daphne, like many other students, lives in the dorm.
  c. Daphne lives in the dorm. But I don't know if she has a roommate.
  d. Daphne probably lives in the dorm. After all, she doesn't have much money, and it costs less to live in the dorm.

6. Football is like rugby. Each team tries to advance a ball to a goal while the other team tries to prevent this.
  a. A prune is just like a plum. So if you don't like plums, you won't like prunes.

b. Belts are just like suspenders. They both serve to keep your pants from falling down to your knees.

c. Ties are as wide as handkerchiefs, these days. That's why they cost so much.

d. Cleveland is just like Columbus. After all, they are both in Ohio.

▲ 7. How was my date with your brother? Well . . . he has a great personality.

a. Hey! When are you going to get rid of that heap and get a car?

b. How do I like my steak? Well, not dripping blood like this specimen here!

c. How do I like the dress? Well, it's very pretty. Say—did you know that black is more slimming than white?

d. How is Sarah's new boyfriend? Gad—I thought it was her father at first.

8. Alberto has a cold, and anybody with a cold should refrain from going to work. Therefore, Alberto should refrain from going to work.

a. I bet Alberto earns more than he did two years ago, since most people earn more than they did two years ago.

b. Alberto works for the university, and most people who work for the university are happy. Therefore, Alberto is probably happy.

c. Since Alberto earns less than he did two years ago, I would be quite surprised if he has a new car.

d. Alberto earns more than anyone else on his floor, which means he earns more than Louis, since Louis works on the same floor as Alberto.

9. Pornography is a problem, but the Constitution gives us a right to free speech.

a. Even though the Constitution gives us a right to free speech, pornography is a problem.

b. The Constitution gives us a right to free speech. However, pornography is a problem.

c. Pornography wouldn't be a problem if the Constitution didn't give us a right to free speech.

d. The Constitution gives us a right to free speech, even though pornography is a problem.

▲ 10. The wind seems to be coming up. Time to head home.

a. Well, they finally arrived. I guess they will order soon.

b. Whenever dinner is late, I get grumpy.

c. The wind seems to be coming up. The boats will be heading home shortly.

d. We shouldn't leave yet. We just got here.

Exercise 1-9 ⎯⎯⎯⎯⎯⎯⎯⎯⎯⎯⎯⎯⎯⎯⎯⎯

Determine which of the following passages contain arguments, and, for any that do, identify the argument's conclusion. Remember that an argument occurs when one or more claims (the premises) are offered in support of a further claim (the conclusion). There aren't many hard-and-fast rules for identifying arguments, so you'll have to read closely and think carefully about some of these.

▲ 1. The *Directory of Intentional Communities* lists more than two hundred groups across the country organized around a wide variety of purposes, including environmentally aware living.

2. Carl would like to help out, but he won't be in town. So we'll have to find someone else who owns a truck.

3. In 1976, Washington, D.C., passed an ordinance prohibiting private ownership of firearms. Since then, Washington's murder rate has shot up 121 percent. Bans on firearms are clearly counterproductive.

▲ 4. Computers will never be able to converse intelligently through speech. A simple example proves that this is so. The sentences "How do you recognize speech?" and "How do you wreck a nice beach?" have entirely different meanings, but they sound similar enough that a computer could not distinguish the two.

5. Recent surveys for the National Science Foundation report that two of three adult Americans believe that alien spaceships account for UFO reports. It therefore seems likely that several million Americans may have been predisposed to accept the report on NBC's *Unsolved Mysteries* that the U.S. military recovered a UFO with alien markings.

6. "Like short-term memory, long-term memory retains information that is encoded in terms of sense modality and in terms of links with information that was learned earlier (that is, *meaning*)."

Neil R. Carlson

▲ 7. Fears that chemicals in teething rings and soft plastic toys may cause cancer may be justified. Last week, the Consumer Product Safety Commission issued a report confirming that low amounts of DEHP, known to cause liver cancer in lab animals, may be absorbed from certain infant products.

8. "It may be true that people, not guns, kill people. But people with guns kill more people than people without guns. As long as the number of lethal weapons in the hands of the American people continues to grow, so will the murder rate."

Susan Mish'alani

9. June 1970: A Miami man gets thirty days in the stockade for wearing a flag patch on the seat of his trousers. March 2000: Miami department stores are selling boxer trunks made up to look like an American flag. Times have changed.

▲ 10. Levi's Dockers are still in style, but pleats are out.

11. There is trouble in the Middle East, there is a recession under way at home, and all the economic indicators have turned downward. It seems likely, then, that the only way the stock market can go is down.

12. Lucy is too short to reach the bottom of the sign.

▲ 13. "Can it be established that genetic humanity is sufficient for moral humanity? I think that there are very good reasons for not defining the moral community in this way."

Mary Anne Warren

14. Pornography often depicts women as servants or slaves, or as otherwise inferior to men. In light of that, it seems reasonable to expect to find more women than men who are upset by pornography.

15. "My folks, who were Russian immigrants, loved the chance to vote. That's probably why I decided that I was going to vote whenever I got the chance. I'm not sure [whom I'll vote for], but I am going to vote. And I don't understand people who don't."

Mike Wallace

▲ 16. "President Clinton's request for $1 billion to create summer jobs for low-income young people was killed in the Senate, forcing him to settle for $166.5 million. Jobs would help make them part of the real community and would represent a beacon of hope—the first step out of poverty and despair."

Christian Science Monitor

17. "Hayek argues that we cannot know enough about each person's situation to distribute to each according to his moral merit (but would justice demand we do so if we did have the knowledge?)."

Robert Nozick

18. The Great Lakes Coastal Commission should prepare regulations that are consistent with the law, obviously. We admit that isn't always easy. But there's no reason for the commission to substitute its judgment for that of the people.

▲ 19. We need to make clear that sexual preference, whether chosen or genetically determined, is a private matter. It has nothing to do with an individual's ability to make a positive contribution to society.

20. "Cinema rarely rises from a craft to an art. Usually it just manufactures sensory blizzards for persons too passive to manage the active engagement of mind that even light reading requires."

George Will

Exercise 1-10

Identify the main issue in each of the following passages.

▲ 1. Police brutality does not happen very often. Otherwise, it would not make headlines when it does happen.

2. We have little choice but to concentrate our crime-fighting efforts on enforcement because we don't have any idea what to do about the underlying causes of crime.

3. A lot of people think that the gender of a Supreme Court justice doesn't make any difference. But now that there are two women on the bench, I'll

bet we'll get some different results on cases dealing with women's issues during the next few years.

▲ 4. "The point is that the existence of an independent world explains our experiences better than any known alternative. We thus have good reason to believe that the world—which seems independent of our minds—really is essentially independent of our minds."

Theodore W. Schick, Jr., and Lewis Vaughn, How to Think About Weird Things

5. Sure, some of the hotdoggers get good grades in Professor Bubacz's class. But my guess is that if Algernon takes it, all it'll get him is flunked out!

6. It is dumb to claim that sales taxes hit poor people harder than rich people. After all, the more money you have, the more you spend; and the more you spend, the more sales taxes you pay. So people with more money are always going to be paying more in sales tax than poor people.

▲ 7. If you're going to buy a computer, you might as well also sign up for some lessons on how to use the thing. After all, no computer ever did any work for its owner until its owner found out how to make it work.

8. Intravenous drug use with nonsterile needles has become one of the leading causes of the spread of AIDS. Many states passed legislation allowing officials to distribute clean needles in an effort to combat this method of infection. But in eleven states, including some of the most populous, possession of hypodermic syringes without a prescription is illegal. The laws in these foot-dragging states have to be changed if we ever hope to bring this awful epidemic to an end.

9. The best way to avoid error—that is, belief in something false—is to suspend judgment about everything except that which is absolutely certain. Because error usually leads to trouble, this shows that suspension of judgment is usually the right thing to do.

▲ 10. "[Readers] may learn something about their own relationship to the earth from a people who were true conservationists. The Indians knew that life was equated with the earth and its resources, that America was a paradise, and they could not comprehend why the intruders from the East were determined to destroy all that was Indian as well as America itself."

Dee Brown, Bury My Heart at Wounded Knee

Exercise 1-11

For each item, identify the issue that the first speaker is addressing. Are the two speakers addressing the same issue? (As a supplementary exercise, you might determine which of these conversations deal with factual matters and which do not.)

Example

THERESA: I think toilet paper looks better if it unwinds from the back side of the spool.

DANIEL: No way! It looks stupid that way. It should unwind from the front side of the spool.

Analysis

The issue for both Theresa and Daniel is whether the toilet paper looks better if it unwinds from the front of the spool. This issue is not a factual matter; it is best seen as subjective.

▲ 1. MR.: Next weekend we go on Standard Time again. We'll have to set the clocks ahead.

MRS.: It isn't next weekend; it's the weekend after. And you set the clocks back one hour, not ahead.

2. BELIEVER: Ghosts exist. People everywhere in all cultures have believed in them. All those people couldn't be wrong.

SKEPTIC: If ghosts exist, it's not for that reason. People once believed Earth was flat, too.

3. SHE: You don't give me enough help around the house; you hardly ever do anything.

HE: That's not true. I mowed the lawn on Saturday and I washed both of the cars on Sunday. What's more, I've been cleaning up after dinner almost every night and I've hauled all that stuff from the garden to the dump. So I don't see how you can say I hardly ever do anything.

SHE: Well, you don't want to hear all that *I* do around here; your efforts are pretty puny compared to mine!

▲ 4. HEEDLESS: When people complain about American intervention in places like Iraq, they tell every tinhorn dictator to go ahead and take over because America will just stand by and watch. I, for one, think people who complain like that ought to just shut up.

CAUTIOUS: Not me. Complaining like that reminds everyone that it isn't in our best interest to get involved in extended wars abroad.

5. ONE SPEAKER: Nothing beats summertime. It's sunny and warm, and you can wear shorts, go on picnics, take hikes, and, best of all, take in a ball game.

ANOTHER SPEAKER: Naw, summer's hot and sticky, and there's no skiing or skating or getting warm 'round a nice cozy fire. Summer's okay—if you're a mosquito.

6. FITNESS BUFF ONE: Look here, the speedometer cable on this exercise bike is starting to squeak. If we don't fix it, the speedometer is going to stop working.

FITNESS BUFF TWO: What we need to do is get a new bike. This old thing is more trouble than it's worth.

7. YOUNG GUY: Baseball players are much better now than they were forty years ago. They eat better, have better coaching, you name it.

OLD GUY: They aren't any better at all. They just seem better because they get more publicity and play with a livelier ball.

8. STUDENT ONE: Studying is a waste of time. Half the time, I get better grades if I don't study.

   STUDENT TWO: I'd like to hear you say that in front of your parents!

9. PHILATELIST: Did you know that U.S. postage stamps are now being printed in Canada?

   PATRIOT: What an outrage! If there is one thing that ought to be made in the United States, it's U.S. postage stamps!

   PHILATELIST: Oh, I disagree. If American printing companies can't do the work, let the Canadians have it.

10. GEORGE: I think the United States ought to pull its troops out of every country they are currently stationed in. We simply cannot afford and do not know how to police the entire globe.

    NEVILLE: Boy, there's a laugh, coming from you. You're the one who thought we should be sending more troops to Vietnam in the early seventies; you cheered the invasions of Grenada and Panama in the eighties; and you were for the action in Somalia in the nineties. It's a little too late to be handing out this isolationist stuff now, isn't it?

11. FIRST NEIGHBOR: Look here. You have no right to make so much noise at night. I have to get up early to get to work.

    SECOND NEIGHBOR: Yeah? Well, you have no right to let your idiot dog run around loose all day long.

12. STUDY PARTNER ONE: Let's knock off for a while and go get some pizza. We'll be able to function better if we have something to eat.

    STUDY PARTNER TWO: Not one of those pizzas you like! I can't stand anchovies.

13. FEMALE STUDENT: The Internet is totally overrated. It takes forever to find something you can actually use in an assignment.

    MALE STUDENT: Listen, it takes a lot longer to drive over to the library, find a place to park, and wait in line to use a terminal.

14. CITIZEN ONE: In 2000 it's going to be George W. Bush for the Republicans and Al Gore for the Democrats, what do you want to bet?

    CITIZEN TWO: I doubt it. Gore's finished. The Democrats will find someone else.

15. CULTURALLY CHALLENGED PERSON: A concert! You think I'm gonna go to a concert when I could be home watching Monday Night Football?

    CULTURALLY CHALLENGED PERSON'S SPOUSE: Yes, if you want dinner this week.

Exercise 1-12 _____

For each of the brief conversations that follow, identify the issue the first speaker is addressing. To what extent does the second speaker address the same issue?

Does he or she miss the point? If so, might the misdirection be intentional? Some of these are best suited to class discussion.

Example

MOORE: I've seen the work of both Thomas Brothers and Vernon Construction, and I tell you Thomas Brothers does a better job.

PARKER: Listen, Thomas Brothers is the highest-priced company in the whole blasted state. If you hire them, you'll pay double for every part of the job.

Analysis

Moore thinks Thomas Brothers does better work than Vernon Construction; Parker thinks Thomas Brothers' work is overpriced. Moore's view is quite compatible with Parker's view: Thomas Brothers may indeed do the best work (i.e., Moore is right) *and* charge wildly excessive prices (i.e., Parker is right, too). However, there is an underlying issue on which Moore and Parker will almost certainly disagree: whether Thomas Brothers should be hired. They have not made this disagreement explicit yet, however.

▲ 1. URBANITE: The new requirements will force people off septic tanks and make them hook up to the city sewer. That's the only way we'll ever get the nitrates and other pollutants out of the ground water.
SUBURBANITE: You call it a requirement, but I call it an outrage! They're going to charge us from five to fifteen thousand dollars each to make the hookups! That's more than anybody in my neighborhood can afford.

2. CRITIC: I don't think it's morally proper to sell junk bonds to anybody without emphasizing the risk involved, but it's especially bad to sell them to older people who are investing their entire savings.
ENTREPRENEUR: Oh, come on. There's nothing the matter with making money.

▲ 3. ONE HAND: What with the number of handguns and armed robberies these days, it's hard to feel safe in your own home.
THE OTHER HAND: The reason you don't feel safe is that you don't have a handgun yourself. It's well known that a criminal would rather hit a house where there's no gun than a house where there is one.

4. ONE GUY: Would you look at the price they want for these digital tape machines? They're making a fortune in profit on every one of these things!
ANOTHER: Don't give me that. I know how big a raise you got last year—you can afford *two* of those players if you want!

▲ 5. FED-UP: This city is too cold in the winter, too hot in the summer, and too dangerous all the time. I'll be happier if I exercise my early retirement option and move to my place in Arkansas.
FRIEND: You're nuts. You've worked here so long you'll be miserable if you retire, and if you move, you'll be back in six months.

Exercise 1-13

Which of the following statements from news reports are neutral statements of fact? Identify and discuss any elements that are subjective in nature.

▲ 1. Family members stood by watching while the fire burned unchecked.

2. The house, an imposing two-story colonial-style building, was completely destroyed.

3. Assad had plainly been pressured into the summit.

▲ 4. Hurricane Fran stranded hundreds of people on barrier islands, and its remnant flooded Virginia hollows Friday.

5. Even the Coors Brewing Company, long a supporter of a right-wing agenda, began offering gay partners the same benefits as spouses in 1995.

6. Castellanos attended the University of North Carolina but dropped out in his final semester to work on Ronald Reagan's 1976 campaign.

▲ 7. In his response to the President, Senator Dole was vigorous and sharp.

8. Representatives of the unions found it difficult not to express pleasure when Senator Byrd announced his proposal to protect pension funds.

9. On August 22 the leader of a Kurdish faction wrote a desperate plea to Saddam Hussein.

▲ 10. After Bennett criticized the senator's campaign as "incoherent and dispassionate," the senator recruited Bennett to join him.

11. The Reverend Jackson, though frank and provocative, has a keen sense of marketing and showmanship.

12. This Sunday, as prescribed by the peace accords, Bosnians are to go to the polls in national elections.

▲ 13. The governor's speeches switch seamlessly from anecdotes told by cops to appropriate quotations from Abe Lincoln.

14. Hard work and creativity have stopped the declining enrollment at Spring Grove Community College.

15. For two years the rapidly expanding global computer matrix had nagged at Gates like a low-level headache.

Exercise 1-14

This exercise is designed to be done as an in-class group assignment. Your instructor will indicate how he or she wants it done. On the basis of a distinction covered in this chapter, divide these items into two groups such that all the items in one group have a feature that none of the items in the second group have. Describe the feature upon which you based your classifications.

1. OROVILLE—A judge Friday ordered an accused gunman held for trial on a felony assault charge stemming from an aborted residential robbery last month during which an Oroville bank executive was wounded.

2. WASHINGTON—As details of a remarkable week of grand jury testimony by President Clinton and a young intern filter into the public domain, Clinton apologists are unwinding a fragile string of explanations to protect him against charges of perjury and obstruction of justice.

3. LHOK SUKON, Indonesia (AP)—Human rights workers on Saturday dug up the skeletons of people activists believe were killed by the Indonesian military. Villagers looking on shouted slogans against former President Suharto.

4. Gunshots were fired at an apartment complex off 10th Street Friday during a "gang bang," which, according to witnesses, may have been contrived to intimidate or retaliate against rival gang members.

5. WASHINGTON—From hideouts in Afghanistan's rugged mountains, Osama bin Laden used his wealth to create cells of Muslim fighters to cleanse the country of its Soviet occupiers. Now bin Laden, who has since become the most significant sponsor of Islamic extremist activities in the world, has declared war on the United States.

6. HARRISBURG, PA. (AP)—With no bathrooms or portable potties in space, NASA has relied on a brand of inexpensive, compressed adult diapers to let astronauts take care of business while they work.

7. WASHINGTON—The attorney general has launched a 90-day investigation to see if she should seek still another independent counsel, this time to check into the truthfulness of the vice president. On the face of it suspicion arises that the investigation might be more a means of dealing with political pressure—another stalling tactic—than of enforcing the law, since the probe won't be finished until after the November elections.

8. SACRAMENTO (AP)—State senators on Thursday approved a bill by Assemblywoman Debra Bowen, D–Marina del Rey, that would give computer owners a way to block unwanted commercial electronic mail, which is commonly known as spam.

9. WASHINGTON—Bill Clinton played kinky games with a girl in a room next to the Oval Office while dignitaries were waiting for him. Independent counsel Kenneth Starr is trying to find out whether Clinton took criminal measures to conceal this weird behavior. Clinton, of course, is merely trying to shield his "family life."

10. Prior to the 1992 national election, President George Bush asked whether character counts. Those who felt character was not important went on to elect the greatest liar and confidence man this nation was ever to suffer under as president.

Writing Exercises

1. Turn to the "Essays for Analysis" section at the back of the book (beginning on page E-1). Identify and write in your own words the principal issues in selections 1 and 2. Your instructor may have other instructions in addition to (or in place of) these.

2. Do people choose which sex they are attracted to? Write a one-page answer to this question, defending your answer with at least one supporting reason. Take about ten minutes to write your answer. Do not put your name on your paper. When everyone is finished, your instructor will collect the papers and redistribute them to the class. In groups of four or five, read the papers that have been given to your group. Divide the drafts into two batches, those that contain an argument and those that do not. Your instructor will ask each group to read to the class a paper that contains an argument and a paper that does not contain an argument (assuming that each group has at least one of each). The group should be prepared to explain why they feel each paper contains or fails to contain an argument.

3. Using the issues you identified in Exercise 1 for each of the selections, choose a side on one of the issues and write a short paper supporting it.

Chapter 2

Critical Thinking and Clear Writing

There you are, with keyboard, pen, or pencil. And there it is, the enemy: a blank screen or piece of paper that you must somehow convert into an essay. If you are like many students we know, the kind of essay that causes you more trouble than any other variety is the argumentative essay, in which the purpose is to support a position on an issue. Successful essays achieve their goal by offering good arguments for their author's position. And because arguments consist of claims, a good argumentative essay contains credible claims.

In the previous chapter, we discussed claims at length and introduced the basics of argument. In this chapter, we show how to apply principles of critical thinking to essay writing: how to organize your thoughts, state your claims clearly, and avoid ineffective and counterproductive language. The chapter is not a substitute for a course in composition or writing, but it provides information that will help you write strong essays based on clearly stated arguments and reasonable claims.

As you progress through this book, you will acquire a working understanding of the various principles by which you can evaluate claims and arguments and, accordingly, argumentative essays. You can also apply these principles of critical thinking to your own writing. So working on your critical-thinking skills will help you get better at both appraising and writing argumentative essays.

The benefits work in reverse, too. You can enlist essay writing in service of critical-thinking objectives. For example, suppose you read an editorial you do not agree with. You might try drafting a response. Doing so will probably help you organize your thoughts and clarify your position; it will almost surely disclose to you considerations you had not thought of or aspects of the issue you did not perceive at first. Your thinking on the subject will probably sharpen.

Organization and Focus

A good argumentative essay must first of all be well organized. Every now and then, you encounter pieces of writing in which the words, claims, and arguments are so strangely assembled that the result is unintelligible. Let's just hope that the piece is nothing you yourself have written.

If you come across an argumentative essay that suffers from such serious organizational defects that it cannot be fully understood, then your only option is to suspend judgment on the unintelligible aspects. If, however, your own writing suffers from these defects, then you can benefit from some simple principles of good organization.

■ Principles of Organization

In an argumentative essay, the most natural and common organizational pattern is to state what you are trying to establish and then proceed to establish it by setting forth the considerations that support your position, adding explanations, illustrations, or other elaboration as needed. Here are some guidelines to help you get organized:

1. *Focus.* Make clear at the outset what issue you intend to address and what your position on the issue will be. Of course, nothing is quite so boring as an essay that begins, "In this essay I shall argue that . . ." and then goes on to itemize everything that's going to be said later. As a matter of style, you should let the reader know what to expect without using trite phrases and without going on at length.

2. *Stick to the issue.* All points you make in an essay should be connected to the issue under discussion and should always either (a) support, illustrate, explain, clarify, elaborate on, or emphasize your position on the

issue or (b) serve as responses to anticipated objections. Rid the essay of irrelevancies and dangling thoughts.

3. *Arrange the components of the essay in a logical sequence.* This is just common sense. Make a point *before* you clarify it, for example, not the other way around. Place support for item B next to item B, not next to item F or G.

When supporting your points, bring in examples, clarification, and the like in such a way that the reader knows what you are doing. Your readers should be able to discern the relationship between any given sentence and your ultimate objective, and they should be able to move from sentence to sentence and from paragraph to paragraph without becoming lost or confused. If a reader cannot outline your essay with ease, you have not properly sequenced your material.

4. *Be complete.* You don't have to be exhaustive in your treatment of the issue; many issues are in fact much too large to be treated exhaustively in a single essay. Remember, finally, this basic principle: The more limited your topic, the easier it is to be complete in your coverage. However, do accomplish what you set out to accomplish, support fully and adequately whatever position you take on the issue, and anticipate and respond to possible objections. Also, be sure that there is closure at every level: Sentences should be complete, paragraphs should be unified wholes (and usually each should stick to a single point), and the essay should reach a conclusion. Reaching a conclusion and summarizing are not the same, incidentally. Short essays do not require summaries.

■ Good Writing Practices

Understanding these principles is one thing—actually employing them may be more difficult. Fortunately, five practices are almost guaranteed to improve the organization of your essay and to help you avoid other problems.

1. At some stage *after* the first draft, outline what you have written. Then make certain that the outline is logical and that every sentence in the essay fits into the outline as it should. Some writers create an informal outline before they begin, but many do not. Our advice: Just start writing and worry about outlining later.

2. Revise your work. Revising is the secret to good writing. Even major league writers revise what they write, and they revise continuously. Unless you are even more gifted than the very best professional writers, then revise, revise, revise. Don't think in terms of two or three drafts. Think in terms of *innumerable* drafts.

3. Have someone else read your essay and offer criticisms of it. Revise as required.

4. If you have trouble with grammar or punctuation, reading your essay out loud may help you detect problems that your eyes have missed.

5. After you are *completely* satisfied with your essay, put it aside. Then come back to it later for still another set of revisions.

■ *Essay Types to Avoid*

Seasoned instructors know that the first batch of essays they get from a class will most likely include several samples of each of the following types. At all costs, try to avoid these pitfalls.

▲ *The Windy Preamble.* Writers of this type of essay avoid getting to the issue and instead go on at length with introductory remarks, often about how important the issue is, how it has troubled thinkers for centuries, how opinions on the issue are many and various, and so on—and on.

▲ *The Stream-of-Consciousness Ramble.* This type of essay results when writers make no attempt to organize their thinking on the issue and instead simply list thoughts more or less in the order they come to mind.

▲ *The Knee-Jerk Reaction.* In this type of essay, writers record their first reaction to an issue without considering the issue in any depth or detail.

▲ *The Glancing Blow.* Writers of this type of essay address the issue obliquely rather than straight on. If they are supposed to evaluate the health benefits of exercise, they will discuss the health benefits of using exercise equipment. If they are supposed to consider the health benefits of using exercise equipment, they will discuss the benefits of bicycling.

▲ *Let the Reader Do the Work.* Writers of this type of essay expect the reader to follow them through non sequiturs, abrupt shifts in direction, and huge gaps in logic.

Exercise 2-1

The sentences in this Associated Press health report have been scrambled. Re-arrange them so that the report makes sense.

1. The men, usually strong with no known vices or ailments, die suddenly, uttering an agonizing groan, writhing and gasping before succumbing to the mysterious affliction.

2. Scores of cases have been reported in the United States during the past decade.

3. In the United States, health authorities call it "Sudden Unexplained Death Syndrome," or "SUDS."

4. Hundreds of similar deaths have been noted worldwide.

5. The phenomenon is known as "lai tai," or "nightmare death," in Thailand.

6. In the Philippines, it is called "bangungut," meaning "to rise and moan in sleep."

7. Health officials are baffled by a syndrome that typically strikes Asian men in their 30s while they sleep.

8. Researchers cannot say what is killing SUDS victims.

▲ Exercise 2-2

The sentences in the following passage have been scrambled. Rearrange them so that the passage makes sense.

1. Weintraub's findings were based on a computer test of 1,101 doctors twenty-eight to ninety-two years old.

2. She and her colleagues found that the top ten scorers aged seventy-five to ninety-two did as well as the average of men under thirty-five.

3. "The test measures memory, attention, visual perception, calculation, and reasoning," she said.

4. "The studies also provide intriguing clues to how that happens," said Sandra Weintraub, a neuropsychologist at Harvard Medical School in Boston.

5. "The ability of some men to retain mental function might be related to their ability to produce a certain type of brain cell not present at birth," she said.

6. The studies show that some men manage to escape the trend of declining mental ability with age.

7. Many elderly men are at least as mentally able as the average young adult, according to recent studies.

Clarity in Writing

In addition to being well organized, a good argumentative essay must be clearly written. If your objective is to support your position, you must write as clearly as possible. Likewise, before you accept what someone else writes (or says), you should be sure you understand what is being expressed.

Consider these examples:

> When I was in the Marine Corps, I was plainly told that many good men died in the uniform that was issued to me.
>
> *—From a letter to the editor*

> Not every framistan has gussets.

> I am glad to be an American, and I appreciate our system of government. Also, I am for a very strong defense. However, the people protesting the war on all sides are out there because they care about life. Now we are in an awful mess. Why? We need to put ourselves in the other guy's shoes. Going out and killing the other guy may be the way to preserve your own.
>
> *—From a newspaper call-in column*

If openness means to "go with the flow," it is necessarily an accommodation to the present. That present is so closed to doubt about so many things impeding the progress of its principles that unqualified openness to it would mean forgetting the despised alternatives to it, knowledge of which makes us aware of what is doubtful in it.

—From ALLAN BLOOM, in *The Closing of the American Mind*

The purpose of extending the kindergarten hours is to provide a thinking meaning appropriately centered-based, academic/social program to meet the diverse needs of the kindergarten students entering at Lewis Elementary. The exposure of the students to the world, due to extended travels, has increased their student based experiences.

—From a California public school proposal for extending kindergarten hours

Maybe Bloom went to Lewis Elementary.

Today, morals are breaking down everywhere. There are no longer any absolutes. That is why the Boy Scouts should not permit gays to be scout leaders. The Boy Scouts stand for values that never change or go out of style.

—From a student paper

I am forty-two years old and I'm conservative. I keep reading and hearing in the news that voters are in a bad mood. No, we are not. We are hopeful and uplifted, but we are mad as hell.

—Reported by William Endicott

Legal laws are fine, but illegal ones should be changed.

—From a student paper

The first example does not mean what it first appears to mean; the second can be understood only by those familiar with framistans, whatever those are. The third example is a set of claims that individually mostly make sense—but the assembled package defies comprehension. The fourth and fifth seem illogical and contradictory. (In the fourth, the second sentence asserts there are no longer any absolutes; the last sentence implies there are. In the fifth, it's hard to see how voters can be mad as hell but not in a bad mood). And the last example is nonsensical.

When we can't tell what someone else is claiming or arguing, or when someone else can't tell what we are claiming or arguing, any number of problems may be causing the difficulty. Here we consider ill-defined terms, poorly chosen words, unintentional ambiguity, vagueness, and faulty comparisons.

■ *Defining Terms*

Any serious attempt to support or sustain a position requires a clear statement of what is at issue. Sometimes stating what is at issue involves a careful definition of key terms.

Perennial Candidate

Dan Quayle, who has been a presidential candidate several times, is notorious for his canny political insight:

- I was recently on a tour of Latin America, and the only regret I have was that I didn't study Latin harder in school so I could converse with these people.
- It isn't pollution that's harming the environment. It's the impurities in our air and water that are doing it.
- I'm confident we can defeat Clinton in 2000.

All the above were attributed to Mr. Quayle, but who knows if he really said them. We are beginning to suspect that his political opponents just make this stuff up.

Purposes and Types of Definitions   Definitions can serve different purposes:

▲ To introduce unusual or unfamiliar words, to coin new words, or to introduce a new meaning to a familiar word (these are called **stipulative definitions**)

▲ To explain, illustrate, or disclose important aspects of difficult concepts (**explanatory definitions**)

▲ To reduce vagueness and eliminate ambiguity (**precising definitions**)

▲ To influence the attitudes of the reader (**persuasive definitions**)

Sometimes definitions are intended just to amuse.

Whatever their purpose, most definitions take various common forms. Three of the most common are **definition by example, definition by synonym,** and **analytical definition:**

1. *Definition by example:* pointing to, naming, or describing one or more examples of something to which the defined term applies. "By 'scripture' I mean books like the Bible or the Koran." "By 'temperate climate' I mean weather in an area like the mid-Atlantic states."

2. *Definition by synonym:* giving another word or phrase that means the same thing. "'Fastidious' means the same as 'fussy.'" "'Prating' is the same as 'chattering.'" "'Pulsatile' means the same as 'throbbing'"; "to be 'lubricous' is to be 'slippery.'"

3. *Analytical definition:* specifying (a) the type of thing the term applies to and (b) the differences between the things the term applies to and other things of the same type. "A mongoose is a ferret-sized mammal native to India that eats snakes and is related to civets."

For more than almost half a century, the Humane Society has led the fight to protect animals.

—Humane Society solicitation sent to one of us

For how long?

More Misstatements . . .

You don't have to be a national political figure to put your foot in your mouth. Ordinary folks can do it too! These are all actual examples from news programs and other published sources.

The President's energy tax won't even be noticed. Besides, it will discourage consumption.

> [Hey, if it won't be noticed, it won't discourage consumption.]

Females score lower on the SAT than males, which right there proves the tests don't show anything. They also demonstrate that teachers do a better job of teaching male students, which is just what you'd expect given the sexual bias that exists in the classroom.

> [If the SATs don't show anything, then they don't show that teachers do a better job teaching males.]

We have to liberate discussion on this campus and not be so restrained by the First Amendment.

> [Right. And we can make people free by sticking them in jail.]

Once your body gets cold, the rest of you will get cold, too.

> [On the other hand, if you can keep your body warm, the rest of you will stay warm, too.]

It's hard to support the President's invasion of Haiti when the American public is so strongly against it. And besides, he's just doing it to raise his standings in the polls.

> [Hmmm. How's it going to raise his standings if the public is so strongly against it?]

"A samovar is an urn with a spigot, used especially in Russia to boil water for tea."

Autobiography Skewers Kansas' Sen. Bob Dole

—Headline in the *Boulder* (Colo.) *Sunday Camera* (reported by Larry Engelmann)

Some terms, especially terms for abstractions (e.g., "goodness," "truth," "knowledge," "beauty") cannot be defined in any complete way, so a writer may have to settle for providing mere hints of their subtle meanings. "By 'reality' I mean the things that most of us agree have independent existence apart from our perceptions of them."

However we define a term, we should be aware that most terms convey meaning beyond the literal sense of the written or spoken words. This "meaning" is a term's **emotive,** or **rhetorical, force**—its tendency to elicit certain feelings or attitudes. The word "dog," for example, has the same literal meaning as "pooch," "mutt," and "cur," but all these terms differ in the attitudes they convey. Or consider the words "child," "dependent minor," "brat," and "little one." What associations do these terms have for you? When people want to manipulate the emotive force of their message, they

"I'd like to take a moment to define what I mean by 'defining moment.'"

frequently substitute euphemisms for more pointed terms. This is the origin of such substitutions as "urban camping" for "homelessness" and "food-insecure" for "starving." The emotive, or rhetorical, force of a term, which is subjective and can vary considerably from one person to another, is usually not taken to be a part of the literal meaning.

Keeping Your Word Choices Simple   Good writing is often simple writing: It avoids redundancy, unnecessary complexity, and prolixity (long-windedness and wordiness). These writing characteristics often confuse readers and listeners, and they sometimes make writers (or speakers) look silly. Why write of *armed* gunmen? Gunmen are automatically armed. Why say that something is *completely* full? If it's full, it's completely full. Michael Jordan, it is often said, is a *famous* superstar. The famous part is pointless, if a person is a superstar. In fact, come to think of it, why say *super*star?

Here's another example:

They expressed their belief that at that point in time it would accord with their desire not to delay their departure.

I'm for abolishing and doing away with redundancy.

—J. Curtis McKay, of the Wisconsin State Elections Board (reported by Ross and Petras)

We ourselves are also for that too.

But all that is necessary is

> They said they wanted to leave.

On the other hand, if the briefest way of making a point is to use words that a reader isn't likely to understand, it is probably better to avoid those words in favor of more familiar ones, even if it takes more of the latter to express the information. "His remarks were obfuscatory and dilatory" will be less clear to most readers than "His remarks confused the issue and were unnecessarily time-consuming." Further, because the world is a complicated place, the language we use to describe it often has to be correspondingly complicated. Sometimes it is necessary to be complicated to be clear. But, in general, simplicity is the best policy.

Exercise 2-3

In groups (or individually if your instructor prefers) determine what term in each of the following is being defined and whether the definition is a definition by example or by synonym or an analytical definition. If it is difficult to tell which kind of definition is present, describe the difficulty.

▲ 1. A piano is a stringed instrument in which felt hammers are made to strike the strings by an arrangement of keys and levers.

2. "Decaffeinated" means without caffeine.

3. Steve Martin is my idea of a successful philosophy major.

▲ 4. The red planet is Mars.

5. "UV" refers to ultraviolet light.

6. The Cheyenne perfectly illustrate the sort of Native Americans who were plains Indians.

7. Data, in our case, is raw information collected from survey forms which is then put in tabular form and analyzed.

▲ 8. "Chiaroscuro" is just a fancy word for shading.

9. Bifocals are glasses with two different prescriptions ground into each lens, making it possible to focus at two different distances from the wearer.

10. Red is the color that we perceive when our eyes are struck by light waves of approximately seven angstroms.

▲ 11. A significant other can be taken to be a person's spouse, lover, long-term companion, or just girlfriend or boyfriend.

12. "Assessment" means evaluation.

13. A blackout is "a period of total memory loss, as one induced by an accident or prolonged alcoholic drinking." When your buddies tell you they loved your rendition of the Lambada on Madison's pool table the other night and you don't even remember being at Madison's, that is a blackout.

Adapted from the CalPoly, San Luis Obispo, Mustang Daily

14. A pearl, which is the only animal-produced gem, begins as an irritant inside an oyster. The oyster then secretes a coating of nacre around the irritating object. The result is a pearl, the size of which is determined by the number of layers with which the oyster coats the object.

15. According to my cousin, who lives in Tulsa, the phrase "bored person" refers to anybody who is between the ages of sixteen and twenty-five and lives in eastern Oklahoma.

■ *Ambiguous Claims*

A claim is an **ambiguous claim** if it can be assigned more than one meaning and if the particular meaning it should be assigned is not made clear by context. If an accountant rises from her desk on Friday afternoon and says, "My work here is finished," she might mean that she has finished the account she was working on, that her whole week's work is done and she's leaving for the weekend, or that she is fed up with her job and is leaving the company.

> *The World Health Organization does not promote a drink a day for health reasons.*
>
> —*Chico Enterprise-Record*
>
> What *do* they promote it for?

Sometimes an ambiguous word or phrase can make the difference in a discussion or a dispute. For example, imagine two people who are disputing whether abortion should be made illegal. Imagine that one person uses the phrase "human being" to refer to any organism that possesses a full complement of human chromosomes and the other person uses the same phrase to refer to a being recognized by statute or Supreme Court decision to have full rights as a citizen under the Constitution. There will be much wasted breath and misunderstanding until they get their two disparate definitions of this crucial phrase sorted out.

Semantic Ambiguity   A claim can be ambiguous for different reasons. Consider these claims:

1. He always lines up on the right side.

2. She is cold.

3. I know a little Greek.

4. She disputed his claim.

5. My brother doesn't use glasses.

I am a marvelous housekeeper. Every time I leave a man I keep his house.

—ZSA ZSA GABOR

The meanings of these claims are unclear because each claim contains an ambiguous word or phrase. For example, "claim" in (4) could mean either a statement or a claim to a gold mine; "glasses" in (5) could mean either eyeglasses or drinking glasses. A claim whose ambiguity is due to the ambiguity of a particular word or phase is called a **semantically ambiguous claim.** Semantic ambiguity can be eliminated by substituting an unambiguous word or phrase, such as "eyeglasses" for "glasses" in (5). Sometimes the substitution may require several extra words.

I wrote a story about a girl making lunch in a skillet.

—GARRISON KEILLOR

A big skillet, perhaps?

Syntactic Ambiguity   Now consider these examples:

1. She saw the farmer with binoculars.

2. Players with beginners' skills only may use court 1.

3. People who protest often get arrested.

4. He chased the girl in his car.

5. There's somebody in the bed next to me.

In contrast with those in the preceding list, these claims are ambiguous because of their structures. Even though we understand the meaning of the phrase "with binoculars," for example, we can't tell whether it pertains to the farmer or to the subject of (1). A claim of this sort is called a **syntactically ambiguous claim.** The only way to eliminate syntactic ambiguity is to rewrite the claim.

The Fallacy of Division in Clinton's Impeachment Trial

Assume two-thirds of a jury thinks a defendant is guilty of having lied about W, X, or Y. Which of these options logically follows?

1. Two-thirds of the jury think the defendant lied about W.
2. Two-thirds of the jury think the defendant lied about X.
3. Two-thirds of the jury think the defendant lied about Y.
4. There is at least one matter, W, X, or Y, that two-thirds of the jury think the defendant lied about.
5. None of the above.

The correct answer is 5. Two-thirds of a jury could think the defendant lied about "W, X, or Y" even though less than two-thirds thought he lied about W, and less than two-thirds thought he lied about X, and less than two-thirds thought he lied about Y!

This confusion, which is actually a subtle example of division, explained later in this chapter, was involved in possibly the most important trial to ever happen in the United States, Bill Clinton's impeachment trial before the U.S. Senate.

Here's how Article I of the impeachment charges read: "William Jefferson Clinton willfully provided perjurious, false, and misleading testimony to the grand jury concerning one or more of the following: [here, four options were listed]."

Here's how the key part of Article II read: "The means used to implement this course of conduct [obstructing justice] included one or more of the following acts: [here several options were listed]."

This presented the Clinton legal defense team with a logical dilemma. The Article I and Article II charges were both worded in such a way that, even if two-thirds of the Senate agreed that Clinton was guilty under one of these two articles of impeachment, it would not follow that there was even a single case of lying or a single case of obstructing justice that two-thirds of the Senate agreed the president committed! In other words, Clinton could have been convicted and removed from office despite not being found guilty *on any specific charge of lying or obstructing justice* by the required two-thirds of the Senate!

This, of course, explains why prosecutors normally make each crime alleged to have been committed by a defendant a separate count.

Sometimes syntactically ambiguous claims result when we do not clearly show what a pronoun refers to. "The boys chased the girls, and they giggled a lot" is an example of this sort of ambiguity; you can't be certain whether "they" refers to the boys or to the girls. "After he removed the trash from the pool, the children played in it" is another example.

Modifying phrases can create syntactic ambiguities if we are careless with them. Consider "He brushed his teeth on the carpet." If you want to avoid suggesting that a carpet might make a good toothbrush, then you

"Grammar Does Some Work!"

Notice in a Help Wanted section of a newspaper:

Wanted. Man to take care of cow that does not smoke or drink.

If the nonsmoking and nondrinking creature is the man, the sentence should say *"who* does not smoke or drink," rather than *"that* does not smoke or drink." That the word "that" is used should tell us that it's the cow the speaker means. A little grammatical knowledge would go a long way—if the writer had it.

FUSCO BROTHERS copyright Lew Little Ent. Reprinted with permission of Universal Press Syndicate. All rights reserved.

▲ *A lot of jokes depend on ambiguity for humor. Unintentional ambiguities can make what you write sort of funny, too.*

should recast the sentence, perhaps as "He brushed his teeth while he was on the carpet." Or take "She wiped up the water with her younger brother." Yes, of course it is unlikely that she used her brother as a towel. But a clear writer will avoid any possibility of misunderstanding—or ridicule—by recasting the sentence, perhaps as "She and her younger brother wiped up the water." "He was bitten while walking by a dog" should be revised either as "While he was walking, he was bitten by a dog" or as "While he was walking by a dog, he was bitten."

Grouping Ambiguity   A peculiar kind of semantic ambiguity, which we'll call **grouping ambiguity,** is illustrated by this claim:

Secretaries make more money than physicians.

Is this claim true or false? We can't say. We don't know *what* the claim is because we don't know exactly what "secretaries" and "physicians" refer to. If the claim is that secretaries *as a group* make more money than

If I said anything which implies that I think that we didn't do what we should have done given the choices we faced at the time, I shouldn't have said that.

—BILL CLINTON
(reported by Larry Engelmann)

Ambiguous Signs

Sign in a Laundromat:

> AUTOMATIC WASHING MACHINES: PLEASE REMOVE ALL YOUR CLOTHES WHEN THE LIGHT GOES OUT

Sign in an office:

> AFTER COFFEE BREAK, PLEASE EMPTY POT AND STAND UPSIDE DOWN ON COUNTER

Sign outside a secondhand shop:

> WE EXCHANGE ANYTHING—BICYCLES, WASHING MACHINES, ETC. WHY NOT BRING YOUR WIFE ALONG AND GET A WONDERFUL BARGAIN?

Sign outside nightclub:

> SMARTS IS THE MOST EXCLUSIVE DISCO IN TOWN. EVERYONE WELCOME.

Sign in safari park:

> ELEPHANTS
> PLEASE STAY IN YOUR CAR

Seen during a conference:

> FOR ANYONE WHO HAS CHILDREN AND DOESN'T KNOW IT, THERE IS A DAY CARE ON THE FIRST FLOOR

Sign in office building:

> TOILET OUT OF ORDER. PLEASE USE FLOOR BELOW.

—We got 'em from JIM WEST, *NIC Architect, MCI Worldcom*

physicians make *as a group*, then the claim is true because there are many more secretaries than physicians. But if the claim is that secretaries individually make more money than physicians individually, then the claim is of course false. Whenever we refer to a collection of individuals, we must clearly show whether the reference is to the collection as a group or as individuals.

The Fallacies of Composition and Division   Related to grouping ambiguities are mistakes, or **fallacies,** known as composition and division. Suppose something holds true of a group of things individually. To think it must therefore necessarily hold true of the same things as a group is to commit the **fallacy of composition.** Here are two examples of this fallacy:

The President will keep the promises he meant to keep.

—Bill Clinton's White House senior adviser, GEORGE STEPHANOPOULOS

Sampras and Agassi are the two best tennis players in the United States, so they'd make the best doubles team.

We don't spend *that* much on military salaries. After all, who ever heard of anyone getting rich in the Army? (In other words, we don't spend that much on service personnel *individually;* therefore, we don't spend much on them *as a group.*)

Conversely, to think that what holds true of a group automatically holds true of all the individuals in that group is to commit the error known as the **fallacy of division.** Here are examples:

Congress is incompetent. Therefore, Congressman Benton is incompetent.

The Eastman School of Music has an outstanding international reputation; therefore, Vladimir Peronepky, who is on the faculty of Eastman, must have a good reputation.

In the 1994 congressional elections, the voters (as a group) made it clear that they did not want a Democratic Congress. Therefore, the voters (individually) made it clear that they did not want a Democratic Congress.

Recognizing and Deciphering Ambiguity   Some claims, such as "Women can fish" and "I will put the sauce on myself," can reasonably be diagnosed as either semantically or syntactically ambiguous. So don't spend much time arguing over which category an ambiguous claim belongs to. What is important is recognizing ambiguities when you encounter them and avoiding them in your own writing.

Some ambiguous claims don't fall into any of the categories we have mentioned. For example, a claim that refers to "the fastest woman on the squad" is ambiguous if two or more women on the squad are equally fast and are faster than anyone else. "I cannot recommend him highly enough" might

More Ambiguous Weirdness

Local High School Dropouts Cut in Half

Astronaut Takes Blame for Gas in Spacecraft

New Study of Obesity Looks for Larger Test Group

Two Soviet Ships Collide, One Dies

Miners Refuse to Work After Death

Enraged Cow Injures Farmer with Ax

Teacher Strikes Idle Kids

Eye Drops off Shelf

Typhoon Rips Through Cemetery; Hundreds Dead

Squad Helps Dog Bite Victim

Some church bulletin bloopers making the rounds on the Web:

This being Easter Sunday, we will ask Mrs. Martin to come forward and lay an egg on the altar.

Next Sunday, a special collection will be taken to defray the cost of the new carpet. All those wishing to do something on the new carpet may come forward and do so.

The United Methodist Women have cast off clothing of every kind. They may be seen in the church basement this Friday from 9 A.M. to 4 P.M.

—*These are courtesy of DAN BARNETT*

mean that he is even better than my highest recommendation, or it might mean that I cannot recommend him very highly at all. The ambiguity, however, is not clearly semantic or syntactic.

Often, but not nearly often enough, the context of a claim will show which possible meaning a speaker or writer intends. If a mechanic says, "Your trouble is in a cylinder," it might be unclear at first whether she means a wheel cylinder or an engine cylinder. Her meaning will probably become clear, though, as you listen to what else she says and consider the entire context in which she is speaking.

Also, common sense often dictates which of two possible meanings a person has in mind. In the example "He brushed his teeth on the carpet," you would probably be safe to assume that "on the carpet" refers to his location and not to an unusual technique of dental hygiene. So, the claim is perhaps not truly ambiguous. But if you wish to be a clear writer (or aren't fond of people laughing at you), you should try to say exactly what you mean and not rely on common sense to make your meaning clear.

Although ambiguous claims can be a fine source of amusement, they can also furnish clever ways of duping people. In advertising, for example, a

We will briefly discuss the history of American Indians on this campus.

—From a flyer advertising "Conversations on Diversity" at the authors' university

"The Biggest Tax Increase in History"

Every presidential election sees somebody link the opposing candidate to "the biggest tax increase in history." What we have here, however, is an ambiguous comparison. Is the increase the biggest in *absolute dollars* or in *dollars adjusted for inflation*? And notice as well the grouping ambiguity in the claim: One and the same tax increase might not be very large as an increase in the *percentage of an individual's income* that he or she pays to taxes, and yet it might still be the largest increase in terms of the total tax revenues it produces.

Somewhere on this globe, every ten seconds, there is a woman giving birth to a child. She must be found and stopped.

—SAM LEVENSON
(1911–1980)

claim might make wild promises for a product when interpreted one way. But under another interpretation, it may say very little, thus giving the manufacturer a loophole against the charge of false advertising.

Unintentional ambiguity has no place in clear writing. It can defeat the purpose of communication by confusing readers, and it can sometimes make the writer look foolish. You'll find other suggestions for improving your writing elsewhere in this chapter. But we want to note here that, aside from simply learning about the problem, proofreading is probably your best guard against unintentional ambiguity. In fact, failure to proofread is a common problem with student writing. It's a good policy to read your work more than once because there are quite a few things you'll be watching for: coherence, grammar, ambiguity, word choice, vagueness, and so on. You want to make sure you find what you want and *don't* find what you *don't* want.

Exercise 2-4

Rewrite the following claims to remedy problems of ambiguity. Do *not* assume that common sense by itself solves the problem. If the ambiguity is intentional, note this fact, and do not rewrite.

Example

Former professional football player Jim Brown was accused of assaulting a thirty-three-year-old woman with a female accomplice.

Answer

This claim is syntactically ambiguous because it isn't clear what the phrase "with a female accomplice" modifies—Brown, the woman who was attacked, or, however bizarre it might be, the attack itself (he might have thrown the accomplice at the woman). To make it clear that Brown had the accomplice, the phrase "with a female accomplice" should have come right after the word "Brown" in the original claim.

▲ 1. The Raider tackle threw a block at the Giants linebacker.

Misleading Comparisons

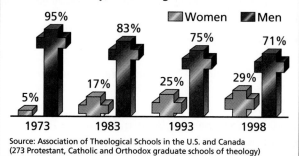

More women of the cloth

Growth in women vs. decline in men studying for a master of divinity degree (usually a precursor to ordained ministry) at theological schools since 1973:

Women   Men

95%
83%
75%
71%
17%   25%   29%
5%

1973   1983   1993   1998

Source: Association of Theological Schools in the U.S. and Canada
(273 Protestant, Catholic and Orthodox graduate schools of theology)

By Anna R. Carey and Quin Tian, USA TODAY

Does this graphic really show that the number of women studying for a master of divinity degree is increasing, whereas the number of men doing so is declining?
Nope.

2. Please close the door behind you.

3. We heard that he informed you of what he said in his letter.

▲ 4. "How Therapy Can Help Torture Victims"

Headline in newspaper

5. Susan sent Ted a cable.

6. They were both exposed to someone who was ill a week ago.

▲ 7. Digital computing began the first time a person counted on his fingers.

8. He was hit by a flying bat.

9. "Tuxedos Cut Ridiculously!"

An ad for formal wear, quoted by Herb Caen

▲ 10. "Police Kill 6 Coyotes After Mauling of Girl"

Headline in newspaper

11. "No shirt, no shoes, no service"

Sign on restaurant door

12. Former governor Pat Brown of California, viewing an area struck by a flood, is said to have remarked, "This is the greatest disaster since I was elected governor."

Quoted by Lou Cannon in the Washington Post

▲ 13. "Besides Lyme disease, two other tick-borne diseases, babesiosis and HGE, are infecting Americans in 30 states, according to recent studies. A single tick can infect people with more than one disease."

Self magazine

14. "Don't freeze your can at the game."

Commercial for Miller beer

15. Volunteer help requested: Come prepared to lift heavy equipment with construction helmet and work overalls.

▲ 16. "GE: We bring good things to life."

Television commercial

17. "Tropicana 100% Pure Florida Squeezed Orange Juice. You can't pick a better juice."

Magazine advertisement

18. "It's biodegradable! So remember, Arm and Hammer laundry detergent gets your wash as clean as can be [pause] without polluting our waters."

Television commercial

▲ 19. If you crave the taste of a real German beer, nothing is better than Dunkelbrau.

20. Independent laboratory tests prove that Houndstooth cleanser gets your bathroom cleaner than any other product.

21. We're going to look at lots this afternoon.

▲ 22. Jordan could write more profound essays.

23. "Two million times a day Americans love to eat, Rice-a-Roni—the San Francisco treat."

Advertisement

24. "New York's first commercial human sperm-bank opened Friday with semen samples from 18 men frozen in a stainless steel tank."

Strunk and White, Elements of Style

▲ 25. She was disturbed when she lay down to nap by a noisy cow.

26. "More than half of expectant mothers suffer heartburn. To minimize symptoms, suggests Donald O. Castell, M.D., of the Graduate Hospital in Philadelphia, avoid big, high-fat meals and don't lie down for three hours after eating."

Self magazine

27. "Abraham Lincoln wrote the Gettysburg address while traveling from Washington to Gettysburg on the back of an envelope."

Richard Lederer

▲ 28. "When Queen Elizabeth exposed herself before her troops, they all shouted 'harrah.'"

Richard Lederer

29. "In one of Shakespeare's famous plays, Hamlet relieves himself in a long soliloquy."

Richard Lederer

30. The two suspects fled the area before the officers' arrival in a white Ford Mustang, being driven by a third male.

31. "To travel to Canada, you will need a birth certificate or a driver's license and other photo ID."

American Automobile Association

▲ 32. "AT&T, for the life of your business."

▲ 33. The teacher of this class might have been a member of the opposite sex.

▲ 34. "Woman gets 9 years for killing 11th husband."

Headline in newspaper

35. "Average hospital costs are now an unprecedented $2,063.04 per day in California. Many primary plans don't pay 20% of that amount."

AARP Group Health Insurance Program advertisement

36. "Drop your trousers here for best results."

Sign in a Bangkok dry cleaner

37. "Visitors are expected to complain at the office between the hours of 9 and 11 A.M. daily."

Sign in an Athens hotel

38. "Order your summers suit. Because is big rush we will execute customers in strict rotation."

Sign in a Rhodes tailor shop

39. "Please do not feed the animals. If you have any suitable food, give it to the guard on duty."

Sign at a Budapest zoo

40. "Our wines leave you with nothing to hope for."

From a Swiss menu

Exercise 2-5

Determine which of the italicized expressions are ambiguous, which are more likely to refer to the members of the class taken as a group, and which are more likely to refer to the members of the class taken individually.

Example

Narcotics are habit-forming.

Answer

In this claim, *narcotics* refers to individual members of the class because it is specific narcotics that are habit-forming. (One does not ordinarily become addicted to the entire class of narcotics.)

▲ 1. *Swedes* eat millions of quarts of yogurt every day.

2. *College professors* make millions of dollars a year.

3. *Our CB radios* can be heard all across the country.

▲ 4. *Students at Pleasant Valley High School* enroll in hundreds of courses each year.

5. *Cowboys* die with their boots on.

6. The *angles of a triangle* add up to 180 degrees.

▲ 7. *The New York Giants* played mediocre football last year.

8. On our airline, *passengers* have their choice of three different meals.

9. On our airline, *passengers* flew fourteen million miles last month without incident.

▲ 10. *Hundreds of people* have ridden in that taxi.

11. *All our cars* are on sale for two hundred dollars over factory invoice.

▲ 12. *Chicagoans* drink more beer than *New Yorkers*.

13. *Power lawn mowers* produce more pollution than *motorcycles*.

14. *The Baltimore Orioles* may make it to the playoffs by the year 2000.

▲ 15. *People* are getting older.

■ *Vague Claims*

Vagueness and ambiguity are often confused. An ambiguous claim has two or more possible meanings, and the context does not make clear which meaning is intended. A **vague claim,** by contrast, has a meaning that is indistinct or imprecise.

The vagueness of a claim is a matter of degree. "He is old" is more vague than "He is at least 70," and "He is at least 70" is more vague than "He is 73 years and 225 days old."

People tend to think that vagueness is something to be avoided. What's to be avoided, however, is *an undesirable degree* of vagueness. Even though a claim may be less precise than it could be, that does not mean that it is less precise than it should be. For example, if you want to move your car and you ask the usher how long you have until the play begins, the reply "Only a minute or two" is less precise than is possible, but it is not less precise than is desirable for your purposes. You don't have time to move your car. But if you are the lead actor in the play and ask the stage manager exactly how much time you have before the curtain goes up, the same answer is probably not precise enough.

The vagueness of some claims is due to the use of "fuzzy" words, words such as "old" and "bald" and "rich," that apply to lots of borderline cases. Bill Gates, for instance, clearly is rich. But is a person who is worth a half million dollars rich? One worth a quarter million? Where does "rich" end and "well-off" begin? Notice, however, that claims with fuzzy words, like vague claims in general, are not always too vague. "Don't take a course from the bald guy in the philosophy department" may well be sufficiently precise to accomplish its intended effect, even though "bald" is not a very precise word.

It's wonderful that we have eight-year-old boys filling sandbags with old women.

—LARRY KING, on attempts to stem Mississippi floods (reported by Larry Engelmann)

But, then, old women filled sandbags with eight-year-old boys, too.

Notice, too, that the absence of fuzzy words does not automatically immunize a claim from undesirable vagueness. "Maria plans to bring her sibling to class on Friday" is probably precise enough, depending on the kind of class we're talking about. But "Maria plans to bring her sibling to the slumber party Friday night" may not be precise enough, especially if it's your teenage daughter who is giving the slumber party and Maria's sibling is her twenty-five-year-old brother. It's not that "sibling" is particularly fuzzy; it's just that in the second of these contexts, the claim in which "sibling" appears is too imprecise for the occasion.

As should be clear by now, it makes little sense to insist that a claim be totally free of vagueness. If we had to be absolutely precise whenever we made a claim, we would say and write very little. The appropriate criticism of a claim is not that it is vague, but that it is too vague relative to what you wish to communicate or know.

■ *Claims That Make Comparisons*

Advertisers and politicians seem to be especially fond of claims like these:

Cut by up to half

Now 25 percent larger

Quietest by far

New and improved

Now better than ever

More than 20 percent richer

Such claims cry out for clarification: What does "up to half" mean? Twenty-five percent larger than what? How far is "by far"? New and improved over what? Better in what way? How much more than 20 percent? And you can ask other questions, too. Remember, though, that the amount of vagueness you can tolerate in a comparative claim depends on your interests and purposes. Knowing that attic insulation will reduce your utility bill "by 15 to 45 percent" may be all it takes for you to know that you should insulate.

Of course, some comparisons may be too vague even to be meaningful: "Have more fun in Arizona." "Gets clothes whiter than white." "Delivers more honest flavor." In other words, have fun in Arizona. Gets clothes white. Can be tasted. On the other hand, "Nothing else is a Pepsi" isn't vague; taken literally, it's necessarily true. Nothing else is a turkey, either. What the claim means, of course, is that no other soft drink tastes as good as Pepsi.

Here are some other questions to ask when you are considering claims that make comparisons:

1. *Is important information missing?* Suppose someone says that only 10 percent of child molestation cases are at the hands of alcoholics. The

Prayer Heals, Vaguely

From a study (reported in Chapter 12) showing that prayer can heal:

> The study found that angioplasty patients with acute heart ailments who were prayed for by seven religious groups did 50 to 100 percent better during their hospital stays than patients who received no prayers.

50 to 100 percent? That's quite a spread, don't you think? Is there a grouping ambiguity here? Are the researchers perhaps looking at the patients individually, rather than collectively? (That is, one patient did 50 percent better—whatever "did better" means—than the patients who received no prayers; another patient did, say, 60 percent better; another 100 percent better, and so on.) At the very least, it's too vague.

person might then say the statement means that alcoholics are less likely to be child molesters than are nonalcoholics because, after all, 90 percent of child molestation cases are at the hands of nonalcoholics. What's missing is important information about the percentage of the general population that is alcoholic. What if, say, only 3 percent of the general population is alcoholic but that 3 percent commits 10 percent of the child molestations? Then it begins to seem that alcoholics are *more* likely than others to molest children.

2. *Is the same standard of comparison being used? Are the same reporting and recording practices being used?* Check to be sure. In February 1994, the unemployment rate suddenly jumped by half a percentage point (a significant jump). Had more people been laid off? Nope. The government had simply changed the way it figured unemployment.

Here's another example. In 1993 the number of people in the United States with AIDS suddenly increased dramatically. Had a new form of the AIDS virus appeared? No; the federal government had expanded the definition of AIDS to include several new indicator conditions. Overnight, 50,000 people were considered to have AIDS who had not been so considered the day before.

3. *Are the items comparable?* Be wary of comparisons between apples and oranges. Don't place undue faith in a comparison between this April's retail business activity and last April's if Easter fell in March in one of the years or the weather was especially cold.

Or suppose someone cites statistics that show you are safer flying than driving because the accident rate for commercial airplane passengers is lower than that for car drivers. What you should note first is that the comparison is between air *passengers* and car *drivers*. A more telling comparison would be between airplane *pilots* and car drivers. And if you are considering going

Cause for Alarm?

According to the National Household Survey on Drug Abuse, cocaine use among Americans twelve to seventeen years of age increased by a whopping 166 percent between 1992 and 1995. Wow, right?

Except that the increase *in absolute terms* was a little less spectacular: In 1992, 0.3 percent of Americans aged twelve to seventeen had used cocaine; in 1995, the percentage was 0.8 percent of that population.

Be wary of comparisons expressed as percentage changes.

Greyhound, an even better comparison would be between commercial airplane pilots and commercial bus drivers. Of course, the claims about the safety of flying versus driving sometimes involve comparisons between air *passengers* and car *passengers*. But such comparisons usually still involve apples and oranges. What you really need to know is the *fatality rate* of air passengers versus that of car passengers in cars *driven by drivers who are as cautious, sober, and skilled as commercial airplane pilots*. After all, that is the kind of person who will be driving you, right?

4. *Is the comparison expressed as an average? Again, be sure important information isn't missing.* The average rainfall in Seattle is about the same as that in Kansas City. But you'll spend more time in rain gear in Seattle because it rains there twice as often as in Kansas City. If Central Valley Components, Inc., reports that average salaries of a majority of its employees have more than doubled over the past ten years, CVC still may not be a great place to work. Perhaps the increases were all due to converting the majority of employees, who worked half time, to full time and firing the rest. Comparisons that involve averages omit details that can be important, simply because they involve averages.

Remember, too, that there are different kinds of averages, or measures of central tendency, as they are also known—the mean, the median, and the mode. Consider, for instance, the average paycheck at Central Valley Components, which happens to be $41,000. That may sound generous enough. But that average is the **mean** (total wages divided by the number of wage earners). The **median** wage, an "average" that is the "halfway" figure (half the employees get more than the figure, and half get less), is $27,000. This average is not so impressive, at least from the perspective of a job seeker. And the **mode,** also an average, the most common rate of pay, is only $17,000. So when someone quotes "the average pay" at CVC, which average is it? At CVC a couple of executives draw fat paychecks, so the mean is a lot higher than the other two figures.

In a class of things in which there are likely to be large or dramatic variations in whatever it is that is being measured, be cautious of figures about an unspecified "average."

Never try to wade a river just because it has an average depth of four feet.

—Martin Friedman

The wrong average can put you under.

Exercise 2-6

The lettered words and phrases that follow each of the following fragments vary in their precision. In each instance, determine which is the most vague and which is the most precise; then rank the remainder in order of vagueness between the two extremes. You will discover when you discuss these exercises in class that they leave some room for disagreement. Further class discussion with input from your instructor will help you and your classmates reach closer agreement about items that prove especially difficult to rank.

Example

Over the past ten years, the median income of wage earners in St. Paul

a. nearly doubled

b. increased substantially

c. increased by 85.5 percent

d. increased by more than 85 percent

Answer

Choice (b) is the most vague because it provides the least information; (c) is the most precise because it provides the most detailed figure. In between, (a) is the second most vague, followed by (d).

▲ 1. Eli and Sarah
   a. decided to sell their house and move
   b. made plans for the future
   c. considered moving
   d. talked
   e. discussed their future
   f. discussed selling their house

2. Manuel
   a. worked in the yard all afternoon
   b. spent the afternoon planting flowers in the yard
   c. was outside all afternoon
   d. spent the afternoon planting salvia alongside his front sidewalk
   e. spent the afternoon in the yard

3. The hurricane that struck South Carolina
   a. caused more than $20 million in property damage
   b. destroyed dozens of structures
   c. was severe and unfortunate
   d. produced no fatalities but caused $25 million in property damage

▲ 4. The recent changes in the tax code
   a. will substantially increase taxes paid by those making more than $200,000 per year
   b. will increase by 4 percent the tax rate for those making more than $200,000 per year; will leave unchanged the tax rate for people making

between $40,000 and $200,000; and will decrease by 2 percent the tax rate
for those making less than $40,000

   c. will make some important changes in who pays what in taxes

   d. are tougher on the rich than the provisions in the previous tax law

   e. raise rates for the wealthy and reduce them for those in the lowest
brackets

5. Smedley is absent because
   a. he's not feeling well
   b. he's under the weather
   c. he has an upset stomach and a fever
   d. he's nauseated and has a fever of more than 103°
   e. he has flulike symptoms

Exercise 2-7

Which of each set of claims is vaguer, if either?

Example

   a. The trees served to make shade for the patio.

   b. He served his country proudly.

Answer

The use of "served" in (b) is more vague than that in (a). We know exactly
what the trees did; we don't know what he did.

▲ 1. a. Rooney served the church his entire life.
     b. Rooney's tennis serve is impossible to return.

   2. a. The window served its purpose.
     b. The window served as an escape hatch.

   3. a. Throughout their marriage, Alfredo served her dinner.
     b. Throughout their marriage, Alfredo served her well.

▲ 4. a. Minta turned her ankle.
     b. Minta turned to religion.

   5. a. These scales will turn on the weight of a hair.
     b. This car will turn on a dime.

   6. a. Fenner's boss turned vicious.
     b. Fenner's boss turned out to be forty-seven.

▲ 7. a. Time to turn the garden.
     b. Time to turn off the sprinkler.

   8. a. The wine turned to vinegar.
     b. The wine turned out to be vinegar.

   9. a. Harper flew around the world.
     b. Harper departed around 3:00 A.M.

▲ 10. a. Clifton turned out the light.
    b. Clifton turned out the vote.

11. a. The glass is full to the brim.
    b. Mrs. Couch has a rather full figure.

12. a. Kathy gave him a full report.
    b. "Oh, no, thank you! I am full."

13. a. Oswald was dealt a full house.
    b. Oswald is not playing with a full deck.

14. a. The pudding sat heavily on Professor Grantley's stomach.
    b. "Set the table, please."

▲ 15. a. Porker set a good example.
    b. Porker set the world record for the 100-meter dash.

Exercise 2-8

Are the italicized words or phrases in each of the following too vague given the implied context? Explain.

▲ 1. Please cook this steak *longer.* It's too rare.

2. If you get ready for bed quickly, Mommy has a *surprise* for you.

3. This program contains language that some viewers may find offensive. It is recommended for *mature* audiences only.

▲ 4. *Turn down the damned noise!* Some people around here want to sleep!

5. Based on our analysis of your eating habits, we recommend that you *lower your consumption of saturated fat.*

6. NOTICE: Hazard Zone. *Small* children not permitted beyond this sign.

▲ 7. SOFAS CLEANED: $48 & *up.* MUST SEE TO GIVE *EXACT* PRICES.

8. And remember, all our mufflers come with a *lifetime guarantee.*

9. CAUTION: To avoid *unsafe levels* of carbon monoxide, do not set the wick on your kerosene stove *too high.*

▲ 10. Uncooked Frosting: Combine 1 unbeaten egg white, ½ cup corn syrup, ½ teaspoon vanilla, and dash salt. Beat with electric mixer until of fluffy spreading consistency. Frost cake. Serve *within a few hours,* or refrigerate.

Exercise 2-9

Read the following passage, paying particular attention to the italicized words and phrases. Determine whether any of these expressions are too vague in the context in which you find them here.

Term paper assignment: "Your paper *should be typed, between eight and twelve pages in length,* and double-spaced. You should *make use of* at least three *sources*. Grading will be based on *organization, use of sources, clarity of expression, quality of reasoning,* and *grammar.*

A *rough draft* is due *before Thanksgiving.* The final version is due *at the end of the semester.*

Exercise 2-10

▲ Read the following passage, paying particular attention to the italicized words and phrases. All of these expressions would be too vague for use in *some* contexts; determine which are and are not too vague in *this* context.

In view of what can happen in twelve months to the fertilizer you apply at any one time, you can see why just one annual application may not be adequate. Here is a guide to timing the *feeding* of some of the more common types of garden flowers.

Feed begonias and fuchsias *frequently* with label-recommended amounts or less frequently with *no more than half* the recommended amount. Feed roses with *label-recommended amounts* as a *new year's growth begins* and as *each bloom period ends.* Feed azaleas, camellias, rhododendrons, and *similar* plants *immediately after bloom* and again *when the nights begin cooling off.* Following these simple instructions can help your flower garden to be as attractive as it can be.

Exercise 2-11

Critique these comparisons, using the questions about comparisons discussed in the text as guides.

Example

You get much better service on Air Atlantic.

Answer

Better than on what? (One term of the comparison is not clear.)
In what way better? (The claim is much too vague to be of much use.)

▲ 1. New improved Morning Muffins! Now with 20 percent more real dairy butter!

2. The average concert musician makes less than a plumber.

3. Major league ballplayers are much better than they were thirty years ago.

▲ 4. What an arid place to live. Why, they had less rain here than in the desert.

5. On the whole, the mood of the country is more conservative than it was in the sixties.

6. Which is better for a person, coffee or tea?

▲ 7. The average GPA of graduating seniors at Wayward State is 3.25, as compared with 2.75 twenty years ago.

8. Women can tolerate more pain than men.

9. Try Duraglow with new sunscreening polymers. Reduces the harmful effect of sun on your car's finish by up to 50 percent.

▲ 10. What a brilliant season! Attendance was up 25 percent over last year.

Exercise 2-12

Critique these comparisons, using the questions discussed in the text as guides.

▲ 1. You've got to be kidding. Paltrow is much superior to Blanchett as an actor.

2. Blondes have more fun.

3. The average chimp is smarter than the average monkey.

▲ 4. The average grade given by Professor Smith is a C. So is the average grade given by Professor Algers.

5. Crime is on the increase. It's up by 160 percent over last year.

6. Classical musicians, on the average, are far more talented than rock musicians.

▲ 7. Long-distance swimming requires much more endurance than long-distance running.

8. "During the monitoring period, the amount of profanity on the networks increased by 45–47 percent over a comparable period from the preceding year. A clear trend toward hard profanity is evident."
   Don Wildmon, founder of the National Federation for Decency

9. "Organizations such as EMILY's List and the Women's Campaign Fund encourage thousands of small contributors to participate, helping to offset the economic power of the special interests. The political system works better when individuals are encouraged to give to campaigns."
   Adapted from the Los Angeles Times

▲ 10. Which is more popular, the movie *Gone with the Wind* or Bing Crosby's version of the song "White Christmas"?

Exercise 2-13

In groups, or individually if your instructor prefers, critique these comparisons, using the questions discussed in the text as guides.

▲ 1. If you worry about the stock market, you have reason. The average stock now has a price-to-earnings ratio of around 25:1.

2. Students are much less motivated than they were when I first began teaching at this university.

3. Offhand, I would say the country is considerably more religious than it was twenty years ago.

And While We're on the Subject of Writing . . .

Don't forget these rules of good style:

1. Avoid clichés like the plague.
2. Be more or less specific.
3. NEVER generalize.
4. The passive voice is to be ignored.
5. Never ever be redundant.
6. Exaggeration is a billion times worse than understatement.
7. Make sure verbs agrees with their subjects.
8. Why use rhetorical questions?
9. Parenthetical remarks (however relevant) are (usually) unnecessary.
10. Proofread carefully to see if you any words out.
11. And it's usually a bad idea to start a sentence with a conjunction.

—This list has been making the rounds on the Internet.

▲ 4. In addition, for the first time since 1960, a majority of Americans now attend church regularly.

5. You really should switch to a high-fiber diet.

6. Hire Ricardo. He's more knowledgeable than Annette.

▲ 7. Why did I give you a lower grade than your roommate? Her paper contained more insights than yours, that's why.

8. Golf is a considerably more demanding sport than tennis.

9. Yes, our prices are higher than they were last year, but you get more value for your dollar.

▲ 10. So, tell me, which do you like more, fried chicken or Volkswagens?

Exercise 2-14 _____

Find two examples of faulty comparisons, and read them to your class. Your instructor may ask other members of the class to critique them.

Persuasive Writing

The primary aim of argumentation and an argumentative essay is to establish something, to support a position on an issue. Good writers, however, write for an audience and hope that their audience will find what they write

Making Ambiguity Work for You

Were you ever asked to write a letter of recommendation for a friend who is, well, incompetent? If you don't want to hurt his or her feelings but also don't want to lie, Robert Thornton of Lehigh University has some ambiguous statements you can use. Here are some examples:

I most enthusiastically recommend this candidate with no qualifications whatsoever.

I am pleased to say that this candidate is a former colleague of mine.

I can assure you that no person would be better for the job.

I would urge you to waste no time in making this candidate an offer of employment.

All in all, I cannot say enough good things about this candidate or recommend the candidate too highly.

In my opinion you will be very fortunate to get this person to work for you.

persuasive. If you are writing for an audience of people who think critically, it is helpful to adhere to these principles:

1. Confine your discussion of an opponent's point of view to issues rather than personal considerations.
2. Anticipate and discuss what opponents might say in criticism of your opinion.
3. When rebutting an opposing viewpoint, avoid being strident or insulting. Don't call opposing arguments absurd or ridiculous.
4. If an opponent's argument is good, concede that it is good.
5. If space or time is limited, be sure to concentrate on the most important considerations. Don't become obsessive about refuting every last criticism of your position.
6. Rebut objections to your position before presenting your own positive case for your side.
7. Present your strongest arguments first.

There is absolutely nothing wrong with trying to make a persuasive case for your position. However, in this book, we place more emphasis on making and recognizing good arguments than simply on devising effective techniques of persuasion. Some people can be persuaded by poor arguments and doubtful claims, and an argumentative essay can be effective as a piece of propaganda even when it is a rational and critical failure. One of the most difficult things you are called upon to do as a critical thinker is to construct and evaluate claims and arguments independently of their power to win a following. The remainder of this book—after a section on writing and diversity—is devoted to this task.

Writing in a Diverse Society

In closing a chapter that deals with writing essays, it seems appropriate to mention how important it is to avoid writing in a manner that reinforces questionable assumptions and attitudes about people's gender, ethnic background, religion, sexual orientation, physical ability or disability, or other characteristics. This isn't just a matter of ethics; it is a matter of clarity and good sense. Careless word choices relative to such characteristics not only are imprecise and inaccurate but also may be viewed as biased even if they were not intended to be, and thus they may diminish the writer's credibility. Worse, using sexist or racist language may distort the writer's own perspective and keep him or her from viewing social issues clearly and objectively.

But language isn't entirely *not* a matter of ethics, either. We are a society that aspires to be just, a society that strives not to withhold its benefits from individuals on the basis of their ethnic or racial background, skin color, religion, gender, or disability. As a people we try to end practices and change or remove institutions that are unjustly discriminatory. Some of these unfair practices and institutions are, unfortunately, embedded in our language.

Some common ways of speaking and writing, for example, assume that "normal" people are all white males. It is still common practice, for instance, to mention a person's race, gender, or ethnic background if the person is *not* a white male, and *not* to do so if the person *is*. Thus, if we are talking about a white male from Ohio, we are apt to say simply, "He is from Ohio." But if the male is Latino, we might tend to mention that fact and say, "He is a Latino from Ohio"—even when the person's ethnic background is irrelevant to whatever we are talking about. This practice assumes that the "normal" person is not Latino and by implication insinuates that if you are, then you are "different" and a deviation from the norm, an outsider.

Of course, it may be relevant to whatever you are writing about to state that this particular man is a Latino from Ohio, and, if so, there is absolutely nothing wrong with writing "He is a Latino from Ohio."

Some language practices are particularly unfair to women. Imagine a conversation among three people, you being one of them. Imagine that the other two talk only to each other. When you speak, they listen politely; but when you are finished, they continue as though you had never spoken. Even though what you say is true and relevant to the discussion, the other two proceed as though you are invisible. Because you are not being taken seriously, you are at a considerable disadvantage. You would have reason to be unhappy.

In an analogous way, women have been far less visible in language than men and have thus been at a disadvantage. Another word for the human race is not "woman," but "man" or "mankind." The generic human has often been referred to as "he." How do you run a project? You *man* it. Who supervises the department or runs the meeting? The chair*man*. Who heads the crew? The fore*man*. Women, like men, can be supervisors, scientists, professors, lawyers, poets, and so forth. But a woman in such a profession is apt to be referred to as a "woman scientist" or "woman supervisor" or as a "lady poet" (or whatever). The implication is that in their primary signification, words like "scientist" and "supervisor" refer to men.

Picture a research scientist to yourself. Got the picture? Is it a picture of a *woman*? No? That's because the standard picture, or stereotype, of a research scientist is a picture of a man. Or, read this sentence: "Research scientists often put their work before their personal lives and neglect their husbands." Were you surprised by the last word? Again, the stereotypical picture of a research scientist is a picture of a man.

A careful and precise writer finds little need to converse in the lazy language of stereotypes, especially those that perpetuate prejudice. As long as the idea prevails that the "normal" research scientist is a man, women who are or who wish to become research scientists will tend to be thought of as out of place. So they must carry an *extra* burden, the burden of showing that they are *not* out of place. That's unfair. If you unthinkingly always write "The research scientist . . . he," you are perpetuating an image that places women at a disadvantage. Some research scientists are men, and some are women. If you wish to make a claim about male research scientists, do so. But if you wish to make a claim about research scientists in general, don't write as though they were all males.

Most often the problem of unintentional gender discrimination arises in connection with pronouns. Note how the use of "he" and "his" in the following two sentences excludes females.

> As *a student* learns to read more critically, *he* usually writes more clearly, too.

> As *a student* learns to read more critically, *his* writing, too, usually becomes clearer.

Obviously, changing "his" and "he" to "her" and "she" would then exclude males. If the writer means to include people of both sexes, one solution is to use two pronouns: for instance, "he or she" (or "his or her").

> As *a student* learns to read more critically, *she or he* usually writes more clearly, too.

> As *a student* learns to read more critically, *his or her* writing, too, usually becomes clearer.

However, a usually less awkward remedy is to change from singular to plural (because plural pronouns do not show gender).

> As *students* learn to read more critically, *they* usually write more clearly, too.

Avoiding Sexist Language

Use the suggestions below to help keep your writing free of sexist language.

Instead of	Use
actress	actor
chairman	chair, chairperson, coordinator, director, head, leader, president, presider
congressman	congressional representative, member of Congress
fathers (of industry, and so on)	founders, innovators, pioneers, trailblazers
housewife	homemaker, woman
man (verb)	operate, serve, staff, tend, work
man (noun)	human beings, individuals, people
man and wife	husband and wife
man-hour	operator-hour, time, work-hour
mankind	human beings, humanity, humankind
manmade	artificial, fabricated, manufactured, synthetic, human-made
manpower	crew, personnel, staff, workers, workforce
newsman	journalist, newscaster, reporter
poetess	poet
policeman	police officer
repairman	repairer
spokesman	representative, spokesperson
statesmanlike	diplomatic, tactful
stewardess	flight attendant
waitress	service person, waiter
weatherman	weather reporter, weathercaster
craftsman	artisan
deliveryman	courier
foreman	supervisor; lead juror
freshman	first-year student
heroine	hero
layman	layperson

You can also refer to any of numerous reference works on bias-free language. See, for example, Marilyn Schwartz, *Guidelines for Bias-Free Writing* (Bloomington: Indiana University Press, 1995).

As *students* learn to read more critically, *their* writing usually becomes clearer, too.

Often the best solution of all is to rephrase the statement entirely, which is almost always possible.

Critical reading leads to clear writing.

Learning to read more critically helps students write more clearly, too.

Frequently a pronoun can simply be deleted or replaced by another word, especially "a" or "the":

The student who develops the habit of reading critically will get more out of *his* college courses.

The student who develops the habit of reading critically will get more out of college courses.

The student who develops the habit of reading critically will get more out of *a* [or *any*] college course.

The rule to follow in all cases is this: Keep writing free of *irrelevant implied evaluation* of gender, race, ethnic background, religion, or any other human attribute.

Recap

An argumentative essay is intended to support a position on some issue. Principles of critical thinking can and should be applied both to essays written by others and to those we ourselves write. Such essays must be soundly organized and clearly written and must truly support the position taken by their author.

Writers can get into trouble in many ways, but you can avoid the most common pitfalls if you are willing to take care. To keep your essay organized, stay focused on your main points, use an outline, and be prepared to revise. To achieve clarity, be sure you clearly define new terms, terms that are especially important to your argument, or terms you are using in an unusual way; and remember to pay attention to the emotive force of your words. Avoid redundancy and unnecessarily complex language. Watch out for ambiguous claims (claims that are insufficiently precise for the purposes at hand). Be especially careful when writing or analyzing claims that make comparisons.

It is acceptable to use persuasive techniques to support a position in an argumentative essay, but don't use them *instead* of reasonable claims and well-constructed arguments. Be careful to avoid irrelevant (and unwarranted) assumptions about people, including those you may overlook because they are embedded in our language.

Remember: If what you want to say is not clear to you, it certainly will remain obscure to your reader.

Having read this chapter and the chapter recap, you should begin to be able to

Check Your Chart

The following are alleged to be actual notations in patients' records. Each has a flagrant ambiguity or other problem. Sometimes the problem interferes with clarity; other times it only produces amusement. Describe what is going on in each case.

- Patient has chest pain if she lies on her left side for over a year.
- She has had no rigors or shaking chills, but her husband states she was very hot in bed last night.
- The patient has been depressed ever since she began seeing me in 1983.
- I will be happy to go into her GI system; she seems ready and anxious.
- The patient is tearful and crying constantly. She also appears to be depressed.
- Discharge status: Alive but without permission. The patient will need disposition, and therefore we will get Dr. Blank to dispose of him.
- Healthy-appearing decrepit 69-year-old male, mentally alert but forgetful.
- The patient refused an autopsy.
- The patient has no past history of suicides.
- The patient expired on the floor uneventfully.
- Patient has left his white blood cells at another hospital.
- Patient was becoming more demented with urinary frequency.
- The patient's past medical history has been remarkably insignificant with only a 40-pound weight gain in the past three days.
- She slipped on the ice and apparently her legs went in separate directions in early December.
- The patient experienced sudden onset of severe shortness of breath with a picture of acute pulmonary edema at home while having sex which gradually deteriorated in the emergency room.
- The patient left the hospital feeling much better except for her original complaints.
- The patient states there is a burning pain in his penis which goes to his feet.

—(These were sent around the Internet after they appeared in a column written by Richard Lederer in the Journal of Court Reporting. Lederer is famous for his collections of remarks taken from student papers, especially papers on historical subjects.)

▲ Create a clear and focused organizational plan for an argumentative essay

▲ Define terms in your essay clearly and choose the words that best suit your purposes

▲ Recognize different types of ambiguity, know the uses and abuses of vagueness, and analyze comparative claims

▲ Make a persuasive case for your positions to an audience of people who can think critically

▲ Avoid sexist, racist, and other inappropriate writing practices

Additional Exercises

Exercise 2-15

Rewrite each of the following claims in gender-neutral language.

Example

We have insufficient manpower to complete the task.

Answer

We have insufficient personnel to complete the task.

▲ 1. A student should choose his major with considerable care.

   2. When a student chooses his major, he must do so carefully.

   3. The true citizen understands his debt to his country.

▲ 4. If a nurse can find nothing wrong with you in her preliminary examination, she will recommend a physician to you. However, in this city the physician will wish to protect himself by having you sign a waiver.

   5. You should expect to be interviewed by a personnel director. You should be cautious when talking to him.

   6. The entrant must indicate that he has read the rules, that he understands them, and that he is willing to abide by them. If he has questions, then he should bring them to the attention of an official, and he will answer them.

▲ 7. A soldier should be prepared to sacrifice his life for his comrades.

   8. If anyone wants a refund, he should apply at the main office and have his identification with him.

   9. The person who has tried our tea knows that it will neither keep him awake nor make him jittery.

▲ 10. If any petitioner is over sixty, he (she) should have completed form E-7.

11. Not everyone has the same beliefs. One person may not wish to put himself on the line, whereas another may welcome the chance to make his view known to his friends.

12. God created man in his own image.

▲ 13. Language is nature's greatest gift to mankind.

14. Of all the animals, the most intelligent is man.

15. The common man prefers peace to war.

▲ 16. The proof must be acceptable to the rational man.

▲ 17. The Founding Fathers believed that all men are created equal.

18. Man's pursuit of happiness has led him to prefer leisure to work.

19. When the individual reaches manhood, he is able to make such decisions for himself.

▲ 20. If an athlete wants to play for the National Football League, he should have a good work ethic.

21. The new city bus service has hired several women drivers.

22. The city is also hiring firemen, policemen, and mailmen; and the city council is planning to elect a new chairman.

23. Harold Vasquez worked for City Hospital as a male nurse.

▲ 24. Most U.S. senators are men.

25. Mr. and Mrs. Macleod joined a club for men and their wives.

26. Mr. Macleod lets his wife work for the city.

▲ 27. Macleod doesn't know it, but Mrs. Macleod is a women's libber.

28. Several coeds have signed up for the seminar.

29. A judge must be sensitive to the atmosphere in his courtroom.

▲ 30. To be a good politician, you have to be a good salesman.

Exercise 2-16 _____

▲ A riddle: A man is walking down the street one day when he suddenly recognizes an old friend whom he has not seen in years walking in his direction with a little girl. They greet each other warmly, and the friend says, "I married since I last saw you, to someone you never met, and this is my daughter, Ellen." The man says to Ellen, "You look just like your mother." How did he know that?

This riddle comes from Janice Moulton's article, "The Myth of the Neutral Man." Discuss why so many people don't get the answer to this riddle straight off.

Writing Exercises

1. Compose a one- to two-page essay in which you respond critically to the position taken and arguments given by the author of "Clean Needles Benefit Society" (page E-15).

2. Recently a district school board adopted a policy that prohibited all "lewd, vulgar or offensive speech by teachers or students in classrooms or at school-sponsored events." Confronted with objections that the policy was too vague, the board revised the part in quotation marks. How would you revise that part? Take about fifteen minutes to write your answer. At the end of the period, your instructor will ask volunteers to read their answers.

3. In exactly twenty-five words define either time or art. One purpose of the exercise is to get you used to the idea of revising and having fun with words. Take eight minutes to write your answer. Your instructor will call on individuals to read their definitions.

Chapter 3

Evaluating Informative Claims

I t's one thing to understand a claim; it's another to accept it. The central task of critical thinking, you'll recall, is determining when it is reasonable to accept claims. In this chapter, we'll consider some general factors that help us determine when claims are acceptable. We'll be concentrating here on claims that are presented without explicit supporting argumentation. Claims offered along with their support—that is, arguments—are discussed in Part 3.

Whether it's a good idea to accept a claim that comes to us without explicit support depends on two things: what the claim is about (its content) and where it comes from (its source). These two general factors are covered in the two numbered portions of the following principle: *Generally speaking, it is reasonable to accept an unsupported claim (1) if it does not conflict with our own observations, our background information, or other credible claims and (2) if it comes from a credible source that offers us no reason to suspect bias.* Keep in mind that the degree of confidence with which we accept a claim can vary quite a bit, from very tentative to thoroughly convinced.

Neither of the categories mentioned is a simple matter, as we'll see, but there is still a lot to be gained from applying a little common sense in both areas. Let's see how the two parts of our principle operate.

Assessing the Content of the Claim

■ Does the Claim Conflict with Our Personal Observations?

Our own observations provide the most reliable source of information about the world. It is therefore only reasonable to be suspicious of any claim that comes into conflict with what we have observed. Let's say that Parker tells

What Americans Find Credible

According to a 1996 *Time*/CNN poll:

- Eighty-two percent of Americans believe in the healing power of personal prayer.
- Seventy-three percent believe that praying for someone else can help cure that person's illness.
- Seventy-seven percent believe that God sometimes intervenes to cure people who have a serious illness.

These poll results, if they reflect reality, say something about some of the claims Americans find credible. One of the things that makes these high percentages interesting is that evidence of the effectiveness of prayer in healing is so difficult to document. More on that subject in Chapter 12.

Moore there will be no mail delivery today. But Moore has just a short while ago seen the mail carrier arrive and deliver the mail. Under such circumstances, obviously, neither Moore, nor you, nor anybody else needs instruction in critical thinking to decide not to accept Parker's claim. Anyone would reject it outright, in fact.

But observations are not infallible, and critical thinkers need to keep this in mind. Our observations may not be reliable if we make them when the lighting is poor or the room is noisy; when we are distracted, emotionally upset, or mentally fatigued; when our senses are impaired; or when our measuring instruments are inexact, temperamental, or inaccurate.

In addition, critical thinkers recognize that people vary in their powers of observation. Some people see and hear better than others and for this reason may be better at making observations than those whose vision or hearing is less acute. Some people have special training or experience that makes them better observers. Customs agents and professional counselors, even those who wear glasses or hearing aids, are better able than most of us to detect signs of nervousness or discomfort in people they observe. Laboratory scientists accustomed to noticing subtle changes in the properties of substances they are investigating are doubtless better than you or I at certain sorts of observations, though perhaps not at certain other sorts. In fact, some professional magicians actually prefer an audience of scientists, believing that such a group is particularly easy to fool.

Our beliefs, hopes, fears, and expectations also affect our observations. Tell someone that a house is infested with rats, and he is likely to believe he sees evidence of rats. Inform someone who believes in ghosts that a house is haunted, and she may well believe she sees evidence of ghosts. At séances staged by the Society for Psychical Research to test the observational powers of people under séance conditions, some observers insist that they see numerous phenomena that simply do not exist. Teachers who are told that

Keeping Up with Politics

Apparently today's college students don't think it's terribly important to keep up with politics. According to the Higher Education Research Institute at UCLA, which conducts a long-standing and fairly comprehensive survey of student attitudes held by hundreds of thousands of first-year students at two- and four-year American colleges and universities, "Keeping up with political affairs" qualifies as a very important or essential life goal to only 25.9 percent of frosh. This compares with 57.8 percent in 1966—way back during the so-called age of turn on and drop out.

According to the survey, more students these days are going to college "to be able to get a better job" (76.9 percent) or "to be able to make more money" (74.6 percent) than "to gain a general education and appreciation of ideas" (62 percent).

Of course, having political and economic data in your background information never hurts when it comes to making money.

A few other interesting findings about many of you who are reading these words:

- A record high of 37.7 percent of new freshmen say they frequently felt "bored in class" during their last year in high school.

- An all-time-high 60.3 percent of students "came late to class" frequently or occasionally, compared with 49.2 percent in 1966.

- Acceptance of casual sex is down, with a record low of 39.6 percent of first-year students agreeing "if two people really like each other, it's all right for them to have sex even if they've known each other for a very short time." This compares with 42.2 percent in 1997 and a high of 51.9 percent in 1987.

- Students starting college in 1998 report the lowest level of beer drinking in the survey's thirty-three-year history. In 1998, 51.6 percent of frosh say they drink beer frequently or occasionally, down from 75.2 percent in 1981. Consumption of wine and liquor has remained steady over the past few years, but the current rate, 54.9 percent, is down substantially from its high, too.

the students in a particular class are brighter than usual are very likely to believe that the work those students produce is better than average, even when it is not.

Maybe most important of all, our personal interests and biases affect our perceptions and the judgments we base on them. We overlook many of the mean and selfish actions of the people we like or love—and when we are infatuated with someone, everything that person does seems wonderful. By contrast, people we detest can hardly do anything that we don't perceive as mean and selfish. If we desperately wish for the success of a project, we are apt to see more evidence for that success than is actually present. On the other hand, if we wish for a project to fail, we are apt to exaggerate flaws that

The Lake Wobegon Effect

In radio humorist and author Garrison Keillor's fictitious town of Lake Wobegon, "the women are strong, the men are good-looking, and all the children are above average." Thus the town lends its name to the utterly reliable tendency of people to believe that they are better than average in a host of different ways. A large majority of the population believe that they are more intelligent than average, more fair-minded, less prejudiced, and better automobile drivers.

A huge study was done not long ago by the Higher Education Research Institute at UCLA on high school seniors, with a million respondents to the survey. Seventy percent of them believed they were above average in leadership ability and only 2 percent thought they were below average. In the category of getting along with others, *fully 100 percent* of those seniors believed they were above average. What's more, in this same category 60 percent believed they were in the top 10 percent, and 25 percent believed they were in the top 1 percent!

People are more than willing to believe—it is probably safe to say *anxious* to believe—that they are better in lots of ways than the objective evidence would indicate. This tendency can make us susceptible to all kinds of trouble, from falling victim to con artists to overestimating our abilities in areas that can cost us our fortunes.

—*Adapted from* THOMAS GILOVICH, How We Know What Isn't So

we see in it or imagine flaws that are not there at all. If a job, chore, or decision is one that we wish to avoid, we tend to draw worst-case implications from it and thus come up with reasons for not doing it. However, if we are predisposed to want to do the job or make the decision, we are more likely to focus on whatever positive consequences it might have.

Finally, the reliability of our observations is no better than the reliability of our memories, except in those cases where we have the means at our disposal to record our observations. And memory, as most of us know, can be deceptive. Critical thinkers are always alert to the possibility that what they remember having observed may not be what they did observe.

But even though firsthand observations are not infallible, they are still the best source of information we have. Any factual report that conflicts with our own direct observations is subject to serious doubt.

Exercise 3-1

Let's compare your powers of observation with those of your classmates. Answer the following sets of questions about your instructor and your classroom. Answer both sets at home, and bring the results to class for checking and comparison with the observations and recollections of others.

Our personal biases often cloud our judgment.

"Surely not guilty. Next case."

Observations of Your Instructor from Your Most Recent Class Meeting

1. Note the following, based on your observations and estimations:
   a. Approximate height _____   c. Eye color _____
   b. Hair color _____

2. Was the instructor wearing . . . ?
   a. a belt _____   d. rings _____
   b. a tie _____   e. a watch _____
   c. glasses _____   f. a hat _____

3. Did the instructor . . . ?
   a. bring a coat to class _____   c. get to class early _____
   b. bring a briefcase _____   d. speak from notes _____

4. State in a sentence the main topic of discussion in the most recent class meeting:

   _____

Observations of Your Classroom

1. Your classroom has how many . . . ?

   a. windows _____   c. chairs or desks _____
   b. doors _____   d. clocks _____

2. What color are the . . . ?

   a. walls _____   b. ceiling _____

3. What kind of floor does the classroom have (e.g., tile, wood, carpet, concrete)? _____

4. Approximately how high is the ceiling? _____

5. Does the room contain . . . ?

   a. a lectern _____   e. pictures on
   b. an overhead projector _____   the walls _____
   c. a chalkboard _____   f. blinds or curtains _____
   d. a movie screen _____

6. As you sit facing the front of the room, which direction of the compass are you facing? _____

Exercise 3-2

Discussion question: Although millions of people have seen professional magicians like David Copperfield and Siegfried and Roy perform in person or on television, it's probably a safe assumption that almost nobody believes they accomplish their feats by means of real magical or supernatural powers—that is, that they somehow "defy" the laws of nature. But, even though they've never had a personal demonstration, a significant portion of the population believe that certain psychics are able to accomplish apparent miracles by exactly such means. How might you explain this difference in belief? (Our answer is given in the *Logical Accessory* instructor's manual.)

Exercise 3-3

1. The text points out that the physical conditions around us can affect our observations. List at least four such conditions.

2. Our own mental state can affect our observations as well. Describe at least three of the ways this can happen, as pointed out in the text.

3. According to the text, it is reasonable to accept an unsupported claim if it does not conflict with (a) _____ , (b) _____ , or (c) _____ , and it comes from a source that is (d) _____ and not (e) _____ .

4. Our most reliable source of information about the world is _____ .

5. The reliability of our observations is no better than the reliability of _____ .

These items were alleged by their Internet source to be true. How much initial plausibility do you give them?

1. In Shakespeare's time, mattresses were secured on bed frames by ropes. When you pulled on the ropes the mattress tightened, making the bed firmer to sleep on. That's where the phrase "Goodnight, sleep tight" came from.
2. In Cleveland, Ohio, it's illegal to catch mice without a hunting license.
3. The first toilet ever seen on television was on *Leave It To Beaver.*
4. The sentence "The quick brown fox jumps over the lazy dog" uses every letter in the alphabet. (It was developed by Western Union to test telex/twx communications.)
5. The only fifteen-letter word that can be spelled without repeating a letter is "uncopyrightable."
6. The only twelve-letter word that is typed with your left hand only is "stewardesses."

7. When opossums are playing possum, they are not playing. They actually pass out from sheer terror.
8. The main library at Indiana University sinks over an inch every year because when it was built, engineers failed to take into account the weight of all the books that would occupy the building.
9. The term "the whole nine yards" came from WWII fighter pilots in the Pacific. When arming their airplanes on the ground, the .50-caliber machine-gun ammo belts measured exactly 27 feet before being loaded into the fuselage. If the pilots fired all their ammo at a target, it got "the whole nine yards."
10. An ostrich's eye is bigger than its brain.
11. The name "Jeep" came from the abbreviation used in the army for the "General Purpose" vehicle, G.P.
12. The cruise liner *Queen Elizabeth II* moves only six inches for each gallon of diesel fuel that it burns.
13. No NFL team that plays its home games in a domed stadium has ever won a Super Bowl.
14. Only one person in two billion will live to be 116 or older.
15. It takes 3,000 cows to supply the NFL with enough leather for a year's supply of footballs.
16. Thirty-five percent of the people who use personal ads for dating are already married.
17. There are an average of 178 sesame seeds on a McDonald's Big Mac bun.
18. The world's termites outweigh the world's humans 10 to 1.
19. When Heinz ketchup leaves the bottle, it travels at a rate of 25 miles per year.
20. Ten percent of the Russian government's income comes from the sale of vodka.
21. On average, 100 people choke to death on ballpoint pens every year.

Conspiracy Theory Web Sites

In case you didn't know it, the Net is teeming with conspiracy theories. Among those we've come across:

- Bill Clinton arranged to have the airplane flown by JFK, Jr., sabotaged to distract people from a remark Hillary Clinton made that turned out to be politically embarrassing to Mrs. Clinton.

- The Third World War was quietly declared by the international elite in 1954 and is being conducted today using biological and other silent weapons, with the object of totally controlling society.

- The Council on Foreign Relations (CFR), a secret society that has tight economic control over Western countries and is run by the Rockefellers and George Bush, is busy setting up a global government. Its plans were discovered by accident when an employee of Boeing Aircraft found details inside an IBM copier he had purchased for scrap parts.

- Top officials of the UN have formed a compact to eliminate individualism, family tradition, religion, and belief in good and evil. One was quoted as saying "No one will enter the New World Order unless he or she will make a pledge to worship Lucifer."

We confess! We are a part of the conspiracy!

■ Does the Claim Conflict with Our Background Information?

Factual claims must always be evaluated against our **background information**—that immense body of justified beliefs that consists of facts we learn from our own direct observations and facts we learn from others. Such information is "background" because we may not be able to specify where we learned it, unlike something we know because we witnessed it this morning. Much of our background information is well confirmed by a variety of sources. Factual claims that conflict with this store of information are usually quite properly dismissed, even if we cannot disprove them through direct observation. We immediately reject the claim "Palm trees grow in abundance near the North Pole," even though we are not in a position to confirm or disprove the statement by direct observation.

Indeed, this is an example of how we usually treat claims when we first encounter them: We begin by assigning them a certain *initial plausibility,* a rough assessment of how credible a claim seems to us. This assessment depends on how consistent the claim is with our background information—how well it "fits" with that information. If it fits very well, we give the claim a high degree of initial plausibility; we lean toward accepting it. If, however, the claim conflicts with our background information, we give it low initial plausibility and lean toward rejecting it unless very strong evidence can be produced on its behalf. The claim "More guitars were sold in the United

Tax the Poor!

How important is it to keep up with current economic and political affairs? Consider this example:

> *Issue:* Should the capital gains tax be cut from 28 percent to 14 percent? (A capital gain is the sale of an asset for more than you paid for it, and the capital gains tax is a tax on your profit.)
> *Con:* The capital gains tax should not be reduced because such a reduction would benefit only the rich.
> *Pro:* The capital gains tax should be reduced because it's an unfairly high tax, not just for the rich but for millions of Americans with modest incomes. More than half the people who pay this tax have incomes of less than $50,000 a year—so it's hardly a tax on the rich.

What isn't stated in this argument is that the capital gains tax rate is a range, with 28 percent at the top. As Michael Gartner of *USA Today* points out, only the wealthiest people pay 28 percent; those with modest incomes generally pay about 15 percent. This little piece of background information can make a big difference in which side you're likely to support in the capital gains tax debate.

States last year than saxophones" fits very well with the background information most of us share, and we would hardly require detailed evidence before accepting it. However, the claim "Charlie's eighty-seven-year-old grandmother swam across Lake Michigan in the middle of winter" cannot command much initial plausibility because of the obvious way it conflicts with our background information about eighty-seven-year-old people, about Lake Michigan, about swimming in cold water, and so on. In fact, short of observing the swim ourselves, it isn't clear just what *could* persuade us to accept such a claim. And even *then* we should consider the likelihood that we're being tricked or fooled by an illusion.

Not every suspicious claim is as outrageous as the one about Charlie's nautical grandmother. Some may not have enough initial plausibility to be immediately acceptable—we may even lean toward rejecting them—but they may still be worth investigating. For example, let's say someone shows up at your door and presents you with what he says is a check for a hundred dollars from an anonymous benefactor. Before you rush right out and spend the hundred, you should, as a critical thinker, consider the possibility that somebody is playing a joke on you. However, even though it's more likely that there is a practical joke going on (practical jokes of this sort are probably more common than actual hundred-dollar surprises, after all), it's worth investigating the possibility that the gift is legitimate. A trip to your bank certainly seems in order. As in most other cases, this is a situation where nothing can take the place of investigating further and gathering more information. Then, depending on how the investigation turns out, one can hope

> There are three types of men in the world. One type learns from books. One type learns from observation. And one type just has to urinate on the electric fence.
> —DR. LAURA SCHLESSINGER (reported by Larry Engelmann)

The authority of experience

Conspiracy Theories

Is the U.S. government conspiring with the United Nations to have the U.N. take over America? Did the CIA and the Mafia engineer John Kennedy's assassination? Did the FBI and the Justice Department stage the Oklahoma City bombing and frame Timothy McVeigh? Did the FBI intentionally start the fire at the Branch Davidian compound near Waco?

We don't know, but in each of these cases the odds are against it. One trouble with conspiracy theories is illustrated by the movie *Wag the Dog,* in which people working for the president fake a war to distract the public's attention from something else. In the movie, the people who know too much have to be silenced (to make sure they won't squeal). The movie does not consider, however, that those who do the silencing also have to be muzzled so they won't let their own secret out; and for the same reason, whoever does the muzzling will have to be silenced as well, and so on, and on.

In our lifetime, most U.S. presidents have been embarrassed by leaks from within their close circle of advisers, leaks they were powerless to prevent. Nixon's advisers, for example, despite their best efforts and having available almost unlimited resources, were unable to keep quiet the Watergate burglary, which initially involved only a few people. Bill Clinton's affair with Monica Lewinsky could not be kept secret despite what may have been monumental efforts on the part of Clinton to prevent it from coming out.

It is difficult to see how a conspiracy requiring the silence of a *large* number of people could be kept quiet for very long. Even the authorship of *Primary Colors,* an anonymously written best-seller presumably about the Clinton presidency, could not be kept secret for very long.

This is not to say it is impossible for a fairly large circle of people to hold their tongues. Various government misdeeds have been kept quiet for a long time.

for a reasonable conclusion to the matter. Unfortunately, there are no neat formulas that can resolve conflicts between what you already believe and new information. Your job as a critical thinker is to trust your background information when considering claims that conflict with that information—that is, claims with low initial plausibility—but at the same time to keep an open mind and realize that further information may cause you to give up a claim you had thought was true. It's a difficult balance, but it's worth getting right.

Finally, keep in mind that you are handicapped in evaluating a factual report on a subject in which you have no background information. This means that the broader your background information, the more likely you are to be able to evaluate any given report effectively. Without some rudimentary knowledge of economics, for example, one is in no position to evaluate claims about the dangers of a large federal deficit; unless we know what cholesterol does in the body, we cannot appreciate the benefits of low-cholesterol foods. The single most effective means of increasing your ability as a critical thinker, regardless of the subject, is to increase what you know: Read widely, converse freely, and develop an inquiring attitude! There is simply no substitute for broad, general knowledge.

Exercise 3-4 _____

This exercise is for written response or, if your instructor indicates, for class-room discussion.

In the text you were asked to consider the claim "Charlie's eighty-seven-year-old grandmother swam across Lake Michigan in the middle of winter." Because of the implausibility of such a claim—that is, because it conflicts with our background information—it is reasonable to reject it. Suppose, however, that instead of just telling us about his grandmother, Charlie brings us a photocopy depicting a page from a Chicago newspaper with a photograph of a person in a wetsuit walking up onto a beach. The caption underneath reads, "Eighty-seven-year-old Grandmother Swims Lake Michigan in January!" Based on this piece of evidence, should a critical thinker decide that the original claim is significantly more likely to be true than if it were backed up only by Charlie's word? Defend your answer.

Assessing the Credibility of the Source

Our guiding principle in evaluating unsupported informational claims re-quires that they come from credible sources. But how do you determine whether a source is credible?

In general, the more knowledgeable a person is about a given subject, the more reason there is to accept what the person says about it. If Parker knows more about automobile mechanics than Moore, for example, you have that much more reason to accept Parker's diagnosis of your car's prob-lem rather than Moore's.

It is sometimes said that observation reports are an exception to this general rule. Observation reports are eyewitness records (or recollections) of events, and that's just what many informative claims are or are based on. Although it may at first appear that one person's observation reports are as acceptable as the next person's, we have seen that this is not true. Suppose two people are both making eyewitness reports; the one who knows more about the subject is the more credible because that person is in general more apt to make accurate and reliable observations about occurrences within his or her sphere of expertise. A musician will generally make more accurate observations than the rest of us about the intonation of the wind instru-ments in last Friday's concert, a carpenter will be more reliable in reporting

Your medical tests are in. You're short, fat, and bald.

—Tom Wilson

For some things, you don't need an expert.

The "Authority" of Experience

. . . a farmer never laid an egg, but he knows more about the process than hens do.

—Henry Darcy Curwen

No one knows more about this mountain than Harry. And it don't dare blow up on him. This goddamned mountain won't blow.

—Harry Truman, 83-year-old owner of a lodge near Mt. St. Helens in Washington, commenting on geologists' predictions that the volcano would erupt. (A few days later it did erupt, killing Harry Truman.)

Through their "observations," the hen and Harry know well enough what it's like to lay an egg or live near a volcano, but these observations are obviously not enough to qualify them as reliable sources about the biological and geological processes involved in egg laying and volcanic eruptions.

on the house being built down the street, and a chef will be better at telling us what herbs and spices were used in a sauce at a new restaurant.

When considering the credibility of the person who asserts a claim, then, an important factor is that person's relevant background information.

Reports from others are subject to "sharpening" and "leveling"* — exaggerating what the speaker thinks is the main point and dropping out or de-emphasizing details that seem peripheral. The result can be a distortion of the story. For example, when you've heard for a while about a person— say, a friend or relative of your college roommate—you sometimes get a distorted picture of that person as *very* smart or *very* sarcastic or *very* good-looking. In other words, you hear more about certain features that your roommate considers trademarks of the person than you do about other features. Typically, when you finally meet the individual, you discover he or she is not really the smartest, the most sarcastic, or the best-looking individual in the world after all but tends to be a lot more like the rest of us than you had been led to believe.

Why do people exaggerate this way? There are probably two reasons. First, we tend to remember things about others that make them different from others rather than things that they have in common with others. That makes their differences play a greater role than their similarities in our image of them. The second reason, which is closely related to the first, is that we want our stories to be interesting to our listeners, and telling about somebody who is *very* this or that is more interesting than telling about somebody who is a lot like the rest of us.

---

*This point comes from Thomas Gilovich, *How We Know What Isn't So,* Chapter 6. We recommend Gilovich's book for a very useful discussion of the psychological mechanisms and confusions that often get in the way of clear thinking.

The Famous Philosophy Exam

We all realize that a story that is secondhand is likely to be more reliable than one that comes from an even more remote source. Stories that are more immediate—that is, more closely related to the speaker or listener—are more interesting than stories about anonymous individuals. And so we often hear tales that are in fact apocryphal but are attributed to actual individuals. Here's an example that we've heard maybe a hundred times: It seems the nephew of a friend (or somebody's cousin, or my former room-mate, or simply this guy) took a philosophy class at UCLA (or the University of North Carolina or Rutgers or Tulane) and the final exam consisted of one word: "Why?" The only person to get an A on the exam, so the story goes, was the one who answered the question with one word: "Because."

We are quite convinced that this story never happened anywhere—and if it did, we trust the instructor did not get tenure and is now in another line of work. But it makes a good story, especially if one is uninformed about philosophy, and the attribution to a specific individual gives it more apparent plausibility than it would otherwise have. And so it gets passed around endlessly.

The point to remember is that a good story may be just that: a good *story* rather than an accurate account.

■ *Experts*

Even if Parker knows more about engines than Moore, he may still not be an expert in the subject. An **expert** is one who, through education, training, or experience, has special knowledge or ability in a subject. The informational claims made by experts are the most reliable of such claims, provided they fall into the area of expertise. This is true even if two conflicting claims are both reports of firsthand observations: If one of the claims is made by an expert and the other by a layperson, there is more reason to accept the claim of the former.

We have to consider the claims of experts carefully, however. We some-times make the mistake of thinking that whatever qualifies someone as an expert in one field automatically qualifies that person in other areas. Even if the intelligence and skill required to become an expert in one field *could* enable someone to become an expert in any field—an assumption that is itself doubtful—possessing the ability to become an expert is entirely different from actually *being* an expert. Thus, informational claims put forth by experts about subjects outside their fields are not automatically more acceptable than claims put forth by nonexperts.

Five main factors establish a person's expertise: (1) education and (2) experience are often the most important factors, followed by (3) accomplishments, (4) reputation, and (5) position, in no particular order. It is not always easy to evaluate the credentials of an expert, and credentials vary

Get a Second Opinion When the Stakes Are High!

The principle we discuss in this chapter is that, *generally speaking,* it's reasonable to accept an unsupported informative claim if it comes from a credible source and does not conflict with your observations, your background information, or other credible claims. We've included the words "generally speaking" because there are exceptions to the principle when there is something very important at stake.

Consider: What if you go to your doctor, and he tells you that the lump on your knee is cancerous and it will be necessary to amputate the leg? Our principle is dependable in most cases, but not in this one. The stakes are high in this case—you could lose a leg—and that makes a big difference. The source (your physician) is credible, and (unless you're an oncologist) the claim probably doesn't conflict with your background information, your observations, or other credible claims; still, the consequences of accepting the doctor's claims are so serious that no reasonable decision can be made without at least a second (and, better, a third) opinion. In short, the principle doesn't always hold when the stakes are high; in such cases the reasonable alternative is to subject the claim to the most stringent tests you can—in the case described, the opinions of other physicians.

considerably from one field to another. Still, there are some useful guidelines worth mentioning.

Education includes but is not strictly limited to formal education—the possession of degrees from established institutions of learning. (Some "doctors" of this and that received their diplomas from mail-order houses that advertise on matchbook covers. The title "doctor" is not automatically a qualification.)

Experience—both the kind and the amount—is an important factor in expertise. Experience is important if it is relevant to the issue at hand, but the mere fact that someone has been on the job for a long time does not automatically make him or her good at it.

Accomplishments are an important indicator of someone's expertise but, once again, only when those accomplishments are directly related to the question at hand. A Nobel Prize winner in physics is not necessarily qualified to speak publicly about toy safety, public school education (even in science), or nuclear proliferation. The last issue may involve physics, it's true, but the political issues are the crucial ones, and they are not taught in physics labs.

A person's reputation always exists only among a particular contingent of people. You may have a strong reputation as a pool player at your local billiards emporium, but that doesn't necessarily put you in the same league as Minnesota Fats. Your friend may consider his friend Mr. Klein the greatest living expert on some particular subject, and he may be right. But you

Of Course He's an Expert. He's My Old Man.

Our assessments of credibility and our willingness to accept the statements of others are often affected by irrelevant considerations. For example, we may treat a claim made by one of our parents as just as credible as a claim made by an expert, even if Mom or Dad is talking about something he or she knows little about. Likewise, people's mannerisms, facial expressions, composure, or even manner of dress can affect how much weight we attach to what they say. And it is well known that all of us unconsciously tend to modify our beliefs to please people who flatter us. The psychological processes that affect the formation of our beliefs are not well understood, but it is clear that logically irrelevant considerations do affect our assessments of credibility and our beliefs in general. That really gives us all the more reason to try to be objective in judging others' credibility.

Psychological research on the effect of "loaded" questions yields a different sort of example of how we modify our beliefs on the basis of irrelevant factors. Loaded questions are questions that make assumptions we have not explicitly agreed to. "Why do you think women are better able to tolerate pain than men?" is an example. The studies show that when asked this type of question, people tend to respond in ways consistent with the assumptions implied in the question—and then modify their system of beliefs to bring it into harmony with their responses. For example, when subjects who have conservative views are asked questions that make liberal assumptions, they tend to answer in ways that are consistent with the implied assumptions. In the process, they become less conservative in their own views.

Rhetoric, which is discussed in Chapters 5 and 6, is effective because unconscious and irrelevant factors affect our beliefs, at least when we are not very careful to think critically.

---

must ask yourself if your friend is in a position to evaluate Mr. Klein's credentials. Most of us have met people who were recommended as experts in some field but who turned out to know little more about that field than we ourselves knew. (Presumably in such cases those doing the recommending knew even less about the subject, or they would not have been so quickly impressed.) By and large, the kind of reputation that counts most is the one a person has among other experts in his or her field of endeavor.

The positions people hold provide an indication of how well *somebody* thinks of them. The director of an important scientific laboratory, the head of an academic department at Harvard, the author of a work consulted by other experts—in each case the position itself is substantial evidence that the individual's opinion on a relevant subject warrants serious attention.

But expertise can be bought. Recall that the last part of our principle cautions us against sources that may be biased on the subject of whatever claim we may be considering. Sometimes a person's position is an indication of what his or her opinion, expert or not, is likely to be. The opinion of a

A Fish Story

Randy Fite of Richards, Texas, boated three bass totaling 22 pounds, 2 ounces Wednesday to take the first-day lead at the Big K-mart BASSMaster Top 150 on Lake Champlain near Burlington, Vt. Shawn Penn of Benton, Ky., is second with 20-15. Rick Lillegard of Atkinson, N.H., had the biggest catch, a 6-pound, 4-ounce largemouth.

—USA Today, 9/16/99

We don't think so. A little arithmetic shows that this story contains either a typographical error or something even worse, because it can't be true as it stands.

lawyer retained by the National Rifle Association, offered at a hearing on firearms and urban violence, should be scrutinized much more carefully (or at least viewed with more skepticism) than that of a witness from an independent firm or agency that has no stake in the outcome of the hearings. It is too easy to lose objectivity where one's interests and concerns are at stake, even if one is *trying* to be objective.

Experts sometimes disagree, especially when the issue is complicated and many different interests are at stake. In these cases, a critical thinker is obliged to suspend judgment about which expert to endorse, unless one expert clearly represents a majority viewpoint among experts in the field or unless one expert can be established as more authoritative or less biased than the others.

Of course, majority opinions sometimes turn out to be incorrect, and even the most authoritative experts occasionally make mistakes. Thus, a claim that you accept because it represents the majority viewpoint or the most authoritative expert may turn out to be thoroughly wrong. Nevertheless, take heart: At the time, you were rationally justified in accepting the majority viewpoint as the most authoritative claim. The reasonable position is one that agrees with the most authoritative opinion but allows for enough open-mindedness to change if the evidence changes.

Finally, do keep in mind that, as noted above, it is sometimes wisest to form no opinion at all. If we are suspicious of our sources and the evidence with which we've been presented, the best course may be to suspend judgment about a claim rather than to accept or reject it prematurely.

You ain't goin' nowhere . . . son. You ought to go back to driving a truck.

—JIM DENNY, Grand Ole Opry manager, firing Elvis Presley after one performance

■ *The News Media*

Our best and most common sources of information about current events are newspapers, newsmagazines, and the electronic media, radio and television. Generally speaking, newspapers offer the broadest coverage of general news, the electronic media the most severely edited and least detailed (with the exception of certain extended-coverage programs and of some Public Broad-

casting System programs); newsmagazines fall somewhere in the middle, although they usually offer extended coverage in their feature stories. News reports, especially those that appear in major metropolitan newspapers (tabloids excepted), national newsmagazines, and television and radio news programs tend to be credible sources of information. This claim is subject to much qualification, though, as we note below.

The breadth of coverage from such news sources is restricted by space, by their audience's interests, and by the concerns of advertisers, pressure groups, and government officials. The accessibility of reliable reports also restricts coverage because governments, corporations, and individuals often simply withhold information.

The location, structure, and headline of a news story in both print and electronic media can be misleading about what is important or essential in the story. The selective presentation of facts is a widely used approach to persuasion in our society, not just by groups with their own agendas but by the supposedly objective news media. There is no guarantee that the media are giving us "the truth, the whole truth, and nothing but the truth." The news they present is subject to shaping by the conscious and unconscious perspectives and purposes of publishers, editors, and owners as well as the groups mentioned above. There are several reasons for this state of affairs, and we'll look at some of the most important ones in the sections that follow.

Because amazing feats are entertaining, the media often plays up amazing events for all (or more than) they are worth, distorts many not-so-amazing events to make them appear extra-ordinary, and sometimes even passes on complete fabrications from unreliable sources.

—THOMAS GILO-VICH, *How We Know What Isn't So*, p. 100)

■ Reporting the News

The popular notion of the hardworking investigative reporter who ferrets out facts, tracks down elusive sources, and badgers people for inside information is largely a creation of the moviemakers. No news service can afford to

"Those are the headlines, and we'll be back in a moment to blow them out of proportion."

devote more than a small portion of its resources to real investigative reporting. Occasionally, this kind of reporting pays off handsomely, as was the case with Bob Woodward and Carl Bernstein's reporting of the Watergate affair in the early 1970s. The *Washington Post* won awards and sold newspapers at a remarkable rate as a result of that series of articles. But such cases are relatively rare. The great bulk of news is *given* to reporters, not dug up after weeks or days or even hours of investigation. Press conferences and press releases are the standard means of getting news from both government and private industry into the mass media. And because spokespeople in neither government nor industry are especially stupid or self-destructive, they tend to produce news items that they and the people they represent *want* to see in the media. Further, because reporters depend on sources in governmental and private institutions to pass items along, reporters who offend those sources are not likely to have them very long. A remarkable example of this interrelationship occurred over a half century ago. Walter Duranty won a Pulitzer Prize for his reporting on the Soviet Union, including his prediction that Josef Stalin would rise to power. According to Eric Newton, in *Crusaders, Scoundrels, Journalists,* "A year later, in a special report in which he purposely lied, he denied the existence of a government-engineered famine that the dictator used to kill 9 million people. He wrote the story to preserve his reputation as a reporter and his access to Soviet officials."

It is important to remember that the news media in this country are private businesses. This situation has both good and bad sides. The good side is that the media are independent of the government, thus making it very difficult for government officials to dictate exactly what gets printed or broadcast. The bad side is that the media, as businesses, have to do whatever

Frank & Ernest reprinted by permission of Newspaper Enterprises Association, Inc.

it takes to make a profit, even if this affects which items make the headlines and which are left out entirely.

Aside from the sources of news, the media must therefore be careful not to overly offend two other powerful constituencies: their advertisers and their audiences. The threat of canceled advertising is difficult to ignore when the great bulk of a business's revenues come from advertising. (This is true of newspapers, which receive more money from advertisers than from those of us who purchase the papers, and of the electronic media as well.) The other constituency, the news-reading and news-watching public, has its own unfortunate effects on the quality of the news that is generally available. The most important of these is the oversimplification of the information presented. Too many people would be bored by a competent explanation of the federal budget deficit or the latest crisis in the Balkans to allow the media to offer such accounts often or in much detail without fearing the loss of their audiences. And, in this context at least, it is not important whether American audiences are unwilling to pay attention to complicated issues or whether they are simply unable to understand them. (In other contexts, however, this distinction is highly significant. Between one-third and one-half of adults in the United States would probably be unable to read and understand the page you're now reading.) Whatever the reason, it is clear that complicated issues are lost on a large percentage of American adults.

Notice the level at which television commercials and political advertisements are pitched. These products are made by highly skilled professionals, who are aware that the projection of an "image" for a candidate or a product goes much further than the coverage of facts and issues. A television network

Springfield, Ore., Pearl, Miss., West Paducah, Ky., Littleton, Colo., Jonesboro, Ark., Edinboro, Pa. School killings certainly appear to be on the increase. Actually, it only seems they are. According to data from the Centers for Disease Control and Prevention, school killings are actually down from the levels reached earlier in the decade and are about what they were in the 1970s.

How Old Did You Say That Intern Was?

Others involved in the scandal have done stupid things, including the president, who in the middle of fighting a court case on sexual harassment, embarked on an affair with a 21-year-old intern.

—*MARY MCGRORY, columnist for the* Washington Post

Ms. McGrory and practically everybody else in the Washington press corps referred to Monica Lewinsky as a twenty-one-year-old intern with whom President Clinton carried on an affair. The truth was that Ms. Lewinsky turned twenty-two in July 1995; when her affair with the president began, she was almost twenty-two and a half. If her age at the time was important enough to report constantly, it was important enough to get correct, but many in the media were still reporting it erroneously over a year later. Some attribute much of the error to the influence of Clinton's political opponents: "That '21-year-old intern' was a year-long invention, a myth created by savvy spinners—and repeated by the obedient press corps over the course of the next thirteen months" (Bob Somerby).

that devotes too much of its prime time to complex social issues in a nonsensationalist way will soon be looking for a new vice president for programming.

■ *Who Listens to the News?*

We come now to another problem with relying on the mass media for a real understanding of events. Much of what goes on in the world, including many of the most important events, is not only complicated but also not very exciting. If a television station advertised that its late news would offer extended coverage of several South American countries' threats to default on loans from United States banks, a considerable part of its audience would either go to bed early or watch reruns on another channel. And they would do so even though loans to other countries have an enormous impact upon the American economy. (How many Americans could explain the connection between Asia recovering from an economic crisis and the danger of a depressed stock market in the United States?) This story is apt to get only fifteen seconds so as not to shortchange the story of the shoot-out at the local convenience store, accompanied by some exciting film. The point is that sensational, unusual, and easily understood subjects can be counted on to receive more attention than the unexciting, the usual, and the complicated, even if the latter are much more important in the long run.

The same kind of mass preference holds for people as well as issues and events. The number of movie stars and celebrities interviewed on talk shows is wildly disproportionate to the effect these individuals have on most of our lives. But they are entertaining in ways that, say, the chairman of the Federal Reserve Board is not.

Tom Toles, from The Buffalo News, 1999. Reprinted by permission.

Although there is nothing wrong with entertainment and our desire to be entertained, the overindulgence of our desire to be entertained comes at the expense of our need to be informed. In the process, we become passive citizens rather than active participants in society. If we count on the media to indulge us, they will give us what we pay for.

A couple of final notes on the news media: Things have changed a lot since we wrote about this topic in the early editions of this book. Competition for readers and viewers has become fierce, and the tactics the media employ to attract an audience have begun to endanger the very idea of an independent, honest, straightforward press. Television in particular has developed new means of coming up with sensational stories, stories that may not have happened at all but for the presence of the television cameras. Here's an example of a nonstory: A film crew in Orlando, Florida, once appeared on the street in front of a house where a dead woman had been discovered. The reporter went on for some time about how police were "dumbfounded" about the cause of death of the woman inside the house and had "put a clamp" on information about the scene. Although the story got several minutes of high-energy coverage, it turned out the woman was in her late sixties and had simply died in bed from a heart attack.

When the decision was made at Time *magazine to darken a cover picture of O. J. Simpson, only the lone nonwhite person in the room objected.*

—Press critic JEFF COHEN, commenting on how the lack of diversity on media staffs can affect the content of the product

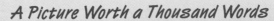

A Picture Worth a Thousand Words

In June 1999, the *New York Times* ran a front-page photograph of Lamar Alexander, at that time a candidate for the Republican presidential nomination. The photograph showed a small group of people listening to remarks by Alexander; about half the people were press photographers. The caption of the photo began, "A Flagging Campaign," and went on to say "Lamar Alexander's campaign has yet to arouse many voters, and his fundraising has fallen below what he hoped."

As it turned out, the scene was not at all as portrayed. In fact, there were at least two hundred people present, but many of them had moved out of the hot sunshine and into some nearby shade. The photograph was made from an angle that did not include any of those so situated.

The next day, the *Times* ran a correction: "A front-page picture yesterday showed Lamar Alexander, a Republican presidential candidate, speaking to a small group of people in Elizabethton, Tenn. In fact, Mr. Alexander was addressing a larger audience—about 200 people, most standing in a shady area just outside camera range. The group had gathered for a town celebration at which Mr. Alexander was invited to speak, and most chose to stand out of the sun, about 20 feet from him. The caption should not have suggested that the scene reflected on his support."

Unfortunately for Mr. Alexander, the correction was much smaller than the original photo and caption, and, more importantly, it was much less prominently displayed, tucked away on page A2.

Evidence of Liberal Bias in Time?

Read My Zipped Lips

George W. Bush opened up about fidelity but has been mute about whether he used cocaine in his youth, thus creating widening ripples of gossip on the matter. Perhaps the candidate doth protest not enough?

—Time, *August 30, 1999*

No one would think this drawing or *Time*'s comment represent straightforward, objective news reporting. Nevertheless, it is a mistake to hold that isolated items like this are evidence of bias on *Time*'s part. To the extent *Time* and other weekly newsmagazines attempt to achieve political neutrality, it is not by deleting points of view from their pages. Rather, it is by trying to balance the number of takes from various political perspectives.

There are some programs that *look* like investigative programs but aren't. Staged dramas like *The X-Files* usually push a point of view that is more gullible than investigative. The large number of cable channels, some with twenty-four hours of news to fill, often have to scrape pretty hard to find anything newsworthy; and when nothing turns up, they may be forced to make something up—or at least make a story out of something that isn't really worth reporting.

The numerous commentators these days are paid to attract attention, not to provide factual information or insight. Thus we see a lot of "in your face" or "scream" television, where people from different parts of the political spectrum spend a half hour yelling at each other and somehow we're supposed to be better informed afterward. Our advice is to be even more skeptical of what you see on television news now than ever before; and there never was reason for too much confidence.

■ *The Internet*

Our newest source of information is the Internet—that amalgamation of electronic lines and connections that allows nearly anyone with a computer and a modem to link up with nearly any other similarly equipped person on the planet. Although the Internet offers great benefits, the information it provides must be evaluated with even *more* caution than information from the print media, radio, or television.

There are basically two kinds of information sources on the Internet. The first consists of commercial and institutional sources; the second, of

In the September 9, 1999, issue of Nature, researchers in physics at Notre Dame developed a method for measuring the average number of links between Web pages. They found that any two randomly chosen Web pages are, on average, only 19 clicks away from one another.

—*Chronicle of Higher Education*

individual and group sites on the World Wide Web. In the first category we include sources like the Lexis-Nexis facility, as well as the online services provided by newsmagazines, large electronic news organizations, and government institutions. The second category includes everything else you'll find on the Web—an amazing assortment of good information, entertainment of widely varying quality, hot tips, advertisements, come-ons, fraudulent offers, outright lies, and even the opportunity to meet the person of your dreams (or your nightmares)! (Rush Limbaugh met his current wife online, and they corresponded via e-mail for a time before meeting in person. On the other hand, in October 1996, a North Carolina man described online to a Pennsylvania woman how, if she would visit him, he would sexually torture her and then kill her. She went, and he did.)

Just as the fact that a claim appears in print or on television doesn't make it true, so it is for claims you run across online. Keep in mind that the information you get from a source is only as good as that source. The Lexis-Nexis information collection is an excellent asset for medium-depth investigation of a topic; it includes information gathered from a wide range of print sources, especially newspapers and magazines, with special collections in areas like the law. But the editorials you turn up there are no more likely to be accurate, fair-minded, or objective than the ones you read in the newspapers—which is where they first appeared anyhow. Remember also

Doing Research on the Web?

According to reliable sources (such as UCLA's Higher Education Research Institute) most college students use the Internet for research. If you are one of these students, you should

- Remember that the slickness of a Web page is no guide to how authoritative it is
- Be wary of Web pages that don't list sources of data
- Remember that Web pages in the organization (.org) domain need even more checking than those in the educational (.edu) and governmental (.gov) domains
- Be especially cautious about data you obtain from an advocacy Web page—one sponsored by an organization whose main purpose is to influence public opinion.

The best guide we know about for evaluating Web resources may be accessed at Widener University's Wolfgram Memorial Library Information Gateway <www2.widener.edu/Wolfgram-Memorial-Library/advoc.htm>. Here are some other useful Web pages for background Information:

- <www.britannica.com> All thirty-two volumes of *Encyclopedia Britannica,* the Cadillac of encyclopedias, are now free and online. Let's hope the *Britannica* people figure out how to make money from this.
- <www.encarta.msn.com/EncartaHome.asp> If you can't get into the *Britannica* Web page
- <www.fac.staff.bucknell.edu/rbeard/diction/html> A web of online dictionaries
- <www.m-w.com/thesaurus.html> Merriam-Webster's *Thesaurus*
- <www.csupomona.edu/~faculty_center/lab> gets you audio help in pronouncing foreign names. This site specializes in Asian names, but links will take you to other languages.

that *any* individual or group can put up a Web site. And they can say *anything* they want to on it. You have about as much reason to believe the claims you find on such sites as you would if they came from any other stranger, except you can't look this one in the eye.

Online Auction Houses   Like everything else on the Internet, it's important to keep a critical eye open when you buy things through an online auction house. It's true that more and more people are buying through the growing number of virtual auction houses, but the number of complaints is growing too. 1999 saw a twentyfold increase in the number of complaints registered

A One-Question Test on Teen Pregnancy

Let's compare your understanding of the problem of teenage pregnancy to that of some other young Americans. What would you say is the percentage of American teenage girls who become pregnant before the age of eighteen?

After you've decided, compare your answer to the numbers in the next box.

with the Federal Trade Commission—a total of over 6,000 for the year, according to an early 2000 story in the Los Angeles Times.

FTC staff attorney Lisa Hone noted that most of the complaints dealt with the nondelivery of goods—you pay and nothing ever shows up. We personally know of a person who bought a computer online and, although it did indeed arrive, it arrived as a box of parts that needed assembly and with no software, not even an operating system. However, there are ways to cut your chances of being the victim of a scam and still take advantage of online bargains. In a moment, we'll remind you of a couple.

Internet auction houses operate in two different ways: some offer direct sales (such as Egghead Auctions, Onsale, and Ubid). Most of the items you'll see for sale at such sites are the result of production overruns or they are rebuilt or refurbished items. The other type of auction is person-to-person (for example, Amazon.com Auctions, EBay, and Yahoo Auctions), which allow independent sellers and buyers to connect with one another. The latter auctions attract both individuals and small businesses as sellers. It shouldn't surprise anyone that person-to-person auctions are riskier. Sellers have been known simply to pocket a buyer's money, sell cheap items that are described as top-of-the-line or otherwise misrepresent their goods, or use shills (accomplices) to artificially drive up the price of items.

Here are a few simple practices that a critical buyer can use to protect him- or herself when buying on the Web:

▲ First, just be cautious. The old saying about a deal that looks too good to be true applies as much here as anywhere else: It probably isn't true.

▲ The auctions themselves offer some information about a seller. Person-to-person auctions provide peer review of sellers by buyers who have dealt with them. For example, eBay offers a "Feedback Rating" where you can read comments from people who have dealt with a seller you're thinking of buying from. Beware, though, because you don't really know who is sending in those words of praise for a seller; they could be his family, his friends, or himself! No system can guarantee that you're dealing with an honest person.

> ### Answers: Teen Pregnancy and Television
> *(If you haven't answered the question in the previous box, do it now, before reading the rest of this box.)*
>
> As it turns out, how young Americans answered the question posed in the previous box seems to have depended on how much they watch television talk shows. According to a study by the Annenberg School for Communication, teens who watch talk shows wildly overestimate the extent of social problems, including the one in question. Viewers who watch talk shows every day, for example, guessed that 55 percent of teen girls become pregnant before the age of eighteen. Those who do not watch such shows overestimated substantially, guessing 30 percent, but this is considerably closer than the TV watchers. The actual rate of pregnancy among teenage girls is only 4 percent.

▲ By all means, pay with a credit card rather than a check or money order. Remember, you're sending money to a complete stranger, and plastic is your best hedge against fraud. You can also use an "escrow" account such as iEscrow, which will charge you about 5 percent but will hold your money until you have received the goods and have indicated satisfaction with them. They then send the money on to the seller. Ebay also has a means of holding your money in escrow.

▲ Keep all documents. Both the original listing and any associated e-mail may be useful later if something goes wrong.

▲ Report problems to the site. If you lose money to a con man, EBay will reimburse you up to $175, Amazon.com up to $250. They'll also kick the con man off their site.

▲ At a minimum, report scams, swindles, and other problems to the FTC (www.ftc.gov). Then the rest of us will have a better idea of how big the problems are.

Remember that nothing's perfect, and things are far from perfect on the Web. It's a wonderful resource, but it also has its spiders lurking in the shadows.

Recap

It is generally reasonable to accept informational claims without supporting arguments provided that they do not conflict with our observations or with our background information—that store of general information we accumulate over the years and on which we constantly depend—and provided that they come from credible, unbiased sources. The less initial plausibility a claim has—that is, the more extraordinary it seems and the less it fits with our background information—the more suspicious of it we should be.

In general, the more knowledgeable someone is in a given field—the more credibility that person has—the more reason there is to accept an informational claim the person makes about subjects in that field. Claims made by experts, those with special knowledge in a subject, are the most reliable, but the claims must pertain to the area of expertise and not conflict with claims made by other experts in the same area. As with any opinion, we should be wary of experts' opinions when we have reason to think they may be biased or subject to prejudicial influence.

Print and electronic media are credible sources in general, but it is necessary to keep an open mind about what we learn from them. Skepticism is even more appropriate when we obtain information from the Internet.

Having read this chapter and the chapter recap, you should be able to

- ▲ Evaluate a claim based on how it accords with your personal observations and background information
- ▲ Evaluate a claim based on the credibility of its source

Additional Exercises

Exercise 3-5

Watch two network television news programs on the same day. Compare the two on the basis of (a) the news stories covered, (b) the amount of air time given to two or three of the major stories, and (c) any difference in the slant of the presentations of a controversial story. From your reading of the chapter, how would you account for the similarities between the two in both the selection and content of the stories?

Exercise 3-6

Listen carefully to a radio or television news broadcast, or read through the national news section of a newspaper, and try to identify as many news items as you can that were supplied by the subjects of the stories rather than found or "dug up" by reporters. Look for phrases that identify the source as a news release, a spokesperson, a representative, and so on.

Exercise 3-7

In groups, decide which is the best answer to each question. Compare your answers with those of other groups and your instructor.

1. "SPACE ALIEN GRAVEYARD FOUND! Scientists who found an extra-terrestrial cemetery in central Africa say the graveyard is at least 500 years old! 'There must be 200 bodies buried there and not a single one of them is human,' Dr. Hugo Schild, the Swiss anthropologist, told reporters." What is the appropriate reaction to this report in the *Weekly World News*?
   a. It's probably true.
   b. It almost certainly is true.
   c. We really need more information to form any judgment at all.
   d. None of these.

2. Is Elvis really dead? Howie thinks not. Reason: He knows three people who claim to have seen Elvis recently. They are certain that it is not a mere Elvis look-alike they have seen. Howie reasons that, since he has absolutely no reason to think the three would lie to him, they must be telling the truth. Elvis must really be alive, he concludes!

   Is Howie's reasoning sound? Explain.

3. VOICE ON TELEPHONE: Mr. Roberts, this is AT&T calling. Have you recently placed several long-distance calls to Lisbon, Portugal?
   MR. ROBERTS: Why, no . . .
   VOICE: This is what we expected. Mr. Roberts, I'm sorry to report that apparently someone has been using your calling card number. However, we are prepared to give you a new number, effective immediately, at no charge to you.
   MR. ROBERTS: Well, fine, I guess . . .
   VOICE: Again let me emphasize that there will be no charge for this service. Now, for authorization, just to make sure that we are calling Mr. Roberts, Mr. Roberts, please state the last four digits of your calling card number, your PIN number, please.

   Question: What should Mr. Roberts, as a critical thinker, do?

4. On Thanksgiving Day 1990, an image said by some to resemble the Virgin Mary was observed in a stained glass window of St. Dominic's Church in Colfax, California. A physicist asked to investigate said the image was caused by sunlight shining through the window and reflecting from a newly installed hanging light fixture. Others said the image was a miracle. Whose explanation is more likely true?
   a. The physicist's
   b. The others'
   c. More information is needed before we can decide which explanation is more likely.

5. It is late at night around the campfire when the campers hear the awful grunting noises in the woods around. They run for their lives! Two campers, after returning the next day, tell others they found huge footprints around the campfire. They are convinced they were attacked by Bigfoot. Which explanation is more likely true?
   a. The campers heard Bigfoot.
   b. The campers heard some animal and are pushing the Bigfoot explanation

to avoid being thought of as chickens, or are just making the story up for unknown reasons.

c. Given this information, we can't tell which explanation is more likely.

6. Megan's aunt says she saw a flying saucer. "I don't tell people about this," Auntie says, "because they'll think I'm making it up. But this really happened. I saw this strange light, and this, well, it wasn't a saucer, exactly, but it was round and big, and it came down and hovered just over my back fence, and my two dogs began whimpering. And then it just, whoosh! It just vanished."

Megan knows her aunt, and Megan knows she doesn't make up stories.

a. She should believe her aunt saw a flying saucer.

b. She should believe her aunt was making the story up.

c. She should believe that her aunt may well have had some unusual experience, but it was probably not a visitation by extraterrestrial beings.

7. According to Dr. Edith Fiore, author of *The Unquiet Dead*, many of your personal problems are really the miseries of a dead soul who has possessed you sometime during your life. "Many people are possessed by earthbound spirits. These are people who have lived and died, but did not go into the afterworld at death. Instead they stayed on Earth and remained just like they were before death, with the fears, pains, weaknesses and other problems that they had when they were alive." She estimates that about 80 percent of her more than 1,000 patients are suffering from the problems brought on by being possessed by spirits of the dead. To tell if you are among the possessed, she advises that you look for such telltale symptoms as low energy levels, character shifts or mood swings, memory problems, poor concentration, weight gain with no obvious cause, and bouts of depression (especially after hospitalization). Which of these reactions is best?

a. Wow! I bet I'm possessed!

b. Well, if a doctor says it's so, it must be so.

c. If these are signs of being possessed, how come she thinks that only 80 percent of her patients are?

d. Too bad there isn't more information available, so we could form a reasonable judgment.

8. **EOC—ENGINE OVERHAUL IN A CAN**

Developed by skilled automotive scientists after years of research and laboratory and road tests! Simply pour one can of EOC into the oil in your crankcase. EOC contains long-chain molecules and special thermoactive metallic alloys that bond with worn engine parts. NO tools needed! NO need to disassemble engine.

Question: Reading this ad, what should you believe?

9. ANCHORAGE, Alaska (AP)—Roped to her twin sons for safety, Joni Phelps inched her way to the top of Mount McKinley. The National Park Service says Phelps, 54, apparently is the first blind woman to scale the 20,300-foot peak.

This report is

a. Probably true

b. Probably false

c. Too sketchy; more information is needed before we can judge

Exercise 3-8

Within each group of observers, are some especially credible or especially not so?

▲ 1. Judging the relative performances of the fighters in a heavyweight boxing match.
   a. the father of one of the fighters
   b. a sportswriter for *Sports Illustrated* magazine
   c. the coach of the American Olympic boxing team
   d. the referee of the fight
   e. a professor of physical education

2. You (or your family or your class) are trying to decide whether you should buy an Apple Macintosh computer or an IBM model. You might consult
   a. a friend who owns either a Macintosh or an IBM
   b. a friend who now owns one of the machines but used to own the other
   c. a dealer for either Macintosh or IBM
   d. a computer column in a big-city newspaper
   e. reviews in computer magazines

▲ 3. The Surgical Practices Committee of Grantville Hospital has documented an unusually high number of problems in connection with tonsillectomies performed by a Dr. Choker. The committee is reviewing her surgical practices. Those present during a tonsillectomy are
   a. Dr. Choker
   b. the surgical proctor from the Surgical Practices Committee
   c. an anesthesiologist
   d. a nurse
   e. a technician

4. The mechanical condition of the used car you are thinking of buying.
   a. the used-car salesperson
   b. the former owner (who we assume is different from the salesperson)
   c. the former owner's mechanic
   d. you
   e. a mechanic from an independent garage

5. A demonstration of psychokinesis (the ability to move objects at a distance by nonphysical means).
   a. a newspaper reporter
   b. a psychologist
   c. a police detective
   d. another psychic
   e. a physicist
   f. a customs agent
   g. a magician

Exercise 3-9

For each of the items below, discuss the credibility and authority of each source relative to the issue in question. Whom would you trust as most reliable on the subject?

▲ 1. Issue: Is Crixivan an effective HIV/AIDS medication?
a. *Consumer Reports*
b. Stadtlander Drug Company (the company that makes Crixivan)
c. the owner of your local health food store
d. the U.S. Food and Drug Administration
e. your local pharmacist

▲ 2. Issue: Should possession of handguns be outlawed?
a. a police chief
b. a representative of the National Rifle Association
c. a U.S. senator
d. the father of a murder victim

▲ 3. Issue: What was the original intent of the Second Amendment to the U.S. Constitution, and does it include permission for every citizen to possess handguns?
a. a representative of the National Rifle Association
b. a justice of the U.S. Supreme Court
c. a constitutional historian
d. a U.S. senator
e. the President of the United States

4. Issue: Is decreasing your intake of dietary fat and cholesterol likely to reduce the level of cholesterol in your blood?
a. *Time* magazine
b. *Runner's World* magazine
c. your physician
d. the National Institutes of Health
e. the *New England Journal of Medicine*

5. Issue: When does a human life begin? (This item is for class discussion.)
a. a lawyer
b. a physician
c. a philosopher
d. a minister
e. you

Exercise 3-10

Each of these items consists of a brief biography of a real or imagined person followed by a list of topics. On the basis of the information in the biography, discuss the credibility and authority of the person described on each of the topics listed.

▲ 1. Jeff Hilgert teaches sociology at the University of Illinois and is the director of its Population Studies Center. He is a graduate of Harvard College, where he received a B.A. in 1965, and of Harvard University, which granted him a Ph.D. in economics in 1968. He taught courses in demography as an assistant professor at UCLA until 1972; then he moved to the sociology department of the University of Nebraska, where he was associate professor and then professor. From 1977 through 1979 he served as acting chief of the Population Trends and Structure Section of the United Nations Population Division. He joined the faculty at the University of Illinois in 1979. He has written books on patterns of world urbanization, the effects of cigarette smoking on international mortality, and demographic trends in India. He is president of the Population Association of America.

Topics

a. The effects of acid rain on humans
b. The possible beneficial effects of requiring sociology courses for all students at the University of Illinois
c. The possible effects of nuclear war on global climate patterns
d. The incidence of poverty among various ethnic groups in the United States
e. The effects of the melting of glaciers on global sea levels
f. The change in death rate for various age groups in all Third World countries between 1960 and 1980
g. The feasibility of a laser-based nuclear defense system
h. Voter participation among religious sects in India
i. Whether the winters are worse in Illinois than in Nebraska

2. Tom Pierce graduated cum laude from Cornell University with a B.S. in biology in 1963. After two years in the Peace Corps, during which he worked on public health projects in Venezuela, he joined Jeffrey Ridenour, a mechanical engineer, and the pair developed a water pump and purification system that is now used in many parts of the world for both regular water supplies and emergency use in disaster-struck areas. Pierce and Ridenour formed a company to manufacture the water systems, and it prospered as they developed smaller versions of the system for private use on boats and motor homes. In 1971, Pierce bought out his partner and expanded research and development in hydraulic systems for forcing oil out of old wells. Under contract with the federal government and several oil firms, Pierce's company was a principal designer and contractor for the Alaskan oil pipeline. He is now a consultant in numerous developing countries as well as chief executive officer and chairman of the board of his own company, and he sits on the boards of directors of several other companies.

Topics

a. The image of the United States in Latin America
b. The long-range effects of the Cuban revolution on South America
c. Fixing a leaky faucet
d. Technology in Third World countries
e. The ecological effects of the Alaskan pipeline

f. Negotiating a contract with the federal government
g. Careers in biology

Exercise 3-11

List as many irrelevant factors as you can think of that people often mistake for signs of a speaker's credibility (for example, the stylishness of his or her clothing).

Exercise 3-12

Watch a debate or panel discussion (e.g., a political debate, a discussion on PBS's *NewsHour with Jim Lehrer*), and decide which participant made the better case for his or her side. When the debate is over, being honest with yourself, list as many irrelevant factors as you can that you think influenced your decision.

Exercise 3-13

1. Members of the U.S. Senate and House of Representatives are subject to a lot of forces as they decide how to cast their votes. They hear from many different people, as well as from their own consciences, as they make their decisions. For this exercise, imagine a member of Congress who is about to vote on a bill that would regulate the manufacture and sale of handguns. Try to identify as many sources as you can that would seek to influence how the member of Congress might vote. (Be as specific as you can.) Which ones do you think he or she should listen to most carefully?

2. Members of Congress have to deal with a wide variety of issues during the course of a year, and no member can become an expert on everything. But a few have nonetheless become much more knowledgeable about some subjects than the average educated person. For this exercise, do some research in the library and try to identify two senators or members of the House who are acknowledged experts in a particular field.

Exercise 3-14

ATTENTION COMMUNITY ALERT
AB 733 WILL MANDATE FLUORIDATION
OF THE MUNICIPAL WATER

Fluoride used in the water system is a highly toxic waste material, a by-product from fertilizer manufacturing. Studies show it will increase hip fractures in senior citizens and has caused death of children. It is associated with cancer, chronic fatigue and other health conditions associated with toxic poisoning.

***This bill will cost taxpayers millions of dollars. Increase tax expenditures at state and federal level. It may increase fees for water service.

Many districts have voted not to fluoridate. However AB 733 will over-rule local control.

***This bill has strong support of the Chemical Industry, AMA, Dental Association and Public Health Association. It is co-sponsored by Willie Brown and Senator Ken Maddy.

***The bill is opposed by California Citizens For Health, National Health Federation, Safe Water Association, Alternative physicians groups, and twelve noble prize winners.

***For information call California Citizens For Health—Frank Cuny at (916) 534-9758. Write letters to Senator TIM LESLIE Capitol Building #4081 Sacramento Ca. 95814 and/or 50 D st.#1 20A, Santa Rosa. His phone there is 576-2771 fax 576-2773. ***Write to Governor Wilson, State Capitol Sacramento Ca. 95814 Phone (916) 445-2841 Fax 445-4633

***Be polite, keep messages short. I am opposed to AB-733 because of 1. Health Danger 2. Increased taxes or rates. 3. against state mandates on local districts.

Which of the claims in the preceding flyer would you be inclined to accept, which to reject, and which to suspend judgment or want further details on? What further details would you want? Discuss your answers with the other members of the class, trying to arrive at a consensus.

Exercise 3-15

From what you know about the nature of each of the following claims and its source, and given your general knowledge, assess whether the claim is one you should accept, reject, or suspend judgment on due to ambiguity, insufficient documentation, vagueness, or subjectivity (e.g., "Tom Cruise is cute"). Compare your judgment with that of your instructor.

▲ 1. "Campbell Soup is hot—and some are getting burned. Just one day after the behemoth of broth reported record profits, Campbell said it would lay off 650 U.S. workers, including 175—or 11% of the work force—at its head-quarters in Camden, New Jersey."

Time

2. [The claim to evaluate is the first one in this passage.] Jackie Haskew taught paganism and devil worship in her fourth-grade classroom in Grand Saline, Texas, at least until she was pressured into resigning by parents of her students. (According to syndicated columnist Nat Hentoff, "At the town meeting on her case, a parent said firmly that she did not want her daughter to read anything that dealt with 'death, abuse, divorce, religion, or any other issue.' ")

3. "By 1893 there were only between 300 and 1,000 buffaloes remaining in the entire country. A few years later, President Theodore Roosevelt persuaded Congress to establish a number of wildlife preserves in which the remaining buffaloes could live without danger. The numbers have increased since, nearly doubling over the past 10 years to 130,000."

Clifford May, in the New York Times Magazine

4. Lee Harvey Oswald, acting alone, was responsible for the death of President John F. Kennedy.

   Conclusion of the Warren Commission on the Assassination of President Kennedy

5. "[N]ewly released documents, including the transcripts of telephone conversations recorded by President Lyndon B. Johnson in November and December 1963, provide for the first time a detailed . . . look at why and how the seven-member Warren [Commission] was put together. Those documents, along with a review of previously released material . . . describe a process designed more to control information than to elicit and expose it."

   "The Truth Was Secondary," Washington Post National Weekly Edition

6. "Short-sighted developers are determined to transform Choco [a large region of northwestern Colombia] from an undisturbed natural treasure to a polluted, industrialized growth center."

   Solicitation letter from the World Wildlife Fund

7. "Frantic parents tell shocked TV audience: space aliens stole our son."

   Weekly World News

▲ 8. "The manufacturer of Sudafed 12-hour capsules issued a nationwide recall of the product Sunday after two people in the state of Washington who had taken the medication died of cyanide poisoning and a third became seriously ill."

   Los Angeles Times

9. "In Canada, smoking in public places, trains, planes or even automobiles is now prohibited by law or by convention. The federal government has banned smoking in all its buildings."

   Reuters

10. "The list of vanishing commodities in Moscow now includes not only sausage and vodka, long rationed, but also potatoes, eggs, bread, and cigarettes."

   National Geographic

11. "Maps, files and compasses were hidden in Monopoly sets and smuggled into World War II German prison camps by MI-5, Britain's counter-intelligence agency, to help British prisoners escape, according to the British manufacturer of the game."

   Associated Press

▲ 12. "Cats that live indoors and use a litter box can live four to five years longer."

   From an advertisement for Jonny Cat litter

13. "A case reported by Borderland Sciences Research Foundation, Vista, California, tells of a man who had attended many of the meetings where a great variety of 'dead' people came and spoke through the body mechanism of Mark Probert to the group of interested persons on a great variety of subjects with questions and answers from 'both sides.' Then this man who had attended meetings while he was in a body, did what is called 'die.' Presumably he had learned 'while in the body' what he might expect at the change

of awareness called death, about which organized religion seems to know little or nothing."

George Robinson, Exploring the Riddle of Reincarnation, undated, no publisher cited

14. "Because of cartilage that begins to accumulate after age thirty, by the time . . . [a] man is seventy his nose has grown a half inch wider and another half inch longer, his earlobes have fattened, and his ears themselves have grown a quarter inch longer. Overall, his head's circumference increases a quarter inch every decade, and not because of his brain, which is shrinking. His head is fatter apparently because, unlike most other bones in the body, the skull seems to thicken with age."

John Tierney (a staff writer for Science '82 magazine), Esquire

15. "Gardenias . . . need ample warmth, ample water, and steady feeding. Though hardy to 20°F or even lower, plants fail to grow and bloom well without summer heat."

The Sunset New Western Garden Book (a best-selling gardening reference in the West)

16. "Exercise will make you feel fitter, but there's no good evidence that it will make you live longer."

Dr. Jordan Tobin, National Institute on Aging

17. "Your bones are still growing until you're 35."

From a national milk ad by the National Fluid Milk Processor Promotion Board

18. "*E. coli* 0157:H7 has become common enough to be the current major cause of acute kidney failure in children." [*E. coli* is a food-borne toxin originally found in the intestines of cows.]

Robin Cook, a physician-turned-novelist. This claim was made by
a fictional expert on food-borne illnesses in the novel Toxin.

19. "A woman employed as a Santa Claus at a Wal-Mart in Kentucky was fired by Wal-Mart when a child pinched her breast and complained to his mother that Santa was a woman. The woman complained to store managers."

Associated Press

▲ 20. "Bill Clinton is the biological son of Jimmy Carter."

A claim alleged to have been made in a suit alleged to
have been filed in the U.S. District Court for the Southern District
of New York. Reported on John E. Schwenkler's home page.

21. "The KGB forged documents to show the CIA was behind the Kennedy assassination. It also 'leaked' the information that the AIDS virus was manufactured by the CIA."

60 Minutes

Writing Exercises

1. Turn to the "Essays for Analysis" section at the back of the book, page E-6, and assess the credibility of the author of Selection 4, "Will Ozone Blob Devour the Earth?" Based on the blurb about the author, say what you can

about his likely expertise and his susceptibility to bias on the subject of the essay.

2. Are our schools doing a bad job educating our kids? Do research in the library or on the Internet to answer this question. Make a list (no more than one page long) of facts that support the claim that our schools are not doing as good a job as they should. Then list facts that support the opposite view (or that rebut the claims of those who say our schools aren't doing a good job). Again, limit yourself to one page. Cite your sources.

    Now think critically about your sources. Are any stronger or weaker than the others? Explain why on a single sheet of paper. Come prepared to read your explanation, along with your list of facts and sources, to the class.

3. Jackson says you should be skeptical of the opinion of someone who stands to profit from your accepting that opinion. Smith disagrees, pointing out that salespeople are apt to know a lot more about products of the type they sell than do most people.

    "Most salespeople are honest, and you can trust them," Smith argues. "Those who aren't don't stay in business long."

    Take about fifteen minutes to defend either Smith or Jackson in a short essay. When everyone is finished, your instructor will collect the essays and read three or more to the class to stimulate a brief discussion. After discussion, can the class come to any agreement about who is correct, Jackson or Smith?

4. Your instructor will survey the class to see how many agree with this claim: The media are biased. Then he or she will ask you to list your reasons for thinking that this claim is true. (If you do not think it is true, list reasons people might have for believing it.) After ten minutes your instructor will collect the lists of reasons and read from several of the lists. Then he or she will give you twenty minutes to defend one of these claims:
    a. The media are biased.
    b. Some of the reasons people have for believing the media are biased are not very good reasons.
    c. It is difficult to say whether the media are biased.

    At the end of the period your instructor may survey the class again to see if anyone's mind has changed, and why.

5. If you haven't done Exercise 4, your instructor will give you twenty minutes to defend an answer to the question, Are the media biased? Put your name on the back of your paper. When everyone is finished, your instructor will collect the papers and redistribute them to the class. In groups of four or five, read the papers that have been given to your group, and decide if any of them are convincing. Do not look at the names of the authors. Your instructor will ask each group to read to the class any essay that the group thinks is convincing.

Chapter 4

Persuasion Through Rhetoric

Brainwashing, drugs, and torture are three effective ways to influence a person's attitudes and behavior. But our concern here is with more subtle attempts to influence, those that are purely linguistic. As explained in previous chapters, one way we try to influence others is through argument—making a case on the basis of evidence and support. Another way is through the use of rhetorical gimmickry, or as it is called in some circumstances, spin. **Rhetoric** usually works through the emotive, or rhetorical, force of words and phrases—the emotional associations they express and elicit, as described in Chapter 2. Have we *reduced* welfare payments or have we *slashed* them? Was the defendant *self-assured* or was he *arrogant*? Are Greenpeace members *devoted* or are they *fanatical*? These phrases are likely to have different impacts on readers by virtue of the differences in their emotive force.

Rhetoric, then, relies on an additional or alternative meaning in a statement to give the statement a certain spin. Consider the difference between the phrases "this original work" and "this so-called original work." We hear a layer of meaning in the second phrase that we do not hear in the first. What difference do you hear between "She still owes over $1,000 on her credit card bill" and "She owes only a little over $1,000 on her credit card bill"?

So rhetoric is used to influence our beliefs and attitudes. Notice, though, that rhetoric often is used as a substitute for argument. Someone who wants to get us to think less of a certain painting may offer an argument to establish its lack of merit—but may also simply use a rhetorical technique, such as referring to the painting as "this so-called painting." In fact, rhetoric can be more effective than argument when it comes to influencing someone's beliefs and attitudes. But it shouldn't be. Rhetoric may be psychologically powerful, but by itself it establishes nothing. If we allow our attitudes and beliefs to be affected by sheer rhetoric, we fall short as critical thinkers.

This isn't to suggest that rhetoric is always used in place of argument. It is also often used *in* argument. The arguments used in political campaigns are often phrased in language that is rhetorically charged. Exactly the same argument without the rhetoric may strike us as weaker somehow, which is precisely why rhetoric is often mixed in with straightforward argument. But an argument's logical force is not enhanced by rhetoric, though its power to persuade psychologically may well be. That's why it is important to recognize rhetoric when we encounter it, so that we do not give more credit to an argument than it is in fact due.

This is not to say, however, that the presence of rhetoric in argument makes the argument weaker. The rhetorical/emotive force of words and sentences does not bear one way or the other on the logical force of the arguments in which they are used. Students in critical-thinking courses sometimes conclude that arguments incorporating rhetorical flourishes are weak and that claims couched in rhetorically charged language are false. Not so. Rhetorically charged language does not in itself offer a reason for accepting a position on an issue, but neither does it give us a reason for rejecting a position.

Furthermore, using **rhetorical devices** is by no means necessarily a bad thing. It would be undesirable—even impossible—to rid our talk and writing of colorful language, except perhaps in the most scientific contexts. It's when rhetoric is used to mislead that we need to be careful.

This being said, let's now consider some common rhetorical techniques. These are designed to give a claim a positive or negative slant regarding a subject, and so they are often known as **slanters,** or "slanting" devices.

Rhetorical Devices and Techniques (Slanters)

■ Euphemisms and Dysphemisms

Language usually offers us a choice of words when we want to say something. Until recently, the term "used car" referred to an automobile that wasn't new, but the trend nowadays is to refer to such a car as "pre-owned." The people who sell such cars, of course, hope that the different terminology will keep potential buyers from thinking about *how* "used" the car might be—maybe it's *used up!* The car dealer's replacement term, "pre-owned," is a **euphemism**—a neutral or positive expression instead of one that carries negative associations. Euphemisms play an important role in affecting our attitudes. People may be less likely to disapprove of an assassination attempt on a foreign leader, for example, if it is referred to as "neutralization." People fighting against the government of a country can be referred to neutrally as "rebels" or "guerrillas," but a person who wants to build support for them may refer to them by the euphemism "freedom fighters." A government is likely to pay a price for initiating a "revenue enhancement," but voters will

Don't Get Carried Away!

Once you're familiar with the ways slanting devices are used to try to influence us, you may be tempted to dismiss a claim or argument *just because it contains strongly slanted language*. But true claims as well as false ones, good reasoning as well as bad, can be couched in such language. Remember that the slanting *itself* gives us no reason to accept a position on an issue; that doesn't mean that there *are* no such reasons. Consider this example, written by someone opposed to using animals for laboratory research:

> It's morally wrong for a person to inflict awful pain on another sensitive creature, one that has done the first no harm. Therefore, the so-called scientists who perform their hideous and sadistic experiments on innocent animals are moral criminals just as were Hitler and his Nazi torturers.

Comment: These are strong words, and you'll find the passage contains more than one of the slanters we've discussed. But before we dismiss the passage as shrill or hysterical, it behooves us as critical thinkers to notice that it contains a piece of reasoning that may shed some light on the issue. A critical thinker who disagrees with the position taken by our speaker should do so because of a problem with the *argument* presented, not because of the strong *language* in which it is presented. (See if you can restate the reasoning in a somewhat less inflammatory way.)

be even quicker to respond negatively to a "tax hike." The U.S. Department of Defense performs the same function it did when it was called the Department of War, but the current name makes for much better public relations.

The opposite of a euphemism is a **dysphemism.** Dysphemisms are used to produce a negative effect on a listener's or reader's attitude toward something or to tone down the positive associations it may have. Whereas "freedom fighter" is a euphemism for "guerrilla" or "rebel," "terrorist" is a dysphemism.

Euphemisms and dysphemisms are often used in deceptive ways or ways that at least hint at deception. All of the examples in the preceding paragraphs are examples of such uses. But euphemisms can at times be helpful and constructive. By allowing us to approach a sensitive subject indirectly—or by skirting it entirely—euphemisms can sometimes prevent hostility from bringing rational discussion to a halt. They can also be a matter of good manners: "Passed on" may be much more appropriate than "dead" if the person to whom you're speaking is recently widowed. Hence, our *purpose* for using euphemisms and dysphemisms determines whether or not those uses are legitimate.

It bears mentioning that some facts just are repellent, and for that reason even neutral reports of them sound horrible. "Lizzy killed her father with an ax" reports a horrible fact about Lizzy, but it does so using neutral

The University of Washington admits that many of its faculty members suffer from what it calls "salary compression." The faculty themselves have a different word for it: "underpaid."

Your Cheatin' Heart?

Here's today's timely if perhaps tasteless question: What's the difference between a rendezvous and an affair?

A rendezvous is what Bill Cosby told Dan Rather he had with the mother of the young woman who allegedly attempted to blackmail him, claiming he was her father.

A rendezvous, not an affair.

"Rendezvous" sounds so much nicer than "affair." So romantic. So pretentious. So French. . . .

An affair is middle class, guilt-ridden and furtive. A rendezvous is urbane, sophisticated and self-conscious. . . .

A rendezvous is twin martinis in the Ritz Bar.

An affair is a couple of Gallo Chardonnays after work.

A rendezvous is the back of a limousine.

An affair is the back of a minivan.

A rendezvous is Bobby Short at the Carlyle.

An affair is Kenny G, wherever. . . .

Basically, though, they boil down to much the same thing.

An affair is what you have if you can't, or won't, admit you're cheating.

A rendezvous is what you have if you can't, or won't, admit you're having an affair.

—From a column by DIANE WHITE

---

language. Neutral reports of unpleasant, evil, or repellent facts do not automatically count as dysphemistic rhetoric.

■ *Persuasive Comparisons, Definitions, and Explanations*

Definitions, explanations, and comparative claims are discussed in other chapters, but the emphasis in those discussions is on uses other than slanting. We want to remind you here that each of these can do quite a bit to prejudice an issue.

Persuasive comparisons are used to express or influence attitudes. You might make the point that a person is of small stature by comparing her to an elf, but you could make the same point in a much less flattering way by comparing her to a gnome or a Chihuahua. You could describe the fairness of a person's complexion by comparing it to either new-fallen snow or whale blubber, but you'd better make the latter comparison out of the individual's hearing. Notice that the argument in the "Don't Get Carried Away!" box on page 119 ends with a persuasive comparison that powerfully underscores the speaker's feelings about the people in question.

Whether you wish to admit it or not, when you approve, morally, of the bombing of foreign targets by the U.S. military, you are approving of acts morally equivalent to the bombing in Oklahoma City.

—A persuasive comparison by TIMOTHY MCVEIGH, Oklahoma City bomber (reported by Larry Engelmann)

—Persuasive comparison. (And a great cartoon.)

Horsey. Reprinted with permission, Seattle Post Intellingencer.

Persuasive definitions smuggle prejudice of one sort or another into the meaning of a term. Abortion and associated issues are fruitful grounds for persuasive definitions. If we define "abortion" as "the murder of an unborn child," there's not much difficulty in arriving at the conclusion that abortion is morally unacceptable. Similarly, "human being" is sometimes taken to refer to any living organism (embryonic, fetal, or post-birth) that is produced by humans. By using this definition, it's easy to conclude that an abortion involves the taking of a human being's life and is thus a homicide. Persuasive definitions used this way are said to "beg the question," a fault discussed in Chapter 6.

Definitions by example can also slant a discussion if the examples are prejudicially chosen. Imagine a liberal who points to a story about a conservative politician found guilty of corruption and says, "*That's* what I mean by conservative politics." Clearly, if we really want to see all sides of an issue, we must be careful to avoid definitions and examples that slant the discussion.

Persuasive explanations are the same kind of slanting device, this time clothed as explanations. "He lost the fight because he's lost his nerve." Is this different from saying that he lost because he was too cautious? Maybe, but maybe not. What isn't in doubt is that the explanation is certainly more unflattering when it's put the former way.

Sex-education classes are like in-home sales parties for abortion.

—PHYLLIS SCHLAFLY, activist

A persuasive comparison.

It was a reasonable proposal. That's why they rejected it.

—Senator BOB DOLE, explaining why the Democrats voted against a Republican proposal

A persuasive explanation.

What Does "Rape" Mean?

In an article for Knight-Ridder Newspapers, Joanne Jacobs of the *San Jose Mercury News* disagreed markedly with the current use of the word "rape" on some university campuses. Notice how language and definition are crucial in the items she reported:

- Swarthmore College's Acquaintance Rape Prevention Workshop training manual asserts that acquaintance rape includes behavior ranging "from crimes legally defined as rape to verbal harassment and inappropriate innuendo."

- A former director of Columbia University's date-rape education program says that "every time you have an act of intercourse there must be explicit consent, and if there's not explicit consent, then it's rape."

- According to Andrea Parrot, a Cornell University psychiatry professor who's written a book on date rape, "Any sexual intercourse without mutual desire is a form of rape." It's as bad to be psychologically pressured into sexual contact by an acquaintance, writes Parrot, as to be "attacked on the streets."

Jacobs believes that defining "rape" in this way trivializes the term and is "a cruel insult to all the women who have been raped" by a man who did more than use "inappropriate innuendos." The definition of "rape" as any sex that goes farther than the woman wants, whether she made that clear or not, is "fantastically broad," she says. She also maintains that this definition makes reports of an epidemic of sexual assault on campuses highly suspect. Were the victims *raped,* she asks, or were they just *nagged*?

Others would say that use of the word "rape" for the behavior described is justified because it draws attention to the seriousness of that behavior.

Note two things: First, the definitions of "rape" given here are *precising definitions,* definitions that serve to specify the applicability of a term. But they are also disguised *persuasive definitions* designed to influence attitudes about a variety of sexual behaviors. Second, notice that "a mere question of semantics" is sometimes a very important matter indeed.

We recently saw a good example of a persuasive explanation in a letter to an editor:

I am a traditional liberal who keeps asking himself, why has there been such a seismic shift in affirmative action? It used to be affirmative action stood for equal opportunity; now it means preferences and quotas. Why the change? It's because the people behind affirmative action aren't for equal rights anymore; they're for handouts.

It's pretty clear that this isn't a dispassionate scholarly explanation but a way of expressing an opinion on and trying to evoke anger at affirmative action policies.

■ *Stereotypes*

When a writer or speaker lumps a group of individuals together under one name or description, especially one that begins with the word "the" (the liberal, the Communist, the right-winger, the Jew, the Catholic, and so on), such labeling generally results in stereotyping. A **stereotype** is a thought or image about a group of people based on little or no evidence. Thinking that women are emotional, that men are insensitive, that lesbians are man haters, that southerners are bigoted, that gay men are effeminate—all count as stereotypes. Language that reduces people or things to categories can induce an audience to accept a claim unthinkingly or to make snap judgments concerning groups of individuals about whom they know little.

Some of the slanters we've already talked about can involve stereotypes. For example, if we use the dysphemism "right-wing extremist" to denigrate a political candidate, we are utilizing a negative stereotype. Commonly, if we link a candidate with a stereotype we like or venerate, we can create a favorable impression of the individual. "Senator Kerry addressed his opponent with all the civility of a gentleman" employs a favorable stereotype, that of a gentleman, in a persuasive comparison.

Our stereotypes come from a great many sources, many from popular literature, and are often supported by a variety of prejudices and group interests. The Native American tribes of the Great Plains were considered noble people by most whites until just before the mid–nineteenth century. But as white people grew more interested in moving them off their lands and as conflicts between the two escalated, popular literature increasingly described Native Americans as subhuman creatures. This stereotype supported

The ventilation fans will be taken care of in a more timely manner because we know that women love to clean.

—General YURI GLAZKOV, expressing the hope that U.S. astronaut Shannon Lucid would clean the fans when she joined the Russians on their space station.

Houston? Are you hearing this, Houston?

the group interests of whites. Conflicts between nations usually produce derogatory stereotypes of the opposition; it is easier to destroy enemies without pangs of conscience if we think of them as less "human" than ourselves. Stereotyping becomes even easier when there are racial differences to exploit.

■ *Innuendo*

The next batch of slanting devices doesn't depend as much on emotional associations as on the manipulation of other features of language. When we communicate with one another, we automatically have certain expectations and make certain assumptions. (For example, when your instructor says, "Everybody passed the exam," she doesn't mean that everybody *in the world* passed the exam. We assume that the scope of the pronoun extends to include only those who took the exam.) These expectations and assumptions help fill in the gaps in our conversations so that we don't have to explain everything we say in minute detail. Because providing such details would be a tedious and probably impossible chore, these underlying conversational factors are crucial to the success of communication.

Consider this statement:

> Ladies and gentlemen, I am proof that there is at least one candidate in this race who does not have a drinking problem.

Notice that this remark does *not* say that any opponent of the speaker *does* have a drinking problem. In fact, the speaker is even allowing for the fact that other candidates may have no such problem by using the words "at least one candidate." But he has still managed to get the idea across that some opponent in the race *may* have a drinking problem. This is an example of **innuendo,** a form of suggestion.

Innuendo from Fox News

We are lucky to have won this action and it's almost miraculous more Americans weren't killed.

—BILL O'REILLY, The O'Reilly Factor, *Fox News Channel, at the end of the bombing siege of Yugoslavia in 1999*

Miraculous that more Americans weren't killed? There weren't any Americans killed at all! 15,000 casualties to none, and the commander in chief just got lucky!

—BOB SOMERBY, The Daily Howler, *commenting on O'Reilly's remark*

O'Reilly's remark is almost too strong to be innuendo, but that's what we'd call it.

Another example, maybe our all-time favorite, is this remark:

I didn't say the meat was tough. I said I didn't see the horse that is usually outside.

—*W. C. Fields*

As you can see, the use of innuendo enables us to insinuate something deprecatory about something or someone without actually saying it. For example, if someone asks you if Ralph is telling the truth, you may reply, "Yes, this time," which would suggest that maybe Ralph doesn't *usually* tell the truth. Or you might say of someone, "She is competent—in many regards," which would insinuate that in some ways she is *not* competent.

Sometimes we condemn somebody with faint praise—that is, by praising a person a small amount when grander praise might be expected, we hint that praise may not really be due at all. This is a kind of innuendo. Imagine, for example, reading a letter of recommendation that says, "Ms. Flotsam has done good work for us, I suppose." Such a letter does not inspire one to want to hire Ms. Flotsam on the spot. Likewise, "She's proved to be useful so far" and "Surprisingly, she seems very astute" manage to speak more evil than good of Ms. Flotsam. Notice, though, that the literal information contained in these remarks is not negative in the least. Innuendo lies between the lines, so to speak.

■ *Loaded Questions*

If you overheard someone ask, "Have you always loved to gamble?" you would naturally assume that the person being questioned did in fact love to gamble. This assumption is independent of whether the person answered yes or no, for it underlies the question itself. Every question rests on assumptions. Even an innocent question like "What time is it?" depends on the

The Mother of All Loaded Questions

Do you admit or deny that when asked on Jan. 17, 1998, in your deposition in the case of Jones vs. Clinton, if you have ever given gifts to Monica Lewinsky, you stated that you did not recall, even though you actually had knowledge of giving her gifts?

One of eighty-one questions submitted to President Clinton by House Judiciary Committee Chairman Henry Hyde, prior to Clinton's impeachment trial before the Senate.

assumptions that the hearer speaks English and has some means of finding out the time, for instance. A **loaded question** is less innocent, however. It rests on one or more *unwarranted* or *unjustified* assumptions. The world's oldest example, "Have you stopped beating your wife?" rests on the assumption that the person asked has in the past beaten his wife. If there is no reason to think that this assumption is true, then the question is a loaded one.

The loaded question is technically a form of innuendo, because it permits us to insinuate the assumption that underlies a question without coming right out and stating that assumption.

■ *Weaselers*

Weaselers are linguistic methods of hedging a bet. When inserted into a claim, they help protect it from criticism by watering it down somewhat, weakening it, and giving the claim's author a way out in case the claim is challenged.

There used to be an advertisement for a brand of sugarless gum that claimed, "three out of four dentists surveyed recommend sugarless gum for their patients who chew gum." This claim contains two weaseling expressions. The first is the word "surveyed." Notice that the ad does not tell us the criteria for choosing the dentists who were surveyed. Were they picked at random, or were only dentists who might not be unfavorably disposed toward gum chewing surveyed? Nothing indicates that the sample of dentists surveyed even remotely represents the general population of dentists. If 99 percent of the dentists in the country disagree with the ad's claim, its authors could still say truthfully that they spoke only about those dentists surveyed, not all dentists.

The second weaseler in the advertisement appears in the last phrase of the claim: "for their patients who chew gum." Notice the ad does not claim that *any* dentist believes sugarless gum chewing is as good for a patient's teeth as no gum chewing at all. Imagine that the actual question posed to the dentists was something like this: "If a patient of yours insisted on chewing gum, would you prefer that he or she chew sugarless gum or gum with sugar in it?" If dentists had to answer that question, they would almost certainly be in favor of sugarless gum. But this is a far cry from recommending that

Overall, Dodge trucks are the most powerful.

—Ad for Dodge

Overall? What does this weaseler mean?

Innocent Until Reported Guilty

In what may be the most obvious indicator of the administration's priorities, Wen Ho Lee and Peter Lee, who reportedly passed the most clamorous secrets, are not even in jail.

—*Boston University professor* ANTHONY CODEVILLA, *in the* Washington Times, *talking about the alleged passing of nuclear secrets to China*

Notice how the weaseler, "reportedly," is used here. We didn't realize that people who have been *reported* to have committed crimes should be put in jail!

any person chew any kind of gum at all. The weaselers allow the advertisement to get away with what *sounds* like an unqualified recommendation for sugarless gum, when in fact nothing in the ad supports such a recommendation.

Let's make up a statistic. Let's say that 98 percent of American doctors believe that aspirin is a contributing cause of Reye's syndrome in children and that the other 2 percent are unconvinced. If we then claim that "some doctors are unconvinced that aspirin is related to Reye's syndrome," we cannot be held accountable for having said something false, even though our claim might be misleading to someone who did not know the complete story. The word "some" has allowed us to weasel the point.

Words that sometimes weasel—such as "perhaps," "possibly," "maybe," and "may be," among others—can be used to produce innuendo, to plant a *suggestion* without actually making a claim that a person can be held to. We can suggest that Berriault is a liar without actually saying so (and thus without making a claim that might be hard to defend) by saying that Berriault *may be* a liar. Or we can say that it is *possible* that Berriault is a liar (which is true of all of us, after all). "*Perhaps* Berriault is a liar" works nicely too. All of these are examples of weaselers used to create innuendo.

Not every use of words and phrases like these is a weaseling one, of course. Words that can weasel can also bring very important qualifications to bear on a claim. The very same word that weasels in one context may not weasel at all in another. For example, a detective considering all the possible angles on a crime who has just heard Smith's account of events may say to an associate, "Of course, it is *possible* that Smith is lying." This need not be a case of weaseling. The detective may simply be exercising due care. Other words and phrases that are sometimes used to weasel can also be used legitimately. Qualifying phrases such as "it is arguable that," "it may well be that," and so on have at least as many appropriate uses as weaseling ones. Others, such as "some would say that," are likely to be weaseling more often than not, but even they can serve an honest purpose in the right context. Our warning, then, is to be watchful when qualifying phrases turn up. Is the speaker or writer adding a reasonable qualification, insinuating a bit

Great Western pays up to 12 percent more interest on checking accounts.

—Radio advertisement

Even aside from the "up to" weaseler, this ad can be deceptive about what interest rate it's promising. Unless you listen carefully, you might think Great Western is paying 12 percent on checking accounts. The presence of the word "more" changes all that, of course. If you're getting 6 percent now and Great Western gives you "up to 12 percent more" than that, they'll be giving you about 6¾ percent—hardly the fortune the ad seems to promise.

of innuendo, or preparing a way out? We can only warn; you need to assess the speaker, the context, and the subject to establish the grounds for the right judgment.

■ *Downplayers*

Downplaying is an attempt to make someone or something look less important or significant. Stereotypes, persuasive comparisons, persuasive explanations, and innuendo can all be used to downplay something. Consider this statement, for example: "Don't mind what Mr. Pierce says in class; he's a liberal." This attempt to downplay Mr. Pierce and whatever views he expresses in class makes use of a stereotype. We can also downplay by careful insertion of certain words or other devices. Let's amend the preceding example like this: "Don't mind what Mr. Pierce says in class; he's just another liberal." Notice how the phrase "just another" denigrates Mr. Pierce's status still further. Words and other devices that serve this function are known as **downplayers.**

Perhaps the words most often used as downplayers are "mere" and "merely." If Kim tells you that she has a yellow belt in the Tibetan martial art of Pujo and that her sister has a mere green belt, you would quite naturally make the assumption that a yellow belt ranks higher than a green belt. We'd probably say that Kim's use of the word "mere" gives you the *right* to make that assumption. Kim has used the word to downplay the significance of her sister's accomplishment. But notice this: It could still be that Kim's sister's belt signifies the higher rank. If called on the matter, Kim might claim that she said "mere" simply because her sister has been practicing the art for much longer and is, after all, not *that* far ahead. Whether Kim has such an out or not, she has used a downplayer to try to diminish her sister's accomplishment.

The term "so-called" is another standard downplayer. We might say, for example, that the woman who made the diagnosis is a "so-called doctor," which downplays her credentials as a physician. Quotation marks can be used to accomplish the same thing:

She got her "degree" from a correspondence school.

Use of quotation marks as a downplayer is different from their use to indicate irony, as in this remark:

John "borrowed" Hank's umbrella, and Hank hasn't seen it since.

The idea in the latter example isn't to downplay John's borrowing the umbrella; it's to indicate that it wasn't really a case of borrowing at all. But the use of quotation marks around the word "degree" and the use of "so-called" in the earlier examples are designed to play down the importance of their subjects. And, like "mere" and "merely," they do it in a fairly unsubtle way.

Many conjunctions—such as "nevertheless," "however," "still," and "but"—can be used to downplay claims that precede them. Such uses are more subtle than the first group of downplayers. Compare the following two versions of what is essentially the same pair of claims:

(1) The leak at the Union Carbide plant in Bhopal, India, was a terrible tragedy, all right; however, we must remember that such pesticide plants are an integral part of the "green revolution" that has helped to feed millions of people.

(2) Although it's true that pesticide plants are an integral part of the "green revolution" that has helped to feed millions of people, it was just such a plant in Bhopal, India, that developed a leak and produced a terrible tragedy.

The differences may not be as obvious as those in the cases of "mere" and "so-called," but the two versions give an indication of where their authors' sympathies lie.

The context of a claim can determine whether it downplays or not. Consider the remark "Claghorn won by only six votes." The word "only" may or may not downplay Claghorn's victory, depending on how thin a six-vote margin is. If ten thousand people voted and Claghorn won by six, then the word "only" seems perfectly appropriate: Claghorn just won by the skin of his teeth. But if the vote was in a committee of, say, twenty, then six is quite a substantial margin (it would be thirteen votes to seven, if everybody voted—almost two-to-one), and applying the word "only" to the result is clearly a slanting device designed to give Claghorn's margin of victory less importance than it deserves.

As mentioned earlier, slanters really can't—and shouldn't—be avoided altogether. They can give our writing flair and interest. What *can* be avoided is being unduly swayed by slanters. Learn to appreciate the effects that subtle and not-so-subtle manipulations of language can have on you. By being aware, you decrease your chances of being taken in unwittingly by a clever writer or speaker.

■ Horse Laugh/Ridicule/Sarcasm

The kind of rhetorical device we call the **horse laugh** includes the use of ridicule of all kinds. Ridicule is a powerful rhetorical tool—most of us really hate being laughed at. So it's important to remember that somebody who simply gets a laugh at the expense of another person's position has not raised any objection to that position.

One may simply laugh outright at a claim ("Send aid to Russia? Har, har, har!"), laugh at another claim that reminds us of the first ("Support the Equal Rights Amendment? Sure, when the ladies start buying the drinks! Ho, ho, ho!"), tell an unrelated joke, use sarcastic language, or simply laugh at the person who is trying to make the point.

The next time you watch a debate, remember that the person who has the funniest lines and who gets the most laughs may be the person who

Sarcasm on the editorial page.

Steve Benson. Reprinted by permission of United Feature Syndicate, Inc.

seems to win the debate, but critical thinkers should be able to see the difference between argumentation on one hand and entertainment on the other. (Notice that we didn't say there's anything *wrong* with entertainment; just like most of you, we wouldn't like to spend *all* of our time watching people be serious, even if they *were* making good arguments.)

■ *Hyperbole*

Hyperbole is extravagant overstatement. A claim that exaggerates for effect is on its way to becoming hyperbole, depending on the strength of its language and the point being made. To describe a hangnail as a serious injury is hyperbole; so is using the word "fascist" to describe parents who insist that their teenager be home by midnight. Not all strong or colorful language is hyperbole, of course. "Oscar Peterson is an unbelievably inventive pianist" is a strong claim, but it is not hyperbolic—it isn't really extravagant. However, "Oscar Peterson is the most inventive musician who ever lived" goes beyond emphasis and crosses over the line into hyperbole. (How could one know that Oscar Peterson is more inventive than, say, Mozart?)

Dysphemisms often involve hyperbole. So do persuasive comparisons. When we use the dysphemisms "traitorous" or "extremist" to describe the secretary of state's recommendations to Congress, we are indulging in hyperbole. If we say that the secretary of state is less well informed than a beet, that's hyperbole in a persuasive comparison. In similar ways, persuasive explanations and definitions can utilize hyperbole.

Hyperbole is also frequently used in ridicule. If it involves exaggeration, a piece of ridicule counts as hyperbole. The example above, saying that the secretary of state is less well informed than a beet, is hyperbole in a persuasive comparison used to ridicule that official.

A claim can be hyperbolic without containing excessively emotive words or phrases. Neither the hangnail nor the Oscar Peterson examples contain such language; in fact, the word "unbelievably" is probably the most emotive word in the two claims about Peterson, and it occurs in the non-hyperbolic claim. But a claim can also be hyperbole as a result of the use of such language. "Parents who are strict about a curfew are fascists" is an example. If the word "mean" were substituted for "fascists," we might find the claim strong or somewhat exaggerated, but we would not call it hyperbole. It's when the colorfulness of language becomes *excessive*—a matter of judgment—that the claim is likely to turn into hyperbole.

Hyperbole is an obvious slanting device, but it can also have more subtle—perhaps unconscious—effects. Even if you reject the exaggeration, you may be moved in the direction of the basic claim. For example, you may reject the claim that Oscar Peterson is the most inventive musician who ever lived, but you may now believe that Oscar Peterson must certainly be an extraordinary musician—otherwise, why would someone make that exaggerated claim about him? Or suppose someone says, "Charlotte Church has the most fabulous voice of any singer around today." Even if you reject the "fabulous" part of the claim, you may still end up thinking Charlotte Church must have a pretty good voice. But be careful: Without support, you have no more reason to accept the milder claims than the wilder ones. Hyperbole can add a persuasive edge to a claim that it doesn't deserve. A hyperbolic claim is pure persuasion.

A feminazi is a woman to whom the most important thing in life is seeing to it that as many abortions as possible are performed.

—Rush Limbaugh

A persuasive definition with hyperbole.

■ Proof Surrogates

An expression used to suggest that there is evidence or authority for a claim without actually citing such evidence or authority is a **proof surrogate.** Sometimes we can't *prove* the claim we're asserting, but we can hint that there *is* proof available, or at least evidence or authority for the claim, without committing ourselves to what that proof, evidence, or authority is. Using "informed sources say" is a favorite way of making a claim more authoritative. Who are the sources? How do we know they're informed? How does the person making the claim know they're informed? "It's obvious that" sometimes precedes a claim that isn't obvious at all. But we may keep our objections to ourselves in the belief that it's obvious to everybody but us, and we don't want to appear more dense than the next guy. "Studies show" crops up in advertising a lot. Note that this phrase tells us nothing about how many studies are involved, how good they are, who did them, or any other important information.

Here's a good example of a proof surrogate from the *Wall Street Journal:*

> We hope politicians on this side of the border are paying close attention to Canada's referendum on Quebec. . . .
>
> Canadians turned out en masse to reject the referendum. There's every reason to believe that voters in the U.S. are just as fed up with the social engineering that lumps people together as groups rather than treating them as individuals.

There *may* be "every reason to believe" that U.S. voters are fed up, but nobody has yet told us what any of those reasons are. Until we hear more evidence, our best bet is to figure that the quotation mainly reflects what the writer at the *Journal* thinks is the proper attitude for U.S. voters. Without a context, such assertions are meaningless.

Remember: Proof surrogates are just that—surrogates. They are not real proof or evidence. Such proof or evidence may exist, but until it has been presented, the claim at issue remains unsupported. At best, proof surrogates suggest sloppy research; at worst, they suggest propaganda.

Exercise 4-1

You will want to recognize when someone is using rhetorical slanting devices to influence your attitudes and beliefs. Let's see if you can identify some of the more common devices. Select the *best* answer.

▲ 1. When President Clinton described alleged phone sex with Monica Lewinsky as "sexual banter," the phrase "banter" might best be viewed as
   a. dysphemism or innuendo
   b. stereotype
   c. hyperbole
   d. downplayer or euphemism
   e. not a slanter

2. "The Republicans weren't interested in finding out the truth about Clinton. They were just engaging in a grotesque orgy of piling on, in order to embarrass the president." In this statement, "grotesque orgy of piling on" might be viewed as
   a. hyperbole
   b. euphemism
   c. downplayer
   d. innuendo
   e. not a slanter

3. In Exercise 2, the phrase "embarrass the president" is best seen as:
   a. hyperbole
   b. dysphemism
   c. innuendo
   d. stereotype
   e. not a slanter

▲ 4. "Isn't the real reason the House of Representatives won't render an impartial finding in any impeachment hearings that it has become a snake pit and war room?" In this statement, the dysphemisms "snake pit and war room" might also be viewed as
   a. downplayer
   b. weaseler
   c. innuendo
   d. persuasive comparison

5. In Exercise 4 the statement *as a whole* might best be viewed as
   a. a loaded question
   b. a persuasive explanation
   c. both a and b
   d. none of the above

6. "'Democrat' equals 'ideologically homeless ex-communist.'"

   Linda Bowles

   This statement might best be viewed as
   a. proof surrogate
   b. weaseler
   c. a persuasive explanation
   d. persuasive definition
   e. none of these

▲ 7. "The obvious truth is bilingual education has been a failure." In this statement, "the obvious truth" might best be viewed as
   a. a proof surrogate
   b. a weaseler
   c. innuendo
   d. dysphemism
   e. not a slanter

8. In Exercise 7, "failure" is
   a. persuasive explanation
   b. innuendo
   c. euphemism
   d. not a slanter

9. "Why do the right-wing zealots want to kill and bury the president? Because clearly they want to have a theocracy in this country, like the one in Iran." In this remark, "kill and bury" might best be viewed as
   a. persuasive explanation
   b. stereotype
   c. weaseler
   d. hyperbole
   e. downplayer

▲ 10. In Exercise 9, "clearly" might best be viewed as
   a. downplayer
   b. innuendo
   c. proof surrogate

> d. weaseler
> e. hyperbole

11. In Exercise 9, "right-wing zealots" might reasonably be viewed as
    a. euphemism
    b. dysphemism
    c. innuendo
    d. persuasive definition
    e. not a slanter

12. The statement in Exercise 9 is or contains a loaded question. (T or F)

▲ 13. The statement in Exercise 9 is or contains a persuasive explanation. (T or F)

14. The statement in Exercise 9 contains a persuasive comparison. (T or F)

15. "You say you are in love with Oscar but are you sure he's right for you? Isn't he a little on the mature side?" This statement contains
    a. loaded question
    b. a euphemism
    c. both A and B
    d. neither A nor B

▲ 16. "Before any more of my tax dollars go to the military, I'd like answers to some questions, such as why are we spending billions of dollars on weapons programs that don't work?" This statement contains an example of
    a. a downplayer
    b. a dysphemism
    c. a proof surrogate
    d. a loaded question
    e. hyperbole and a loaded question

17. "Newt Gingrich had to go [i.e., be removed from office] because the left feared all the political, economic, relational, cultural and moral havoc they had brought upon this nation was about to be reversed. They turned him into a grinch who wanted to starve children and kill the elderly. . . . Some in his own party joined the opposition because they feared being exposed as weak leaders. Newt Gingrich speaks like a leader. How many of the incumbent sissies will come forward and follow his lead, not only with tough talk, but with a bold agenda?"

    Cal Thomas

    This quotation contains an example of
    a. persuasive explanation
    b. hyperbole
    c. dysphemism
    d. all of the above

18. "Can Governor Davis be believed when he says he will fight for the death penalty? You be the judge." This statement contains
    a. dysphemism
    b. proof surrogate
    c. innuendo

      d. hyperbole

      e. no slanters

▲ 19. "Which is it George W. Bush lied about, whether he used cocaine, when he used cocaine, or how much cocaine he used?" This statement contains

      a. hyperbole

      b. dysphemism

      c. loaded question

      d. proof surrogate

      e. no slanter

20. "Studies confirm what everyone knows: smaller classes make kids better learners."

Bill Clinton

    This statement contains:

      a. proof surrogate

      b. weaseler

      c. hyperbole

      d. innuendo

      e. no slanter

21. MAN SELLING HIS CAR: "True, there's a little wear and tear, but what are a few dents?" This statement contains what might best be called

      a. loaded question

      b. innuendo

      c. dysphemism

      d. euphemism

▲ 22. MAN THINKING OF BUYING THE CAR IN EXERCISE 21, TO HIS WIFE: "Okay, okay, so it's got a few miles on it. Still, it may be the only Mustang in the whole country for that price." In this item, "few" and "still" could be said to belong to the same category of slanter. (T or F)

23. In Exercise 22, "it may be" is

      a. a weaseler

      b. a proof surrogate

      c. downplayer

      d. not a slanter

24. Still in Exercise 22, "in the whole country" is an example of

      a. innuendo

      b. hyperbole

      c. a euphemism

      d. none of these

Exercise 4-2

▲ Determine which of the numbered, italicized words and phrases are used as rhetorical devices in the following passage. If the item fits one of the text's categories of rhetorical devices, identify it as such.

The National Rifle Association's campaign *to arm every man, woman, and child in America*[1] received a setback when the President signed the Brady Bill. But the *gun-pushers*[2] know that the bill was only *a small skirmish in a big war*[3] over guns in America. They can give up some of their more *fanatic*[4] positions on such things as *assault weapons*[5] and *cop-killer bullets*[6] and still win on the one that counts: regulation of manufacture and sale of handguns.

Exercise 4-3

▲ Follow the directions for Exercise 4-2.

The *big money guys*[1] who have *smuggled*[2] the Rancho Vecino development onto the November ballot *will stop at nothing to have this town run just exactly as they want.*[3] *It is possible*[4] that Rancho Vecino will cause traffic congestion on the east side of town, and *it's perfectly clear that*[5] the number of houses that will be built will overload the sewer system. *But*[6] a small number of individuals have taken up the fight. *Can the developers be stopped in their desire to wreck our town?*[7]

Exercise 4-4

Follow the directions for Exercise 4-2.

The U.S. Congress has cut off funds for the superconducting supercollider that the *scientific establishment*[1] wanted to build in Texas. The *alleged*[2] virtues of the supercollider proved no match for the *huge*[3] *cost-overruns*[4] that had piled up *like a mountain alongside a sea of red ink.*[5] Despite original estimates of five to six billion dollars, the latest figure was over eleven billion and *growing faster than weeds.*[6]

Exercise 4-5

Identify as many rhetorical devices as you can in the following passage.

Not to contribute to millennial paranoia, but we do live in strange times. The president is being tried over an extramarital affair.

I know, I know. I have heard Republican after Republican solemnly declaim that this is not about sex—it is about the rule of law, about the sanctity of oaths, about the preservation of the nation and about the retention of the very concept of virtue.

I have heard from Republicans that this is about absolute truth vs. relative truth; it is about where we went wrong in the '60s; it is about high crimes and misdemeanors; and it is about the law treating the mightiest in the land with the same impartial hand as the lowliest among us.

I have never listened to so much bilge in my life, and I have covered the Texas Legislature for 30 years. New records for overreaching are set hourly.

—*from a column by Molly Ivins* (Fort Worth Star-Telegram)

Exercise 4-6

Identify each italicized rhetorical technique.

▲ 1. *It may well be* that many faculty members deserve *some sort* of pay increase. *Nevertheless,* it *is clearly true* that others are already amply compensated.

2. What do I think of Hillary Clinton's health care plan? *I think Hillary is an excellent mother for Chelsea.*

3. What do I think of Hillary Clinton's *ignominious* health care plan? The idea of *turning all HMOs over to the government* is pretty absurd, I'd say.

▲ 4. I wouldn't say he copied her answers. I'd say he *adjusted* his own answers.

5. Here we are in the first presidential election of the new century. Once again we find *the extreme wing* of the Republican Party in *clear* control of party machinery.

Exercise 4-7

Identify any rhetorical devices you find in the following selections, and classify those that fit the categories described in the text. For each, explain its function in the passage.

▲ 1. I trust you have seen Janet's file and have noticed the "university" she graduated from.

2. The original goal of the Milosovic government in Belgrade was ethnic cleansing in Kosovo.

3. "National Health Care: The compassion of the IRS and the efficiency of the post office, all at Pentagon prices."

From a letter to the editor, Sacramento Bee

▲ 4. Although it has always had a bad name in the United States, socialism is nothing more or less than democracy in the realm of economics.

5. We'll have to work harder to get Representative Burger reelected because of his little run-in with the law.

▲ 6. It's fair to say that, compared with most people his age, Mr. Beechler is pretty much bald.

7. During World War II, the U.S. government resettled many people of Japanese ancestry in internment camps.

▲ 8. "Overall, I think the gaming industry would be a good thing for our state."

From a letter to the editor, Plains Weekly Record

9. Morgan has decided to run for state senator. I'm sorry to hear that he's decided to become a politician.

10. I'll tell you what capitalism is: Capitalism is Charlie Manson sitting in Folsom Prison for all those murders and still making a bunch of bucks off T-shirts promoted by Guns n' Roses.

Exercise 4-8

Identify any rhetorical devices you find in the following passages, and explain their purposes. Note: some items may contain *no* rhetorical devices.

▲ 1. "If the United States is to meet the technological challenge posed by Japan, Inc., we must rethink the way we do everything from design to manufacture to education to employee relations."

Harper's

2. According to UNICEF reports, several thousand Iraqi children die each month because of the U.N. sanctions.

3. Maybe Professor Lankirshim's research hasn't appeared in the first-class journals as recently as that of some of the other professors in his department; that doesn't necessarily mean his work is going downhill. He's still a fine teacher, if the students I've talked to are to be believed.

▲ 4. "Let's put it this way: People who make contributions to my campaign fund get access. But there's nothing wrong with constituents having access to their representatives, is there?"

Loosely paraphrased from an interview with a California state senator

5. In the 1996 presidential debates, Bill Clinton and Vice President Al Gore consistently referred to their own tax proposal as a "tax plan" and to their opponents' tax proposal as a "tax scheme."

6. "By defending Clinton's 'degrading' of Serbia's military capability, pro-war liberals are degrading their own moral capability to serve as critical watchdogs."

Tom Hayden in The Nation

▲ 7. [*Note:* Dr. Jack Kevorkian was instrumental in assisting a number of terminally ill people in committing suicide during the 1990s.] "We're opening the door to Pandora's Box if we claim that doctors can decide if it's proper for someone to die. We can't have Kevorkians running wild, dealing death to people."

Larry Bunting, assistant prosecutor, Oakland County, Michigan

8. "LOS ANGELES—Marriott Corp. struck out with patriotic food workers at Dodger Stadium when the concession-holder ordered them to keep working instead of standing respectfully during the National Anthem. . . . Concession stand manager Nick Kavadas . . . immediately objected to a Marriott representative.

"Marriott subsequently issued a second memo on the policy. It read: 'Stop all activities while the National Anthem is being played.'

"Mel Clemens, Marriott's general manager at the stadium, said the second memo clarified the first memo."

Associated Press

9. These so-called forfeiture laws are a serious abridgment of a person's constitutional rights. In some states, district attorneys' offices only have to *claim* that a person has committed a drug-related crime to seize the person's assets. So fat-cat DAs can get rich without ever getting around to proving that anybody is guilty of a crime.

▲ 10. "A few years ago, the deficit got so horrendous that even Congress was embarrassed. Faced with this problem, the lawmakers did what they do best. They passed another law."

Abe Mellinkoff, in the San Francisco Chronicle

11. "[U]mpires are baseball's designated grown-ups and, like air-traffic controllers, are paid to handle pressure."

George Will

12. "Last season should have made it clear to the moguls of baseball that something still isn't right with the game—something that transcends residual fan anger from the players' strike. Abundant evidence suggests that baseball still has a long way to go."

Stedman Graham, Inside Sports

▲ 13. "As you know, resolutions [in the California State Assembly] are about as meaningful as getting a Publishers' Clearinghouse letter saying you're a winner."

Greg Lucas, in the San Francisco Chronicle

14. The entire gain in the stock market in the first four months of the year was due to a mere fifty stocks.

15. "The continuing saga of Whitewater . . . reminds me of some people's obsession with UFOs and the Hale-Bopp comet some days."

Hillary Rodham Clinton, quoted in the Los Angeles Times

▲ 16. "The future of the National Basketball Association is Dennis Rodman."

Leigh Montville, in Sports Illustrated

17. "[Supreme Court Justice Antonin] Scalia's ideology is a bald and naked concept called 'Majoritarianism.' Only the rights of the majority are protected."

Letter to the editor of the San Luis Obispo Telegram-Tribune

18. "Mimi Rumpp stopped praying for a winning lottery ticket years ago. . . . But after a doctor told her sister Miki last year that she needed a kidney transplant, the family began praying for a donor. . . . Less than a year later, Miki has a new kidney, courtesy of a bank teller in Napa, Calif., to whom she had told her story. The teller was the donor; she was so moved by Miki's plight she had herself tested and discovered she was a perfect match. Coincidence? Luck? Divine intervention? Rumpp is sure: 'It was a miracle.'"

Newsweek

▲ 19. "We are about to witness an orgy of self-congratulation as the self-appointed environmental experts come out of their yurts, teepees, and grant-maintained academic groves to lecture us over the impending doom of the planet and agree with each other about how it is evil humanity and greedy 'big business' that is responsible for it all."

Tim Worstall, in New Times

20. "In the 1980s, Central America was awash in violence. Tens of thousands of people fled El Salvador and Guatemala as authoritarian governments seeking to stamp out leftist rebels turned to widespread arrests and death squads."

USA Today

Exercise 4-9

Discuss the following stereotypes in class. Do they invoke the same kind of images for everyone? Which are negative and which are positive? How do you think they came to be stereotypes? Is there any "truth" behind them?

1. soccer mom
2. Religious Right
3. dumb blonde
4. tax-and-spend liberal
5. homosexual agenda
6. redneck
7. radical feminist
8. contented housewife
9. computer nerd
10. tomboy
11. interior decorator
12. Washington insider
13. Earth mother
14. frat rat
15. Deadhead

Exercise 4-10

Your instructor will give you three minutes to write down as many positive and negative stereotypes as you can. Are there more positive stereotypes on your list or more negative ones? Why do you suppose that is?

Exercise 4-11

Write two brief paragraphs describing the same person, event, or situation—that is, both paragraphs should have the same informative content. The first paragraph should be written in a *purely* informative way, using language that is as neutral as possible; the second paragraph should be slanted as much as possible either positively or negatively (your choice).

Exercise 4-12

Explain the difference between a weaseler and a downplayer. Find a clear example of each in a newspaper, magazine, or other source. Next find an example of a phrase that is sometimes used as a weaseler or downplayer but that is used appropriately or neutrally in the context of your example.

Exercise 4-13

Explain how persuasive definitions, persuasive comparisons, and persuasive explanations differ. Find an example of each in a newspaper, magazine, or other source.

Advertising

> Advertising [is] the science of arresting the human intelligence long enough to get money from it.
>
> —*Stephen Leacock*

One place rhetorical devices find a happy home in our society is advertising. Ads are used to sell many products other than toasters, television sets, and toilet tissue. They can encourage us to vote for a candidate, agree with a political proposal, take a tour, give up a bad habit, or join the army. They can also be used to make announcements (for instance, about job openings, lectures, concerts, or the recall of defective automobiles) or to create favorable climates of opinion (for example, toward labor unions or offshore oil drilling).

Advertising firms understand our fears and desires at least as well as we understand them ourselves, and they have at their disposal the expertise to exploit them.* Such firms employ trained psychologists and some of the world's most creative artists and use the most sophisticated and well-researched theories about the motivation of human behavior. Maybe most important, they can afford to spend whatever is necessary to get each detail of an advertisement exactly right. (On a per-minute basis, television ads are the most expensively produced pieces that appear on your tube.) A good ad is a work of art, a masterful blend of word and image often composed in accordance with the exacting standards of artistic and scientific genius (some ads, of course, are just plain silly). Can untrained lay people even hope to evaluate such psychological and artistic masterpieces intelligently?

Fortunately, it is not necessary to understand the deep psychology of an advertisement to evaluate it in the way that's most important to us. When confronted with an ad, we should ask simply: Does this ad give us a good reason to buy this product? And the answer, in general terms, can be simply put: Because the only good reason to buy anything in the first place is to improve our lives, the ad justifies a purchase only if it establishes that we'd be better off with the product than without it (or that we'd be better off with the product than with the money we would trade for it).

However, do we always know when we'll be better off with a product than without it? Do we really want, or need, a videocassette rewinder or an exercise bike? Do people even recognize "better taste" in a cigarette? Advertisers spend vast sums creating within us new desires and fears—and hence a need to improve our lives by satisfying those desires or eliminating those fears through the purchase of advertised products. They are often successful, and we find ourselves needing something we might not have known existed before. That others can instill in us through word and image a desire for something we did not previously desire may be a lamentable fact, but it *is*

---

*For an excellent treatment of this and related subjects, we recommend *Age of Propaganda: The Everyday Use and Abuse of Persuasion*, by Anthony R. Pratkanis and Elliot Aronson (New York: W. H. Freeman and Co., 1992).

How Powerful Are the Images That Advertising Can Create?

Demetrick James Walker was just seventeen when he was sentenced to life in prison for killing sixteen-year-old Johnny Bates. The reason for the slaying: Demetrick so wanted a pair of Nikes like the ones he had seen on TV that he put a .22-caliber pistol to Bates's head, pulled the trigger, and walked off with a new pair of high-tops. During the trial, Houston prosecutor Mark Vinson placed some of the blame on the images created by advertising. Said Vinson, "It's bad when we create such an image of luxury about athletic gear that it forces people to kill over it."

—*Quoted from* Age of Propaganda, *by Anthony R. Pratkanis and Elliot Aronson*

clearly a fact. Still, *we* decide what would make us better off, and *we* decide to part with our money. So it is only with reference to what in *our* view would make life better for us that we properly evaluate advertisements.

There are basically two kinds of ads: those that offer reasons and those that do not. Those that offer reasons for buying the advertised product almost always promise that certain hopes will be satisfied, certain needs met, or certain fears eliminated. (You'll be more accepted, have a better image, be a better parent, and so on.)

Those ads that do not rely on reasons fall mainly into three categories: (1) those that bring out pleasurable *feelings* in us (e.g., through humor, glad tidings, pretty images, beautiful music, heartwarming scenes); (2) those that depict the product being used or endorsed by *people* we admire or think of ourselves as being like (sometimes these people are depicted by actors, sometimes not); and (3) those that depict the product being used in *situations* in which we would like to find ourselves. Of course, some ads go all out and incorporate elements from all three categories—and for good measure also state a reason or two why we should buy the advertised item.

Buying a product (which includes joining a group, deciding how to vote, and so forth) on the basis of reasonless ads is, with one minor exception that we'll explain shortly, never justified. Such ads tell you only that the product exists and what it looks like (and sometimes where it is available and how much it costs); if an ad tells you much more than this, then it begins to qualify as an ad that gives reasons for buying the product. Reasonless ads do tell us what the advertisers think of our values and sense of humor (not always a pleasant thing to notice, given that they have us pegged so well), but this information is irrelevant to the question of whether we should buy the product.

Ads that submit reasons for buying the product might have been treated in Part 3 of this book, which is devoted to arguments. However, so little need be said about argumentative ads that we will discuss them here. Such "promise ads," as they have been called, usually tell us more than that a certain

Celebrity Endorsements We Can Live With

One of America's greatest humorists was once asked to write an endorsement for a certain brand of piano. Because he would not speak on behalf of a product he had not tried, he wrote the following:

> Dear Sirs,
> I guess your pianos are the best I ever leaned against.
>
> Yours truly,
> Will Rogers

Opera singer Giovanni Martinelli, when questioned by a reporter about cigarette smoking, replied, "Tobacco, cigarettes, bah! I would not think of it!" The reporter then reminded Martinelli that he had appeared in an advertisement for a particular brand of cigarette and had said that those cigarettes did not irritate his throat. "Yes, yes, of course I gave that endorsement," Martinelli said impatiently. "How could they irritate my throat? I have never smoked."

product exists—but not much more. The promise, with rare exception, comes with no guarantees and is usually extremely vague (Gilbey's gin promises "more gin taste," Kleenex is "softer").

Such ads are a source of information about what the *sellers* of the product are willing to claim about what the product will do, how well it will do it, how it works, what it contains, how well it compares with similar products, and how much more wonderful your life will be once you've got one. However, to make an informed decision on a purchase, you almost always need to know more than the seller is willing to claim, particularly because no sellers will tell you what's wrong with their products or what's right with those of their competitors.

Further, the claims of advertisers are notorious not only for being vague but also for being ambiguous, misleading, exaggerated, and sometimes just plain false. Even if a product existed that was so good that an honest, unexaggerated, and fair description of it would justify our buying it without considering competing items (or other reports on the same item), and even if an advertisement for this product consisted of just such a description, we would still not be justified in purchasing the product on the basis of that advertisement alone. For we would be unable to tell, simply by looking at the advertisement, that it was uninflated, honest, fair, and not misleading. Our suspicions about advertising in general should undercut our willingness to believe in the honesty of any particular advertisement.

Thus, even advertisements that present reasons for buying an item do not by themselves justify our purchase of the item. Sometimes, of course, an advertisement can provide you with information that can clinch your decision to make a purchase. Sometimes the mere existence, availability, or

Persuasive Comparisons

When the government sued Microsoft for monopolistic practices, persuasive comparisons filled network news and business programs. This sampling from *Time* includes the best ones—along with how the comparisons break down:

Sounds Like, Smells Like, Feels Like . . .

If the antitrust suit against Microsoft shows anything, it's that nobody has a monopoly on analogies. Both sides in the complicated legal case filed last week have latched on to similes and metaphors to make their positions clear. But do they work? Maybe up to a point:

METAPHOR	Yeah but . . .
BILL GATES: "Forcing Microsoft to include Netscape's competing software in our operating system is like requiring Coca-Cola to include three cans of Pepsi in every six-pack it sells."	*. . . Coke doesn't control the system that distributes all drinks.*
A SENIOR GOVERNMENT OFFICIAL: "If Coca-Cola owned the only store in town, you can bet it would be required to sell Pepsi too."	*. . . it would get a bit messy if the government got into the business of telling stores what to sell.*
ROBERTA KATZ, LAWYER FOR NETSCAPE: "It's as if one of the networks was also producing the inner workings of the TV set, and every TV was wired so that that network was the one you saw."	*. . . at least the Windows user can stick the Microsoft browser in the trash and download Netscape.*
JOEL KLEIN, JUSTICE DEPARTMENT ANTITRUST CHIEF: "This is like having someone with a monopoly in CD players forcing consumers to take its CDs in order to get the machine."	*. . . at least you're getting some free CDs. Besides, you can always get other CDs elsewhere.*
GATES: "It's like ordering Ford to sell autos fitted with Chrysler engines."	*. . . you have the choice of a lot of competing cars and different engines.*
JEFF RAIKES OF MICROSOFT: "When you go into McDonald's anywhere in the world, you have a sense of what that customer experience is going to be . . . It's very important that Microsoft . . . make[s] sure that customers have a consistent user experience."	*. . . McDonald's does offer a consistent user interface. It also hasn't had a successful innovation in years. And it has competition.*

affordability of a product—all information that an ad can convey—is all you need to make a decision to buy. But if the purchase is justifiable, you must have some reasons apart from those offered in the ad for making it. If, for some reason, you already know that you want or need and can afford a car with an electric motor, then an ad that informs you that a firm has begun marketing such a thing would supply you with the information you need to buy one. If you can already justify purchasing a particular brand of microwave oven but cannot find one anywhere in town, then an advertisement informing you that the local department store stocks them can clinch your decision to make the purchase.

For people on whom good fortune has smiled, those who don't care what kind of whatsit they buy, or those to whom mistaken purchases simply don't matter, all that is important is knowing that a product is available. Most of us, however, need more information than ads provide to make reasoned purchasing decisions. Of course, we all occasionally make purchases solely on the basis of advertisements, and sometimes we don't come to regret them. In such cases, though, the happy result is due as much to good luck as to the ad.

Exercise 4-14 ⎯⎯⎯⎯⎯⎯⎯⎯⎯⎯⎯⎯⎯⎯⎯⎯⎯⎯⎯⎯⎯⎯⎯⎯⎯

Find five advertisements that give no reasons for purchasing the products they are selling. Explain how each ad attempts to make the product seem attractive.

Exercise 4-15 ⎯⎯⎯⎯⎯⎯⎯⎯⎯⎯⎯⎯⎯⎯⎯⎯⎯⎯⎯⎯⎯⎯⎯⎯⎯

Find five advertisements that give reasons for purchasing the products they are selling. Which of the reasons are promises to the purchaser? Exactly what is being promised? What is the likelihood that the product will fulfill that promise?

Recap

Speakers and writers sometimes win acceptance for a claim or influence a person's attitude or behavior without presenting reasons. We call this rhetoric. A primary means of wielding such influence is the use of rhetorical devices—words or phrases that have positive or negative emotional associations, suggest favorable or unfavorable images, or manipulate the assumptions or expectations that always underlie communication. Common rhetorical devices include euphemisms and dysphemisms; persuasive comparisons, definitions, and explanations; stereotypes; innuendo; loaded questions; weaselers; downplayers; horse laugh, ridicule, or sarcasm; hyperbole; and proof surrogates. Such devices are often used deliberately, but subtle uses can creep into people's speech or writing even when they think they are being objective. Some such phrases, especially euphemisms and weaselers, have both valuable, nonprejudicial uses and slanting ones. Only by speaking, writing, listening, and reading carefully can we use this type of language appropriately and distinguish prejudicial from nonprejudicial uses of these devices.

Advertising assaults us at every turn with nonargumentative persuasion, attempting to sell us goods, services, beliefs, and attitudes. Because substantial talent and resources are employed in this effort, we need to ask ourselves constantly whether the products in question will really make the differences in our lives that their advertising claims or hints they will make.

After reading this chapter and the chapter recap, you should be able to

▲ Describe some legitimate uses of rhetorical devices
▲ Identify and give examples of ten common rhetorical devices
▲ Describe the tools and techniques advertisers use to persuade us to buy their products, and explain how critically thinking consumers can resist persuasive advertising

Additional Exercises

Exercise 4-16

Look through an issue of *Time, Newsweek,* or another newsmagazine, and find a photograph that portrays its subject in an especially good or bad light—that is, one that does a nonverbal job of creating slant regarding the subject.

Exercise 4-17

In groups invent two newspaper or magazine headlines to go with this photograph of Steve Forbes. Make one headline create a favorable impression in combination with the photo and make the other create an unfavorable impression.

Exercise 4-18

Read the following passage and, in groups, answer the questions that follow. Then compare your answers with those of other groups and your instructor.

> "It is not the job of the state, and it is certainly not the job of the school, to tell parents when to put their children to bed," declared David Hart of the National Association of Head Teachers, responding to David Blunkett's idea that parents and teachers should draw up "contracts" (which you could be fined for breaching) about their children's behaviour, timekeeping, homework and bedtime. Teachers are apparently concerned that their five-to-eight-year-old charges are staying up too late and becoming listless truants the next day.
>
> While I sympathise with Mr. Hart's concern about this neo-Stalinist nannying, I wonder whether it goes far enough. Is it not high time that such concepts as Bathtime, Storytime and Drinks of Water were subject to regulation as well? I for one would value some governmental guidance as to the number of humorous swimming toys (especially Hungry Hippo) allowable per gallon of water. Adopting silly voices while reading Spot's Birthday or Little Rabbit Foo-Foo aloud is something crying out for regulatory guidelines, while the right of children to demand and receive wholly unnecessary glasses of liquid after lights-out needs a Statutory Minimum Allowance.
>
> *John Walsh,* The Independent

1. What issue is addressed in the passage?
2. What position does the author take on that issue?
3. If the author supports his position with an argument, state that argument in your own words.
4. Does the author use rhetorical devices? If so, identify the main type of devices used.

Writing Exercises

1. Turn to Selection 4 in Essays for Analysis, "Will Ozone Blob Devour the Earth?" and identify as many rhetorical devices as you can find. (Your instructor may narrow the scope of the assignment to just certain paragraphs.)
2. Write a brief paragraph about an object, an event, or a person using language that is as neutral as you can make it. Then write a second version (with the same factual content) but with a definite positive or negative slant. Try to use more than one of the rhetorical devices described in this chapter. Then, in groups, select the two versions that are the most effective to share with the class.
3. The following paragraph was part of an article on Al Gore, written by David Maraniss and Ellen Nakashima for the *Washington Post* early during Gore's presidential campaign of 1999–2000. Read it and note your impressions.

> During his early years as a senator's son in Washington, Al Gore was often the smallest one in the crowd, a pint-size boy with dark hair and freckles

who lived with his prominent parents in Suite 809 atop the Fairfax Hotel along Embassy Row. If this experience made him different from you and me, to borrow F. Scott Fitzgerald's phrase, it was not from being rich, but rather from being apart. He grew up in a singularly odd world of old people and bellhops, separated from the child-filled neighborhoods of his class-mates at St. Albans and further still from his summertime pals at the family farm in Tennessee.

Do you get the impression that Gore was rich as a youngster? The second sentence, which uses the word "rich," is ambiguous. Do you see the two possible meanings? Do you detect any innuendo? What is not mentioned here is that the Fairfax Hotel was owned by a rich uncle of Gore's, who allowed young Al Gore's family to stay there for no charge. Does knowing this extra piece of information affect how one takes the original passage? Explain your answers in a brief paragraph.

With thanks to Robert Somerby

Chapter 5

More Rhetorical Devices

In the previous chapter, we began discussing rhetorical techniques—ways people attempt to influence or persuade by using the rhetorical, or emotive, content of words, phrases, and grammatical constructs. This and the next chapter cover additional rhetorical devices.

The rhetorical devices we talk about here (and in Chapter 6) are especially apt to be dressed up to look like reasonable arguments. For that reason we refer to this type of rhetoric as *pseudoreasoning*. As such, pseudoreasoning comprises a large and varied catalog of emotional appeals, factual irrelevancies, and persuasive devices that sometimes move people to accept or reject claims when they have no good grounds for doing so. Since the techniques discussed here so often are couched in the language of arguments, we also refer to them occasionally as "fallacies"—a fancy word for "defective arguments."

So don't look for a technical definition of pseudoreasoning; it isn't a technical concept. It's just our name for the grab bag of rhetorical ploys that we cover in this and the next chapter. These techniques include appeals to emotion and other psychological gimmicks, distracting irrelevancies, bogus dichotomies, appeals to vanity, and the like. What they all have in common is that none of them should affect our beliefs. That's because, just like the devices considered in Chapter 4, they lack power to prove or establish what they may seem to prove or establish. A good argument provides us with some justification for accepting its conclusion. A piece of pseudoreasoning may have some connection with an issue, often an emotional connection, but at bottom it provides no grounds for accepting the claim it seems to support.

Finally, bear this in mind: Don't place everything that *reminds* you of a category of "pseudoreasoning" into that category. Many cases that *resemble* pseudoreasoning actually are reasonable arguments, as we'll explain.

Smokescreen/Red Herring

In most devices covered in this chapter, the inducement that erroneously leads one to accept or reject a claim is in fact irrelevant to the truth of the claim. Here's an example:

MOORE: What do you think of coal-fired power plants, Parker? Do you think we ought to have more of them?

PARKER: Well, frankly, I agree with some of the environmentalists . . .

MOORE: Well, we should build more coal-fired plants, and I'll tell you why. I'm sick and tired of these environmentalists, always complaining about something or other. What a bunch of troublemakers. They find something wrong with everything.

PARKER: I hate to tell you, Moore, but you haven't said anything about coal-fired power plants.

> We admit that this measure is popular. But we also urge you to note that there are so many bond issues on this ballot that the whole concept is getting ridiculous.
>
> A generic red herring (unclassifiable irrelevance) from a California ballot pamphlet.

Parker is exactly right, of course. Moore hasn't said anything relevant to the issue of whether more coal-fired plants should be built. This sort of irrelevance is typical of most pseudoreasoning. Moore is putting up a **smokescreen;** he's bringing in another topic—one that many people may think of when they consider the coal-fired plants issue, but one that is in fact a wholly separate matter. This irrelevant topic, the "environmentalists," diverts our attention from the original issue, which then gets lost in the fog generated by the irrelevant topic. Hence the label "smokescreen." Another name for an irrelevant consideration brought into a discussion is **red herring.** The term "red herring" has an interesting background: A herring cured in salt (which is reddish in color) has a powerful odor before it is cooked. If one is dragged across the trail of an animal that dogs are tracking, the dogs will give up the original scent and follow the herring.*

Remember, the point of any smokescreen or red herring is to *distract* the reader or listener from the issue at hand. Here's an example from Senator Peckingham, who is dining with some fellow Republicans:

> Could somebody please show me one hospital built by a dolphin? Could somebody show me one highway built by a dolphin? Could someone show me one automobile invented by a dolphin?
>
> —RUSH LIMBAUGH, responding to the *New York Times*'s claim that dolphins' "behavior and enormous brains suggest an intelligence approaching that of human beings."
>
> Good point. Anyone know of a hospital or highway built by Rush Limbaugh, or an automobile invented by him?

I think this gun-control plan the administration has produced is a pretty good idea. You know, the gun-control issue is getting linked to the crime-fighting issue these days. So if we Republicans are going to keep our reputation as the number-one crime-fighting party, we're going to have to get behind this gun-control plan.

---

*Thanks to Robert Claiborne, *Loose Cannons and Red Herrings* (New York: Ballantine Books, 1988), for this bit of word lore.

Doing the Old Side-Step . . .

Here's an exchange between Tim Russert, of NBC's *Meet the Press,* and Senator Christopher Dodd of Connecticut:

> Russert: Senator Dodd, can we afford to continue the war [in Yugoslavia]?
> Dodd: Can we afford not to?

The Senator's side-step, or dodge, is a case of red herring. But it can also be seen as an attempt to shift the burden of proof from one side of the issue to the other. We'll have a close look at burden-of-proof issues in the next chapter.

Anyone who thinks Peckingham has given a relevant reason for believing the gun-control plan has any merit is mistaken. His statement that Republicans should be in favor of gun control may be true, but it is certainly irrelevant to the merits of the administration's plan. Peckingham's remark may well help support the claim that Republicans should begin to favor gun control, but it doesn't support claims about the *merits* of any particular plan.

Many of the techniques covered in this and the next chapter introduce irrelevant appeals of one kind or another, but we reserve the smokescreen or red herring label for cases in which none of the narrower, more descriptive categories seem to apply and for instances in which the irrelevant issue is intentionally brought up to distract one's audience. The important thing is that you recognize when the subject has been changed and the discussion thrown off course.

The Subjectivist Fallacy

How many times have you heard people say, with a rhetorical flourish, "Well, that may be true for you, but it isn't true for me" when they've been confronted with a claim that they don't want to accept? In almost every case, such a remark provides no reason for rejecting the claim. To think that it does is to commit the **subjectivist fallacy.** All one accomplishes by saying "true for you but not for me" is to say that "maybe you accept the claim, but I don't." That's quite a bit different, of course, from the claim's actually being true for someone else and its being false for you. Claims about factual matters don't work that way, by and large: If they're true, they're true, period. What would it mean for the claim "The door is closed" to be true for one person and false for another? It doesn't make any difference to the door whether anybody believes that it's closed; the door is simply where it is, and either it's closed or it's not.

Claims may be true *about* one person and false *about* another. Look at this example:

MOORE: You know, I've come to the conclusion that a person really needs at least seven hours of sleep every night in order to feel healthy.

PARKER: That may be true for you, but it certainly isn't true for me.

Parker has made a perfectly reasonable remark, as long as we take him to mean simply that *he* doesn't need seven hours of sleep every night, even though *Moore* may need that much. Notice that Parker has not given a reason for his claim or for anything else. But, once again, people will sometimes use the "true for you; not true for me" remark to insist that it's acceptable for you to believe a claim about a matter of fact and equally acceptable for them to reject the same claim. And when they do, they haven't given a reason for anything at all.

The view that underlies the subjectivist fallacy is sometimes called *relativism,* and it seems to be a common view among many students. Simply put, this view maintains that truth is relative. Now, lots of things are relative among individuals (fear of going to the dentist, for example) and among cultures (e.g., the acceptability of going about without clothes). Some people argue that morality is relative, that what is right and wrong depends on one's culture or society. (This is a controversial point, and there are sophisticated arguments on both sides.) But most claims, certainly those about straightforward matters of fact (provided they are reasonably free of vagueness and ambiguity) are simply true or false independent of any particular person's acceptance of them.

It's likely that people often use some version of the subjectivist fallacy not because they somehow really deny the objectivity of truth, but because they simply want to put an end to rational discussion—they use the fallacy as a conversation stopper. In general, it would be better simply to admit that one doesn't wish to discuss a subject than to cloak one's wish in the subjectivist fallacy.

One source of confusion on this topic is a failure to distinguish *respect* for other people's opinions from a refusal to *question* those opinions. These are very different things. When we say that we should respect the beliefs of others, we are really saying that we should respect the people, and such respect involves taking their views seriously. But taking their views seriously means, among other things, subjecting them to critical assessment. Here's an example: Each year, about two million young women around the world are subjected to painful genital surgery as the result of a variety of cultural belief systems about women and sex. From the fact that we respect *people* from such cultures, does it follow that we should agree with their beliefs about such matters? Of course not. Does it mean we should find it perfectly acceptable that they continue to hold such beliefs? Not necessarily. If we think the beliefs lead to harm, it is at least acceptable (if not our duty) to try to convince these people to change those beliefs. In brief, we can respect a person and still believe that person is mistaken.

Appeal to Popularity (ad populum)

There are several varieties of appeal to popularity, but all have one thing in common: They encourage the acceptance of a claim (or practice) on the basis of its acceptance by some substantial number of others. Of course, there are times when it's perfectly reasonable to believe what others believe; their belief may be based on truth. But we need to know that at least some of those who believe the claim are credible sources, as we discussed in Chapter 3, or we need independent evidence for the claim. A claim's acceptance by others all by itself does not generally warrant our accepting it; certainly the mere fact that most people believe a claim does not guarantee its truth. When we accept other people's opinions without such reason, we are being taken in by an **appeal to popularity.** Here are a couple of examples:

> Free will? Of course, people have free will. Everyone believes that. It hardly seems possible *not* to believe it.

> A job in management is surely better than a job as, say, a bus driver. Just ask anybody. They'll tell you that it's better to get an education and go into management.

The fact that nearly everybody believes in free will—or even, were it true, that everybody without exception believes in it—does not assure us there is any such thing. This pseudoreason is no more to the point than the argument in medieval times that because everyone believed the earth was the center of the universe, it had to be true.

Most people seem to assume that bus driving and similar jobs are somehow less desirable than white-collar jobs. The widespread acceptance of this assumption creates its own momentum—that is, we tend to accept it because everybody else does, and we don't stop to think about whether it actually has anything to recommend it. For a lot of people, a job driving a bus might make for a much happier life than a job as a manager.

In *some* instances, we should point out, what people think actually *determines* what is true. The meanings of most words, for example, are determined by popular usage. In addition, it would not be pseudoreasoning to conclude that the word "ain't" is out of place in formal speech because most speakers of English believe that it is out of place in formal speech.

There are other cases where what people think is an *indication* of what is true, even if it cannot *determine* truth. If several Bostonians of your acquaintance think that it is illegal to drink beer in their public parks, then you have some reason for thinking that it's true. And if you are told by several

A Subtle Version of Appeal to Popularity

[M]any baseball people believe that baseball's biggest on-field problem is not the impulsive misbehavior of players in the heat of competition but the incompetence, confrontational surliness and premeditated misbehavior of some umpires, factors that threaten the integrity of the competition.

—GEORGE WILL, in Newsweek

The first five words of this passage are a fine piece of subtle manipulation. They are a proof surrogate (Chapter 4), but they also illustrate a specialized kind of appeal to popularity, where the appeal is to a large number (or "many" or "most") of people *in a certain category*. In this case, it's "baseball people," who, presumably, are especially knowledgeable about the game and who, naturally, agree with the writer. In other words, if this view is popular among the experts, then it certainly should be acceptable to you.

Europeans that it is not gauche to eat with your fork in your left hand in Europe, then it is not pseudoreasoning to conclude that European manners allow eating with your fork in your left hand. The situation here is one of credibility, which we discussed in Chapter 3. Natives of Boston in the first case and Europeans in the second case can be expected to know more about the two claims in question, respectively, than others know. In a watered-down sense, they are "experts" on the subjects, at least in ways that many of us are not. In general, when the "everyone" who thinks that X is true includes experts about X, then what they think is indeed a good reason to accept X.

Thus it would be incorrect to automatically label as a fallacy or as pseudoreasoning any instance in which a person cites people's beliefs to establish a point. (No "argument" fitting a pattern in this chapter should *unthinkingly* be dismissed.) But it is important to view such references to people's beliefs as red alerts. These are cautionary signals that warn you to look closely for genuine reasons in support of the claim asserted.

There are several variants of the appeal to popularity. We'll describe three of them in the following pages: common practice, peer pressure, and bandwagon pseudoreasoning. As its name implies, common practice always involves a defense of a *practice* rather than a claim. Peer pressure results from our desire to be accepted by our friends (whether they be right or wrong!), and bandwagon rests on our preference for winners over losers, even sometimes when the winners are in the wrong and the losers in the right.

■ Common Practice

Common practice pseudoreasoning is the justification or defense of an action on the grounds that it is a common *practice*—that everybody does it, that most people do it, or that most people in a particular category do it. (Thus, most people must believe that it's all right to do it.) Some people might argue that they shouldn't be given a ticket for speeding because almost everybody drives over the limit or that they shouldn't be punished for fudging on their taxes because nearly everybody does it. But the fact that other people do X doesn't make X an acceptable thing to do, of course. Now, there is something to watch out for here: When a person defends an action by saying that other people do the same thing, we can take the claim as a request for fair play. And, indeed, if others *are* doing the same thing, we must remember that *their* actions are as wrong as those of the person we're criticizing. If it's proper to criticize *one* person for doing X, then, lacking any relevant difference between the two, it's proper to criticize another for doing X as well.

■ *Peer Pressure*

We all want to be accepted by our friends and associates, and there is often nothing wrong with doing things to win their approval. But sometimes we do things because we desire the approval of others even though it is not reasonable to do those things—when the desire for approval is irrelevant to the issue. In other words, we succumb to **peer pressure.** Here are two examples; pay careful attention to what issues the desire for approval *is* relevant to and what issues it is *not* relevant to.

> You're trying to decide whether you're a good enough skier to tackle the South Face. You're pretty sure that you are not, but then one of your friends changes your mind. "C'mon," he says, "you don't see any of the rest of us holding back, do you?" You decide that you're as good as your friends, and they're going to tackle it, so you figure you're good enough to give it a try.

> You and your friends are talking about an upcoming concert at which the opening band is Pavement. You think they're a good group, but when you express your opinion, your friends burst out laughing. "They've been around forever, and they just never make it," one friend says. You make a mental note to hide your Pavement CDs before anyone comes over on the weekend.

In the first of these examples, you have been given no reason at all for altering your initial assessment of your skiing abilities; you've been induced to alter them through peer pressure—that is, through rhetoric—which plays on a person's desire not to be disliked or disrespected. But your abilities are what they are, and what they are is not affected by what your friends think or do. (If your initial assessment of your skiing ability was right, and it's true that you ski as well as your friends, there may be a busy hour ahead for the ski patrol.)

In the second example, you do have a reason for hiding your Pavement CDs, assuming you don't want your friends laughing at you again (though in fact you could well win some respect for independence if you stick with your preference). But if you are like many of us, you may do more than hide your

CDs; you may conclude that Pavement isn't that great after all. You may even start looking for reasons for thinking that they're inferior, though your friends haven't given you any reasons for that opinion. In this case, you have been peer pressured. (And if you are like a lot of people, you'll feel peer pressure on issues much more important than this.)

■ Bandwagon

In times gone by in the United States, political rallies used to be preceded by a wagon carrying a band drawn through the center of town to attract people to the rally. When a candidate looked as though he or she (generally "he" in those days) was going to be successful, a lot of people would join in support just because they wanted to be on the side of a winner. This was—and still is—known as "jumping on the bandwagon." Our notion of **bandwagon** pseudoreasoning is similar: If you try to win support for a candidate, a position, or a policy merely on the grounds that he or she or it is going to win (rather than on whatever merits he or she or it may have), then you commit bandwagon pseudoreasoning.

Our desire to be on the winning side functions like our desire for approval. It is usually irrelevant to the merits of a position, and, generally speaking, we should judge a position on its merits. However, there are times when the opportunity to vote for a candidate or proposal that has a chance of winning can take on more importance. Let's say, for example, that there are three candidates running for office. You believe that Abercrombie is the best candidate, slightly better than Burkhart, and that Chislink is absolutely awful. Unfortunately, Abercrombie is given very little chance of winning, trailing far behind Burkhart and Chislink, who are neck-and-neck in the polls. In such a case, it might be quite reasonable to vote for Burkhart rather than Abercrombie simply because the former has a chance of winning and the latter does not. Notice that this is not a case of bandwagon pseudoreasoning; we fall for bandwagon rhetoric when it's our *desire* to be on the winning side (whatever side that is) that motivates us.

Wishful Thinking

Sometimes the idea of a claim's being false is *so* unpleasant that we decide the claim must be true simply because the alternative is so awful. For example:

> I don't believe that we cease entirely to exist when our bodies die. I mean, if I thought it was all going to be *over,* I just couldn't stand it.

Unfortunately, our fear of its "being over," or our desire not to contemplate such a thing, is not evidence that it isn't over when we die. To think that the awful consequences of a claim's being true—or our believing it to be true—

provide a reason for rejecting it is to fall prey to what everybody recognizes as **wishful thinking.** It happens the other way too: To think that the awful consequences of its being false—or our *not* believing it—provide a reason for accepting it is the other side of this pseudoreasoning coin.

Not only do our concerns about a claim's wonderful (or awful) consequences not provide reasons for accepting (or rejecting) it, but they also cannot make the claim the least bit more or less likely. Consider:

> It would be so *great* to win the lottery. I've imagined all week how I would spend the money! I just really think I've got a chance this week.

He does have a chance, the same chance as everybody else—in our state, that's about one in fourteen million. So, the basic idea is simple: Wanting something doesn't make it so, unfortunately, nor even more likely.

This kind of error is very obvious when discussed in the abstract or observed in another person, but it is much more difficult to recognize and admit to when we ourselves are guilty of it. Most of us are willing to go to some lengths to avoid discomfort, after all, and that's what this kind of pseudoreasoning achieves for us, at least in the short run. A desire for an afterlife helps convince a person that there is one; a smoker discounts reports on smoking's ill effects because she finds it so unpleasant to contemplate coming down with them; an individual with a serious disease refuses to get treatment because he refuses to believe that he has the disease. All such thinking is designed to promote comfort, but it does not promote good reasoning, and it can be dangerous.

We typically perpetrate this variety of pseudoreasoning on ourselves rather than on one another, but even this kind of comfort can be packaged and sold. Wishful-thinking pseudoreasoning underlies much of the empty rhetoric of "positive thinking"—rhetoric that claims "you are what you want to be" and other such slogans. To believe in your dreams—that is, to believe that they will come true *for no better reason than that you hope they will*—may provide solace to the soul, but it is not to think critically.

Scare Tactics

Dear Professor Moore:

I'd like to make an appointment to see you tomorrow about my final grade. I think it was unfair and I should have gotten a better one. My telephone number is below, so please call me.

By the way, I believe you know my aunt. She's your dean.

Sincerely yours,
Cassandra Petrel

Impeachment Fallout

We need to send a strong signal to the president by impeaching him.

—DAN QUAYLE

[That would get his attention, all right.]

Clinton should be removed from office, and speedily. He perjured himself and that makes it impossible for him to deal effectively with foreign and domestic issues.

—Representative BILL McCOLLUM

[Of course, removal from office might make it even more difficult to deal with those issues.]

When they are considering whether Bill Clinton should be impeached, Republicans should be wary of what voters will say when they get their chance.

—JAMES CARVILLE, Democratic strategist

[Just good, old-fashioned scare tactics here.]

In this example, the student provides no reason for believing she was misgraded, but she does manage to threaten Professor Moore with retaliation via her aunt, the dean. She's using **scare tactics** to induce fear in her professor to get him to revise her grade.

The underlying structure of this example, and of all pseudoreasoning based on psychological inducements, is the same. Something is said in connection with a claim that elicits or is intended to elicit a psychological response of some sort—a desire, a fear, some feeling or emotion—that may well induce acceptance of the claim. But neither what is said nor the psychological response elicited is a reason for accepting the claim because neither is logically related to the claim. To accept a claim on the basis of such irrelevant psychological inducements is to fall victim to pseudoreasoning.

The distinction may be obvious, but we still want to point out the difference between scare tactics on the one hand and warnings on the other. If someone says, "You should be careful of that snake—it's deadly poisonous," we might be scared, all right, but that doesn't mean we have a case of scare tactics in our sense of the phrase. Only when the scare is irrelevant to the issue do we get pseudoreasoning, and the scare and the issue here (i.e., whether one should be careful of the snake) are very closely connected indeed.

Here is another, somewhat more subtle, example of scare tactics. Imagine that you've been shopping for a house. You find one that comes close to suiting your needs, but the kitchen is much too small and the house needs more repairs than you would care to contend with. So you conclude that you really don't want this house. When you explain your concerns to the real estate agent, she observes that the seller already has four offers that he is considering and will probably sell very soon. This moves you to make an offer on the house after all. "The kitchen isn't that small," you think. "And not that many things really need repairing." The real estate agent in this example is using a form of scare tactic to get you to make an offer. Let's identify the issues to which her assertion is relevant.

What you have learned is that the value of the house as determined by what others might pay for it may be greater than you had previously believed. This new information is indeed a reason for considering whether to try to live with the defects you have identified in the house. It isn't a very good reason, of course, for you have no information on the amount that has been offered, if indeed anything has been offered (mentioning "other offers" is a common sales gimmick). Still, it is a reason for considering whether to try to live with the defects of the house. *But the new information is not a reason, not even a bad one, for changing your mind about the size of the kitchen or the need for repairs.* To avoid pseudoreasoning, you need to recognize to which issues your feelings are relevant and to which they are not. Fear of the house being sold to someone else is not a reason for thinking that the kitchen is acceptably large or that the repairs are less serious than you first believed. Learning that the house *may* be more valuable than you thought is a reason for reconsidering whether you wish to put up with the problems of the house.

Appeal to Pity

Helen is running for a seat on the city council. Though you like her, you have doubts about her qualifications and in fact believe that an opposing candidate would make a better member of the council. When you communicate your concerns about her qualifications to a mutual friend, the friend counters by saying that Helen would be terribly hurt if she were to lose the election. After thinking this over, you conclude that maybe Helen's qualifications are not so bad after all.

The mutual friend has evoked compassion in you for Helen, but she has not given you a reason for changing your opinion of Helen's qualifications. This pattern of pseudoreasoning is called **appeal to pity.** Clearly, the issue—whether Helen's qualifications are sufficient—is unaffected by the fact that her feelings will be hurt if she loses the election.

Notice that even if the mutual friend had told you Helen would be terribly hurt to learn what you think of her credentials, she would still have failed to give you a reason for changing your evaluation of them—though she would have given you a reason for not sharing your opinion with Helen.

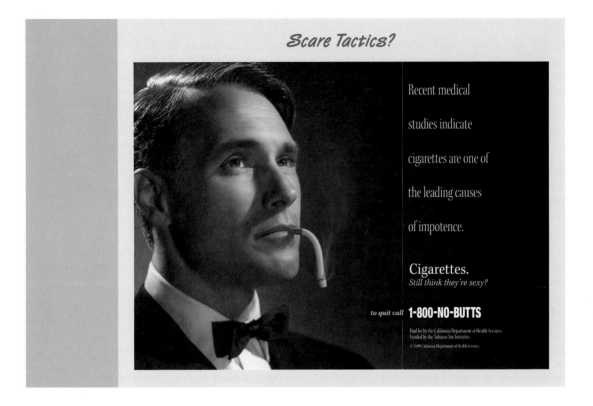

Does your compassion for Helen enter the picture at all? Certainly, but only in this way: You now have to weigh Helen's hurt at losing the election against the consequences of having her as a council member instead of the better-qualified candidate. Which, you have to decide, is more important?

Let's look at another example:

ROOFER: I'm positive that my work will meet your requirements.
I really need the money, what with my wife being sick
and all.

The roofer seems to be giving a reason for thinking that his work will meet your requirements. But of course he is not; that issue is unaffected by the fact that he really needs the money. This fact is not a reason, not even a bad reason, for concluding anything at all about the quality of his work.

Notice, though, that actions performed out of concern for others are often rationally and ethically justified. Indeed, in some instances they count as among the noblest of human deeds. If the roofer is qualified and needs the money for his wife's illness, and you are willing to take a chance on his work, then by all means hire him! Just don't think that he has given you a reason for thinking that his work will meet your specifications; whether it will or not is something you must establish on other grounds.

Apple Polishing

> Hannah, I'd be proud if you'd support me in my campaign for city council. People know they can trust you, and I know it too. I need an honest, reliable person on my side, and they don't come much better than you.

This is an old-fashioned case of **apple polishing** (there are more graphic names for it, too). We can hope that Hannah doesn't think she's been given a *reason* for supporting the speaker.

> Dear Professor Parker:
>
> If it's not too much trouble, please send my final grade on the attached postcard and drop it in the mail. I've already addressed the card.
>   I certainly enjoyed your course. You are a wonderful instructor and did an excellent job of making the class interesting and useful. There is one thing, though: Would you mind taking another look at my grade on the second exam? With one more point I would have made an A.
>
> Sincerely,
> Fawn Wheedle

The issue, whether the student earned an A, is unaffected by the fact that he likes (or gives the appearance of liking) his professor. So that fact is no reason for changing his grade. Again, the attempted inducement is through an appeal to the instructor's vanity.

You shouldn't think, of course, that you have spotted a case of apple polishing every time somebody says something nice about another person. Apple polishing occurs only when the nice words are illegitimately used in connection with an issue to which they are irrelevant.

Appeal to Anger or Indignation

"It's your money," the political ad begins, "and the folks in Washington want to spend it on—midnight basketball leagues!"

What's going on here? The people who wrote this ad want you to get angry. They want you to rise up in indignation and declare yourself mad as heck.

This is a typical example of an **appeal to indignation,** which is just another word for anger, especially the type of anger you feel when you think you have been treated unjustly. By arousing your anger, a politician (or anyone, for that matter) may hope that you won't think too clearly.

But now, look. If someone else is wasting your money, then you have a right to get angry; there's no pseudoreasoning involved in doing so. However,

Sleaze and Anger

One of the more startling (that's sometimes a euphemism for "sleazy") political ads of recent times was a fifteen-second television spot by one Tim LeFever attacking incumbent Representative Vic Fazio of California. In the ad, harsh black-and-white footage of Richard Allen Davis appeared on the screen, while a voice identified Fazio as one of those "who have built their entire political career defending people like Richard Allen Davis from the death penalty." California viewers knew well the face of Davis, who had recently been found guilty of kidnapping and murdering teenager Polly Klaas. Few criminals in the history of the state had offended public sensibilities to a greater degree than Davis, who calmly made a gesture with his middle finger at Polly Klaas's family during the trial.

The ad was a fairly obvious attempt to direct public outrage about the Polly Klaas case against Fazio. In fact, Fazio had voted on several occasions to expand the death penalty, though he had expressed doubts about capital punishment as a matter of principle. But opposing the death penalty as a matter of principle is not quite the same as defending some particular individual from execution. In their anger at Davis, however, viewers might take scant notice of such a subtle—but vitally important—distinction.

when we are angry (especially if we are in a "blind rage"), it is easy to become illogical, in various ways. For one thing, we may think that we have been given a reason for being angry when in fact we have not. Is spending money on midnight basketball leagues a waste of money? Well, let's talk about it and see. If a midnight basketball league reduces crime in a neighborhood, then maybe it isn't such a waste of money. It is illogical to think that something is wrong simply because it makes us angry: Presumably we are angry because it is wrong, not the other way around.

Another mistake we can make is to let the anger we feel as the result of one thing influence our evaluation of an unrelated thing. That one person has done something to anger us isn't normally in itself a reason for upgrading our evaluation of another person or that person's deeds. Nor is it a reason for downgrading the first person's performance on some other matter.

Suppose, for example, a coworker didn't recommend you for a promotion and now is up for one herself. It may anger you that she didn't recommend you, but the fact that she didn't isn't logically related to the question of whether she has earned a promotion herself. Similarly, if she had recommended you, that too would be logically unrelated to the question of whether she deserved a promotion herself. Notice how it is that people we don't like have to be exceptionally good for us to praise them, whereas a friend wins our admiration for being merely competent. It takes careful thinking to keep our general feelings about others from coloring our evaluation of some specific accomplishment or action on their part.

Radio talk show hosts often seem to attempt to arouse and feed indignation (and even outrage) on the part of listeners; some politicians do the same. Regardless of who does it, if we find ourselves rising up in righteous indignation, it's probably good to remember that anger does not provide the clearest lens through which to view the world.

Two Wrongs Make a Right

Two wrongs make a right is a form of pseudoreasoning that is intended to justify the claim that it is all right for A to do something harmful to B. It occurs when somebody tries to justify illegitimate retaliation. It is somewhat controversial whether every case of this type of "two wrongs make a right" thinking should be classified as pseudoreasoning. There is a well-known and widely held theory known as *retributivism*, according to which it *is* acceptable to do harm to someone in return for a similar harm he or she has done to you. But we certainly may distinguish between what may be legitimate retaliation, as for instance in the case of capital punishment, which retributivists may be able to defend successfully, and what is illegitimate retaliation.

Pseudoreasoning clearly occurs when we are urged to consider a wrong to be justification for *any* retaliatory action, as would be the case if Moore burned down Parker's house to repay him for denting the fender of his car. It is also pseudoreasoning when the second "wrong" is misdirected—if, for example, A does wrong to B, so B then does wrong to C. B may say rhetorically that he has "evened his scorecard," but here the second wrong is clearly illegitimate. We also use "two wrongs" pseudoreasoning to defend A's doing harm to B on the grounds that B *would* (or might) do the same to A. An example:

> After leaving the local supermarket, Serena notices that the sales clerk has given her too much change. "Oh well," she says, "if I had given him too much money, he wouldn't have returned it to me."

Serena is indeed rationalizing. She is trying to excuse her dishonesty with a pseudoreason. Even assuming that the clerk wouldn't have returned the money to her had the situation been reversed, that fact does not justify a similar action by another person, herself included.

Notice, though, another scheme very similar to this pattern of pseudoreasoning that is not pseudoreasoning but is, rather, quite acceptable: It is *not* illogical or "pseudoreasoning" to defend A's doing X to B *on the grounds that doing so is necessary to prevent B from doing X to A.* Thus, for instance,

most people would agree that it is not wrong for you to injure a mugger if doing so is necessary to prevent that person from injuring you. To take another example, near the end of World War II, the United States dropped two atomic bombs on Japanese cities, killing tens of thousands of civilians. It was argued that the bombing was justified because it helped end the war and thus prevented more casualties from the fighting, including the deaths of more Americans. People have long disagreed on whether this argument provides *sufficient* justification for the bombings, but there is no disagreement about its being a real argument and not empty rhetoric.

People can be moved to take a position on an issue by language that plays on feelings such as fear, compassion, guilt, loyalty, pride, wishful thinking, or what-have-you. In many cases the feelings are irrelevant to the issue at hand. Using language in this way, when the feelings have no bearing on the issue, counts as what we call pseudoreasoning; language so used is really just empty rhetoric.

In this chapter, we examined twelve categories of pseudoreasoning:

Smokescreen/red herring—bringing up an irrelevant topic to draw attention away from the issue at hand

Subjectivist fallacy—asserting that a claim may be true for one person but not for another

Appeal to popularity—urging acceptance of a claim simply because some selection of other people believe it (when those believers have no more knowledge or expertise in the subject than you do). Variants of appeal to popularity include

> Common practice—justifying an action or practice on the grounds that lots of people (or a significant number within a certain category) engage in it

> Peer pressure—urging acceptance of a claim on the grounds it will gain the listener approval from friends or associates, where that approval is irrelevant to the truth of the claim

> Bandwagon—supporting a position, candidate, or policy on the grounds it is going to win or become the dominant alternative

Wishful thinking—urging acceptance of a claim on the basis of the listener's desire that it be true

Scare tactics—accepting or urging acceptance of a claim on grounds of fear, when the threat is not relevant to the issue addressed by the claim

Appeal to pity—accepting or urging acceptance of a claim on grounds of pity, when the appeal is not relevant to the issue addressed by the claim

Apple polishing—accepting or urging acceptance of a claim on grounds of vanity; allowing praise of oneself to substitute for judgment about the truth of a claim

Appeal to anger or indignation—substituting anger or indignation for reason and judgment when taking a side on an issue

Two wrongs make a right—justifying doing X to somebody because they would do X to you given the chance, or justifying an action against someone as "making up" for something bad that happened to you. Instances of this occur that are not pseudoreasoning.

Having read this chapter and the chapter recap, you should be able to

▲ Identify the kinds of pseudoreasoning we cover in this chapter when you encounter it, whether in someone else's writing or speaking, or in your own writing, speaking, or thinking

▲ Explain and give examples of the types of pseudoreasoning described in this chapter

Exercises

In daily life it is not terribly important that you be able to label a case of pseudoreasoning as, say, "subjectivist fallacy" or "appeal to popularity." What is important is being able to identify pseudoreasoning wherever it occurs and to recognize why the would-be reasons are irrelevant to the point at issue. Nevertheless, in the exercises that follow, we will ask you to name patterns of pseudoreasoning, and your instructor may do the same on an exam. The objective is to help you become familiar with and remember these common patterns so that you will be alert to pseudoreasoning when it occurs in daily life.

Exercise 5-1 ———————————————————

Working in groups, invent a simple, original, and clear illustration of each pattern of pseudoreasoning covered in this chapter. Then in the class as a whole select the illustrations that are clearest and most straightforward. Go over these illustrations before doing the remaining exercises in this chapter, and review them before you take a test on this material.

Exercise 5-2 ———————————————————

Identify any instances of pseudoreasoning that occur in the following passages, either by naming them or, where you think they do not conform to any of the patterns we have described, by explaining in one or two sentences why the pseudoreasons are irrelevant to the point at issue. (There are a few passages that contain no pseudoreasoning. Be sure you don't find it where it doesn't exist!)

▲ 1. The tax system in this country is unfair and ridiculous! Just ask anyone!

2. SHE: I think it was exceedingly boorish of you to finish off the last of their expensive truffles like that.
   HE: Bosh. They certainly would have done the same to us, if given the chance.

3. Overheard:
   "Hmmmm. Nice day. Think I'll go catch some rays."
   "Says here in this magazine that doing that sort of thing is guaranteed to get you a case of skin cancer."
   "Yeah, I've heard that, too. I think it's a bunch of baloney, personally. If that were true, you wouldn't be able to do anything—no tubing, skiing, nothing. You wouldn't even be able to just plain lay out in the sun. Ugh!"

▲ 4. I've come before you to ask that you rehire Professor Johnson. I realize that Mr. Johnson does not have a Ph.D., and I am aware that he has yet to publish his first article. But Mr. Johnson is over forty now, and he has a wife and two high-school-aged children to support. It will be very difficult for him to find another teaching job at his age, I'm sure you will agree.

5. JUAN: But, Dad, I like Horace. Why shouldn't I room with him, anyway?
   JUAN'S DAD: Because I'll cut off your allowance, that's why!

6. That snake has markings like a coral snake. Coral snakes are deadly poisonous, so you'd better leave it alone!

▲ 7. RALPH: He may have done it, but I don't hold him responsible. I'm a determinist, you know.
   SHARON: What's that?
   RALPH: A determinist? Someone who doesn't believe in free will. There's no free will.
   SHARON: Oh. Well, I disagree.
   RALPH: Why's that?
   SHARON: Because. Determinism may be real for you, but it certainly isn't for me.

8. The animal rights people shouldn't pick on rodeos. If they'd come out and see the clowns put smiles on kids' faces and see horses buck off the cowboys and hear the crowd go "ooh" and "ahh" at the bull riding, why then they'd change their minds.

9. HE: Tell you what. Let's get some ice cream for a change. Sunrise Creamery has the best—let's go there.
   SHE: Not that old dump! What makes you think their ice cream is so good, anyway?
   HE: Because it is. Besides, that old guy who owns it never gets any business any more. Every time I go by the place I see him in there all alone, just staring out the window, waiting for a customer. He can't help it that he's in such an awful location. I'm sure he couldn't afford to move.

▲ 10. Student speaker: "Why, student fees have jumped by more than 300 percent in just two years! This is outrageous! The governor is working for a balanced budget, but it'll be on the backs of us students, the people who have the very least to spend! It seems pretty clear that these increased student fees are undermining higher education in this state. Anybody who isn't mad about this just doesn't understand the situation."

Exercise 5-3

Answer the following questions and, where relevant, explain your answers.

▲ 1. Is the fact that a brand of toothpaste is advertised as a best-seller relevant to the issue of whether to buy that brand?

   2. Is the fact that a brand of toothpaste *is* best-selling relevant to the issue of whether to buy that brand?

▲ 3. Is the fact that an automobile is a best-seller in its class relevant to the issue of whether to buy that kind of automobile?

   4. Is the fact that a movie is a smash hit relevant to the issue of whether to see it?

   5. Is the fact that a movie is a smash hit a reason for liking it?

   6. Is the fact that your friends like a movie relevant to the issue of whether to see it?

▲ 7. Is the fact that your friends like a movie a reason for liking it?

   8. Is the fact that your friends like a movie relevant to the issue of whether to say that you like it?

   9. Is the fact that movie critics like a movie relevant to the issue of whether to see it?

▲ 10. Is it bandwagon pseudoreasoning to advertise a product as best-selling?

Exercise 5-4

The acceptability of laws banning discrimination against gay men and lesbians has been fairly controversial in recent years. Many arguments about it stem from a point made in the following dialogue. Read it and discuss the question that follows.

> UNDECIDED: I'm trying to decide whether to vote for or against that voter initiative on civil rights for gay men and lesbians. I understand that the initiative would prohibit cities from passing laws that forbid discriminating against them.
> DECIDED: I didn't have any trouble with that one; I'm voting for it. I don't think gay men and lesbians should be given special rights that nobody else has.

Has Decided brought in a red herring, or not?

Exercise 5-5

For each of the passages that follow, determine whether pseudoreasoning is present and, if so, whether it fits one of the categories described in this chapter. In particular, notice whether there is an appeal to emotion and, if so, whether it is relevant to the main issue. (You'll have to make sure you know what the main issue *is*, of course!)

▲ 1. Boss to employee: "I'll be happy to tell you why this report needs to be finished by Friday. If it isn't ready by then, you'll be looking for another job. How's that for a reason?"

2. Mother: "I think he has earned an increase in his allowance. He doesn't have any spending money at all, and he's always having to make excuses about not being able to go out with the rest of his friends because of that."

3. Mother to father: "You know, I really believe that our third-grader's friend Joe comes from an impoverished family. He looks to me as though he doesn't get enough to eat. I think I'm going to start inviting him to have dinner at our house once or twice a week."

▲ 4. "Aw, c'mon, Jake, let's go hang out at Dave's. Don't worry about your parents; they'll get over it. You know, the one thing I really like about you is that you don't let your parents tell you what to do."

5. Overheard: "You're telling me that you actually believe that this battery will last twenty-five years? Well, I've got some nice oceanfront property in Nebraska that you might like to buy, too."

6. FRED: I think we should just buy the new truck and call it a business expense so we can write it off on our taxes.
ETHEL: I don't know, Fred. That sounds like cheating to me. We wouldn't really use the truck very much in the business, you know.
FRED: Oh, don't worry about it. This kind of thing is done all the time.

▲ 7. I'm going to use the textbook that's on reserve in the library. I'll have to spend more time on the campus, but it's sure better than shelling out over a hundred bucks for one book.

8. Imagine yourself alone beside your broken-down car at the side of a country road in the middle of the night. Few pass by and no one stops to help. Don't get caught like that—don't get caught without your Polytech cellular phone!

9. One political newcomer to another: "I tell you, Sam, you'd better change those liberal views of yours. I know there has been a temporary pause, but the general slant toward conservatism is not over yet. You'll be left behind unless you change your mind about some things."

▲ 10. Reporter COKIE ROBERTS: Mr. Cheney, aside from the legal issues that stem from the various United Nations resolutions, isn't there an overriding moral dimension to the suffering of so many Kurdish people in Iraq? (Former) Secretary of Defense DICK CHENEY: Well, we recognize that's a tragic situation, Cokie, but there are tragic situations occurring all over the world.

Adapted from an interview on National Public Radio's Morning Edition

Exercise 5-6 ————————————————————————————

For each of the following passages: (a) briefly state the main issue; (b) identify the feeling or sentiment, if any, the speaker or writer is trying to express or elicit; and (c) state whether that feeling or sentiment, or any claim made in the effort to elicit it, is relevant to the main issue. In addition, (d) if the passage illustrates a type of pseudoreasoning that has a name, give its name.

▲ 1. "Grocers are concerned about *sanitation problems* from beverage residue that Proposition 11 could create. Filthy returned cans and bottles—*over 11 billion a year*—don't belong in grocery stores, where our food is stored and sold. . . . Sanitation problems in other states with similar laws have caused increased use of *chemical sprays* in grocery stores to combat rodents and insects. Vote no on 11."

Argument against Proposition 11, California ballot pamphlet

2. Overheard: "I'm not going to vote for Tomley for governor, and you shouldn't either. I lived in L.A. when Tomley was mayor, and the crime was so bad we had to leave. You couldn't walk around alone, for fear of your life, and I mean this was the middle of the day!"

3. STUDENT: I think I deserve a better grade than this on the second question.
PROF: Could be. Why do you think so?
STUDENT: You think my answer's wrong.
PROF: Well, your answer *is* wrong.
STUDENT: Maybe you think so, but I don't. You can't mark me wrong just because my answer doesn't fit your opinion.

▲ 4. C'mon, George, the river's waiting and everyone's going to be there. You want me to tell 'em you're gonna worry on Saturday about a test you don't take 'til Tuesday? What're people going to think?

5. ATTENDANT: I'm sorry, sir, but we don't allow people to top off their gas tanks at this station. There's a state law against it, you know.
RICHARD: What? You've got to be kidding! I've never heard of a place that stopped people from doing that!

6. One roommate to another: "I'm telling you, George, you shouldn't take Highway 50 this weekend. In this weather, it's going to be icy and danger-ous. Somebody slides off that road and gets killed nearly every winter. And you don't even have any chains for your car!"

▲ 7. That, in sum, is my proposal, ladies and gentlemen. You know that I trust and value your judgment, and I am aware I could not find a more astute panel of experts to evaluate my suggestion. Thank you.

8. Letter to the editor: "So Joanne Edwards wishes that the Army Reserves would not use Walnut Park for exercises, does she? Well, Ms. Edwards, par-

don me, but I hardly think that the Reserves disturb the solitude of the park. After all, we should be proud of our armed forces who stand ever-prepared to defend flag, nation, and American honor."

Tri-County Observer

9. Businessman to partner: "I'm glad Brownell has some competition these days. That means when we take estimates for the new job, we can simply ignore his, no matter what it is. That'll teach him a lesson for not throwing any business our way last year."

▲ 10. One local to another: "I tell you, it's disgusting. These college students come up here and live for four years—and ruin the town—and then vote on issues that will affect us long after they've gone somewhere else. This has got to stop! I say, let only those who have a genuine stake in the future of this town vote here! Transient kids shouldn't determine what's going to happen to local residents. Most of these kids come from Philadelphia . . . let them vote there."

Exercise 5-7 _____

For each of the following passages: (a) briefly state the main issue; (b) identify the feeling or sentiment, if any, the speaker or writer is trying to express or elicit; and (c) state whether that feeling or sentiment, or any claim made in the effort to elicit it, is relevant to the main issue. In addition, (d) if the passage illustrates a type of pseudoreasoning that has a name, give its name.

▲ 1. Chair, Department of Rhetoric (to department faculty): "If you think about it, I'm certain you'll agree with me that Mary Smith is the best candidate for department secretary. I urge you to join with me in recommending her to the administration. Concerning another matter, I'm now setting up next semester's schedule, and I hope that I'll be able to give you all the classes you have requested."

2. NELLIE: I really don't see anything special about Sunquist grapefruit. They taste the same as any other grapefruit to me.
   NELLIE'S MOM: Hardly! Don't forget that your Uncle Henry owns Sunquist. If everyone buys his fruit, you may inherit a lot of money some day!

3. Letter to the editor: "It's unfortunate that there are so many short-sighted people who want to cut the military budget even further than the administration wants to cut it. There may be less of a threat from Russia these days (although you can bet they'll be back!), but they aren't the only ones we have to worry about. Most of the countries of the world are jealous of our success and would like to take what we've got for themselves. It'll be our military that keeps them from doing it."

Miltonville Gazette

▲ 4. *"Don't risk letting a fatal accident rob your family of the home they love—on the average more than 250 Americans die each day because of accidents.* What would happen to your family's home if you were one of them?

Your home is so much more than just a place to live. It's a community you've chosen carefully . . . a neighborhood . . . a school district . . . the way of life you and your family have come to know. And you'd want your family to continue sharing its familiar comforts, even if suddenly you were no longer there. . . . Now, as a Great Western mortgage customer, you can protect the home you love. . . . Just complete the Enrollment Form enclosed for you."

Advertisement from Colonial Penn Life Insurance Company

5. "You've made your mark and your scotch says it all."

Glen Haven Reserve

6. Dear Senator Jenkins,
   I am writing to urge your support for higher salaries for state correctional facility guards. I am a clerical worker at Kingsford Prison, and I know whereof I speak. Guards work long hours, often giving up weekends, at a dangerous job. They cannot afford expensive houses or even nice clothes. Things that other state employees take for granted, like orthodontia for their children and a second car, are not possibilities on their salaries, which, incidentally, have not been raised in five years. Their dedication deserves better.
   Very truly yours, . . .

▲ 7. In *Shelley v. Kraemer*, 334 U.S.1 (1948), the "argument" was put before the Supreme Court that "state courts stand ready to enforce restrictive covenants excluding white persons from the ownership or occupancy of property covered by such agreements," and that therefore "enforcement of covenants excluding colored persons may not be deemed a denial of equal protection of the laws to the colored persons who are thereby affected." The court decided that "this contention does not bear scrutiny." In fact, the contention seems to be an example of what form of pseudoreasoning?

8. The suggestion was once made to replace the word "manpower" in the course description of Dartmouth's Business Administration 151, Management of Human Resources, because of the sexist connotation of the word. This brought delighted responses in the press. Shouldn't they get rid of "management" in the course title, wrote someone, in favor of "personagement"? Shouldn't "human" in the title give way to "huperson," asked another? Is the course open to "freshpersons?" a third wondered. In fact, is the course open to any person? the same individual queried. "Son" is a masculine word; therefore "person" itself is sexist.

9. There are very good reasons for the death penalty. First, it serves as a deterrent to those who would commit capital offenses. Second, it is just and fair punishment for the crime committed. Third, reliable opinion polls show that over 70 percent of all Americans favor it. If so many people favor it, it has to be right.

▲ 10. Two famous political opponents are said to have had this exchange in the English Parliament:
   GLADSTONE: You, sir, will either die upon the gallows or succumb to a horrible social disease!

DISRAELI: That will depend, I suppose, upon whether I embrace your principles or your mistress.

11. Frankly, I think the Salvation Army, the Red Cross, and the Wildlife Fund will put my money to better use than my niece Alison and her husband would. They've wasted most of the money I've given them. So I think I'm going to leave a substantial portion of my estate to those organizations instead of leaving it all to my spendthrift relatives.

12. "The President's jobs bill is an excellent idea. He wasn't elected to do nothing!"

13. Student to teacher: "I've had to miss several classes and some quizzes because of some personal matters back home. I know you have a no-make-up policy, but there was really no way I could avoid having to be out of town; it really was not my fault."

▲ 14. BUD: So here's the deal. I'll arrange to have your car "stolen," and we'll split the proceeds from selling it to a disposer. Then you file a claim with your insurance company and collect from it.
   LOU: Gee, this sounds seriously illegal and dangerous.
   BUD: Illegal, yeah, but do you think this is the first time an insurance company ever had this happen? Why, they actually expect it—they even budget money for exactly this sort of thing.

15. Kibitzer, discussing the job Lamar Alexander did as secretary of education: "It was absolutely clear to me that Alexander was not going to do any good for American education. He was way too involved in money-making schemes to give any attention to the job *we* were paying him for. Do you know that back before he was appointed, he and his wife invested five thousand dollars in some stock deal, and four years later that stock was worth over eight hundred thousand dollars? Tell me there's nothing fishy about a deal like that!"

16. My opponent, the evolutionist, offers you a different history and a different self-image from the one I suggest. While I believe that you and I are made in the image of God and are only one step out of the Garden of Eden, he believes that you are made in the image of a monkey and are only one step out of the zoo.

▲ 17. "EPA study—Environmental Protection Agency officials have launched a new study to assess the risks of—brace yourself—taking showers. Seems someone in the EPA worries people might be injured by inhaling water vapor while taking a shower. No, we didn't make it up. It's true, according to a publication called EPA Watch.

   "Doubtless, several bureaucrats will take home paychecks for months while the imagined hazard is studied. Unfortunately, there's probably a 50-50 chance someone in Washington will decide showers really are dangerous.

   "Wonder if anyone at the EPA ever has studied the hazards of pouring billions of dollars into overregulation?"

   Charleston *(W.Va.)* Gazette

18. "Boomers beware! The 76 million people born between 1946 and 1964 are entering their prime working years. They'd better listen carefully. Douglas Bernheim, an economics professor at Princeton, says current retirees were 'extraordinarily lucky' in that their home values climbed, high inflation took the sting out of their fixed-rate mortgages, and there were big increases in private and public pensions. 'The average baby boomer must triple his or her rate of savings to avoid a precipitous decline of living standards during retirement,' Bernheim said. . . .

  "To be on the safe side, baby boomers should have an aggressive savings plan and not rely on government assurances of cushy retirement years. It is always best to err on the side of caution."

  Charleston (W. Va.) Daily Mail

19. [*Note:* A short time before the 1994 Olympics, figure skater Tonya Harding was accused of being involved in an effort to injure her principal competitor, Nancy Kerrigan. As of this date (2000) Tonya's back and skating again.] Overheard: "Should Tonya Harding resign from the United States Olympic Team? No way. Why, I feel sorry for her. Just imagine how *you'd* feel if everyone in the country was against you, accusing you of stuff like this. There's no need for people to pile it on like this."

Writing Exercises

1. Find an example of pseudoreasoning in a newspaper editorial or opinion magazine (substitute an example from an advertisement or a letter to the editor only as a last resort and only if your instructor permits it). Identify the issue and what side of the issue the writer supports. Explain why the passage you've chosen does not really support that position—that is, why it involves pseudoreasoning. If the writer's claims do support some other position (possibly on a different, related issue), describe what position they do support.

2. Should there be an amendment to the U.S. Constitution prohibiting desecration of the U.S. flag? Write a one-page essay defending a "yes" answer to this question. Take about fifteen minutes to write it. Put your name on the back of your paper. Avoid pseudoreasoning. When everyone is finished, your instructor will collect the papers and redistribute them to the class. In groups of four or five, read the papers that have been given to your group, looking for instances of pseudoreasoning. Do not look at the names of the authors. (Everyone will have tried to avoid pseudoreasoning, so you should not find many instances of it.) Your instructor will ask each group to select one paper to read to the class, the paper the group believes is the best. The group should be prepared to say what they like about the paper and how they think it might be improved.

3. Follow the instructions for Exercise 2, this time defending a "no" answer to the question, Should it be illegal to desecrate the U.S. flag?

Chapter 6

More Pseudoreasoning and Other Rhetorical Ploys

In Chapter 4 we explored some of the ways the rhetorical content of words and phrases can be used to manipulate belief and attitude; in Chapter 5 we examined some common appeals to emotions and related techniques. Obviously there is considerable overlap here; people frequently utilize the rhetorical content of words and phrases *to* appeal to emotions, desires, or fears.

Many rhetorical patterns in this next group are so common that their names frequently occur in popular speech, just as do "apple polishing" and "scare tactics" from Chapter 5. Likewise, many patterns from this chapter exploit the rhetorical content of words and phrases, using devices like those discussed earlier. Frequently, too, many of these patterns are dressed in the clothing of argument, and for this reason we refer to them as patterns of "pseudoreasoning," or "fallacies." (Once again, "fallacy" is the traditional word for a tempting but defective argument, and "pseudoreasoning" is our name for the various rhetorical techniques listed in this and the previous chapter.)

Sometimes pseudoreasoning and other rhetorical techniques are used *in place of* argument, and other times they are used *in addition to* argument. Still other times they are used *as if they were* legitimate argument, and this last is especially true of many patterns discussed in this chapter. The point to bear in mind about all the techniques we are discussing is this: They can all tempt us to accept a claim or modify our position on an issue without our having a good reason for doing so.

Ad Hominem

A common rhetorical move is to attempt to refute or rebut someone's opinion by criticizing the person himself or herself. However, logically, the faults of the person are one thing, and defects in what he or she says are quite another; and the faults of the individual don't automatically attach them-selves to what he or she says. This means that whenever we try to use a person's shortcomings as evidence of shortcomings in his or her claims, we had better be prepared to explain how the shortcomings of the person trans-fer to the person's claim. If such an explanation can't be made, we are guilty of **ad hominem** pseudoreasoning. In short, ad hominem pseudoreasoning al-most always results from saying, in effect,

> "So-and-so's claim should be rejected because so-and-so is _____ ," where nearly any term with presumably negative impact is placed in the blank (for example, "ignorant," "a liar," "a Republican," "a Democrat," "just saying that to get rich," and so on).

Rare exceptions can occur in which a person's shortcomings do auto-matically transfer to the person's claim, but such a transaction takes a pecu-liar kind of circumstance. "Moore's claim should be rejected because Moore has been paid to lie about this matter" might qualify as an example. But such exceptions are rare. True, when we have doubts about the credibility of a source, we must be careful before we *accept* a claim from that source. But the doubts are rarely sufficient grounds for *rejecting* the claim. No matter what claim Ms. Crete might make and no matter what Ms. Crete's faults might be, we are rarely justified in rejecting the claim as false simply because Ms. Crete has those faults.

■ *Personal Attack*

"Ad hominem" is Latin for "to the man," indicating that it is the person and not the subject matter that's being addressed. There are several subspecies of ad hominem pseudoreasoning. The first, illustrated by the examples above, is the **personal attack.** We engage in it when we make abusive remarks about a person and use them as grounds for rejecting what that person says. (We are also guilty of this type of pseudoreasoning when we reject the claims of people whom we simply dislike, as indicated in our discussion of bias in Chapter 3.)

■ *Circumstantial Ad Hominem*

A slightly different form of ad hominem is an attack, not on the person, but on the person's circumstances, inferring that a claim this person makes is false because somebody in that position could be expected to make such claims. Example:

> John says that we should reject what Father Hennesy says about the dangers of abortion because, "After all, he's a Catholic priest, and priests are required to hold such views."

It may be true that Father Hennesy is a priest and that his views on abor-tion represent those of the Catholic Church. That does not make his views false, however. John has given us an example of a **circumstantial ad hominem.**

The circumstantial variety of ad hominem is closely related to the personal attack variety. Sometimes, in fact, a person may intend to attack a speaker or writer by referring to the individual's circumstances—as when a conservative dismisses a writer's views on the grounds that the writer is a "bleeding-heart liberal." Notice, though, that in the example above, John may think very highly of Catholic priests in general and of Father Hennesy in particular and that John isn't really mounting a personal attack on Father Hennesy. Because the personal attack and circumstantial ad hominem categories overlap, trying to determine whether a particular example qualifies as one or the other can be an exercise in futility.

■ *Pseudorefutation*

Another type of ad hominem is based on claims of inconsistency. When we say that a person's claim is false because it's inconsistent with something else the person has said or done, we are guilty of **pseudorefutation.** It is one thing to charge someone with accepting claims that conflict with one another, because claims that conflict with one another cannot all be true. (For a discussion of this topic, see Appendix 1.) But the fact that a person may not act (or may not always have acted) as if the claim before us is true does not allow us to infer that the claim is false—or even that the person *thinks* the claim is false. We must allow people the opportunity to change their minds; sometimes we make claims that conflict with something we said earlier simply because we've learned that the earlier claim is false. Suppose, for example, the President changes course on welfare: He now supports a type of reform he used to oppose. Do we demonstrate some defect in his support by pointing out that he used to have a different opinion? Of course not. To refuse to allow a change of mind is to require that we carry our earliest opinions to the grave.

Sometimes a person's behavior seems inconsistent with what the person says. For example, Wright makes claims about the merits of generosity and urges others to be generous. But his own behavior is that of a very stingy, ungenerous person. We might quite correctly accuse Wright of hypocrisy, but it would be pseudoreasoning to give his behavior as a reason for rejecting his claims about generosity. Another example: Let's say your doctor tells you that you should not use tobacco. We engage in pseudorefutation if we discount her advice because she herself smokes. Again: Her behavior is not a reason for rejecting her claims about tobacco. (She may be seriously addicted to tobacco and simply has been unable to quit, even though she knows that her health would benefit from quitting.) Notice that charges of inconsistency can also amount to a type of personal attack—another instance of overlap among the varieties of ad hominem.

Pseudorefutation includes what has traditionally been known as *tu quoque* (or "you too") pseudoreasoning. Many times pseudorefutations boil down to nothing more than saying, "You too!" or "You do it, too!"

There were 750,000 people in New York's Central Park recently for Earth Day. They were throwing Frisbees, flying kites, and listening to Tom Cruise talk about how we have to recycle everything and stop corporations from polluting. Excuse me.

Didn't Tom Cruise make a stock-car movie in which he destroyed thirty-five cars, burned thousands of gallons of gasoline, and wasted dozens of tires? If I were given the opportunity, I'd say to Tom Cruise, "Tom, most people don't own thirty-five cars in their life, and you just trashed thirty-five cars for a movie. Now you're telling other people not to pollute the planet? Shut up, sir."

—RUSH LIMBAUGH

A pseudorefutation (ad hominem).

I get calls from nutso environmentalists who are filled with compassion for every snail darter that is threatened by some dam somewhere. Yet, they have no interest in the 1.5 million fetuses that are aborted every year in the United States. I love to argue with them and challenge their double standard.

—RUSH LIMBAUGH

Often a pseudorefutation will accuse someone of having a double standard. Notice how this example is combined with ridicule.

■ Poisoning the Well

Poisoning the well can be thought of as an ad hominem in advance. If someone dumps poison down your well, you don't drink from it. Similarly, when A poisons your mind about B by relating unfavorable information about B, you may be inclined to reject what B says to you.

Well-poisoning is easier to arrange than you might think. You might suppose that to poison someone's thinking about Mrs. Jones, you would have to say or at least insinuate something depreciatory or derogatory about her. In fact, recent psycholinguistic research suggests you can poison someone's thinking about Mrs. Jones by doing just the opposite! If we don't know Mrs. Jones, even a sentence that expresses an outright denial of a connection between her and something unsavory is apt to make us form an unfavorable impression of her. Psychological studies indicate that people are more apt to form an unfavorable impression of Mrs. Jones from a sentence like "Mrs. Jones is not an ax murderer" than from a sentence like "Mrs. Jones has a sister."

Moral: Because it might be easy for others to arrange for us to have a negative impression of someone, we must be extra careful not to reject what a person says *just because* we have an unfavorable impression of the individual.

Genetic Fallacy

Ad hominem types of attack can be directed at organizations, groups, or other entities as well as at specific individuals. For example, if we urge people to reject a policy *just* because it was put forth as part of the Republican or Democratic party platform, we commit pseudoreasoning. Similarly, it's a mistake to reject a policy *just* because it was formerly adopted, let's say, by a slave-holding state in the South back in the nineteenth century. The policy may have nothing to do with slavery, after all, and we should not rationally hold its background or history against it.

In general, when we reject a claim, policy, or position just because of its source, associations, or history, we commit the **genetic fallacy.** If this sounds to you a lot like what we said about ad hominem pseudoreasoning, you are perfectly correct. You can think of ad hominem as being a specific variety of the genetic fallacy; just remember that the genetic fallacy also includes cases where the source is not a specific individual.

Burden of Proof

To say that we put the burden of proof on one side of an issue is just to say that we're inclined at the outset to agree with the other side, unless of course the first side can convince us to change our minds. Listen to these two:

MOORE: If you rub red wine on your scalp, it will help your hair to grow back.

PARKER: Oh, baloney. That's not true at all.

Do you think one of these speakers is more likely to be correct than the other? If so, then that means you would be inclined to put the "burden of proof" on the other speaker. Say, for example, that you agree with Parker. In that case, you put the burden of proof on Moore. This is sort of like saying to Moore, "Oh, yeah? Then prove it!" Why would one ask Moore to prove his side rather than ask Parker to prove his side? Answering that question is what understanding the burden of proof is all about.

The **burden of proof** type of pseudoreasoning (its unabridged name is "inappropriate burden of proof") occurs when the burden of proof is placed on the *wrong* side of an issue or is placed too *heavily* on one side compared with the other. (Make sure you understand this.) Misplacing the burden of proof is a common rhetorical technique and is one of the most important that we'll cover in our discussions in this chapter.

Let's ask first, What reasonable grounds would make us place the burden of proof more on one side of an issue than the other? There are a variety of such grounds, but they fall mainly into three kinds of categories. We can express them as a set of rules of thumb:

1. *Initial plausibility.* In Chapter 3, we said that the more a claim coincides with our background information, the greater its initial plausibility. The general rule that most often governs the placement of the burden of proof is simply this: The less initial plausibility a claim has, the greater the burden of proof we place on someone who asserts that claim. This is just good sense,

▲   *Paleological pseudoreasoning!*

of course. We are quite naturally less skeptical about the claim that Charlie's now-famous eighty-seven-year-old grandmother drove a boat across Lake Michigan than we are about the claim that she swam across Lake Michigan. Unfortunately, this rule is a rule of thumb, not a rule that can be applied precisely. We are unable to assess the specific degree of a claim's plausibility and then determine with precision just exactly how much evidence its advocates need to produce to make us willing to accept the claim. But, as a rule of thumb, the initial plausibility rule can keep us from setting the requirements unreasonably high for some claims and allowing others to slide by unchallenged when they don't deserve to.

2. *Affirmative/negative.* Other things being equal, the burden of proof falls automatically on those supporting the affirmative side of an issue rather than on those supporting the negative side. In other words, we generally want to hear reasons why something *is* the case before we require reasons why it is *not* the case. Consider this conversation:

MOORE: The car won't start.

PARKER: Yeah, I know. It's a problem with the ignition.

MOORE: What makes you think that?

PARKER: Well, why not?

Parker's last remark seems strange because we generally require the affirmative side to assume the burden of proof; it is Parker's job to give reasons for thinking that the problem *is* in the ignition.

This rule applies to cases of existence versus nonexistence, too. Most often, the burden of proof should fall on those who claim something exists rather than on those who claim it doesn't. There are people who believe in ghosts, not because of any evidence that there *are* ghosts, but because nobody has shown there are no such things. (When someone claims that we should believe in such-and-such because nobody has proved that it *isn't* so, we have a subtype of burden of proof known as **appeal to ignorance.**) This is burden-of-proof pseudoreasoning because it mistakenly places the requirement of proving their position on those who do not believe in ghosts. (Of course, the first rule applies here, too, because ghosts are not part of background knowledge for most of us.)

In general, the affirmative side gets the burden of proof because it tends to be much more difficult—or at least much more inconvenient—to prove the negative side of an issue. Imagine a student who walks up to the ticket window at a football game and asks for a discounted student ticket. "Can you prove you're a student?" he is asked. "No," the student replies, "can you prove I'm not?" Well, it may be possible to prove he's not a student, but it's no easy chore, and it would be unreasonable to require it.

Incidentally, some people say it's *impossible* to "prove a negative." But difficult is not the same as impossible. And some "negatives" are even easy to prove. For example, "There are no elephants in this classroom."

3. *Special circumstances.* Sometimes getting at the truth is not the only thing we want to accomplish, and on such occasions we may purposely place the burden of proof on a particular side. Courts of law provide us with the most obvious example. Specific agreements can also move the burden of proof from where it would ordinarily fall. A contract might specify, "It will be presumed that you receive the information by the tenth of each month unless you show otherwise." In such cases, the rule governing the special circumstances should be clear and acceptable to all parties involved.

One important variety of special circumstances occurs when the stakes are especially high. For example, if you're thinking of investing your life savings in a company, you'll want to put a heavy burden of proof on the person who advocates making the investment. However, if the investment is small, one you can afford to lose, you might be willing to lay out the money even though it has not been thoroughly proved that the investment is safe. In short, it is reasonable to place a higher burden of proof on someone who advocates a policy that could be dangerous or costly if he or she is mistaken.

These three rules cover most of the ground in placing the burden of proof properly. Be careful about situations where people put the burden of proof on the side other than where our rules indicate it should fall. Take this example:

PARKER: I think we should invest more money in expanding the interstate highway system.

MOORE: I think that would be a big mistake.

Innocent Until Proved Guilty

We must point out that sometimes there are specific reasons why the burden of proof is placed entirely on one side. The obvious case in point is in criminal court, where it is the prosecution's job to prove guilt. The defense is not required to prove innocence; it must only try to keep the prosecution from succeeding in its attempt to prove guilt. We are, as we say, "innocent until proved guilty." As a matter of fact, it's possible that more trials might come to a correct conclusion (i.e., the guilty get convicted and the innocent acquitted) if the burden of proof were equally shared between prosecution and defense. But we have wisely decided that if we are to make a mistake, we would rather it be one of letting a guilty person go free than one of convicting an innocent person. Rather than a kind of pseudoreasoning, then, this lopsided placement of the burden of proof is how we guarantee a fundamental right: the presumption of innocence.

PARKER: How could anybody object to more highways?

With his last remark, Parker has attempted to put the burden of proof on Moore. Such tactics can put one's opponent in a defensive position; Moore now has to show why we should *not* spend more on roads rather than Parker having to show why we *should* spend more. This is an inappropriate burden of proof.

You should always be suspicious when an inability to *disprove* a claim is said to show that one is mistaken in doubting the claim or in saying that it's false. It does no such thing, unless the burden was on that person to disprove the claim. Inability to disprove that there is extrasensory perception (ESP) is no reason to think that one is mistaken in doubting that ESP exists. But psychics' repeated failure to prove that ESP exists *does* weaken *their* case because the burden of proof is on them.

Straw Man

We get a case of **straw man** rhetoric when someone ignores an opponent's actual position and presents in its place a distorted, oversimplified, or misrepresented version of that position. A distorted version of the opposition's views is more easily attacked, much like a straw man is more easily knocked over than a real one. Here are some examples:

Senator Peckingham says she's against tightening the immigration laws. Clearly she doesn't mind the idea of having the country overrun by illegal aliens, who soak up resources and pay next to nothing in taxes.

Mr. and Mrs. Herrington are arguing about cleaning out their attic. "Why, we just went through all that old stuff last year," Mr. Herrington exclaims. "Do we have to clean it out every day?"

"There you go again," his wife retorts, "exaggerating as usual. Nobody said anything about doing it every day—it's just that you want to keep everything around forever, and that's ridiculous."

The Herringtons are each stating distorted versions of the other's position. Presumably Mrs. Herrington does not want to clean the attic out on a daily basis, nor is it likely that Mr. Herrington wants to keep every old thing around forever. In the first example, the speaker has distorted the senator's position. Who said anything about allowing illegal aliens to overrun the country? Not the senator—leaving the immigration laws as they are is a far cry from allowing illegal aliens to overrun the country. Immigration laws deal with *legal* immigration, after all. (Notice that the speaker has used a red herring to create the straw position.)

I'm a very controversial figure to the animal rights movement. They no doubt view me with some measure of hostility because I am constantly challenging their fundamental premise that animals are superior to human beings.

—RUSH LIMBAUGH, setting up another straw man for the kill

False Dilemma

The pattern of pseudoreasoning known as **false dilemma** results from limiting consideration to only two alternatives when in fact there are others that deserve consideration. Take a look at these examples:

CONGRESSMAN CLAGHORN: Guess we're going to have to cut back expenditures on social programs again this year.

YOU: Why's that?

CLAGHORN: Well, we either do that or live with this high deficit, and that's something we can't allow.

DANIEL: Theresa and I both endorse this idea of allowing prayer in public schools, don't we, Theresa?

THERESA: I never said any such thing!

DANIEL: Hey, I didn't know you were an atheist!

In the first example, Claghorn maintains that either we live with the high deficit or we cut social programs, and that therefore, because we can't live with the high deficit, we have to cut social programs. But this reasoning works only if cutting social programs is the *only* alternative to a high deficit. Of course, that is not the case (taxes might be raised, or military spending cut, for example).

In the other example, Daniel's "argument" amounts to this: Either you endorse prayer in public schools, or you are an atheist; therefore, because you do not endorse school prayer, you must be an atheist. But a person does not

Guns are not the issue. Hate, what pulled the trigger of violence, is the issue.

—VIKKI BUCKLEY, *secretary of state of Colorado, speaking at the 1999 National Rifle Association annual meeting in Denver, a few weeks after two teenagers had killed fifteen people, including themselves, at a high school in Littleton, Colorado*

Does this strike you as a false dilemma?

have to be an atheist in order to feel unfavorable toward prayer in public schools. The alternatives Daniel presents, in other words, could both be false. Theresa might not be an atheist and still not endorse school prayer.

The example Daniel provides us shows how this type of pseudoreasoning and the preceding one can work together: A straw man is often used as part of a false dilemma. A person who wants us to accept X may not only ignore other alternatives besides Y but also exaggerate or distort Y. In other words, this person leaves only *one* "reasonable" alternative because the only other one provided is really a straw man. You can also think of a false dilemma as a false dichotomy.

It might help in understanding false dilemmas to look quickly at a *real* dilemma. Consider: You know that the Smiths heat their house in the winter. You also know that the only heating options available in their location are gas and electricity. Under these circumstances, if you find out that they do *not* have electric heat, it must indeed be true that they have gas heat because that's the only alternative remaining. False dilemma pseudoreasoning occurs only when reasonable alternatives are ignored. In such cases, both X and Y may be false, and some other alternative may be true.

Therefore, before you accept X because some alternative, Y, is false, make certain that X and Y cannot *both* be false. Look especially for some third alternative, some way of rejecting Y without having to accept X. Example:

DANIEL: Look, Theresa, you're going to have to make up your mind. Either you decide that you can afford this stereo, or you decide that you're going to do without music for a while.

Theresa could reject both of Daniel's alternatives (buying this stereo and going without music) because of some obvious third possibilities. One, she might find a less expensive stereo. Or, two, she might buy a part of this stereo now—just the CD player, amplifier, and speakers, say—and postpone until later purchase of the rest.

▲ *Has Mom fallen for a false* trilemma?

Before moving on, we should point out that there is more than one way to present a pair of alternatives. Aside from the obvious "either X or Y" version we've described so far, we can use the form "if not X, then Y." For instance, in the example at the beginning of the section, Congressman Claghorn can say, "Either we cut back on expenditures, or we'll have a big deficit," but he can accomplish the same thing by saying, "If we don't cut back on expenditures, then we'll have a big deficit." These two ways of stating the dilemma are equivalent to one another. Claghorn gets the same result: After denying that we can tolerate the high deficit, he concludes that we'll have to cut back expenditures. Again, it's the artificial narrowness of the alternatives—the falsity of the claim that says "if not one, then surely the other"—that makes this pseudoreasoning.

■ *Perfectionist Fallacy*

A particular subspecies of false dilemma and common rhetorical ploy is something we call the **perfectionist fallacy.** It comes up when a plan or policy is under consideration, and it goes like this:

> If policy X will not meet our goals as well as we'd like them met (i.e., "perfectly"), then policy X should be rejected.

This principle downgrades policy X simply because it isn't perfection. It's a version of false dilemma because it says, in effect, "Either the policy is perfect, or else we must reject it."

An excellent example of the perfectionist fallacy comes from the National Football League's experience with the instant replay rule, which allows an off-field official to review videotape of a play to determine whether the on-field official's ruling was correct. To help the replay official, tape from several angles can be viewed, and the play run in slow motion.

One of the most often heard arguments against the use of videotape replays goes like this: "It's a mistake to use replays to make calls because no matter how many cameras you have following the action on the field, you're still going to miss some calls. There's no way to see everything that's going on."

According to this type of reasoning, we should not have police unless they can prevent *every* crime or apprehend *every* criminal. You can probably think of other examples that show perfectionist reasoning to be very unreliable indeed.

■ Line-Drawing Fallacy

Another version of the false dilemma is called the line-drawing fallacy. An example comes from the much-publicized Los Angeles case in which four police officers were acquitted of beating Rodney King. After the trial, one of the jurors indicated that an argument like the following finally convinced her and at least one other juror to vote "not guilty":

> Everybody agrees that the first time one of the officers struck King with a nightstick it did not constitute excessive force. Therefore, if we are to conclude that excessive force was indeed used, then sometime during the course of the beating (during which King was hit about fifty times) there must have been a moment—a particular blow—at which the force *became* excessive. Since there is no point at which we can determine that the use of force changed from warranted to excessive, we are forced to conclude that it did not become excessive at any time during the beating; and so the officers did not use excessive force.

These jurors accepted the **line-drawing fallacy,** the fallacy of insisting that a line must be drawn at some precise point when in fact it is not necessary that such a line be drawn.

To see how this works, consider another example: Clearly, it is impossible for a person who is not rich to become rich by our giving her one dollar. But, equally clearly, if we give our lucky person a million dollars, one at a time (very quickly, obviously—maybe we have a machine to deal them out), she will be rich. According to the line-drawing argument, however, *if we cannot point to the precise dollar that makes her rich, then she can never get rich, no matter how much money she is given!*

The problem, of course, is that the concepts referred to by "rich" and "excessive force" (and many others) are vague concepts. We can find cases where the concepts clearly apply and cases where they clearly do not apply. But it is not at all clear exactly where the borderlines are.

Many logicians interpret line drawing as a variety of slippery slope (discussed next). The King case might be seen this way: If the first blow struck against King did not amount to excessive violence, then there's nothing in

[People] who are voyeurs, if they are not irredeemably sick, . . . feel ashamed at what they are witnessing.

—IRVING KRISTOL, "Pornography, Obscenity, and the Case for Censorship"

Do you find any pseudoreasoning here? (In fact, you might identify either false dilemma or begging the question.)

the series of blows to change that fact. So there's no excessive violence at the end of the series, either.

Our own preference is to see line-drawing fallacies as a version of false dilemma. They present the following alternatives: Either there is a precise place where we draw the line, or else there is no line to be drawn (no difference) between one end of the scale and the other. Either there is a certain blow at which the force used against King became excessive, or else the force never became excessive.

Again, remember that our pseudoreasoning categories sometimes overlap. When that happens, it doesn't matter as much which way we classify a case as that we see that an error is being made.

Slippery Slope

We've all heard people make claims of this sort: "If we let X happen, the first thing you know Y will be happening." This is one form of the **slippery slope.** Such claims amount to pseudoreasoning when in fact there is no reason to think that X will lead to Y. Sometimes X and Y can be the same kind of thing or can bear some kind of similarity to one another, but that doesn't mean that one will inevitably lead to the other.

Opponents of handgun control sometimes use a slippery slope argument, saying that if laws to register handguns are passed, the next thing we know there will be laws to make owning any kind of gun illegal. This is pseudoreasoning if there is no reason to think that the first kind of law will make the second kind more likely. It's up to the person who offers the slippery slope claim to show *why* the first action will lead to the second.

It is also argued that one should not experiment with certain drugs because experimentation is apt to lead to serious addiction or dependence. In the case of drugs that are known to be addictive, there is no pseudoreasoning present—the likelihood of the progression is clear.

The other version of slippery slope occurs when someone claims we must continue a certain course of action simply because we have already begun that course. It was said during the Vietnam War that because the United States had already sent troops to Vietnam, it was necessary to send more troops to support the first ones. Unless there is some reason supplied to show that the first step *must* lead to the others, this is pseudoreasoning. (Notice that it's easy to make a false dilemma out of this case as well; do you see how to do it?)

Sometimes we take the first step in a series, and then we realize that it was a mistake. To insist on taking the remainder when we could admit our mistake and retreat is to fall prey to slippery slope pseudoreasoning. (If you insist on following one bad bet with another one, we'd like to invite you to a friendly poker game.)

Slippery slope pseudoreasoning has considerable force because *psychologically* one item does often lead to another even though *logically* it does no such thing. When we think of X, say, we may be led immediately to think of Y. But this certainly does not mean that X itself is necessarily followed by Y. Once again, to think that Y has to follow X is to engage in slippery slope thinking; to do so when there is no particular reason to think Y must follow X is to commit slippery slope pseudoreasoning.

Begging the Question

Here's a version of a simple example of begging the question, one that's been around a long time (we'll return to it later):

> Two gold miners roll a boulder away from its resting place and find three huge gold nuggets underneath. One says to the other, "Great! That's one nugget for you and two for me," handing one nugget to his associate.
> "Wait a minute!" says the second miner. "Why do you get two and I get just one?"
> "Because I'm the leader of this operation," says the first.
> "What makes you the leader?" asks miner number two.
> "I've got twice the gold you do," answers miner number one.

Gay marriages should not be legal because if there wasn't anything wrong with them they would already be legal, which they aren't.
—From a student essay

If you examine this "reasoning" closely, it says that gay marriages shouldn't be legal because they aren't legal. This is not quite "X is true just because X is true," but it's close. The issue is whether the law should be changed. So giving the existence of the law as a "reason" for its *not* being changed can carry no weight, logically.

This next example is quite famous: Some people say they can prove God exists. When asked how, they reply, "Well, the Scriptures say very clearly that God must exist." Then, when asked why we should believe the Scriptures, they answer, "The Scriptures are divinely inspired by God himself, so they must be true."

The problem with such reasoning is that the claim at issue—whether it's the case that God exists—turns out to be one of the very premises the argument is based on. If we can't trust the Scriptures, then the argument isn't any good, but the reason given for trusting the Scriptures requires the existence of God, the very thing we were arguing for in the first place! Examples like this are sometimes called circular reasoning or arguing in a circle because they start from much the same place as they end up.

Persuasive definitions can beg questions. Consider an example from an earlier chapter: If we define abortion as "the murder of innocent children," then it's obvious that abortion is morally wrong. But of course anyone who doubts that abortion is morally wrong is certainly not going to accept the definition just given. That person will most likely refuse to recognize an embryo or early-stage fetus as a "child" at all and will certainly not accept the word "murder" in the definition.

And this brings us to the real problem in cases of question begging: a misunderstanding of what premises (and definitions) it is reasonable for one's audience to accept. We are guilty of **begging the question** when we ask our audience to accept premises that are as controversial as the conclusion we're arguing for and are controversial on the same grounds. The sort of

"I believe the President is telling the truth because he
says he's telling the truth."

grounds on which people would disagree about the morality of abortion are much the same as those on which they would disagree about the definition of abortion above. The person making the argument has not "gone back far enough," as it were, to find common ground with the audience whom he or she wishes to convince.

Let's return to our feuding gold miners to illustrate what we're talking about. Clearly, the two disagree about who gets the gold, and, given what being the leader of the operation means, they're going to disagree just as much about that. But what if the first miner says, "Look, I picked this spot, didn't I? And we wouldn't have found anything if we'd worked where you wanted to work." If the second miner agrees, they'll have found a bit of common ground. Maybe—*maybe*—the first miner can then convince the second that this point, on which they agree, is worth considering when it comes to splitting the gold. At least there's a chance of moving the discussion forward when they proceed this way.

In fact, if you are ever to hope for any measure of success in trying to convince somebody of a claim, you should always try to argue for it based on whatever common ground you can find between the two of you. Indeed, the attempt to find common ground from which to start is what underlies the entire enterprise of rational debate.

Recap

The patterns of pseudoreasoning covered in this chapter, like some of those in Chapter 5, may resemble legitimate arguments, but none can give us a reason for accepting or rejecting a claim.

The discussion in these chapters should help make you sensitive to the difference between considerations that are truly relevant to a conclusion and the emotional appeals, factual irrelevancies, and other devices that often take the place of good reasoning.

In this chapter we examined the following types of pseudoreasoning:

Ad hominem—attacking the person offering a claim or argument rather than attacking the claim or argument

> Personal attack—saying bad things about the individual's character, history, and so forth
>
> Circumstantial ad hominem—basing the attack on the individual's situation, job, or other special circumstance
>
> Pseudorefutation—basing the attack on the claim that the individual has spoken or otherwise acts as if he or she doesn't believe the claim; a charge of inconsistency
>
> Poisoning the well—committing an ad hominem before the individual even has a chance to make the claim in question; an "ad hominem in advance"

Genetic fallacy—denying a claim because of its origins; includes ad hominem attacks but also includes attacks on groups, political parties, organizations

Burden of proof—requiring the wrong side of an issue to make its case

Straw man—offering or accepting a distorted or exaggerated version of a position in place of the actual, more reasonable version

False dilemma—erroneously narrowing down the range of alternatives; saying we have to do X or Y when in reality we might choose Z

> Perfectionist fallacy—allowing only the alternatives of adopting a policy that will solve a problem perfectly and completely or doing nothing at all
>
> Line-drawing fallacy—requiring that a precise line be drawn someplace on a scale or continuum when no such precise line can be drawn; usually occurs when a vague concept is treated like a precise one

Slippery slope—refusing to take the first step in a progression on unwarranted grounds that doing so will make taking the remaining steps

Issue Advocacy Advertising

Recently, Citizens for Better Medicare sponsored a TV ad campaign featuring likable older people (especially a hip white-haired woman named "Flo") warning senior citizens that "big government" was set to dictate what medicines they could take. Pretty scary, huh? And, if you can't trust Citizens for Better Medicare, whom can you trust? In fact, "Citizens for Better Medicare" is not your everyday group of concerned citizens, but an advocacy group sponsored by the pharmaceutical industry. The drug companies were worried about price controls on drugs under Medicare reform proposed by Bill Clinton, and they spent $30 million on TV ads to get us to worry about them, too.

Ads like this are examples of "issue advocacy ads," which try to influence public opinion on proposals being considered in Congress or state legislatures. Usually such ads appear merely to be giving unbiased information on important issues and often seem to be sponsored by concerned citizens' groups. In fact, they usually present only one side of an issue, the side advocated by some particular business interest. Frequently they play on our fears or get us to rise up in indignation (which is why we mention them here in our chapters on pseudoreasoning). A famous example was the "Harry and Louise" campaign paid for by the health insurance industry, which featured two real-life people expressing their worries that a Clinton health reform package would limit people's choice of doctors. After the ads aired, public opinion, which had favored the Clinton proposals, reversed itself; reform never did see the light of day. (Interestingly enough, with no reform, people now have even less choice in their doctors than they had at the time.) More recently, a coalition of HMOs sponsored an ad blitz intended to defeat a (bipartisan) bill that would allow patients to sue health plans. The ads claimed the bill would make lawyers rich by drowning the courts with new lawsuits that "could cost 2 million Americans their health insurance." (Portraying the bill as enriching lawyers was good strategy: Surveys indicate people dislike lawyers even more than health plans.)

When you see an issue advocacy ad, remember you are seeing only one side of the picture, and be alert for plays on emotions.

inevitable; or insisting erroneously on taking the remainder of the steps simply because the first one was taken

Begging the question—assuming as true the very claim that is at issue

Having read this chapter and the chapter recap, you should be able to

▲ Identify further instances of pseudoreasoning when you encounter it

▲ Explain and give examples of the types of pseudoreasoning described in this chapter

Exercises

Exercise 6-1

Working in groups, invent a simple, original, and clear illustration of each pattern of pseudoreasoning covered in this chapter. Then in the class as a whole select the illustrations that are clearest and most straightforward. Go over these illustrations before doing the remaining exercises in this chapter, and review them before you take a test on this material.

Exercise 6-2

Classify each of the following cases of ad hominem pseudoarguments as personal attack, circumstantial ad hominem, pseudorefutation, poisoning the well, or genetic fallacy. Identify the cases, if any, in which it might be difficult or futile to assign the item to any single one of these categories, as well as those cases, if any, where the item doesn't fit comfortably into any of these categories at all.

▲ 1. The proponents of this spend-now–pay-later boondoggle would like you to believe that this measure will cost you only one billion dollars. That's NOT TRUE. In the last general election some of these very same people argued against unneeded rail projects because they would cost taxpayers millions more in interest payments. Now they have changed their minds and are willing to encourage irresponsible borrowing. Connecticut is already awash in red ink. Vote NO.

2. Rush Limbaugh argues that the establishment clause of the First Amendment should not be stretched beyond its intended dimensions by precluding voluntary prayer in public schools. This is a peculiar argument, when you consider that Limbaugh is quite willing to stretch the Second Amendment to include the right to own assault rifles and Saturday night specials.

3. I think you can safely assume that Justice Scalia's opinions on the cases before the Supreme Court this term will be every bit as flaky as his past opinions.

▲ 4. Harvard now takes the position that its investment in urban redevelopment projects will be limited to projects that are environmentally friendly. Before you conclude that that is such a swell idea, stop and think. For a long time Harvard was one of the biggest slumlords in the country.

5. REPUBLICAN: Finally! Finally the governor is getting around to reducing taxes—as he promised. What do you think of his plan?
DEMOCRAT: Not much. He's just doing it so the Democrats won't get all the credit.

6. Dear Editor—
I read with amusement the letter by Leslie Burr titled "It's time to get tough." Did anyone else notice a little problem in her views? It seems a

little odd that somebody who claims that she "loathes violence" could also say that "criminals should pay with their life." I guess consistency isn't Ms. Burr's greatest concern.

▲ 7. YOU: Look at this. It says here that white males still earn a lot more than minorities and women for doing the same job.
YOUR FRIEND: Yeah, right. Written by some woman, no doubt.

8. "Steve Thompson of the California Medical Association said document-checking might even take place in emergency rooms. That's because, while undocumented immigrants would be given emergency care, not all cases that come into emergency rooms fall under the federal definition of an emergency.

   "To all those arguments initiative proponents say hogwash. They say the education and health groups opposing the initiative are interested in protecting funding they receive for providing services to the undocumented."

   Article in Sacramento Bee

9. Horace, you're new to this town, and I want to warn you about the local newspaper. It's in cahoots with all them left-wing environmental nutcakes that are wrecking the economy around here. You can't believe a thing you read in it.

▲ 10. WASHINGTON (AP)—A California ballot measure that would eliminate most public services for illegal immigrants drew its first opposition from national Republican leaders Wednesday, as conservatives Jack Kemp and William Bennett denounced it.

   The former Republican cabinet secretaries issued a statement criticizing Proposition 187 as contrary to conservative principles and likely to encourage racial discrimination.

   "For some, immigrants have become a popular political social scapegoat," the two said.

   "But concerns about illegal immigration should not give rise to a series of fundamentally flawed, constitutionally questionable 'solutions' which are not consonant with our history."

   California's Gov. Pete Wilson, also a Republican, has made support for Proposition 187 a cornerstone of his re-election campaign. At an appearance in Los Angeles, Wilson said, "My response is those are two guys in Washington and it's clear they've been there too long. I think when you spend too much time in an ivory tower think tank, you begin to lose touch with reality."

   Associated Press

11. Creationism cannot possibly be true. People who believe in a literal interpretation of the Bible just never outgrew the need to believe in Santa Claus.

12. "Americans spend between $28 billion and $61 billion a year in medical costs for treatment of hypertension, heart disease, cancer and other ill-

nesses attributed to consumption of meat, says a report out today from a pro-vegetarian doctor's group.

"Dr. Neal D. Barnard, lead author of the report in the *Journal of Preventive Medicine*, and colleagues looked at studies comparing the health of vegetarians and meat eaters, then figured the cost of treating illnesses suffered by meat eaters in excess of those suffered by vegetarians. Only studies that controlled for the health effects of smoking, exercise and alcohol consumption were considered.

"The American Medical Association, in a statement from Dr. M. Roy Schwarz, charged that Barnard's group is an 'animal rights front organization' whose agenda 'definitely taints whatever unsubstantiated findings it may claim.'"   USA Today

Exercise 6-3

In groups, vote on which option best depicts the pattern of pseudoreasoning found in each passage; then compare results with other groups in the class. *Note:* The patterns include those found in Chapter 5 and Chapter 6.

▲ 1. The Health Editor for *USA Today* certainly seems to know what she is talking about when she recommends we take vitamins, but I happen to know she works for Tishcon, Inc., a large manufacturer of vitamin supplements.
   a. smokescreen/red herring
   b. subjectivist fallacy
   c. appeal to popularity
   d. circumstantial ad hominem
   e. no pseudoreasoning

  2. The City Council wants to raise fees for sanitary disposal service. Well, that's pretty ridiculous when you think about it, the idea of milking people for every last cent they earn to pick up their garbage.
   a. common practice
   b. peer pressure
   c. bandwagon
   d. straw man
   e. begging the question

  3. Well, I for one think the position taken by our union is correct, and I'd like to remind you before you make up your mind on the matter that around here we employees have a big say in who gets rehired.
   a. wishful thinking
   b. ad hominem
   c. scare tactics
   d. apple polishing
   e. begging the question

▲ 4. On the whole, I think global warming is a farce. After all, most people think winters are getting colder, if anything. How could that many people be wrong?

    a. appeal to indignation
    b. appeal to popularity
    c. straw man
    d. no pseudoreasoning

5. MARCO: I think global warming is a farce.
    CLAUDIA: Oh, gad. How can you say such a thing, when there is so much evidence behind the theory?
    MARCO: Because. Look. If it isn't a farce, then how come the world is colder now than it used to be?
    a. begging the question
    b. subjectivist fallacy
    c. red herring
    d. circumstantial ad hominem
    e. no pseudoreasoning

6. Of course you should buy a life insurance policy! Why shouldn't you?
    a. smokescreen/red herring
    b. wishful thinking
    c. scare tactics
    d. peer pressure
    e. burden of proof

▲ 7. My opponent, Mr. London, has charged me with having cheated on my income tax. My response is, When are we going to get this campaign out of the gutter? Isn't it time we stood up and made it clear that vilification has no place in politics?
    a. smokescreen/red herring
    b. wishful thinking
    c. common practice
    d. appeal to popularity
    e. circumstantial ad hominem

8. Either we impeach the man or we send a message to the kids of this country that it's all right to lie under oath. Seems like an easy choice to me.
    a. smokescreen/red herring
    b. straw man
    c. false dilemma
    d. pseudorefutation
    e. none of these

9. If cigarettes aren't bad for you, then how come it's so hard on your health to smoke?
    a. circumstantial ad hominem
    b. genetic fallacy
    c. slippery slope
    d. begging the question

▲ 10. Global warming? I don't care what the scientists say. Just 'cause it's true for them doesn't make it true for me.

    a. smokescreen/red herring
    b. subjectivist fallacy
    c. appeal to popularity
    d. common practice

Exercise 6-4 _____

In groups, vote on which option best depicts the pattern of pseudoreasoning found in each passage, and compare results with other groups. (It is all right with us if you ask anyone who is not participating in the discussions in your group to leave.) *Note:* The patterns include those found in Chapter 5 and Chapter 6.

▲ 1. So what if the senator accepted a little kickback money—most politicians are corrupt, after all.
    a. appeal to popularity
    b. bandwagon
    c. common practice
    d. subjectivist fallacy
    e. no pseudoreasoning

  2. Me? I'm going to vote with the majority on this one. After all, their proposal is going to win. I don't want to be on the losing side.
    a. genetic fallacy
    b. bandwagon
    c. slippery slope
    d. no pseudoreasoning

  3. Public opinion polls? They're rigged. Just ask anyone.
    a. common practice
    b. bandwagon
    c. begging the question
    d. appeal to popularity
    e. no pseudoreasoning

▲ 4. Hey! It can't be time for the bars to close. I'm having too much fun.
    a. false dilemma
    b. burden of proof
    c. wishful thinking
    d. appeal to popularity
    e. no pseudoreasoning

  5. A mural for the municipal building? Excuse me, but why should public money, *our* tax dollars, be used for a totally unnecessary thing like art? There are potholes that need fixing. Traffic signals that need to be put up. There are a *million* things that are more important. It is an *outrage,* spending taxpayers' money on unnecessary frills like art. Give me a break!
    a. ad hominem
    b. appeal to indignation
    c. slippery slope

   d. perfectionist fallacy
   e. no pseudoreasoning

6. Mathematics is more difficult than sociology, and I *really* need an easier
   term this fall. So I'm going to take a sociology class instead of a math class.
   a. ad hominem
   b. appeal to pity
   c. false dilemma
   d. begging the question
   e. no pseudoreasoning

▲ 7. Parker says Macs are better than PCs, but what would you expect him to
   say? He's owned Macs for years.
   a. personal attack
   b. circumstantial ad hominem
   c. pseudorefutation
   d. perfectionist fallacy
   e. no pseudoreasoning

8. The congressman thought the president's behavior was an impeachable
   offense. But that's nonsense, coming from the congressman. He had an
   adulterous affair himself, after all.
   a. pseudorefutation
   b. poisoning the well
   c. circumstantial ad hominem
   d. genetic fallacy
   e. no pseudoreasoning

9. Your professor wants you to read Moore and Parker? Forget it. Their book is
   so far to the right it's falling off the shelf.
   a. poisoning the well
   b. pseudorefutation
   c. burden of proof
   d. appeal to popularity
   e. no pseudoreasoning

▲ 10. How do I know God exists? Hey, do you know he doesn't?
   a. perfectionist fallacy
   b. pseudorefutation
   c. burden of proof
   d. slippery slope
   e. begging the question

Exercise 6-5

In groups, vote on which option best depicts the pattern of pseudoreasoning
found in each pattern, and compare results with other groups. *Note:* The patterns
include those found in Chapter 5 and Chapter 6.

▲ 1. Laws against teenagers drinking?—They are a total waste of time, frankly. No matter how many laws we pass, there are always going to be some teens who drink.
  a. burden of proof
  b. perfectionist fallacy
  c. line-drawing fallacy
  d. no pseudoreasoning

2. Even though Sidney was old enough to buy a drink at the bar, he had no identification with him and the bartender would not serve him.
  a. perfectionist fallacy
  b. pseudorefutation
  c. burden of proof
  d. slippery slope
  e. no pseudoreasoning

3. Just how much sex has to be in a movie before you call it pornographic? Seems to me the whole concept makes no sense.
  a. perfectionist fallacy
  b. line-drawing fallacy
  c. straw man
  d. slippery slope
  e. no pseudoreasoning

▲ 4. Studies confirm what everyone already knows: Smaller classes make students better learners.
  a. common practice
  b. begging the question
  c. burden of proof
  d. appeal to popularity
  e. no pseudoreasoning

5. The trouble with impeaching Bill Clinton is this: Going after every person who occupies the presidency will take up everyone's time and the government will never get anything else done.
  a. pseudorefutation
  b. straw man
  c. burden of proof
  d. appeal to popularity
  e. red herring

6. The trouble with impeaching Bill Clinton is this. If we start going after Clinton, next we'll be going after senators, representatives, governors. Pretty soon no elected official will be safe from partisan attack.
  a. pseudorefutation
  b. slippery slope
  c. straw man
  d. false dilemma
  e. burden of proof

▲ 7. MR. IMHOFF: That does it. I'm cutting down on your peanut butter cookies. Those things blimp me up.
   MRS. IMHOFF: Oh, Imhoff, get real. What about all the ice cream you eat?
   a. circumstantial ad hominem
   b. subjectivist fallacy
   c. straw man
   d. slippery slope
   e. smokescreen/red herring

8. KEN: I think I'll vote for Andrews. She's the best candidate.
   ROBERT: Why do you say she's best?
   KEN: Because she's my sister-in-law. Didn't you know that?
   a. apple polishing
   b. appeal to pity
   c. scare tactics
   d. bandwagon
   e. none of the above

9. MOE: You going to class tomorrow?
   JOE: I s'pose. Why?
   MOE: Say, don't you get tired of being a Goody Two-shoes? You must have the most perfect attendance record of anyone who ever went to this school— certainly better than the rest of us; right, guys?
   a. poisoning the well
   b. appeal to pity
   c. scare tactics
   d. no pseudoreasoning
   e. none of the above

▲ 10. Morgan, you're down to earth and I trust your judgment. That's why I know I can count on you to back me up at the meeting this afternoon.
   a. apple polishing
   b. appeal to pity
   c. scare tactics
   d. bandwagon
   e. no pseudoreasoning

11. "Do you want to sign this petition to the governor?"
   "What's it about?"
   "We want him to veto that handgun registration bill that's come out of the legislature."
   "Oh. No, I don't think I want to sign that."
   "Oh, really? So are you telling me you want to get rid of the Second Amendment?"
   a. false dilemma
   b. personal attack
   c. genetic fallacy
   d. burden of proof
   e. no pseudoreasoning

12. Outlaw gambling? Man, that's a strange idea coming from you. Aren't you the one who plays the lottery all the time?
    a. pseudorefutation
    b. circumstantial ad hominem
    c. genetic fallacy
    d. scare tactics
    e. no pseudoreasoning

Exercise 6-6

Most of the following passages contain pseudoreasoning from Chapter 5 or Chapter 6. Identify the pseudoreasoning and try to place it in one of the categories we have described.

▲ 1. "People in Hegins, Pennsylvania, hold an annual pigeon shoot in order to control the pigeon population and to raise money for the town. This year, the pigeon shoot was disrupted by animal rights activists who tried to release the pigeons from their cages. I can't help but think these animal rights activists are the same people who believe in controlling the human population through the use of abortion. Yet, they recoil at a similar means of controlling pigeons. What rank hypocrisy."

    Rush Limbaugh

2. Dear Mr. Swanson: I realize I'm not up for a salary increase yet, but I thought it might make my review a bit more timely if I pointed out to you that I have a copy of all the recent e-mail messages between you and Ms. Flood in the purchasing department.

3. I don't care if Nike has signed up Michael Jordan, Tiger Woods, and even Santa Claus to endorse their shoes. They're a crummy company that makes a crummy product. The proof is the fact that they pay poor women a dollar sixty for a long day's work in their Vietnamese shoe factories. That's not even enough to buy a day's worth of decent meals!

▲ 4. I don't care if Nike has signed up Michael Jordan, Tiger Woods, and even Santa Claus to endorse their shoes. They're a crummy company, and I wouldn't buy their shoes no matter what the circumstance. You don't need any reason beyond the fact that they pay poor women a dollar sixty for a long day's work in their Vietnamese shoe factories. That's not even enough to buy a day's worth of decent meals!

5. ANNE: It's a safe bet those new neighbors of ours do drugs.
   DENNIS: Yeah? Do you have proof?
   ANNE: Yeah, well do you have proof they don't?

6. ANNE: It's a safe bet Clinton is a liar.
   DENNIS: Yeah? Do you have any proof?
   ANNE: Certainly. He said he doesn't lie, and we know that's false because the man never tells the truth.

▲ 7. I know the repair guy in the bookstore screwed up my computer; he's the only one who's touched it since it was working fine last Monday.

8. If you give the cat your leftover asparagus, next thing you know you'll be feeding him your potatoes, maybe even your roast beef. Where will it all end? Pretty soon that wretched animal will be sitting up here on the table for dinner. He'll be eating us out of house and home.

9. Look, either we refrain from feeding the cat table scraps, or he'll be eating us out of house and home. So don't go giving him your asparagus.

▲ 10. We have a simple choice. Saving Social Security is sure as hell a lot more important than giving people a tax cut. So write your representative now and let him or her know how you feel.

11. Let gays join the military? Give me a break. God created Adam and Eve, not Adam and Steve.

12. So my professor told me if he gave me an A for getting an 89.9 on the test, next he'd have to give people an A for getting an 89.8 on the test, and pretty soon he'd have to give everyone in the class an A. How could I argue with that?

▲ 13. Those blasted Democrats! They want to increase government spending on education again. This is the same outfit that gave us $10,000 toilets and government regulations up the yin-yang.

14. All this yammering about Clinton lying—spare me! Every president known to man has lied—Reagan, Bush, Kennedy, Nixon, probably even Jimmy Carter.

15. Lauren did a better job than anyone else at the audition, so even if she has no experience, we've decided to give her the part in the play.

▲ 16. TERRY: I failed my test but I gave my prof this nifty argument. I said, "Look, suppose somebody did 0.0001 percent better than I, would that be a big enough difference to give him a higher grade?" And he had to say "no," so then I said, "And if someone did 0.0001 percent better than that second person, would that be a big enough difference?" And he had to say "no" to that, too, so I just kept it up, and he never could point to the place where the difference was big enough to give the other person a higher grade. He finally saw he couldn't justify giving anyone a better grade.
TERRI: Well? What happened?
TERRY: He had to fail the whole class.

17. What's wrong with lying under oath? Kids will think it's okay to lie, too. Everybody knows that.

18. Look, maybe you think it's okay to legalize tribal casinos, but I don't. Letting every last group of people in the country open a casino is a ridiculous idea, bound to cause trouble.

▲ 19. What, you of all people complaining about violence on TV? You, with all the pro football you watch?

20. You have three Fs and a D on your exams, and your quizzes are on the borderline between passing and failing. I'm afraid you don't deserve to pass the course.

Exercise 6-7

Identify any examples of pseudoreasoning in the following passages. Tell why you think pseudoreasoning is present, and identify which category it belongs in, if it fits any of those we've described. Instances of pseudoreasoning are all from the patterns in Chapter 6.

▲ 1. Suspicious: "I would forget about whatever Moore and Parker have to say about pay for college teachers. After all, they're both professors themselves; what would you *expect* them to say?"

2. It's obvious to me that abortion is wrong—after all, everybody deserves a chance to be born.

3. Overheard: Well, I think that's too much to tip her. It's more than 15 percent. Next time it will be 20 percent, then 25 percent—where will it stop?

▲ 4. CARLOS: Four A.M.? Do we really have to start that early? Couldn't we leave a little later and get more sleep?
JEANNE: C'mon, don't hand me that! I know you! If you want to stay in bed until noon and then drag in there in the middle of the night, then go by yourself! If we want to get there at a reasonable hour, then we have to get going early and not spend the whole day sleeping.

5. I know a lot of people don't find anything wrong with voluntary euthanasia, where a patient is allowed to make a decision to die and that wish is carried out by a doctor or someone else. What will happen, though, is that if we allow voluntary euthanasia, before you know it we'll have the patient's relatives or the doctors making the decision that the patient should be "put out of his misery."

6. "Congress was elected to make laws, not Dr. David Kessler, commissioner of the Food and Drug Administration, who convinced Clinton to have the FDA regulate nicotine. What's next? Will Dr. Kessler have Clinton regulate coffee and Coca-Cola? Will Big Macs be outlawed and overeating prohibited?"

▲ 7. Whenever legislators have the power to raise taxes, they will always find problems that seem to require for their solution doing exactly that. This is an axiom, the proof of which is that the power to tax always generates the perception on the part of those who have that power that there exist various ills the remedy for which can only lie in increased governmental spending and hence higher taxes.

8. Don't tell me I should wear my seat belt, for heaven's sake. I've seen you ride a motorcycle without a helmet!

9. People who own pit bulls show a lack of respect for their friends, their neighbors, and anybody else who might come in contact with their dogs. They don't care if their dogs chew other people up.

▲ 10. When it comes to the issue of race relations, either you're part of the solution or you're part of the problem.

11. What! So now you're telling me we should get a new car? I don't buy that at all. Didn't you claim just last month that there was nothing wrong with the Plymouth?

12. Letter to the editor: "The Supreme Court decision outlawing a moment of silence for prayer in public schools is scandalous. Evidently the American Civil Liberties Union and the other radical groups will not be satisfied until every last man, woman and child in the country is an atheist. I'm fed up."

    Tri-County Observer

▲ 13. We should impeach the attorney general. Despite the fact that there have been many allegations of unethical conduct on his part, he has not done anything to demonstrate his innocence.

14. What do you mean, support Amnesty International? They only defend criminals.

15. Overheard: "Hunting immoral? Why should I believe that coming from you? You fish, don't you?"

16. "Will we have an expanding government, or will we balance the budget, cut government waste and eliminate unneeded programs?"

    Newt Gingrich, in a Republican National Committee solicitation

Exercise 6-8

Identify any examples of pseudoreasoning in the following passages. Tell why you think pseudoreasoning is present, and identify which category from Chapter 6 it belongs in, if it fits any of those we've described.

▲ 1. Despite all the studies and the public outcry, it's still true that nobody has ever actually *seen* cigarette smoking cause a cancer. All the antismoking people can do is talk about statistics; as long as there isn't real proof, I'm not believing it.

2. There is only one way to save this country from the domination by the illegal drug establishment to which Colombia has been subjected, and that's to increase tenfold the funds we spend on drug enforcement and interdiction.

3. I believe that the great flood described in the Bible really happened. The reason is simple: Noah would not have built the ark otherwise.

▲ 4. In 1996 a University of Chicago study gave evidence that letting people carry concealed guns appears to sharply reduce murders, rapes, and other violent crimes. Gun-control backer Josh Sugarman of the Violence Policy Center commented: "Anyone who argues that these laws reduce crime either doesn't understand the nature of crime or has a preset agenda."

5. Letter to the editor: "I strongly object to the proposed sale of alcoholic beverages at County Golf Course. The idea of allowing people to drink wher-

ever and whenever they please is positively disgraceful and can only lead to more alcoholism and all the problems it produces—drunk driving, perverted parties, and who knows what else. I'm sure General Stuart, if he were alive today to see what has become of the land he deeded to the county, would disapprove strenuously."

Tehama County Tribune

6. Letter to the editor: "I'm not against immigrants or immigration, but something has to be done soon. We've got more people already than we can provide necessary services for, and, at the current rate, we'll have people standing on top of one another by the end of the century. Either we control these immigration policies or there won't be room for any of us to sit down."

Lake County Recorder

▲ 7. Letter to the editor: "So now we find our local crusader-for-all-that-is-right, and I am referring to Councilman Benjamin Bostell, taking up arms against the local adult bookstore. Is this the same Mr. Bostell who owns the biggest liquor store in Chilton County? Well, maybe booze isn't the same as pornography, but they're the same sort of thing. C'mon, Mr. Bostell, aren't you a little like the pot calling the kettle black?"

Chilton County Register

8. Letter to the editor: "Once again the *Courier* displays its taste for slanted journalism. Why do your editors present only one point of view?

"I am referring specifically to the editorial of May 27, regarding the death penalty. So capital punishment makes you squirm a little. What else is new? Would you prefer to have murderers and assassins wandering around scot-free? How about quoting someone who has a different point of view from your own, for a change?"

Athens Courier

9. "Clinton oughta be thrown in jail for immoral behavior. Just look at all the women he has had affairs with since he left the presidency."

"Hey, wait a minute. How do you know he has had affairs since he was president?"

"Because if he didn't, then why would he be trying to cover up the fact that he did?"

▲ 10. It's practically a certainty that the government is violating the law in the arms deals with Saudi Arabians. When a reporter asked officials to describe how they were complying with the law, he was told that details about the arms sales were classified.

Exercise 6-9

Where we (Moore and Parker) teach, the city council recently debated relaxing the local noise ordinance. One student (who favored relaxation) appeared before the council and stated: "If 250 people are having fun, one person shouldn't be able to stop them."

We asked our students to state whether they agreed or disagreed with that student and to support their position with an argument. Here are some of the responses.

Divide into groups that are either all male or all female, and then identify any instances of pseudoreasoning you find in any answers, drawing from the materials in the last two chapters. Compare your results with those of other groups. After the instructor gives out what he or she thinks are the correct answers, see whose groups do better, the male groups or the female.

1. I support what the person is saying. If 250 people are having fun, one person shouldn't be able to stop them. Having parties and having a good time are a way of life for Chico State students. The areas around campus have always been this way.

2. A lot of people attend Chico State because of the social aspects. If rules are too tight, the school could lose its appeal. Without the students, local businesses would go under. Students keep the town floating. It's not just bars and liquor stores, but gas stations and grocery stores and apartment houses. This town would be like Orland.

3. If students aren't allowed to party, the college will go out of business.

4. We work hard all week long studying and going to classes. We deserve to let off steam after a hard week.

5. Noise is a fact of life around most college campuses. People should know what they are getting into before they move there. If they don't like it, they should just get earplugs or leave.

6. I agree with what the person is saying. If 250 people want to have fun, what gives one person the right to stop them?

7. I am sure many of the people who complain are the same people who used to be stumbling down Ivy Street twenty years ago doing the same thing that the current students are doing.

8. Two weeks ago I was at a party and it was only about 9:00 P.M. There were only a few people there and it was quiet. And then the police came and told us we had to break it up because a neighbor complained. Well, that neighbor is an elderly lady who would complain if you flushed the toilet. I think it's totally unreasonable.

9. Sometimes the noise level gets a little out of control, but there are other ways to go about this problem. For example, if you are a neighbor and you are having a problem with the noise level, why don't you call the "party house" and let them know, instead of going way too far and calling the police.

10. I'm sure that these "narcs" have nothing else better to do than to harass the "party people."

11. You can't get rid of all the noise around a college campus no matter what you do.

12. The Chico noise ordinance was put there by the duly elected officials of the city and is the law. People do not have the right to break a law that was put in place under proper legal procedures.

13. The country runs according to majority rule. If the overwhelming majority want to party and make noise, under our form of government they should be given the freedom to do so.

14. Students make a contribution to the community, and in return they should be allowed to make noise if they want.

15. Your freedom ends at my property line.

16. A majority rule must recognize individual rights. A majority does not have the freedom to invade another person's home with anything, whether it's noise, litter, smoke, garbage, their bodies, or anything else.

Exercise 6-10

Identify any examples of pseudoreasoning in the following passages. Tell why you think pseudoreasoning is present, and identify which category it belongs in, if it fits any category we've described.

▲ 1. Letter to the editor: "I would like to express my feelings on the recent conflict between county supervisor Blanche Wilder and Murdock County Sheriff Al Peters over the county budget.

    "I have listened to sheriffs' radio broadcasts. Many times there have been dangerous and life-threatening situations when the sheriff's deputies' quickest possible arrival time is 20 to 30 minutes. This is to me very frightening.

    "Now supervisor Wilder wants to cut two officers from the Sheriff's Department. This proposal I find ridiculous. Does she really think that Sheriff Peters can run his department with no officers? How anyone can think that a county as large as Murdock can get by with no police is beyond me. I feel this proposal would be very detrimental to the safety and protection of this county's residents."

2. Letter to the editor: "Andrea Keene's selective morality is once again showing through in her July 15 letter. This time she expresses her abhorrence of abortion. But how we see only what we choose to see! I wonder if any of the anti-abortionists have considered the widespread use of fertility drugs as the moral equivalent of abortion, and, if they have, why they haven't come out against them, too. The use of these drugs frequently results in multiple births, which leads to the death of one of the infants, often after an agonizing struggle for survival. According to the rules of the pro-lifers, isn't this murder?"

North-State Record

3. In one of her columns, Abigail Van Buren printed the letter of "I'd rather be a widow." The letter writer, a divorcée, complained about widows who said they had a hard time coping. Far better, she wrote, to be a widow than to be

a divorcée, who are all "rejects" who have been "publicly dumped" and are avoided "like they have leprosy." Abby recognized the pseudoreasoning for what it was, though she did not call it by our name. What is our name for it?

▲ 4. Overheard: "Should school kids say the Pledge of Allegiance before class? Certainly. Why shouldn't they?"

5. Letter to the editor: "Once again the Park Commission is considering closing North Park Drive for the sake of a few joggers and bicyclists. These so-called fitness enthusiasts would evidently have us give up to them for their own private use every last square inch of Walnut Grove. Then anytime anyone wanted a picnic, he would have to park at the edge of the park and carry everything in—ice chests, chairs, maybe even grandma. I certainly hope the Commission keeps the entire park open for everyone to use."

6. "Some Christian—and other—groups are protesting against the placing, on federal property near the White House, of a set of plastic figurines representing a devout Jewish family in ancient Judaea. The protestors would of course deny that they are driven by any anti-Semitic motivation. Still, we wonder: Would they raise the same objections (of unconstitutionality, etc.) if the scene depicted a modern, secularized Gentile family?"

National Review

▲ 7. "It's stupid to keep on talking about rich people not paying their fair share of taxes while the budget is so far out of balance. Why, if we raised the tax rates on the wealthy all the way back to where they were in 1980, it would not balance the federal budget."

Radio commentary by Howard Miller

8. From a letter to the editor: "The counties of Michigan clearly need the ability to raise additional sources of revenue, not only to meet the demands of growth but also to maintain existing levels of service. For without these sources those demands will not be met, and it will be impossible to maintain services even at present levels."

9. In February 1992, a representative of the Catholic Church in Puerto Rico gave a radio interview (broadcast on National Public Radio) in which he said that the Church was against the use of condoms. Even though the rate of AIDS infection in Puerto Rico is much higher than on the U.S. mainland, the spokesman said that the Church could not support the use of condoms because they are not absolutely reliable in preventing the spread of the disease. "If you could prove that condoms were absolutely dependable in preventing a person from contracting AIDS, then the Church could support their use."

▲ 10. A 1991 book by a former member of the National Security Council indicated that supporters of Ronald Reagan may have made a deal with the Iranians who had been holding American hostages for months. The Iranians agreed not to release the hostages until after the 1980 election (in which Reagan defeated Jimmy Carter), and, it was alleged, the new administration promised to make weapons available to Iran. Here's one reaction to the announcement of the deal:

> "I'm not surprised about Reagan's using trickery to get himself elected president. After all, he was nothing but an old actor, and he was used to using Hollywood trickery to fool people during his first career."

Exercise 6-11

Identify any examples of pseudoreasoning in the following passages. Tell why you think pseudoreasoning is present, and identify which category it belongs in, if it fits any category we've described.

▲ 1. The U.S. Congress considered a resolution criticizing the treatment of ethnic minorities in a Near Eastern country. When the minister of the interior was asked for his opinion of the resolution, he replied, "This is purely an internal affair in my country, and politicians in the U.S. should stay out of such affairs. If the truth be known, they should be more concerned with the plight of minority peoples in their own country. Thousands of black and Latino youngsters suffer from malnutrition in the United States. They can criticize us after they've got their own house in order."

2. It doesn't make any sense to speak of tracing an individual human life back past the moment of conception. After all, that's the beginning, and you can't go back past the beginning.

3. MOE: The death penalty is an excellent deterrent for murder.
JOE: What makes you think so?
MOE: Because there's no evidence that it's *not* a deterrent.
JOE: Well, states with capital punishment have higher murder rates than states that don't have it.
MOE: Yes, but that's only because there are so many legal technicalities standing in the way of executions that convicted people hardly ever get executed. Remove those technicalities, and the rate would be lower in those states.

▲ 4. Overheard: "The new sculpture in front of the municipal building by John Murrah is atrocious and unseemly, which is clear to anyone who hasn't forgotten Murrah's mouth in Vietnam right there along with Hayden and Fonda calling for the defeat of America. I say: Drill holes in it so it'll sink and throw it in Walnut Pond."

5. Overheard: "Once we let these uptight guardians of morality have their way and start censoring *Playboy* and *Penthouse,* the next thing you know they'll be dictating everything we can read. We'll be in fine shape when they decide that *Webster's* should be pulled from the shelves."

6. It seems the biggest problem the nuclear industry has to deal with is not a poor safety record, but a lack of education of the public on nuclear power. Thousands of people die each year from pollution generated by coal-fired plants. Yet to date, there has been no death directly caused by radiation at a commercial nuclear power plant in the United States. We have a clear choice: an old, death-dealing source of energy or a safe, clean one. Proven

through the test of time, nuclear power is clearly the safest form of energy and the least detrimental to the environment. Yet it is perceived as unsafe and an environmental hazard.

▲ 7. A high school teacher once told my class that if a police state ever arose in America, it would happen because we freely handed away our civil rights in exchange for what we perceived would be security from the government. We are looking at just that in connection with the current drug crisis.

For almost thirty years we've seen increasing tolerance, legally and socially, of drug use. Now we are faced with the very end of America as we know it, if not from the drug problem, then from the proposed solutions to it.

First, it was urine tests. Officials said that the innocent have nothing to fear. Using that logic, why not allow unannounced police searches of our homes for stolen goods? After all, the innocent would have nothing to fear.

Now we're looking at the seizure of boats and other property when even traces of drugs are found. You'd better hope some drug-using guest doesn't drop the wrong thing in your home, car, or boat.

The only alternative to declaring real war on the real enemies—the Asian and South American drug families—is to wait for that knock on the door in the middle of the night.

8. The mayor's argument is that because the developers' fee would reduce the number of building starts, ultimately the city would lose more money than it would gain through the fee. But I can't go along with that. Mayor Tower is a member of the Board of Realtors, and you know what *they* think of the fee.

9. Letter to the editor: "Next week the philosopher Tom Regan will be in town again, peddling his animal rights theory. In case you've forgotten, Regan was here about three years ago arguing against using animals in scientific experimentation. As far as I could see then and can see now, neither Regan nor anyone else has managed to come up with a good reason why animals should not be experimented on. Emotional appeals and horror stories no doubt influence many, but they shouldn't. I've always wondered what Regan would say if his children needed medical treatment that was based on animal experiments."

▲ 10. Not long before Ronald and Nancy Reagan moved out of the White House, former Chief of Staff Don Regan wrote a book in which he depicted a number of revealing inside stories about First Family goings-on. Among them was the disclosure that Nancy Reagan regularly sought the advice of a San Francisco astrologer. In response to the story, the White House spokesman at the time, Marlin Fitzwater, said, "Vindictiveness and revenge are not admirable qualities and are not worthy of comment."

Exercise 6-12

In addition to a very serious weaseler (see Chapter 4) and some errors of omission, the radio ad against Proposition 111, analyzed here by the *Sacramento Bee*,

Proposition 111 Foes Take to Airwaves

Opponents of Proposition 111, which would raise gasoline taxes and the state's government spending limit, have begun running radio and television advertisements against the measure. Here is the text of their radio ad, which is set in an imaginary newsroom, with an analysis of its contents by Amy Chance of *The Bee* Capitol Bureau.

Editor, answering a telephone: Newsroom. Yeah, we'll have that story by press time. . . .   Hey, Carl and Bob, have you finished that story on Proposition 111, the so-called gas tax proposition?

Carl: We just got this report in from Sacramento. It says that if 111 passes, a family of four may have to pay over $9,000 in new taxes.

Analysis: *The $9,000 figure, which opponents say is the total of new taxes that could be imposed over a 10-year period, assumes that two-thirds of both houses of the Legislature and the governor would raise taxes to the maximum level allowed under the revised spending limit. Proposition 111 itself does not impose those increases.*

Editor: You're sure 111 could cost a family of four over $9,000 in new taxes?

Bob: You got it, Chief. 111 eliminates the Gann spending limit.

Analysis: The measure does not eliminate the limit but alters the way it is calculated to allow a higher level of state spending on a variety of state programs.

Carl: But that's not all, Chief. It looks like traffic will actually get worse if 111 passes.

Analysis: The measure is designed to raise $15.5 billion over 10 years for a variety of transportation improvements, including projects aimed specifically at reducing traffic congestion. An accompanying bond measure, Proposition 108, would raise $1 billion for transit projects.

Editor: How's that?

Bob: Loopholes in the law let developers off the hook for the traffic congestion they cause with new development.

Analysis: Legislation accompanying the measure seeks to make local governments take transportation into account when they make land-use decisions. Details of the plan were negotiated by developers and environmental organizations and accepted by representatives of both groups.

Carl: Us taxpayers are going to have to pick up the tab again.

Editor: Is there anything good about Proposition 111?

Carl: Well, here's something just in. This report says Exxon is a major contributor to the "Yes on 111" campaign.

Analysis: Opponents of the measure say Exxon contributed $25,000 to the measure. Proponents have said they expect to raise at least $5 million for the campaign. Backers also include a broad range of public interest and business groups, including the California Taxpayers Association and the California Chamber of Commerce.

Editor: Hmmm. That's not good.

Announcer: Send the big spenders a message they'll understand. Vote "No" on Proposition 111 for the sake of your pocketbook.

---

contains two instances of pseudoreasoning introduced in this chapter. Can you spot them? (The sections labeled "Analysis" are not a part of the ad. They are part of the *Bee's* analysis of the ad.)

Exercise 6-13 _____

Identify any examples of pseudoreasoning in the following passages. Tell why you think pseudoreasoning is present, and identify which category it belongs in, if it fits any category we've described.

▲ 1. Of course Chinese green tea is good for your health. If it weren't, how could it be so beneficial to drink it?

2. Overheard: "No, I'm against this health plan business. None of the proposals are gonna fix everything, you can bet on that."

3. You have a choice: Either you let 'em out to murder and rape again and again, or you put up with a little prison overcrowding. I know what I'd choose.

▲ 4. "The legalization of drugs will not promote their use. The notion of a widespread hysteria sweeping across the nation as every man, woman, and child instantaneously becomes addicted to drugs upon their legalization is, in short, ridiculous."

From a student essay

5. Way I figure is, giving up smoking isn't gonna make me live forever, so why bother?

6. "The trouble with [syndicated columnist Joseph] Sobran's gripe about Clinton increasing the power of the federal government is that Sobran is the one who wants the government to tell women they can't have abortions."

From a newspaper call-in column

▲ 7. Aid to Russia? Gimme a break! Why should we care more about the Russians than about our own people?

8. Clinton's crime bill stinks. He's just trying to get Republican votes.

9. I believe Tim is telling the truth about his brother because he just would not lie about that sort of thing.

▲ 10. I think I was treated unfairly. I got a ticket out on McCrae Road. I was doing about sixty miles an hour, and the cop charged me with "traveling at an unsafe speed." I asked him what would have been a *safe* speed on that particular occasion—fifty? forty-five?—and he couldn't tell me. Neither could the judge. I tell you, if you don't know what speeds are unsafe, you shouldn't give tickets for "unsafe speeds."

Exercise 6-14 _____

Go through a newspaper, newsmagazine, or opinion journal looking for examples of the pseudoreasoning types discussed in this chapter. Clip out, photocopy, or write down any good examples and bring them to class for discussion. Your instructor may ask you to explain in writing why you think the example contains pseudoreasoning.

Exercise 6-15

Watch one of the news/public affairs programs on television (*NewsHour with Jim Lehrer, Nightline, Face the Nation*, and so on), and make a note of any examples of pseudoreasoning that occur. Explain in writing why you think the examples contain pseudoreasoning.

Alternatively, watch *Politically Incorrect* with Bill Maher. It usually doesn't take long to find a case of pseudoreasoning there.

Exercise 6-16

The following passages contain pseudoreasoning from both this and the preceding chapter. Identify the category in which each item belongs.

▲ 1. "I can safely say that no law, no matter how stiff the consequence is, will completely stop illegal drug use. Outlawing drugs is a waste of time."

      From a student essay

   2. "If we expand the commuter bus program, where is it going to end? Will we want to have a trolley system? Then a light rail system? Then expand Metrolink to our area? A city this size hardly needs and certainly cannot afford all these amenities."

      From a newspaper call-in column

   3. YAEKO: The character Dana Scully on *The X-Files* really provides a good role model for young women. She's a medical doctor and an FBI agent, and she's intelligent, professional, and devoted to her work.
      MICHAEL: Those shows about paranormal activities are so unrealistic. Alien abductions, government conspiracies—it's all ridiculous.

   4. Overheard: "The reason I don't accept evolution is that ever since Darwin, scientists have been trying to prove that we evolved from some apelike primate ancestor. Well, they still haven't succeeded. Case closed."

▲ 5. Ladies and gentlemen, as you know, I endorsed Council Member Morrissey's bid for reelection based on his outstanding record during his first term. Because you are the movers and shakers in this community, other people place the same high value on your opinions that I do. Jim and I would feel privileged to have your support.

   6. It's totally ridiculous to suppose that creationism is true. If creationism were true, then half of what we know through science would be false, which is complete nonsense.

   7. KIRSTI: I counted my CDs this weekend, and out of twenty-seven, ten of them were by REM. They are such a good band! I haven't heard anything by Michael Stipe for a long time. He has such a terrific voice!
      BEN: Isn't he bisexual?

   8. Was Graybosch a good committee chair? Well, I for one think you have to say he was excellent, especially when you consider all the abuse he put up with. Right from the start people went after him—they didn't even give him

a chance to show what he could do. It was really vicious—people making fun of him right to his face. Yes, under the circumstances he has been quite effective.

▲ 9. Medical research that involves animals is completely unnecessary and a waste of money. Just think of the poor creatures! We burn and blind and torture them, and then we kill them. They don't know what is going to happen to them, but they know something is going to happen. They are scared to death. It's really an outrage.

10. Dear Editor—
If Christians do not participate in government, only sinners will.

From a letter to the Chico Enterprise Record

11. The HMO people claim that the proposal will raise the cost of doing business in the state to such a degree that insurers will be forced to leave the state and do business elsewhere. What nonsense. Just look at what we get from these HMOs. I know people who were denied decent treatment for cancer because their HMO wouldn't approve it. There are doctors who won't recommend a procedure for their patients because they are afraid the HMO will cancel their contract. And when an HMO does cancel some doctor's contract, the patients have to find a new doctor themselves—*if* they can. Everybody has a horror story. Enough is enough.

12. HOWARD: Dad, I really appreciate your letting me borrow the Chevy. But Melanie's parents just bought her a brand new Mercedes!
DAD: Some people just refuse to buy American!

▲ 13. [Dole campaign chairman] SCOTT REID: There is a clear pattern of campaign finance abuse by the [Clinton] administration. Indonesian business interests have steered millions into the President's campaign using a gardener as a front, and [Democratic fund raiser] John Huang, who apparently laundered money at a fund-raiser at a Buddhist temple in California, is suddenly nowhere to be found.
[White House Senior Adviser] GEORGE STEPHANOPOULOS: I can't let these charges go unrefuted. Dole has received millions from foreign supporters like José Fanjul, and his vice chairman for finance, Simon Fireman, had to pay the largest fine in the history of the country for massive violations of campaign-finance laws.

On NBC's Meet the Press

14. The proposal to reduce spending for the arts just doesn't make any sense. We spend a paltry $620 million for the NEA [National Endowment for the Arts], while the deficit is closing in on $200 billion. Cutting support for the arts isn't going to eliminate the deficit; that's obvious.

15. Year-round schools? I'm opposed. Once we let them do that, the next thing you know they'll be cutting into our vacation time and asking us to teach in the evenings and on the weekends and who knows where it will end. We teachers have to stand up for our rights.

▲ 16. [NBC's *Meet the Press* host] TIM RUSSERT: Mr. Perot, Bob Dole says that every vote for Ross Perot is a vote for Bill Clinton. True?

ROSS PEROT: Of course that's not true. They've been programmed from birth to say that if they are a Republican.

17. Even if we outlaw guns we're still going to have crime and murder. So I really don't see much point in it.

From a student essay

18. Do you think affirmative action programs are still necessary in the country? *Answers:*
   a. Yes, of course. I don't see how you, a woman, can ask that question. It's obvious we have a very long way to go still.
   b. No. Because of affirmative action, my brother lost his job to a minority who had a lot less experience than he did.
   c. Yes. The people who want to end affirmative action are all white males who just want to go back to the good-old-boy system. It's always the same: Look out for number one.
   d. No. The people who want it to continue know a good deal when they see one. You think I'd want to end it if I were a minority?

Exercise 6-17

Explain in a sentence or two how each of the following passages involves a type of pseudoreasoning mentioned in either this or the preceding chapter. *Many of these examples are difficult* and should serve to illustrate how pseudoreasoning sometimes conforms only loosely to the standard patterns.

▲ 1. I believe that the companies that produce passenger airliners should be more strictly supervised by the FAA. I mean, good grief, everybody knows that you can make more money by cutting corners here and there than by spending extra time and effort getting things just right, and you know there have got to be airlines that are doing exactly that.

2. From a letter to a college newspaper editor: "I really appreciated the fact that your editorial writer supports the hike in the student activity fee that has been proposed. Since the writer is a senior and won't even be here next year, he will escape having to pay the fee himself, so of course there's no downside to it as far as he's concerned. I'm against the fee, and I'll be one of those who pay it if it passes. Mine is an opinion that should count."

3. "'There's a certain sameness to the news on the Big Three [ABC, NBC, and CBS] and CNN,' says Moody, . . . who is in charge of Fox News's day-to-day editorial decisions. That's the message, Moody says, that 'America is bad, corporations are bad, animal species should be protected, and every cop is a racist killer. That's where "fair and balanced" [Fox's slogan] comes in. We don't think all corporations are bad, every forest should be saved, every government spending program is good. We're going to be more inquisitive.'"

From an interview with John Moody, vice president for news editorial at Fox News Network, in Brill's Content *magazine*

▲ 4. During the Reagan and Bush administrations, Democratic members of Congress pointed to the two presidents' economic policies as causing huge deficits that could ultimately ruin the country's economy. President Bush dismissed such charges as "the politics of doom and gloom." "These people will find a dark cloud everywhere," he has said. Was this response pseudoreasoning?

▲ 5. "Louis Harris, one of the nation's most influential pollsters, readily admits he is in the polling business to 'have some impact with the movers and shakers of the world.' So poll questions are often worded to obtain answers that help legitimize the liberal Establishment's viewpoints."

Conservative Digest

6. "At a White House meeting in February of 1983 with Washington, D.C., anchormen, Ronald Reagan was asked to comment on 'an apparent continuing perception among a number of black leaders that the White House continues to be, if not hostile, at least not welcome to black viewpoints.' President Reagan replied as follows: 'I'm aware of all that, and it's very disturbing to me, because anyone who knows my life story knows that long before there was a thing called the civil-rights movement, I was busy on that side. As a sports announcer, I didn't have any Willie Mayses or Reggie Jacksons to talk about when I was broadcasting major league baseball. The opening line of the Spalding Baseball Guide said, "Baseball is a game for Caucasian gentlemen." And as a sports announcer I was one of a very small fraternity that used that job to editorialize against that ridiculous blocking of so many fine athletes and so many fine Americans from participating in what was called the great American game.' Reagan then went on to mention that his father refused to allow him to see *Birth of a Nation* because it was based on the Ku Klux Klan and once slept in a car during a blizzard rather than stay at a hotel that barred Jews. Reagan's 'closest teammate and buddy' was a black, he said."

James Nathan Miller, The Atlantic

7. From a letter to the editor of the *Atlantic Monthly:* "In all my reading and experience so far, I have found nothing presented by science and technology that precludes there being a spiritual element to the human being. . . . The bottom line is this: Maybe there are no angels, afterlife, UFOs, or even a God. Certainly their existence has not yet been scientifically proved. But just as certainly, their *nonexistence* remains unproved. Any reasonable person would therefore have to reserve judgment."

8. Stop blaming the developers for the fact that our town is growing! If you want someone to blame, blame the university. It brings the new people here, not the developers. Kids come here from God knows where, and lots of them like what they find and stick around. All the developers do is put roofs over those former students' heads.

▲ 9. Two favorite scientists of the Council for Tobacco Research were Carl Seltzer and Theodore Sterling. Seltzer, a biological anthropologist, believes smoking has no role in heart disease and has alleged in print that data in the huge 45-year, 10,000-person Framingham Heart Study—which found otherwise—have been distorted by anti-tobacco researchers. Framingham Director William Castelli scoffs at Seltzer's critique but says it "has had some impact in keeping the debate alive."

Sterling, a statistician, disputes the validity of population studies linking smoking to illness, arguing that their narrow focus on smoking obscures the more likely cause—occupational exposure to toxic fumes.

For both men, defying conventional wisdom has been rewarding. Seltzer says he has received "well over $1 million" from the Council for research. Sterling got $1.1 million for his Special Projects work in 1977–82, court records show.

> From "How Tobacco Firms Keep Health Questions 'Open' Year After Year,"
> by Alix Freedman and Laurie Cohen. The article originally appeared in
> the Wall Street Journal and was reprinted in the Sacramento Bee.

10. We have had economic sanctions in effect against China ever since the Tienanmen Square massacre. Clearly they haven't turned the Chinese leadership in Beijing into a bunch of good guys. All they've done, in fact, is cost American business a lot of money. We should get rid of the sanctions and find some other way to make them improve their human rights record.

Writing Exercises

1. Turn to any of the following selections from the Essays for Analysis section at the back of the book, and follow the instructions: 5A,B; 6A,B; 7; 9A,B; 10A,B; 11A,B; 12A,B; or 13A,B. You might also turn to Selections 14 or 15, and follow the second set of instructions of each.

2. Should same-sex marriages be illegal? Write a one-page essay defending a "yes" answer to this question. Take about twenty minutes to write it. Put your name on the back of your paper. Avoid pseudoreasoning. When everyone is finished, your instructor will collect the papers and redistribute them to the class at random. In groups of four or five, read the papers that have been given to your group, looking for instances of pseudoreasoning. Do not look at the names of the authors. (Because everyone will have tried to avoid pseudoreasoning, you should not find many instances of it.) The instructor will ask each group to select the paper the group believes is the best and read it to the class. The group should be prepared to say what they like about the paper and how they think it might be improved.

3. Follow the instructions for Exercise 3, this time defending a "no" answer to the question, Should same-sex marriages be illegal?

Chapter 7

Explanations

When we provide reasons for believing that a claim is true, we offer an argument. However, when we try to explain how something came to be or what made it what it is, we present an **explanation.** There are many kinds of explanations: We explain what things are, how they work, what they are good for, why they cost so much, what they are like, who invented them, why we don't have one, why people like them, and who knows what. There is a big difference in principle between arguments and explanations, and before we examine arguments in detail, we must say something about explanations.

Explanations and Arguments

Arguments try to show that something is, or will be, or should be the case. Explanations try to show *how* or *why* something is or will be. Unfortunately, arguments and explanations can look a lot like each other, a problem we'll get to later. First, though, here are Moore and Parker discussing whether Parker's dog has fleas. Moore: "Look, Parker, I told you your dog has fleas. Look how it's scratching."

Moore has just given an argument *that* the dog has fleas. The issue here is *whether* the dog has fleas, and Moore has advanced an *argument* that bears on this issue.

Now let's suppose that Moore and Parker *agree* that Parker's dog has fleas; let's assume the issue of whether the dog has fleas has been settled. Moore and Parker might then consider a further question, of *why* the dog has fleas. Moore then might say: "The reason the dog has fleas is that the weather has been cool and damp." In this case, Moore has given an *explanation* of why the dog has fleas.

As shown by this example, we give an argument if we try to settle whether some claim is true. We propose an explanation, if, instead, we try to explain what makes it true.

Let's take another example. Here are Parker and Moore again, debating whether Henry Hyde dyes his hair. Parker says: "I'm sure he doesn't dye his hair. His hair is gray. There's no point in dyeing your hair gray."

Has Parker given Moore an argument or an explanation? The answer is an *argument* that Hyde doesn't dye his hair. But suppose Parker assumes that he and Moore both agree that Hyde doesn't dye his hair. Parker might then speculate as to *why* it is that Hyde doesn't dye his hair—after all, a lot of men Hyde's age do dye their hair, especially those who are in the public eye. So Parker might then propose an *explanation* of why Hyde does not dye his hair and say, "He probably thinks gray hair makes him look more authoritative—that's why he doesn't dye it."

Unfortunately, in real life, it is often difficult to tell whether we are dealing with an argument or with an explanation. There are four reasons for this difficulty. First, people often aren't clear themselves whether they are arguing for something or explaining something. The result of this confusion may be a statement that is hard to classify. Second, the same words and phrases are used in presenting arguments and in offering explanations. For example, this is an argument:

The reason you should vote Republican is that Republicans are fiscal conservatives.

But the following, in most contexts, would be an explanation:

The reason big business favors Republicans is that Republicans are fiscal conservatives.

Notice how similar they are in form and language. Here's another argument:

Republicans are fiscal conservatives. That's why you should vote for them.

But the following, in many contexts, would be an explanation:

Republicans are fiscal conservatives. That's why big business favors Republicans.

We could go on with similar examples, the point being that much of the vocabulary used in arguments is also used in explanations. Consequently, you have to use some common sense in figuring out whether someone is offering an argument or setting forth an explanation.

A third reason it is easy to confuse explanations and arguments is that, unfortunately, the word "explanation" and its derivatives are themselves used in arguments! Look at this:

Republicans are fiscal conservatives. This explains why you should vote for them.

Keeping Secrets

▲   *If somebody told you that cows stand up and talk to each other, you'd say he or she was nuts, right? After all, nobody has ever seen cows doing that. But suppose the person were to respond by telling you that cows stand up only when nobody can see them? Or suppose a psychic were to explain that his or her psychic abilities disappear when threatened or contaminated by the skepticism of an investigating scientist?*

What's wrong with those explanations? Read the rest of the chapter to find out.

This is an argument because the writer is offering reasons for believing that you should vote for Republicans. But the following *is* an explanation:

Republicans are fiscal conservatives. This is the explanation of why big business votes for Republicans.

Remember: You are offering an argument if and only if you are trying to *establish that* such-and-such is true.

The fourth reason it is easy to confuse arguments and explanations is that explanations are sometimes used *in* arguments, and, even worse, they are sometimes used *as* arguments. For example, a stage magician might explain *how* a so-called psychic bends spoons using sleight of hand in order to prove (i.e., to argue) *that* we shouldn't credit the psychic with mystical powers. A Ford ad might explain *why* Ford trucks are best-sellers in order to establish (i.e., to argue) *that* they are great trucks. You might explain *why* Dianne Feinstein will never become president in order to convince your reader *that* she should not vote for Feinstein. A writer might explain *how* a bolt-action rifle can be fired three times in 5.2 seconds in order to argue *that* Lee Harvey Oswald could have shot John F. Kennedy.

Consider the following additional example:

> You won't be able to see the comet from here tonight. The reason is that we're too close to the lights of the city to see anything that faint in the sky.

This passage does indeed supply a reason for believing *that* you won't be able to see the comet, which indicates the presence of an argument; but the passage also tells us why this is (or will be) so. Whether it would be better to call this an argument or an explanation depends on the context and the interests of the parties concerned. It could be offered *both* as an argument *and* as an explanation.

Explanations and Justifications

A justification of an action is an argument given in defense of it, an attempt to show that the action is justified. Sometimes explanations are used as justifications. For example, in attempting to justify her theft of a loaf of bread, a person might explain her motives (e.g., to feed her hungry family).

It is equally important to notice when an explanation is *not* an attempt to justify. For example, someone may try to explain why many Germans adopted the vicious anti-Semitic views of the Nazi party during the 1930s. The speaker may point out that the German economy was in a mess, that the country still suffered from terms imposed on it at the end of World War I, and, furthermore, that people often look for scapegoats on whom they can blame their troubles. These remarks may help us understand why the German people were easily led into anti-Semitism, but an uncritical listener may believe that the speaker is trying to muster sympathy for those people and their actions. As a matter of fact, just such an explanation was given by Phillipp Jenniger in the German parliament on the fiftieth anniversary of the *Kristallnacht*, a night when Nazis attacked Jewish neighborhoods and shops. Many of Jenniger's fellow Germans misunderstood his account, thinking it was a justification for the Nazis' actions. But it does not follow that a person proposing explanations has any sympathy at all for the views or actions being explained.

In sum, explanations themselves can be entirely neutral with regard to approval or disapproval of X, even though we might include an explanation of X as part of an attempt to justify it. It is important to see the difference between explaining an event and justifying it, for otherwise we may find ourselves stifling attempts to explain bad behavior for fear we will be seen as defending it. And unless we are able to explain and understand such behavior, we will be hampered in our attempts to discourage it.

Exercise 7-1

For each of the following, determine whether the speaker is more likely presenting an argument or an explanation. If your answer assumes an unusual context for the utterance, describe that context.

▲ 1. Collins is absent again today because she's ill.

2. I told you Collins was ill. Just look at her color.

3. Did Bobbie have a good time last night? Are you kidding? She had a *great* time! She stayed up all night, she had such a good time.

▲ 4. The reason Collins was ill is that she ate and drank more than she should have.

5. For a while there, Jazzercise was really popular. But you don't hear much about it anymore. That's probably because rock makes you feel more like moving than jazz. Jazz just makes you feel like moving into another room.

6. How come light beer has fewer calories than real beer? It has less alcohol, that's why.

▲ 7. The senator's popularity goes up and down, up and down. That's because sometimes he says things that make sense, and other times he says things that are totally outrageous.

8. VIKKI: Say, remember the California Raisins? Whatever happened to them, anyway?
NIKKI: They faded. I guess people got tired of them or something.

9. Programs of preferential treatment may seem unfair to white males, but a certain amount of unfairness to individuals can be tolerated for the sake of the common good. Therefore, such programs are ethically justified.

▲ 10. I'm telling him, "Let's book!" and he's like, "Relax, dude," and since it's his wheel, what can I do? That's why we're late, man.

Exercise 7-2

Some of these items have a feature, discussed in this chapter, that is not shared by the remaining items. Identify the items and describe the feature. Your instructor may assign this exercise to small groups.

1. What a winter! And to think it's all just because there's a bunch of cold water off the California coast.

2. Hmmmm. I'm pretty sure you have the flu. You can tell because if you had a cold you wouldn't have aches and a fever. Aches and fever are a sure sign you have the flu.

3. You know, it occurs to me the reason the band sounded so bad is the new director. They haven't had time to get used to him or something.

4. For a while there it seemed like every male under thirty was shaving his head. It was probably the Michael Jordan influence.

5. If you ever want to get good at cross-country skiing, you better learn how to do a telemark.

6. "A year ago, Sue Spiegel, 33, a television producer, didn't know a blitz from a blintz and assumed 'first and 10' was a Manhattan street address. Ms. Spiegel now has a good idea how hard football players work, thanks to a football program run by Bob Shaw, a personal trainer and the owner of Physical Structure, a New York City health club."

    —*Wendy Marston*

7. Today's amusement park rides are faster, scarier, and more elaborate than ever, and as a result some theme park visitors are clutching their stomachs and opting for the sidelines.

8. "A practice that could pass as a Draconian punishment for perjury, tongue piercing, has pushed its way into youth culture—and the trend is alarming many dentists. . . . Enthusiasts pay piercers, who are unlicensed and are trained by apprenticing with senior colleagues, $50 or more to punch a hole through their lips, cheeks, or tongue (the most common site) with the mouth jewelry of the customer's choice, usually a 12-gauge needle tipped with two balls like a barbell."

    —*Alisa Tang*

9. Believe it or not, couples who regard each other as relatively equal are more likely to suffer from high blood pressure than are couples who perceive one or the other as dominant. This is an excellent reason for marrying someone you think is beneath (or above) you.

10. Believe it or not, couples who regard each other as relatively equal are more likely to suffer from high blood pressure than are couples who perceive one or the other as dominant. The reason seems to be that couples who see their partners as relatively equal tend to argue more often and more vigorously, pushing up blood pressure.

Exercise 7-3

Some of these items have a feature, discussed in this chapter, that is not shared by the remaining items. Identify the items and describe the feature. Your instructor may assign this exercise to small groups.

1. I got sick because I didn't get enough rest over the weekend.

2. You shouldn't buy that computer because it doesn't have very much memory.

3. The president should resign because foreign leaders are going to lose faith in his leadership skills.

4. Pine trees are called "evergreens" because they don't lose their leaves in the fall.

5. You are making a mistake to wear that outfit because it makes you look too old.

6. Stephanie won't wear outfits like that because she thinks they are tacky.

7. Used couches are so plentiful here because the students give them away at the end of each school year.

8. If I were you, I wouldn't open up a furniture store in this town, because students give good furniture away at the end of each school year.

9. Freestone peaches are better than clingstone, because they are easier to eat and have a crisper texture.

10. The sky appears blue because of the way light reflects off the atmosphere.

Exercise 7-4

Can you identify an explanation when you see one? For each of the following, mark a if the item is an explanation; if it is not, mark b.

▲ 1. If you ask a person to pick a number between 12 and 5, he'll probably say 7. That's because his brain automatically subtracts 5 from 12.

2. Ask a person to name a vegetable, and the first thing to come to mind is a carrot. Don't believe me? Ask someone.

3. To be acid-free, take Pepcid AC.

▲ 4. Why, just look at all the dog hair on this keyboard. Where do you let your dog sleep, anyway? No wonder your computer isn't working right.

5. On September 19, Mike Tyson will make the holy trek to Las Vegas, to ask the Nevada Athletic Commission to reinstate his boxing license, and chances are they will. Why would they do that for a man who bit another boxer, attacked a sixty-two-year-old man, and kicked another older man in the groin? The answer can be stated in a sentence: Vegas likes big money.

6. Feet hurt? Really hurt? Chances are you have weak or fallen arches.

▲ 7. "Let me explain to you why you know the public opinion polls are all rigged. Everybody I know hates Clinton, and if you listen to talk radio you can tell that most people agree with us."

—Adapted from a newspaper call-in column

8. Linda takes care of two youngsters, puts in a forty-hour week at her job, is troop leader for the local chapter of the Girl Scouts, serves half a day each

week as a teacher's aide, and is almost finished with a book on time management. So it shouldn't surprise you that she hasn't been able to come out to the coast for a visit lately.

9. I believe God exists because my parents brought me up that way.

10. I believe God exists because there obviously had to be a first cause for everything, and that first cause was God.

Exercise 7-5 _____

For each of the following passages, determine whether the writer or speaker is most likely presenting an argument or an explanation, or both. Determine also whether any argument present attempts to justify an action or practice. If more information about the context is needed to answer, or if your answer assumes some unusual context for the passage, explain.

▲ 1. I can't understand how the garage got this cluttered. Must be we just never throw anything away.

2. When the sun reaches its equinox, it is directly over the equator, a fact that explains why the days are exactly the same length every place on the globe at that time.

3. Awww, don't get on her, Mom. The reason she didn't rake the leaves is that her stomach began hurting. She *had* to go lie down.

▲ 4. Watch out! Parker's giving a test today. I saw him carrying a big manila folder into the classroom.

5. Moore gave a test on Friday because he wanted to surprise everyone.

6. They get so many fires in southern California in the fall because that's when you get the Santa Ana winds, which blow in from the desert and make everything hot and extremely dry.

7. LATE SLEEPER: Those idiot garbage collectors. Why do they have to make so much noise so early in the morning, anyway?
   EARLY RISER: Give 'em a break. They gotta make noise when they work, and they gotta start work early to get done on time.

▲ 8. HOSTESS: You know, I really think you should shave. The company's coming in less than an hour and you look like a hairy pig.
   HOST: Hey, I told you! I can't shave because my razor is broken. What am I supposed to do, shave with my pocket knife?

9. So you actually believe he knows the names of the people in the audience because God tells him? Here's how he really does it. He's got a wireless radio receiver in his ear, okay? And the people fill out prayer cards before the show. Then his wife collects them and radios the details to him during the show.

▲ 10. Let me explain to you why that was a great movie. The acting was good, the story was interesting, the photography was a knockout, and the ending was a killer.

11. Harold must be rich. Just look at the car he's driving.

▲ 12. I agree that the water contamination around here is getting worse and worse. It's because we've allowed people to install septic systems whenever and wherever they want.

13. "I could never endure to shake hands with Mr. Slope. A cold, clammy perspiration always exudes from him, the small drops are ever to be seen standing on his brow, and his friendly grasp is unpleasant."

Anthony Trollope, Barchester Towers

14. I know you think I wasted my vote by voting for Ross Perot in the '96 election, but that isn't so. I didn't approve of either of the main candidates, and if I'd voted for one of them and he had won, then my vote would have counted as an endorsement of him and his views. I don't want to add my endorsement to what I think are bad policies.

▲ 15. It could be that you're unable to sleep because of all that coffee you drink in the evening.

16. The coffee I drink in the evening can't be why I'm not sleeping, because I drink only decaffeinated coffee.

17. Of *course* the real estate industry depends on tax benefits. Just look at how hard the real estate lobby fought to preserve those benefits.

▲ 18. Although the computer case is double-insulated, the pins in the cable connections are not insulated at all. In fact, they are connected directly to the logic board inside the machine. So if you are carrying a charge of static electricity and you touch those connector pins, you can fry the logic circuits of your computer.

19. The orange is sour because it didn't have a chance to ripen properly.

20. "In 1970 Chrysler abandoned reverse-thread lug bolts on the left-hand side of its cars and trucks. One of those engineers must have realized, after about fifty years of close observation, that sure enough, none of the wheels were falling off the competition's cars, which had your ordinary, right-hand wheel fastenings."

John Jerome, Truck

▲ 21. "Economically, women are substantially worse off than men. They do not receive any pay for the work that is done in the home. As members of the labor force their wages are significantly lower than those paid to men, even when they are engaged in similar work and have similar educational backgrounds."

Richard Wasserstrom, "On Racism and Sexism," in Today's Moral Problems

22. Some people think that Iowa has too much influence in determining who becomes a leading presidential candidate, but I don't agree. Having early caucuses in a relatively small state makes it possible for a person to begin a run at the presidency without spending millions and millions of dollars. And it may as well be Iowa as any other state.

23. "The handsome physical setting of Los Angeles is more threatened than the settings of most of the world's major cities. All the region's residents are

affected by the ever-present threat of earthquakes, foul-smelling and chemical-laden tap water, and the potential for water shortages by the year 2000."

Charles Lockwood and Christopher Leinberger, "Los Angeles Comes of Age,"
in the Atlantic Monthly

24. She appears hard-hearted, but in reality she is not. She maintains strict discipline because she believes that if her children learn self-discipline, in the long run they will lead happier, more productive lives.

▲ 25. Letter to the editor: "Many people are under the impression that the Humane Society is an animal rights organization. Let me correct this misconception. Our purpose is that of an animal welfare organization. Animal rights groups have some excellent ideas but they are too broad of scope for us. We focus our attention on the care and welfare of the animals in our community. It is our primary purpose to provide humane care for homeless and owner-surrendered animals. However, we are against mistreatment of animals and we assist the State Humane Officer who investigates cases of animal abuse."

▲ 26. "American Airlines, United Airlines and TWA confirmed to the *Los Angeles Times* that some of their crews bypass passenger metal detectors. They said their current security procedures are effective and argued that switching to metal detectors would be costly and inefficient. Furthermore, they said, their security policies have been approved by the Federal Aviation Administration."

Los Angeles Times

Exercise 7-6

Can you tell when an explanation is used as an argument? For each of the following, mark a if the item is an explanation used as an argument (remember, justifications are arguments). Mark b if it is an explanation not used as an argument. Mark c if it is something else entirely, such as an argument with no explanation involved.

▲ 1. The reason the door keeps banging is that the windows are open on the south side of the house and there is a strong south breeze.

2. Moore always starts his class exactly on the hour, because he has a lot to cover, and he can't afford to waste time.

3. Moore always starts his class exactly on the hour. Don't believe me? Just ask anyone.

▲ 4. The Rotary Club provides free dinners on Thanksgiving, the reason being that they want to help the poor.

5. So you think the lawnmower won't start because it's too old? Here's what's really going on. We let gas sit in the carburetor all winter and it gums up the works—that's why it won't start. It has nothing to do with its being too old.

6. "If slavery had been put to a vote, slavery never would have been over-turned. We don't accept that you can put civil rights to a vote in a sexist and racist society."

Heather Bergman, member of the Coalition to Defend Affirmative Action
by Any Means Necessary

▲ 7. Rejecting a last-minute bid by Democrats to give President Clinton's law-yers a few days for review, House Republican leaders on Thursday arranged to make public today 445 pages of Independent Counsel Kenneth Starr's re-port on possible impeachable offenses by the president. It may seem as if the Republicans are seeking to embarrass the president as much as they can, but in fact they called for the release because they feel the public de-serves to know as soon as possible why Starr believes he has credible evi-dence that Clinton committed several crimes.

8. The share of public-school budgets devoted to regular education plummeted from 80 percent in 1967 to less than 59 percent in 1996. The rest goes to students with special needs. This at least partially accounts for declines in test scores among America's average students.

9. Just as Mary Shelley's Frankenstein monster fascinated us, computer viruses have come to do the same because they are much like a man-made life-form. Because of this fascination, you'll see more and more viruses turn up in hoaxes, urban legends, television shows, and movies.

Adapted from Scientific American

▲ 10. It is becoming more and more clear that child molestation is passed down from one generation to another. What isn't clear is whether the tendency is actually an inherited trait or whether a young child's being molested by a parent psychologically conditions the child to be a molester when he be-comes an adult. Either way, it looks as though a child with a molester for a parent is not the same as the rest of us; he has something to overcome that we don't, and it may be impossible for us to understand what a difficult problem he may have in avoiding the forbidden behavior.

Kinds of Explanations

Many kinds of things require explanations, so it shouldn't be surprising that many kinds of explanations exist. Here we briefly explain three important and common types of explanations to help you recognize and understand an explanation when you see it.

■ Physical Explanations

How did we get this flat tire?

Why did the rocket explode just after liftoff?

How did I get to have such high blood pressure?

How come there's been so much snow this winter?

What caused the thinning of the ozone layer?

Why did the dinosaurs die out?

Each of these questions asks for a **physical explanation.** Such explanations give us the physical background of the event in question to elucidate the causes of the event. "Physical" here is used in the broad sense, which includes not only the domain of the discipline physics, but also those of chemistry, geology, biology, neuroscience, and the other natural sciences.

The physical background, of course, includes the general conditions under which the event occurred—in the case of the question asked about the rocket, for example, the physical background includes such meteorological facts as the ambient temperature, atmospheric pressure, relative humidity, and so on. However, these general conditions are usually left unstated in an explanation if they are normal for the situation; we simply take them for granted. It's when they are unusual that they might be worth noting. For example, if we have been driving on a blisteringly hot day, we'd probably note that as a part of our explanation of why we had a flat tire.

More important, the physical background of an event includes whatever events we determine to be the *direct* or *immediate* cause of the phenomenon in question. But here there is a complication: More than one chain of causes contributes to an event's happening. For example, the home run clears the right field fence; depending on our interests and knowledge, we might focus on the chain of causation that accounts for the *bat's* arrival at the point of impact, or, if we are students of pitching, we might focus on the causal chain that accounts for the *ball's* arriving. Our interests and knowledge also determine which link in a causal chain we identify as *the* cause of an event. Whether we say the home run's direct cause was a good swing, a bad pitch, or both depends on our interests; each way of putting it can be useful for different purposes.

Under normal circumstances, a short explanation of the cause of an event may suffice. How did Moore get this flat tire? Ordinarily a brief explanation—"The tire has a nail in it"—would be enough. But under unusual circumstances, a more complete explanation may be required. If the tire had been in Moore's garage rather than on an automobile, he might require another link in the causal chain, one that would tell him how the nail got in the tire. This event might be explained, in turn, by the claim that the tire fell off the garage wall and onto the nail. Moore might be satisfied with stopping there; then again, he might want to find a further link in the chain—the cause of the tire's falling. He might well not request any further links if he learns that the hook on which the tire hung pulled out of the garage wall or that an earthquake shook the whole town and caused the tire to fall.

Pushing a line of questioning in this way can lead to the first of three general kinds of mistakes that we can make regarding physical explanations.

1. If we continue to require that a causal chain be traced further and further back, we eventually find ourselves being unreasonable, much like

Admit It. Your Sexual Adjustment Has Presented Problems for You

Have you ever wondered why astrological descriptions of your personality—descriptions based on your horoscope—often seem so absolutely right on? Here are two explanations.

First, the *astrological explanation*: The movements of the celestial bodies influence human affairs and determine the course of events. The position of the stars, the planets, the sun, and the moon at the time of your birth endow you with your temperament, tendencies, and future prospects for better or worse. These can be read by a trained astrologer from your horoscope—a map of the heavens at the time of your birth that shows the positions of the celestial bodies in relation to each other and to the "signs," or zones of the heavens, through which they pass. (Each zone is named for an ascendant constellation, such as Aries, Taurus, Gemini.)

Second, the *"Barnum-effect" explanation* (named in honor of P. T. Barnum's shrewd remark that a sucker is born every minute): An astrological description contains "elastic" statements that can seem accurate and specific relative to different individuals, such as, "Security is one of your major goals in life," or "You have found it unwise to be too frank in revealing yourself to others."

The elasticity of Barnum-effect statements can result from different causes. One such statement may be vague, such as the title of this box (does it apply to you?); another may be favorable to the reader (e.g., "You do not accept others' statements without satisfactory proof"); another may depict common personality traits (e.g., "You find that study is not always easy"); yet another may be two-headed (e.g., "At times you are extroverted, affable, and sociable, whereas at other times you are introverted, wary, and reserved"). Research has shown that subjects, regardless of their familiarity with astrology, tend to be even more impressed with the accuracy of Barnum-effect personality descriptions relative to themselves than they are with "genuine" horoscopes. (These examples of Barnum-effect statements are from Christopher C. French, Mandy Fowler, Katy McCarthy, and Debbie Peers, "Belief in Astrology," in *The Skeptical Inquirer*.)

So, which explanation is the better one, and why?

four-year-olds, who sometimes ask "Why?" until they become exasperating. But it is not easy to identify the precise point at which a demand to extend a causal chain becomes unreasonable. Sometimes the causal chain takes us too far afield from the original phenomenon; at that point, we have grounds for bringing the search for further links to a halt. (Moore is worried about getting more flats and about fixing this one; for these purposes, he doesn't care what caused the earthquake that shook the wall and caused the tire to fall on the nail.) At other times, the causal chain can become so complex that sorting it out would make the explanation more involved than the original event justifies. (A person needn't learn what causes earthquakes to

"This Book Isn't Fun to Read Because of All the Stupid Examples in It."

In Chapter 2, we warned you about syntactical ambiguities, claims that are ambiguous because of their structure or syntax. Sometimes people give explanations that take the form "Not-P because Q." Frequently such accounts are syntactically ambiguous, as in this example:

He didn't marry her because she was flirtatious.

Does this mean that he didn't marry her, and the reason he didn't is that she was flirtatious? Or does it mean that he did marry her, but not because she was flirtatious?

Examples of this sort are common: "The engine didn't stall because of the new design"; "The ride wasn't rough because the tires were low on air"; "They weren't nervous because the test was a surprise." And so on.

explain why the tire is flat.) Fortunately, our needs and curiosity being what they are, we generally do reach a point at which we are satisfied and stop searching for further links in the causal chain.

2. A second mistake we can make when dealing with physical explanations is to expect a reason or motive behind a causal chain. For example, we can legitimately ask why electrons take up certain orbits around an atom's nucleus if we are asking for the physical cause of the phenomenon only. But physical accounts cannot help us if we mean by our question, "What are the orbits for? What is the reason behind the electron's behavior?" The vocabulary of physics does not officially include references to desires, intentions, goals, and the like.

3. A third kind of mistake we can make in giving a physical explanation is to give it at the wrong technical level for our audience. In general discourse, a commonsense explanation usually suffices. If we wish to know why the water in a pan is boiling, we are ordinarily satisfied by learning that the pan is sitting on an electric burner. In an elementary physics class, a more detailed explanation involving the movement of excited molecules in the burner, pan, and water may be appropriate. Even though both explanations are equally correct, each can be inappropriate in the wrong context. A good explanation is always given at a level appropriate to the context in which it is given.

It is worth noting that not all physical explanations deal with the causes of specific events. Why do gases expand when heated? How do species evolve? Why do unsupported objects in the proximity of the earth always fall to its surface? Questions like these refer not to some specific event, but to apparent regular occurrences in nature. Ordinarily such occurrences must be explained by reference to a theory: molecular theory, gravitational theory, genetics, plate tectonics, and so on.

■ *Behavioral Explanations*

A second kind of explanation is called for by questions like these:

Why did Pete leave early last night?

Why did the union vote to approve the contract?

Why is the governor asking the legislature to approve a state lottery?

Why does Adrian let Melinda treat him that way?

Why do people watch so much television?

Why are people moving away from the inner cities?

Why can't we reduce the deficit?

These are requests for **behavioral explanations,** explanations that attempt to clarify the causes of behavior in terms of psychology, political science, sociology, history, economics, and the other behavioral and social sciences. Also included are explanations for behavior in terms of "commonsense psychology"—that is, in terms of someone's reasons or motives. (Within some contexts, it would be appropriate to distinguish reasons from motives, but for purposes of this discussion we need not do so.)

Like physical explanations, many behavioral explanations provide the relevant background information and, in addition, attempt to identify the immediate or direct cause of the behavior in question. In this case, however, the causal background is of a historical nature and includes political, economic, social, or psychological factors. *Which* factors are important depends on our interests and knowledge; one and the same event may have different explanations at the hands of psychologists, economists, and sociologists. If we want to explain Bill Clinton's reelection in 1996, for example, we might discuss the economy, or people's concern about the opposition's policies, or even the way Clinton's mannerisms and speech affect people. It really makes little sense to suppose that there is a single correct explanation of any instance of voluntary behavior.

Recurring patterns of behavior also seem to beg for explanation—for example, the tendency of people to distrust strangers, to sympathize with others in need, or to be inspired by nationalist sentiments. Like recurring patterns in nature, recurring patterns of behavior need to be explained in terms of a theory: economic, psychological, sociological, and so on. Of course, the theories we know about and accept affect our analysis of the causes of specific behaviors as well, and these theories help determine which factors we deem relevant in our explanations of them.

Because human behavior is less than fully predictable, at least given current knowledge, we should expect more exceptions to generalizations about behavior than to statements about regular occurrences in nature. We should similarly anticipate that theories of the behavioral and social sciences will be less rigid, more qualified, and more probabilistic (and sometimes

Proof That There's an Afterlife?

That a theory offers a good explanation of certain facts is a legitimate reason for accepting the theory—if indeed it does offer a good explanation. An interviewer from the *San Francisco Chronicle* asked passersby the question, What is proof to you that there's an afterlife? Most of the people interviewed think the theory of an afterlife gives a good explanation for certain facts. As an exercise, think up alternative explanations of the facts these people believe are explained by the existence of an afterlife.

- *Déjà vu.* That feeling that something has happened before or you've been someplace before. I believe in reincarnation, the soul going on to another life.

- It's a feeling I get from talking to other people about it. Like someone saying they've lived as a warrior in another life. I haven't experienced those memories myself, but from what people say, I get a feeling they're right.

- I think we're on Earth to learn things for our souls. When you die, you go into limbo and if you didn't learn certain things, you come back again. Once you accomplish everything, you go with God.

- When a baby is born and you spank it on the bottom, it cries. How would it know to cry if it didn't know about pain from another life? Crying is a natural reaction, because of previous lives where the person learned to cry.

- People make movies about coming back as someone else. People have feelings that could be from another life. People have certain dreams over and over again, like dying in a car accident. That could be because they died in a car accident. It just seems logical that a person can come back.

- I've just come to accept it from what I've been taught through religion. It's just a conclusion that this can't just be it. Think about nature. A plant grows up and lives and dies and goes into the ground and regenerates. That's probably a clue. It's a cycle.

- Because the world is here. Somebody—God, something—had to create it. It didn't just happen. There has to be a creator. The main thing about life is surviving and that survival goes on after we die. Survival is the strongest thing in us. Your spirit goes on to heaven or hell.

—*from* The San Francisco Chronicle

more philosophical) than many physical theories. It would be incorrect to automatically regard this looseness as a shortcoming in a behavioral explanation.

Like physical explanations, behavioral explanations can be pitched at the wrong technical level for the audience. Likewise, we can pursue the chain of causation in a behavioral explanation beyond the point that is reasonable for the purposes at hand; we don't require a history of civilization to explain why the Democrats lost control of New York City.

Unlike physical explanations and other behavioral explanations, explanations of behavior in terms of an agent's motives or reasons make reference not to the past, but to the future. Why did Pete leave early last night? He wanted to get home in time to watch *Mystery!* on PBS. Why did the union vote not to approve the contract? The contract contained provisions that were not in the interest of the union members (that is, they did not want to be governed by this set of provisions). Why is the governor asking the legislature to approve a state lottery? Because she thinks the lottery will decrease the need for a tax increase. Explanations in terms of reasons and motives are forward-looking, not backward-looking.

One mistake is peculiar to this type of explanation—namely, failing to see the difference between *a reason* for doing something and a *particular person's reason* for doing it. For example, there might be a reason for aiding homeless people, but that reason might not be a political leader's reason for helping them. We have to be careful to make clear whether we are requesting (or giving) reasons for doing something or whether we are requesting (or giving) some individual person's reasons for doing it. When we give a reason for doing something, we are presenting an *argument* for doing it. When we cite an individual person's reason for doing it, we are *explaining why* she or he did it.

■ *Functional Explanations*

Consider these requests for explanations:

> What's a carburetor?
>
> What do antibodies do?
>
> Why do skunks smell so awful?
>
> What in the world are those bells for?

Each of these questions asks about the function of something, and its answer will explain that thing's function or purpose. Ordinarily, a **functional explanation** requires putting the thing to be explained in a wider context and indicating its role in that context. For example:

> Carburetors mix fuel and air for combustion engines.
>
> Antibodies attack foreign bodies and thus help prevent infection.
>
> Skunks use a foul-smelling spray to ward off predators.
>
> The cats keep killing birds, so I put bells on their collars to give the birds a fair chance.

An object's actual function may be different from its originally intended function, if indeed any function was ever intended for it. More than one piece of sculpture winds up as a doorstop; our noses serve very well as supports for eyeglasses while they keep the rain out of our breathing apparatuses. Note that an item may have more than one function, as shown by the latter example. To be helpful, a functional explanation must be given in terms of the correct context.

Functional explanations can be as simple as those in the preceding examples, or they can be extremely complicated. An explanation of the Constitution of the United States will be relatively complex—just how complex, however, will depend on the audience and the circumstances in which the explanation is called for.

The function or purpose of many things (maybe all things) is determined by the reasons and motives of conscious beings, so for any behavioral explanation that refers to an agent's reasons or motives, you can usually find close at hand a functional explanation that refers to something's purpose or function. For example, a reasons/motives explanation of the voters' support for a state lottery is that they think the lottery will decrease the need for a tax increase. But you could also give a functional explanation of the state lottery by saying that its purpose is to decrease the need for a tax increase. A functional explanation is rather like a reasons/motives explanation stated in the passive voice. It is not inaccurate to think of a reasons/motives explanation as a sort of functional explanation of an instance of behavior.

To give a good account of a phenomenon, we must sometimes use more than one kind of explanation. For example, if the nail in the tire had gotten there, not because the tire fell on it, but because a neighbor pounded it in with a hammer, a thorough account of the event would have to include mention of whatever reason was behind the neighbor's action. Similarly, if a functional explanation needs detailed elaboration, some amount of physical explanation may be required; it may be appropriate to explain not only *what* a carburetor does but also *how* it does it as well. Even though understanding the different kinds of explanations is important, we do not need to be careful to use only one at a time. Using different kinds of explanations in combination may provide the best understanding of the phenomenon for our audience.

Exercise 7-7

State what is explained in the following passages and then determine whether each explanation is (a) a physical explanation, (b) a behavioral explanation, (c) a functional explanation, or (d) none of the above. Some passages may contain more than one explanation or fit into more than one category. This is especially true of some behavioral explanations, which might also be analyzed as functional explanations.

▲ 1. Francis uses artificial sweetener because he doesn't want to gain weight.

2. Why would anyone be an informer for the Drug Enforcement Agency? Money, that's why.

3. The purpose of the new steering column is to prevent theft. Here's how it works. You take the key out of the ignition, and the steering wheel disconnects from the steering mechanism. The result is that the car can't be steered.

▲ 4. It isn't clear why the Macintosh computer lost so much of its share of the market, especially because a lot of experts in personal computing claim it's better than most of its competition. Probably its competitors just do a better job marketing and advertising their products.

5. Television caused the defeat of the voter initiative. The opponents aired three times as many ads as the supporters of the measure, and the public votes for what it hears most often.

6. "American investors are increasingly taking a second look at Brazil, because it is a nation with an economy larger than Russia's and almost twice the size of Mexico's. With the bloom off of Eastern Europe as an investment opportunity, Brazil is emerging as the last major Latin country in line for a free-market revival."

New York Times

▲ 7. In Southern California the grass turns brown in the summer because there is no rain.

8. Even though cold air sinks, refrigerators with freezers on the bottom cost more to run than models with their freezers on top. That's because the motor is on the bottom and it heats up the freezer compartment.

9. That black rubber is around the tailgate to prevent water from leaking into the back of the station wagon.

▲ 10. Bruce Weitz, who played a detective on NBC's *Hill Street Blues*, explained the decline in the ratings of the series during its sixth year: "I think there's no reason in the sixth year of an episodic series that you can't take some chances. And [the producers] are not taking any chances; they're being very conservative."

11. At the outbreak of World War I, [Charles Edward] Montague dyed his gray hair black in order to conceal his age and join the army. H. W. Nevinson remarked that Montague was the "only man on record whose hair turned black in a single night from fearlessness."

Clifton Fadiman

12. The reason spring came so late this year is that people just forget how long winter really is around here.

13. Natasha lost the piano competition because she forgot to repeat the andante section. But she forgot because she didn't really want to win.

▲ 14. "The trouble started a fortnight ago—and by last week thousands of people in five Midwestern states were suffering from abdominal pain, diarrhea, nausea and dehydration. Illinois reported most of the cases, and it didn't take local health officials long to discover the cause: *Salmonella typhimu-*

▲ *Who has the better explanation?*

rium, a bacterium sometimes found in meat and dairy products. By the weekend more than 3,600 cases had been confirmed in one of the worst outbreaks of food poisoning ever. The source of the salmonella was quickly traced to two brands of milk sold by the giant Jewel Food Stores chain—specifically, milk processed and packaged at the company's main processing plant in the Chicago suburb of Melrose Park. . . . What puzzles both the company and health officials is how the salmonella could possibly survive the pasteurization process, which heats raw milk to 160 degrees and should destroy pathogenic bacteria."

Newsweek

15. Sales figures show that Pictionary remains one of the best-selling games in the country. The reason, according to a spokesperson for the company that makes it, is that "it's a game the whole family can enjoy."

▲ 16. The Supreme Court recently decided to allow a family to sue the U.S. government. A youngster in the family contracted a severe case of polio as a result of having been vaccinated against polio with a government-approved vaccine.

17. "Question: I've driven past petroleum refineries and noticed flares of gas burning 24 hours a day. Why, considering these times of fuel shortages, isn't this gas used to make gasoline or some other useful product? Answer: Most

refineries do recycle gaseous by-products of catalytic crackers, but it is nei- ther physically possible nor economical to save 100 percent of the gas. Some of it is flared as unsalvageable."

New York Times

Spotting Weak Explanations

It certainly is beyond the scope of this book (not to mention our abilities) to tell you how to evaluate the theoretical explanations of physicists, psychol- ogists, economists, and other natural and social/behavioral scientists. What we can do, however, is suggest criteria useful for spotting problems in many everyday explanations, including those that many people mistake for genu- ine science.

Although the following criteria are useful for spotting *problems* in ex- planations, bear in mind that an explanation that is *not* defective with re- spect to any of these criteria might still be inadequate or unacceptable for other reasons. There is no finite list of hard-and-fast rules that can be applied automatically when you are evaluating explanations.

■ Testability

An explanation must be subject to testing; if there is no way to test it for correctness, then there is no way to know whether it is in fact correct. An account that cannot be verified or refuted under any circumstances is one that should be viewed with suspicion. Some untestable explanations are known as "rubber" explanations (or *ad hoc hypotheses*): They can stretch around any objection. The only reason offered for believing an untestable explanation is the presence of the phenomenon it was produced to explain; no other evidence can be brought to bear on it. An example:

> Parker explains why his pocket watch works by telling you that a very small gremlin lives inside it and cranks away at the movement, thus causing motion in the gears. If you ask to see this wonderful thing, he explains that it is invisible. It also cannot be felt; neither does it show up in X-ray images; and if you listen closely, you'll find it is absolutely silent.

On the other hand, the fact that an explanation is difficult—even very difficult—to test does not mean it is not a good one. Some perfectly good scientific hypotheses are enormously difficult to test. But we are justified in being suspicious when there seem to be *no* means to test the explanatory claim:

> Poor Horace! Why did he die at such a young age? I guess it was due to fate.

Therapeutic Touch Healing

Do you know about therapeutic touch healing? By holding or moving their hands a few inches above a patient's body, practitioners claim to treat various physical ailments, from arthritis to cancer. One theory holds that the practice realigns a patient's energy fields.

Reportedly, thousands of people claim to have been helped by therapeutic touch, and among its advocates are health care professionals with impressive credentials. According to news reports, over eighty hospitals in North America offer the treatment. Nevertheless, the practice has never been confirmed scientifically, although anecdotes abound (see Chapters 11 and 12 for a discussion of anecdotal evidence).

In 1998, a nine-year-old girl named Emily Rosa recruited twenty-one practitioners to participate in a little experiment. Each therapist sat across from Ms. Rosa at a table and laid his or her arms out flat, with palms up. A piece of cardboard with armholes was placed over the therapist's forearms so neither his nor her hands nor Emily was visible. Emily would then place one of her hands a few inches above the therapist's right or left hand—a coin flip would determine which. Therapists then tried to detect which hand Emily was holding her hand above. Overall the average correct score was nearly 50 percent, exactly what would be expected by chance alone.

Emily, with her parents and a physician who specializes in uncovering medical fraud, published her research in the *Journal of the American Medical Association.* She wrote that, taken together, her findings and the lack of supportive studies suggest that therapeutic touch claims are groundless and that further use of the technique by health care professionals is unjustified.

Not bad critical thinking for a nine-year-old. (But see next box.)

Proponents of therapeutic touch reportedly disputed the importance of Emily Rosa's study (see nearby box) on the grounds that Emily's mother, Linda Rosa, is a well-known critic of therapeutic touch who has spent years lobbying against the procedure.

Is this a good reason for discounting or dismissing the study? If you think so, read Chapter 6 right away.

Is there any conceivable way we could test to see whether Horace's death was due to fate? Another cause for suspicion is the substitution of a new, less vulnerable explanation for a previous explanation that is giving way under attack:

> Of course you've never heard of watch gremlins. They're very shy and avoid gatherings of any kind. That's why people think they don't exist.

■ *Noncircularity*

An explanation is circular if it merely restates the phenomenon it was intended to explain. Such an explanation *looks* like an explanation, but in reality it is describing the phenomenon in different words. In untestable or ad hoc explanations, the phenomenon explained is the *only evidence* for the explanation; in a circular explanation, the phenomenon and its explanation are the *same thing.* Example:

Did Emily Show That Therapeutic Touch Doesn't Work?

If you read the previous box, you might have concluded that Emily showed that therapeutic touch has no therapeutic value. But such a conclusion would be incorrect. The extra attention given to a patient by a nurse using the technique might be beneficial. Some patients might improve through a placebo effect.

However, some therapeutic touch practitioners claim that they can sense a patient's "energy field" with their own hands. Emily's subjects couldn't even sense which of their own hands was in contact with Emily's energy field (assuming Emily's energy field was near Emily's body). Of course, it is possible that therapeutic touch practitioners can sense a patient's energy field with their hands without being aware *which* hand is doing the sensing, but this begins to make the claim (to be able to sense a patient's energy field) look untestable.

If the practice has therapeutic value, it is probably not due to a practitioner's sensing an "energy field" that is out of alignment.

He sits at the typewriter, but he simply cannot think of a thing to write. It's because he has writer's block.

We may as well say that he can't write because he can't write.

■ Relevance

Obviously, an explanation has to connect somehow with the thing or event being explained. But how do we characterize what is relevant and what is not? We noted earlier that a good physical or psychological explanation allows us to predict the phenomenon it explains with some degree of confidence. In general, we can say that an explanation is relevant to the extent that it enables us to make such predictions. Example:

Moore's car misses, sputters, and backfires. He explains that the battery is low.

It's true that low batteries can cause trouble in cars, but they cannot make an engine miss and backfire. Having a low battery does not allow us to predict the phenomena we need to explain. Thus, the explanation is not relevant to the phenomena.

A second example:

When asked why Trish always orders peppermint at the ice cream shop, Parker explains that she is allergic to chocolate.

Parker's explanation does explain why Trish doesn't order chocolate, but it fails to account for her ordering peppermint. On the basis of knowing about

Of course, they came up with excuses. One said the room was too cold. Another complained that the air conditioning blew the force field away.
—EMILY ROSA (see nearby boxes), on why therapeutic touch therapists could not detect her energy field

Remember: an explanation of why some effect was not observed is not evidence that the effect actually happened.

her allergy alone, we cannot predict her flavor selection with any confidence at all. (Note: If there were only two selections available, chocolate and peppermint, it would be a strange ice cream shop, but the explanation would be a good one.)

■ Freedom from Excessive Vagueness

Like any other claim or set of claims, an explanation can suffer from vagueness (see the section on vagueness in Chapter 2). Notice how little explaining is accomplished in this example:

> Moore is rude and snappish on the telephone. When Parker asks another acquaintance why, he is told that Moore is out of sorts today.

This does tell Parker something, but not very much—"out of sorts" is a vague phrase and could apply to Moore in a great number of circumstances.

■ Reliability

If an explanation leads to predictions that turn out to be false, then it is unreliable. Example:

> All the lights in your house suddenly go out. Someone suggests that the utility company has suffered a power failure. Looking out the window, however, you see that lights are on in other houses in your neighborhood.

We cannot tell if the explanation in this example is bad until we come to the last sentence of the passage, where we find that the explanation leads to a false prediction—namely, that the neighbors' lights should be out but they aren't. Notice that unlike some of the other criteria, reliability cannot be tested at first glance. We must first make predictions based on the explanation; the reliability of the explanation hinges on whether such predictions turn out to be true. In effect, we are testing the explanation. In the example above, the explanation failed the test because, had it been true, there would have been no lights in other houses in the neighborhood.

■ Explanatory Power

Other things being equal, the more phenomena an explanation explains, the better. This criterion is especially important when the explanation comes in the form of a scientific theory.

For example, let's say that according to the archeological evidence, there were two tribes of people living in southern Mexico hundreds of years ago and that they seem to have disappeared at about the same time. Anthropologist A comes up with a theory that explains what may have happened to one tribe, but this theory is irrelevant to the other tribe. Anthropologist B comes up with a theory that explains what may have happened to both tribes. Even if both theories are equal on all other grounds and both are equally supported by the physical evidence, the explanation offered by anthropologist B has the edge over that of anthropologist A on the grounds of greater explanatory power—it simply explains more.

Another example:

> Bill plants a new variety of tulip in his garden, and it comes up earlier than is usual. The earlier development may indeed be due to the characteristics of the new variety. But Bill notices that nearly every one of his flowers is up earlier than normal this year. Then he remembers that January and February have been much warmer than usual.

In this case, the warm weather provides a better explanation for the early bloom than do the genetic characteristics of the new tulips—because the weather accounts for the early development of the other plants as well. (Notice that the tulips' genetic features may indeed contribute to their early development; these two explanations are not incompatible.)

■ Freedom from Unnecessary Assumptions

One explanation is generally considered better than another if it requires fewer assumptions than the second. Such assumptions can include the existence of dubious entities or of especially unusual events involving familiar entities. (A dubious entity is one that we have reason to be skeptical about because it is not part of our background knowledge.) Example:

> A medium (or "psychic") comes up with surprising information about the participants at a séance—family nicknames, facts about friends and relatives, and so on. Aside from "natural" explanations about how this is done (e.g., subconscious cuing), observers might come up with these two explanations: (1) the medium acquired the information telepathically from the people at the table, or (2) the medium acquired the information through telepathic communication with spirits of deceased people.

The second of these explanations is more complicated; it requires that we assume the existence of departed spirits. Both explanations require unusual and even dubious activities—telepathic communication—but the first requires *only* this assumption. (One reason natural explanations are generally preferable is that they require fewer such assumptions.)

■ Consistency with Well-Established Theory

Sometimes a time-tested theory turns out to be defective. Newtonian physics, for example, was well established before Einstein and other twentieth-

Astrological Explanations and Other Psychic Happenings

In an episode of *Nova* telecast on PBS in 1993, magician James Randi distributed horoscopes to a classroom filled with students, each of whom was then asked to rate the accuracy of the horoscope he or she received. Almost all of them found the horoscopes highly accurate and uniquely applicable to their own individual situations. Then Randi had the students exchange horoscopes, and to their amazement, they discovered that every student had received the same horoscope, one that Randi had concocted for the experiment. They learned from the experiment that you don't need to invoke astrological theory to account for the apparent accuracy of horoscopes.

But one fellow was not impressed. "You didn't disprove astrology," he scolded Randi.

Randi agreed. "I can't disprove astrology," he said. "But I also can't prove there is no Santa Claus or Easter Bunny."

Randi was right. He didn't disprove astrology. What he did do was show that it isn't necessary to believe in astrology to explain the success of horoscopes.

In the same episode of *Nova,* Randi attempted to test the claims of Russian psychics that water standing around in a psychic hospital (where psychical cures were supposedly effected) became psychically charged. Unfortunately, the only people who could detect the psychic charge were psychics, so you just had to take their word for whether or not a container of water had become charged. But Randi thought of a solution to that problem: Could the psychics tell which of two *unmarked* containers held the charged water? Unfortunately, they could not, they said. This was due to the fact, they said, that regular water in the presence of charged water itself picks up the charge.

Randi concluded that the most amazing property of the charged water was its complete lack of any discernible qualities that would serve to distinguish it from regular water.

QUESTION: Why isn't more serious research being done on ESP? Is it because the scientific community believes that it's pure hokum?

—MARV BENSEND, Atkins, Iowa

ANSWER: I certainly hope so.

—"Ask Marilyn" by MARILYN VOS SAVANT

We hope so too.

century physicists discovered its limitations. Still, we cannot take such theories lightly; we need very powerful evidence before we consider giving them up. So, if an explanation conflicts with such a theory, we have good reason to look for an alternative account. Example:

> Ian Stevenson is both one of America's foremost psychical researchers and a strong believer in reincarnation. But he admits that reincarnation challenges standard biological theory on certain fundamental details.

If Stevenson is right in allowing this conflict, then we should be suspicious of reincarnation as an explanation for anything because standard biology is widely confirmed and accepted.

Supernatural . . . Or Just a Coincidence?

These days it's common for people to explain any event whose cause is not instantaneously understood as the result of supernatural forces. We're a bit more skeptical. Let's just note that some everyday occurrences attributed to the supernatural are better explained as matters of coincidence. What people tend to forget is that coincidences happen to someone or other all the time, and they really aren't anything special.

For example, Parker once dreamed that a friend of his was in an accident. Later he learned his friend really was in an accident at almost the exact time Parker had the dream. Looking at this from Parker's point of view, you might be inclined to think the odds against this happening by chance are just too long to take seriously. In other words, some telepathic or extrasensory processes seem to have been at work.

But were they? What you really must do is ask this question: What are the chances that, *some time or other* during the history of civilization, *someone or other* among the world's billions of people would find, among *one or another* of his or her (almost innumerable) dreams, a dream about *something or other* happening to *one or another* of the hundreds of people he or she had been acquainted with, something that was *similar,* in *some respect or other,* to what actually happened to that individual? When we look at things this way, we should be less amazed at Parker's experience. In fact, we should be totally *unamazed.* There are so many people and so many dreams that we'd expect coincidences like this to happen *frequently,* to someone or other—just as we expect someone to win the Pennsylvania lottery.

The point is, the chances for coincidences happening similar to the one experienced by Parker are pretty good, when you consider the population as a whole. We don't have to resort to supernatural explanations to understand them.

■ Absence of Alternative Explanations

It pays always to be on the lookout for alternative explanations of things. Example: Parker loses his appetite one day and explains that it is the result of a bad headache. Maybe. But then maybe Parker's loss of appetite and his headache are not causally related to each other at all. Perhaps each is an independent result of some common cause—did he celebrate too much the night before? Is he coming down with the flu?

Another example: When President Jimmy Carter raised taxes, double-digit inflation followed. Some commentators, in opposing Bill Clinton's tax increases, explained Carter's inflation problem as a result of the tax hike. Were the Carter tax increases responsible for Carter-era inflation? Maybe. But just before the inflation, OPEC (Organization of Petroleum Exporting Countries) also raised the price of oil to unprecedented levels. Maybe that was the explanation.

In Part 3, when we discuss the arguments that are used to support causal claims, we'll be taking a closer look at various types of alternative explanations as well.

Explanatory Comparisons (Analogies)

When we compare two or more objects, events, or other phenomena, we can have any of several purposes in mind. One of these is explanation. If X is more familiar than Y, then we may be able to communicate information about Y by comparing it to X—provided the two have significant features in common. For example, we might explain to a European what the climate is like in California by comparing it with that of the Mediterranean region of Europe.

Explanatory comparisons (or **analogies,** as they are often called) are sometimes hard to label as "true" or "correct." Suppose we try to explain to an English person what American football is like. We might want to compare it to a game with which our listener is familiar, so we choose rugby because this game resembles football more than, say, soccer or darts. But it is neither "true" to say that football is like rugby nor "false" to say that it is like soccer (or even darts—it isn't *much* like darts, but there may be *something* useful in making such a comparison). What we are trying to do in making such statements is to enlighten, to be helpful. And we succeed to one degree or another—or we fail entirely if, for example, our listener understands no more when we're finished than when we began.

The goal of this comparison is to explain how the game of football is played. This matter is relatively complicated, so it will be most helpful if the game chosen to compare to football resembles football in as many aspects as possible. This, of course, is what makes rugby a better candidate than darts. But notice that the two items do not have to resemble one another in some precise number of respects for the comparison to be "correct." Nor do the resemblances themselves have to be exact. Because it is unclear just what will be the most helpful in getting across the idea we want to communicate, we opt for the comparison that will give us the greatest number of close resemblances and the shortest list of important differences. In the example at hand, we begin with the game of rugby, assuming for the moment that football is just like it, and then we point out differences between the two. Rugby is a better choice than darts precisely because the list of differences between football and the latter is so much longer.

In general, our success in getting the idea across to our audience is more important than the "correctness" of our comparison. This is especially true when the features of the items compared are vague, complicated, or numerous. When the features we identify as common to the items compared are clear, relatively simple, and few, and the comparison itself is literal, we can evaluate the comparison with regard to correctness. In the statement "John's car is the same color as your hat," it is clear which features of the car and hat

Bigfoot: Is It Real?

Skeptics have questions. If members of a species of North American ape actually exist, how can they be so elusive? Why hasn't one wandered onto a highway or into a town? Why haven't hunters killed any? Why aren't so-called sightings more reliable? Why haven't bones been found? Or bodies? Why have DNA tests of alleged hair samples been inconclusive? Why is there no fossil evidence that nonhuman primates ever inhabited North America? Why is the photographic evidence so scanty and inconclusive?

Idaho State University professor of anatomy Jeff Meldrum (shown with the plaster cast of a gorilla's foot) thinks the questions are reasonable. However, he thinks there is evidence for a North American ape that cannot be overcome by such questions, in the form of numerous plaster casts he and others have taken from tracks. Meldrum has considered what the foot muscles and bones in a towering primate weighing a thousand pounds would have to be like. Some of the tracks, he maintains, have anatomical details incorrect for an enlargement of a human foot but consistent with a large primate. He finds it exceedingly difficult to believe a hoaxer could have the anatomical knowledge required to produce tracks of the sort he has seen and casted.*

Skeptical scientists are unimpressed and, according to Meldrum, refuse even to look at these data. Associated Press writer Dan Gallagher quotes Mercyhurst College biology professor David Hyland as saying, "An organism which lives that long requires a breeding population of a certain size . . . there is no evidence but footprints and anecdotal accounts. It begs the question of whether they do exist."

Actually, footprints (and anecdotal accounts, for that matter) do not beg the question. Crediting them as evidence of a North American ape does not require us to *assume* such a thing exists. Nevertheless, they are not hard evidence in the way in which bones and dead bodies are hard evidence.

The question seems to come down to this: Given the population size requirements for species sustenance, if there were Bigfeet, it might seem likely that bones and bodies and other traces would have been found by now and reliable sightings made. On the other hand, assuming the anatomical details of the footprints are as described by a professor of anatomy, it might seem likely the footprints weren't planted by pranksters. Which likelihood seems greater?

---

*Professor Meldrum sent us photographs of castings in which dermal ridges are evident (dermal ridges are those little ridges that you see on finger and palm prints). But the ridges in the castings are vertical, whereas the ridges in human footprints aren't.

Watch Out for This Kind of "Proof"!

Recently we heard a psychologist defend the theory that TV violence causes violent behavior. He spoke vigorously and said something like this:

> Of course TV violence causes violent behavior! It's like smoking and lung cancer. If you want to deny that smoking causes lung cancer, you would have to ignore an impressive accumulation of evidence. Not everyone who smokes will get cancer, and not everyone who gets cancer smoked. But the evidence that the one causes the other is overwhelming. It shows that a far greater number of smokers than nonsmokers get cancer, and it shows that a far greater number of people who are exposed to secondary smoke get cancer, too.

Did the psychologist show that TV violence causes violent behavior in viewers? Not at all. His persuasive analogy made it clear that he believed there was strong evidence for his claim. But he did not provide any evidence for this claim in his statement.

are being compared—the comparison is between one definite color and another (in this case, the same color). Similarly, one can explain something of how a rocket engine works by comparing it to what happens when a balloon is blown up and released to fly around the room. In this case, the balloon exemplifies Newton's third law of motion, a principle on which rocket engines work. In both cases the respect in which the two items are being compared is quite definite and literal.

The same is true of the comparison between football and rugby—if we select a certain narrow aspect of both for comparison. We can say, for example, that carrying the ball across the goal line counts as a score in football just as it does in rugby. This claim is either correct or it is not, for it is sufficiently precise and simple to permit such evaluation. But if we are trying to communicate the general idea of football and do not mean to take a lifetime to do it, we are better off not identifying every possible feature of the game for comparison with some feature of rugby. The economy we gain by having rugby as a comparative of football is lost in such a scheme—we get more for our efforts by leaving the comparison rather vague and ignoring the standard of correctness. We can still hope for some degree of success with our explanation by giving our audience at least a general idea of what football is like.

We have a different situation if we consider the poet Robert Burns's comparison "O my luve is like a red, red rose." Now, his love is probably not *literally* like a red rose in any respect at all. This is not to say, though, that the poet has said something false. He may have told us something about his love, but he has done it in an indirect, nonliteral way that we call metaphorical. His intention was to get us to react in a certain way—to evoke a certain

The Wrong Initials Can Shorten Your Life

Researchers at the University of California, San Diego, looking at twenty-seven years of California death certificates, found that men with "indisputably positive" initials like JOY and WOW and ACE and GOD and WIN and VIP lived 4.48 years longer than a control group of men with neutral initials and ambiguous initials, like DAM and WET and RAY and SUN, that had both a positive and a negative interpretation. Further, men with "plainly negative" initials like ASS and DUD died on average 2.8 years earlier than did the men in the control group.

As an exercise, propose an explanation for these findings that isn't defective in terms of the criteria discussed in this chapter. Explain how you would test the explanation.

feeling, perhaps—and in that fashion give us a kind of understanding that we may not have had before. He might succeed or fail in this. One person may indeed understand something new as a result of the line of poetry; another may walk away puzzled about how Burns's love could resemble a flower.

A point worth noting here is that only a person who is familiar with both terms of an explanatory comparison is in a position to evaluate it. The individual for whom the comparison is made, because he or she is familiar with only one term, is in a position to determine only if his or her new understanding makes sense, not whether it is accurate with regard to the phenomenon at issue. Our English person may have a very clear picture in mind as a result of our comparison of football to rugby but might still be thoroughly surprised upon seeing a football game for the first time. The clarity of his or her mental image, which was all this individual was in a position to evaluate, is no guarantee of its accuracy or completeness.

Often a comparison is made not to explain but to illustrate a point that is not explicitly stated. Consider: "I'd rather beat my head against the wall than go jogging," or "James has about as much imagination as a bridge abutment." These are simply colorful ways of saying that the speaker has a distaste for jogging and that James has no imagination; in neither case is any explanation being offered. In such cases, the comparisons themselves are less important than the point that is implicit in them. In such cases as the football/rugby example, the comparison, and the terms being compared, are very important. But one could substitute barbells or any number of things for the bridge abutment in the other example; the success or failure of the remark hinges on whether the listener takes notice of what the real point is (which is probably to influence the listener's attitude). In this case, the speaker is likening James to something with no imagination at all. These examples are called persuasive comparisons and take their place beside persuasive definitions (see Chapter 4). Besides conveying information, they are intended to express or evoke an attitude by means of their colorful language.

Yuppies have a low birth rate because they have to go to Aspen to mate.

—Dave Barry

Some "explanations" are just made in good fun.

When women are depressed they either eat or go shopping. Men invade another country. It's a whole different way of thinking.

—Elayne Boosler

So are some comparisons.

Recap

Although there are times when a set of claims counts as both an explanation and an argument, these are two separable functions. Explanations are designed to show *how* or *why* something is or will be; arguments are designed to show *that* something is or was or will or should be. Some explanations are used as justifications. However, to explain an event is not necessarily to attempt to justify it, though some people automatically assume that it is.

Three kinds of explanation are especially important to understand. Physical explanations explain a phenomenon by providing cause-and-effect relationships among elements in its physical background; which elements we determine to be most important depends mainly on our interests and knowledge. Behavioral explanations attempt to elucidate behavior in terms of social, economic, political, historical, or psychological causes. Functional explanations place an object or event in a context and show what role it plays there.

The following criteria can help us spot problems in explanations: The *presence* of testability, relevance, reliability, and explanatory power are desirable qualities in an explanation; also desirable is the *absence* of circularity, vagueness, and unnecessary assumptions. We should also consider alternative explanations and whether the explanation under scrutiny conflicts with well-established theory.

Explanatory comparisons, or analogies, make use of common features in a familiar and an unfamiliar item in order to explain the latter. We often evaluate such comparisons more in terms of their success in conveying a conception of an object or event than in terms of their correctness.

Having read this chapter and the chapter recap, you should be able to

▲ Distinguish an explanation from an argument and give examples of each

▲ Describe three kinds of explanation and discuss how they are used

▲ Describe nine common criteria that can be used in evaluating explanations

▲ Discuss explanatory comparisons and the strengths and weaknesses of this kind of explanation

Additional Exercises

Exercise 7-8

Review: Answer the questions based on your reading of the text.

▲ 1. Can more than one causal chain be important in explaining the cause of an event?

2. What determines our selection of the most important causal chain leading to an event and the most important links in that chain?

3. What are three mistakes that can be made in dealing with physical explanations?

4. What is the usual basis for explanations of regularities in nature?

▲ 5. We often have somewhat less confidence in behavioral explanations than in physical explanations. What might the reason be?

6. Can an object have more than one function?

7. Does the current function of an object depend on the intentions of the creator or designer of that object?

8. Without going back to the section on spotting weak explanations, list as many of the nine criteria for explanations as you can.

▲ 9. If you want to explain what X is like to someone who is unfamiliar with it, how might you do so using a comparison or an analogy?

▲ 10. Why might we say that success is more important than correctness in an explanatory comparison?

11. A reasons/motives behavioral explanation is closely related to what other type of explanation?

12. Is there usually a single correct explanation of voluntary behavior?

13. An explanation of a recurring pattern of behavior usually involves reference to what?

▲ 14. Should we expect behavioral generalities to be more likely or less likely to hold without exceptions than natural regularities?

15. What is the difference between a reason for doing something and some individual person's reason for doing it?

Exercise 7-9

▲ What kinds of explanations do you find in the article on the following page? How would you evaluate them?

Exercise 7-10

Here are some findings from studies of heart attacks, reported by the Associated Press. Propose explanations for them that are not defective in terms of criteria discussed in this chapter.

Alternative group assignment: In groups propose explanations for each finding that are not defective in terms of criteria discussed in this chapter. Two neighboring groups then form a supergroup and compare their explanations and, if there are any differences, vote on which explanation for each item seems the most likely. Two supergroups then compare their explanations, and so on until the class reaches consensus as to the most likely explanation.

Indians Flock to See Statues "Drink" Milk

NEW DELHI, India—Millions rushed to Hindu temples across India on Thursday after reports of a miracle—the statues of one of their gods were drinking milk.

The faithful—bearing milk in everything from earthen and steel pots to tumblers and jugs—converged on temples that had reproductions of the elephant-headed Lord Ganesha.

"It is a miracle," said A. K. Tiwari, a priest at a temple in southern New Delhi.

Scientists dismissed that explanation, saying the offered milk trickled down the granite or marble idols in a thin film that was not easily visible.

Crowds thronged temples in dozens of cities, including New Delhi, Bombay, Calcutta, and Madras.

Police and paramilitary soldiers were called out to guard temples across India. In the northern town of Jamshedpur, police waved bamboo canes to control a crowd of 500 that tried to storm a temple.

Tiwari, the priest, said the excitement began early Thursday when a devotee dreamed that the deity wanted milk. When the man, who wasn't identified, held a spoonful of milk near the statue's trunk, the milk disappeared.

Word spread quickly, and people began lining up at temples as early as 4 a.m.

The faithful dismissed suggestions of a hoax.

"It cannot be a hoax. Where would all the milk being offered go? It is such a small idol, it can't take in so much," said Parmesh Soti, a business executive who stood in line. "The gods have come down to earth to solve our problems."

So widespread were the reports of a miracle that the federal Department of Science and Technology was asked to investigate.

Their scientists offered milk mixed with colored pigment to an idol in a New Delhi temple. Although it disappeared from the spoon, it soon coated the idol. The scientists credited the "miracle" to surface tension, saying molecules of milk were pulled from the spoon by the texture of the statues.

Associated Press, in *The Sacramento Bee*

1. The chance of having a heart attack is significantly higher in the morning.

2. People who have a heart attack at night are twice as likely to die as those who have a heart attack at some other time.

3. The risk of having a heart attack is 33 percent higher in the winter than in the summer, even in Los Angeles.

4. For every 18 degrees Fahrenheit that readings fall in the day's average temperature, the risk of a first heart attack rises by 13 percent.

5. The risk of having a heart attack on a Monday is nearly 40 percent higher than on any other day.

Exercise 7-11

Using the criteria listed in the text, criticize the following explanations. In cases where the criteria do not apply, explain in your own words what is wrong with the explanation. If you can think of a better explanation of the phenomenon in question than the one given, state what it is.

▲ 1. The reason he has blue eyes is that he acquired them in a previous incarnation.

2. The Kings did much better in the second half of the game. That's because they gained momentum.

3. "Men are biologically weaker than women and that's why they don't live as long, a leading expert declares."

Weekly World News

▲ 4. PARKER: Gad, there are a lot of lawyers in this country today.
MOORE: That's because there are so many lawsuits that there's a huge demand for lawyers.

5. Why did he come down with the flu? He's just prone to that sort of thing, I guess.

6. If God had meant for people to fly, he'd have given them wings.

▲ 7. Alcoholics find it so difficult to give up drinking because they have become physiologically and psychologically addicted to it.

8. Alcoholics find it so difficult to give up drinking because they have no willpower.

9. The reason *Pulp Fiction* was a box-office hit is that Roger Ebert, one of the most influential movie critics, gave it a good review.

▲ 10. According to some psychologists, we catch colds because we want to. Most of the time we are not aware of this desire, which may, therefore, be said to be subconscious. Viruses are present when we have a cold, but unless we desire to catch cold, the viruses do not affect us.

11. Why does she sleep so late? I guess she's just one of those people who have a hard time waking up in the morning.

12. I wonder what made me choose Budweiser. Maybe I've been subjected to subliminal advertising.

▲ 13. The area along this part of the coast is especially subject to mudslides because of the type of soil that's found on the slopes and because there is not enough mature vegetation to provide stability with root systems.

14. How did he win the lottery twice? I'd have to say he's psychic.

15. "Parapsychologist Susan Blackmore failed to find evidence of ESP in numerous experiments over more than a decade. *Fate* magazine's consulting editor D. Scott Rogo explained her negative results as follows: 'In the course of my conversations with Blackmore I have come to suspect that she resists—at a deeply unconscious level—the idea that psychic phenomena exist. . . . *If* Blackmore is ever fortunate enough to witness a poltergeist or see some other striking display of psychic phenomena, I am willing to bet that her experimental results will be more positive.'"

The Skeptical Inquirer

16. According to a report by Scotty Paul, writing in *Weekly World News*, thousands of tourists who defied an ancient curse and took home souvenir chunks of lava rock from Hawaii's Volcanoes National Park have felt the bitter wrath of a vengeful volcano goddess. The curse explains why a

Michigan man tumbled to his death down a stairway and why a Canadian tourist died in a head-on auto accident, as well as why a Massachusetts widow lost her life savings in the stock market. The three suffered their misfortunes after taking lava rocks from the volcano and defying the curse of Madame Pele, the volcano goddess.

▲ 17. Why is there so much violence these days? Rap music, that's why. That and the fact that there's so much violence on TV and in the movies.

18. The reason I got into so much trouble as a kid is that my father became a heavy drinker.

▲ 19. "Why do so many professors write bad prose? Ten years ago I heard a classics professor say the single most important thing—in my opinion—that anyone has said about professors: 'We must remember,' he declared, 'that professors are the ones nobody wanted to dance with in high school.' This is an insight . . . that helps to explain the problem of academic writing. What one sees in professors, repeatedly, is exactly the manner that anyone would adopt after a couple of sad evenings sidelined under the crepe-paper streamers in the gym, sitting on a folding chair while everyone else danced. Dignity, for professors, perches precariously on how well they can convey this message: 'I am immersed in some very important thoughts, which unsophisticated people could not even begin to understand. Thus, I would not *want* to dance, even if one of you unsophisticated people were to ask me.'

"Think of this, then, the next time you look at an unintelligible academic text. 'I would not want the attention of a wide reading audience, even if a wide audience were to *ask* for me.' "

Patricia Nelson Limerick

20. In their book *The Gulf Breeze Sightings: The Most Astounding Multiple Sightings of UFOs in U.S. History,* authors Ed and Frances Walters provide photographs of UFOs. According to the *Pensacola News Journal,* the man who now lives in the house the Walters family occupied at the time they photographed the UFOs discovered a flying saucer hidden under some insulation in the attic of the garage. With this model, news photographers were able to create photos of "UFOs" that looked like the Walterses' photos. Walters denies the model was his, but the paper in which it was wrapped contains part of a house plan Walters drew up (Walters is a building contractor). Walters says that model was planted by someone who wished to discredit him.

A Gulf Breeze youngster named Tom Smith also has come forth, admitting that he and Walters's son helped produce the fake saucer photos. He has five UFO photos of his own to substantiate his claim. Walters says Smith's photos are genuine. Which of the two explanations given for the original UFO photos is most plausible, and why? (This report is from *The Skeptical Inquirer.*)

▲ 21. According to mathematician and science writer Martin Gardner, in Shivpuri, a village near Poona, India, there is a large stone ball weighing about 140 pounds in front of a mausoleum containing the remains of

Kamarali Darvesh, a Muslim saint. It is possible for five men to stand around the ball and touch it with a forefinger at spots on or below the ball's equator. After they recite in unison "Kamarali Darvesh," an attendant gives a signal, and the ball slowly rises. The explanation of this phenomenon, according to devout Muslims, is that it is a miracle of Allah's.

Exercise 7-12

Before the 1996 presidential election, Bob Dole trailed Bill Clinton in the polls by a sizable margin. Three generally conservative columnists offered alternative explanations. George Will said that voters understood that under Clinton the rates of inflation and unemployment were very low, federal spending was down, and the federal deficit had declined. Joseph Sobran said that voters sensed insincerity and opportunism on the part of Dole because Dole had traditionally opposed tax cuts but was now suddenly promising to lower everyone's taxes. Linda Bowles said that the poll results were selectively reported by a biased media determined to defeat Dole.

  Which explanation seems to you to be simplest? Is the explanation that seems simplest on the surface really the simplest? Explain why or why not.

Exercise 7-13

The first paragraph below describes a phenomenon of recent interest to paleontologists and astronomers. Two possible explanations, A and B, are given afterward. After reading about the phenomenon and both explanations, answer the questions at the end of the exercise.

> *The Phenomenon:* The age of dinosaurs came to an end approximately sixty-five million years ago. Nearly every species of dinosaur, and countless other species as well, became extinct in a very short period of time. Recently, two scientists at the University of Chicago, John Sepkoski and David Raup, completed an exhaustive study of the earth's fossil record for the last 250 million years. Their study turned up evidence that mass extinctions like that of the dinosaurs have happened on a regular, cyclical basis every twenty-six million years.
>
> *Common Evidence:* Two explanations have been produced to explain these regular catastrophes, based in large part on Berkeley geologist Walter Alvarez's discovery of a layer of clay containing large amounts of the rare element iridium, which is often found in extraterrestrial bodies such as asteroids. This clay was laid down at about the time of the passing of the dinosaurs, giving scientists reason to think that the impact of one or more asteroids on the planet and the consequent raising of massive dust clouds in the atmosphere caused the extinctions. This problem remained: What might cause the pelting of Earth by asteroids in twenty-six-million-year cycles?
>
> *Explanation A:* One view holds that the sun, like many stars, has a smaller companion star in a binary orbit, one that brings it into the

vicinity of the solar system and a nearby cloud of asteroids every twenty-six million years. The star, nicknamed "Nemesis," is presumed to be quite small, which fact, in combination with its huge orbit, would make it very difficult to spot. But it is of sufficient size and gravitational attraction to dislodge asteroids from their ordinary paths and send them flying through the solar system, where some of them would fall into the earth's gravitational field and be pulled to the surface of the planet. Hence the impacts, the dust clouds, and the extinctions.

Explanation B: The second theory, from astronomer Daniel Whitmore, hypothesizes, *not* an as-yet undiscovered companion star, but an undiscovered new planet, dubbed "Planet X." This planet, it is suggested, orbits the sun about once every one thousand Earth years in a region far beyond the farthest known planet, Pluto. The orbit of Planet X would bring it into proximity with the asteroid cloud every twenty-six million years, with the same result as suggested for the star, Nemesis. Planet X might also account for the mysterious wobbles that exist in the orbits of Pluto and Uranus.*

Questions

▲ 1. Do the two explanatory theories seem evenly matched to you, given the information supplied, or does one seem any more likely than the other?

▲ 2. An orbit as large as that of Nemesis, some scientists believe, would be sufficiently unstable to prevent its being absolutely regular in a twenty-six-million-year cycle. How much damage, if any, does this do to explanation A?

▲ 3. What effect, if any, would there be on explanation B if Pluto and Uranus did not wobble in their orbits?

▲ 4. If no iridium had been found in the clay layer, would the likelihood of either A or B be affected?

▲ 5. If the extinctions occurred in a less regular fashion, would either A or B be affected?

Exercise 7-14

Read the following passage, and answer the questions at the end.

[Recently] some unusual events occurred in the household of John and Joan Resch of Columbus, Ohio. They live in a two-story house with their twenty-five-year-old son John, their fourteen-year-old adopted daughter Tina, and four young foster children. The following are excerpts from a story that describes the incidents:

> [Joan] had turned off the lights in the empty dining room, but now they were on again. So were lights in the deserted and previously unlighted hallway. With no one upstairs, the shower began to run.

---

*A third theory, which is not germane to this exercise, is that volcanic activity declined, causing carbon dioxide levels to fall, causing plant life to decline, causing oxygen to diminish, causing the dinosaurs to wheeze to death.

Back in the kitchen, the washer and dryer sounded odd, and Joan could see by the dials that they were going through their cycles too fast. The hands on the electric clock raced wildly.

John, a man of impressive girth and few words, listened to their story of household appliances apparently gone haywire. When he called an electrician, there was an odd noise on the phone—according to both men, "almost like a howl."

To veteran electrician Bruce Claggett, the Resches' problem sounded like a faulty main breaker-switch. But he found the switch in perfect working order. Maybe some electronic interference, he guessed. But individual lights still seemed to be controlled by their respective wall switches, which went from off to on by themselves. He went from room to room taping the switches down. But before he could make a full sweep through the house, the first lights were on again and the tape had disappeared.

After three hours, Claggett gave up. "I had a strange feeling I never want to have again," he says. That evening, he called John Resch. "The lights seem to be okay now," John told him. "But something worse is happening. Things are flying through the air."

Pictures tumbled from their hooks. A treasured set of stemware crashed, piece by piece, from its display shelf. Chairs seemed to move on their own, and couches upended themselves. Bewildered, the Resches called the police, and two officers arrived to hear their story. "You need help," one officer said, "but it's not the kind we can give." That night the family stayed together, some sleeping on convertible sofas in the family room and the others in sleeping bags on the floor.

The next day, the Resches thought they had a clue. John remembered that, on Saturday, there had been an hour of calm while Tina was out visiting a friend. On Sunday morning, the trouble started again when she awoke.

"I'm not making it happen," Tina insisted. "I'm not doing it on purpose." And they hadn't seen her do anything. Saturday, in fact, a candlestick had taken flight and hit Tina on the head.

Was it a poltergeist? "I don't believe in such things," Joan said, finding another name for it. "A force," she called it. "Maybe Tina can't control it, but that's what it is."

On Monday morning, Joan Resch called Mike Harden, a Columbus *Dispatch* columnist who had written about the family and their foster children. She hoped Harden would know where she could turn for help.

"I don't believe in the supernatural," Harden told Joan when he arrived at the house. For a while, he talked quietly with the family. Then a mug of hot coffee seemed to move on its own, spilling into Tina's lap. Magazines fell mysteriously from a table. Mike telephoned for a photographer.

Fred Shannon arrived for "the most bizarre assignment of my life." While Tina was perched on the arm of a chair, he saw a loveseat move toward her, "as if to attack her." When she shifted to the loveseat, an afghan rug flew up from the floor and draped itself over Tina's head. Fred snapped the picture. Tina was about four feet away from a tissue box when Fred saw it take off from a table and fly across the room.

Again and again a white phone seemed to hurl itself at Tina. Fred wanted a picture of the flying phone, but it apparently was camera-shy. To outwit "the force," he readied his camera, and then turned away, watching only out of the corner of his eye. At the first flash of movement, he clicked the shutter. The result was a photograph of the phone flying across Tina's body, "the picture of a lifetime," published in newspapers around the world.

The Columbus *Dispatch* story and picture of the flying phone made other journalists clamor for access to the house, and Drew Hadwal, of WTVN-TV in Columbus, had his camera focused when a large lamp seemed to hurl itself to the floor. Triumphantly, Drew raced back to the studio.

Rolling the tape in slow motion, he found that the camera had caught what the human eye had missed. Tina, on tape, was looking around as if to check if anyone was watching. There was her hand, reaching up to tip the shade and knock over the lamp.

The next day, Tina explained. "I was tired and angry. I did it so the reporters could have what they came for and leave." The explanation seemed plausible. Still, if Tina played a trick once, had she done so other times?

The family invited a team from the Psychical Research Foundation of Chapel Hill, N.C., into their home. Director William Roll says that, of the "poltergeist" cases he has investigated, he's found about one-third to be trickery or natural phenomena (such as house settling), another third to be "inconclusive," and a final third to be "genuine." Roll does not, however, believe in poltergeists as "noisy spirits," in the literal meaning of the word. Phenomena attributed to poltergeist activity are, he says, the product of something he calls Recurrent Spontaneous Psychokinesis (RSPK), a power some individuals possess that causes objects to fly around by themselves.

According to Roll, RSPK is usually involuntary and is most often an affliction of teen-agers. He believes it's an energy that comes out of the turmoil so many teen-agers feel.

At the time of the disturbances in her house, Tina Resch had been feeling more stress than most teen-agers. Along with problems in school that had led to her staying home and working with a tutor, she had just broken up with her first boyfriend. And she was beginning to wonder about finding her birth mother, who had brought Tina to a hospital when she was ten months old and never returned for her.

Roll and an assistant lived with the Resches for a week, checking for natural causes and for wires and trick devices. They found nothing. All the while, Roll kept Tina under close observation. Objects still seemed to move on their own.

Investigators from the Committee for the Scientific Investigation of Claims of the Paranormal (CSICOP), with headquarters in Buffalo, N.Y., were turned away. "One group at a time is enough," Joan said.

The CSICOP team—two university scientists (an astronomer and an astrophysicist) and James Randi, a noted magician who has revealed trickery in many cases of claimed paranormal events—had to settle for interviews with witnesses. Their key question: "Did you see the phone or the glass or any other object actually take off and begin to fly?"

Again and again, witnesses admitted they'd missed the takeoff, the point at which a human hand might have started the object on its flight. Photographer Fred Shannon, however, insisted that he had seen a telephone and also a tissue box as they rose into the air and began to fly.

"The hand," says Prof. Steven Shore, the astrophysicist on the team, "is always quicker than the eye." He believes that's the explanation for all the recorded events.

Tina's is the most publicized case of suspected paranormal phenomena in recent years, and one of the best-documented. Yet the events are hard to prove or disprove. Odd things happened when Tina went with Roll to North Carolina—a door seemed to open by itself, a telephone flew from a desk and struck Tina in the back.

By the time she was back home, two months had passed since the curious events had begun. The house has remained calm since Tina's return.

It is *eerie* to think that a young girl might have the uncontrollable power to make objects fly through the air. But it is also hard to accept that an average teen-ager, with no special skills or knowledge or dexterity, could beguile and hoodwink so many adults.

Both skeptics and believers agree on one thing. Whether the events in the Resch household were paranormal or a prank, the energy for them came from the storms and stresses of being a teen-ager.

"There are things that can't be explained," their minister told the Resch family. One of them is poltergeists. Another is teen-agers.

Excerpted from Claire Safran, "Poltergeist, Or Only a Teen-ager," Reader's Digest

Questions

▲ 1. How many different explanations were suggested by the people who appear in the story?

▲ 2. Does the writer of the story seem to prefer one explanation over the rest?

3. Of the people who suggested explanations, who seems to you to be the most credible? Why?

▲ 4. William Roll does not believe in poltergeists, it was said. He attributes the phenomena to "recurrent spontaneous psychokinesis." Does either of these accounts—poltergeists or RSPK—seem more credible than the other when measured against the criteria listed in the "Spotting Weak Explanations" section of the text?

5. Measured against the same criteria, how does the RSPK explanation compare with the "natural" explanation made by Professor Shore of the CSICOP team?

6. Look back to the third paragraph from the end. Are the two explanations given there *equally* hard to accept? Keep in mind your answer to the preceding question.

Writing Exercises —————————————————————————————

1. Why is it that athletes get paid so much more than classical musicians in American society? Propose a serious explanation for this phenomenon. Take about twenty minutes to write it. Put your name on the back of your paper. When everyone is finished, your instructor will collect the papers and redistribute them to the class. In groups of four or five, read the papers that have been given to your group. Do not look at the names of the authors. Then rank-order the papers. Your instructor will read the papers that have been top-ranked by two (or more) groups, for discussion.

2. Follow the instructions for Exercise 1, but this time explain why so many drivers become insanely enraged over even trifling inconveniences caused by other drivers.

Chapter 8

Understanding and Evaluating Arguments

Sometimes the reasons for accepting a claim are explicitly set forth in an argument; other times they are not. When they are not—when we are dealing with unsupported or nonargued claims—we have to determine for ourselves whether there are reasons for accepting them. In Part 2 we discussed unsupported claims. We now turn to arguments and their evaluation.

The Anatomy of Arguments

An argument consists of a conclusion (the claim that the speaker or writer is arguing for) and premises (the claims that he or she offers in support of the conclusion). Here are two examples of arguments:

> [Premise] Every officer on the force has been certified, and [premise] nobody can be certified without scoring above 70 percent on the firing range. Therefore, [conclusion] every officer on the force must have scored above 70 percent on the firing range.

> [Premise] Mr. Conners, the gentleman who lives on the corner, comes down this street on his morning walk every day, rain or shine. So [conclusion] something must have happened to him, because [premise] he has not shown up today.

Notice that sometimes the conclusion of one argument can serve as the premise of another:

> [Premise] Every student who made 90 percent or better on the midterms has already been assigned a grade of A. [Premise] Since Margaret made 94 percent on her midterms, [conclusion] she already has her A.

Conclusion Indicators

When the words in the following list are used in arguments, they usually indicate that a premise has just been offered and that a conclusion is about to be presented. (The three dots represent the claim that is the conclusion.)

Thus . . .	Consequently . . .
Therefore . . .	So . . .
Hence . . .	Accordingly . . .
This shows that . . .	This implies that . . .
This suggests that . . .	This proves that . . .

Example:

Stacy drives a Porsche. This suggests that either she is rich or her parents are.

The conclusion is

Either she is rich or her parents are.

The premise is

Stacy drives a Porsche.

[Premise] All those students who have been assigned A's are excused from the final exam. [Premise] Margaret got an A, so [conclusion] she is excused from the final.

The claim that Margaret has a grade of A is the conclusion in the first argument but a premise in the second.

Notice also that arguments can have unstated premises:

[Premise] You can't check books out of the library without an ID card. So [conclusion] Bill won't be able to check any books out.

The unstated premise must be "Bill has no ID card." We'll have more to say about unstated premises later.

Arguments can have unstated conclusions as well:

[Premise] The political party that best reflects mainstream opinion will win the most seats in the next election, and [premise] the Republicans certainly best reflect mainstream opinion.

The unstated conclusion is "The Republicans will win the most seats in the next election."

Notice finally that there is a difference between **independent premises** and **dependent premises** for a conclusion.

Premise Indicators

When the words in the following list are used in arguments, they generally introduce premises. They often occur just *after* a conclusion has been given. A premise would replace the three dots in an actual argument.

Since . . .

Because . . .

For . . .

In view of . . .

This is implied by . . .

Example:

Either Stacy is rich or her parents are, since she drives a Porsche.

The premise is the claim that Stacy drives a Porsche; the conclusion is the claim that either Stacy is rich or her parents are.

[Premise] Raising the speed limit will wear out the highways faster. In addition, [premise] doing so will result in more highway deaths. Therefore, [conclusion] we should not raise the speed limit.

[Premise] Raising the speed limit will waste gas. [Premise] We don't have any gas to waste. Therefore, [conclusion] we should not raise the speed limit.

The first example gives two independent premises for the conclusion that we should not raise the speed limit (doing so would wear out the highways; doing so would waste lives). The premises are independent of one another because the falsity of one would not cancel the support the other provides for the conclusion.

But the premises in the second example (raising the speed limit will waste gas; we don't have any gas to waste) are dependent on one another. The falsity of either premise would automatically cancel the support the other provides for the conclusion that the speed limit should not be raised.

If you want, you can think of an argument with two independent premises as *two arguments for the same conclusion:*

Raising the speed limit will wear out the highways faster. In addition, doing so will result in more highway deaths. Therefore, we should not raise the speed limit.

You can view this either as one argument with two independent premises, or as two separate arguments for one conclusion (the conclusion that we should not raise the speed limit). There are subtle theoretical differences between

Distinguish Arguments from Explanations!

As we explain in Chapter 7, people often use similar language in arguments and explanations. For example:

Bill had a family emergency yesterday; thus he was unable to be here.

Is what follows "thus" a conclusion? Well, maybe. *If* the speaker is trying to establish *that* Bill was unable to be here, then she is presenting an argument, and "thus" indicates her conclusion.

But the speaker may be explaining *why* Bill was unable to be at the meeting, and if she is doing this, then "thus" is not a conclusion indicator. It means "that's why." In other words, in an explanation "thus" is an indicator that the *explanation of something* is about to be presented. Other words that are conclusion-indicators in arguments have similar functions in explanations. Chapter 7 treats this important source of confusion in more detail. Fortunately, we usually have some idea at the outset what speakers and writers are up to: that is, whether they are arguing for a point, explaining— or doing something else entirely.

these views, but these differences are of little consequence to the practical task of evaluating arguments.

Exercise 8-1

Indicate which blanks would ordinarily contain premises and which would ordinarily contain conclusions.

▲ 1. ____a____, and ____b____. Therefore, ____c____.

▲ 2. ____a____. So, since ____b____, ____c____.

▲ 3. ____a____, because ____b____.

▲ 4. Since ____a____ and ____b____, ____c____.

▲ 5. ____a____. Consequently, ____b____, since ____c____ and ____d____.

Exercise 8-2

Identify the premises and conclusions in each of the following arguments.

▲ 1. Since all Communists are Marxists, all Marxists are Communists.

2. The Lakers almost didn't beat the Jazz. They'll never get past Dallas.

3. If the butler had done it, he could not have locked the screen door. Therefore, since the door was locked, we know that the butler is in the clear.

▲ 4. That cat is used to dogs. Probably she won't be upset if you bring home a new dog for a pet.

5. Hey, he can't be older than his mother's daughter's brother. His mother's daughter has only one brother.

6. Moscone will never make it into the state police. They have a weight limit, and he's over it.

▲ 7. Presbyterians are not fundamentalists, but all born-again Christians are. So no born-again Christians are Presbyterians.

8. I guess he doesn't have a thing to do. Why else would he waste his time watching daytime TV?

9. "There are more injuries in professional football today than there were twenty years ago," he reasoned. "And if there are more injuries, then today's players suffer higher risks. And if they suffer higher risks, then they should be paid more. Consequently, I think today's players should be paid more," he concluded.

▲ 10. Let's see . . . If we've got juice at the distributor, the coil isn't defective, and if the coil isn't defective, then the problem is in the ignition switch. So the problem is in the ignition switch.

Exercise 8-3

Identify the premises and the conclusions in the following arguments.

▲ 1. The darned engine pings every time we use the regular unleaded gasoline, but it doesn't do it with super. I'd bet that there is a difference in the octane ratings between the two in spite of what my mechanic says.

2. Kera, Sherry, and Bobby were all carded at JJ's, and they all look as though they're about thirty. Chances are I'll be carded too.

3. Seventy percent of freshmen at Wharfton College come from wealthy families; therefore, probably about the same percentage of all Wharfton College students come from wealthy families.

▲ 4. When blue jays are breeding, they become very aggressive. Consequently, scrub jays, which are very similar to blue jays, can also be expected to be aggressive when they're breeding.

5. A cut in the capital gains tax will benefit wealthy people. Marietta says her family would be much better off if capital gains taxes were cut, so I'm sure her family is wealthy.

6. According to *Nature*, today's thoroughbred racehorses do not run any faster than their grandparents did. But human Olympic runners are at least 20 percent faster than their counterparts of fifty years ago. Most likely, racehorses have reached their physical limits but humans have not.

▲ 7. It's easier to train dogs than cats. That means they're smarter than cats.

8. "Let me demonstrate the principle by means of logic," the teacher said, holding up a bucket. "If this bucket has a hole in it, then it will leak. But it doesn't leak. Therefore, obviously it doesn't have a hole in it."

9. I know there's a chance this guy might be different, but the last person we hired from Alamo Polytech was a rotten engineer, and we had to fire him. Thus I'm afraid that this new candidate is somebody I just won't take a chance on.

▲ 10. If she were still interested in me, she would have called, but she didn't.

Exercise 8-4

In any of the following arguments that have more than one premise, determine whether the premises provide dependent or independent reasons for the conclusion.

▲ 1. I gave you a five-dollar bill this morning, and I gave you a ten-dollar bill this afternoon. So I have already given you fifteen dollars today.

2. Jim is going to ride with Mary to the party, and Sandra is going to ride with her too. So Mary won't be driving all by herself to the party.

▲ 3. Michael should go ahead and buy another car. The one he's driving is just about to fall apart, and he just got a new job and he can certainly afford another car now.

4. If Parker goes to Las Vegas, he'll wind up in a casino; and if he winds up in a casino, it's a sure thing he'll spend half the night at a craps table. So you can be sure: If Parker goes to Las Vegas, he'll spend half the night at a craps table.

5. It's going to be rainy tomorrow, and Moore doesn't like to play golf in the rain. It's going to be cold as well, and he *really* doesn't like to play when it's cold. So you can be sure Moore will be someplace other than the golf course tomorrow.

▲ 6. Hey, you're overwatering your lawn. See? There are mushrooms growing around the base of that tree—a sure sign of overwatering. Also, look at all the worms on the ground. They come up when the earth is oversaturated.

7. "Will you drive me to the airport?" she asked. "Why should I do that?" he wanted to know. "Because I'll pay you twice what it takes for gas. Besides, you said you were my friend, didn't you?"

8. If you drive too fast, you're more likely to get a ticket, and the more likely you are to get a ticket, the more likely you are to have your insurance premiums raised. So, if you drive too fast, you are more likely to have your insurance premiums raised.

▲ 9. If you drive too fast, you're more likely to get a ticket. You're also more likely to get into an accident. So you shouldn't drive too fast.

10. MARVIN: If Bob Dole had been elected president, we'd be a lot happier.
ALEXI: What, you think so?

MARVIN: Yes. If he were president, he'd have lowered taxes by now; then we'd have more money. And if we had more money, we'd have more to spend. And if we had more money to spend, we'd be a lot happier.

11. DANIEL: Where did that cat go, anyway?
    THERESA: I think she ran away. Look, her food hasn't been touched in two days. Neither has her water.

▲ 12. There are several reasons why you should consider installing a solarium. First, you can still get a tax credit. Second, you can reduce your heating bill. Third, if you build it right, you can actually cool your house with it in the summer.

13. From a letter to the editor: "By trying to eliminate Charles Darwin from the curriculum, creationists are doing themselves a great disservice. When read carefully, Darwin's discoveries only support the thesis that species change, not that they evolve into new species. This is a thesis that most creationists can live with. When read carefully, Darwin actually supports the creationist point of view."

14. Editorial comment: "The Supreme Court's ruling that schools may have a moment of silence but not if it's designated for prayer is sound. Nothing stops someone from saying a silent prayer at school or anywhere else. Also, even though a moment of silence will encourage prayer, it will not favor any particular religion over any other. The ruling makes sense."

▲ 15. We must paint the house now! Here are three good reasons: (a) If we don't, then we'll have to paint it next summer; (b) if we have to paint it next summer, we'll have to cancel our trip; and (c) it's too late to cancel the trip.

Exercise 8-5

In any of the following arguments that have more than one premise, determine whether the premises provide dependent or independent reasons for the conclusion.

▲ 1. All mammals are warm-blooded creatures, and all whales are mammals. Therefore, all whales are warm-blooded creatures.

2. Jones won't plead guilty to a misdemeanor, and if he won't plead guilty, then he will be tried on a felony charge. Therefore, he will be tried on a felony charge.

3. John is taller than Bill, and Bill is taller than Margaret. Therefore, John is taller than Margaret.

▲ 4. Rats that have been raised in enriched environments, where there are a variety of toys and puzzles, have brains that weigh more than the brains of rats raised in more barren environments. Therefore, the brains of humans will weigh more if humans are placed in intellectually stimulating environments.

5. From a letter to the editor: "In James Kilpatrick's July 7 column it was stated that Scientology's 'tenets are at least as plausible as the tenets of

Southern Baptists, Roman Catholics . . . and prayer book Episcopalians.' Mr. Kilpatrick seems to think that all religions are basically the same and fraudulent. This is false. If he would compare the beliefs of Christianity with the cults he would find them very different. Also, isn't there quite a big difference between Ron Hubbard, who called himself God, and Jesus Christ, who said 'Love your enemies, bless them that curse you, do good to them that hate you'?"

6. We've interviewed two hundred professional football players, and 60 percent of them favor expanding the season to twenty games. Therefore, 60 percent of all professional football players favor expanding the season to twenty games.

7. Exercise may help chronic male smokers kick the habit, says a study published today. The researchers, based at McDuff University, put thirty young male smokers on a three-month program of vigorous exercise. One year later, only 14 percent of them still smoked, according to the report. An equivalent number of young male smokers who did not go through the exercise program were also checked after a year and it was found that 60 percent still smoked. Smokers in the exercise program began running three miles a day and gradually worked up to eight miles daily. They also spent five and a half hours each day in modestly vigorous exercise such as soccer, basketball, biking, and swimming.

▲ 8. Letter to the editor: "I was enraged to learn that the mayor now supports the initiative for the Glen Royale subdivision. Only last year he himself proclaimed 'strong opposition' to any further development in the river basin. Besides, Glen Royale will only add to congestion, pollution, and longer lines at the grocery store, not that the grocers will mind."

9. Believe in God? Yes, of course I do. The universe couldn't have arisen by chance, could it? Besides, I read the other day that more and more physicists believe in God, based on what they're finding out about the Big Bang and all that stuff.

▲ 10. From an office memo: "I've got a good person for your opening in Accounting. Jesse Brown is his name, and he's as sharp as they come. Jesse has a solid background in bookkeeping, and he's good with computers. He's also reliable, and he'll project the right image. Best of all, he's a terrific golfer. As you might gather, I know him personally. He'll be contacting you later this week."

Good and Bad, Valid and Invalid, Strong and Weak

When we say that an argument is a **good argument,** we are saying that it gives us grounds for accepting its conclusion. "Good" and "bad" are relative terms: Arguments can be better or worse depending on the degree to which they furnish support for their conclusions.

There is more than one way in which an argument might qualify as good; before we explain them, however, we need to describe some important technical distinctions.

An argument whose premises provide absolutely conclusive support for the conclusion is "valid." In other words:

> A **valid argument** has this characteristic: It is necessary, on the assumption that the premises are true, that the conclusion be true.

This is merely a precise way of saying that the premises of a valid argument, if true, absolutely guarantee a true conclusion. Here's an example:

> [Premise] Every philosopher is a good mechanic, and [premise] Emily is a philosopher. So, [conclusion] Emily is a good mechanic.

Valid? Yes. These premises, if true, guarantee that the conclusion is true.

But notice this: Although the argument about Emily is valid, it so happens the premises aren't true. Not every philosopher is a good mechanic, and Emily is no philosopher; she's Parker's cat. So the argument is not a good one, from the standpoint of offering us justification for accepting the claim that Emily is a good mechanic. However, the argument is valid nonetheless, because the conclusion *must* follow from the premises. Thus, an argument's being valid does not depend on its premises being true. What determines whether an argument is valid is whether the conclusion *absolutely follows* from the premises. (Once again: When we say that a conclusion absolutely follows from the premises, we mean that, *if* the premises were true, the conclusion would then *have to be* true as well.) If the conclusion does absolutely follow from the premises, the argument is valid, whether or not the premises are true.

Now, a valid argument whose premises *are* true is called a "sound" argument:

> A **sound argument** has these two characteristics: It is valid, and its premises are all true.

And here is an example:

> [Premise] Some pesticides are toxic for humans, and [premise] anything that is toxic for humans is unsafe for most humans to consume. Therefore, [conclusion] some pesticides are unsafe for most humans to consume.

This is a sound argument: It is valid, because the conclusion absolutely follows from the premises, and its premises (and hence its conclusion) are true.

It should be clear, then, that an argument can be valid without necessarily being a good argument. The argument about Emily isn't good because,

Abe Lincoln Knew His Logic
Validity and Soundness in the Lincoln-Douglas Debates

Here's Abraham Lincoln speaking in the fifth Lincoln-Douglas debate:

I state in syllogistic form the argument:
Nothing in the Constitution . . . can destroy a right distinctly and expressly affirmed in the Constitution.

The right of property in a slave is distinctly and expressly affirmed in the Constitution.

Therefore, nothing in the Constitution can destroy the right of property in a slave.

Lincoln goes on to say:

There is a fault [in the argument], but the fault is not in the reasoning; but the falsehood in fact is a fault of the premises. I believe that the right of property in a slave is *not* distinctly and expressly affirmed in the Constitution.

In other words, the argument is valid, Lincoln says, but unsound, and thus not a good argument.
Syllogisms, by the way, are covered in Chapter 9.

even though it's valid, it doesn't justify accepting the conclusion: Its premises are false.

A sound argument, by contrast, normally does justify accepting the conclusion. We say "normally" because cases can arise in which even sound arguments aren't particularly good. Arguments that beg the question, as explained in Chapter 6, fall in this category. Or consider the argument:

If a person travels in the same direction far enough, he or she will arrive back at the place he or she started from. Therefore, if Kotar travels in the same direction far enough, he will arrive back at the place he started from.

This is a sound argument; but, if Kotar happened to live in the middle of Europe in the tenth century, it seems odd to suppose *he* would have been justified in believing that if he traveled far enough in the same direction, he would arrive back where he started.

Arguments can be useful—they can qualify as good arguments—even though we don't intend them to be valid or sound. Look at this example, in which Moore says to Parker:

[Premise] Every year as far back as I can remember my roses have developed mildew in the spring. [Conclusion] Therefore, my roses will develop mildew this spring, too.

Everyday English Definitions

In everyday English, "valid argument," "sound argument," and "strong argument" are used interchangeably and often just mean "good argument." Other terms people use to praise arguments include "cogent," "compelling," and "telling." Further, people often apply "valid," "sound," "cogent," and "compelling" to things other than arguments—claims, theories, and explanations, for example. So before you pounce on someone for using these words incorrectly, consider the context in which you hear them.

In everyday English, "weak argument" includes arguments that are invalid and unsound and has numerous synonyms, including "poor," "faulty," "fallacious," "specious," "unreasonable," "illogical," "stupid," and so forth.

This argument doesn't qualify as valid (or sound) because it is *possible* that the conclusion is false even assuming the premise is true (it might be an incredibly dry winter). Nevertheless, this isn't a bad argument. In fact, it's really quite good: It may not be absolutely impossible that Moore's roses won't get mildew this spring, but, given the premise, it is very, very likely that they will. Moore is certainly justified in believing his conclusion.

Arguments like this one, which only show that the conclusion is *probably* true, are said to be relatively *strong*. More precisely:

> A **strong argument** has this distinguishing characteristic: It is *unlikely*, on the assumption that the premises are true, that the conclusion is false.

Again, notice that the premises don't actually have to be true for the argument to be strong.

When someone advances an argument like Moore's, an argument that he or she intends only to be a strong argument, it is somewhat inappropriate to discuss whether it is valid. Yes, technically, Moore's argument is invalid, but because Moore is only trying to demonstrate that the conclusion is *likely*, the criticism doesn't amount to much—he never intended that the argument be valid.

Let's summarize these various points:

1. A *good* argument justifies acceptance of the conclusion.
2. A *valid* argument has this defining characteristic: It is necessary, on the assumption that the premises are true, that the conclusion be true.
3. A valid argument whose premises are all true is called a *sound* argument.

4. A *strong* argument has this defining characteristic: It is unlikely, on the assumption that the premises are true, that the conclusion is false.

5. Normally, sound arguments and strong arguments are good arguments.

6. The best policy is not to speak of valid arguments as strong or weak; speak of them as sound or unsound. Likewise, the best policy is not to speak of strong or weak arguments as valid or invalid; just refer to them as strong or weak.

Finally, notice that the terms "valid" and "invalid" are absolute terms. Either an argument is valid, or it is not, and that's that. By contrast, "strong" and its opposite, "weak" (like "good" and "bad"), are relative terms. Arguments can be evaluated as stronger or weaker depending on how likely the premises show the conclusion to be.

Deduction and Induction

Philosophers have traditionally distinguished deductive arguments from inductive arguments, though the best way of defining the difference is controversial. One way to view them is to say that **deductive arguments** are those that are either valid or intended by their author to be so. **Inductive arguments** are neither valid nor intended to be so by their authors; nevertheless, such arguments can be quite strong.

Exercise 8-6

Fill in the blanks where called for, and answer true or false where appropriate.

1. Valid arguments are said to be strong or weak.

2. Valid arguments are always good arguments.

▲ 3. Sound arguments are _____ arguments whose premises are all _____ .

4. The premises of a valid argument are never false.

5. If a valid argument has a false conclusion, then not all its premises can be true.

▲ 6. If a strong argument has a false conclusion, then not all its premises can be true.

7. A sound argument cannot have a false conclusion.

8. A true conclusion cannot be derived validly from false premises.

▲ 9. "Strong" and "weak" are absolute terms.

Deductive and Inductive; General and Specific

A lot of people, including a few authors of articles and books on logic, think it's possible to explain the difference between deductive arguments and inductive arguments by referring to whether they go from general to particular or vice versa. In the words of one such author, "Deductive arguments involve reasoning from general premises to specific conclusions, while inductive arguments involve reasoning from specific instances to general conclusions."

It's true that *many* arguments fit this scheme, but many do not. Here's an argument that is clearly deductive (and valid, in fact):

> Maria scored higher on the logic exam than Ron did, and Ron scored higher than Kenneth. So Maria must have scored higher than Kenneth.

Notice that there are no general claims at all in this argument; each one is about a specific relationship, and so it is false that all deductive arguments proceed from general claims to specific ones.

Now look at this argument:

> I've watched the Dennis Miller television show four or five times recently, and I've really liked it each time. So it's a safe bet that I'll enjoy it again when I watch it tonight.

This argument is inductive (of a type called arguments by analogy, which are described in Chapter 11), but it too contains no general claims at all; it proceeds from particular cases to a further particular case. And so it is also false that all inductive arguments proceed from specific instances to general conclusions.

10. The following argument is valid: All swans are orange. You're a swan, so you're orange.

11. The following argument is *both* valid *and* sound: Jesse Helms is one of New York's U.S. senators, and he is a Democrat. Therefore, he is a Democrat.

12. A strong argument with true premises has a conclusion that probably is true.

Exercise 8-7

Go back to Exercises 8-2 and 8-3, and determine which arguments are valid. In the answer section at the back of the book, we have answered items 1, 4, 7, and 10 in each set.

Exercise 8-8

Given the premises, discuss whether the conclusion of each argument that follows is (a) true beyond a reasonable doubt, (b) probably true, or (c) possibly true or possibly false. You should expect disagreement on these items, but the closer your answers are to your instructor's, the better.

▲ 1. The sign on the parking meter says "Out of Order," so the meter isn't working.

2. The annual rainfall in California's north valley averages twenty-three inches. So the rainfall next year will be about twenty-three inches.

3. You expect to get forty miles to the gallon in *that?* Why, that old wreck has a monster V8; besides, it's fifty years old and needs an overhaul.

4. In the last two presidential races, the winner of the Iowa Republican primary has not captured the Republican nomination. Therefore, the winner of the next Iowa Republican primary will not capture the Republican nomination.

▲ 5. The New York steak, the Maine lobster, and the beef stroganoff at that restaurant are all exceptionally good. You can probably count on all the entrees being excellent.

6. The number of cellular telephones has increased dramatically in each of the past few years. It's a safe bet that there will be even more of them in use this coming year.

7. Since the graduates of Harvard, Yale, Princeton, and other Ivy League schools generally score higher on the Graduate Record Examination than students from Central State, it follows that the Ivy League schools do more toward educating their students than Central State does.

8. Hey, my dad wants to try out for the Green Bay Packers. I told him to forget it. They'd never sign him. He's fifty-five years old.

▲ 9. Although Max bled profusely before he died, there was no blood on the ground where his body was found. Therefore, he was killed somewhere else and brought here after the murder.

10. When liquor was banned in 1920, hospitalizations for alcoholism and related diseases plummeted; in 1933, when Prohibition was repealed, alcohol-related illnesses rose sharply again. Legalization of cocaine, heroin, and marijuana would not curb abuse of those substances.

11. Relax. The kid's been delivering the paper for, how long? Three, four years maybe? And not once has she missed us. The paper will be here, just wait and see. She's just been delayed for some reason.

▲ 12. First, it seems clear that even if there are occasional small dips in the consumption of petroleum, the general trend shows no sign of a real permanent decrease. Second, petroleum reserves are not being discovered as fast as petroleum is currently being consumed. From these two facts we can conclude that reserves will eventually be consumed and that the world will have to do without oil.

Unstated Premises

As we've noted, arguments can have unstated premises. Suppose a husband and wife are dining out, and she says to him: "It's getting very late, so we should call for the check." For this little argument to be valid, this principle must be assumed: *"If it is getting very late, then we should call for the check."* The wife, no doubt, is assuming this principle (among many other things), and even if *she* is not assuming it, *we* must assume it if we are to credit her with a valid argument.

Most real-life arguments are like this argument in that some unstated proposition must be assumed for the argument to be valid. And it is useful to be able to specify what must be assumed for a given argument to be valid. What, for example, must be assumed for the following argument to be valid?

> Moore's dog is a bloodhound, so it has a keen sense of smell.

What must be assumed, of course, is that all bloodhounds have a keen sense of smell. We are also assuming here that we know nothing about the dog in question except that it is a bloodhound. The argument is valid if and only if we assume that all bloodhounds have a keen sense of smell. Further, since it is questionable whether *all* bloodhounds have a keen sense of smell, we see that the validity of this argument depends on a questionable assumption.

However, recall that an argument need not necessarily be valid to be a good argument. Invalid arguments may still be strong; that is, their premises may provide strong support, though less than absolutely conclusive support, for their conclusions. Let's therefore ask, Is there an unstated premise that would make the bloodhound argument a strong one? The answer is that if we plug into the argument the premise that *most* bloodhounds have a keen sense of smell, which is certainly a reasonable premise, the result is quite a strong argument:

> Moore's dog is a bloodhound.
> [Unstated: Most bloodhounds have a keen sense of smell.]
> Therefore, Moore's dog has a keen sense of smell.

If you can spot what must be assumed for an argument to be valid or to be strong, you'll be in a much better position to evaluate it. If a plausible assumption suffices to make an argument valid, then it is a good argument. If a plausible assumption can at best only make an argument strong, then it may still be a good argument, depending on how strong it is and how plausible the stated premises and unstated assumption are.

Let's consider another example:

> He's related to Edward Kennedy, so he's rich.

For the argument to be valid, one must assume that *everyone* related to Kennedy is rich, and that's not a very plausible assumption. For the argument

Unstated Arguments

There aren't any. An argument can contain unstated premises or an unstated conclusion, but the argument *itself* cannot be entirely unstated. A masked bandit who waves you against a wall with a gun is not presenting you with an argument, though his actions give you a good reason for moving; if you do not want to get shot, then you need to construct an argument in your own mind—and quickly, too—with the conclusion "I'd better move" and the premise "If I don't move, I may get my head blown off."

There is no such thing, then, as an unstated argument, though an argument can have unstated premises or an unstated conclusion. Further, it isn't possible for *all* the premises in an argument to be unstated. If the bandit waves his gun and says "Better move over against that wall," he has given you a reason for moving, but he hasn't given you an argument. Maybe you think that waving a gun around *implies* a premise such as "If you don't move, I'll shoot you." But no, implication is a relationship that holds only between claims: Only a claim can imply a claim.

to be strong, one must assume that *most* people related to Kennedy are rich, and although that assumption is a good bit more plausible than the first assumption, it still isn't very plausible. The most plausible relevant assumption is that *many* people related to Kennedy are rich, but with that assumption plugged into the argument, the argument is not particularly strong.

Another example:

It's March, so the apple trees will bloom by the end of the month.

This argument is valid only if it is assumed that the apple trees *always* bloom by the end of March. Maybe that's true where you live, but it's not true where we live. Still, where we live it's true that the apple trees *almost always* bloom by the end of March, and with this assumption plugged into the argument, the argument turns out to be pretty strong.

Identifying Unstated Premises

When someone produces an argument, it isn't productive to ask, What is this person assuming? No doubt the person is assuming many things, such as that you can hear (or read), that you understand English, that what he or she is saying is worth saying, that you aren't comatose or dead, and who knows what else. There are two better questions to ask, and the first is, "Is there a reasonable assumption I could make that would make this argument valid?" And if what you must assume for the argument to be valid isn't plausible, then you ask the second question: "Is there a reasonable assumption I could make that would make this argument strong?"

As may be clear from the preceding section, an argument can be made valid by adding to it a general claim that appropriately connects the stated premises to the conclusion and says, in effect, that if the stated premises are true, then the conclusion is true. For example, take this argument:

> It's raining, so there is a south wind.

This argument is automatically valid if you add to it the general claim "Any time it is raining, there is a south wind." (Any variation of this claim will do equally well, such as "Whenever it is raining, there is a south wind," or "Only in the presence of a south wind is there rain.") But this claim isn't particularly plausible, at least where Moore and Parker live. And thus we should modify the claim by asking the second question, "What must I assume for this argument to be strong?" When we do this, we obtain a more plausible premise: "When it rains, there is usually a south wind." This is a reasonable claim (in our neck of the woods), and including it in the argument makes the argument a strong one.

Here's another example:

> You shouldn't let her pass. After all, this is the second time you caught her cheating.

A general claim that ties the stated premise to the conclusion and yields a valid argument would be "No person caught cheating two times should be permitted to pass." We'd accept this claim and, consequently, we'd also accept the conclusion of the argument, assuming that the stated premise (that this is the second time she was caught cheating) is true.

Here's one final example:

> Yes, Stacy and Harold are on the brink of divorce. They're remodeling their house.

When we try to make the argument valid by connecting the premise to the conclusion with a general claim, we get something like "A couple that remodels their house must be on the brink of divorce." But we can suppose that nobody would seriously subscribe to such a claim. So we attempt to make the argument strong, rather than valid, by modifying the claim to "Most couples remodeling their house are on the brink of divorce." However, this claim is also implausible. The only plausible thing to say is that *some* couples who remodel are on the brink of divorce. But this claim doesn't justify a conclusion that states unqualifiedly that Stacy and Harold are on the brink of divorce.

To summarize: Formulate a general claim that connects the stated premise with the conclusion in such a way as to make the argument valid, as explained above. If that premise isn't plausible, modify or qualify it as necessary to make the argument strong. If the argument just can't be made either valid or strong except by using an implausible premise, then you really shouldn't accept the argument—or use it yourself.

In your own essays, it is good practice always to consider exactly what your readers must accept if they are to agree with your reasoning. You shouldn't require them to accept any claim that is implausible or unreasonable, whether you actually state that claim or not.

Exercise 8-9

For each passage, supply a claim that turns it into a valid argument.

Example

The fan needs oil. It's squeaking.

Claim That Makes It Valid

Whenever the fan squeaks, it needs oil.

▲ 1. Jamal is well mannered, so he had a good upbringing.

2. Bettina is pretty sharp, so she'll get a good grade in this course.

3. It must have rained lately because there are puddles everywhere.

▲ 4. He'll drive recklessly only if he's upset, and he's not upset.

5. Let's see . . . they have tons of leftovers, so their party could not have been very successful.

6. I think we can safely conclude that the battery is still in good condition. The lights are bright.

▲ 7. Either the dog has fleas, or its skin is dry. It's scratching a lot.

8. Melton was a good senator. He'd make an excellent president.

9. Gelonek doesn't own a gun. He's sure to be for gun control.

▲ 10. The Carmel poet Robinson Jeffers is one of America's most outstanding poets. His work appears in many Sierra Club publications.

Exercise 8-10

Go back to Exercise 8-9, and supply a claim that will produce a strong (but not valid) argument. In the answer section at the back of the book, we have answered items 1, 4, 7, and 10.

Example

The fan needs oil. It's squeaking.

Claim That Makes It Strong

When the fan squeaks, it usually needs oil.

Exercise 8-11

For each passage, supply a claim that turns it into a valid argument.

▲ 1. Prices in that new store around the corner are going to be high, you can bet. All they sell are genuine leather goods.

2. I had a C going into the final exam, but I don't see how I can make less than a B for the course because I managed an A on the final.

3. He's a good guitarist. He studied with Pepe Romero, you know.

▲ 4. That plant is an ornamental fruit tree. It won't ever bear edible fruit.

5. The Federal Reserve Board will make sure that inflation doesn't reach 10 percent again. Its chair is an experienced hand at monetary policy.

6. Murphy doesn't stand a chance of getting elected in this county. His liberal position on most matters is well known.

▲ 7. Washington, D.C., mayor Marion Barry was convicted of cocaine use; he could not have been a very effective mayor while he was using drugs.

8. Half the people in the front row believe in God; therefore, half the entire class believes in God.

9. Montezuma State students are all career-oriented. I say this because every Montezuma State student I ever met was career-oriented.

▲ 10. Population studies show that smoking causes lung cancer; therefore, if you smoke, you will get lung cancer.

Exercise 8-12

Do Exercise 8-11 again, making the arguments strong but not valid. In the answer section at the back of the book, we have answered items 1, 4, 7, and 10.

Techniques for Understanding Arguments

A good argument provides justification for accepting its conclusion. To do this, its premises must be reasonable—that is, it must be likely that they are true—and they must support the conclusion—that is, the argument must be either valid or strong. So, to evaluate an argument, we must answer these two questions:

1. Are the premises reasonable (i.e., is it likely that they are true)?
2. Do the premises support the conclusion (i.e., is the argument either valid or strong)?

Before we can proceed with the evaluation of an argument, we have to understand it. Many arguments are difficult to understand because they are

Don't Forget Pseudoreasons

In Chapters 5 and 6 we say that people will sometimes make statements in order to establish a claim when in reality their remarks have nothing to do with the claim. For example, "Margaret's qualifications are really quite good; after all, she'd be terribly hurt to think that you didn't think highly of them." Although Margaret's disappointment would no doubt be a reason for *something* (e.g., for keeping your views to yourself), it would not be a reason for altering your opinion of her qualifications. Her feelings are, in fact, thoroughly irrelevant to her qualifications. Extraneous material of all sorts can often be eliminated as argumentative material if you ask yourself simply, "Is this really relevant to the conclusion? Does this matter to what this person is trying to establish?" If you have worked through the exercises in Chapters 5 and 6, you have already had practice in spotting irrelevances. If you haven't done these exercises, it would be useful to go back and do them now.

spoken and thus go by so quickly that we cannot be sure of the conclusion and the premises. Others are difficult to understand because they have a complicated structure. Still others are difficult to understand because they are embedded in nonargumentative material consisting of background information, prejudicial coloring, illustrations, parenthetical remarks, digressions, subsidiary points, and other window dressing. And some arguments are difficult to understand because they are confused or because the reasons they contain are so poor that we are not sure whether to regard them as reasons.

In understanding any argument, the first task is to find the conclusion— the main point or thesis of the passage. The next step is to locate the reasons that have been offered for the conclusion—that is, to find the premises. Next, we look for the reasons, if any, given for these premises. To proceed through these steps, you have to learn both to spot premises and conclusions when they occur in spoken and written passages and to understand the interrelationships among these claims—that is, the structure of the argument.

■ Clarifying an Argument's Structure

Let's begin with how to understand the relationships among the argumentative claims, because this problem is sometimes easiest to solve. If you are dealing with written material that you are free to mark up, one useful technique is to number the premises and conclusions and then use the numbers to lay bare the structure of the argument. Let's start with this argument as an example:

I don't think we should get Peter his own car. As a matter of fact, he is not responsible, because he doesn't care for his things. And anyway, we don't have enough money for a car, since even now we have trouble making ends meet. Last week you yourself complained about our financial situation, and you never complain without really good reason.

We want to display the structure of this argument clearly. First, circle all premise and conclusion indicators. Thus:

I don't think we should get Peter his own car. As a matter of fact, he is not responsible (because) he doesn't care for his things. And anyway, we don't have enough money for a car, (since) even now we have trouble making ends meet. Last week you yourself complained about our financial situation, and you never complain without really good reason.

Next, bracket each premise and conclusion, and number them consecutively as they appear in the argument. So what we now have is this:

① [I don't think we should get Peter his own car.] As a matter of fact, ② [he is not responsible] because ③ [he doesn't care for his things.] And anyway, ④ [we don't have enough money for a car], since ⑤ [even now we have trouble making ends meet.] ⑥ [Last week you yourself complained about our financial situation], and ⑦ [you never complain without really good reason.]

And then we diagram the argument as follows: Using an arrow to mean "therefore" or "is intended as evidence [or as a reason or as a premise] for," the first three claims in the argument can be diagrammed as follows:

Now ⑥ and ⑦ together support ④; that is, they are *dependent* reasons for ④. To show that ⑥ and ⑦ are dependent reasons for ④, we simply draw a line under them, put a plus sign between them, and draw the arrow from the line to ④, like this:

Because ⑤ and ⑥ + ⑦ are *independent* reasons for ④, we can represent the relationship between them and ④ as follows:

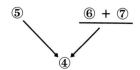

Finally, because ④ and ② are *independent* reasons for ①, the diagram of the entire argument is this:

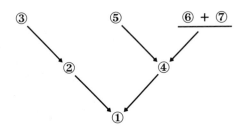

So, the conventions governing this approach to revealing argument structure are very simple: First, circle all premise- and conclusion-indicating words. Then, assuming you can identify the claims that function in the argument (a big assumption, as you will see before long), simply number them consecutively. Then display the structure of the argument using arrows for "therefore" and plus signs over a line to connect together two or more dependent premises.

Some claims, incidentally, may constitute reasons for more than one conclusion. For example:

① [Peter continues to be irresponsible.] ② [He certainly should not have his own car], and, as far as I am concerned, ③ [he can forget about that trip to Hawaii this winter, too.]

Structure:

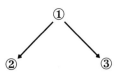

Frequently, too, we evaluate counterarguments to our positions. For example:

① We really should have more African Americans on the faculty. ② That is why the new diversity program ought to be approved. True, ③ it may involve an element of unfairness to whites, but ④ the benefits to society of having more black faculty outweigh the disadvantages.

Notice that claim ③ introduces a consideration that runs counter to the conclusion of the argument, which is stated in ②. We can indicate counterclaims by crossing the "therefore" arrow with lines, thus:

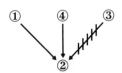

Beer Makes You Smarter

Can you diagram this argument from Tony Graybosch? (The answer is in the answer section at the back of the book.)

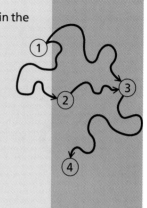

> A herd of buffalo can only move as fast as the slowest buffalo and when the herd is hunted, it is the slowest and weakest ones at the back that are killed first. This natural selection is good for the herd as a whole, because the general speed and health of the whole group keeps improving by the regular attrition of the weakest members.
>
> In much the same way, the human brain can only operate as fast as the slowest brain cells. Excessive intake of alcohol, we all know, kills brain cells; but naturally it attacks the slowest and weakest brain cells first. In this way, regular consumption of beer eliminates the weaker brain cells, making the brain a faster and more efficient machine. This shows that you always are smarter after a few beers.

This diagram indicates that item ③ has been introduced by the writer as a consideration that runs counter to ②.

Of course, one might adopt other conventions for clarifying argument structure—for example, circling the main conclusion and drawing solid lines under supporting premises and wavy lines under the premises of subarguments. The technique we have described is simply one way of doing it; any of several others might work as well for you. However, *no* technique for revealing argument structure will work if you cannot spot the argumentative claims in the midst of a lot of background material.

■ *Distinguishing Arguments from Window Dressing*

We should point out that it is not always easy to isolate the argument in a speech or a written piece. Often, speakers and writers think that because their main points are more or less clear to them, they will be equally apparent to their listeners or readers. But it doesn't always work that way.

If you are having trouble identifying a conclusion in what you hear or read, it *could* be that the passage is not an argument at all. Make sure that the passage in question is not a report, a description, an explanation, or something else altogether, rather than an argument. The key here is determining whether the speaker or writer is offering reasons intended to convince you of one or more of the claims made in the passage.

The problem could also be that the conclusion is left unstated. Sometimes it helps simply to put the argument aside and ask yourself, "What is this person trying to prove?" In any case, the first and essential step in understanding an argument is to spot the conclusion.

If you are having difficulty identifying the *premises*, consider the possibility that you have before you a case of rhetoric (see Chapter 4). (You

Stupid Liberal!

The employer introduced himself to his new gardener.

"I am a professor of logic," the employer said.

"Oh. What's that?" the gardener asked.

"I shall give you a demonstration," announced the professor. "Do you own a wheelbarrow?"

"Yes," replied the gardener.

"Then I infer you are a hard worker," the professor continued. "And from that fact I infer you have a family. And from that I infer you are conscientious and responsible. And from that I infer you are a conservative. Am I right?"

"Wow!" exclaimed the gardener. "That's right! So that's logic?"

"That's logic," preened the professor.

Later the gardener met up with one of his buddies and told him he had a job with a professor of logic.

"Logic?" his friend asked, "What's that?"

"I'll show you," the gardener said. "Do you own a wheelbarrow?"

"No."

"Stupid liberal."

can't find premises in a piece of rhetoric because there *are* no premises.) You have an advantage over many students in having learned about nonargumentative persuasion in Part 2. By this time you should be getting pretty good at recognizing it.

In the remainder of this book, we are concerned primarily with argument evaluation rather than argument clarification, so most of the arguments we present are straightforward and unconfusing; you probably won't need to use diagrams to clarify their structure. However, as you apply what you learn in this book to arguments you encounter in real life, you are apt to encounter arguments and argumentative essays whose organization is difficult to comprehend. When you do, you may find diagramming a useful technique. We also suggest that you attempt to diagram your own essays—if you find that you have difficulty, it is a good indication that you need to reorganize your essay and make the structure of your reasoning clearer.

Evaluating Arguments

Once you understand an argument, you need to evaluate it. Your mechanic can often tell if there is something wrong with your car engine simply by plugging it into a machine and reading a meter or dial. Unfortunately, you can't plug an argument into a machine. To tell if there is something wrong with an argument, you have to determine if (a) the premises support the conclusion and (b) the premises are reasonable. This may sound simple enough, but it in fact involves this entire book.

■ *Do the Premises Support the Conclusion?*

The question "Do the premises support the conclusion" means, Is the argument either (a) valid or (b) relatively strong? Do not expect to be able to answer these questions just yet, for that is what much of the remainder of this book is about.

■ *Are the Premises Reasonable?*

Any premises for which reasons have been presented in the argument are the conclusions of subarguments and should be evaluated according to the principles in Part 3. Unsupported premises should be evaluated in accordance with the guidelines and questions provided in Parts 1 and 2. Let us review these guidelines in summary fashion:

1. It is reasonable to accept a premise if it comes from a credible source and does not conflict with what you have observed, your background knowledge, or other credible claims.
2. You shouldn't accept a premise that conflicts with what you have observed or otherwise have reason to believe, unless you have a very good reason for doing so.
3. You also shouldn't accept a premise that conflicts with the claims of another credible source unless the question of which source to believe has been resolved.
4. Premises that are vague, ambiguous, or otherwise unclear require clarification before acceptance.

It is reasonable to believe that baseball will still be around in thirty years, and it is also reasonable to believe that the sun will still be around in thirty years. But although it is reasonable to believe both claims, there is a greater chance that the sun will be around than that baseball will be. So we can see that, although the premises of an argument might both be reasonable, one argument might be better than another because its premises are *more* likely to be true. Comparing premises as to likelihood requires knowledge, experience, and good judgment, as well as inclination.

Alternatively, one argument might be better than another, not because its premises are more likely to be true, but because they produce a stronger argument. For example, compare these two arguments:

[Premise] Sixty percent of a random sample of two hundred residents of Minneapolis believe in God; [conclusion] therefore, approximately 60 percent of all residents of Minneapolis believe in God.

[Premise] Sixty percent of a random sample of five hundred residents of Minneapolis believe in God; [conclusion] therefore, approximately 60 percent of all residents of Minneapolis believe in God.

The second argument is a better argument because its premise provides a greater justification for believing the conclusion. Weighing the relative strengths of inductive arguments is something we'll consider in Chapters 11 and 12.

Recap

An argument consists of a conclusion and premises. Valid arguments (arguments whose conclusions absolutely follow from the premises) are either sound or unsound, depending on whether or not their premises are all true. On the other hand, conclusions of some arguments are not even intended to follow absolutely from their premises; the premises are supposed to show only that it is likely that the conclusion is true. We speak of such arguments as being to varying degrees strong or weak.

Before you can evaluate an argument, you must understand it; to do this, find the conclusion. Then locate the reasons that have been offered in support of the conclusion—these reasons are stated in the premises. One technique for clarifying the structure of a written argument—if you can identify the claims that function in the argument—is to number the claims consecutively as they are written and then use the numbers to lay out the structure of the argument.

Whatever method helps you to understand an argument, make sure that the premises are reasonable and that they support the conclusion. In Chapters 9–12, we consider more carefully when the premises of an argument do support the conclusion.

Having read this chapter and the chapter recap, you should be able to

- ▲ Explain what the parts of an argument are and identify premises and conclusions in a variety of arguments
- ▲ Discuss the distinctions among good, valid, and strong arguments and relate them to inductive and deductive arguments
- ▲ Explain what unstated premises are and supply premises in a variety of arguments with unstated premises that make those arguments valid
- ▲ Describe techniques for understanding arguments and for evaluating arguments

Additional Exercises

Exercise 8-13

Diagram the following "arguments," using the method explained in the text.

▲ 1. ①, because ② and ③. [Assume that ② and ③ are dependent.]

2. ① and ②; therefore ③. [Assume that ① and ② are independent.]

3. Since ①, ②; and since ③, ④. And since ② and ④, ⑤. [Assume that ② and ④ are independent.]

▲ 4. ①; therefore ② and ③. But because ② and ③, ④. Consequently, ⑤. Therefore, ⑥. [Assume ② and ③ are independent.]

5. ①, ②, ③; therefore ④. ⑤, in view of ①. And ⑥, since ②. Therefore ⑦. [Assume ①, ②, and ③ are dependent.]

Exercise 8-14

Go back to Exercises 8-2, 8-3, 8-4, and 8-5, and diagram the arguments using the method explained in the text. In the answer section at the back of the book, we have answered items 1, 4, 7, and 10 in Exercises 8-2 and 8-3; items 6, 9, 12, and 15 in Exercise 8-4; and items 1, 4, 8, and 10 in Exercise 8-5.

Exercise 8-15

Diagram the arguments contained in the following passages, using the method explained in the text.

▲ 1. Dear Jim,

   Your distributor is the problem. Here's why. There's no current at the spark plugs. And if there's no current at the plugs, then either your alternator is shot, or your distributor is defective. But if the problem were in the alternator, then your dash warning light would be on. So, since the light isn't on, the problem must be in the distributor. Hope this helps.

   Yours,
   Benita Autocraft

2. The federal deficit must be reduced. It has contributed to inflation, and it has hurt American exports.

3. It's high time professional boxing was outlawed. Boxing almost always leads to brain damage, and anything that does that ought to be done away with. Besides, it supports organized crime.

▲ 4. They really ought to build a new airport. It would attract more business to the area, not to mention the fact that the old airport is overcrowded and dangerous.

5. Vote for Jackson? No way. He's too radical, and he's too inexperienced, and his lack of experience would make him a dangerous council member.

Exercise 8-16

Diagram the arguments contained in the following passages, using the method explained in the text.

▲ 1. Cottage cheese will help you to be slender, youthful, and more beautiful. Enjoy it often.

2. If you want to listen to loud music, do it when we are not at home. It bothers us, and we're your parents.

3. If you want to see the best version of *The Three Musketeers*, try the 1948 version. Lana Turner is luscious; Vincent Price is dastardly; Angela Lansbury is exquisitely regal; and nobody ever has or ever will portray D'Artagnan with the grace, athleticism, or skill of Gene Kelly. Rent it. It's a must.

▲ 4. From a letter to the editor: "The idea of a free press in America today is a joke. A small group of people, the nation's advertisers, control the media more effectively than if they owned it outright. Through fear of an advertising boycott they can dictate everything from programming to news report content. Politicians as well as editors shiver in their boots at the thought of such a boycott. This situation is intolerable and ought to be changed. I suggest we all listen to National Public Radio and public television."

5. Too many seniors, disabled veterans, and families with children are paying far too much of their incomes for housing. Proposition 168 will help clear the way for affordable housing construction for these groups. Proposition 168 reforms the outdated requirement for an election before affordable housing can even be approved. Requiring elections for every publicly assisted housing venture, even when there is no local opposition, is a waste of taxpayers' money. No other state constitution puts such a roadblock in front of efforts to house senior citizens and others in need. Please support Proposition 168.

6. More than thirty-five years after President John F. Kennedy's assassination, it's no easier to accept the idea that a loser like Lee Harvey Oswald committed the crime of the century all by himself with a $12.78 mail-order rifle and a $7.17 scope. Yet even though two-thousand-plus books and films about the episode have been made, there is no credible evidence to contradict the Warren Commission finding that "the shots which killed President Kennedy and wounded Governor Connally were fired by Lee Harvey Oswald" and that "Oswald acted alone."

   After all these years, it's time to accept the conclusion. The nation pays a heavy price for chronic doubts and mistrust. Confidence in the government has declined. Participation in the voting process has steadily slid downward. The national appetite for wild theories encourages peddlers to persist. Evil is never easy to accept. In the case of JFK, the sooner we let it go, the better.

▲ 7. "Consumers ought to be concerned about the Federal Trade Commission's dropping a rule that supermarkets must actually have in stock the items they advertise for sale. While a staff analysis suggests costs of the rule outweigh the benefits to consumers, few shoppers want to return to the practices that lured them into stores only to find the advertised products they sought were not there.

"The staff study said the rule causes shoppers to pay $200 million to receive $125 million in benefits. The cost is a low estimate and the benefits a high estimate, according to the study.

"However, even those enormously big figures boil down to a few cents per shopper over a year's time. And the rule does say that when a grocer advertises a sale, the grocer must have sufficient supply of sale items on hand to meet reasonable buyer demand."

The Oregonian

8. "And we thought we'd heard it all. Now the National Rifle Association wants the U.S. Supreme Court to throw out the ban on private ownership of fully automatic machine guns.

"As the nation's cities reel under staggering murder totals, as kids use guns simply to get even after feuds, as children are gunned down by random bullets, the NRA thinks it is everybody's constitutional right to have their own personal machine gun.

"This is not exactly the weapon of choice for deer hunting or for a homeowner seeking protection. It is an ideal weapon for street gangs and drug thugs in their wars with each other and the police.

"To legalize fully automatic machine guns is to increase the mayhem that is turning this nation—particularly its large cities—into a continual war zone. Doesn't the NRA have something better to do?"

Capital Times, *Madison, Wisconsin*

9. From a letter to the editor: "Recently the California Highway Patrol stopped me at a drunk-drive checkpoint. Now, I don't like drunk drivers any more than anyone else. I certainly see why the police find the checkpoint system effective. But I think our right to move about freely is much more important. If the checkpoint system continues, then next there will be checkpoints for drugs, seat belts, infant car seats, drivers' licenses. We will regret it later if we allow the system to continue."

▲ 10. "Well located, sound real estate is the safest investment in the world. It is not going to disappear, as can the value of dollars put into savings accounts. Neither will real estate values be lost because of inflation. In fact, property values tend to increase at a pace at least equal to the rate of inflation. Most homes have appreciated at a rate greater than the inflation rate (due mainly to strong buyer demand and insufficient supply of newly constructed homes)."

Robert Bruss, The Smart Investor's Guide to Real Estate

11. "The constitutional guarantee of a speedy trial protects citizens from arbitrary government abuse, but it has at least one other benefit, too. It prevents crime.

    "A recent Justice Department study found that more than a third of those with serious criminal records—meaning three or more felony convictions—are arrested for new offenses while free on bond awaiting federal court trial. You don't have to be a social scientist to suspect that the longer the delay, the greater the likelihood of further violations. In short, overburdened courts mean much more than justice delayed; they quite literally amount to the infliction of further injustice."

    Scripps Howard Newspapers

12. "There is a prevailing school of thought and growing body of opinion that one day historians will point to a certain television show and declare: This is what life was like in small-town America in the mid-20th century.

    "We like to think those future historians will be right about *The Andy Griffith Show.* It had everything, and in rerun life still does: humor, wisdom, wholesomeness and good old red-blooded American entertainment.

    "That's why we are so puzzled that a group of true-blue fans of the show want to rename some suitable North Carolina town Mayberry. The group believes there ought to be a real-live city in North Carolina called Mayberry, even though everybody already knows that Mayberry was modeled on Mount Airy, sort of, since that is Sheriff Taylor's, uh, Andy Griffith's hometown.

    "No, far better that the group let the whole thing drop. For one thing, we don't know of anyplace—hamlet, village, town, or city—that could properly live up to the name of Mayberry. Perhaps the best place for Mayberry to exist is right where it is—untouched, unspoiled and unsullied by the modern world. Ain't that right, Ernest T. Bass?"

    Greensboro *(N.C.)* News & Record

▲ 13. As we enter a new century, about 100 million Americans are producing data on the Internet as rapidly as they consume it. Each of these users is tracked by technologies ever more able to collate essential facts about them—age, address, credit rating, marital status, etc.—in electronic form for use in commerce. One Web site, for example, promises, for the meager sum of seven dollars, to scan "over two billion records to create a single comprehensive report on an individual." It is not unreasonable, then, to believe that the combination of capitalism and technology pose a looming threat to what remains of our privacy.

    Loosely adapted from Harper's

14. Having your car washed at the carwash may be the best way to go, but there are some possible drawbacks. The International Carwashing Association (ICA) has fought back against charges that automatic carwashes, in recycling wash water, actually dump the salt and dirt from one car onto the next. And that brushes and drag cloths hurt the finish. Perhaps there is some truth to these charges.

The ICA sponsored tests that supposedly demonstrated that the average home car wash is harder on a car than an automatic wash. Maybe. But what's "the average" home car wash? And you can bet that the automatic carwashes in the test were in perfect working order.

There is no way you or I can tell for certain if the filtration system and washing equipment at the automatic carwash are properly maintained. And even if they are, what happens if you follow some mud-caked pickup through the wash? Road dirt might still be caught in the bristles of the brushes or strips of fabric that are dragged over your car.

Here's my recommendation: Wash your own car.

15. Letter to the editor: "The worst disease of the next decade will be AIDS, Acquired Immune Deficiency Syndrome.

"AIDS has made facing surgery scary. In the last ten years several hundred Americans got AIDS from getting contaminated blood in surgery, and it is predicted that within a few years more hundreds of people will receive AIDS blood each year.

"Shouldn't we be tested for AIDS before we give blood? As it is now, no one can feel safe receiving blood. Because of AIDS, people are giving blood to themselves so they will be safe if they have to have blood later. We need a very sensitive test to screen AIDS donors."

North State Record

▲ 16.   **Argument in Favor of Measure A**

"Measure A is consistent with the City's General Plan and City policies directing growth to the City's non-agricultural lands. A 'yes' vote on Measure A will affirm the wisdom of well-planned, orderly growth in the City of Chico by approving an amendment to the 1982 Rancho Arroyo Specific Plan. Measure A substantially reduces the amount of housing previously approved for Rancho Arroyo, increases the number of parks and amount of open space, and significantly enlarges and enhances Bidwell Park.

"A 'yes' vote will accomplish the following: • Require the development to dedicate 130.8 acres of land to Bidwell Park • Require the developer to dedicate seven park sites • Create 53 acres of landscaped corridors and greenways • Preserve existing arroyos and protect sensitive plant habitats and other environmental features • Create junior high school and church sites • Plan a series of villages within which, eventually, a total of 2,927 residential dwelling units will be developed • Plan area which will provide onsite job opportunities and retail services. . . ."

County of Butte Sample Ballot

17.   **Rebuttal to Argument in Favor of Measure A**

"Villages? Can a project with 3,000 houses and 7,000 new residents really be regarded as a 'village'? The Sacramento developers pushing the Rancho Arroyo project certainly have a way with words. We urge citizens of Chico to ignore their flowery language and vote no on Measure A.

"These out-of-town developers will have you believe that their project protects agricultural land. Hogwash! Chico's Greenline protects valuable farmland. With the Greenline, there is enough land in the Chico area available for development to build 62,000 new homes. . . .

"They claim that their park dedications will reduce use of our overcrowded Bidwell Park. Don't you believe it! They want to attract 7,000 new residents to Chico by using Rancho Arroyo's proximity to Bidwell Park to outsell other local housing projects.

"The developers imply that the Rancho Arroyo project will provide a much needed school site. In fact, the developers intend to sell the site to the school district, which will pay for the site with taxpayers' money.

"Chico doesn't need the Rancho Arroyo project. Vote no on Measure A."

County of Butte Sample Ballot

18. Letter to the editor: "A relative of mine is a lawyer who recently represented a murderer who had already had a life sentence and broke out of prison and murdered someone else. I think this was a waste of the taxpayers' money to try this man again. It won't do any good. I think murderers should be executed.

"We are the most crime-ridden society in the world. Someone is murdered every 27 minutes in the U.S., and there is a rape every ten minutes and an armed robbery every 82 seconds. According to the FBI, there are 870,000 violent crimes a year, and you know the number is increasing.

"Also according to the FBI, only 10 percent of those arrested for the crimes committed are found guilty, and a large percentage are released on probation. These people are released so they can just go out and commit more crimes.

"Why are they released? In the end it is because there aren't enough prisons to house the guilty. The death sentence must be restored. This would create more room in prisons. It would also drastically reduce the number of murders. If a robber knew before he shot someone that if he was caught his own life would be taken, would he do it?

"These people deserve to die. They sacrificed their right to live when they murdered someone, maybe your mother. It's about time we stopped making it easy for criminals to kill people and get away with it."

Cascade News

▲ 19. Letter to the editor: "In regard to your editorial, 'Crime bill wastes billions,' let me set you straight. Your paper opposes mandatory life sentences for criminals convicted of three violent crimes, and you whine about how criminals' rights might be violated. Yet you also want to infringe on a citizen's right to keep and bear arms. You say you oppose life sentences for three-time losers because judges couldn't show any leniency toward the criminals no matter how trivial the crime. What is your definition of trivial, busting an innocent child's skull with a hammer?"

North State Record

▲ 20. Freedom means choice. This is a truth antiporn activists always forget when they argue for censorship. In their fervor to impose their morality, groups like Enough Is Enough cite extreme examples of pornography, such as child porn, suggesting that they are easily available in video stores.

This is not the way it is. Most of this material portrays, not actions such as this, but consensual sex between adults.

The logic used by Enough Is Enough is that if something can somehow hurt someone, it must be banned. They don't apply this logic to more harmful substances, such as alcohol or tobacco. Women and children are more adversely affected by drunken driving and secondhand smoke than by pornography. Few Americans would want to ban alcohol or tobacco even though they kill hundreds of thousands of people each year.

Writing Exercises

1. Write a one-page essay in which you determine whether, and why, it is better (you get to define "better") to look younger than your age, older than your age, or just your age. Then number the premises and conclusions in your essay and diagram it.

2. Should there be a death penalty for first-degree murder? On the top half of a sheet of paper, list considerations supporting the death penalty, and on the bottom half, list considerations opposing it. Take about ten minutes to compile your two lists. (Selection 1, at the back of the book, may give you some ideas. Your instructor may provide extra time for you to read this selection.)

   After everyone is finished, your instructor will call on people to read their lists. He or she will then give everyone about twenty minutes to write a draft of an essay that addresses the issue, Should there be a death penalty for first-degree murder? Put your name on the back of your paper. After everyone is finished, your instructor will collect the papers and redistribute them to the class. In groups of four or five, read the papers that have been given to your group. Do not look at the names of the authors. Select the best essay in each group. Your instructor will ask each group to read the essay they have selected as best.

   As an alternative, your instructor may have each group rank-order the papers. He or she will have neighboring groups decide which of their top-ranked papers is the best. The instructor will read the papers that have been top-ranked by two (or more) groups, for discussion.

3. Follow the instructions for Exercise 2, but this time address the question, Are free-needle programs a good idea? (Selections 9A and 9B at the end of the book may give you some ideas. Your instructor may provide extra time for you to read those selections.)

4. If you have not done so already, turn to Selection 2, 7, 14, or 15 at the end of the book and follow the first set of instructions.

5. Turn to Selection 3 or 8 at the end of the book and follow the instructions.

6. Turn to Selections 5A,B; 6A,B; 9A,B; 10A,B; 11A,B; 12A,B; or 13A,B at the end of the book and discuss which side has the stronger argument and why.

Chapter 9

Deductive Arguments I: Categorical Logic

M any of the deductive arguments we come across can be clarified and evaluated using the techniques of categorical logic, which is a way of studying inferences that dates back to the time of Aristotle. During more than two thousand years of history, all manner of embellishments were developed and added to the basic theory, especially by monks and other scholars during the medieval period. Although some of these developments are interesting, we don't want to weight you down with lots of fine distinctions that are best appreciated by professional logicians. So, we'll be content to set forth the basics of the subject in this chapter.

Categorical logic is a system of logic based on the relations of inclusion and exclusion among classes ("categories"). Like truth-functional logic (the subject of Chapter 10), categorical logic is useful in clarifying and analyzing arguments. But this is only one reason to study the subject: There is no better way to understand the underlying logical structure of our everyday language than learning to put it into the kinds of formal terms we'll introduce in these two chapters. Just exactly what is the difference between the claim (1) "Everybody who is ineligible for physics 1A must take physical science 1" and (2) "No students who are required to take physical science 1 are eligible for physics 1A"? Here's another pair of claims: (3) "Harold won't attend the meeting unless Vanessa decides to go" and (4) "If Vanessa decides to go, then Harold will attend the meeting." You might be surprised how many college students have a very hard time trying to determine whether the claims in each pair say the same thing or something different. In this chapter and the next, we'll show you a foolproof method for determining how to unravel the logical implications of such claims and for seeing how any two such claims relate to one another. [Incidentally, in case it wasn't obvious, claims (1) and (2) do not say the same thing at all, and neither do (3) and (4).] If you're signing a lease or entering into a contract of any kind, it pays to be able to figure out just what is being said in it and what is not;

people who have trouble with claims like those just stated are at risk when there is more at stake.

Studying categorical and truth-functional logic can teach us that being careful and precise is possible; it can also give us some ways to become more careful and precise in our own thinking. Getting comfortable with this type of thinking can be helpful in general, but for those who will someday be applying to law school, medical school, or graduate school, it has the added advantage that many admittance exams for such programs deal with the kinds of reasoning discussed in this chapter.

Let's start by looking at the four basic kinds of claims on which all of categorical logic is based.

Categorical Claims

A **categorical claim** says something about classes (or "categories") of things. Our interest lies in categorical claims of certain standard forms. A **standard-form categorical claim** is a claim that results from putting names or descriptions of classes into the blanks of the following structures:

A: All _____ are _____.
(*Example:* All Presbyterians are Christians.)

E: No _____ are _____.
(*Example:* No Muslims are Christians.)

I: Some _____ are _____.
(*Example:* Some Christians are Presbyterians.)

O: Some _____ are not _____.
(*Example:* Some Christians are not Presbyterians.)

The phrases that go in the blanks are **terms;** the one that goes into the first blank is the **subject term** of the claim, and the one that goes into the second blank is the **predicate term.** Thus, "Presbyterians" is the subject term of the first example above and the predicate term of the third and fourth examples. In many of the examples and explanations that follow, we'll use the letters S and P (for "subject" and "predicate") to stand for terms in categorical claims. And we'll talk about the subject and predicate *classes*, which are just the classes that the terms refer to.

But first a caution: Only nouns and noun phrases will work as terms. An adjective alone, such as "red," won't do. "All fire engines are red" does *not* produce a standard-form categorical claim because "red" is not a noun or noun phrase. To see that it is not, try switching the places of the terms: "All red are fire engines." This doesn't make sense, right? But "red vehicles" (or even "red things") will do because "All red vehicles are fire engines" makes sense (even though it's false).

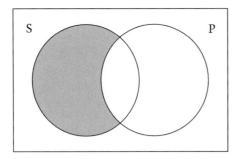

FIGURE 1 A-claim: All S are P.

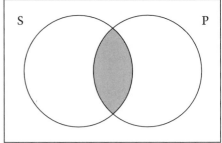

FIGURE 2 E-claim: No S are P.

Looking back at the standard-form structures given above, notice that each one has a letter to its left. These are the traditional names of the four types of standard-form categorical claims. The claim "All Presbyterians are Christians" is an A-claim, and so are "All idolators are heathens," "All people born between 1946 and 1964 are baby boomers," and any other claim of the form "All S are P." The same is true for the other three letters and the other three kinds of claims.

■ *Venn Diagrams*

Each of the standard forms has its own graphic illustration in a **Venn diagram,** as shown in Figures 1 through 4. Named after British logician John Venn, these diagrams exactly represent the four standard-form categorical claim types. In the diagrams, the circles represent the classes named by the terms, shaded areas represent areas that are empty, and areas containing Xs represent areas that are not empty—that contain at least one item. An area that is blank is one that the claim says nothing about; it may be occupied, or it may be empty.*

Notice that in the diagram for the A-claim, the area that would contain any members of the S class that were not members of the P class is shaded—that is, it is empty. Thus, that diagram represents the claim "All S are P," since there is no S left that isn't P. Similarly, in the diagram for the E-claim, the area where S and P overlap is empty; any S that is also a P has been eliminated. Hence: "No S are P."

For our purposes in this chapter, the word "some" means "at least one." So, the third diagram represents the fact that at least one S is a P, and the X in the area where the two classes overlap shows that at least one thing inhabits this area. Finally, the last diagram shows an X in the area of the S circle that is outside the P circle, representing the existence of at least one S that is not a P.

---

*There is one exception to this, but we needn't worry about it for a few pages yet.

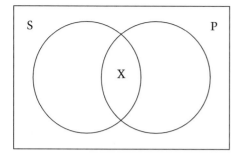

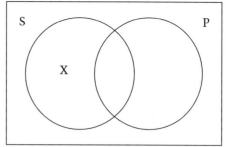

FIGURE 3   I-claim: Some S are P.   **FIGURE 4**   O-claim: Some S are not P.

We'll try to keep technical jargon to a minimum, but here's some terminology we'll need: The two claim types that *include* one class or part of one class within another, the A-claims and I-claims, are **affirmative claims;** the two that *exclude* one class or part of one class from another, the E-claims and O-claims, are **negative claims.**

Although there are only four standard-form claim types, it's remarkable how versatile they are. A large portion of what we want to say can be rewritten, or "translated," into one or another of them. Because this task is sometimes easier said than done, we'd best spend a little while making sure we understand how to do it.

■ *Translation into Standard Form*

The main idea is to take an ordinary claim and turn it into a standard-form categorical claim that is exactly equivalent. We'll say that two claims are **equivalent claims** if, and only if, they would be true in all and exactly the same circumstances—that is, under no circumstances could one of them be true and the other false. (You can think of such claims as "saying the same thing," more or less.)

Lots of ordinary claims in English are easy to translate into standard form. A claim of the sort "Every X is a Y," for example, more or less automatically turns into the standard-form A-claim "All Xs are Ys." And it's easy to produce the proper term to turn "Minors are not eligible" into the E-claim "No minors are eligible people."

All standard-form claims are in the present tense, but even so we can use them to talk about the past. For example, we can translate "There were creatures weighing more than four tons that lived in North America" as "Some creatures that lived in North America are creatures that weighed more than four tons."

What about a claim like "Only sophomores are eligible candidates"? It's good to have a strategy for attacking such translation problems. First, identify the terms. In this case, the two classes in question are "sophomores" and "eligible candidates." Now, which do we have on our hands, an A-, E-, I-, or

© 2000 by Sidney Harris.

▲ *Aristotle was interested in a lot of subjects besides logic—practically everything, in fact. Fortunately for his reputation, these remarks (which he* did *make!) are not typical of him.*

O-claim? Generally speaking, nothing but a careful reading can serve to answer this question. So, you'll need to think hard about just what relation between classes is being expressed and then decide how that relation is best turned into a standard form. Fortunately, we can provide some rules of thumb that help in certain frequently encountered problems, including one that applies to our current example. If you're like most people, you don't have too much trouble seeing that our claim is an A-claim, but *which* A-claim? There are two possibilities:

> All sophomores are eligible candidates

and

> All eligible candidates are sophomores.

If we make the wrong choice, we can change the meaning of the claim significantly. (Notice that "All sophomores are students" is very different from "All students are sophomores.") In the present case, notice that we are saying something about *every* eligible candidate—namely, that he or she must be a sophomore. (*Only* sophomores are eligible—i.e., no one else is eligible.) In an

A-claim, the class so restricted is always the subject class. So, this claim should be translated into

> All eligible candidates are sophomores.

In fact, *all claims of the sort "Only Xs are Ys" should be translated as "All Ys are Xs."*

But there are other claims in which the word "only" plays a crucial role and which have to be treated differently. Consider, for example, this claim: "The only people admitted are people over twenty-one." In this case, a restriction is being put on the class of people admitted; we're saying that *nobody else is admitted* except those over twenty-one. Therefore, "people admitted" is the subject class: "All people admitted are people over twenty-one." And, in fact, *all claims of the sort "The only Xs are Ys" should be translated as "All Xs are Ys."*

The two rules of thumb that govern most translations of claims that hinge on the word "only" are these:

> The word "only," used by itself, introduces the *predicate* term of an A-claim.

> The phrase "the only" introduces the *subject* term of an A-claim.

Note that, in accordance with these rules, we would translate both of these claims

> Only matinees are half-price shows

and

> Matinees are the only half-price shows

as

> All half-price shows are matinees.

The kind of thing a claim directly concerns is not always obvious. For example, if you think for a moment about the claim "I always get nervous when I take logic exams," you'll see that it's a claim about *times*. It's about getting nervous and about logic exams indirectly, of course, but it pertains directly to times or occasions. The proper translation of the example is "All times I take logic exams are times I get nervous." Notice that the word "whenever" is often a clue that you're talking about times or occasions, as well as an indication that you're going to have an A-claim or an E-claim. "Wherever" works the same way for places: "He makes trouble wherever he goes" should be translated as "All places he goes are places he makes trouble."

English's Most Versatile Word

Question:

There's only one word that can be placed successfully in any of the 10 numbered positions in this sentence to produce 10 sentences of different meaning (each sentence has 10 words): (1) *I* (2) *helped* (3) *my* (4) *dog* (5) *carry* (6) *my* (7) *husband's* (8) *slippers* (9) *yesterday* (10). What is that word?

—GLORIA J., Salt Lake City, Utah

Answer:

The word is "only," which makes the following 10 sentences:
1. Only *I* helped my dog carry my husband's slippers yesterday. (Usually the cat helps too, but she was busy with a mouse.)
2. I only *helped* my dog carry my husband's slippers yesterday. (The dog wanted me to carry them all by myself, but I refused.)
3. I helped only *my* dog carry my husband's slippers yesterday. (I was too busy to help my neighbor's dog when he carried them.)
4. I helped my only *dog* carry my husband's slippers yesterday. (I considered getting another dog, but the cat disapproved.)
5. I helped my dog only *carry* my husband's slippers yesterday. (I didn't help the dog eat them; I usually let the cat do that.)
6. I helped my dog carry only *my* husband's slippers yesterday. (My dog and I didn't have time to help my neighbor's husband.)
7. I helped my dog carry my only *husband's* slippers yesterday. (I considered getting another husband, but one is enough.)
8. I helped my dog carry my husband's only *slippers* yesterday. (My husband had two pairs of slippers, but the cat ate one pair.)
9. I helped my dog carry my husband's slippers only *yesterday.* (And now the dog wants help again; I wish he'd ask the cat.)
10. I helped my dog carry my husband's slippers yesterday only. (And believe me, once was enough—the slippers tasted *terrible.*)

—MARILYN VOS SAVANT, author of the "Ask Marilyn" column (Reprinted with permission from Parade and Marilyn vos Savant. Copyright © 1994, 1996.)

There are two other sorts of claims that are a bit tricky to translate into standard form. The first is a claim about a single individual, such as "Aristotle is a logician." It's clear that this claim specifies a class, "logicians," and places Aristotle as a member of that class. The problem is that categorical claims are always about *two* classes, and Aristotle isn't a class. (We certainly couldn't talk about *some* of Aristotle being a logician.) What we want to do is treat such claims as if they were about classes with exactly one member—in the present case, Aristotle. One way to do this is to use the term "people who are identical with Aristotle," which of course has only Aristotle as a member. (Everybody is identical with himself or herself, and nobody else is.) The important thing to remember about such claims can be summarized in the following rule of thumb:

> Claims about single individuals should be treated as A-claims or E-claims.

"Aristotle is a logician" can therefore be translated into "All people identical with Aristotle are logicians," an A-claim. Similarly, "Aristotle is not left-handed" becomes the E-claim "No people identical with Aristotle are left-handed people." (Your instructor may prefer to leave the claim in its original form and simply *treat* it as an A-claim or an E-claim. This avoids the awkward "people identical with Aristotle" wording and is certainly okay with us.)

It isn't just people that crop up in individual claims. Often this kind of treatment is called for when we're talking about objects, occasions, places, and other kinds of things. For example, the preferred translation of "St. Louis is on the Mississippi" is "All cities identical with St. Louis are cities on the Mississippi."

Other claims that cause translation difficulty contain what are called *mass nouns.* Consider this example: "Boiled okra is too ugly to eat." This claim is about a *kind of stuff.* The best way to deal with it is to treat it as a claim about *examples* of this kind of stuff. The present example translates into an A-claim about *all* examples of the stuff in question: "All examples of boiled okra are things that are too ugly to eat." An example such as "Most boiled okra is too ugly to eat" translates into the I-claim "Some examples of boiled okra are things that are too ugly to eat."

As we noted, it's not possible to give rules or hints about every kind of problem you might run into when translating claims into standard-form categorical versions. Only practice and discussion can bring you to the point where you can handle this part of the material with confidence. The best thing to do now is to turn to some exercises.

Exercise 9-1

Translate each of the following into a standard-form claim. Make sure that each answer follows the exact form of an A-, E-, I-, or O-claim and that each term you use is a noun or noun phrase that refers to a class of things. Remember that you're trying to produce a claim that's equivalent to the one given; it doesn't matter whether the given claim is actually true.

▲   1. Every salamander is a lizard.

2. Not every lizard is a salamander.

3. Only reptiles can be lizards.

▲   4. Snakes are the only members of the suborder Ophidia.

    5. The only members of the suborder Ophidia are snakes.

    6. None of the burrowing snakes is poisonous.

▲ 7. Anything that's an alligator is a reptile.

    8. Anything that qualifies as a frog qualifies as an amphibian.

    9. There are frogs wherever there are snakes.

▲ 10. Wherever there are snakes, there are frogs.

  11. Whenever the frog population decreases, the snake population decreases.

  12. Nobody arrived except the cheerleaders.

▲ 13. Except for vice presidents, nobody got raises.

  14. Unless people arrived early, they couldn't get seats.

  15. Home movies are often as boring as dirt.

▲ 16. Socrates is a Greek.

  17. The bank robber is not Jane's fiancé.

  18. If an automobile was built before 1950, it's an antique.

▲ 19. Salt is a meat preservative.

  20. Most corn does not make good popcorn.

Exercise 9-2

Follow the instructions given in the preceding exercise.

▲ 1. Students who wrote poor exams didn't get admitted to the program.

    2. None of my students is failing.

    3. If you live in the dorms, you can't own a car.

▲ 4. There are a few right-handed first basemen.

    5. People make faces every time Joan sings.

    6. The only tests George fails are the ones he takes.

▲ 7. Nobody passed who didn't make at least 50 percent.

    8. You can't be a member unless you're over fifty.

    9. Nobody catches on without studying.

▲ 10. I've had days like this before.

  11. Roofers aren't millionaires.

  12. Few holidays fall on Saturday.

▲ 13. A few holidays fall on Saturday.

  14. Only outlaws own guns.

  15. You have nothing to lose but your chains.

▲ 16. Unless you pass this test you won't pass the course.

  17. If you cheat, your prof will make you sorry.

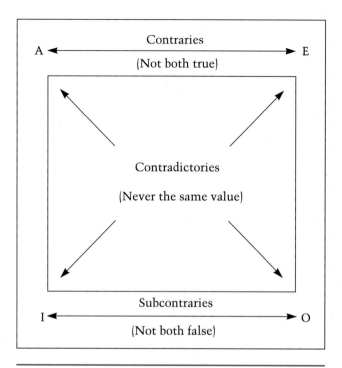

A

Contraries

(Not both true)

E

Contradictories

(Never the same value)

I

Subcontraries

(Not both false)

O

FIGURE 5 The square of opposition.

18. If you cheat, your friends couldn't care less.

▲ 19. Only when you've paid the fee will they let you enroll.

20. Nobody plays who isn't in full uniform.

■ *The Square of Opposition*

Two categorical claims *correspond* to each other if they have the same subject term and the same predicate term. So, "All Methodists are Christians" corresponds to "Some Methodists are Christians": In both claims, "Methodists" is the subject term, and "Christians" is the predicate term. Notice, though, that "Some Christians are not Methodists" does *not* correspond to either of the other two; it has the same terms but in different places.

We can now exhibit the logical relationships between corresponding A-, E-, I-, and O-claims. The **square of opposition,** in Figure 5, does this very concisely. The A- and E-claims, across the top of the square from each other, are **contrary claims**—they can both be false, but they cannot both be true. The I- and O-claims, across the bottom of the square from each other, are **subcontrary claims**—they can both be true, but they cannot both be false. The A- and O-claims and the E- and I-claims, which are at opposite diagonal corners from each other, respectively, are **contradictory claims**—they never have the same truth values.

Notice that these logical relationships are reflected on the Venn diagrams for the claims (see Figures 1 through 4). The diagrams for corresponding A- and O-claims say exactly opposite things about the left-hand area of the diagram, namely, that the area *has* something in it and that it *doesn't*; those for corresponding E- and I-claims do the same about the center area. Clearly, exactly one claim of each pair is true no matter what—either the relevant area is empty, or it isn't.

The diagrams show clearly how both subcontraries can be true: There's no conflict in putting X's in both left and center areas. In fact, it's possible to diagram an A-claim and the corresponding E-claim on the same diagram; we just have to shade out the entire subject class circle. This amounts to saying that *both* an A-claim and its corresponding E-claim can be true *as long as there are no members of the subject class.* We get an analogous result for subcontraries: They can both be false as long as the subject class is empty.*
We can easily avoid this result by making an assumption: When making inferences from one contrary (or subcontrary) to another, we'll assume that the classes we're talking about are not entirely empty. On this assumption, the A-claim or the corresponding E-claim (or both) must be false, and the I-claim or the corresponding O-claim (or both) must be true.

If we have the truth value of one categorical claim, we can often deduce the truth values of the other three corresponding claims by using the square of opposition. For instance, if we hear "All aluminum cans are recyclable items," we can immediately infer that its contradictory, "Some aluminum cans are not recyclable items," is false; the corresponding E-claim, "No aluminum cans are recyclable items," is also false because it is the contrary of the original A-claim and cannot be true if the A-claim is true. The corresponding I-claim, "Some aluminum cans are recyclable items," must be true because we just determined that *its* contradictory, the E-claim, is false.

However, we cannot *always* determine the truth values of the remaining three standard-form categorical claims. For example, if we know only that the A-claim is false, all we can infer is the truth value (true) of the corresponding O-claim. Nothing follows about either the E- or the I-claim. Because the A- and the E-claim can both be false, knowing that the A-claim is false does not tell us anything about the E-claim—it can still be either true or false. And if the E-claim remains undetermined, then so must its contradictory, the I-claim.

So here are the limits on what can be inferred from the square of opposition: Beginning with a *true* claim at the top of the square (either A or E), we can infer the truth values of all three of the remaining claims. The same is true if we begin with a *false* claim at the bottom of the square (either I or O): We can still deduce the truth values of the other three. But if we begin with

---

*It is quite possible to interpret categorical claims this way. By allowing both the A- and the E-claims to be true and both the I- and the O-claims to be false, this interpretation reduces the square to contradiction alone. We're going to interpret the claims differently, however; at the level at which we're operating, it seems much more natural to see "All Cs are Ds" as conflicting with "No Cs are Ds."

a false claim at the top of the square or a true claim at the bottom, all we can determine is the truth value of the contradictory of the claim in hand.

Exercise 9-3 _____

Translate the following into standard-form claims, and determine the three corresponding standard-form claims. Then, assuming the truth value in parentheses for the given claim, determine the truth values of as many of the other three as you can.

Example

Most snakes are harmless. (True)
Translation (I-claim): Some snakes are harmless creatures. (True)
Corresponding A-claim: All snakes are harmless creatures. (Undetermined)
Corresponding E-claim: No snakes are harmless creatures. (False)
Corresponding O-claim: Some snakes are not harmless creatures. (Undetermined)

▲ 1. Not all anniversaries are happy occasions. (True)

2. There's no such thing as a completely harmless drug. (True)

3. There have been such things as just wars. (True)

▲ 4. There are allergies that can kill you. (True)

5. Woodpeckers sing really well. (False)

6. Mockingbirds can't sing. (False)

7. Some herbs are medicinal. (False)

8. Logic exercises are easy. (False)

Three Categorical Operations

The square of opposition allows us to make inferences from one claim to another, as you were doing in the last exercise. We can think of these inferences as simple valid arguments, because that's exactly what they are. We'll turn next to three operations that can be performed on standard-form categorical claims. They, too, will allow us to make simple valid arguments and, in combination with the square, some not-quite-so-simple valid arguments.

■ Conversion

You find the **converse** of a standard-form claim by switching the positions of the subject and predicate terms. The E- and I-claims, but not the A- and O-claims, contain just the same information as their converses; that is,

All E- and I-claims, but not A- and O-claims, are equivalent to their converses.

Each member of the following pairs is the converse of the other:

E: No Norwegians are Slavs.
   No Slavs are Norwegians.

I: Some state capitals are large cities.
   Some large cities are state capitals.

Notice that the claims that are equivalent to their converses are those with symmetrical Venn diagrams.

■ *Obversion*

To discuss the next two operations, we need a couple of auxiliary notions. First, there's the notion of a *universe of discourse*. With rare exceptions, we make claims within contexts that limit the scope of the terms we use. For example, if your instructor walks into class and says, "Everybody passed the last exam," the word "everybody" does not include everybody in the world. Your instructor is not claiming, for example, that your mother and the President of the United States passed the exam. There is an unstated but obvious restriction to a smaller universe of people—in this case, the people in your class who *took* the exam. Now, for every class within a universe of discourse, there is a *complementary class* that contains everything in the universe of discourse that is *not* in the first class. Terms that name complementary classes are complementary terms. So, "students" and "nonstudents" are **complementary terms.** Indeed, putting the prefix "non" in front of a term is often the easiest way to produce its complement. Some terms require different treatment, though. The complement of "people who took the exam" is probably best stated as "people who did not take the exam" because the universe is pretty clearly restricted to people in such a case. (We wouldn't expect, for example, the complement of "people who took the exam" to include *everything* that didn't take the exam, including your shoes and socks!)

Now, we can get on with it: To find the **obverse** of a claim, (a) change it from affirmative to negative, or vice versa (i.e., go horizontally across the square—an A-claim becomes an E-claim; an O-claim becomes an I-claim, and so on); then (b) replace the predicate term with its complementary term.

All categorical claims of all four types, A, E, I, and O, are equivalent to their obverses.

Here are some examples; each claim is the obverse of the other member of the pair:

A: All Presbyterians are Christians.
   No Presbyterians are non-Christians.

E: No fish are mammals.
All fish are nonmammals.

I: Some citizens are voters.
Some citizens are not nonvoters.

O: Some contestants are not winners.
Some contestants are nonwinners.

■ *Contraposition*

You find the **contrapositive** of a categorical claim by (a) switching the places of the subject and predicate terms, just as in conversion, and (b) replacing both terms with complementary terms. Each of the following is the contrapositive of the other member of the pair:

A: All Mongolians are Muslims.
All non-Muslims are non-Mongolians.

O: Some citizens are not voters.
Some nonvoters are not noncitizens.

All A- and O-claims, but not E- and I-claims, are equivalent to their contrapositives.

The operations of conversion, obversion, and contraposition are important to much of what comes later, so make sure you can do them correctly and that you know which claims are equivalent to the results.

"You should say what you mean," the March Hare went on.
"I do," Alice hastily replied; "at least—at least I mean what I say— that's the same thing, you know."
"Not the same thing a bit!" said the Hatter. "Why, you might just as well say that 'I see what I eat' is the same thing as 'I eat what I see!'"
—LEWIS CARROLL, *Alice's Adventures in Wonderland*

The Mad Hatter is teaching Alice *not* to convert A-claims.

Exercise 9-4 _____

Find the claim described, and determine whether it is equivalent to the claim you began with.

▲ 1. Find the contrapositive of "No Sunnis are Christians."

2. Find the obverse of "Some Arabs are Christians."

3. Find the obverse of "All Sunnis are Muslims."

▲ 4. Find the converse of "Some Kurds are not Christians."

5. Find the converse of "No Hindus are Muslims."

6. Find the contrapositive of "Some Indians are not Hindus."

▲ 7. Find the converse of "All Shiites are Muslims."

8. Find the contrapositive of "All Catholics are Christians."

9. Find the converse of "All Protestants are Christians."

▲ 10. Find the obverse of "No Muslims are Christians."

Exercise 9-5

Follow the directions given in the preceding exercise.

▲ 1. Find the obverse of "Some students who scored well on the exam are students who wrote poor essays."

2. Find the obverse of "No students who wrote poor essays are students who were admitted to the program."

3. Find the contrapositive of "Some students who were admitted to the program are not students who scored well on the exam."

▲ 4. Find the contrapositive of "No students who did not score well on the exam are students who were admitted to the program."

5. Find the contrapositive of "All students who were admitted to the program are students who wrote good essays."

6. Find the obverse of "No students of mine are unregistered students."

▲ 7. Find the contrapositive of "All people who live in the dorms are people whose automobile ownership is restricted."

8. Find the contrapositive of "All commuters are people whose automobile ownership is unrestricted."

9. Find the contrapositive of "Some students with short-term memory problems are students who do poorly in history classes."

▲ 10. Find the obverse of "No first basemen are right-handed people."

Exercise 9-6

For each of the following, find the claim that is described.

Example

Find the contrary of the contrapositive of "All Greeks are Europeans." First, find the contrapositive of the original claim. It is "All non-Europeans are non-Greeks." Now, find the contrary of that. Going across the top of the square (from an A-claim to an E-claim), you get "No non-Europeans are non-Greeks."

1. Find the contradictory of the converse of "No clarinets are percussion instruments."

▲ 2. Find the contradictory of the obverse of "Some encyclopedias are definitive works."

3. Find the contrapositive of the subcontrary of "Some English people are Celts."

▲ 4. Find the contrary of the contradictory of "Some sailboats are not sloops."

5. Find the obverse of the converse of "No sharks are freshwater fish."

Exercise 9-7

For each of the numbered claims below, determine which of the lettered claims that follow are equivalent. You may use letters more than once if necessary. (Hint: This is a lot easier to do after all the claims are translated, a fact that indicates at least one advantage to putting claims into standard form.)

1. Some people who have not been tested can give blood.
▲ 2. People who have not been tested cannot give blood.
3. Nobody who has been tested can give blood.
▲ 4. Nobody can give blood except those who have been tested.
  a. Some people who have been tested cannot give blood.
  b. Not everybody who can give blood has been tested.
  c. Only people who have been tested can give blood.
  d. Some people who cannot give blood are people who have been tested.
  e. If a person has been tested, then he or she cannot give blood.

Exercise 9-8

Try to make the claims in the following pairs correspond to each other—that is, arrange them so that they have the same subject and the same predicate terms. Use only those operations that produce equivalent claims; for example, don't convert A- or O-claims in the process of trying to make the claims correspond. You can work on either member of the pair or both. (The main reason for practicing on these is to make the problems in the next two exercises easier to do.)

Example

  a. Some students are not unemployed people.
  b. All employed people are students.

These two claims can be made to correspond by obverting claim (a) and then converting the result (which is legitimate because the claim has been turned into an I-claim before conversion). We wind up with "Some employed people are students," which corresponds to (b).

▲ 1. a. Some Slavs are non-Europeans.
    b. No Slavs are Europeans.
2. a. All Europeans are Westerners.
    b. Some non-Westerners are non-Europeans.
3. a. All Greeks are Europeans.
    b. Some non-Europeans are Greeks.
▲ 4. a. No members of the club are people who took the exam.
    b. Some people who did not take the exam are members of the club.

5. a. All people who are not members of the club are people who took the exam.
   b. Some people who did not take the exam are members of the club.

6. a. Some cheeses are not products high in cholesterol.
   b. No cheeses are products that are not high in cholesterol.

▲ 7. a. All people who arrived late are people who will be allowed to perform.
   b. Some of the people who did not arrive late will not be allowed to perform.

8. a. No nonparticipants are people with name tags.
   b. Some of the people with name tags are participants.

9. a. Some perennials are plants that grow from tubers.
   b. Some plants that do not grow from tubers are perennials.

▲ 10. a. Some decks that play digital tape are not devices equipped for radical oversampling.
   b. All devices that are equipped for radical oversampling are decks that will not play digital tape.

Exercise 9-9

Which of the following arguments is valid? (Remember, an argument is valid when the truth of its premises guarantees the truth of its conclusion.)

▲ 1. Whenever the battery is dead, the screen goes blank; that means, of course, that whenever the screen goes blank, the battery is dead.

2. For a while there, some students were desperate for good grades, which meant some weren't, right?

3. Some players in the last election weren't members of the Reform Party. Obviously, therefore, some members of the Reform Party weren't players in the last election.

▲ 4. Since some of the students who failed the exam were students who didn't attend the review session, it must be that some students who weren't at the session failed the exam.

5. None of the people who arrived late were people who got good seats, so none of the good seats were occupied by latecomers.

6. Everybody who arrived on time was given a box lunch, so the people who did not get a box lunch were those who didn't get there on time.

▲ 7. None of the people who gave blood are people who were tested, so everybody who gave blood must have been untested.

8. Some of the people who were not tested are people who were allowed to give blood, from which it follows that some of the people who were *not* allowed to give blood must have been people who were tested.

9. Everybody who was in uniform was able to play, so nobody who was out of uniform must have been able to play.

▲ 10. Not everybody in uniform was allowed to play, so some people who were not allowed to play must not have been people in uniform.

Exercise 9-10

For each pair of claims, assume that the first has the truth value given in parentheses. Using the operations of conversion, obversion, and contraposition along with the square of opposition, decide whether the second claim is true, false, or remains undetermined.

Example

 a. No aardvarks are nonmammals. (True)
 b. Some aardvarks are not mammals.

Claim (a) can be obverted to "All aardvarks are mammals." Because all categorical claims are equivalent to their obverses, the truth of this claim follows from that of (a). Because this claim is the contradictory of claim (b), it follows that claim (b) must be false.

Note: If we had been unable to make the two claims correspond without performing an illegitimate operation (such as converting an A-claim), then the answer is automatically *undetermined*.

▲ 1. a. No mosquitoes are poisonous creatures. (True)
 b. Some poisonous creatures are mosquitoes.

2. a. Some students are not ineligible candidates. (True)
 b. No eligible candidates are students.

▲ 3. a. Some sound arguments are not invalid arguments. (True)
 b. All valid arguments are unsound arguments.

4. a. Some residents are nonvoters. (False)
 b. No voters are residents.

▲ 5. a. Some automobile plants are not productive factories. (True)
 b. All unproductive factories are automobile plants.

Many of the following will have to be rewritten as standard-form categorical claims before they can be answered.

6. a. Most opera singers take voice lessons their whole lives. (True)
 b. Some opera singers do not take voice lessons their whole lives.

7. a. The hero gets killed in some of Gary Brodnax's novels. (False)
 b. The hero does not get killed in some of Gary Brodnax's novels.

8. a. None of the boxes in the last shipment are unopened. (True)
 b. Some of the opened boxes are not boxes in the last shipment.

▲ 9. a. Not everybody who is enrolled in the class will get a grade. (True)
 b. Some people who will not get a grade are enrolled in the class.

10. a. Persimmons are always astringent when they have not been left
       to ripen. (True)
    b. Some persimmons that have been left to ripen are not astringent.

Categorical Syllogisms

A **syllogism** is a two-premise deductive argument. A **categorical syllogism** (in standard form) is a syllogism whose every claim is a standard-form categorical claim and in which three terms each occur exactly twice in exactly two of the claims. Study the following example:

> All Americans are consumers.
> Some consumers are not Democrats.
> Therefore, some Americans are not Democrats.

Notice how each of the three terms "Americans," "consumers," and "Democrats" occurs exactly twice in exactly two different claims. The *terms of a syllogism* are sometimes given the following labels:

> *Major term:* the term that occurs as a predicate term of the syllogism's conclusion

> *Minor term:* the term that occurs as the subject term of the syllogism's conclusion

> *Middle term:* the term that occurs in both of the premises but not at all in the conclusion

The most frequently used symbols for these three terms are *P* for major term, *S* for minor term, and *M* for middle term. We use these symbols throughout to simplify the discussion.

In a categorical syllogism, each of the premises states a relationship between the middle term and one of the others, as shown in Figure 6. If both premises do their jobs correctly—that is, if the proper connections between S and P are established via the middle term M—then the relationship between S and P stated by the conclusion will have to follow—that is, the argument is valid.

In case you're not clear about the concept of validity, remember: An argument is valid if, and only if, it is not possible for its premises to be true while its conclusion is false. This is just another way of saying that *were the premises of a valid argument true (whether they are in fact true or false), then the truth of the conclusion would be guaranteed.* In a moment we'll begin developing the first of two methods for assessing the validity of syllogisms.

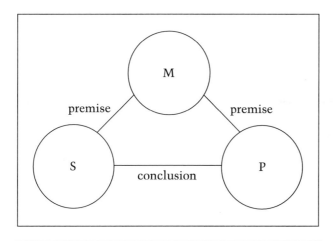

FIGURE 6   Relationship of terms in categorical syllogisms.

First, though, let's look at some candidates for syllogisms. In fact, only one of the following qualifies as a categorical syllogism. Can you identify which one? What is wrong with the other two?

1. All cats are mammals.
   Not all cats are domestic.
   Therefore, not all mammals are domestic.

2. All valid arguments are good arguments.
   Some valid arguments are boring arguments.
   Therefore, some good arguments are boring arguments.

3. Some people on the committee are not students.
   All people on the committee are local people.
   Therefore, some local people are nonstudents.

We hope it was fairly obvious that the second argument is the only proper syllogism. The first example has a couple of things wrong with it: Neither the second premise nor the conclusion is in standard form—no standard-form categorical claim begins with the word "not"—and the predicate term must be a noun or noun phrase. The second premise can be translated into "Some cats are not domestic creatures" and the conclusion into "Some mammals are not domestic creatures," and the result is a syllogism. The third argument is okay up to the conclusion, which contains a term that does not occur anywhere in the premises: "nonstudents." However, because "nonstudents" is the complement of "students," this argument can be turned into a proper syllogism by obverting the conclusion, producing "Some local people are not students."

© 2000 by Sidney Harris.

Once you're able to recognize syllogisms, it's time to learn how to determine their validity. We'll turn now to our first method, the Venn diagram test.

■ The Venn Diagram Method of Testing for Validity

Diagramming a syllogism requires three overlapping circles, one representing each class named by a term in the argument. To be systematic, in our diagrams we put the minor term on the left, the major term on the right, and the middle term in the middle, but lowered a bit. We will diagram the following syllogism step by step:

> No Republicans are collectivists.
> All socialists are collectivists.
> Therefore, no socialists are Republicans.

In this example, "socialists" is the minor term, "Republicans" is the major term, and "collectivists" is the middle term. See Figure 7 for the three circles required, labeled appropriately.

We fill in this diagram by diagramming the premises of the argument just as we diagrammed the A-, E-, I-, and O-claims earlier. The premises in the above example are diagrammed like this: First: No Republicans are collectivists (Figure 8). Notice that in this figure we have shaded the entire area where the Republican and collectivist circles overlap.

Paradoxes

The first claim in this box is false.

If the preceding claim is true, then it must be false, right? But if it's false, then what it says is true. So if it's true, it's false, and if it's false, it's true. Which is it?

This is an example of a liar paradox. Logicians are not entirely agreed as to what is the best thing to say about this type of problem. Neither are we. (Although the most frequently said thing about such paradoxes is that they show you can't let a claim refer to itself.)

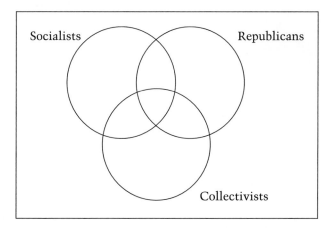

FIGURE 7   Before either premise has been diagrammed.

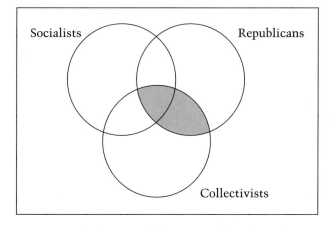

FIGURE 8   One premise diagrammed.

Bizarro © Dan Piraro. Reprinted with permission of Universal Press Syndicate.

Second: All socialists are collectivists (Figure 9). Because diagramming the premises resulted in the shading of the entire area where the socialist and Republican circles overlap, and because that is exactly what we would do to diagram the syllogism's conclusion, we can conclude that the syllogism is valid. In general, a syllogism is valid if and only if diagramming the premises automatically produces a correct diagram of the conclusion. (The one exception is discussed later.)

When one of the premises of a syllogism is an I- or O-premise, there can be a problem about where to put the required X. The following example presents such a problem (see Figure 10 for the diagram). Note in the diagram that we have numbered the different areas in order to refer to them easily.

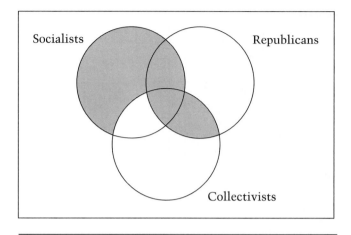

FIGURE 9   Both premises diagrammed.

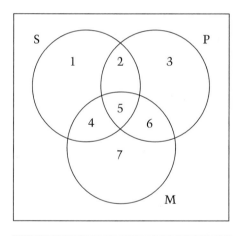

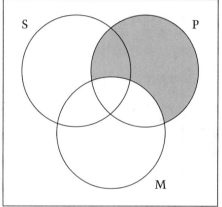

FIGURE 10   **FIGURE 11**

Some S are not M.
All P are M.
———————————
Some S are not P.

(The horizontal line separates the premises from the conclusion.)

An X in either area 1 or area 2 of Figure 10 makes the claim "Some S are not M" true, because an inhabitant of either area is an S but not an M. How do we determine which area should get the X? In some cases, the decision can be made for us: *When one premise is an A- or E-premise and the other is an I- or O-premise, diagram the A- or E-premise first.* (Always shade before putting in X's.) Refer to Figure 11 to see what happens with the current example when we follow this rule.

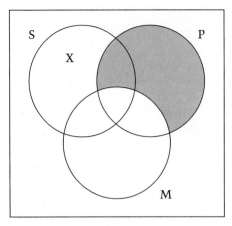

FIGURE 12

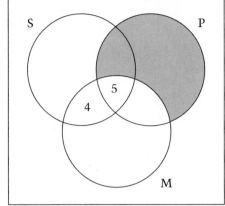

FIGURE 13

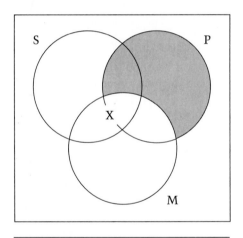

FIGURE 14

Once the A-claim has been diagrammed, there is no longer a choice about where to put the X—it has to go in area 1. Hence, the completed diagram for this argument looks like Figure 12. And from this diagram we can read the conclusion "Some S are not P," which tells us that the argument is valid.

In some syllogisms, the rule just explained does not help. For example:

All P are M.
Some S are M.

Some S are P.

A syllogism like this one still leaves us in doubt about where to put the X, even after we have diagrammed the A-premise (Figure 13): Should the X go in area 4 or 5? When such a question remains unresolved, here is the rule to follow: *An X that can go in either of two areas goes on the line separating the areas*, as in Figure 14.

In essence, an X on a line indicates that the X belongs in one or the other of the two areas, maybe both, but we don't know which. When the time comes to see whether the diagram yields the conclusion, we look to see whether there is an X *entirely* within the appropriate area. In the current example, we would need an X entirely within the area where S and P overlap; because there is no such X, the argument is invalid. An X *partly* within the appropriate area fails to establish the conclusion.

Please notice this about Venn diagrams: When both premises of a syllogism are A- or E-claims and the conclusion is an I- or O-claim, diagramming the premises cannot possibly yield a diagram of the conclusion (because A- and E-claims produce only shading, and I- and O-claims require an X to be read from the diagram). In such a case, remember our assumption that every class we are dealing with has at least one member. This assumption justifies our looking at the diagram and determining whether any circle has all but one of its areas shaded out. *If any circle has only one area remaining unshaded, an X should be put in that area.* This is the case because any member of that class has to be in that remaining area. Sometimes placing the X in this way will enable us to read the conclusion, in which case the argument is valid (on the assumption that the relevant class is not empty); sometimes placing the X will not enable us to read the conclusion, in which case the argument is invalid, with or without any assumptions about the existence of a member within the class.

■ *Categorical Syllogisms with Unstated Premises*

Many "real-life" categorical syllogisms have unstated premises. For example, suppose somebody says:

> You shouldn't give chicken bones to dogs. They could choke on them.

The speaker's argument rests on the unstated premise that you shouldn't give dogs things they could choke on. In other words, the argument, when fully spelled out, is this:

> All chicken bones are things dogs could choke on.
> [No things dogs could choke on are things you should give dogs.]
> Therefore, no chicken bones are things you should give dogs.

The unstated premise appears in brackets.

To take another example:

> Driving around in an old car is dumb, since it might break down in a dangerous place.

Our Coach, the Expletive

Exasperated with his team's losing, coach Dick Motta of the Sacramento Kings threatened to trade his star player, Wayman Tisdale, because Motta doubted Tisdale's ability to be a leader.

"You almost have to be a bad guy to be a great leader in this league," Motta said. "Very few guys can do it. There's no way Wayman Tisdale is ever going to be a bad guy."

You can put this argument into standard form, can't you?

Motta also said, "The great ones turn into pieces of [expletive] when they assume leadership. Wayman is a preacher's son. He's not going to be an [expletive]."

Same type of argument, right? Roughly:

All great leaders are pieces of expletive.
Tisdale is not a piece of expletive.
Therefore, Tisdale is not a great leader.

(When he was told what Motta said about him, Tisdale said he thought Motta should know, since Motta was a leader: All great leaders are pieces of expletive; Motta is a great leader; therefore, Motta is a piece of expletive.)

Here the speaker's argument rests on the unstated premise that it's dumb to risk a dangerous breakdown. In other words, when fully spelled out, the argument is this:

All examples of driving around in an old car are examples of risking dangerous breakdown.
[All examples of risking dangerous breakdown are examples of being dumb.]
Therefore, all examples of driving around in an old car are examples of being dumb.

When you hear (or give) an argument that looks like a categorical syllogism that has only one stated premise, usually a second premise has been assumed and not stated. Ordinarily this unstated premise remains unstated because the speaker thinks it is too obvious to bother stating. The unstated premises in the arguments above are good examples: "You shouldn't give dogs things they could choke on," and "It is dumb to risk a dangerous breakdown."

When you encounter (or give) what looks like a categorical syllogism that is missing a premise, ask: Is there a reasonable assumption I could make that would make this argument valid? We covered this question of unstated premises in more detail on pages 273–274, and you might want to look there for more information on the subject.

At the end of this chapter, we have included a few exercises that involve missing premises.

■ *Real-Life Syllogisms*

We'll end this section with a word of advice. Before you use a Venn diagram or the rules method for determining the validity of real-life arguments, it helps to use a letter to abbreviate each category mentioned in the argument. This is mainly just a matter of convenience: It is easier to write down letters than to write down long phrases.

Take the first "real-life" categorical syllogisms given above:

You shouldn't give chicken bones to dogs because they could choke on them.

The argument spelled out, once again, is this:

All chicken bones are things dogs could choke on.
[No things dogs could choke on are things you should give dogs.]
Therefore, no chicken bones are things you should give dogs.

Abbreviating each of the three categories with a letter, we get:

C = chicken bones; D = things dogs could choke on; and S = things you should give dogs.

Then, the argument is:

All C are D
[No D are S]
Therefore, no C are S.

Likewise, the second argument was this:

Driving around in an old car is dumb, since it might break down in a dangerous place.

When fully spelled out, the argument is:

All examples of driving around in an old car are examples of risking dangerous breakdown.
[All examples of risking dangerous breakdown are examples of being dumb.]
Therefore, all examples of driving around in an old car are examples of being dumb.

Abbreviating each of the three categories we get:

D = examples of driving around in an old car; R = examples of risking dangerous breakdown; S = examples of being dumb.

Then, the argument is:

All D are R
[All R are S]
Therefore, all D are S.

A final tip: Take the time to write down your abbreviation key clearly.

Exercise 9-11

Use the diagram method to determine which of the following syllogisms are valid and which are invalid.

▲ 1. All paperbacks are books that use glue in their spines.
    No books that use glue in their spines are books that are sewn in signatures.
    No books that are sewn in signatures are paperbacks.

   2. All sound arguments are valid arguments.
    Some valid arguments are not interesting arguments.
    Some sound arguments are not interesting arguments.

   3. All topologists are mathematicians.
    Some topologists are not statisticians.
    Some mathematicians are not statisticians.

▲ 4. Every time Louis is tired he's edgy. He's edgy today, so he must be tired today.

   5. Every voter is a citizen, but some citizens are not residents. Therefore, some voters are not residents.

   6. All the dominant seventh chords are in the mixolydian mode, and no mixolydian chords use the major scale. So, no chords that use the major scale are dominant sevenths.

▲ 7. All halyards are lines that attach to sails. Painters do not attach to sails, so they must not be halyards.

   8. Only systems with removable disks can give you unlimited storage capacity of a practical sort. Standard hard disks never have removable disks, so they can't give you practical, unlimited storage capacity.

   9. All citizens are residents. So, since no noncitizens are voters, all voters must be residents.

▲ 10. No citizens are nonresidents, and all voters are citizens. So all residents must be nonvoters.

Exercise 9-12

Put the following arguments in standard form (you may have to use the obversion, conversion, or contraposition operations to accomplish this); then determine whether the arguments are valid by means of diagrams.

▲ 1. No blank disks contain any data, although some blank disks are formatted. Therefore, some formatted disks do not contain any data.

2. All ears of corn with white tassels are unripe, but some ears are ripe even though their kernels are not full-sized. Therefore, some ears with full-sized kernels are not ears with white tassels.

3. Prescription drugs should never be taken without a doctor's order. So, no over-the-counter drugs are prescription drugs, because all over-the-counter drugs can be taken without a doctor's order.

▲ 4. All tobacco products are damaging to people's health, but some of them are addictive substances. Some addictive substances, therefore, are damaging to people's health.

5. A few compact disc players use 24x sampling, so some of them must cost at least a hundred dollars, because you can't buy any machine with 24x sampling for less than a hundred dollars.

6. Everything that Pete won at the carnival must be junk. I know that Pete won everything that Bob won, and all the stuff that Bob won is junk.

▲ 7. Only people who hold stock in the company may vote, so Mr. Hansen must not hold any stock in the company, because I know he was not allowed to vote.

8. No off-road vehicles are allowed in the unimproved portion of the park, but some off-road vehicles are not four-wheel-drive. So some four-wheel-drive vehicles are allowed in the unimproved part of the park.

9. Some of the people affected by the new drainage tax are residents of the county, and many residents of the county are already paying the sewer tax. So, it must be that some people paying the sewer tax are affected by the new drainage tax, too.

▲ 10. No argument with false premises is sound, but some of them are valid. So some unsound arguments must be valid.

■ *The Rules Method of Testing for Validity*

The diagram method of testing syllogisms for validity is intuitive, but there is a faster method that makes use of three simple rules. These rules are based on two ideas, the first of which has been mentioned already: affirmative and negative categorical claims. (Remember, the A- and I-claims are affirmative; the E- and O-claims are negative.) The other idea is that of *distribution*. Terms that occur in categorical claims are either distributed or undistributed: Either the claim says something about every member of the class the

A-claim: All (S) are P.
E-claim: No (S) are (P).
I-claim: Some S are P.
O-claim: Some S are not (P).

FIGURE 15   Distributed terms

term names, or it does not.* Three of the standard-form claims distribute one or more of their terms. In Figure 15, the circled letters stand for distributed terms, and the uncircled ones stand for undistributed terms. As the figure shows, the A-claim distributes its subject term, the O-claim distributes its predicate term, the E-claim distributes both, and the I-claim distributes neither.

We can now state the three *rules of the syllogism.* A syllogism is valid if and only if all of these conditions are met:

1. **The number of negative claims in the premises must be the same as the number of negative claims in the conclusion.** (Because the conclusion is always one claim, this implies that no valid syllogism has two negative premises.)

2. **At least one premise must distribute the middle term.**

3. **Any term that is distributed in the conclusion of the syllogism must be distributed in its premises.**

These rules are easy to remember, and with a bit of practice, you can use them to determine quickly whether a syllogism is valid.

Which of the rules is broken in this example?

All pianists are keyboard players.
Some keyboard players are not percussionists.
Some pianists are not percussionists.

---

*The above is a rough-and-ready definition of distribution. If you'd like a more technical version, here's one: A term is *distributed* in a claim if, and only if, on the assumption that the claim is true, the class named by the term can be replaced by *any* subset of that class without producing a false claim. Example: In the claim "All senators are politicians," the term "senators" is distributed because, assuming the claim is true, you can substitute *any* subset of senators (Democratic ones, Republican ones, tall ones, short ones . . .) and the result must also be true. "Politicians" is not distributed: The original claim could be true while "All senators are honest politicians" was false.

© 2000 by Sidney Harris

▲   *Nope. 'Fraid it's none of the above. Is it clear what error our logician is making?*

The term "keyboard players" is the middle term, and it is undistributed in both premises. The first premise, an A-claim, does not distribute its predicate term; the second premise, an O-claim, does not distribute its subject term. So, this syllogism breaks rule 2.

Another example:

> No dogs up for adoption at the animal shelter are pedigreed dogs.
> Some pedigreed dogs are expensive dogs.
> _____
> Some dogs up for adoption at the animal shelter are expensive dogs.

This syllogism breaks rule 1 because it has a negative premise but no negative conclusion.

A last example:

> No mercantilists are large landowners.
> All mercantilists are creditors.
> _____
> No creditors are large landowners.

The minor term, "creditors," is distributed in the conclusion (because it's the subject term of an E-claim) but not in the premises (where it's the predicate term of an A-claim). So, this syllogism breaks rule 3.

Recap

In this chapter, we have developed the basics of categorical logic. There are four types of standard-form categorical claims (A: "All S are P"; E: "No S are P"; I: "Some S are P"; and O: "Some S are not P"). These can be represented by Venn diagrams. Translation of ordinary English claims into standard-form categorical ones is made somewhat easier by a few rules of thumb: "Only" introduces a predicate term; "the only" introduces a subject term; "whenever" means we're probably talking about times or occasions; "wherever" means we're probably talking about places. Claims about individuals should be treated as A- or E-claims.

The square of opposition displays the relations of contradiction, contrariety, and subcontrariety among corresponding standard-form claims. Conversion, obversion, and contraposition are three operations that can be performed on categorical claims—depending on the kind of claim on which you perform the operation, the result can be an equivalent claim.

Categorical syllogisms are standardized deductive arguments. We can test them for validity by two methods, one of which relies on Venn diagrams and one of which relies on rules about affirmative/negative claims and about the distribution of terms.

Having read this chapter and the chapter recap, you should be able to

▲ Define categorical logic and explain the four kinds of standard-form categorical claims

▲ Diagram standard-form categorical claims using Venn diagrams and translate claims into equivalent claims

▲ Exhibit the logical relationships among corresponding claims and determine the truth value of those claims using the square of opposition

▲ Make inferences about claims using the operations conversion, obversion, and contraposition

▲ Explain categorical syllogisms and determine their validity using both the diagram method and the rules method

Additional Exercises

Exercise 9-13

In each of the following items, identify whether A, B, or C is the middle term.

▲ 1. All A are B.
   All A are C.
   All B are C.

2. All B are C.
 No C are D.
 _____
 No B are D.

3. Some C are not D.
 All C are A.
 Some D are not A.

▲ 4. Some A are not B.
 Some B are C.
 _____
 Some C are not A.

5. No C are A.
 Some B are A.
 _____
 Some A are not B.

Exercise 9-14 _____

Which terms are distributed in each of the following?

▲ 1. All A are B.
 a. A only
 b. B only
 c. Both A and B
 d. Neither A nor B

2. No A are B.
 a. A only
 b. B only
 c. Both A and B
 d. Neither A nor B

3. Some A are B.
 a. A only
 b. B only
 c. Both A and B
 d. Neither A nor B

▲ 4. Some A are not B.
 a. A only
 b. B only
 c. Both A and B
 d. Neither A nor B

Exercise 9-15 _____

How many negative claims appear in the premises of each of the following arguments? (In other words, how many of the premises are negative?) Your options
are 0, 1, or 2.

▲ 1. All A are B.
   All A are C.
   Therefore, all B are C.

2. All B are C.
   No C are D.
   Therefore, no B are D.

3. Some C are not D.
   All C are A.
   Therefore, some D are not A.

▲ 4. Some A are not B.
   Some B are C.
   Therefore, some C are not A.

5. No A are B.
   Some B are not C.
   Some A are C.

Exercise 9-16 _____

Which rules (if any) are broken in each of the following? Select from these options:
   a. Breaks rule 1 only
   b. Breaks rule 2 only
   c. Breaks rule 3 only
   d. Breaks more than one rule
   e. Breaks no rule

▲ 1. All A are B.
   All A are C.
   Therefore, all B are C.

2. All B are C.
   No C are D.
   Therefore, no B are D.

3. Some C are not D.
   All C are A.
   Therefore, some D are A.

▲ 4. Some A are not B.
   Some B are C.
   Therefore, some C are not A.

5. Some A are C.
   Some C are B.
   Therefore, some A are B.

6. Some carbostats are framistans.
   No framistans are arbuckles.
   Some arbuckles are not carbostats.

▲ 7. All framistans are veeblefetzers.
   <u>Some veeblefetzers are carbostats.</u>
   Some framistans are carbostats.

8. No arbuckles are framistans.
   <u>All arbuckles are carbostats.</u>
   No framistans are carbostats.

9. All members of the class are registered students.
   <u>Some registered students are not people taking fifteen units.</u>
   Some members of the class are not people taking fifteen units.

▲ 10. All qualified mechanics are people familiar with hydraulics.
   <u>No unschooled people are people familiar with hydraulics.</u>
   No qualified mechanics are unschooled people.

Exercise 9-17

Which rules (if any) are broken in each of the following?

Note: If an argument breaks a rule, *which* rule is broken depends on how you translate the claims in the argument. For example, the claim "Dogs shouldn't be given chicken bones" could be translated as an *E-claim:* "No dogs are animals that should be given chicken bones." But it also could be translated as an *A-claim:* "All dogs are animals that shouldn't be given chicken bones." If the original claim appeared in an invalid argument, one rule would be broken if you translated it as the E-claim. A different rule would be broken if you translated it as the A-claim.

▲ 1. All tigers are ferocious creatures. Some ferocious creatures are zoo animals. Therefore, some zoo animals are tigers. (For this and the following items, it will help if you abbreviate each category with a letter. For example, let T = tigers, F = ferocious creatures, and Z = zoo animals.)

2. Some pedestrians are not jaywalkers. Therefore, some jaywalkers are not gardeners, since no gardeners are pedestrians.

3. Because all shrubs are ornamental plants, it follows that no ornamental plants are cacti, since no cacti qualify as shrubs.

▲ 4. Weightlifters aren't really athletes. Athletics requires the use of motor skills; and few, if any, weightlifters use motor skills.

5. The trick to finding syllogisms is to think categorically, as well as to focus on the key argument in a passage. For example, some passages contain a good bit of rhetoric, and some passages that do this make it hard to spot syllogisms, with the result that it is hard to spot syllogisms in some passages.

6. Every broadcast network has seen its share of the television audience decline during the past six years. But not every media outlet that has a decline in television audience share has lost money. So not every broadcast network has lost money.

▲ 7. Many students lift papers off the Internet, and this fact is discouraging to teachers. However, it must be noted that students who do this are only cheating themselves, and anyone who cheats himself or herself loses in the long run. Therefore, lifting papers off the Internet is a losing proposition in the long run.

8. When he was Speaker of the House, Mr. Newt Gingrich could be counted on to advance Republican causes. At the time nobody who would do that could be accused of being soft on crime, which explains why at the time Gingrich could hardly be accused of being soft on crime.

9. It would be in everyone's interest to amend the Constitution to permit school prayer. And it is obviously in everyone's interest to promote religious freedom. It should be no surprise, then, that amending the Constitution to permit school prayer will promote religious freedom.

▲ 10. If you want to stay out all night dancing, it is fine with me. Just don't cry about it if you don't get good grades. Dancing isn't a total waste of time, but dancing the whole night certainly is. There are only so many hours in a day, and wasting time is bound to affect your grades negatively. So, fine, stay out dancing all night. It's your choice. But you have to expect your grades to suffer.

Exercise 9-18

Refer back to Exercises 9-11 and 9-12 and check the arguments for validity using the rules. We recommend abbreviating each category with a letter.

Once again, remember: If an argument breaks a rule, *which* rule is broken depends on how you translate the claims in the argument. For example, the claim "Dogs shouldn't be given chicken bones" could be translated as an E-claim: "No dogs are animals that should be given chicken bones." But it also could be translated as an A-claim (the obverse of the other version): "All dogs are animals that shouldn't be given chicken bones." If the original claim appeared in an invalid argument, one rule would be broken if you translated it as an E-claim. A different rule would be broken if you translated it as an A-claim.

Answers to 2, 5, 7, and 8 are given in the answer section.

Exercise 9-19

Refer to Exercise A3-4 in Appendix 3. Ignore the directions given there as well as any "hints" given in parentheses. Rewrite the passages as required so as to make syllogisms of them; then, test for validity by using diagrams or the rules, according to your instructor's directions.

Exercise 9-20

For each of the following items: Abbreviate each category with a letter, then translate the argument into standard form using the abbreviations. Then test the argument for validity using either the diagram method or the rules method.

    Note: For many of these items it can be difficult to translate the arguments into standard form.

▲ 1. Some athletes are not baseball players, and some baseball players are not basketball players. Therefore, some athletes are not basketball players.

   2. Rats are disease-carrying pests, and as such should be eradicated, because such pests should all be eradicated.

▲ 3. This is not the best of all possible worlds, because the best of all possible worlds would not contain mosquitoes, and *this* world contains plenty of mosquitoes!

   4. From time to time, the police have to break up parties here on campus, since some campus parties get out of control, and when a party gets out of control, well, you know what the police have to do.

   5. I know that all fundamentalist Christians are evangelicals, and I'm pretty sure that all revivalists are also evangelicals. So, if I'm right, at least some fundamentalist Christians must be revivalists.

▲ 6. "Their new lawn furniture certainly looks cheap to me," she said. "It's made of plastic, and plastic furniture just looks cheap."

   7. None of our intramural sports are sports played in the Olympics, and some of the intercollegiate sports are not Olympic sports either. So some of the intercollegiate sports are also intramural sports.

   8. The moas were all Dinornithidae, and no moas exist anymore. So there aren't any more Dinornithidae.

▲ 9. Everybody on the district tax roll is a citizen, and all eligible voters are also citizens. So everybody on the district tax roll is an eligible voter.

  10. Any piece of software that is in the public domain may be copied without permission or fee. But that cannot be done in the case of software under copyright. So software under copyright must not be in the public domain.

  11. None of the countries that have been living under dictatorships for these past few decades are familiar with the social requirements of a strong democracy—things like widespread education and a willingness to abide by majority vote. Consequently, none of these countries will make a successful quick transition to democracy, since countries where the abovementioned requirements are unfamiliar simply can't make such a transition.

▲ 12. Trust Senator Cobweb to vote with the governor on the new tax legislation. Cobweb is a liberal, and liberals just cannot pass up an opportunity to raise taxes.

  13. Investor-held utilities should not be allowed to raise rates, since all public utilities should be allowed to raise rates, and public utilities are not investor-held.

14. Masterpieces are no longer recorded on cassettes. This is because masterpieces belong to the classical repertoire, and classical music is no longer recorded on cassettes.

15. It isn't important to learn chemistry, since it isn't very useful, and there isn't much point in learning something that isn't useful.

16. Stockholders' information about a company's worth must come from the managers of that company, but in a buy-out, the managers of the company are the very ones who are trying to buy the stock from the stockholders. So, ironically, in a buy-out situation, stockholders must get their information about how much a company is worth from the very people who are trying to buy their stock.

▲ 17. All of the networks devoted considerable attention to reporting poll results during the last election, but many of those poll results were not especially newsworthy. So, the networks have to admit that some unnewsworthy items received quite a bit of their attention.

▲ 18. If a person doesn't understand that the earth goes around the sun once a year, then that person can't understand what causes winter and summer. Strange as it may seem, then, there are many American adults who don't know what causes winter and summer, because a survey a year or so ago showed that many such adults don't know that the earth goes around the sun.

19. Congress seems ready to impose trade sanctions on China, and perhaps it should. China's leaders cruelly cling to power. They flout American interests in their actions in Tibet, in their human-rights violations, in their weapons sales, and in their questionable trade practices. Any country with a record like this deserves sanctions.

▲ 20. Since 1973, when the U.S. Supreme Court decided *Miller v. California,* no work can be banned as obscene unless it contains sexual depictions that are "patently offensive" to "contemporary community standards" and unless the work as a whole possesses no "serious literary, artistic, political or scientific value." As loose as this standard may seem when compared with earlier tests of obscenity, the pornographic novels of "Madame Toulouse" (a pseudonym, of course) can still be banned. They would offend the contemporary standards of *any* community, and to claim any literary, artistic, political, or scientific value for them would be a real joke.

Exercise 9-21

This exercise is a little different, and you may need to work one or more such items in class in order to get the hang of them. Your job is to try to prove each of the following claims about syllogisms true or false. You may need to produce a general argument—that is, to show that *every* syllogism that does *this* must also do *that*—or you may need to produce a counterexample, that is, an example that proves the claim in question false. The definition of categorical syllogism and the rules of the syllogism are of crucial importance in working these examples.

▲ 1. Every valid syllogism must have at least one A- or E-claim for a premise.

2. Every valid syllogism with an E-claim for a premise must have an E-claim for a conclusion.

3. Every valid syllogism with an E-claim for a conclusion must have an E-claim for a premise.

▲ 4. It's possible for a syllogism to break two of the rules of the syllogism.

5. No syllogism can break three of the rules of the syllogism.

Exercise 9-22

The following is an anonymous statement of opinion that appeared in a newspaper call-in column.

> This is in response to the person who called in that we should provide a shelter for the homeless, because I think that is wrong. These people make the downtown area unsafe because they have nothing to lose by robbing, mugging, etc. The young boy killed by the horseshoe pits was attacked by some of these bums, assuming that witnesses really saw people who were homeless, which no doubt they did, since the so-called homeless all wear that old worn-out hippie gear, just like the people they saw. They also lower property values. And don't tell me they are down and out because they can't find work. The work is there if they look for it. They choose for themselves how to live, since if they didn't choose, who did?

A lot of things might be said in criticism of this tirade, but what we want you to notice is the breakdown of logic. The piece contains, in fact, a gross logic error, which we ask you to make the focus of a critical essay. Your audience is the other members of your class; that is, you are writing for an audience of critical thinkers.

Exercise 9-23

> Pornography violates women's rights. It carries a demeaning message about a woman's worth and purpose and promotes genuine violence. This is indeed a violation of women's civil rights and justifies the Minneapolis City Council in attempting to ban pornography.

This letter to the editor is, in effect, two syllogisms. The conclusion of the first is that pornography violates women's rights. This conclusion also functions as a premise in the second syllogism, which has as its own conclusion the claim that the Minneapolis City Council is justified in attempting to ban pornography. Both syllogisms have unstated premises. Translate the entire argument into standard-form syllogisms, supplying missing premises, and determine whether the reasoning is valid.

Exercise 9-24

Each of the following arguments contains an unstated premise, which, together with the stated premise, makes the argument in question valid. Your job is to identify this unstated premise, abbreviate each category with a letter, and put the argument in standard form.

▲ 1. Ladybugs eat aphids; therefore, they are good to have in your garden.

2. CEOs have lots of responsibility; therefore, they should be paid a lot.

3. Anyone who understands how a computer program works knows how important logic is. Therefore, anyone who understands how a computer program works understands how important unambiguous writing is.

▲ 4. Self-tapping screws are a boon to the construction industry. They make it possible to screw things without drilling pilot holes.

5. No baseball player smokes anymore. Baseball players all know that smoking hampers athletic performance.

6. You really ought to give up jogging. It is harmful to your health.

7. Camping isn't much fun. It requires sleeping on the hard ground and getting lots of bug bites.

8. Having too much coffee makes you sleep poorly. That's why you shouldn't do it.

9. Do you have writer's block? No problem. You can always hire a secretary.

10. "You think those marks were left by a—snake? That's totally crazy. Snakes don't leave footprints."

Writing Exercises

1. Should dogs be used in medical experiments, given that they seem to have the capacity to experience fear and feel pain? Write a short paper defending a negative answer to this question, taking about five minutes to do so. When you have finished, exchange your argument with a friend and rewrite each other's argument as a categorical syllogism or a combination of categorical syllogisms. Remember that people often leave premises unstated.

2. Follow the instructions for Exercise 1, but this time defend the position that it is not wrong to use dogs in medical experiments.

3. Turn to Selection 1 at the end of the book and follow the instructions for the alternative assignment.

4. Turn to Selection 2 at the end of the book and follow the second set of instructions.

5. Turn to Selection 9A, 9B, 10A, 10B, 11A, or 11B and follow the second alternative assignment.

Chapter 10

Deductive Arguments II: Truth-Functional Logic

*T*he earliest development of truth-functional logic took place among the Stoics, who flourished from about the third century B.C.E. until the second century C.E. But it was in the late nineteenth and twentieth centuries that the real power of **truth-functional logic** (known also as *propositional* or *sentential logic*) became apparent.

The "logic of sentences" is one of the bases on which modern symbolic logic rests, and as such it is important in such intellectual areas as set theory and the foundations of mathematics. It is also the model for electrical circuits of the sort that are the basis of digital computing. But truth-functional logic is also a useful tool in the analysis of arguments.

The study of truth-functional logic can benefit you in several ways. For one thing, you'll learn something about the structure of language that you wouldn't learn any other way. For another, you'll get a sense of what it's like to work with a very precise, nonmathematical system of symbols that is nevertheless very accessible to nearly any student willing to invest a modest amount of effort. The model of precision and clarity that such systems provide can serve you well when you communicate with others in ordinary language.

If you're not comfortable working with symbols, the upcoming sections on truth-functional arguments and deductions might look intimidating. But they are not as forbidding as they may appear. We presume that the whole matter of a symbolic system is unfamiliar to you, so we'll start from absolute scratch. Keep in mind, though, that everything builds on what goes before. It's important to master each concept as it's explained and not fall behind. Catching up can be very difficult. If you find yourself having difficulty with a section or a concept, put in some extra effort to master it before moving ahead. It will be worth it in the end.

Truth Tables and the Truth-Functional Symbols

Our "logical vocabulary" will consist of claim variables and truth-functional symbols. Before we consider the real heart of the subject, truth tables and the symbols that represent them, let's first clarify the use of letters of the alphabet to symbolize terms and claims.

■ Claim Variables

In Chapter 9, we used uppercase letters to stand for terms in categorical claims. Here we use uppercase letters to stand for claims. Our main interest is now in the way that words such as "not," "and," "or," and so on affect claims and link them together to produce compound claims out of simpler ones. So don't confuse the Ps and Qs, called **claim variables,** that appear in this chapter with the term variables used in Chapter 9.*

■ Truth Tables

Let's now consider truth tables and symbols. In truth-functional logic, any given claim, P, is either true or false. The following little table, called a **truth table,** displays both possible truth values for P:

P
T
F

*Whichever truth value the claim P might have, its negation or contradictory, which we'll symbolize ~P, will have the other. Here, then, is the truth table for **negation:***

P	~P
T	F
F	T

The left-hand column of this table sets out both possible truth values for P, and the right-hand column sets out the truth values for ~P based on P's values. This is a way of defining the negation sign, ~, in front of the P. The symbol means "change the truth value from T to F or from F to T, depending on P's values." Because it's handy to have a name for negations that you can

---

*It is customary to use one kind of symbol, usually lowercase letters or Greek letters, as *claim variables* and plain or italicized uppercase letters for *specific claims*. Although this use has some technical advantages and makes possible a certain theoretical neatness, students often find it confusing. Therefore, we'll use uppercase letters for both variables and specific claims and simply make it clear which way we're using the letters.

say aloud, we read ~P as "not-P." So, if P were "Parker is at home," then ~P would be "It is not the case that Parker is at home," or, more simply, "Parker is not at home." In a moment we'll define other symbols by means of truth tables, so make sure you understand how this one works.

Because any given claim is either true or false, two claims, P and Q, must both be true, both be false, or have opposite truth values, for a total of four possible combinations. Here are the possibilities in truth-table form:

P	Q
T	T
T	F
F	T
F	F

A **conjunction** is a compound claim made from two simpler claims, called *conjuncts. A conjunction is true if and only if both of the simpler claims that make it up (its conjuncts) are true.* An example of a conjunction is the claim "Parker is at home and Moore is at work." We'll express the conjunction of P and Q by connecting them with an ampersand (&). The truth table for conjunctions looks like this:

P	Q	P & Q
T	T	T
T	F	F
F	T	F
F	F	F

P & Q is true in the first row only, where both P and Q are true. Notice that the "truth conditions" in this row match those required in the italicized remark above.

Here's another way to remember how conjunctions work: If either part of a conjunction is false, the conjunction itself is false. Notice finally that although the word "and" is the closest representative in English to our ampersand symbol, there are other words that are correctly symbolized by the ampersand: "but" and "while," for instance, as well as phrases such as "even though." So if we let P stand for "Parsons is in class" and Q stand for "Quincy is absent," then we should represent "Parsons is in class even though Quincy is absent" by P & Q. The reason is that the compound claim is true only in one case: where both parts are true. And that's all it takes to require an ampersand to represent the connecting word or phrase.

A **disjunction** is another compound claim made up of two simpler claims, called *disjuncts. A disjunction is false if and only if both of its disjuncts are false.* Here's an example of a disjunction: "Either Parker is at home or Moore is at work." We'll use the symbol v ("wedge") to represent disjunction when we symbolize claims—as indicated in the example, the

"VERY CREATIVE. VERY IMAGINATIVE. LOGIC... THAT'S WHAT'S MISSING."

© 2000 by Sidney Harris

closest word in English to this symbol is "or." The truth table for disjunctions is this:

P	Q	P v Q
T	T	T
T	F	T
F	T	T
F	F	F

Notice here that a disjunction is false only in the last row, where both of its disjuncts are false. In all other cases a disjunction is true.

The third kind of compound claim made from two simpler claims is the **conditional claim.** In ordinary English, the most common way of stating conditionals is by means of the words "if . . . then . . . ," as in the example "If Parker is at home, then Moore is at work."

We'll use an arrow to symbolize conditionals: P → Q. The first claim in a conditional, the P in the symbolization, is the **antecedent,** and the second— Q in this case—is the **consequent.** *A conditional claim is false if and only if its antecedent is true and its consequent is false.* The truth table for conditionals looks like this:

P	Q	P → Q
T	T	T
T	F	F
F	T	T
F	F	T

Only in the second row, where the antecedent P is true and the consequent Q is false, does the conditional turn out to be false. In all other cases it is true.

Of the four types of truth-functional claims—negation, conjunction, disjunction, and conditional—the conditional typically gives students the most trouble. Let's have a closer look at it by considering an example that may shed light on how and why conditionals work. Let's say that Moore promises you that, if his paycheck arrives this morning, he'll buy you lunch. So now we can consider the conditional,

If Moore's paycheck arrives this morning, then Moore will buy you lunch.

We can symbolize this using P (for the claim about the paycheck) and L (for the claim about lunch): P → L. Now let's try to see why the truth table above fits this claim.

The easiest way to see this is by asking yourself what it would take for Moore to break his promise. A moment's thought should make this clear: Two things have to happen before we can say that Moore has fibbed to you. The first is that his paycheck must arrive this morning. (After all, he didn't say what he was going to do if his paycheck *didn't* arrive, did he?) Then, it being true that his paycheck arrives, he must then *not* buy you lunch. Together, these two items make it clear that Moore's original promise was false. Notice: Under no other circumstances would we say that Moore broke his promise. And *that* is why the truth table has a conditional false in one and only one case, namely, where the antecedent is true and the consequent is false. Basic information about all four symbols is summarized in Figure 1.

Our truth-functional symbols can work in combination. Consider, for example, the claim "If Paula doesn't go to work, then Quincy will have to work a double shift." We'll represent the two simple claims in the obvious way, as follows:

P = Paula goes to work.
Q = Quincy has to work a double shift.

Negation (~)	Conjunction (&)
Truth table:	Truth table:
P ~P T F F T	P Q (P & Q) T T T T F F F T F F F F
Closest English counterparts: "not," or "it is not the case that"	Closest English counterparts: "and," "but," "while"
Disjunction (v)	Conditional (→)
Truth table:	Truth table:
P Q (P v Q) T T T T F T F T T F F F	P Q (P → Q) T T T T F F F T T F F T
Closest English counterparts: "or," "unless"	Closest English counterparts: "if . . . . then," "provided that"

FIGURE 1   The Four Basic Truth-Functional Symbols

And we can symbolize the entire claim like this:

$$\sim P \rightarrow Q$$

Here is a truth table for this symbolization:

P	Q	~P	~P → Q
T	T	F	T
T	F	F	T
F	T	T	T
F	F	T	F

Notice that the symbolized claim $\sim P \rightarrow Q$ is false in the *last* row of this table. That's because here and only here the antecedent, $\sim P$, is true and its consequent, Q, is false. Notice that we work from the simplest parts to the most complex: The truth value of P in a given row determines the truth value of $\sim P$, and that truth value in turn, along with the one for Q, determines the truth value of $\sim P \rightarrow Q$.

Consider another combination: "If Paula goes to work, then Quincy and Rogers will get a day off." This claim is symbolized this way:

P → (Q & R)

This symbolization requires parentheses to prevent confusion with (P → Q) & R, which symbolizes a different claim and has a different truth table. Our claim is a conditional with a conjunction for a consequent, whereas (P → Q) & R is a conjunction with a conditional as one of the conjuncts. The parentheses are what make this clear.

You need to know a few principles to produce the truth table for the symbolized claim P → (Q & R). First you have to know how to set up all the possible combinations of true and false for the three simple claims P, Q, and R. In claims with only one letter, there were two possibilities, T and F. In claims with two letters, there were four possibilities. *Every time we add another letter, the number of possible combinations of T and F doubles, and so, therefore, does the number of rows in our truth table.* The formula for determining the number of rows in a truth table for a compound claim is $r = 2^n$, where r is the number of rows in the table and n is the number of letters in the symbolization. Because the claim we are interested in has three letters, our truth table will have eight rows, one for each possible combination of T and F for P, Q, and R. Here's how we do it:

P	Q	R
T	T	T
T	T	F
T	F	T
T	F	F
F	T	T
F	T	F
F	F	T
F	F	F

The systematic way to construct such a table is to alternate Ts and Fs in the right-hand column, then alternate *pairs* of Ts and *pairs* of Fs in the next column to the left, then sets of *four* Ts and sets of *four* Fs in the next, and so forth. The leftmost column will always wind up being half Ts and half Fs.

The second thing we have to know is that the truth value of a compound claim in any particular case (i.e., any row of its truth table) depends entirely upon the truth values of its parts; and if these parts are themselves compound, their truth values depend upon those of their parts; and so on, until we get down to letters standing alone. The columns under the letters, which you have just learned to construct, will then tell us what we need to know. Let's build a truth table for P → (Q & R) and see how this works.

Test Yourself

See these cards? They obey the following rule: "If there is a vowel on one side then the card has an even number on the other side."

Question: To see that the rule has been kept, how many cards must be turned over and checked?

P.S. Most university students flunk this simple test of critical thinking.

P	Q	R	Q & R	P → (Q & R)
T	T	T	T	T
T	T	F	F	F
T	F	T	F	F
T	F	F	F	F
F	T	T	T	T
F	T	F	F	T
F	F	T	F	T
F	F	F	F	T

The three columns at the left, under P, Q, and R, are our *reference columns*, set up just as we discussed above. They determine what goes on in the rest of the table. From the second and third columns, under the Q and the R, we can fill in the column under Q & R. Notice that this column contains a T only in the first and fifth rows, where both Q and R are true. Next, from the column under the P and the one under Q & R, we can fill in the last column, which is the one for the entire symbolized claim. It contains Fs in only rows two, three, and four, which are the only ones where its antecedent is true and its consequent is false.

What our table gives us is a *truth-functional analysis* of our original claim. Such an analysis displays the compound claim's truth value, based on the truth values of its simpler parts.

If you've followed everything so far without problems, that's great. If you've not yet understood the basic truth table idea, however, as well as the truth tables for the truth-functional symbols, then by all means stop now and go back over this material. You should also understand how to build a truth table for symbolizations consisting of three or more letters. What comes later builds on this foundation, and like any construction project, without a strong foundation the whole thing collapses.

A final note before we turn to tips for symbolizing compound claims: Two claims are **truth-functionally equivalent** if they have exactly the same truth table—that is, if the Ts and Fs in the column under one claim are in the same arrangement as those in the column under the other. Generally speaking, when two claims are equivalent, one can be used in place of another—truth-functionally, they each imply the other.*

■ *Symbolizing Compound Claims*

Most of the things we can do with symbolized claims are pretty straightforward; that is, if you learn the techniques, you can apply them in a relatively clear-cut way. What's less clear-cut is how to symbolize a claim in the first place. We'll cover a few tips for symbolization in this section, and then give you a chance to practice with some exercises.

Remember, when you symbolize a claim, you're displaying its truth-functional structure. The idea is to produce a version that will be truth-functionally equivalent to the original informal claim—that is, one that will be true under all the same circumstances as the original and false under all the same circumstances. Let's go through some examples that illustrate some standard symbolization problems.

"If" and "Only If"   In symbolizing truth-functional claims, as in translating categorical claims in Chapter 9, nothing can take the place of a careful reading of what the claim in question says. It always comes down to a matter of exercising careful judgment. Nonetheless, there are some tips we can give you that should make the job a little easier.

Of all the basic truth-functional types of claim, the conditional is probably the most difficult for students to symbolize correctly. There are so many ways to make these claims in ordinary English that it's not easy to keep track. Fortunately, the phrases "if" and "only if" account for a large number of conditionals, so you'll have a head start if you understand their uses. Here are some rules of thumb to remember:

1. The word "if," used alone, introduces the antecedent of a conditional.
2. The phrase "only if" introduces the consequent of a conditional.

---

*The exceptions to this remark are due to *non*-truth-functional nuances that claims sometimes have. Most compound claims of the form P & Q, for example, are interchangeable with what are called their commutations, Q & P. That is, it doesn't matter which conjunct comes first. (Note that this is also true of disjunctions but *not* of conditionals.) But at times "and" has more than a truth-functional meaning, and in such cases which conjunct comes first can make a difference. In "Daniel got on the train and bought his ticket," the word "and" would ordinarily mean "and then." So "Daniel bought his ticket and got on the train" turns out to be a different claim from the previous one; it says that he did the two things in a different order from that stated in the first claim. This temporal-ordering sense of "and" is part of the word's occasional non-truth-functional meaning.

Truth-Functional Trickery

Using what you know about truth-functional logic, can you identify how the sender of this encouraging-looking notice can defend the claim (because it *is* true) even though the receiver is not really going to win one nickel?

You Have Absolutely Won
$1,000,000.00

If you follow the instructions inside
and return the winning number!

Answer: Because there is not going to be any winning number inside (there are usually several *losing* numbers, in case that makes you feel better), the conjunction "You follow the instructions inside and [you] return the winning number" is going to be false, even if you do follow the instructions inside. Therefore, because this conjunction is the antecedent of the whole conditional claim, the conditional claim turns out to be true.

Of course, uncritical readers will take the antecedent to be saying something like "If you follow the instructions inside *by returning the winning number inside* (as if there were a winning number inside). These are the people who may wind up sending their own money to the mailer.

To put it another way: It's not the location of the part in a conditional that tells us whether it is the antecedent or the consequent; it's the logical words that identify it. Consider this example:

> Moore will get wet *if* Parker capsizes the boat.

The "Parker" part of the claim is the antecedent, even though it comes *after* the "Moore" part. It's as though the claim had said,

> If Parker capsizes the boat, Moore will get wet.

We would symbolize this claim as P → M. Once again, it's the word "if" that tells us what the antecedent is.

> Parker will beat Moore at 9-ball *only if* Moore has a bad day.

This claim is different. In this case, the "Parker" part is the antecedent because "only if" introduces the consequent of a conditional. This is truth-functionally the same as

> If Parker beats Moore at 9-ball (P), then Moore had (or must have had) a bad day (B).

Hell Hath Enlarged Herself

The fearful, and unbelieving, and the abominable, and murderers, and whoremongers, and sorcerers, and idolaters, and all liars, shall have their part in the lake which burneth with fire and brimstone.

—*(Revelation 21:8)*

This came to us in a brochure from a religious sect offering salvation for the believer. Notice, though, that the passage from the Bible doesn't say that if you believe you won't go to hell. It says, if you don't believe, you will go to hell.

Using the letters indicated in parentheses, we'd symbolize this as

   P → B

Don't worry about the grammatical tenses; we'll adjust those in whatever way necessary so that the claims make sense. We can use "if" in front of a conditional's antecedent, or we can use "only if" in front of its consequent; we produce exactly equivalent claims in the two cases. As in the case with "if," it doesn't matter where the "only if" part of the claim occurs. The part of this claim that's about Moore is the consequent, even though it occurs at the beginning of this version:

   Only if Moore has a bad day will Parker beat him at 9-ball.

Exercise 10-1

Symbolize the following using the claim variables P and Q. (You can ignore differences in past, present, and future tense.)

▲ 1. If Quincy learns to symbolize, Paula will be amazed.
▲ 2. Paula will teach him if Quincy pays her a big fee.
▲ 3. Paula will teach him only if Quincy pays her a big fee.
▲ 4. Only if Paula helps him will Quincy pass the course.
▲ 5. Quincy will pass if and only if Paula helps him.

Claim 5 in the preceding exercise introduces a new wrinkle, the phrase "if and only if." Remembering our rules of thumb about how "if" and "only if" operate separately, it shouldn't surprise us that "if and only if" makes both antecedent and consequent out of the claim it introduces. We can make P both antecedent and consequent this way:

(P → Q) & (Q → P)

There are other ways to produce conditionals, of course. In one of its senses, the word "provided" (and the phrase "provided that") works like the word "if" in introducing the antecedent of a conditional. "Moore will buy the car, provided the seller throws in a ton of spare parts" is equivalent to the same expression with the word "if" in place of "provided."

Necessary and Sufficient Conditions   Conditional claims are sometimes spelled out in terms of necessary and sufficient conditions. Consider this example:

The presence of oxygen is a necessary condition for combustion.

This tells us that we can't have combustion without oxygen, or "If we have combustion (C), then we must have oxygen (O)." Notice that the necessary condition becomes the consequent of a conditional: C → O.

A sufficient condition *guarantees* whatever it is a sufficient condition for. Being born in the United States is a sufficient condition for U.S. citizenship—that's *all* one needs to be a U.S. citizen. Sufficient conditions are expressed as the antecedents of conditional claims, so we would say, "If John was born in the United States (B), then John is a U.S. citizen (C)": B → C.

You should also notice the connection between "if" and "only if" on the one hand and necessary and sufficient conditions on the other. The word "if," by itself, introduces a sufficient condition; the phrase "only if" introduces a necessary condition. So, the claim "X is a necessary condition for Y" would be symbolized "Y → X."

From time to time, one thing will be both a necessary and a sufficient condition for something else. For example, if Jean's payment of her dues to the National Truth-Functional Logic Society (NTFLS) guaranteed her continued membership (making such payment a sufficient condition) and there was no way for her to continue membership *without* paying her dues (making payment a necessary condition as well), then we could express such a situation as "Jean will remain a member of the NTFLS (M) if and only if she pays her dues (D)": (M → D) & (D → M).

We often play fast and loose with how we state necessary and sufficient conditions. A parent tells his daughter, "You can watch television only if you clean your room." Now, the youngster would ordinarily take cleaning her room as both a necessary and a sufficient condition for being allowed to watch television, and probably that's what a parent would intend by those words. But notice that the parent actually stated only a necessary condition; technically, he would not be going back on what he said if room cleaning turned out not to be sufficient for television privileges. Of course he'd better be prepared for more than a logic lesson from his daughter in such a case, and most of us would be on her side in the dispute. But, literally, it's the necessary condition that the phrase "only if" introduces, not the sufficient condition.

Okay, Lew, the deal is, you can use the car tonight only if you wash and wax it this afternoon.

▲ *Comment: We often use "only if" when we mean to state both necessary and sufficient conditions, even though, literally speaking, it produces only the former. If Lew were a critical thinker, he'd check this deal more carefully before getting out the hose and bucket.*

"Unless" Consider the claim "Paula will foreclose unless Quincy pays up." Asked to symbolize this, we might come up with $\sim Q \rightarrow P$ because the original claim is equivalent to "If Quincy doesn't pay up, then Paula will foreclose." But there's an even simpler way to do it. Ask yourself, what is the truth table for $\sim Q \rightarrow P$? If you've gained familiarity with the basic truth tables by this time, you realize that it's the same as the table for P v Q. And, as a matter of fact, you can treat the word "unless" exactly like the word "or" and symbolize it with a "v."

"Either . . ." Sometimes we need to know exactly where a disjunction begins; it's the job of the word "either" to show us. Compare the claims

    Either P and Q or R

and

    P and either Q or R.

These two claims say different things and have different truth tables, but the only difference between them is the location of the word "either"; without that word, the claim would be completely ambiguous. "Either" tells us that the disjunction begins with P in the first claim and Q in the second claim. So we would symbolize the first (P & Q) v R and the second P & (Q v R).

The word "if" does much the same job for conditionals as "either" does for disjunctions. Notice the difference between

> P and if Q then R

and

> If P and Q then R.

"If" tells us that the antecedent begins with Q in the first example and with P in the second. Hence, the second must have P & Q for the antecedent of its symbolization.

In general, the trick to symbolizing a claim correctly is to pay careful attention to exactly what the claim says—and this often means asking yourself just exactly what would make this claim false (or true). Then try to come up with a symbolization that says the same thing—that is false (or true) in exactly the same circumstances. There's no substitute for practice, so here's an exercise to work on.

Exercise 10-2 ———————————————————————————

When we symbolize a claim, we're displaying its truth-functional structure. Show that you can figure out the structures of the following claims by symbolizing them. Use these letters for the first ten items:

> P = Parsons objects.
> Q = Quincy turns (or will turn) the radio down.
> R = Rachel closes (or will close) her door.

Use the symbols ~, &, v, and →. We suggest that, at least at first, you make symbolization a two-stage process: First, replace simple parts of claims with letters; then, replace logical words with logical symbols, and add parentheses as required. We'll do an example in two stages to show you what we mean.

Example

> If Parsons objects, then Quincy will turn the radio down but Rachel will not close her door.
>
> Stage 1: If P, then Q but ~R.
> Stage 2: P → (Q & ~R)

▲ 1. If Parsons objects then Quincy will turn the radio down, and Rachel will close her door.

▲ 2. If Parsons objects, then Quincy will turn the radio down and Rachel will close her door.

3. If Parsons objects and Quincy turns the radio down then Rachel will close her door.

4. Parsons objects and if Quincy turns the radio down Rachel will close her door.

▲ 5. If Parsons objects then if Quincy turns the radio down Rachel will close her door.

6. If Parsons objects Quincy turns the radio down, and if Rachel closes her door Quincy turns the radio down.

7. Quincy turns the radio down if either Parsons objects or Rachel closes her door.

8. Either Parsons objects or, if Quincy turns the radio down, then Rachel will close her door.

9. If either Parsons objects or Quincy turns the radio down then Rachel will close her door.

10. If Parsons objects then either Quincy will turn the radio down or Rachel will close her door.

For the next ten items, use the following letters:

C = My car runs well.
S = I will sell my car.
F = I will have my car fixed.

▲ 11. If my car doesn't run well, then I will sell it.

▲ 12. It's not true that if my car runs well, then I will sell it.

13. I will sell my car only if it doesn't run well.

14. I won't sell my car unless it doesn't run well.

15. I will have my car fixed unless it runs well.

▲ 16. I will sell my car, but only if it doesn't run well.

17. Provided my car runs well, I won't sell it.

18. My car's running well is a sufficient condition for my not having it fixed.

19. My car's not running well is a necessary condition for my having it fixed.

▲ 20. I will neither have my car fixed nor sell it.

Exercise 10-3

Construct truth tables for the symbolizations you produced for Exercise 10-2. Determine whether any of them are truth-functionally equivalent to any others. (Answers to items 1, 5, and 12 are provided in the answer section at the end of the book.)

Truth-Functional Arguments

Categorical syllogisms (discussed in Chapter 9) have a total of 256 forms. A truth-functional argument, by contrast, can take any of an infinite number of forms. Nevertheless, we have methods for testing for validity that are flexible enough to encompass every truth-functional argument. In the remainder of this chapter, we'll look at three of them: the truth-table method, the short truth-table method, and the method of deduction.

Before doing anything else, though, let's quickly review the concept of validity. An argument is *valid*, you'll recall, if and only if the truth of the premises guarantees the truth of the conclusion—that is, if the premises were true, the conclusion could not then be false. (In logic, remember, it doesn't matter whether the premises are *actually* true.)

The *truth-table test for validity* requires familiarity with the truth tables for the four truth-functional symbols, so go back and check yourself on those if you think you may not understand them clearly. Here's how the method works: We present all of the possible circumstances for an argument by building a truth table for it, then we simply look to see if there are any circumstances in which the premises are all true and the conclusion false. If there are such circumstances—one row of the truth table is all that's required—then the argument is invalid.

Let's look at a simple example. Let P and Q represent any two claims. Now look at the following symbolized argument:

P → Q
~P
Therefore, ~Q

We can construct a truth table for this argument by including a column for each premise and one for the conclusion:

P	Q	~P	P → Q	~Q
T	T	F	T	F
T	F	F	F	T
F	T	T	T	F
F	F	T	T	T

The first two columns are reference columns; they list truth values for the letters that appear in the argument. The third and fourth columns appear under the two premises of the argument, and the fifth column is for the conclusion. Note that in the third row of the table, both premises are true and the conclusion is false. This tells us that it is possible for the premises of this argument to be true while the conclusion is false; thus, the argument is invalid. Because it doesn't matter what claims P and Q might stand for,

A Real-Life Example

Sometimes it takes effort to see the truth-functional logic in a passage. To illustrate, consider the letter to Marilyn vos Savant in the column printed below:

If homosexuality is a product of nature and not chosen, are fewer homosexuals being born every year? As homosexuality becomes more acceptable, it seems logical that passing genetic material to offspring should be declining.

—*Wes Alexander, Lilburn, Ga.*

We don't know how many gay people there were in the past any more than we know how many gay people there are now. Estimates of today's gay population range from 1% to 10%, but we don't know whether the number is up, down or stable.

The genetic situation is also unknown. For example, genes can be passed on by people who are themselves unaffected by them. And gay people could be born that way for reasons other than strictly genetic ones: Conditions during pregnancy play an important role in the development of the unborn baby.

Even the social situation is unclear. Gay people may want to have families as much (or as little) as straight people do. After all, when heterosexual couples make love, they usually aren't trying to conceive. A desire for a heterosexual relationship is definitely not the same thing as a desire to become a parent.

Anyway, population is determined by women—heterosexual *and* homosexual. A gay woman is just as capable of having a baby and, if she wants to be a mother, that's what she'll do. And like a straight woman, she has a choice of straight and gay partners. The main difference is that she's less likely to live with him afterward. Either way, the population statistics are unaffected.

Can you see that the letter has this form?

H = Homosexuality is becoming more acceptable
P = Homosexuality is a product of nature and not chosen
F = Fewer homosexuals are born every year

H
H → (P → F)
~ F
/∴ ~ P

Be sure to notice which premises Ask Marilyn disputes (and why).

the same is true for *every* argument of this pattern. Here's an example of such an argument:

> If the Saints beat the Forty-Niners, then the Giants will make the playoffs. But the Saints won't beat the Forty-Niners. So the Giants won't make the playoffs.

Using S for "The Saints beat (or will beat) the Forty-Niners," and G for "The Giants make (or will make) the playoffs," we can symbolize the argument like this:

$$S \rightarrow G$$
$$\frac{\sim S}{\sim G}$$

The first premise is a conditional, and the other premise is the negation of the antecedent of that conditional. The conclusion is the negation of the conditional's consequent. It has exactly the same structure as the argument for which we just did the truth table; accordingly, it too is invalid.

Let's do another simple one:

> We're going to have large masses of arctic air (A) flowing into the Midwest unless the jet stream (J) moves south. Unfortunately, there's no chance of the jet stream's moving south. So you can bet there'll be arctic air flowing into the Midwest.

Symbolization gives us

$$A \lor J$$
$$\frac{\sim J}{A}$$

Here's a truth table for the argument:

1	2	3	4
A	J	A v J	~J
T	T	T	F
T	F	T	T
F	T	T	F
F	F	F	T

Note that the first premise is represented in column 3 of the table, the second premise in column 4, and the conclusion in one of the reference columns, column 1. Now, let's recall what we're up to. We want to know whether this argument is valid—that is to say, is it possible for the premises to be true and the conclusion false? If there is such a possibility, it will turn up in the truth table because, remember, the truth table represents every possible situation with respect to the claims A and J. We find that the premises are both true in only one row, the second, and when we check the conclusion, A, we find it is true in that row. Thus, there is *no* row in which the premises are true and the conclusion false. So the argument is valid.

Here's an example of a rather more complicated argument:

> If Scarlet is guilty of the crime, then Ms. White must have left the back door unlocked and the colonel must have retired before ten o'clock. However, either Ms. White did not leave the back door unlocked, or the colonel did not retire before ten. Therefore, Scarlet is not guilty of the crime.

Let's assign some letters to the simple claims so that we can show this argument's pattern.

> S = Scarlet is guilty of the crime.
> W = Ms. White left the back door unlocked.
> C = The colonel retired before ten o'clock.

Now we symbolize the argument to display this pattern:

> S → (W & C)
> ~W v ~C
> —————————
> ~S

Let's think our way through this argument. As you read, refer back to the symbolized version above. Notice that the first premise is a conditional, with "Scarlet is guilty of the crime" as antecedent and a conjunction as consequent. In order for that conjunction to be true, both "Ms. White left the back door unlocked" and "The colonel retired before ten o'clock" have to be true, as you'll recall from the truth table for conjunctions. Now look at the second premise. It is a disjunction that tells us *either* Ms. White did not leave the back door unlocked *or* the colonel did not retire before ten. But if either or both of those disjuncts are true, at least one of the claims in our earlier conjunction is false. So it cannot be that *both* parts of the conjunction are true. This means the conjunction symbolized by W & C must be false. And so the consequent of the first premise is false. How can the entire premise be true, in that case? The only way is for the antecedent to be false as well. And that means that the conclusion, "Scarlet is not guilty of the crime," must be true.

All of this reasoning (and considerably more that we don't require) is implicit in the following truth table for the argument:

If Saddam doesn't back down, the U.S. should launch an air strike. He backed down. Therefore, we shouldn't launch a strike.

—RICHARD COHEN, Secretary of Defense

Whoops, a mistake in logic. See Appendix 3 for the name of the mistake.

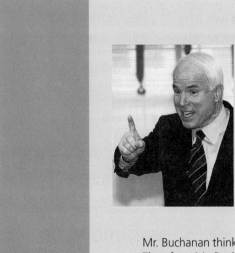

Rule 1

Hitler was clearly intent on taking over the world. Mr. Buchanan thinks we should have stood by silently watching, and so, no, I would not say he belongs in the Republican Party.

The remark by Senator John McCain of Arizona is actually Rule 1 (page 357) with an unstated premise, in effect:

[If Mr. Buchanan thinks we should have stood by silently watching, then Mr. Buchanan does not belong in the Republican Party.]

Mr. Buchanan thinks we should have stood by silently watching.
Therefore, Mr. Buchanan does not belong in the Republican Party.

1 S	2 W	3 C	4 ~W	5 ~C	6 W & C	7 S → (W & C)	8 ~W v ~C	9 ~S
T	T	T	F	F	T	T	F	F
T	T	F	F	T	F	F	T	F
T	F	T	T	F	F	F	T	F
T	F	F	T	T	F	F	T	F
F	T	T	F	F	T	T	F	T
F	T	F	F	T	F	T	T	T
F	F	T	T	F	F	T	T	T
F	F	F	T	T	F	T	T	T

We've numbered the columns at the top to make reference somewhat easier. The first three are our reference columns, columns 7 and 8 are for the premises of the argument, and column 9 is for the argument's conclusion. The remainder—4, 5, and 6—are for parts of some of the other symbolized claims; they could be left out if we desired, but they make filling in columns 7 and 8 a bit easier.

Once the table is filled in, evaluating the argument is easy. Just look to see whether there is any row in which the premises are true and the conclusion is false. One such row is enough to demonstrate the invalidity of the argument.

In the present case, we find that both premises are true only in the last three rows of the table. And in those rows, the conclusion is also true. So there is no set of circumstances—no row of the table—in which both premises are true and the conclusion is false. Therefore, the argument is valid.

Although filling out a complete truth table always produces the correct answer regarding a truth-functional argument's validity, it can be quite a tedious chore—in fact, life is much too short to spend much of it filling in truth tables. Fortunately, there are shorter and more manageable ways of finding such an answer. The easiest systematic way to determine the validity or invalidity of truth-functional arguments is the *short truth-table method.* Here's the idea behind it: Because, if an argument is invalid, there has to be at least one row in the argument's truth table where the premises are true and the conclusion is false, we'll look directly for such a row. Consider this symbolized argument:

$P \rightarrow Q$
$\sim Q \rightarrow R$
_____
$\sim P \rightarrow R$

We begin by looking at the conclusion. Because it's a conditional, it can be made false only one way, by making its antecedent true and its consequent false. So we do that, by making P false and R false.

Can we now make both premises true? Yes, as it turns out, by making Q true. This case,

P	Q	R
F	T	F

makes both premises true and the conclusion false and thus proves the argument invalid. What we've done is produce the relevant row of the truth table without bothering to produce all the rest. Had the argument been valid, we would not have been able to produce such a row.

Here's how the method works with a valid argument. Consider this example:

$(P \vee Q) \rightarrow R$
$S \rightarrow Q$
_____
$S \rightarrow R$

The only way to make the conclusion false is to make S true and R false. So we do that:

P	Q	R	S
		F	T

Now, with S true, the second premise requires that we make Q true. So we do that next:

P	Q	R	S
T	F	T	

But now, there is no way at all to make the first premise true, because P v Q is going to be true (because Q is true) and R is already false. Because there is no other way to make the conclusion false and the second premise true and because this way fails to make the first premise true, we can conclude that the argument is *valid.*

In some cases, there may be more than one way to make the conclusion false. Here's a symbolized example:

P & (Q v R)
R → S
P → T
—————
S & T

Because the conclusion is a conjunction, it is false if either or both of its conjuncts are false, which means we could begin by making S true and T false, S false and T true, or both S and T false. This is trouble we'd like to avoid if possible, so let's see if there's someplace else we can begin making our assignment. (Remember: The idea is to try to assign true and false to the letters so as to make the premises true and the conclusion false. If we can do it, the argument is invalid.)

In this example, to make the first premise true, we *must* assign true to the letter P. Why? Because the premise is a conjunction and both of its parts must be true for the whole thing to be true. That's what we're looking for: places where we are *forced* to make an assignment of true or false to one or more letters. Then we take those assignments and see where they lead us. In this case, once we've made P true, we see that, to make the third premise true, we are forced to make T true (because a true antecedent and a false consequent would make the premise false, and we're trying to make our premises true).

After making T true, we see that, to make the conclusion false, S must be false. So we make that assignment. At this point we're nearly done, needing only assignments for Q and R.

P	Q	R	S	T
T			F	T

Are there any other assignments that we're forced to make? Yes: We must make R false to make the second premise true. Once we've done that, we see that Q must be true to preserve the truth of the first premise. And that completes the assignment:

P	Q	R	S	T
T	T	F	F	T

This is one row in the truth table for this argument—the only row, as it turned out—in which all the premises are true and the conclusion is false; thus, it is the row that proves the argument invalid.

In the preceding example, there was a premise that forced us to begin with a particular assignment to a letter. Sometimes neither the conclusion nor any of the premises forces an assignment on us. In that case we must use trial and error: Begin with one assignment that makes the conclusion false (or some premise true) and see if it will work. If not, try another assignment. If all fail, then the argument is valid.

Often, several rows of a truth table will make the premises true and the conclusion false; any one of them is all it takes to prove invalidity. Don't get the mistaken idea that, just because the premises are all true in one row and so is the conclusion, the conclusion follows from the premises—that is, that the argument must be valid. To be valid, the conclusion must be true in *every* row in which all the premises are true.

To review: Try to assign Ts and Fs to the letters in the symbolization so that all premises come out true and the conclusion comes out false. There may be more than one way to do it; any of them will do to prove the argument invalid. If it is impossible to make the premises and conclusion come out this way, the argument is valid.

Exercise 10-4

Construct full truth tables or use the short truth-table method to determine which of the following arguments are valid.

▲ 1. P v ~Q
   ~Q
   ―――――
   ~P

2. P → Q
   ~Q
   ―――――
   ~P

3. ~ (P v Q)
   R → P
   ―――――
   ~R

▲ 4. P → (Q → R)
   ~ (P → Q)
   ―――――
   R

5. $P \lor (Q \rightarrow R)$
   $\underline{Q \,\&\, \sim R}$
   $\sim P$

6. $(P \rightarrow Q) \lor (R \rightarrow Q)$
   $\underline{P \,\&\, (\sim P \rightarrow \sim R)}$
   Q

▲ 7. $(P \,\&\, R) \rightarrow Q$
   $\underline{\sim Q }$
   $\sim P$

8. $P \,\&\, (\sim Q \rightarrow \sim P)$
   $\underline{R \rightarrow \sim Q }$
   $\sim R$

9. $L \lor \sim J$
   $\underline{R \rightarrow J }$
   $L \rightarrow \sim R$

10. $\sim F \lor (G \,\&\, H)$
    $\underline{P \rightarrow F }$
    $\sim H \rightarrow \sim P$

Exercise 10-5

Use either the long or short truth-table method to determine which of the following arguments are valid.

▲ 1. $K \rightarrow (L \,\&\, G)$
   $M \rightarrow (J \,\&\, K)$
   $\underline{B \,\&\, M }$
   $B \,\&\, G$

▲ 2. $L \lor (W \rightarrow S)$
   $P \lor \sim S$
   $\underline{\sim L \rightarrow W }$
   P

▲ 3. $M \,\&\, P$
   $R \rightarrow \sim P$
   $F \lor R$
   $\underline{G \rightarrow M }$
   $G \,\&\, F$

▲ 4. (D & G) → H
   M & (H → P)
   M → G
   _____

   D & P

▲ 5. R → S
   (S & B) → T
   T → E
   _____

   (R v B) → E

Deductions

The next method we'll look at is less useful for proving an argument *invalid* than the truth-table methods, but it has some advantages in proving that an argument is valid. The method is that of **deduction.**

When we use this method, we actually deduce (or "derive") the conclusion from the premises by means of a series of basic truth-functionally valid argument patterns. This is a lot like "thinking through" the argument, taking one step at a time to see how, once we've assumed the truth of the premises, we eventually arrive at the conclusion. We'll consider some extended examples showing how the method works as we explain the first few basic argument patterns. We'll refer to these patterns as truth-functional rules because they govern what steps we're allowed to take in getting from the premises to the conclusion. (Your instructor may ask that you simply learn some or all of the basic valid argument patterns. It's a good idea to be able to identify these patterns whether you go on to construct deductions from them or not.)

■ *Group I Rules: Elementary Valid Argument Patterns*

This first group of rules should be learned before you go on to the Group II rules. Study them until you can work Exercise 10-6 with confidence.

Rule 1: Modus ponens (MP), also known as affirming the antecedent   Any argument of the pattern

   P → Q
   P
   _____

   Q

is valid. If you have a conditional among the premises and if the antecedent of that conditional occurs as another premise, then by **modus ponens** the consequent of the conditional follows from those two premises. The claims involved do not have to be simple letters standing alone—it would have made no difference if, in place of P, we had had something more complicated, such as (P v R), as long as that compound claim appeared everywhere that P appears in the pattern above. For example:

1. (P v R) → Q   Premise
2. P v R   Premise

3. Q   From the premises, by modus ponens

The idea, once again, is that if you have *any conditional whatsoever* on a line of your deduction and if you have the antecedent of that conditional on some other line, you can write down the consequent of the conditional on your new line.

If the consequent of the conditional is the conclusion of the argument, then the deduction is finished—the conclusion has been established. If it is not the conclusion of the argument you're working on, the consequent of the conditional can be listed just as if it were another premise to use in deducing the conclusion you're after. An example:

1. P → R
2. R → S
3. P   Therefore, S

We've numbered the three premises of the argument and set its conclusion off to the side. (Hereafter we'll use a slash and three dots [/∴] in place of "therefore" to indicate the conclusion.) Now, notice that line 1 is a conditional, and line 3 is its antecedent. Modus ponens allows us to write down the consequent of line 1 as a new line in our deduction:

4. R   1, 3, MP

At the right we've noted the abbreviation for the rule we used and the lines the rule required. These notes are called the *annotation* for the deduction. We can now make use of this new line in the deduction to get the conclusion we were originally after, namely, S.

5. S   2, 4, MP

Again, we used modus ponens, this time on lines 2 and 4. The same explanation as that for deriving line 4 from lines 1 and 3 applies here.

Notice that the modus ponens rule and all other Group I rules can be used only on whole lines. This means that you can't find the items you need for MP as *parts* of a line, as in the following:

P v (Q → R)
Q

P v R   (erroneous!)

THE BORN LOSER reprinted by permission of Newspaper Enterprise Association, Inc.

This is *not* a legitimate use of MP. We do have a conditional as *part* of the first line, and the second line is indeed the antecedent of that conditional. But the rule cannot be applied to parts of lines. The conditional required by rule MP must take up the entire line, as in the following:

$$P \rightarrow (Q \vee R)$$
$$\underline{P}$$
$$Q \vee R$$

Rule 2: Modus tollens (MT), also known as **denying the consequent**   The **modus tollens** pattern is this:

$$P \rightarrow Q$$
$$\underline{\sim Q}$$
$$\sim P$$

If you have a conditional claim as one premise and if one of your other premises is the negation of the consequent of that conditional, you can write down the negation of the conditional's antecedent as a new line in your deduction. Here's a deduction that uses both of the first two rules:

1. $(P \,\&\, Q) \rightarrow R$
2. S

3. S → ~R   /∴ ~(P & Q)
4. ~R   2, 3, MP
5. ~(P & Q)   1, 4, MT

In this deduction we derived line 4 from lines 2 and 3 by modus ponens, and then 4 and 1 gave us line 5, which is what we were after, by modus tollens. The fact that the antecedent of line 1 is itself a compound claim, (P & Q), is not important; our line 5 is the antecedent of the conditional with a negation sign in front of it, and that's all that counts.

Rule 3: Chain argument (CA)

P → Q
Q → R
―――
P → R

The **chain argument** rule allows you to derive a conditional from two you already have, provided the antecedent of one of your conditionals is the same as the consequent of the other.

Rule 4: Disjunctive argument (DA)

P v Q   P v Q
~P   ~Q
――   ――
Q   P

From a disjunction and the negation of one disjunct, the other disjunct may be derived.

Rule 5: Simplification (SIM)   This one is obvious, but we need it for obvious reasons:

P & Q   P & Q
―――   ―――
P   Q

If the conjunction is true, then of course the conjuncts must all be true. You can pull out one conjunct from any conjunction and make it the new line in your deduction.

Rule 6: Conjunction (CONJ)

P
Q
―――
P & Q

If the Dollar Falls...

The valid argument patterns are in fact fairly common. Here's one in an article in *Time* as to why a weakening dollar is a threat to the stock market:

> Why should we care? . . . If the dollar continues to droop, investors may be tempted to move their cash to currencies on the upswing. That would drive the U.S. market lower. . . . because foreigners hold almost 40% of U.S. Treasury securities, any pullout would risk a spike in interest rates that would ultimately slaughter the bull market.

The chain argument here is reasonably obvious. In effect: If the dollar falls, then investors move their cash to currencies on the upswing. If investors move their cash to currencies on the upswing, then the U.S. market goes lower. If the U.S. market goes lower, then interest rates on U.S. Treasury securities rise. If interest rates on U.S. Treasury securities rise, then the bull market dies. [Therefore, if the dollar falls, then the bull market dies.]

This rule allows you to put any two lines of a deduction together in the form of a conjunction.

Rule 7: Addition (ADD)

$$\frac{P}{P \vee Q} \qquad \frac{Q}{P \vee Q}$$

Clearly, no matter what claims P and Q might be, if P is true then *either* P or Q must be true. The truth of one disjunct is all it takes to make the whole disjunction true.

Rule 8: Constructive dilemma (CD)

$$\frac{\begin{array}{l} P \to Q \\ R \to S \\ P \vee R \end{array}}{Q \vee S}$$

The disjunction of the antecedents of any two conditionals allows the derivation of the disjunction of their consequents.

Rule 9: Destructive dilemma (DD)

$$P \rightarrow Q$$
$$R \rightarrow S$$
$$\underline{\sim Q \vee \sim S}$$
$$\sim P \vee \sim R$$

The disjunction of the negations of the consequents of two conditionals allows the derivation of the disjunction of the negations of their antecedents. (Refer to the pattern above as you read this, and it will make a lot more sense.)

Exercise 10-6

For each of the following groups of symbolized claims, identify which of the Group I rules was used to derive the last line.

▲ 1. $P \rightarrow (Q \ \& \ R)$
$(Q \ \& \ R) \rightarrow (S \vee T)$
$P \rightarrow (S \vee T)$

▲ 2. $(P \ \& \ S) \vee (T \rightarrow R)$
$\sim (P \ \& \ S)$
$T \rightarrow R$

▲ 3. $P \vee (Q \ \& \ R)$
$(Q \ \& \ R) \rightarrow S$
$P \rightarrow T$
$S \vee T$

▲ 4. $(P \vee R) \rightarrow Q$
$\sim Q$
$\sim (P \vee R)$

▲ 5. $(Q \rightarrow T) \rightarrow S$
$\sim S \vee \sim P$
$R \rightarrow P$
$\sim (Q \rightarrow T) \vee \sim R$

Exercise 10-7

Construct deductions for each of the following using the Group I rules. Each can be done in just a step or two (except number 10, which takes more).

▲ 1. 1. $R \rightarrow P$
   2. $Q \rightarrow R$ $/ \therefore Q \rightarrow P$

  2. 1. $P \rightarrow S$
   2. $P \vee Q$
   3. $Q \rightarrow R$ $/ \therefore S \vee R$

God and Evil

An age-old argument that God is either not all powerful or not all good goes like this:

> If God is all powerful, then he would be able to abolish evil.
> If God is all good, then he would not allow evil to be.
> Either God is not able to abolish evil, or God allows evil to be.
> Therefore, either God is not all powerful, or God is not all good.

This argument, you can see, is just an instance of Rule 9 (see page 362).

3. 1. R & S
   2. S → P   /∴ P

▲ 4. 1. P → Q
   2. ~P → S
   3. ~Q   /∴ S

5. 1. (P v Q) → R
   2. Q   /∴ R

6. 1. ~P
   2. ~(R & S) v Q
   3. ~P → ~Q   /∴ ~(R & S)

▲ 7. 1. ~S
   2. (P & Q) → R
   3. R → S   /∴ ~(P & Q)

8. 1. P → ~(Q & T)
   2. S → (Q & T)
   3. P   /∴ ~S

9. 1. (P v T) → S
   2. R → P
   3. R v Q
   4. Q → T   /∴ S

▲ 10. 1. (T v M) → ~Q
   2. (P → Q) & (R → S)
   3. T   /∴ ~P

■ Group II Rules: Truth-Functional Equivalences

A claim or part of a claim may be replaced by any claim or part of a claim to which it is equivalent by one of the following equivalence rules. Don't despair if this sounds complicated. The way such replacement works will become clear after a few examples.

There are a few differences between these rules about equivalences and the Group I rules. First, these rules allow us to go two ways instead of one—from either claim to its equivalent. Second, these rules allow us to replace part of a claim with an equivalent part, rather than having to deal with entire lines of a deduction all at once. In the examples that follow the first few rules, watch for both of these differences.

We'll use a double-headed arrow ($\leftrightarrow$) to indicate the equivalence of two claims.

Rule 10: Double negation (DN)

$$P \leftrightarrow \sim\sim P$$

This rule allows you to add or remove two negation signs in front of any claim, whether simple or compound. For example, this rule allows the derivation of either of the following from the other

$$P \rightarrow (Q \vee R) \qquad P \rightarrow \sim\sim(Q \vee R)$$

because the rule guarantees that (Q v R) and its double negation, $\sim\sim$(Q v R), are equivalent. This in turn guarantees that $P \rightarrow (Q \vee R)$ and $P \rightarrow \sim\sim(Q \vee R)$ are equivalent, and hence that each implies the other.

Here's an example of DN at work:

1. $P \vee \sim(Q \rightarrow R)$
2. $(Q \rightarrow R)$ /∴ P
3. $\sim\sim(Q \rightarrow R)$ 2, DN
4. P   1, 3, DA

Rule 11: Commutation (COM)

$$(P \,\&\, Q) \leftrightarrow (Q \,\&\, P)$$
$$(P \vee Q) \leftrightarrow (Q \vee P)$$

This rule simply allows any conjunction or disjunction to be "turned around," so that the conjuncts or disjuncts occur in reverse order. Here's an example:

$$P \rightarrow (Q \vee R) \qquad P \rightarrow (R \vee Q)$$

Notice that commutation is used on *part* of the claim—just the consequent.

Rule 12: Implication (IMPL)
This rule allows us to change a conditional into a disjunction and vice versa.

$$(P \rightarrow Q) \leftrightarrow (\sim P \vee Q)$$

Notice that the antecedent always becomes the negated disjunct, or vice versa, depending on which way you're going. Another example:

$(P \vee Q) \rightarrow R \leftrightarrow \sim(P \vee Q) \vee R$

Rule 13: Contraposition (CONTR)   This rule may remind you of the categorical operation of contraposition (see Chapter 9)—this rule is its truth-functional version.

$(P \rightarrow Q) \leftrightarrow (\sim Q \rightarrow \sim P)$

This rule allows us to exchange the places of a conditional's antecedent and consequent, but only by putting on or taking off a negation sign in front of each. Here's another example:

$(P \& Q) \rightarrow (P \vee Q) \leftrightarrow \sim(P \vee Q) \rightarrow \sim(P \& Q)$

Sometimes you want to perform contraposition on a symbolization that doesn't fit either side of the equivalence because it has a negation sign in front of either the antecedent or the consequent but not both. You can do what you want in such cases, but it takes two steps, one applying double negation and one applying contraposition. Here's an example:

$(P \vee Q) \rightarrow \sim R$
$\sim\sim(P \vee Q) \rightarrow \sim R$ Double negation
$R \rightarrow \sim(P \vee Q)$ Contraposition

Your instructor may allow you to combine these steps (and refer to both DN and CONTR in your annotation).

Rule 14: DeMorgan's Laws (DEM)

$\sim(P \& Q) \leftrightarrow (\sim P \vee \sim Q)$
$\sim(P \vee Q) \leftrightarrow (\sim P \& \sim Q)$

Notice that when the negation sign is "moved inside" the parentheses, the & changes into a v, or vice versa. It's important not to confuse the use of the negation sign in DeMorgan's Laws with that of the minus sign in algebra. Notice that when you take $\sim(P \vee Q)$ and "move the negation sign in," you do *not* get $(\sim P \vee \sim Q)$. The wedge must be changed to an ampersand or vice versa whenever DEM is used. You can think of $\sim(P \vee Q)$ and $(\sim P \& \sim Q)$ as saying "neither P nor Q," and you can think of $\sim(P \& Q)$ and $(\sim P \vee \sim Q)$ as saying "not both P and Q."

Rule 15: Exportation (EXP)

$[P \rightarrow (Q \rightarrow R)] \leftrightarrow [(P \& Q) \rightarrow R]$

Square brackets are used exactly as parentheses are. In English, the exportation rule says that "If P, then if Q, then R" is equivalent to "If both P and Q, then R." (The commas are optional in both claims.) If you look back to Exercise 10-2, items 3 and 5 (page 347), you'll notice that, according to the exportation rule, each of these can replace the other.

Rule 16: Association (ASSOC)

[P & (Q & R)] ↔ [(P & Q) & R]
[P v (Q v R)] ↔ [(P v Q) v R]

Association simply tells us that, when we have three items joined together with wedges or with ampersands, it doesn't matter which ones we group together. If we have a long disjunction with more than two disjuncts, it still requires only one of them to be true for the entire disjunction to be true; if it's a conjunction, then all the conjuncts have to be true, no matter how many of them there are, in order for the entire conjunction to be true. Your instructor may allow you to drop parentheses in such symbolizations, but if you're developing these rules as a formal system, he or she may not.

Rule 17: Distribution (DIST)

This rule allows us to "spread a conjunct across a disjunction" or to "spread a disjunct across a conjunction." In the first example below, look at the left-hand side of the equivalence. The P, which is conjoined with a disjunction, is picked up and dropped (distributed) across the disjunction by being conjoined with each part. (This is easier to understand if you see it done on a chalkboard than by trying to figure it out from the page in front of you.) The two versions of the rule, like those of DEM, allow us to do exactly with the wedge what we're allowed to do with the ampersand.

[P & (Q v R)] ↔ [(P & Q) v (P & R)]
[P v (Q & R)] ↔ [(P v Q) & (P v R)]

Rule 18: Tautology (TAUT)

(P v P) ↔ P
(P & P) ↔ P

This rule allows a few obvious steps; they are sometimes necessary to "clean up" a deduction.

Here are some deductions that use rules from both Group I and Group II. Look at them carefully, covering up the lines with a piece of paper and uncovering them one at a time as you progress. This gives you a chance to figure out what you might do before you see the answer. In any case, make sure you understand how each line was achieved before going on. If necessary, look up the rule used to make sure you understand it.

Group I

1. Modus ponens (MP) $P \rightarrow Q$ <u>P</u> Q	2. Modus tollens (MT) $P \rightarrow Q$ <u>$\sim Q$</u> $\sim P$	3. Chain argument (CA) $P \rightarrow Q$ <u>$Q \rightarrow R$</u> $P \rightarrow R$
4. Disjunctive argument (DA) $P \vee Q$ $P \vee Q$ <u>$\sim P$</u> <u>$\sim Q$</u> Q P	5. Simplification (SIM) <u>$P \& Q$</u> <u>$P \& Q$</u> P Q	6. Conjunction (CONJ) P <u>Q</u> $P \& Q$
7. Addition (ADD) <u>P</u> <u>Q</u> $P \vee Q$ $P \vee Q$	8. Constructive dilemma (CD) $P \rightarrow Q$ $R \rightarrow S$ <u>$P \vee Q$</u> $R \vee S$	9. Destructive dilemma (DD) $P \rightarrow Q$ $R \rightarrow S$ <u>$\sim Q \vee \sim S$</u> $\sim P \vee \sim R$

Group II

10. Double negation (DN) $P \longleftrightarrow \sim\sim P$	11. Commutation (COM) $(P \& Q) \longleftrightarrow (Q \& P)$ $(P \vee Q) \longleftrightarrow (Q \vee P)$	12. Implication (IMPL) $(P \rightarrow Q) \longleftrightarrow (\sim P \vee Q)$
13. Contraposition (CONTR) $(P \rightarrow Q) \longleftrightarrow (\sim Q \rightarrow \sim P)$	14. DeMorgan's Laws (DEM) $\sim(P \vee Q) \longleftrightarrow (\sim P \& \sim Q)$ $\sim(P \& Q) \longleftrightarrow (\sim P \vee \sim Q)$	15. Exportation (EXPORT) $[P \rightarrow (Q \rightarrow R)] \longleftrightarrow [(P \& Q) \rightarrow R]$
16. Association (ASSOC) $[P \& (Q\&R)] \longleftrightarrow [(P \& Q) \& R]$ $[P \vee (Q \vee R)] \longleftrightarrow [(P \vee Q) \vee R]$	17. Distribution (DIST) $[P \& (Q \vee R)] \longleftrightarrow [(P \& Q) \vee (P \& R)]$ $[P \vee (Q \& R)] \longleftrightarrow [(P \vee Q) \& (P \vee R)]$	18. Tautology (TAUT) $(P \vee P) \longleftrightarrow P$ $(P \& P) \longleftrightarrow P$

FIGURE 2   Truth-Functional Rules for Deductions

The first example is long, but fairly simple. Length is not always proportional to difficulty.

1. $P \rightarrow (Q \rightarrow R)$
2. $(T \rightarrow P) \& (S \rightarrow Q)$
3. $T \& S$ $/\therefore R$

4. T → P	2, SIM
5. S → Q	2, SIM
6. T	3, SIM
7. S	3, SIM
8. P	4, 6, MP
9. Q	5, 7, MP
10. P & Q	8, 9, CONJ
11. (P & Q) → R	1, EXP
12. R	10, 11, MP

It's often difficult to tell how to proceed when you first look at a deduction problem. One strategy is to work backward. Look at what you want to get, look at what you have, and see what you would need in order to get what you want. Then determine where you would get *that,* and so on. We'll explain in terms of the following problem.

1. P → (Q & R)		
2. S → ~Q		
3. S		/∴~P
4. ~Q	2, 3, MP	
5. ~Q v ~R	4, ADD	
6. ~(Q & R)	5, DEM	
7. ~P	1, 6, MT	

We began by wanting ~P as our conclusion. If we're familiar with modus tollens, it's clear from line 1 that we can get ~P if we can get the negation of line 1's consequent, which would be ~(Q & R). That in turn is the same as ~Q v ~R, which we can get if we can get either ~Q or ~R. So now we're looking for someplace in the first three premises where we can get ~Q. That's easy: from lines 2 and 3, by modus ponens. A little practice and you'll be surprised how easy these strategies are to work, at least *most* of the time!

Exercise 10-8

The annotations that explain how each line was derived have been left off the following deductions. For each line, supply the rule used and the numbers of any earlier lines the rule requires.

▲ 1.   1. P → Q   (Premise)
        2. R → S   (Premise)
        3. Q → ~S   (Premise) /∴P → ~R
        4. P → ~S
        5. ~S → ~R
        6. P → ~R

2. 1. ~P   (Premise)
    2. (Q → R) & (R → Q)   (Premise)
    3. R v P   (Premise) / ∴ Q
    4. R
    5. R → Q
    6. Q

3. 1. P → Q   (Premise)
    2. R → (~S v T)   (Premise)
    3. ~P → R   (Premise) / ∴ (~Q & S) → T
    4. ~Q → ~P
    5. ~Q → R
    6. ~Q → (~S v T)
    7. ~Q → (S → T)
    8. (~Q & S) → T

▲4. 1. (P & Q) → T   (Premise)
    2. P   (Premise)
    3. ~Q → ~P   (Premise) / ∴ T
    4. P → Q
    5. Q
    6. P & Q
    7. T

5. 1. ~(S v R)   (Premise)
    2. P → S   (Premise)
    3. T → (P v R)   (Premise) / ∴ ~T
    4. ~S & ~R
    5. ~S
    6. ~P
    7. ~R
    8. ~P & ~R
    9. ~(P v R)
    10. ~T

Exercise 10-9

Derive the indicated conclusions from the premises supplied.

▲ 1. 1. P & Q
      2. P → R   / ∴ R

▲ 2. 1. R → S
      2. ~P v R   / ∴ P → S

  3. 1. P v Q
     2. R & ~Q   / ∴ P

▲ 4. 1. ~P v (~Q v R)
      2. P   / ∴ Q → R

5. 1. T v P
   2. P → S   /∴~T → S

6. 1. Q v ~S
   2. Q → P   /∴S → P

7. 1. ~S v ~R
   2. P → (S & R)   /∴~P

▲ 8. 1. ~Q & (~S & ~T)
   2. P → (Q v S)   /∴~P

9. 1. P v (S & R)
   2. T → (~P & ~R) /∴~T

10. 1. (S & P) → R
    2. S   /∴P → R

Exercise 10-10

Derive the indicated conclusions from the premises supplied.

▲ 1. 1. P → R
   2. R → Q   /∴~P v Q

2. 1. ~P v S
   2. ~T → ~S   /∴P → T

3. 1. F → R
   2. L → S
   3. ~C
   4. (R & S) → C /∴~F v ~L

▲ 4. 1. P v (Q & R)
   2. (P v Q) → S /∴S

5. 1. (S & R) → P
   2. (R → P) → W
   3. S   /∴W

6. 1. ~L → (~P → M)
   2. ~(P v L)   /∴M

▲ 7. 1. (M v R) & P
   2. ~S → ~P
   3. S → ~M   /∴R

8. 1. Q → L
   2. P → M
   3. R v P
   4. R → (Q & S) /∴~M → L

9. 1. Q → S
   2. P → (S & L)
   3. ~P → Q
   4. S → R   /∴R & S

▲ 10. 1. P v (R & Q)
      2. R → ~P
      3. Q → T   /∴ R → T

■ *Conditional Proof*

Conditional proof (CP) is both a rule and a strategy for constructing a deduction. It is based on the following idea: Let's say we want to produce a deduction for a conditional claim, P → Q. If we produce such a deduction, what have we proved? We've proved the equivalent of "If P were true, then Q would be true." One way to do this is simply to *assume* that P is true (that is, to add it as an additional premise) and then to prove that, on that assumption, Q has to be true. If we can do that—prove Q after assuming P—then we'll have proved that if P then Q, or P → Q. Let's look at an example of how to do this; then we'll explain it again.

Here is the way we'll use CP as a new rule: Simply write down the antecedent of whatever conditional we want to prove, drawing a circle around the number of that step in the deduction; in the annotation write "CP Premise" for that step. Here's what it looks like:

    1. P v (Q → R)   Premise
    2. Q   Premise   /∴ ~P → R
    ③. ~P   CP Premise

Then, after we've proved what we want—the consequent of the conditional—in the next step, we write the full conditional down. Then we draw a line in the margin to the left of the deduction from the premise with the circled number to the number of the line we deduced from it. (See below for an example.) In the annotation for the last line in the process, list *all the steps from the circled number to the one with the conditional's consequent*, and give CP as the rule. Drawing the line that connects our earlier CP premise with the step we derived from it indicates we've stopped making the assumption that the premise, which is now the antecedent of our conditional in our last step, is true. This is known as *discharging the premise*. Here's how the whole thing looks:

    1. P v (Q → R)   Premise
    2. Q   Premise   /∴ ~P → R
    ③. ~P   CP Premise
    4. Q → R   1,3, DA
    5. R   2,4, MP
    6. ~P → R   3–5, CP

Here's the promised second explanation. Look at the example. Think of the conclusion as saying that, given the two original premises, *if* we had ~P, we could get R. One way to find out if this is so is to *give ourselves* ~P and then see if we can get R. In step 3, we do exactly that: We give ourselves ~P. Now, by circling the number, we indicate that *this is a premise we've given our-selves* (our "CP premise") and therefore that it's one we'll have to get rid of before we're done. (We can't be allowed to invent, use, and keep just any old premises we like—we could prove *anything* if we could do that.) But once we've given ourselves ~P, getting R turns out to be easy! Steps 4 and 5 are pretty obvious, aren't they? (If not, you need more practice with the other rules.) In steps 3 through 5 what we've actually proved is that *if we had ~P, then we could get R.* So we're justified in writing down step 6 because that's exactly what step 6 says: If ~P, then R.

Once we've got our conditional, ~P → R, we're no longer dependent on the CP premise, so we draw our line in the left margin from the last step that depended on the CP premise back to the premise itself. We *discharge* the premise.

Here are some very important restrictions on the CP rule:

1. CP can be used only to produce a conditional claim: After we discharge a CP premise, the very next step must be a conditional with the preceding step as consequent and the CP premise as antecedent. [Remember that lots of claims are equivalent to conditional claims. For example, to get (~P v Q), just prove (P → Q), and then use IMPL.]

2. If more than one use is made of CP at a time—that is, if more than one CP premise is brought in—they must be discharged in exactly the reverse order from that in which they were assumed. This means that the lines that run from different CP premises must not cross each other. See examples below.

3. Once a CP premise has been discharged, no steps derived from it—those steps encompassed by the line drawn in the left margin—may be used in the deduction. (They depend on the CP premise, you see, and it's been discharged.)

4. All CP premises must be discharged.

This sounds a lot more complicated than it actually is. Refer back to these restrictions on CP as you go through the examples, and they will make a good deal more sense.

Here's an example of CP in which two additional premises are assumed and discharged in reverse order.

1. P → [Q v (R & S)]	Premise	
2. (~Q → S) → T	Premise	/∴ P → T
⌐ ③ P	CP Premise	
4. Q v (R & S)	1,3, MP	
⌐ ⑤ ~Q	CP Premise	
6. R & S	4,5, DA	
7. S	6, SIM	
8. ~Q → S	5–7, CP	
9. T	2,8, MP	
10. P → T	3–9, CP	

Notice that the additional premise added at step 5 is discharged when step 8 is completed, and the premise at step 3 is discharged when step 10 is completed. Once again: Whenever you discharge a premise, you must make that premise the antecedent of the next step in your deduction. (You might try the preceding deduction without using CP; doing so will help you appreciate having the rule, however hard to learn it may seem at the moment. Using CP makes many deductions shorter, easier, or both.

Here are three more examples of the correct use of CP:

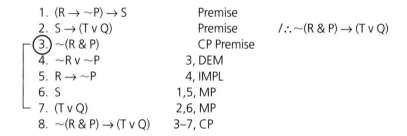

1. (R → ~P) → S   Premise
2. S → (T v Q)   Premise   /∴ ~(R & P) → (T v Q)
3. ~(R & P)   CP Premise
4. ~R v ~P   3, DEM
5. R → ~P   4, IMPL
6. S   1,5, MP
7. (T v Q)   2,6, MP
8. ~(R & P) → (T v Q)   3–7, CP

In this case, one use of CP follows another:

1. (P v Q) → R   Premise
2. (S v T) → U   Premise   /∴ (~R → ~P) & (~U → ~T)
3. ~R   CP Premise
4. ~(P v Q)   1,3, MT
5. ~P & ~Q   4, DEM
6. ~P   5, SIM
7. ~R → ~P   3–6, CP
8. ~U   CP Premise
9. ~(S v T)   2,8, MT
10. ~S & ~T   9, DEM
11. ~T   10, SIM
12. ~U → ~T   8–11, CP
13. (~R → ~P) & (~U → ~T)   7,12, CONJ

In this case, one use of CP occurs "inside" another:

1. R → (S & Q)   Premise
2. P → M   Premise
3. S → (Q → ~M)   Premise
4. (J v T) → B   Premise   /∴ R → (J → (B & ~P))

(5.) R	CP Premise
(6.) J	CP Premise
7. J v T	6, ADD
8. B	4,7, MP
9. (S & Q)	1,5, MP
10. (S & Q) → ~M	3, EXP
11. ~M	9,10, MP
12. ~P	2,11, MT
13. B & ~P	8,12, CONJ
14. J → (B & ~P)	6–13, CP
15. R → (J → (B & ~P))	5–14, CP

Recap

This chapter has been concerned with the truth-functional structures of claims and arguments. These structures result from the logical connections between claims, connections that are represented in English by words such as "and," "or," "if . . . then," and so forth.

Truth-functional connections are explained by truth tables, which display the conditions under which a claim is true and those under which it is false. Truth tables are used to define truth-functional symbols, which stand for logical connections between claims in symbolizations. To symbolize a claim is simply to reduce it to its truth-functional structure.

To evaluate truth-functional arguments—which are just arguments that depend on truth-functional connections for their validity—we learned first about the full truth-table method. This method requires that we set out a truth table for an argument and then check to see whether there are circumstances in which the premises are true and the conclusion false. In the short truth-table method, we look directly for such rows: If we find one, the argument is invalid; if we don't, it is valid.

We can improve our efficiency in determining the validity of many truth-functional arguments by learning to recognize certain elementary valid argument patterns. These patterns can be linked up to produce deductions, which are sequences of valid truth-functional inferences.

Having read this chapter and the chapter recap, you should be able to

▲ Explain truth tables and the four types of truth-functional claims

▲ Use truth tables to produce truth-functional analyses of claims

▲ Symbolize compound claims to display their truth-functional structure

▲ Evaluate truth-functional arguments using both the full truth-table method and the short truth-table method

▲ Explain the truth-functional rules that govern the basic valid argument patterns in deductive reasoning

▲ Demonstrate an understanding of the conditional proof strategy of deduction

Additional Exercises

Exercise 10-11

Display the truth-functional structure of the following claims by symbolizing them. Use the letters indicated.

D = We do something to reduce the deficit.
B = The balance of payments gets worse.
C = There is (or will be) a financial crisis.

▲ 1. The balance of payments will not get worse if we do something to reduce the deficit.

2. There will be no financial crisis unless the balance of payments gets worse.

3. Either the balance of payments will get worse or, if no action is taken on the deficit, there will be a financial crisis.

▲ 4. The balance of payments will get worse only if we don't do something to reduce the deficit.

5. Action cannot be taken on the deficit if there's a financial crisis.

6. I can tell you about whether we'll do something to reduce the deficit and whether our balance of payments will get worse: Neither one will happen.

▲ 7. In order for there to be a financial crisis, the balance of payments will have to get worse and there will have to be no action taken to reduce the deficit.

8. We can avoid a financial crisis only by taking action on the deficit and keeping the balance of payments from getting worse.

9. The *only* thing that can prevent a financial crisis is our doing something to reduce the deficit.

Exercise 10-12

For each of the numbered claims below, there is exactly one lettered claim that is equivalent. Identify the equivalent claim for each item. (Some lettered claims are equivalent to more than one numbered claim, so it will be necessary to use some letters more than once.)

▲ 1. Oil prices will drop if the OPEC countries increase their production.

2. Oil prices will drop only if the OPEC countries increase their production.

3. Neither will oil prices drop nor will the OPEC countries increase their production.

▲ 4. Oil prices cannot drop unless the OPEC countries increase their production.

5. The only thing that can prevent oil prices dropping is the OPEC countries' increasing their production.

6. A drop in oil prices is necessary for the OPEC countries to increase their production.

▲ 7. All it takes for the OPEC countries to increase their production is a drop in oil prices.

8. The OPEC countries will not increase their production while oil prices drop; each possibility excludes the other.
    a. It's not the case that oil prices will drop, and it's not the case that the OPEC countries will increase their production.
    b. If OPEC countries increase their production, then oil prices will drop.
    c. Only if OPEC countries increase their production will oil prices drop.
    d. Either the OPEC countries will not increase their production, or oil prices will not drop.
    e. If the OPEC countries do not increase production, then oil prices will drop.

Exercise 10-13

Construct deductions for each of the following. (Try these first without using conditional proof.)

▲ 1. 1. P
       2. Q & R
       3. (Q & P) → S   / ∴ S

   2. 1. (P v Q) & R
       2. (R & P) → S
       3. (Q & R) → S   / ∴ S

   3. 1. P → (Q → ~R)
       2. (~R → S) v T
       3. ~T & P   / ∴ Q → S

▲ 4. 1. P v Q
       2. (Q v U) → (P → T)
       3. ~P
       4. (~P v R) → (Q → S)   / ∴ T v S

   5. 1. (P → Q) & R
       2. ~S
       3. S v (Q → S)   / ∴ P → T

   6. 1. P → (Q & R)
       2. R → (Q → S)   / ∴ P → S

▲ 7. 1. P → Q   /∴ P → (Q v R)

   8. 1. ~P v ~Q
      2. (Q → S) → R   /∴ P → R

   9. 1. S
      2. P → (Q & R)
      3. Q → ~S   /∴ ~P

▲ 10. 1. (S → Q) → ~R
      2. (P → Q) → R   /∴ ~Q

Exercise 10-14

Use the rule of conditional proof to construct deductions for each of the following.

▲ 1. 1. P → Q
      2. P → R   /∴ P → (Q & R)

   2. 1. P → Q
      2. R → Q   /∴ (P v R) → Q

   3. 1. P → (Q → R)   /∴ (P → Q) → (P → R)

▲ 4. 1. P → (Q v R)
      2. T → (S & ~R)   /∴ (P & T) → Q

   5. 1. ~P → (~Q → ~R)
      2. ~(R & ~P) → ~S   /∴ S → Q

   6. 1. P → (Q → R)
      2. (T → S) & (R → T)   /∴ P → (Q → S)

▲ 7. 1. P v (Q & R)
      2. T → ~(P v U)
      3. S → (Q → ~R)   /∴ ~S v ~T

   8. 1. (P v Q) → R
      2. (P → S) → T   /∴ R v T

   9. 1. P → ~Q
      2. ~R → (S & Q)   /∴ P → R

▲ 10. 1. (P & Q) v R
      2. ~R v Q   /∴ P → Q

Exercise 10-15

Display the truth-functional form of the following arguments by symbolizing them; then use the truth-table method, the short truth-table method, or the method of deduction to prove them valid or invalid. Use the letters provided. (We've used underscores in the example and in the first two problems to help you connect the letters with the proper claims.)

Example

> If Maria does not go to the movies, then she will help Bob with his logic homework. Bob will fail the course unless Maria helps him with his logic homework. Therefore, if Maria goes to the movies, Bob will fail the course. (M, H, F)

Symbolization

1. ~M → H   (Premise)
2. ~H → F   (Premise)   /∴ M → F

Truth Table

M	H	F	~M	~H	~M → H	~H → F	M → F
T	T	T	F	F	T	T	T
T	T	F	F	F	T	T	F

We need to go only as far as the second row of the table, since both premises came out true and the conclusion comes out false in that row.

▲ 1. If it's cold, Dale's motorcycle won't start. If Dale is not late for work, then his motorcycle must have started. Therefore, if it's cold, Dale is late for work. (C, S, L)

2. If profits depend on unsound environmental practices, then either the quality of the environment will deteriorate, or profits will drop. Jobs will be plentiful only if profits do not drop. So, either jobs will not be plentiful, or the quality of the environment will deteriorate. (U, Q, D, J)

3. The new road will not be built unless the planning commission approves the funds. But the planning commission's approval of the funds will come only if the environmental impact report is positive, and it can't be positive if the road will ruin Mill Creek. So, unless they find a way for the road not to ruin Mill Creek, it won't be built. (R, A, E, M)

▲ 4. The message will not be understood unless the code is broken. The killer will not be caught if the message is not understood. Either the code will be broken, or Holmes's plan will fail. But Holmes's plan will not fail if he is given enough time. Therefore, if Holmes is given enough time, the killer will be caught. (M, C, K, H, T)

5. If the senator votes against this bill, then he is opposed to penalties against tax evaders. Also, if the senator is a tax evader himself, then he is opposed to penalties against tax evaders. Therefore, if the senator votes against this bill, he is a tax evader himself. (V, O, T)

6. If you had gone to class, taken good notes, and studied the text, you'd have done well on the exam. And, if you'd done well on the exam, you'd have passed the course. Since you did not pass the course and you did go to class, you must not have taken good notes and not studied the text.

▲ 7. Either John will go to class, or he'll miss the review session. If John misses the review session, he'll foul up the exam. If he goes to class, however, he'll miss his ride home for the weekend. So John's either going to miss his ride home or foul up the exam.

8. If the government's position on fighting crime is correct, then if more people are locked up, then the crime rate should drop. But the crime rate has not dropped despite the fact that we've been locking up record numbers of people. It follows that the government's position on fighting crime is not correct.

9. The creation story in the Book of Genesis is compatible with the theory of evolution, but only if the creation story is not taken literally. If, as most scientists think, there is plenty of evidence for the theory of evolution, the Genesis story cannot be true if it is not compatible with evolution theory. Therefore, if the Genesis story is taken literally, it cannot be true.

▲ 10. The creation story in the Book of Genesis is compatible with the theory of evolution, but only if the creation story is not taken literally. If there is plenty of evidence for the theory of evolution, which there is, the Genesis story cannot be true if it is not compatible with evolution theory. Therefore, if the Genesis story is taken literally, it cannot be true.

11. If there was no murder committed, then the victim must have been killed by the horse. But the victim could have been killed by the horse only if he, the victim, was trying to injure the horse before the race; and, in that case, there certainly was a crime committed. So, if there was no murder, there was still a crime committed.

12. Holmes cannot catch the train unless he gets to Charing Cross Station by noon; and if he misses the train, Watson will be in danger. Because Moriarty has thugs watching the station, Holmes can get there by noon only if he goes in disguise. So unless Holmes goes in disguise, Watson will be in danger.

▲ 13. It's not fair to smoke around nonsmokers if secondhand cigarette smoke really is harmful. If secondhand smoke were not harmful, the American Lung Association would not be telling us that it is. But they are telling us that it's harmful. That's enough to conclude that it's not fair to smoke around nonsmokers.

14. If Jane does any of the following, she's got an eating disorder: If she goes on eating binges for no apparent reason, if she looks forward to times when she can eat alone, or if she eats sensibly in front of others and makes up for it when she's alone. Jane does in fact go on eating binges for no apparent reason. So it's clear that she has an eating disorder.

15. The number of business majors increased markedly during the past decade; and if you see that happening, you know that younger people have developed a greater interest in money. Such an interest, unfortunately, means that greed has become a significant motivating force in our society; and if greed has become such a force, charity will have become insignificant. We can predict that charity will not be seen as a significant feature of this past decade.

Writing Exercises

1. a. In a one-page essay, evaluate the soundness of the argument in the box on page 363. Alternatively, in a one-page essay evaluate the soundness of the argument in the letter to Ask Marilyn (page 349). Write your name on the back of your paper.

   b. When everyone is finished, your instructor will collect the papers and re-distribute them to the class. In groups of four or five, read the papers that have been given to your group and select the best one. The instructor will select one group's top-rated paper to read to the class for discussion.

2. Take about fifteen minutes to write an essay responding to the paper the instructor has read to the class in Exercise 1. When everyone is finished, the members of each group will read each other's responses and select the best one to share with the class.

Chapter 11

Inductive Arguments

he premises of an inductive argument are not offered as definitive evidence for the truth of their conclusion, but rather as evidence for the likelihood of the conclusion's truth.* Remember, deductive arguments are either valid or invalid. But inductive arguments can fall anywhere on the scale from very strong to very weak. An inductive argument's premises can give powerful support for its conclusion, no support at all, or anything in between.

There are three main kinds of inductive arguments, and in this chapter we look at two of them.

Inductive Generalizations

In an **inductive generalization,** we generalize from a sample to an entire class. We reason that, because many (or most or all or some percentage) of a sample of the members of a class or "population" have a certain property or characteristic, many (or most or all or some percentage) of the members of the class or population also have that property or characteristic. Examples always help:

Example 1

Premise: Most Republicans I know are conservative.
Conclusion: Most Republicans are conservative.

---

*As we noted in Chapter 8, there is more than one way to distinguish deductive from inductive arguments.

Example 2

Premise: Many of the students in this class are over thirty.
Conclusion: Many of the students in this university are over thirty.

Example 3

Premise: Every transformer we have tested from this batch of transformers has been defective.
Conclusion: All the transformers in this batch of transformers are defective.

Example 4

Premise: Thirty percent of a random sample of registered voters say they would not vote for a woman president.
Conclusion: Thirty percent of all registered voters would say they would not vote for a woman president.

In the premise of each of these examples, the members of a **sample** are said to have a property. This is the **property in question.** In the conclusion, the property in question is attributed to many (or most or all or some percentage) of the entire class or population, called the **target** or **target class** (or population).

So, in the first example ("Most Republicans I know are conservative; therefore, most Republicans are conservative"), the sample is Republicans I know, the property in question is being conservative, and the target class is the entire class of Republicans.

In the second example ("Many of the students in this class are over thirty; therefore, many of the students at this university are over thirty"), the sample is students in this class, the property in question is being over thirty, and the target class is the entire class of students at this university.

In the third example ("Every transformer we have tested from this batch of transformers has been defective; therefore, all the transformers in this batch of transformers are defective"), the sample is transformers we have tested, the property in question is being defective, and the target or target class is the entire class of transformers in this batch.

In the last example ("Thirty percent of a random sample of registered voters say they would not vote for a woman president; therefore, thirty percent of all registered voters would say they would not vote for a woman president"), the sample is the random sample of registered voters, the property in question is the property of saying that they wouldn't vote for a woman president, and the target class or population is the entire class of registered voters.

■ *Representativeness and Bias*

In an inductive generalization we use a sample to reach a conclusion about a target class. Therefore, the sample must *represent* the target class. This is a crucially important idea. A sample represents a target class (is a **representa-**

tive sample) to the extent it possesses all features of the target relevant to the property in question and possesses them in the same proportions as the target. If a sample consists of unusual or atypical members of the target class, then we can't infer much about the target class by considering that sample. If you ask two opera buffs in between acts at an opera what they think of public funding for orchestras, you would be unwise to think their views represent general sentiment across the country.

The first thing to remember about generalizations, therefore, is this:

> **The less confidence we have that the sample of a class or population accurately represents the entire class or population, the less confidence we should have in the inductive generalization based on that sample.**

Whether an inductive generalization is strong or weak depends on whether or not the sample accurately represents the target class. A sample that doesn't accurately represent its class is a **biased sample.** It should be clear that the word "biased" is used here in a different sense from that in which we refer to a prejudiced person as biased (although the two meanings are related).

Look back at our first example ("Most Republicans I know are conservative; therefore, most Republicans are conservative"). The sample in the argument consists of Republicans the speaker knows. How well does that sample represent the entire class or population of Republicans? Well, if the speaker is Moore, probably a disproportionate number of Moore's Republican acquaintances are teachers, since Moore is a teacher. Unless a person's circumstances are rather unusual, his or her friends are not likely to accurately represent the entire class of Republicans.

Five out of four people have trouble with fractions.

So, again, a sample argument accurately represents a target class to the extent it has all relevant features of the target class in the same proportion as the target.

What features are relevant? A feature or property P is **relevant** to another feature or property Q if it is reasonable to suppose the presence or absence of P could affect the presence or absence of Q. Here's what we mean. Suppose we want to know what percentage of the registered voters in our state approve of a state lottery. Suppose we have a sample of registered voters whose religious convictions differed from those of the entire population of registered voters in the state. Are the religious convictions of the state's registered voters a relevant feature of that population, with respect to attitude on a state lottery? Yes, because it is reasonable to suppose a person's religious convictions could affect his or her view on gambling. Therefore, because the religious convictions of the sample are different from the religious convictions of the target population, the sample is biased. In contrast, what letter a person's name begins with is not relevant to attitude on a state lottery. Therefore, if in our sample the percentage of people whose names begin with M isn't the same as in the general population of registered voters in the state, that difference wouldn't matter. It is highly unlikely the letter a person's name begins with affects his or her views on gambling.

Or does it? Obviously our knowledge of what features affect what other features is limited. As a result, it can be difficult to have confidence that a sample of things accurately represents the entire target class or population. Fortunately, there are a couple of ways to get around this problem. First, if a class of things is homogeneous, then we can be confident in the representativeness of our sample. For example, if we had a batch of water molecules in a sterile beaker, then we could be confident that a sample of those water molecules—say, a couple of drops of water—would accurately represent the entire population. Or if we had a box of bolts all manufactured from the same raw materials by the same device, then we could be confident in the representativeness of a sample consisting of just a few of the bolts, though our confidence would be less than in the water example.

When we are dealing with heterogeneous populations (populations that are diverse in character), the most widely known method for achieving a representative sample is to select the sample at random from the target population. Statisticians have complicated ways of defining randomness, but we can get along with this simple version: A **random sample** of a population is one in which every individual in the population has an equal chance of being selected.

Devising a procedure by which members of a population are chosen randomly often requires careful thought. And it doesn't do much good to randomly select a sample from a subpopulation which itself doesn't accurately represent the target population. For example, suppose we want to know what percentage of the students in our university pray before final exams. Shall we take a random sample of student members of the campus Baptist Prayer Club? Obviously not. The sample is biased despite being random. It may be a random sample of the campus Baptist Prayer Club, but that doesn't make it a random sample of students in our university. Or suppose you want to know what percentage of voters in your state like the Republican candidate for governor. Will you take a random sample of voters in a wealthy neighborhood? You shouldn't. Random or not, the sample is still biased: It is a random sample of voters in that neighborhood, but not a random sample of voters in the state.

■ *Random Variation*

Another source of error in inductive generalizations is due to random variation. This needs explanation. Consider all the marbles in a large bin of marbles. (To simplify the example, we'll assume the marbles in the bin are well mixed.) Let's suppose that in fact 30 percent of these marbles are black. Now, if you grabbed a handful of the marbles, would you be surprised if, say, only 29 percent of the marbles in this particular sample were black? Of course not. You'd expect random variation from sample to sample. And if in the next handful 32 percent of the marbles were black, again you'd not be surprised. If you took a large series of samples, they would *average* very close to 30 percent, but you wouldn't expect *exactly* 30 percent of each and every sample to be black marbles.

Now suppose you don't know how many marbles in a bin of marbles are black, but you want to find out. This is what we do when we make an inductive generalization. We look at a sample of a population or class, and draw a conclusion about the whole population or class. Suppose, then, you reach into the bin, take out a handful, and find that 30 percent of your sample are black marbles. Would you conclude that *exactly* 30 percent of all the marbles in the bin were black? Of course not. You'd remember that there will be random variations in the percentage of black marbles found in a series of samples of the marbles. You'd allow room for the error that can creep in through purely random variation. You'd conclude not that *exactly* 30 percent of all the marbles in the bin are black, but that *around* 30 percent of all the marbles in the bin *probably* are black.

When you generalize from a sample of a population to the entire population, you must allow room for the random variation that can occur from sample to sample. This "room" is called the **error margin.** If 30 percent of a random sample of things has some feature, you can at best conclude only that, in the target population, 30 percent *plus or minus (±) a few points* have that feature. The range of percentage points expresses the error margin.

The larger the sample, the smaller the error margin. This isn't complicated: If we have a large sample, we need not allow as much room for error due to random variation.

Also, if we have a wide error margin, we can be more confident in our inductive generalization. Again, this is not really complicated. Suppose we find that 30 percent of a handful of marbles from the bin are black. We can be more confident that 30 percent ± *10* points of all the marbles in the bin are black than we can that 30 percent ± *2* points have that feature.

So, the level of confidence we have in the conclusion of our inductive generalization depends on the size of the random sample and on the error margin we allow for random variation. The larger the sample *or* the more room we allow for random variation (i.e., the larger the error margin we allow), the more confidence we can have in the conclusion.

Let's review these important concepts. Suppose x percent of a population has some feature. The error margin is the range of random variation in this percentage that can occur from random sample to random sample. The larger the random samples, the smaller this range. And, the larger the range, the more probable it is that the percentage of things having the feature in any given random sample will fall within this range. The probability that the percentage of things in any given random sample will fall within the error margin is called the **confidence level.** For example, if the confidence level is 95 percent, that means that 95 percent of random samples of a certain size will fall within the error margin for that size sample. If the random sample size were increased, the confidence level would go up, or the error margin would shrink (or both).

Now, an inductive generalization occurs when *we don't know* what percentage of a class or population has a given feature and want to find out. So we make an inference from a sample. But our inference must make an allowance for the random variation that will occur from sample to sample.

"I Don't Know Enough to Have an Opinion . . ."

A . . . fascinating recent survey showed the direction in which polling should head. The NPR–Kaiser–Kennedy School poll conducted an intriguing experiment. The poll asked voters to state their views on two current education issues. Robert Siegel explained the procedure:

> SIEGEL: Now an interesting finding about polls . . . It's about the answer that we often too hastily discard, the answer, "I don't know." The folks who designed the education poll did something special with two of the questions, one about school vouchers and one about charter schools. Half the people surveyed were asked . . . "Are you in favor or opposed to vouchers or charter schools?" And half were given the third option, "I haven't heard enough about that to have an opinion."

The results of the experiment were remarkable. Among respondents asked simply if they favored or opposed charter schools, here was the breakdown:

> Favor charter schools: 62%
> Oppose charter schools: 29%
> Don't know: 9%

The 9 percent had voluntarily said they didn't know. But for the second group of respondents, "I don't know" was given as an explicit third choice. Here was the new breakdown in opinion:

> Favor charter schools: 25%
> Oppose charter schools: 12%
> Don't know: 63%

Obviously, when the poll is conducted in the first way, it produces a completely misleading impression. But that is the way opinion polls are routinely conducted and reported. Poll stories routinely give the impression that an informed electorate has weighed in on a policy question. It's a pleasing image, straight from our civics texts—but one that is frequently wrong.

—The Daily Howler <*www.dailyhowler.com*>

In other words, we must allow for an error margin. So, if x percent of the sample have some feature, we can only conclude that somewhere around x percent of the total population will have the feature in question. The greater the margin of error we allow, the higher our confidence level is. Looking at things this way, then, the confidence level is the probability that, given a random sample of a certain size, the percentage of things in the entire population will fall within the error margin for a random sample of that size.

Okay. Let's sum all this up in a general principle—one that's important enough for some boldface type:

When we generalize from the percentage of a random sample that has a certain feature to the percentage of the target class that has that

Watch Their Language

Poll results can be misunderstood when reports do not reveal the actual language used in the poll. In their book, *Unreliable Sources,* Martin A. Lee and Norman Solomon cite the results of a Roper poll that were widely reported as follows:

> ROPER FINDS THREE OUT OF FOUR AMERICANS APPROVE COMMERCIAL SPONSORSHIP FOR CHILDREN'S TV PROGRAMS.

The question the Roper organization asked, however, was this:

> How do you feel—that there should be NO commercials on any children's programs or that it is all right to have them if they don't take unfair advantage of the children?

> Given the phrasing of the question, we can't say we're surprised by the results.

feature, **the larger the sample size, the higher the confidence level or the smaller the error margin (or both).**

Now let's apply all this to a hypothetical case. In the year 2000, Hillary Clinton runs for the U.S. Senate in New York. Suppose that before election day she wants to know her approval rating among women voters over the age of fifty-five in the state. We might imagine her pollster surveying a random sample of 500 such people and finding that 50 percent of the sample approve of Clinton (we'll ignore how "approval" is defined).

POLLSTER: "Ms. Clinton, there is a 95 percent probability that, in New York, between 46 and 54 percent of registered women voters over fifty-five like you."

MS. CLINTON: "What? Can't you narrow that 46–54 percent margin down a bit?"

POLLSTER: "Yes, but then we can no longer be 95 percent confident of our findings."

MS. CLINTON: "But I want to be *more* than 95 percent confident, not less."

POLLSTER: "Well, I am almost 100 percent confident that between 10 and 90 percent of registered women voters over fifty-five in this state like you."

MS. CLINTON: "You're some help. Isn't there some way to narrow that spread without lowering our confidence level?"

POLLSTER: "Well, the only way to do that is to survey more
women, but that will cost you."

If you understand the principles expressed in this dialogue, you know much of what you need to know about error margins and confidence levels.

Table 11-1, on page 389, gives some indication of the error margins for various random sample sizes at the 95 percent confidence level, which is the level at which most surveys are conducted. Again, it is important to remember that "error margin" is merely a measure of *random variation*. It has nothing whatsoever to do with other types of errors such as ambiguously worded surveys, poorly constructed samples, incorrectly administered procedures, or whatever.

If you pay close attention to the reported error margins in the well-known popular opinion polls (e.g., the Gallup poll), you'll notice that the sample sizes and error margins do not correspond exactly to those in Table 11-1. The reason is that most of these surveys do not use polls that are absolutely random. To make collecting the sample more convenient and less expensive, they often use a form of "cluster sampling," which produces a slightly wider error margin for a given size of sample or which requires a somewhat larger sample to produce a given error margin.* The figures in the table can serve, however, as guideposts for the kind of statistical arguments we hear about most often. For example, most polls are designed to have a confidence level of 95 percent, and that's what you can generally presume when a poll from a respectable organization is reported without mention of a confidence level. But if you should hear of a survey of, say, 400 individuals and the error margin is said to be ± 3 percent, you know this is not a survey you can have 95 percent confidence in. Random samples of 400 don't produce results that are within ± 3 percent of the truth 95 percent of the time.

■ *Everyday Inductive Generalizations*

The possibility of random variation and the concepts associated with it (error margin and confidence level) are always taken into account when precise statistical inferences are made. But in ordinary affairs, we rarely worry about what the exact percentage is of a sample of things that has a feature. Home-grown inductive generalizations are fast and loose: We don't generally say things to each other like, "Ed, the chances of your catching a three-pound fish in that lake are 37 percent, plus or minus 4 percent" or "My sample indicates that 66.6 percent of the callers to that talk show are conservatives, with an error margin of 8 percentage points." Rather than calculating exact percentages, we use imprecise concepts like *many, most, several, a heck of a lot,* and so on.

---

*See George Gallup, *The Sophisticated Poll Watcher's Guide* (Princeton, N.J.: Princeton Opinion Press, 1972). For a general account of statistical arguments, we recommend David S. Moore, *The Basic Practice of Statistics* (New York: W. H. Freeman, 1998).

TABLE 11-1   Approximate Error Margins for Random Samples of Various Sizes

Confidence level of 95 percent in all cases.

Sample Size	Error Margin (%)	Corresponding Range (Percentage Points)
10	±30	60
25	±22	44
50	±14	28
100	±10	20
250	±6	12
500	±4	8
1,000	±3	6
1,500	±2	4

The error margin decreases rapidly as the sample size begins to increase, but this decrease slows markedly as the sample gets larger. It is usually pointless to increase the sample beyond 1,500 unless there are special requirements of precision or confidence level.

(We presume, both here and in the text, that the target population is large—that is, 10,000 or larger. When the target is small, there is a correction factor that can be applied to determine the appropriate error margin. But most reported polls have large enough targets that we need not concern ourselves with the calculation methods for correcting the error margin here.)

Nevertheless, although "error margin" and "confidence level" are technical concepts, the idea that underlies them is applicable to ordinary, nontechnical inductive generalizations. The basic idea amounts to this:

Except in populations known to be homogeneous, the smaller the sample in an inductive generalization, the more guarded the conclusion should be.

A conclusion can be made more guarded in various ways, including the following two. The first way is to decrease the precision of the conclusion. If you say that "most" of the marbles in this box are black, you are being less precise than if you say "exactly 60 percent" of the marbles are. Therefore "most" is more guarded than "60 percent." If you say that "many" of the marbles are black, you are being less precise than if you say that "most" are black, and therefore you are being even more guarded. Decreasing the precision of the conclusion of an inductive generalization is an informal way of increasing the error margin.

A second way to make a conclusion more guarded is to express a lower degree of probability that it is true. Saying "it is highly likely" most of the marbles in this box are black expresses a lower degree of probability (and is more guarded) than saying "it is certain" most of them are. Saying "it is likely" that most of the marbles are black expresses an even lower degree of

The polls, concerning Clinton, are phony and contrived. With few exceptions, everyone I talk to do not approve of his job performance.

—From a letter to the editor in our local newspaper

His own "poll" may not be phony, but it sure has other problems.

And How Do You Feel About Undressing in Front of the Mirror?

Not all opinion surveys are devoted to the popularity of presidents, government policies, and television programs. If you want to know Americans' thoughts on some *really* important subjects, you have to consult *The First Really Important Survey of American Habits,* by Mel Poretz and Barry Sinrod. Their findings—inductive generalizations based on a nationwide survey of adults over twenty-one—include the following percentages:

Percentage of those surveyed who like the way they look in the nude	41
Percentage who don't	59
Percentage of men who like the way they look in the nude	68
Percentage of women who don't like the way they look in the nude	78
Percentage of men who perceive themselves as overweight and like the way they look in the nude	55
Percentage of women who perceive themselves as overweight and like the way they look in the nude	59
Percentage of those surveyed who like their appearance in clothes	72
Percentage who don't	24
Percentage of men who don't like their appearance in clothes	8
Percentage of women who don't like their appearance in clothes	35

What might be some reasons the women in this survey report more dissatisfaction with their own appearance than men do with theirs?

Poretz and Sinrod conducted the survey by questionnaires that were mailed out to and returned by respondents. How does this fact affect the reliability of the survey?

probability (and is even more guarded). Informally expressing a lower degree of probability for the conclusion is an informal way of lowering the confidence level of the conclusion.

If you listen to a talk radio station for twenty minutes one day, and during that time three people call in and all three have extreme political views, you might be tempted to say "the callers to this show all have extreme political views." But in fact your sample is too small to warrant inferring much about the entire class of callers. You certainly would not be warranted in concluding that *all* the callers to the show have extreme political views. You would not even be warranted in thinking that *most* do. Anything you inferred would have to express a low "confidence level" or a large "error margin," perhaps something along the lines that *"it's possible* that *many* callers to this show have extreme political views." The phrase "it's possible" expresses a low level of confidence, and the word "many" allows a wide margin for error.

Of course, the less guarded the conclusion of an inductive generalization, the larger the sample should be, unless the population is known to be homogeneous. If Parker concludes, on the basis of inductive generalizing from a sample, that "three-quarters" of students at his university believe in astrology, then he needs a larger sample than he would if he concludes, say, "a large majority" do. If he concludes without qualification that a large majority do, he needs a larger sample than if he concludes "possibly a large majority do." If Moore says it is "very certain" the students at his university believe in astrology, then he had better have a sizable sample, or he should allow a large margin of error—for example, "It is very certain that *some* students at this university believe in astrology." The term "some" allows much room for error.

■ *The Two Key Questions We Should Ask of Any Inductive Generalization*

Finally, we can put all this together into two key questions we should ask of any inductive generalization:

1. **How well does the sample represent the target population?** (If the population is nonhomogeneous, then the sample should be random or otherwise constituted so as to represent the target population.)

2. **Are the size and representativeness of the sample appropriate for how guarded the conclusion is?**

Armed with these two questions, we should be suspicious of many inductive arguments found in everyday life:

Herb notices the price of canned peaches is lower at the local warehouse supermarket than at Kroger's. Fearlessly, he concludes "they charge more for things at Kroger's." But Herb's sample (the canned peaches) doesn't accurately represent the entire population of things sold at the stores, and it is too small for the confidence level and error margin expressed in the conclusion.

Jennifer encounters two rude people her first time in Minneapolis. Two. "The people here are so rude!" she exclaims. Jennifer's sample does not represent the people in Minneapolis very well and is too small to warrant such an unguarded conclusion.

In fact, if you apply these principles carefully, you may find many everyday inductive generalizations wanting.

> ### But Aren't We Guilty of Weaseling When We Make a Conclusion Guarded?
>
> Weaseling a claim (see Chapter 4) is attempting to immunize it from refutation. Here we are trying to make the "confidence level" and "error margin" of the conclusion of an inductive generalization appropriate to the size of the sample.

Analogical Arguments

Inductive generalizations are one important kind of inductive argument. **Analogical arguments** are another important kind.

Melody and her sister are alike in many ways. They both are fond of classical music, romance novels, and tennis. They have the same taste in clothes and both have the same friends. Given these similarities, we would expect there to be other similarities. For example, if we learn that Melody likes a certain movie, we might predict that Melody's sister would like it, too.

This is an analogical argument. Such arguments are also called **inductive analogical arguments** and **arguments from analogy.** The idea is simple enough. The more ways two or more things are alike, the more likely it is they'll be alike in some further way.

For example, dogs, cats, and people are similar in that all three are warm-blooded, have a heart and lungs, propagate by live birth, and share other features common to mammals. If, therefore, we find that a certain substance causes cancer in dogs and cats, we suspect it could cause cancer in people.

The pattern these arguments have is this:

X, Y, and Z (etc.) have features, *a, b, c,* etc.
Further, X and Y have additional feature *f.*
Therefore, Z has feature *f* too.

The feature mentioned in the conclusion of an analogical argument (feature *f* in the above pattern) is the **feature** (or property or characteristic) **in question.** The things that we know have the feature in question (X and Y) are the sample, and the thing that we conclude must also have this feature (Z) is the **target item.**

Here are three more examples of analogical arguments:

Example 1

Premises: Two of Jean's friends own Rapide motorbikes, and both of the bikes leak oil. Jean recently bought a Rapide motorbike.
Conclusion: Jean's new motorbike will also leak oil.

The sample: Jean's friends' Rapides. The target item: Jean's Rapide. The feature in question: leaking oil.

Example 2

Premises: Parker's tenants haven't paid their rent on time three of the last four months.
Conclusion: Parker's tenants are apt to be late in their rent next month.

The sample: the past four occasions on which Parker's tenants paid rent. The target item: the next occasion on which Parker's tenants pay rent. The feature in question: paying the rent late.

Example 3

Premises: Jake is good at basketball, baseball, and soccer; and despite some differences, these three sports are similar in many, many ways to football.
Conclusion: Jake is probably good at football, too.

The sample in this case is Jake's performance in basketball, baseball, and soccer. The target item is Jake's performance in football. The feature in question is being good (i.e., being a good performer).

As you can see, the difference between analogical arguments and inductive generalizations is this:

- ▲ In an inductive generalization, we generalize from a sample of a class or population to the entire class or population.

- ▲ In an analogical argument, we "generalize" from a sample of a class or population to another member of the class or population.

This is good news. It means the same evaluation questions apply to both types of argument. All you have to do is spot the class to which the sample items and target item belong. Let's refer to that class as the **implied target class** (or implied target population).

Look at Example 1 again: Jean's friends' Rapides leak oil, so Jean's Rapide will leak oil. The implied target class? Rapides.

Example 2: Moore's tenants have paid their rent late three of the last four times, so they will probably pay their rent late next month. The implied target class is Moore's tenants' rent payments.

Example 3: Jake is good at basketball, baseball, and soccer, and those three sports are similar to football. So Jake is probably good at football, too. The implied target class? Jake's performance in all sports.

Having spotted the implied target class, we can treat the analogical argument as an inductive generalization from a sample to the implied target class or population. Here, then, are the two questions we ask of analogical arguments:

1. **How well does the sample represent the implied target class or population?** (If the population is nonhomogeneous, then the sample

Welcome to Saint Simpson's

There are many ways that statistical reports can be misleading. The following illustrates one of the stranger ways, known to statisticians as "Simpson's Paradox":

Let's say you need a fairly complicated but still routine operation, and you have to pick one of the two local hospitals, Mercy or Saint Simpson's, for the surgery. You decide to pick the safer of the two, based on their records for patient survival during surgery. You get the numbers: Mercy has 2,100 surgery patients in a year, of which 63 die—a 3 percent death rate. Saint Simpson's has 800 surgery patients, of whom 16 die—a 2 percent death rate. You decide it's safer to have your operation done at Saint Simpson's.

The fact is, you could actually be *more* likely to die at Saint Simpson's than at Mercy Hospital, despite the former hospital's lower death rate for surgery patients. But you would have no way of knowing this without learning some more information. In particular, you need to know how the total figures break down into smaller, highly significant categories.

Consider the categories of high-risk patients (older patients, victims of trauma) and low-risk patients (e.g., those who arrive in good condition for elective surgery). Saint Simpson's may have the better looking overall record, not because it performs better, but because *Saint Simpson's gets a higher proportion of low-risk patients than does Mercy.* Let's say Mercy had a death rate of 3.8 percent among 1,500 high-risk patients, whereas Saint Simpson's, with 200 high-risk patients, had a death rate of 4 percent. Mercy and Saint Simpson's each had 600 low-risk patients, with a 1 percent death rate at Mercy and a 1.3 percent rate at Saint Simpson's.

So, as it turns out, it's a safer bet going to Mercy Hospital whether you're high risk or low, even though Saint Simpson's has the lower overall death rate.

The moral of the story is to be cautious about accepting the interpretation that is attached to a set of figures, especially if they lump together several categories of the thing being studied.

—*Adapted from a story in the* Washington Post, *which quoted extensively from* DAVID S. MOORE, *professor of statistics at Purdue University*

should be random or otherwise constituted so as to represent the implied target population.)

2. **Are the size and representativeness of the sample appropriate for how guarded the conclusion is?**

Applying these two questions to the three analogical arguments given above, we get results like this:

Example 1

Jean's friends' Rapides leak oil, so Jean's Rapide will leak oil, too.

Typical Sample Cases: Deduction in Disguise

Let's say you want to know whether gold is denser than lead. To find out, you take exactly one cubic centimeter of gold and the same volume of lead, and you place them on the two sides of a balance scale. The weighing shows that the cubic centimeter of gold is heavier than the lead (in fact, the weight of the lead is about 59 percent of that of the gold). You then conclude that, as a matter of fact, gold in general is more dense than lead—that is, that *every instance* of gold is more dense than *every instance* of lead.

Are you committing the fallacy of hasty generalization by basing your conclusion on only one case? No, of course not. The reason is that you can safely assume that every instance of gold is similar in density to every other instance of gold and that instances of lead are likewise similar with regard to properties like density, because gold and lead are elements.

Reasoning such as this is often made out to be a peculiar kind of inductive argument, one where a little sample goes a long way, as it were. In fact, though, arguments like this are really *deductive* arguments in disguise. The assumption that makes the argument inductively strong (namely, that in the matter of density, gold is all alike and so is lead) also makes the argument deductively valid! The argument turns out to be this:

General assumption: All gold is alike with regard to density, and so is all lead.

Result of weighing: This gold is denser than this lead.

Conclusion: Gold is denser than lead.

Question 1: How well does the sample represent the implied target class—that is, all Rapides? Answer: We'd expect any group of mass-produced items to be pretty homogeneous, and the sample therefore represents Rapides *of the same type.* But is Jean's Rapide the same type? Is it the same model with the same size engine produced at the same plant? Without knowing more, it would be unwise to assume this sample represents all Rapides.

Question 2: Are the size and representativeness of the sample appropriate for how guarded the conclusion is? Answer: The conclusion is not guarded at all.

Summary: But if the sample of Rapides and Jean's Rapide are all the same model produced at the same plant, Jean should not be in the least bit surprised if her Rapide leaks oil.

Example 2

Moore's tenants have paid their rent late three of the last four times, so they will probably pay their rent late next month.

The implied target class is Moore's tenants' rent payments.

Question 1: How well does the sample represent the implied target class? That class includes the four "sample" payments plus any future payments made by those tenants in conditions like those that existed when the sample payments were made. Moore's sample represents that class fairly well, though it would not do so if the class included payments the tenants make under different circumstances.

Question 2: Are the size and representativeness of the sample appropriate for how guarded the conclusion is? Yes. Assuming these are the only four payments Moore has received, Moore should anticipate trouble unless the tenants' circumstances change.

Example 3

Jake is good at basketball, baseball, and soccer, and those three sports are similar to football. So Jake is probably good at football, too.

Question 1: Does the sample (Jake's performance in basketball, baseball, and soccer) represent the class of Jake's performance in all sports? Answer: It's a pretty representative sample.

Question 2: Is the size of the sample appropriate for how guarded the conclusion is? Answer: We'd say it is.

Summary: We'd bet Jake *is* good at football.

Fallacies

Various types of mistakes in generalizing and reasoning by analogy are common enough to have earned names. Four in particular stand out.

To base a generalization (or conclusion of an analogical argument) on a sample that is too small is to commit the fallacy of **hasty generalization.** If you think all the marbles in an urn are black on the grounds that a sample of one was black, you commit this fallacy. You also commit the fallacy if you think the next marble will be black because a sample of one was black.

Often hasty generalizations are presented in the form of an anecdote. Anecdote? That's an interesting story or account of an experience or incident. This type of hasty generalization has earned its own name: **appeal to anecdotal evidence.** Let's say Parker tells a story about a time he played a joke on his friend Fred, who is an accountant. Fred, according to the story, didn't take it very well. Parker concludes that accountants in general (or the next accountant one might run into) don't take jokes very well. Parker has committed the version of hasty generalization known as appeal to anecdotal evidence.

You can probably see why statisticians are fond of saying "anecdotes prove nothing" or "stories prove nothing." What they mean is that a story about a couple of Xs that have some feature doesn't prove anything about Xs *in general* (unless the class of Xs is known to be very homogeneous). An anecdote that shows that one or two Xs have feature *f* proves only that one

Teenage Drug Use

According to a recent survey of 4,600 teenagers conducted by the Department of Health and Human Services, the number of kids who reported using cocaine increased from 14 to 37 over the year before, the number who reported using heroin increased from 14 to 32, and the number who reported using marijuana increased from 276 to 377. In absolute terms, none of these increases looks like much: 23 more kids using cocaine, 18 more using heroin, and 101 more using marijuana? No big deal, right? It's probably because these numbers look so unimpressive that Peter Jennings (ABC News) reported that the figures showed that "not many kids" used heroin or cocaine, and that "the drug crisis is really based on a big increase in the use of marijuana, not cocaine, or heroin."

If we look at the increases in percentage terms, however, Jennings's second claim seems inaccurate: The increase in cocaine use was 164 percent, and the increase in heroin use was 130 percent, but the increase in marijuana use was only 37 percent.

Further, we must remember that this is just a sample. If it is representative of the entire teen population (some 18 million people), then there were 72,000 more teenage heroin users this year than last, and that would strike many as rather a lot of new teenage heroin users. From this point of view, Jennings's first claim, that the survey shows that "not many kids" used heroin, seems inaccurate.

On the other hand, the percentage of teenagers using heroin in the sample (and also in the general population if the sample can reliably be projected) increased from only 0.3 percent to 0.69 percent, which means that more than 99 percent of teenagers don't use heroin.

Moral: Is the increase in drug use a major problem? The same figures could support both an affirmative and a negative answer to the question. When possible, look at the figures, and don't rely simply on other people's reports of what they mean.

or two Xs have feature *f.* Thus, the phrase "anecdotes prove nothing" is well worth remembering; appeals to anecdotal evidence are quite common.

Incidentally, there is no hard and fast line between a hasty generalization that is presented as an anecdote and one that isn't.

Sometimes we ask someone to reject a general claim on the basis of an example or two that run counter to the claim. When we do this, we commit the fallacy known as **refutation via hasty generalization.** And it doesn't matter whether or not the refutation is in the form of an anecdote; as long as it is a refutation based on a sample that is too small, it counts as this fallacy.

For example, suppose Moore has claimed that most professional musicians have perfect pitch. If Parker endeavors to refute this claim by saying he knows several professional musicians who don't have perfect pitch, Parker has committed the fallacy of refutation via hasty generalization. You cannot demonstrate the falsity of the claim that most professional musicians have perfect pitch by citing an example or two who don't.

Notice, however, that a *universal* general claim *can* be refuted by a single counterexample. The claim *"all* professional musicians have perfect pitch" is refuted by Parker's identification of one who doesn't. But the claim that many, or most, or a majority, or several do cannot be refuted by an example or two.

The fourth and last common fallacy is known as **biased generalization.** This occurs when the problem isn't the size of the sample but the sample's representativeness. For example, suppose you conclude most Republicans are against gay rights because most of a huge sample of Republicans at a convention of the Christian Coalition are against gay rights. The sample's size isn't the problem; the problem is that the sample does not represent the target class very well. (Note that the analogical argument version is also a fallacy: If you conclude that some specific Republican is apt to be against gay rights because most of the sample of Republicans at a convention of the Christian Coalition are against gay rights, you would also commit a version of the fallacy known as biased analogy.)

Please take note: Hasty generalization involves making inference from too small a sample. A small sample can, of course, be biased (and almost always is). But let's reserve the three names "hasty generalization," "appeal to anecdotal evidence," and "refutation via hasty generalization" for arguments based on samples that are too small. And let's reserve the name "biased generalization" for an argument whose sample is biased, however large it might be.

■ *Untrustworthy Polls*

As mentioned earlier, generalizations are often encountered in the form of public opinion polls. To what we said about generalizations, we might add a word of caution about some common types of poll.

1. Polls based on self-selected samples   The members of a self-selecting sample put themselves in the sample. For example, if a TV station conducts a poll by having viewers call in to express their opinion on some subject, the sample is composed entirely of people who put themselves in it by calling in. Thus, in this type of survey, people who have strong enough feelings about the subject to take the time and trouble (and maybe money, if the call costs something) to respond will be oversampled, and those who don't will be undersampled. In addition, people who call in more than once are oversampled. So we cannot say that the sample is representative.

Another common self-selecting sample is found in newspaper column surveys. A few years ago Abigail Van Buren ("Dear Abby") asked her female readers to write in answering the question, Which do you like more, tender cuddling or "the act" (sex)? When she published her result, which was that her readers preferred tender cuddling to sex, columnist Mike Royko asked his male readers which *they* liked more, tender cuddling or bowling. Royko's

Ask Us No [Loaded] Questions; We'll Tell You No Lies

In the spring of 1993, H. Ross Perot did a nationwide survey that received a lot of publicity. But a survey is only as good as the questions it asks, and loaded questions can produce a biased result. *Time* and CNN hired the Yankelovich Partners survey research firm to ask a split random sample of Americans two versions of the questions; the first was Perot's original version, the second was a rewritten version produced by the Yankelovich firm. Here is what happened for three of the topics covered.

Question 1

PEROT VERSION: "Do you believe that for every dollar of tax increase there should be two dollars in spending cuts with the savings earmarked for deficit and debt reduction?"

YANKELOVICH VERSION: "Would you favor or oppose a proposal to cut spending by two dollars for every dollar in new taxes, with the savings earmarked for deficit reduction, even if that meant cuts in domestic programs like Medicare and education?"

RESULTS: Perot version: 67 percent yes; 18 percent no
Yankelovich version: 33 percent in favor; 61 percent opposed

Question 2

PEROT VERSION: "Should the President have the Line Item Veto to eliminate waste?"

YANKELOVICH VERSION: "Should the President have the Line Item Veto, or not?"

RESULTS: Perot version: 71 percent in favor; 16 percent opposed
Yankelovich version: 57 percent in favor; 21 percent opposed

Question 3

PEROT VERSION: "Should laws be passed to eliminate all possibilities of special interests giving huge sums of money to candidates?"

YANKELOVICH VERSION: "Should laws be passed to prohibit interest groups from contributing to campaigns, or do groups have a right to contribute to the candidate they support?"

RESULTS: Perot version: 80 percent yes; 17 percent no
Yankelovich version: 40 percent for prohibition; 55 percent for right to contribute

The Gap Between Rich and Poor

According to the U.S. Census Bureau, the disparity between the income of the richest segment of society and the poorest is huge. Specifically, in 1997 the census showed that the bottom quintile received only 3.6 percent of income while the top quintile received almost 50 percent.

However, in an article in the *Los Angeles Times,* Robert Rector and Rea Hederman note reasons for being suspicious of the comparison:

- The census quintiles count households, not population. Low-income families are smaller on the average because they contain single-person "households" like retirees and teenagers just entering the work force. The result: Though the quintiles have the same number of households, the highest quintile contains over 64.2 million people and the bottom quintile 39.1 million people.

- Related to this point, the bottom quintile contains only 11.5 percent of all working-age adults and the top quintile 27.6 percent. The bottom quintile can't generate as much work as the top quintile.

- The census does not subtract taxes from the income of the top quintile or add welfare, food stamps, or public housing to the income of the bottom.

In other words, according to Rector and Hederman, the census compares apples and oranges. When they corrected for these considerations, they found the figure for income controlled by the bottom quintile went up to 9.4 percent, and the figure for the top quintile went down to 39.7 percent. (Still a big gap, but not nearly as big as that reported by the census.)

males preferred bowling. Although both surveys were good fun, neither could be taken to reflect accurately the views of either columnist's readership (let alone society as a whole).

2. Person-on-the-street interviews   Surveys of this type oversample people who are out and about on foot and undersample people who drive most places. They also oversample people who frequent the neighborhood where the survey is conducted. They undersample people who seem to be in a hurry or look unfriendly or for whatever other reason are not questioned by the interviewer.

3. Telephone surveys   A lot of surveying of public opinion is done by telephone. However, bias can creep into such samples unless they are constructed carefully. The potential exists to undersample people who have no phone or have an unlisted number and to oversample people who have more than one listed number.

What Global Warming?

For the worrywarts still concerned about the global warming hoax, Elko experienced two record low temperatures this month—including a 32-degree reading Aug. 7. That chilly reading in the heart of summer should be enough to encourage everyone to return to aerosol deodorants, and maybe even give an extra shot into the air each morning for the ozone hole.

—Elko (Nevada) Daily Free Press

A little anecdotal evidence from northern Nevada.

4. Questionnaires   Surveys that depend on a sample of people to return a questionnaire may have a "nonresponse problem": Many people find it easier just to chuck the questionnaire in the wastebasket. If the nonrespondents are atypical with respect to their views on the question asked, the survey results are unreliable.

5. Polls commissioned by advocacy groups   Polls of this sort can be legitimate, but questions might be worded in such a way as to elicit responses favorable to the group in question. These two questions, for example, ask essentially the same thing, but the second question might tend to evoke a response more to the liking of a teachers' union.

> Do you think the school board should agree to teachers' demands for higher pay?
>
> Do you think it is unreasonable for the local public school teachers to seek raises?

Also, the sequence in which questions are asked can affect results:

> Are you AWARE or UNAWARE that local school teachers have not had a salary increase for the past six years?
>
> Do you APPROVE or DISAPPROVE efforts by the local school teachers for salary increases?

Having been primed by the first question, a respondent might have a greater tendency to choose the APPROVE option in the second question.

Note as well that the second question apparently does not have an option for "no opinion," and that, of course, can affect results.

Survey questions can be "loaded" in other ways, too:

Do you think education will be subject to further decline if local teachers do not receive raises?

The question is loaded: It insinuates that education has been in a decline.

As another example, in recent discussions of health care reform, it was widely reported that the public didn't like the idea of health care alliances. However, as it turned out, the surveys that produced the negative public reaction were sponsored in part by physicians' organizations and had asked respondents whether they favored "huge, government-sponsored" insurance-buying groups. The words may have prejudiced the survey; we're pretty sure most people wouldn't even go for huge, government-sponsored apple pie.

In general, it's not a bad idea to look at the actual wording of poll questions if you can.

6. Push-polling   A fairly recent innovation in polling is so-called push-polling, when a survey is used not to gauge public opinion but to influence it. Here's how it works. You get a call from a pollster who asks you a negative question about a candidate or an issue: for example, "Would you be more likely or less likely to vote for Michael McDunn if you knew that he has voted for privatizing city waste collection in return for campaign contributions from North Highlands Disposal Company?" This technique is intended to push the listener away from an individual—hence the name "push-polling." Of course, it is not really polling at all, but marketing. The National Council on Public Polls has denounced the practice as unethical, but even reputable political pollsters have admitted to using "negative" questions about an opponent as long as the question implies something true. It is impossible to estimate how widespread the practice is, though common sense suggests that it is more likely to happen in local campaigns, where it could reach a significant percentage of voters.

Studies indicate that more brunettes than blondes or redheads have high-paying corporate jobs.

—From a letter in the *San Francisco Chronicle*

Is this evidence of discrimination against blondes and redheads, as the writer of the letter thought?

Nope; there are more brunettes to begin with. We'd be suspicious if *fewer* brunettes had high-paying corporate jobs.

Playing by the Numbers

What if your instructor were to flip a coin ten times, and it came up heads seven times out of that ten? Would this make you think your teacher is a wizard or a sleight-of-hand artist? Of course not. There's nothing unusual in the coin coming up heads seven times out of ten, despite the fact that we all know the chance of heads in a fair coin flip is 50-50 (or 1 in 2, or, as the statisticians put it, 0.5). But what if your instructor were to get heads 70 percent of the time after flipping the coin a *hundred* times? This would be much more unexpected, and if he or she were to flip the coin a *thousand* times and get 70 percent heads—well, the whole class should leave right now for Las Vegas, where your instructor will make you all rich.

Why is 70 percent heads so unsurprising in the first case and so nearly miraculous in the last? The answer lies in what we call the **law of large numbers,** which says,

The larger the number of chance-determined repetitious events considered, the closer the alternatives will approach predictable ratios.

This is not as complicated as it sounds; metaphorically, it just says that large numbers "behave" better than small numbers. Here's the idea: Because a single fair coin flip (i.e., no weighted coin, no prestidigitation) has a 50 percent chance of coming up heads, we say that the **predictable ratio** of heads to tails is 50 percent. The law of large numbers says that the more flips you include, the closer to 50 percent the heads-to-tails ratio will get.

The reason smaller numbers don't fit the percentages as well as bigger ones is that any given flip or short series of flips can produce nearly any kind of result. There's nothing unusual about several heads in a row or several tails—in fact, if you flip a thousand times, you'll probably get several "streaks" of heads and tails (and a sore thumb, too). Such streaks will balance each other out in a series of a thousand flips, but even a short streak can skew a small series of flips. The idea is that when we deal with small numbers, every number counts for a very large number of percentage points. Just two extra cases of heads can produce a 70:30 ratio in ten flips, a ratio that would be astounding in a large number of flips.

The law of large numbers operates in many circumstances. It is the reason we need a minimum sample size even when our method of choosing a sample is entirely random. To infer a generalization with any confidence, we need a sample of a certain size before we can trust the numbers to "behave" as they should. Smaller samples increase the likelihood of random sampling error.

The law of large numbers also keeps knowledgeable gamblers and gambling establishments in business. They know that if they make a bet that gives them even a modest advantage in terms of a predictable ratio, then all they have to do is make the bet often enough (or, more frequently, have some chump make the opposing bet against them often enough) and they will come out winners.

Almost no one in Las Vegas believes the Gambler's fallacy is in fact a fallacy.

—From an anonymous reviewer of this book

Let's consider an example. A person who plays roulette in an American casino gives away an advantage to the house of a little over 5 percent. The odds of winning are 1 in 38 (because there are slots for thirty-six numbers plus a zero and a double-zero), but when the player wins, the house pays off only at the rate of 1 in 36 (as if there were no zeros). Now, this advantage to the house doesn't mean you might not walk up to a table and bet on your birthday and win four times in a row. But the law of large numbers says that if you pull up a chair and play long enough, eventually the house will win it all back—and the rent money, too.

A final note while we're speaking about gambling. There is a famous error known as the **gambler's fallacy,** and it is as seductive as it is simple. Let's say that you're flipping a coin, and it comes up heads four times in a row. You succumb to the gambler's fallacy if you think that the odds of its coming up heads the next time are anything except 50 percent. It's true that the odds of a coin coming up heads five times in a row are small—only a little over 3 in 100—but once it has come up heads four times in a row, the

Reverse Gambler's Fallacy

If you want to get tails, your chances are greater if you flip after there's been a run of heads, right? Well, no—that's the gambler's fallacy.

And if you *don't* want to get tails, you are better off if you flip *before* there's been a run of heads—Whoops! That's the gambler's fallacy in reverse.

odds are still 50-50 that it will come up heads the next time. Past performance may give you a clue about a horse race, but not about a coin flip (or any other event with a predictable ratio).

Recap

Inductive arguments include inductive generalizations, analogical arguments, and a third kind we'll discuss in the next chapter.

Inductive generalizations are made when we infer that an entire class or population of things (a target class or population) has a property or feature (the property or feature in question) because a sample of those things has that property or feature. Analogical arguments are made when we infer that some specific thing or things have a property or feature because some other similar things have that property or feature. An analogical argument contains an inference that an implied target class or population has a feature because a sample of that class or population has the feature. This means we can evaluate analogical arguments and inductive generalizations by asking two questions:

1. How well does the sample represent the target class or implied target class? (If the population is nonhomogeneous, then the sample should be random or otherwise constituted so as to represent the target class or implied target class.)
2. Are the size and representativeness of the sample appropriate for how guarded the conclusion is?

Four fallacies are common when people reason by inductive generalization or by analogy:

1. Hasty generalization: Sample too small.
2. Appeal to anecdotal evidence: A type of hasty generalization based on an anecdote.

3. Refutation via hasty generalization: A type of hasty generalization or appeal to anecdotal evidence that attempts to refute a generalization.

4. Biased generalization: Sample large enough, but biased.

The results of random events such as flips of a coin or spins of a roulette wheel are much less predictable when the numbers of events considered are small; as the numbers get larger and larger, the results approximate the predictable ratios more and more closely.

The gambler's fallacy results from thinking that the preceding events in a repetitious series can affect the odds of the next such event—that because a coin comes up heads three times in a row, it is less likely that the coin will come up heads the next time.

Having read this chapter and the chapter recap, you should be able to

▲ Explain argument by analogy and inductive generalization and describe the factors that affect the strength of each of these types of inductive reasoning

▲ Describe and explain four fallacies of inductive reasoning

▲ Discuss the pitfalls of public opinion polls

▲ Explain the law of large numbers and the gambler's fallacy

▲ Evaluate whether or not conclusions of inductive generalizations and analogical arguments are appropriate to their premises

Exercises

Exercise 11-1

In groups (or individually if the instructor prefers) decide whether each of the following is (a) an analogical argument or (b) an inductive generalization.

▲ 1. Paulette, Georgette, Babette, and Brigitte are all Miami University English majors, and they are all atheists. Therefore Janette, who is a Miami University English major, probably is also an atheist.

2. Paulette, Georgette, Babette, and Brigitte are all Miami University English majors, and they are all atheists. Therefore, probably all the English majors at Miami University are atheists.

3. Gustavo likes all the business courses he has taken at Harvard to date. Therefore, he'll probably like all the business courses he takes at Harvard.

▲ 4. Gustavo likes all the business courses he has taken at Harvard to date. Therefore, he'll probably like the next business course he takes at Harvard.

5. Gustavo likes all the business courses he has taken at Harvard to date. Therefore, his brother, Sergio, who also attends Harvard, will probably like all the business courses he takes there, too.

6. Forty percent of Moore's 8:00 A.M. class are atheists. Therefore, 40 percent of all Moore's students are atheists.

▲ 7. Forty percent of Parker's 8:00 A.M. class are atheists. Therefore, probably 40 percent of Parker's 9:00 A.M. class are atheists.

8. Forty percent of Moore's 8:00 A.M. class are atheists. Therefore, probably 40 percent of all the students at Moore's university are atheists.

9. Bill Clinton lied to the American public about his relationship with Monica Lewinsky; therefore, he probably lied to the American public about Iraq, too.

▲ 10. Bill Clinton lied to the American public about his relationship with Monica Lewinsky; therefore, he probably lied to the American public about most things.

Exercise 11-2

In groups (or individually, if the instructor prefers) decide whether each of the following is (a) an analogical argument or (b) an inductive generalization.

▲ 1. With seven out of the last nine El Niños, we saw below-average rainfall across the northern United States and southern Canada. Therefore, chances are we'll see the same with the next El Niño.

2. I've been to at least twenty Disney movies in my lifetime, and not one of them has been especially violent. I guess the Disney people just don't make violent movies.

3. Most of my professors wear glasses; it's a good bet most professors everywhere do the same.

▲ 4. Seems like the Christmas decorations go up a little earlier each year. I bet next year they're up by Halloween.

5. The conservatives I've met dislike Colin Powell. Based on that, I'd say most conservatives feel the same way.

6. FIRST PROF: I can tell after just one test exactly what a student's final grade will be.
SECOND PROF: How many tests do you give, just a couple?
FIRST PROF: As a matter of fact I give a test every week of the semester.

▲ 7. MRS. BRUDER: Bruder! Bruder! Guess what! The music department is selling two of their grand pianos!
MR. BRUDER: Well, let's check it out, but remember the last pianos they sold were way overpriced. Probably it'll be the same this time.

8. A 60 percent approval rating? Those polls are rigged by the liberal media. Most of the people I know say the man ought to be impeached.

9. The New England Patriots have won six of their last seven home games. They're playing at home on Sunday. Don't bet against them.

▲ 10. You're going out with a Georgette? Well, don't expect much because I've known three Georgettes and all of them have been stuck up, spoiled yuckheads. I'll bet this one will be a yuckhead, too.

Exercise 11-3

Go through the preceding exercise and for each item identify (1) the sample, (2) the target or implied target class or population, and (3) the feature or property in question.

Exercise 11-4

In groups (or individually, if the instructor prefers) decide whether each of the following comments is (a) an analogical argument or (b) an analogy that isn't in an argument.

▲ 1. These shrubs look rather similar to privet. I bet they keep their leaves in the winter, just like privet.

2. Working in this office is just about exactly as much fun as driving in Florida without air conditioning.

3. The last version of Word was filled with bugs; that's why I know the new version will be the same way.

▲ 4. If you ask me, Dr. Walker has as much personality as a piece of paving concrete.

5. I hate math, and soon as I saw all those formulas and junk, I knew I'd hate this symbolic logic stuff too.

6. Your new boyfriend has been married five times?! Say—do you seriously think it'll work out better the next time?

▲ 7. Too much sun will make your face all wrinkly; I suppose it would have that effect on your hands, too.

8. A CEO who had sex with an intern would be fired on the spot. A senior officer who slept with a recruit would be court-martialed. That's why Bill Clinton should have been impeached.

9. I go, "Mom, don't buy me any more Levi's"; and she's like, "What?" So I told her, "they're for people your age," and she's like, "Well, I'll just give them to your sister"; and so I told her you're just like me and you won't want them either.

▲ 10. Here, you can use your screwdriver just like a chisel, if you want. Just give it a good whack with this hammer.

11. In elections during economic hard times, the party out of the White House has always made major gains in the Congress. That's why we can expect the president's party to suffer losses in the next election.

12. "Those thinkers in whom all stars move in cyclic orbits are not the most profound. Whoever looks into himself as into vast space and carries galaxies in himself, also knows how irregular all galaxies are; they lead into the chaos and labyrinth of existence."

Friedrich Nietzsche

▲ 13. "Religion . . . is the *opium* of the people. To abolish religion as the *illusory* happiness of the people is to demand their *real* happiness."

Karl Marx

14. "Publishing is to thinking as the maternity ward is to the first kiss."

Friedrich Von Schlegel

15. She's not particularly good at tennis, so I doubt she'd be good at racquetball.

▲ 16. "A book is like a mirror. If an ape looks in, a saint won't look out."

Ludwig Wittgenstein

17. As odd as it sounds, historically the stock market goes up when there is bad news on unemployment, and the latest statistics show the unemployment rate is skyrocketing. This could be a good time to buy stocks.

18. I never met anyone from North Carolina who didn't have an accent thicker than molasses.

▲ 19. Yamaha makes great motorcycles, so I'll bet their pianos are pretty good, too.

20. The last time we played Brazil in soccer we got run through the washer and hung out to dry.

Exercise 11-5

In groups (or individually, if the instructor prefers) determine in which of the following inductive generalizations or analogical arguments the target classes or implied target classes are excessively vague or ambiguous.

▲ 1. The tests in this class are going to be hard, judging from the first midterm.

2. Judging from my experience, technical people are exceedingly difficult to communicate with sometimes.

3. The transmissions in 1999 Chrysler minivans tend to fail prematurely, if my Voyager is any indication.

▲ 4. Women can tolerate more stress than can men. My husband even freaks when the newspaper is a little late.

5. Movies are much too graphic these days. Just go to one—you'll see what I mean.

6. Violent scenes in the current batch of movies carry a message that degrades women. Just go see any of the movies playing downtown right now.

▲ 7. You'll need to get better clothing than that if you're going to Iowa. In my experience, the weather there sucks much of the year.

8. Entertainment is much too expensive these days, judging from the cost of movies.

9. Art majors sure are weird! I roomed with one, once. Man.

▲ 10. Artsy people bug me. They're all like, aaargh, you know what I mean?

11. The French just don't like Americans. Why, in Paris, they won't give you the time of day.

12. All the research suggests introverts are likely to be well-versed in computer skills.

▲ 13. Suspicious people tend to be quite unhappy, judging from what I've seen.

Exercise 11-6

In groups (or individually, if the instructor prefers), determine in which of the preceding thirteen arguments the feature in question is excessively vague or ambiguous.

Exercise 11-7

How well does the sample in each of the following arguments represent the target class (or implied target class)? In groups (or individually) choose from the following options:

a. Very well

b. Pretty well

c. Not very well

d. Very poorly

▲ 1. The coffee in that pot is lousy—I just had a cup.

2. The coffee at that restaurant is lousy—I just had a cup.

3. The food in that restaurant is lousy—I just ate there.

▲ 4. This student doesn't write very well, judging from how poorly she wrote on the first paper.

5. Terrence didn't treat her very well on their first date; I can't imagine he will treat her better next time.

6. I expect I'll have trouble sleeping after this huge feast. Whenever I go to bed on a full stomach, I never sleep very well.

▲ 7. Lupe's sister and mother both have high blood pressure; chances are Lupe does too.

8. Every movie Courtney Cox Arquette has been in has been great! I bet her next movie will be great, too!

9. If you hit Control-Shift-Return this computer will bomb. It did for me.

▲ 10. Women don't play trombones; leastwise, I never heard of one who did.

11. I'm sure Blue Cross will cover that procedure because I have Blue Cross and they covered it for me.

12. Cocker spaniels are nice dogs, but they eat like pigs. When I was a kid, we had this little cocker that ate more than a big collie we had.

▲ 13. Cadillacs are nice cars, but they are gas hogs. When I was a kid, we owned this Cadillac that got around ten miles per gallon.

14. Cockatoos are great birds, but they squawk. A lot. Had one when I was a kid, and even the neighbors complained, it was so raucous.

15. The parties at the university always turn into drunken brawls. Why, just last week the police had to go out and break up a huge party at Fifth and Ivy.

Exercise 11-8

Arrange the alternative conclusions of the following arguments in order of increasing guardedness, and then compare your rankings with those of three or four classmates. Some options are pretty close to being tied. Don't get in feuds with classmates or the teacher over close calls.

▲ 1. Not once this century has this city gone Republican in a presidential election. Therefore . . .
   a. I wouldn't count on it happening this time.
   b. it won't happen this time.
   c. in all likelihood it won't happen this time.
   d. there's no chance whatsoever it will happen this time.
   e. it would be surprising if it happened this time.
   f. I'll be a donkey's uncle if it happens this time.

2. Byron doesn't know how to play poker, so . . .
   a. he sure as heck doesn't know how to play blackjack.
   b. it's doubtful he knows how to play blackjack.
   c. there's a possibility he doesn't know how to play blackjack.
   d. don't bet on him knowing how to play blackjack.
   e. you're nuts if you think he knows how to play blackjack.

3. Every time I've used the Beltway, the traffic has been heavy, so I figure that . . .
   a. the traffic is almost always heavy on the Beltway.
   b. frequently the traffic on the Beltway is heavy.
   c. as a rule, the traffic on the Beltway is heavy.
   d. the traffic on the Beltway can be heavy at times.
   e. the traffic on the Beltway is invariably heavy.
   f. typically, the traffic on the Beltway is heavy.
   g. the traffic on the Beltway is likely to be heavy most of the time.

Exercise 11-9

In which of the following arguments is the conclusion too guarded or unguarded, given the premises? After you have decided, compare results with three or four classmates.

▲ 1. We spent a day on the Farallon Islands last June, and was it ever foggy and cold! So dress warmly when you go there this June. Based on our experience, it is 100 percent certain to be foggy and cold.

2. We've visited the Farallon Islands on five different days, two during the summer and one each during fall, winter, and spring. It's been foggy and cold every time we've been there. So dress warmly when you go there. Based on our experience, there is an excellent chance it will be foggy and cold whenever you go.

3. We've visited the Farallon Islands on five different days, all in June. It's been foggy and cold every time we've been there. So dress warmly when you go there in June. Based on our experience, it could well be foggy and cold.

▲ 4. We've visited the Farallon Islands on five different days, all in June. It's been foggy and cold every time we've been there. So dress warmly when you go there in June. Based on our experience, there is a small chance it will be foggy and cold.

5. We've visited the Farallon Islands on five different days, all in January. It's been foggy and cold every time we've been there. So dress warmly when you go there in June. Based on our experience, it almost certainly will be foggy and cold.

Exercise 11-10

For the past four years, Clifford has gone on a hundred-mile bicycle ride on the Fourth of July. He has always become too exhausted to finish the entire hundred miles. He decides to try the ride once again, but thinks, "Well, I probably won't finish it this year, either, but no point in not trying."

▲ 1. Does the conclusion seem appropriate given the size and representativeness of the sample?

▲ 2. Suppose the past rides were done in a variety of different weather conditions. Does this information warrant a more or a less guarded conclusion than that stated above?

3. Suppose the past rides were done on a variety of different kinds of bike (e.g., ten-speed road bikes, mountain bikes, racing bikes, etc.), and Clifford hasn't yet decided what kind of bike to ride in this year's ride. Does that information warrant a more or a less guarded conclusion than the original?

4. Suppose the past rides were all done on exactly the same bike Clifford will ride this year. Does this information warrant a more or a less guarded conclusion than the original?

▲ 5. Suppose the past rides were all done on the same bike, but that bike is not the bike Clifford will ride this year. Does this information warrant a more or a less guarded conclusion than the original?

6. Suppose the past rides were done on a variety of terrain and Clifford doesn't know where this year's ride will be. Does this information warrant a more or a less guarded conclusion than the original?

7. Suppose the past rides were all done on flat ground and Clifford's ride this year will also be on flat ground. Does this information warrant a more or a less guarded conclusion than the original?

8. Suppose the past rides were all done on flat ground and Clifford's ride this year will be on hills. Does this information warrant a more or a less guarded conclusion than the original?

9. Suppose the past rides were all done on hills and Clifford's ride this year will be on flat ground. Does this information warrant a more or a less guarded conclusion than the original?

Exercise 11-11

During three earlier years Kirk has tried to grow artichokes in his backyard garden, and each time his crop has been ruined by mildew. Billie prods him to try one more time, and he agrees to do so, though he secretly thinks: "This is probably a waste of time. Mildew is likely to ruin this crop, too."

▲ 1. Suppose this year Kirk plants the artichokes in a new location. Does this information warrant a more or a less guarded conclusion than the original?

2. Suppose on the past three occasions Kirk planted his artichokes at different times of the growing season. Does this information warrant a more or a less guarded conclusion than the original?

3. Suppose this year Billie plants marigolds near the artichokes. Does this information warrant a more or a less guarded conclusion than the original?

▲ 4. Suppose the past three years were unusually cool. Does this information warrant a more or a less guarded conclusion than the original?

5. Suppose only two of the three earlier crops were ruined by mildew. Does this information warrant a more or a less guarded conclusion than the original?

6. Suppose one of the earlier crops grew during a dry year, one during a wet year, and one during an average year. Does this information warrant a more or a less guarded conclusion than the original?

▲ 7. Suppose this year, unlike the preceding three, there is a solar eclipse. Does this information warrant a more or a less guarded conclusion than the original?

8. Suppose this year Kirk fertilizes with lawn clippings for the first time. Does this information warrant a more or a less guarded conclusion than the original?

9. Suppose this year Billie and Kirk acquire a large dog. Does this information warrant a more or a less guarded conclusion than the original?

▲ 10. Suppose this year Kirk installs a drip irrigation system. Does this information warrant a more or a less guarded conclusion than the original?

Exercise 11-12

For each of the following, identify (1) the sample, (2) the target item, (3) the implied target class, and (4) the property or feature in question. *Hint:* The sample in many cases is not explicitly stated. *Additional hint:* The implied target class is the class of things having features a, b, c in the pattern on page 392.

1. Senator Claghorn has been an excellent senator, so he would make an excellent president.

▲ 2. Beatrice likes the representative from Tri-State Investments. He is polite, well informed, and kind. She decides, therefore, that he will not mislead her and agrees to purchase the life insurance policy he recommends.

3. The Barneses are traveling to Europe for a year and decide to find a student to house-sit for them. They settle on Homer because he is neat and tidy in his appearance. "If he takes such good care of his personal appearance," Mrs. Barnes thinks, "he's likely to take good care of our house, too."

4. Tiger Woods began playing golf at the age of two, and look what he's accomplished. I'm starting golf lessons for my two-year-old so maybe he can achieve the same result.

▲ 5. Record company executive to record producer: "Look, I want this record done just the way you did their last hit. In fact, just take their last hit and rework it a bit; use different lyrics, but the same beat, the same backup, the same sound. It'll sell if the sound's the same."

6. A household that does not balance its budget is just asking for trouble. It's the same, therefore, with the federal government. Balance the federal budget, or watch out!

7. There's no way I can actually feel a pain that you're experiencing. But, because we're so much alike in other ways, I figure you must have experiences much like the ones I have.

▲ 8. First it was cyclamates. They were taken out of soft drinks because they caused cancer. Then it was saccharin. It too was discovered to be carcinogenic. So I don't care what they call this new artificial sweetener. It'll probably be carcinogenic, too.

9. Oregon has a bottle-return law just like the one proposed here in Michigan, and the Oregon law works! It's cleaned up the highways, provided extra jobs. It will do the same here.

10. ". . . if a body and an environment were supposed [in which we might exist after our present body dies] . . . of a kind radically different from bodies of flesh and their material environment, then it is paradoxical to suppose that,

under such drastically different conditions, a personality could remain the same as before. . . . To take a crude but telling analogy, it is past belief that, if the body of any one of us were suddenly changed into that of a shark or an octopus and placed in the ocean, his personality could, for more than a very short time, if at all, recognizably survive so radical a change of environment."

> *C. J. Ducasse,* A Critical Examination of the Belief in a Life After Death

Exercise 11-13

Every student I've met from Ohio State believes in God. My conclusion is that most of the students from Ohio State believe in God.

▲ 1. Suppose (as is the case) that Ohio State has no admission requirements pertaining to religious beliefs. Suppose further the students in the sample were all interviewed as they left a local church after Sunday services. Does this supposition warrant a more or a less guarded conclusion than the original?

2. Suppose all those interviewed were first-year students. Does this supposition warrant a more or a less guarded conclusion than the original?

3. Suppose all students interviewed were on the Ohio State football team. Does this supposition warrant a more or a less guarded conclusion than the original?

▲ 4. Suppose the speaker selected all the students interviewed by picking every tenth name on an alphabetical list of students' names. Does this supposition warrant a more or a less guarded conclusion than the original?

5. Suppose the students interviewed all responded to a questionnaire published in the campus newspaper entitled "Survey of Student Religious Beliefs." Does this supposition warrant a more or a less guarded conclusion than the original?

6. Suppose the students interviewed were selected at random from the record office's list of registered automobile owners. Does this supposition warrant a more or a less guarded conclusion than the original?

Exercise 11-14

You want to find out what percentage of residents of your local community believe the sheriff's department is adequately staffed, so you conduct a survey. Name four characteristics of the sample that would bias the survey—characteristics that would reduce our confidence that your findings applied to the community at large. For example, if the people in the sample were all interviewed in a local bar, that characteristic should diminish our confidence that your findings can be extended to the community in general.

Now name four characteristics of a sample that would increase our confidence that your findings applied to the community at large. For example, if the people surveyed belonged to a wide range of economic backgrounds, that fact would increase our confidence that your findings applied to the entire community.

Now name four characteristics of your sample that would not affect our confidence one way or the other. In other words, name four characteristics that are irrelevant to the issue.

Exercise 11-15

Suppose that you are interested in finding out what percentage of people in your community lift weights. Name four characteristics of your sample that would decrease our confidence that your results were generalizable to the whole population, four that would increase our confidence, and four that would be irrelevant.

Exercise 11-16

Suppose you want to determine what percentage of people in your state believe that gasoline taxes for road repairs should be increased. Name four characteristics of your sample that would decrease our confidence that your results were generalizable to the whole population, four that would increase our confidence, and four that would be irrelevant.

Exercise 11-17

Read the following Associated Press newspaper story; then decide how the last sentence should be completed.

> WASHINGTON—More Americans than ever support a ban on handgun sales, saying it is needed for the safety of children in an increasingly violent society, according to a poll released Thursday.
>
> The poll of 1,250 adults conducted April 3–12 by Louis Harris of LH Research Inc. found 52 percent in favor of a ban and 43 percent opposed.
>
> That would be the first time a majority of Americans expressed support for a ban, Harris said. But the margin of error was plus or minus 3 percentage points . . .

Exercise 11-18

George's class is doing a survey of student opinion on social life and drinking. One of the questions is "Do you believe that students who are members of fraternities and sororities drink more alcohol than students who are not members of such organizations?" Let's say that George would only wager a large sum on a bet if he had a 95 percent chance of winning. Answer the following questions for him. (Use Table 11-1 on page 389 to help you with this exercise.)

▲ 1. Exactly 60 percent of a random sample of 250 students at George's college believe that students in fraternities and sororities drink more than others. Should George bet that exactly 60 percent of the student population hold the same belief?

2. Should he bet that *at least* 60 percent hold the belief?

3. Should he bet that *no more than* 66 percent hold the belief?

▲ 4. According to the text, the largest number that he can safely bet hold the belief mentioned is _____ percent.

5. Let's change the story a bit. Let's make the sample size 100 and once again say that exactly 60 percent of it hold the belief in question. Should George bet that at least 55 percent of the total student population hold the belief?

6. Should he bet that at least 50 percent of the total hold it?

▲ 7. It is safe for George to bet that no more than _____ percent of the total population share the belief in question. What's the smallest number that can be placed in the blank?

Exercise 11-19 _____

Read the passage below, and answer the questions that follow.

> In the Sunrise University History Department, students are invited to submit written evaluations of their instructors to the department's personnel committee, which uses those evaluations to help determine whether history instructors should be recommended for retention and promotion. In his three history classes, Professor Ludlum has a total of one hundred students. Six students turned in written evaluations of Professor Ludlum; four of these evaluations were negative, and two were positive. Professor Hitchcock, who sits on the History Department Personnel Committee, argued against recommending Ludlum for promotion. "If a majority of the students who bothered to evaluate Ludlum find him lacking," he stated, "then it's clear to me that a majority of all his students find him lacking."

▲ 1. What is the sample in Professor Hitchcock's reasoning?

2. What is the target?

3. What is the property in question?

▲ 4. Is this an analogical argument or a generalization?

5. Are there possibly important differences between the sample and the target that should reduce our confidence in Professor Hitchcock's conclusion?

6. Does Professor Hitchcock have any information concerning the diversification of the sample?

▲ 7. Is the sample random?

8. How about the size of Professor Hitchcock's sample? Is it large enough to help ensure that the sample and target classes won't be too dissimilar?

▲ 9. Based on the analysis of Professor Hitchcock's reasoning that you have just completed in the foregoing questions, how strong is his reasoning?

Exercise 11-20

Identify any fallacies that are present in the following passages:

▲ 1. From a letter to the editor: "I read with great interest the May 23 article on the study of atheists in federal prisons, according to which most of these atheists identify themselves as socialists, communists, or anarchists. That most atheists, along with all their other shortcomings, turn out to be political wackos surprises yours truly not one bit."

2. I ordered a packet of seeds from Hansen Seed Company last year, and only half of them germinated. I'll bet you get only half the plants you're expecting from the order you just sent them.

3. My cousin has a Dodge truck that he drives around on the ranch and back and forth to town as well. It now has 120,000 miles on it without any major overhaul. I've started to believe the commercials: Dodge does build tough trucks!

▲ 4. Drug abuse among professional athletes is a serious and widespread problem. Three players from a single team admitted last week that they had used cocaine.

5. Most Americans favor a national lottery to reduce the federal debt. In a poll taken in Las Vegas, more than 80 percent said they favored such a lottery.

6. I think collies are one of the easiest breeds of dog to train. I had one when I was young, and she was really easy to teach. Of course, if you need more evidence, there's Lassie.

7. Wow! I just got one of those CD-ROM readers for my computer setup at home. It's incredible how much information those things can hold. The first CD-ROM disk I got has an entire encyclopedia on it.

8. From a letter to the editor: "Last week, members of the Animal Liberation Front stole several hours of videotapes of experiments done to animals at the University of Pennsylvania's Head Injury Clinical Research Center. According to reliable reports, one of the tapes shows baboons having their brains damaged by a piston device that smashed into their skulls with incredible force. The anesthetic given the baboons was allegedly insufficient to prevent serious pain. Given that this is what animal research is all about, Secretary of Health and Human Services Margaret Heckler acted quite properly in halting federal funding for the project. Federal funding for animal research ought to be halted, it seems to me, in the light of these atrocities."

9. FIRST PERSON: I don't go out of my way to get a suntan anymore. There's just too much evidence that you can pay for it in the long run with skin cancer. SECOND PERSON: My father worked outdoors most of his life, and he doesn't have skin cancer. I think this stuff about suntans being dangerous is just some fad.

▲ 10. Overheard: "You're not going to take a course from Harris, are you? I know at least three people who say he's terrible. All three flunked his course, as a matter of fact."

11. A majority of Ohio citizens consider the problem of air pollution critical. According to a survey taken in Cleveland, more than half the respondents identified air pollution as the most pressing of seven environmental issues, and as having either "great" or "very great" importance.

▲ 12. Comment: What are we getting for the billions we spend on these new weapons? Absolutely nothing. Just look at the Apache helicopter. I read where they can't fly one of them for more than ten hours without grounding it for major repairs.

13. The IRS isn't interested in going after the big corporations, just middle-class taxpayers like you and me. I was audited last year, and I know several people who have been audited. You ever hear of Exxon getting nailed?

14. I am totally outraged by the ethics of our elected representatives. Just look around: Bill Clinton accepted illegal campaign donations; Newt Gingrich was fined $300,000 for misusing money. I tell you, they are all just a bunch of crooks.

▲ 15. When he was president, Ronald Reagan occasionally would wave a copy of the "Help Wanted" section of some newspaper to demonstrate that U.S. unemployment wasn't really so bad. What was the fallacy in this "argument"?

Exercise 11-21

1. In the text, it is said that a person playing roulette has a disadvantage of about 5 percent compared with the house. Explain what this means.

2. Choose two or three other gambling bets for which you can calculate or look up the odds against the bettor. (Stick with games of pure chance; those that can involve a bit of skill, such as twenty-one—also known as blackjack—are much more difficult to deal with.) Determine which bet gives the house the smallest advantage.

3. Choose a state lottery and determine the odds against winning for a given ticket. Can you determine what kind of advantage the "house" has in such a gamble?

Exercise 11-22

1. Explain in your own words what the law of large numbers says.

2. "Over the long term, human births will approximate 50 percent males and 50 percent females." Is this a reasonable application of the law of large numbers? What facts can you think of that are relevant to determining whether this is a reasonable application of the law?

3. A person is betting on flips of a coin. He always bets on heads. After he loses three in a row, you hear him say, "Okay, I'm due for one now!" as he raises his bet. Write a brief note in which you give him some friendly advice.

Writing Exercises

1. Which of the following general claims do you accept? Select one that you accept and write a one-page essay presenting evidence (giving arguments) for the claim. When you are finished, write down on a separate piece of paper a number between 1 and 10 that indicates how strong you think your overall "proof" of the general claim is, with 10 = very strong and 1 = very weak. Take about two minutes to complete your essay. Write your name on the back of your paper.

   General claims:

   You get what you pay for.
   Nice guys finish last.
   Everything else being equal, men prefer blondes.
   Women are more gentle and nurturing than men.
   Politicians are untrustworthy.
   Government intrudes into our private lives/business affairs too
      much.
   Too many welfare recipients don't deserve assistance.
   College teachers are liberals.
   Jocks are dumb.
   The superwealthy pay less in taxes than they should.

2. When everyone is finished, the instructor will collect the papers and redistribute them to the class. In groups of four or five, read the papers and assign a number from 1 to 10 to each one (10 = very strong; 1 = very weak). When all groups are finished, return the papers to their authors. When you get your paper back, compare the number you assigned to your work with the number the group assigned to it. The instructor may ask volunteers to defend their own judgment of their work against the judgment of the group. Do you think there is as much evidence for the claim you selected as you did when you argued for it initially?

Chapter 12

Causal Arguments

A causal argument attempts to support a causal claim or hypothesis. A **causal claim** says or implies that one thing caused or causes another. A **causal hypothesis** is a causal claim put forth to explain the cause or effect of something, when the cause or effect hasn't yet been conclusively established. Here are some examples of causal claims:

Smoking causes birth defects.

The reception is bad because the cable came loose.

At high concentrations, the enzyme damages healthy tissue.

The new treatment prevents infections.

Pressing the two surfaces together produces a permanent bond.

DNase significantly improved lung function.

Vitamin C does not cure colds.

Potash stimulates root development.

In this chapter we turn to the arguments that are most commonly used to support causal claims or hypotheses.

Causation Among Specific Events

Frequently we reason that one specific event caused another specific event. This morning Moore's coffee tasted better than usual. Why? Well, this morning Moore used a different brand of coffee. Maybe, we hypothesize, using the new brand resulted in the coffee's tasting better. Using a new brand of coffee was one event, the coffee's tasting better was another event, and maybe the first event caused the second event.

Parker's car was running just fine—until he took it in for the 50,000-mile service prescribed in the owner's manual. When he got the car back, it pinged and lost power when going uphill. Parker figured (this is his hypothesis) they did something to the car during the service that evidently caused the problem. One specific event—something done when servicing the car—apparently caused another specific event—the car's performing poorly on hills.

How do we reach a conclusion (confirm a causal hypothesis) that one specific event or occurrence caused some other specific event or occurrence? In this section we discuss the two most frequently employed types of arguments (patterns of reasoning) designed to reach such conclusions.

■ Only-Relevant-Difference Reasoning

Parker's car began performing badly on hills. Why? Well, it was running fine until something *different* happened to it: It was serviced. Servicing was the *only relevant difference* between the car's running fine and its not running fine. Naturally Parker suspected the servicing.

Moore's coffee never tasted especially good—until this morning. And then it tasted much better. Why? Well—this morning Moore used a new brand of coffee. The new coffee brand was the *only relevant difference* between this morning's great coffee and past mornings' mediocre coffee. The new brand caused this morning's coffee to taste good, Moore concludes.

Not too long ago, Moore's daughter stuck two identical pink roses in two separate vases. She placed an aspirin in the water in one vase. The rose in that vase lasted longer than the rose in the other vase. Moore's daughter concluded that the aspirin caused the rose to last longer. She reached this conclusion because the aspirin was the *only relevant difference* between the rose that lasted longer and the rose that lasted less long.

The type of reasoning illustrated by these three examples has an obvious name: only-relevant-difference reasoning. The reasoning is this:

1. One item has a feature other similar items lack.
2. There is only one other relevant difference between the item that has the feature in question and the other items that don't have the feature in question.
3. Therefore, the difference before us is the cause of the feature in question.

Perhaps it wouldn't hurt to review the three examples above to see that they fit this formula:

1. One cut rose lasted longer than another cut rose. The longer-lasting one was treated with aspirin. Therefore, the aspirin caused the first rose to last longer.

The feature in question? The longer-lastingness of the one rose. The difference that supposedly caused the feature in question? The one rose's being treated with aspirin.

2. This morning's coffee tasted better than previous mornings' coffee. It also was made using a new brand of coffee. Therefore, the new brand was responsible for the coffee's tasting good.

The feature in question? The new coffee's tasting better. The difference that supposedly caused the feature in question? The brand used to brew this morning's coffee.

3. Parker's car before the service didn't ping or lose power on hills. Parker's car after the service did. The after-service car also had been serviced. The only relevant difference between the "two" cars (apart from the pinging and losing of power) was the service. Therefore, the service caused the bad performance.

The feature in question? The after-service car's pinging and losing power on hills. The difference? The service.

As you can see, to employ only-relevant-difference reasoning, we need at least two things to compare. The things must be the same except for (1) the feature in question that we wish to know the cause of and (2) the difference that produced the feature.

As you can also see, only-relevant-difference reasoning is used in before-after comparisons—Parker's car and Moore's coffee were cases like this. And it can be used in side-by-side comparisons—Moore's daughter's roses gave us that kind of case.

Obviously, for only-relevant-difference reasoning to work, the difference we consider must be *relevant* to the feature in question. And it must be the *only* relevant difference between the things we are comparing, apart from the feature in question. Was the car's being serviced relevant to its bad performance? Certainly. But was the service the *only* relevant difference between after-service car and before-service car? For example, did Parker also fill up the after-service car with a new brand of gasoline? Did his son work on the engine after the service? Critical thinking requires consideration of important alternative differences that may have been overlooked.

Only-relevant-difference reasoning can be conclusive—at least in experimental conditions. If a piece of litmus paper turns red when Moore dips it in a liquid, it is very safe to think the liquid caused the alteration. That's because the litmus paper prior to dipping and the litmus paper during dipping were exactly the same, except for the liquid. That means the liquid was the only relevant difference that could explain the feature in question.

Even apart from carefully controlled experimental conditions, this pattern of reasoning can yield conclusions that are certain by everyday stan-

Speed Saves Lives

When Congress ended the national 55-mph speed limit in 1995, many thought the result would be increased carnage on the highways. As it has turned out, the traffic death rate has dropped substantially nationwide, and in California it declined to its lowest level since 1959. It looks as if eliminating the speed limit did *not* diminish highway safety after all, right? In fact (using only-relevant-difference reasoning), it looks as if ending the speed limit may actually have made the highways safer—which is exactly what some advocates of the higher speed limits had predicted.*

In fact, according to statistics reported in the *Sacramento Bee,* on the freeways where California raised the speed limit from 55 to 65, the rate of fatal accidents increased 8.7 percent. And where the state raised the limit to 75, the rate went up 9.7 percent.

We don't know what caused the overall decline in traffic fatalities, but it doesn't seem to be raising the speed limit.[†]

---

*The argument, as we recall, was this: A low speed limit increases the disparities in velocity between those who obey the limit and those who don't, and that produces hazardous conditions.

[†]On the other hand, columnist George Will argued that the reason there were more fatal accidents on the highways was because before the limits were raised, the police had to concentrate on the highways, leaving people free to drive recklessly on back roads. After the limits were raised, police devoted more energy to back roads (where, he said, there collectively is more traffic), and that produced an overall decline in the rate of fatalities. So, he concluded, raising the speed limits did reduce the fatality rate after all! Whatever. Personally, we'd agree with the *Bee* and suspect air bags and increased seat belt usage caused the decline.

dards of rigor. If Parker's friends become violently ill immediately upon eating a lunch he made for them, it would be unwise not to attribute the problem to the lunch. True, in real life it is possible that Parker's friends' distress is due to something else besides the lunch, since their before- and after-lunch conditions are probably not nearly as similar as the conditions of the litmus paper before and after dipping. So the reasoning isn't as strong as in the litmus case. But it's strong enough for him to conclude that his lunch caused the problem and maybe to consider taking his friends to a restaurant next time he wants to treat them.

Many important cases aren't as conclusive as the lunch example, because often we cannot be certain that the difference in question is the only relevant difference between the cases we are comparing. The rose with aspirin might also have come from a hardier bush, or it might have been fresher to begin with. There may be all sorts of relevant differences between this morning's cup of coffee and previous mornings' cups, besides their having been made with a different brand of coffee. The temperature of the water, the cleanliness of the pot and cup, or the condition of Moore's taste buds could all be different.

It is NOT the mark of a critical thinker to pretend to know nothing about anything.

What do we mean when we say a difference is "relevant"? We mean that it is not unreasonable to suppose the difference might have caused the feature in question. Obviously, the more you know about a subject, the better able you are to say whether a given difference is relevant to a feature in question. When the mechanics serviced Parker's car, they also washed it. If you know *nothing* about *anything*, you could not exclude the washing as irrelevant or nonmajor. However, it is *not* the mark of a critical thinker to *pretend* to know nothing about anything. If Parker says he thinks something they did during servicing caused his car to perform badly because that was the only difference prior to the car's misbehaving, it is *not* thinking critically to say, "How do you know it isn't because you washed it?"

Please notice again: To say a factor is relevant is only to say it is not unreasonable to suppose it caused some feature. If you learn that, in fact, it did not cause the feature, that doesn't necessarily mean you were mistaken to think it was relevant. Even though it did not cause the feature, it might not have been unreasonable to suppose it did.

■ *Only-Relevant-Common-Thread Reasoning*

Sometimes we confront multiple occurrences of something. Five friends simultaneously are afflicted with acute intestinal discomfort. What caused it? If there is a single common thread among the friends' various activities, we regard this common thread as the cause. If the five all ate at Anne's Soup Kitchen, we suspect the food at Anne's. If we have reason to think eating at Anne's is the *only* relevant thing the five had in common, then we make a point not to dine at Anne's ourselves.

Suppose you play a variety of sports. Sometimes your knee hurts when you play; other times it doesn't. You begin to notice that when it hurts, you are always wearing your Nike shoes. *Voila!* You have found a likely culprit for your discomfort.

The pattern of reasoning here is this:

1. Multiple occurrences of a feature (the feature in question) are united by a single relevant common thread (the common thread in question)
2. Therefore, the common thread in question is the cause of the feature in question.

Of course, dining at Anne's is not really the only feature the friends had in common. They were all friends. They had all experienced breathing air, living on earth, being creatures with heads, and so forth. But these common experiences were not relevant to the feature in question. Further, these experiences were had by others who did not suffer acute intestinal discomfort. We look for a common experience restricted to these five.

However, what if these five are the *only* people on earth who belong to a secret club, which they formed while dining at Anne's? Isn't this common thread restricted to the five? Yes—but it isn't relevant to acute intestinal distress. So we can ignore it. The more we know about human illness, the better able we are to weed out common threads that are irrelevant.

What if more than a single (relevant) common thread can be found? Then we have more than one possible cause. For example, perhaps the five friends ate at Anne's, but also went to a movie and shared a box of popcorn. Then Anne's food and the popcorn are both suspect.

For brevity, let's refer to only-relevant-common-thread reasoning as common-thread reasoning, and only-relevant-difference reasoning as relevant-difference reasoning. Common-thread reasoning is best suited as a method for forming hypotheses to be tested in some other way, usually through experimentation involving relevant-difference reasoning. Why? First of all, multiple occurrences of a feature in question could always have resulted from different causes. For instance, the five people eating at Anne's might have suffered intestinal distress for different reasons, and then it would just be coincidence that they all ate at Anne's. The second reason common-thread reasoning is best suited as a method for forming hypotheses is that, even if we are dealing with multiple occurrences of an effect somehow known to have been caused by one and the same thing, these multiple occurrences are likely to have many other things in common besides whatever it was that caused them—common-thread reasoning by itself cannot tell us which of these common things was the actual cause of the multiple occurrences of the effect.

Common Mistakes Found in Causal Reasoning

The strength of causal reasoning of the two varieties just considered depends on the extent to which we can be sure important possibilities have been eliminated.

■ Possible Mistakes in Relevant-Difference Reasoning

The likely mistakes in relevant-difference reasoning are as follows. To understand them, recall (one last time!) the story of Moore's coffee:

> Moore's coffee today has the feature of tasting especially good. The only relevant difference between today's coffee and previous cups Moore has brewed, apart from the feature in question, is that today's cup was made using a new brand of coffee. Therefore, using the new brand was the cause of the feature in question.

Now, the difference we take to be the cause of the feature in question might not really be a *difference*. That is, Moore might be mistaken in thinking he used a new brand. Maybe he just dreamed he used a new brand. But, since this is not a problem in reasoning, we won't dwell on it. The problems we are concerned with are the following:

1. The major difference we take to be the cause of the feature in question might not be a *relevant* difference. (Remember, to say a difference is relevant is merely to say it isn't unreasonable to think it played a role in causing the feature in question. It is *not* to state that it definitely did play a role in causing the feature in question.) If Moore had focused not on the new brand of coffee but on the color of the coffee cup, he would have focused on an irrelevant difference. The fact that the latest and great-tasting coffee was served in a yellow cup would merely be coincidental. (On the other hand, maybe taste is influenced by what something is served in. Moore was once served coffee in a cup that looked as if it had most recently been used to make mud pies. He did not wish to taste the coffee.)

2. The difference we take to have caused the feature in question might be a relevant difference, but not the *only* relevant difference. (Again, to say that a difference is relevant is to say that it isn't unreasonable to think it played a role in causing the occurrence or feature in question. It is *not* to say that it did play a role.) Using a different brand for today's coffee is a relevant difference, but was it the only relevant difference between today's coffee and previous days' coffee? Was today's coffee brewed with a different filter? Was the condition of Moore's mouth different? Was the temperature of the water different? The condition of the cup? If the major difference is not the only relevant difference, then it may not be the cause of the feature in question.

3. Sometimes the difference we're looking at is the effect rather than the cause of the feature in question. George seems unusually jittery and remarks that he didn't sleep well. His wife thinks George's insomnia (the feature about George in question) was caused by his jitters (the only relevant difference). She may fail to consider the possibility that George's being jittery was the effect of his poor sleeping rather than the cause.

4. Perhaps the difference did not cause the feature in question, but rather the difference and feature in question are both effects of a third underlying cause. In the example above, maybe George's jitters and his insomnia are both the result of too much coffee.

Mixing the Patterns

Researchers did follow-up studies on twenty individuals who had been identified as carriers of the AIDS virus. After three years, it was discovered that
fourteen of the carriers had developed AIDS and six still showed no symptoms of the disease.

New experimental techniques were used to isolate and analyze the
virus in all of the patients with symptoms and in one of those with no
symptoms. The results of the tests showed that the virus from the asymptomatic carrier was of a new strain with an altered p24 antigen. The researchers concluded that this difference in strain was the cause of the lack of
symptoms in this patient.

In an attempt to confirm their hypothesis, the scientists analyzed the
virus from the other five asymptomatic carriers. Sure enough, they too were
infected with the virus that has an altered p24 antigen. Said one of the
scientists, "This establishes with reasonable certainty that the cause of AIDS
patients' failure to develop symptoms over time is that they carry a different
strain of the virus than the one we're accustomed to finding in victims of
the disease."

Notice that in the first of these hypothetical experiments, the researchers, in analyzing virus from seven symptomatic patients and one
asymptomatic carrier, used the only-relevant-difference pattern of reasoning. The confirming experiment (checking the remaining asymptomatic patients) made use of the common-thread pattern. These two patterns are
often used this way—one is applied to check results first obtained by the
other.

The two patterns can also be used simultaneously, as would have been
the case had all twenty patients been checked at once, with the same conclusions drawn.

Thus, when we have a case of relevant-difference reasoning, we must
consider not only whether it is truly the *only relevant* difference (apart from
the feature in question), but also

- ▲ Could we have reversed cause and effect?
- ▲ Have we overlooked a possible common cause?

■ Possible Mistakes in Common-Thread Reasoning

Similar questions need be asked with regard to common-thread reasoning.
Here again is the case of the sour stomachs:

After dining at Anne's, five people suffered from acute intestinal distress. Since
dining at Anne's was the only relevant common thread among the five (apart
from the illness itself), we conclude that Anne's food caused them to become ill.

Assuming we aren't mistaken in thinking all five dined at Anne's, we need ask the following:

1. Is the common thread *relevant* to the feature in question? (For example, if all five had worn white shirts, that common thread would not be relevant to the five becoming sick.)

2. Is the common thread the *only* relevant common thread? (For example, did all go to the movies and eat popcorn?) If there are other relevant common threads, the common thread we have focused on (eating at Anne's) may only be a part of the explanation. Or it may not have anything at all to do with the feature in question.

3. Could we have reversed cause and effect? In this example there is no danger that cause and effect could have been reversed, because the effect (getting sick) came later than the suspected cause (eating at Anne's). But consider a different example: An educator notices that countries that have strong economies are united by a common thread: They all spend generously on public education. "Therefore," he or she reasons, "spending generously on public education caused their economies to be strong." This educator may well have reversed cause and effect. Did spending on education promote economic strength? Or did the strong economy make it possible for the country to spend on education?

4. Have we overlooked a possible common cause of the common thread and the feature in question? Let's say Moore notices a common thread among the students who do well on his exams: They all complete the homework assignments. "See what doing your homework can do for you?" Moore asks his class. Moore thinks the students do well on exams because they do their homework. But that might be a mistake. Perhaps they do well on exams because they are smart, and perhaps they also do their homework because they are smart. Being smart might be a common cause both of the common thread and of the feature in question.

Or, to take another example of the same problem, a man from southern Florida moves to Boston and notices a curious thing. Every fall the trees lose their leaves and shortly thereafter the branches become brittle. "Aha!" the man reasons, "Losing their leaves is the common thread in the branches becoming brittle. Therefore, it must be that losing their leaves makes the branches brittle." This example, which Nickolas Pappas gave to us, is a case in which someone has overlooked the possibility that the common thread (branches losing leaves) and the feature in question (branches becoming brittle) both were caused by some third thing (cold weather and low sunlight).

Thus, to return to the five people who dined at Anne's—perhaps they all did so because they were coming down with something and showed up at Anne's because she stocks Rolaids. In this case, dining at Anne's and suffering intestinal distress later were both caused by a third, underlying factor, the illness in question.

In theory, a careful application of the second question above (Is the common thread we are focusing on the only common thread?) should disclose possible candidates for underlying causation by some third thing. However, it is extremely important to be alert to the possibility of underlying causation by some third thing. So consider the question in its own right: Were the feature in question and the common thread we have focused on both the result of some underlying third factor?

5. Is the feature in question such that it might not have required a common cause to begin with? For example, five people who become ill might have become so for different reasons, a virus in one instance, too much apple cider in another, and so forth. True, all five ate at Anne's—but *that* common thread may have been coincidence. We should not unthinkingly assume multiple occurrences of something have a common cause—even if there is a common thread present. A common thread might induce us to assume that a single thing caused the feature in question, and that might be a mistake.

To summarize: With common-thread reasoning, we must be certain the common thread is the *only relevant one,* and we must consider the following questions:

▲ Were the cause and the effect reversed?

▲ Have we overlooked a possible common cause of the common thread and the feature in question?

▲ Did we mistakenly assume there was a common cause when in fact there wasn't one?

■ *Post Hoc, Ergo Propter Hoc*

We have listed several questions to consider when we are confronted with relevant-difference or common-thread reasoning. When we don't consider one or more of these questions, our reasoning could commit the mistake or fallacy known as ***post hoc, ergo propter hoc.***

Post hoc, ergo propter hoc means "After that, therefore because of that," or, more loosely, "*This* happened about the same time *that* happened, therefore *this* happened because *that* happened." Just because one thing happened about the same time another thing happened doesn't mean that the first thing *caused* the second. Moore's birthday happened the day after Parker's, but that doesn't mean Parker's birthday caused Moore's birthday to happen.

So, it is a mistake to suppose that, just because X happened around the time Y happened, that X happened *because* Y happened. You dip a piece of litmus paper in a liquid and the paper turns red. It is fine to conclude the fluid caused the paper to turn red, *if* you have reason to suppose (as you might well have) the only thing that could have made the paper turn red was being dipped in the liquid. But it is another thing, and a mistake in reasoning, to conclude the liquid caused the paper to turn red if your conclusion rests on nothing more than the fact the paper turned red after it was dipped in the liquid.

Thus, when you hear people saying something like

John got a heart attack while sprinting, so we know the sprinting caused the heart attack

I think you're going to have a lot of politicians spending time in gyms now.

—Tongue-in-cheek post hoc from BILL CLINTON, commenting on Jesse "The Body" Ventura's election as governor of Minnesota

The Spotted Owl

After logging in old-growth forests was halted in the Pacific Northwest to save the spotted owl, the general economy in that area went into a dramatic tailspin. To conclude from this fact that the measures taken to save the spotted owl *caused* the economic decline is to be guilty of *post hoc* reasoning. To have caused the economic decline, these measures would have to have been the *only relevant thing to happen before the decline*. (In fact, the most severe economic recession since the Great Depression also happened at the same time, throughout the American economy. Maybe the attempt to save the spotted owl caused that, too.)

this is *post hoc* reasoning. We could argue with equal force:

> John got a heart attack while sweating profusely. Therefore, we know sweating profusely caused the heart attack.

Or to take another example, you can see the difference between arguing

> Five people dined at Anne's and all got sick. Therefore, eating at Anne's caused them to get sick.

and

> Five people got sick. They had only one relevant thing in common: They all earlier had dined at Anne's. Further, because nobody else dined at Anne's that night, we know nobody who dined at Anne's who didn't get sick. We have (somehow) eliminated the possibility that getting sick and dining at Anne's could both be the result of the same underlying cause. In addition, getting sick later could not have caused them to have dined at Anne's earlier, so we haven't reversed cause and effect. Finally, we have no reason to suppose they got sick for independent reasons. Therefore, eating at Anne's caused them to get sick.

The second argument here is strong. The first argument is *post hoc, ergo propter hoc.*

■ Overlooking the Possibility of Coincidence

Sometimes the connection between events is coincidental, not causal. There are three common types of coincidence we sometimes overlook.

Count the Post Hocs

The following is excerpted from an article in the *Orange County Register,* August 1999, entitled "The union's unfair share." The article was written by Mark Clark and Edward Erler, who are professors of political science at California State University, San Bernardino. At the time of the article, the California Legislature was considering a "Fair Share" bill that would require California State University faculty who were not members of the California Faculty Association (CFA) either to pay 85% of the amount CFA members pay in dues to the union or to pay a similar amount to charity. The authors consider several related issues in the article, including the following:

> One union official argues that "free loaders" are simply "selfish" because they refuse to "pay for the union expenses that protect all of our rights." But how has CFA protected the rights of all faculty? Prior to collective bargaining, faculty salaries were among the highest in the nation among comparable institutions. After collective bargaining, salaries have lagged significantly behind.
>
> Prior to collective bargaining tenure could be awarded after four years; after collective bargaining it is six years. Since collective bargaining, working conditions have precipitously declined; faculty-student ratios have increased, faculty morale has declined; support for research has been eviscerated; and academic freedom has been threatened by assaults from the minions of political correctness.

We get a series of *post hoc* fallacies if we take the authors as saying that collective bargaining caused the bad effects listed. If they mean only that collective bargaining failed to prevent the circumstances described, then of course there could be no *post hoc.* In that case we'd suspect the use of innuendo.

First, we might think two events are related as cause and effect when in fact they are not causally related to one another at all. Parker washed his car, and shortly afterward he had a flat tire. It would be silly (and *post hoc*) to think the wash job caused the flat, and probably nobody would think that. Or would they? People are superstitious, and what underlies many superstitions is thinking of coincidental events as causally related to one another. Do you have a lucky number? People who believe in a lucky number generally do so because they once won something with that number. What they think is that the number caused them to win. In fact, selecting the number and then winning something was just a matter of coincidence.

This kind of coincidence crops up in relevant-difference reasoning when we haven't made sure the "only relevant difference" we are thinking about truly is the *only relevant difference* that might account for the feature in question.

The other two kinds of coincidence crop up in common-thread reasoning: Sometimes we think multiple occurrences of an effect are due to a common thread shared by all the occurrences, when in fact *some other* common thread caused the occurrences. In this case, it's just coincidence the first common thread is present. For example, the illness of the five people who ate at Anne's may have been due to a common virus they were all exposed to last week. The common thread of eating at Anne's may have nothing at all to do with their illness. Or, to take another example, every time your hay fever acts up, you have just mowed the lawn. "Aha!" you reason. "There is a common thread here. Every time my hay fever acts up, gas fumes have been present. Gas fumes must activate my hay fever." In fact, the gas-fume common thread is present only by coincidence. The mower also kicks up pollen, and that common thread is the one that activated your hay fever.

The last way in which people overlook coincidence is to assume multiple occurrences of an effect are due to the common thread shared by all the occurrences, when in fact the occurrences were not caused by a single thing. The illness of the five people who dined at Anne's may not have been due to Anne's food or any other common factor. One person's illness might have been caused by one thing, another's by another thing, and so forth, with the result that it was just coincidence that they all dined at Anne's.

Keeping in mind the questions listed above helps to avoid mistaking coincidence for cause and effect.

■ *Questions to Ask About Causal Reasoning*

To summarize: If the reasoning ("argument") is relevant difference, ask these questions:

1. Is the difference in question *relevant?* (A strong argument requires the difference be relevant.)

2. Are there *other relevant differences?* (If there are, the difference in question is at best a partial explanation of the feature in question.)

3. Could the difference in question and feature in question *be effects of an underlying cause?* (Unless you can discount this possibility, you can't have much confidence in the argument.)

4. Could *cause and effect be reversed?* (Unless you can discount this possibility, you can't have much confidence in the argument.)

If the reasoning ("argument") is common thread, ask these questions:

1. Is the common thread *relevant?* (A strong argument requires the common thread be relevant.)

2. Are there *other relevant common threads?* (If there are, the common thread in question is at best a partial explanation of the feature in question.)

3. Could common thread and feature in question *both be effects of an underlying cause?* (Unless you can discount the possibility, you can't have much confidence in the argument.)

"Teen Smoking Surge Reported After Joe Camel's 1988 Debut"

Rise in youth smoking
The incidence of youths becoming regular smokers jumped 50 percent between 1988 and 1996. A look at the rate of youths who started smoking daily, age 12–17:

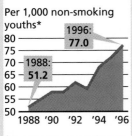

Per 1,000 non-smoking youths*

1996: 77.0

1988: 51.2

80
75
70
65
60
55
50

1988 '90 '92 '94 '96

*Considered non-smokers at start of year
Source: Centers for Disease Control and Prevention

So said the Associated Press headline that accompanied this graphic. The article, however, stated that the Centers for Disease Control *attributed* the surge in part to kid-friendly cartoon advertising like the Joe Camel ads. It also noted that President Clinton had blamed the increase on the Joe Camel ad campaign.

It is true that the CDC studies showed that the rate for beginning smokers had been *declining* steadily for over a decade before it started increasing again in 1988. It is also true that *something* caused the rate to start increasing again, beginning in 1988. And finally, it is true that R. J. Reynolds introduced *Joe Camel* in its advertising for Camel cigarettes in 1988.

But *this* information, while suspicious, does not show that the increase was *caused,* even in part, *by* the ad campaign. For example, reportedly there was a notable increase in the appearance of cigarette smoking in movies beginning about then, too. As it stands, this is *post hoc, ergo propter hoc.*

4. Could *cause and effect be reversed?* (Unless you can discount this possibility, you can't have much confidence in the argument.)

5. Could there possibly *not even be a common cause,* despite the presence of a common thread? (Unless you are sure there is a common cause, you cannot have much confidence in the argument.)

Exercise 12-1

We want to further pinpoint the cause of the illness of the five friends who ate at Anne's by looking for common threads in what they ate.

▲ 1. Suppose three ate tuna sandwiches and two ate pastrami sandwiches. Which is more likely to have been the cause of the illness?
   a. The tuna sandwiches
   b. The pastrami sandwiches
   c. Neither of these is more likely, based on the given information.

2. Instead, suppose only four of your five friends became sick. But suppose all five ate tuna sandwiches. Which is the best hypothesis?
   a. The tuna sandwiches caused the four to become sick.

b. If the tuna sandwiches caused the four to get sick, they did so only in connection with other factors.

c. The tuna sandwiches did not cause the four to become sick.

▲3. Suppose the five all ate tuna sandwiches and all drank lemonade. Which is the best hypothesis?

a. The sandwiches and lemonade both might have played a role in the illness.

b. Neither the sandwiches nor lemonade played a role in the illness.

c. The sandwiches made some of the individuals sick; the lemonade made the others sick.

d. The information given does not favor a, b, or c.

4. Suppose we can find no common thread in what the five friends ate, but the five did arrive in the same car. Which is the best hypothesis?

a. The car must have had something to do with their illness.

b. The car might have had something to do with their illness.

c. The car definitely had nothing whatsoever to do with their illness.

5. Suppose all of the following are common threads among the five sick friends. Which are relevant?

a. They all drank water from the same pitcher.

b. They all joined in singing "Happy Birthday" to some other diner.

c. They all had the salad bar.

d. They all knew the waitperson.

e. They all knew each other.

f. They had all just come from the same party.

g. They had all just played soccer.

h. They all had ice in their drinks.

Exercise 12-2

Identify each reasoning pattern as (a) only relevant difference or (b) only relevant common thread.

▲ 1. Pat never had trouble playing that passage before. I wonder what the problem is. It must have something to do with the piano she just bought.

2. Sometimes the fishing is pretty good around here; sometimes it isn't. When I try to pin down why, it seems like the only variable is the wind. Strange as it sounds, the fish just don't bite when it's windy.

3. The price of gas has gone up more than 40 cents a gallon in the past three or four weeks. It all started when they had that fire down there in that refinery in Texas. Must have really depleted supplies somehow.

▲ 4. You know, it has occurred to me, whenever we have great roses like this, it's always after a long period of cloudy weather. I'll bet they don't like direct sun.

5. All of a sudden he's all, "Let's go to Beano's for a change." Right. Am I supposed to think it's just coincidence his old girlfriend started working there?

6. You really want to know what gets into me and makes me be so angry? It's you! You and your stupid habit of never lifting up the toilet seat.

▲ 7. Why in heck am I so tired today? Must be all the studying I did last night. Thinking takes a lot of energy.

8. The computer isn't working again. Every time it happens the dang kids have been playing with it. Why can't they just use the computers they have down at school?

9. What makes your dog run away from time to time? I bet it has to do with that garbage you feed him. You want him to stay home? Feed him a better brand of dog food.

▲ 10. I'll tell you what caused all these cases of kids taking guns to school and shooting people. Every single one of those kids liked to play violent video-games, that's what caused it.

11. Gag! What did you do to this coffee, anyway—put Ajax in it?

12. Can you beat that? I set this battery on the garage floor last night and this morning it was dead. I guess the old saying about cement draining a battery is still true.

▲ 13. Clinton was impeached. Then his standing went up in the opinion polls. Just goes to show: No publicity is bad publicity.

14. Why did the dog yelp? Are you serious? You'd yelp if someone stomped on your foot, too.

15. Dennis certainly seems more at peace with himself these days. I guess starting up psychotherapy was good for him.

▲ 16. Every time we have people over, the next morning the bird is all squawky and grumpy. The only thing I can figure is it must not get enough sleep when people are over in the evening.

17. The lawn mower started up just fine last week. Could the fact I let it stand out in the rain have something to do with it?

18. Every time Moore plays soccer, his foot starts to hurt. It also hurts right after he goes jogging. But when he bicycles, or uses an elliptical trainer, he doesn't have a problem. He decides to avoid exercise that involves pounding his feet on the ground.

▲ 19. You know, all of a sudden she's been, like, cool toward me? A bit, you know, icy? I don't think she liked it when I told her I was going to start playing poker with you guys again.

20. Your Chevy Suburban is hard to start. My Chevy Suburban starts right up. You always use Chevron gas; I use Texaco. You'd better switch to Texaco.

Exercise 12-3

In each of the following, the speaker might be making an unwarranted assumption as represented by the three lettered statements. State which kind of unwarranted assumption the speaker might be making.

a. Assuming two things are related as cause and effect when in fact they may well be unrelated

b. Attributing causation of multiple events or features to a common cause when in fact they may not have a common cause

c. Attributing causation of multiple events or features to a common cause when they may well have a common cause, but a cause different from that which has been cited

▲ 1. Whenever I mow the lawn I end up sneezing a lot more than normal. Must be the gas fumes from the mower.

2. Chris had that heart attack right after he drank a big cup of Minute Maid. Next time he'd better pass on the Minute Maid.

3. My Chevy Suburban is hard to start, and I've been using Texaco. Maybe I'd better switch.

▲ 4. The Chinese minister criticizes the United States, and NATO "mistakenly" bombs the Chinese embassy in Belgrade? You think that's coincidence?

5. I flunk the final. I sprain my ankle. Someone puts a huge dent in my car. I'll tell you what it is. I'm a Sagittarius and the alignment of the stars was awful for me today.

6. Moore's heart races when he plays soccer. It also races when he plays football or volleyball. But it doesn't race when he rides his bicycle. The excitement from the competition in competitive sports must really affect him.

▲ 7. Edna's tumor miraculously disappeared right after the saint prayed for her. If that doesn't demonstrate the power of prayer, I don't know what does.

8. First, Rodrigo gets a large inheritance. Then Charles meets the girl of his dreams. And Amanda gets the job she was hoping for. What did they all have in common? They all thought positively. It can work for you, too.

9. All seven of the lung cancer patients in this wing of the hospital were overweight. I'll bet carrying around all that extra weight placed a strain on their respiratory systems.

▲ 10. Sharon, Tadd, and Jonathan are in the chess club and are extremely nearsighted, while Tim, Chris, and Nick are on the tennis squad and have perfect eyesight. Playing chess must have been detrimental to Sharon, Tadd, and Jonathan's eyesight.

11. Every time Seth gets a headache he takes vitamin A, and the headache goes away. That's why he takes vitamin A. He's learned from experience it cures a headache.

12. See, what I think is you can see the future in your dreams. Last night I dreamed my mother won the lottery, and today she won it! She won $100!

▲ 13. The lights won't go on, the wipers won't run, and the radio doesn't work. This all happened less than a week after I had new spark plugs put in. Maybe the plugs messed up the electrical system somehow.

14. Can you beat that? You and I were born on the same day thousands of miles apart. Then we found each other and fell in love! It's fate, that's what it is.

15. When I went to Munich last summer I went to this bar and who was there? This guy I went to school with and hadn't seen in 15 years! There's no way that could happen by chance. I wonder what the explanation is.

Exercise 12-4

Classify each of the following passages as either

a. Overlooking the possibility that two or more events might have a common cause

b. Thinking of two events as cause and effect when they may not be related at all

c. Assuming two or more events have a common cause when in fact they may not

d. Overlooking the possibility that cause and effect have been reversed.

If a passage fits into more than one category, be sure to say so.

▲ 1. It's odd. I've seen a huge number of snails this year, and the roses have mildew. Don't know which caused which, but one of them obviously caused the other.

2. Maybe the reason he's sick is all the aspirin he's been taking.

3. I was just sitting there listening to the radio. The engine was off. Then I turned on the overhead light, and it wouldn't go on. Next thing you know, the radio died. A short in the light must have caused the light to malfunction and the radio to die.

▲ 4. That big business deal was signed right then while they were drinking all that champagne. Looks like that's a pretty good way to get a deal to close successfully.

5. The only thing that could possibly account for Clark and his two brothers all having winning lottery tickets is that all three had been blessed by the Reverend Dim Dome just the day before. I'm signing up for the Reverend's brotherhood.

6. Her boyfriend is in a bad mood, you say? I'll bet it's because she's trying just a bit too hard to please him. It probably gets on his nerves.

▲ 7. Well, if you ask me, I think she got an A in chemistry because the prof plays golf with her dad. And I bet she got an A in math because the stupid teacher likes her. And I know the only reason she got an A in philosophy is she's just plain lucky.

8. Whenever there's a hurricane, the barometer is extremely low. This suggests that an extremely low barometer can cause hurricanes.

9. Perhaps Jason is so nearsighted because he reads so many books.

▲ 10. George Mallory died on Mt. Everest. They found his body in 1999, along with the broken rope that must have caused his fall.

11. Yes, they're saying electric blankets aren't a health threat, but I know better. A friend had cancer and know what? He slept with an electric blanket.

12. At finals time, the bearded man on the front campus offers prayers in return for food. Donald is thinking, "Sure. Why not?—can't hurt anything." He approaches the bearded man with a tidbit. Later: The bearded man prays. Donald passes his finals. To skeptical friends: "Hey, you never know. I'll take all the help I can get."

▲ 13. Ever notice how all them Democrats favor liberal causes—murdering babies, taking away our guns, you name it? I sure ain't gonna let my kid become a Democrat and end up way over there on the left.

14. Darby is talking on the telephone. Suddenly the line goes dead and the lights go out. She thinks perhaps the power outage caused the phone to go dead.

15. In 1962 the Supreme Court outlawed prayer in public schools. America then spent a decade losing the most devastating war the country has ever been in. At the same time the moral fabric of the country dissolved. Teenage pregnancies. Homosexuality. Crime. Drugs. Welfare. Filthy movies. God's message is clear.

▲ 16. Why did Uncle Ted live such a long time? He had a good attitude, that's why.

Exercise 12-5

Identify the supposed cause and the supposed effect in each of the following items.

▲ 1. "That terrible call by the officials at the end of the third quarter triggered a 21-point explosion for Houston, Al. That call won this game for them."

ABC's Monday Night Football

2. Ever since this country lost its moral direction, the crime rate has gone through the ceiling. What more proof do we need that the cause of the sky-rocketing crime rate is the breakdown in traditional family values?

3. Wow, is Brown hot or what? After that rocky start, he has struck out the last nine batters to face him. That's what happens when you get your confidence back.

▲ 4. It's an unusually warm evening, and the birds are singing with exceptional vigor. "Hot weather does make a bird want to sing," Uncle Irving observes.

5. The three times Grimsley has eaten at the Zig Zag Pizza House he has become ill. The first time he ate a large pizza and a side order of hot peppers; the second time he had the all-you-can-eat ravioli special and the hot peppers; and the third time he had the giant meatball sandwich and the hot

peppers. Concluding that the hot peppers were the offending item, Grimsley determines never to order them again.

6. On your trip across the country, you note that the traffic is awful at the first intersection you come to in Hawthorne, Nevada. "They certainly didn't do anybody a favor by putting a traffic light at this place," you think. "Look at all the congestion it caused."

▲ 7. Whenever the Democrats have won a second term in the White House, hemlines on women's skirts have gone down. Must be something about Democratic presidencies that depresses people's spirits or something.

8. Lack of self-confidence can be difficult to explain, but common sense suggests that stuttering is among the causes, judging from how often the two things go together.

9. Statistics show that people who are older when they become sexually active don't experiment with drugs. That to me is a very good reason to keep youngsters from having sex.

▲ 10. I've had a lot more energy since I started taking vitamins. They really work for me.

11. You'll notice that the top executives drive the best cars around here. My advice is, if you want to advance, get a better car.

12. I didn't study at all for the last test and guess what? I aced it. Now I know what to do for the final.

▲ 13. People with eating disorders were often the victims of child abuse, which reveals yet another terrible outcome of child abuse.

▲ 14. Caroline's face has broken out since she started her new, high-pressure job. She figures it must be all the pressure she's under.

15. Studies show that people who are insecure about their relationship with their partners have a notable lack of ability to empathize with others. That's why we recommend that partners receive empathy training before they get married.

16. After the Brady Bill was passed, murders in this town decreased by a whopping 33 percent, so don't tell me that the Brady Bill didn't reduce violent crime.

▲ 17. ". . . and let's not underestimate the importance of that home field advantage, guys."

"Right, Dan. Six of the last seven teams that had the home field advantage went on to win the Super Bowl."

ABC's Monday Night Football

Exercise 12-6

▲ In which of the items in the preceding exercise is it reasonable to wonder if the cause and the effect have been reversed?

Exercise 12-7 ──────────────────────────────────

In which of the items in Exercise 12-5 is it reasonable to wonder if the cause and the effect are both the effects of an underlying cause?

Exercise 12-8 ──────────────────────────────────

Identify those items in Exercise 12-5 that attempt to use only-relevant-common-thread reasoning. In which of those items is it reasonable to wonder if there even is a single cause despite the presence of a common thread?

Exercise 12-9 ──────────────────────────────────

Identify the supposed cause and the supposed effect in each of the following items.

▲   1. Each Monday and Friday, Hubert jogs up Skyline Road to the top of Thompson Peak. This Friday he doesn't have the stamina to go more than halfway up and can't figure out why. Finally he remembers that he went to sleep earlier than usual the previous night. "Aha," he thinks. "That's the problem. Too much sleep."

2. Mr. Mahlman has observed earthworms appearing on his lawn from time to time. Puzzled, he thinks about possible causes. "One day they're there," he says to his wife, "and the next day they're not. Sometimes they come out early, sometimes late, sometimes right in the middle of the day. I wonder what brings them out?"

   Mrs. Mahlman is not puzzled. "I've seen them, too," she says. "And if you were paying attention you'd notice that every time you see them it's just after you've been watering, or after a heavy rain. It's the water that brings them out."

3. Stacia and Megan just got back from dining at Anne's Soup Kitchen, and Megan begins to look a little green around the gills.

   "Megan, are you all right?" asks Stacia.

   "No, as a matter of fact, my stomach is a little upset," Megan replies.

   "Didn't the food agree with you?"

   "I guess not. It must have been that stupid fishhead soup. It's the only thing I ate that was unusual, and I felt just fine until after I ate it."

▲   4. The only time in my entire life that I've had a backache was right after I tried lifting weights. I'll never do that again!

5. The cat won't eat, so Mrs. Quinstartle searches her mind for a reason. "Now, could it be that I haven't heard mice scratching around in the attic lately?" she thinks. "Yes, that's it!" she concludes.

6. Ten abnormally wet winters on the Pacific Coast have been preceded by El Niños, a periodic heating of the equatorial Pacific Ocean. El Niños, therefore, caused the wet winters.

See What Happens If You Watch the Tube?

Recent research indicates that people who watch several hours of TV each day, as compared with those who don't watch very much, express more racially prejudiced attitudes, perceive women as having more limited abilities and interests than men, overestimate the prevalence of violence in society, and underestimate the number of old people. Does this suggest to you that these attitudes and misconceptions are the *result* of watching a lot of TV, that TV *causes* people to have these attitudes and misconceptions? If so, that's fine. But remembering not to overlook possible underlying common causes should lead you to contemplate another idea. It's possible that what accounts for these attitudes and misconceptions isn't too much TV, but rather *ignorance*, and that ignorance is also what makes some people happy spending hours in front of the tube.

▲ 7. Each time one of the burglaries occurred, observers noticed a red Mustang in the vicinity. The police, of course, want to find the driver of the car, believing that he or she may have something to do with the crimes.

▲ 8. Harold has spent his last three spring vacations in Florida, and each time he has come down with a cold a few days after arriving. Figuring that being cooped up in a car with his friends on the long nonstop drive down from Boston is exposing him to too many germs, Harold decides to stay home this spring. Because he doesn't get a cold, he concludes that his hypothesis was correct.

9. Mallory, who is on the field hockey team, is annoyed with her knee. "I wonder why it goes out on me sometimes and not other times," she reflects. Suddenly it dawns on her! "Why, I only have trouble after Coach has us do those backwards running drills. That's got to be it."

10. Judith's contact lenses have been bothering her for the past three days. Because she has just started using some new brands of rinsing and disinfecting solution, she suspects that one of them is the cause of her problems. Thinking back, she remembers that the day after she let the lenses soak in the new disinfecting solution an extra long time, she was especially bothered by the lenses. So she concludes that it is the disinfecting solution that caused her problem.

11. Delmer has had a run of hard luck lately: His car battery died, leaving him stranded; his boss announced that Delmer's salary would have to be cut because of the increase in the price of heating oil; and, to top it off, his house was burglarized. He wishes now that he hadn't thrown out that chain letter he received; the thing had warned him of bad luck if he didn't send it on.

12. Hong is puzzled by the smell of burning electrical wiring in the cab of his pickup. Figuring that the problem has to be in the windshield wiper motor,

radio, air conditioner, heater, or lights, he remembers that the problem seems unrelated to the weather or time of day or night. He then concludes that the radio is the source of the problem, because it is the only thing that could be running at any time of the day or night, in any weather, and in any season.

▲ 13. Violette is a strong Cowboys fan. Because of her work schedule, however, she has been able to watch their games only once this season, and that was the only time they lost. She resolved not to watch any more Dallas games even if she has the chance. "It's bad luck," she thinks.

▲ 14. The recent volcanic eruptions in Hawaii were preceded by earthquakes around the Pacific Rim. Evidently, therefore, the earthquakes caused the eruptions.

15. What explains all the violence in society today? TV. Just look at all the violence on TV these days.

▲ 16. On Monday, Mr. O'Toole came down with a cold. That afternoon, Mrs. O'Toole caught it. Later that evening, their daughter caught it, too.

▲ 17. The males incarcerated for sexual assault in the Duluth, Minnesota, jail during a thirty-six-hour period were interviewed as part of a study, and it was discovered that all seven of them had listened to rap music within twenty-four hours of the alleged assault. This was considered evidence that rap music helped trigger the assaults.

18. Elroy had chest pains for about two months. Recently, though, when he had a cold, the pains stopped. Soon after the cold was over, the pains returned. "Odd," he thought. "There seem to be just two possible explanations. Maybe *not* having a cold causes my chest pain. But that's absurd. So the pains must be due to something that I didn't have or wasn't doing when I had the cold." Thinking further, Elroy recalls that when he had the cold he temporarily stopped drinking coffee and refrained from working out every day with his basketball league. He then reasons that either the coffee or the basketball is the cause of his pains.

19. When he was twelve years old, Sean Marsee, of Ada, Oklahoma, began dipping snuff, and by the time he entered high school he had developed an addiction that led him to consume up to ten cans of snuff each week. In his senior year, Marsee developed a painful sore on his tongue that refused to heal and that turned out to be malignant. Neither extensive surgery nor radiation contained the cancer, and the next year he died. Many believed the snuff caused his death.

20. Retail sales are down this year. That's because unemployment is so high.

Exercise 12-10

▲ Do any of the items in Exercise 12-9 attempt to use only-relevant-common-thread reasoning? If so, which ones?

Exercise 12-11

▲ In which of the items you identified in Exercise 12-9 as common-thread arguments is it reasonable to wonder if there even is a single common cause?

Exercise 12-12

In which of the items in Exercise 12-9 is it reasonable to wonder if the cause and the effect have been reversed?

Exercise 12-13

In which of the items in Exercise 12-9 is it reasonable to wonder if the cause and the effect are both the effects of an underlying cause?

Causation in Populations

Many causal claims do not apply in any straightforward way to individuals but rather apply to populations.* The claim "Drinking causes cancer of the mouth," for example, should not be interpreted as meaning that drinking will cause mouth cancer for any given individual, or even that drinking will cause mouth cancer for the majority of individuals. The claim is that drinking is a *causal factor* for mouth cancer—that is, there would be more cases of mouth cancer if everyone drank than if no one did. And so it is with other claims about causation in populations: To say that X causes Y in population P is to say that there would be more cases of Y in population P if every member of P were exposed to X than if no member of P were exposed to X.

The evidence on which such claims may be soundly based comes principally from three kinds of studies, or "arguments."

■ Controlled Cause-to-Effect Experiments

In **controlled cause-to-effect experiments,** a random sample of a target population is itself randomly divided into two groups: (1) an experimental group, all of whose members are exposed to a suspected causal factor, C (e.g., exposure of the skin to nicotine), and (2) a control group, whose members are all treated exactly as the members of the experimental group, except that they are not exposed to C. Both groups are then compared with respect

---

*For our analysis of causal factors in populations, we are indebted to Ronald N. Giere, *Understanding Scientific Reasoning*, 3d ed. (Fort Worth: Holt, Rinehart, and Winston, 1991).

Carrots Can Kill!

A few orange and green ruminations about life, death and vegetables from the Miner Institute, Chazy, New York

Nearly all sick people have eaten carrots. Obviously, the effects are cumulative.

An estimated 99.9 percent of all people who die from cancer have eaten carrots.

Another 99.9 percent of people involved in auto accidents ate carrots within 60 days before the accident.

Some 93.1 percent of juvenile delinquents come from homes where carrots are served frequently.

Among the people born in 1839 who later dined on carrots, there has been a 100 percent mortality rate.

All carrot eaters born between 1900 and 1910 have wrinkled skin, brittle bones, few teeth, and failing eyesight . . . if the perils of carrot consumption have not already caused their deaths.

—*Priorities* magazine, Summer 1990

What errors in causal reasoning can you find in these "arguments"?

to frequency of some effect, E (e.g., skin cancer). If the difference, *d*, in the frequency of E in the two groups is sufficiently large, then C may justifiably be said to cause E in the population.

This probably sounds complicated, but the principles involved are matters of common sense. You have two groups that are essentially alike, except that the members of one group are exposed to the suspected causal agent. If the effect is then found to be sufficiently more frequent in that group, you conclude that the suspected causal agent does indeed cause the effect in question.

Familiarizing yourself with these concepts and abbreviations will help you understand cause-to-effect experiments:

Experimental group—the sample of the target population whose members are all exposed to the suspected causal agent

Control group—the sample of the target population whose members are treated exactly as the members of the experimental group are except that they are not exposed to the suspected causal agent

C—the suspected causal agent

E—the effect whose cause is being investigated

d—the difference in the frequency of this effect in the experimental group and in the control group

Hey, Couch Potato—Read This!

You sometimes hear people say they avoid exercise because they know of someone who had a heart attack while working out. We trust you now recognize such reasoning as *post hoc:* To show that Uncle Ned's heart attack was caused by lifting weights, or whatever, you have to do more than show that the one thing happened and then the other thing happened.

There is a further problem here. To wonder whether strenuous exercise causes heart attacks is to wonder whether such exercise is a causal factor for heart attacks. And you can't really answer such questions by appealing to specific incidents, as we explain in the text. To think that you can show that something is (or isn't) a causal factor in a population by referring to isolated, specific events is to appeal illegitimately to anecdotal evidence, as we discuss at the end of this chapter.

(For the record: According to research published in the *New England Journal of Medicine* at the end of 1993, males who undertake heavy physical exertion increase their risk of a heart attack by around 100 times *if* they are habitually sedentary—out of shape. For those who do exercise regularly, strenuous exertion doesn't increase their risk of heart attack.)

Let us suppose that the frequency of the effect in the experimental group is found to be greater than in the control group. *How much greater* must the frequency of the effect in the experimental group be for us to say that the suspected causal agent actually is a causal factor? That is, how great must *d* be for us to believe that C is really a causal factor for E? After all, even if nicotine does *not* cause skin cancer, the frequency of skin cancer found in the experimental group *might* exceed the frequency found in the control group because of some chance occurrence.

Suppose that there are one hundred individuals in our experimental group and the same number in our control group, and suppose that *d* was greater than 13 percentage points—that is, suppose the frequency of skin cancer in the experimental group exceeded the frequency in the control group by more than 13 percentage points. Could that result be due merely to chance? Yes, but there is a 95 percent probability that it was *not* due to chance. If the frequency of skin cancer in the experimental group were to exceed the frequency in the control group by more than 13 percentage points (given one hundred members in each group), then this finding would be *statistically significant at the 0.05 level*, which simply means that we could say with a 95 percent degree of confidence that nicotine is a cause of skin cancer. If we were content to speak with less confidence, or if our samples were larger, then the difference in the frequency of skin cancer between the experimental group and control group would not have to be as great to qualify as statistically significant.

Thus, saying that the difference in frequency of the effect between the experimental and control groups is **statistically significant** at some level (e.g., 0.05) simply means that it would be unreasonable to attribute this difference in frequency to chance. Just how unreasonable it would be depends on what level is cited. Recall from Chapter 11 that if no level is cited—as in reports of controlled experiments that stipulate only that the findings are "significant"—it is customary to assume that the results were significant at the 0.05 level, which simply means that the result could have arisen by chance in about five cases out of one hundred.

Media reports of controlled experiments usually state or clearly imply whether the difference in frequency of the effect found in the experimental and control groups is significant. However, if, as occasionally happens, there is a question about whether the results are statistically significant (i.e., are unlikely to have arisen by chance), it is important not to assume uncritically or automatically

If you look at the new cases of death from AIDS, the fastest growing category could be ladies over the age of 70. If last year one woman over 70 died from AIDS and this year two do, you get a 100 percent increase in AIDS deaths for that category.

—JOHN ALLEN PAULOS

Percentage increases from a small baseline can be misleading.

1. That the sample is large enough to guarantee significance. A large sample is no guarantee that the difference (*d*) in the frequency of the effect in the experimental group and in the control group is statistically significant. (However, the larger the sample, the smaller *d*—expressed as a difference in percentage points—need be to count as significant.) People are sometimes overly impressed by the mere size of a study.

2. That the difference in frequency is great enough to guarantee significance. The fact that there seems to be a pronounced difference in the frequency of the effect in the experimental group and in the control group is no guarantee that the difference is statistically significant. If the sample size is small enough, it may not be. If there are fifty rats in an experimental group and fifty more in a control group, then even if the frequency of skin cancer found in the experimental group exceeds the frequency of skin cancer found in the control group by as much as 18 percentage points, this finding would not be statistically significant (at the 0.05 level). If each group contained a thousand rats, a difference in frequency of 3 points would not qualify as significant. (And remember that a 3-point difference can be referred to as a "whopping" 50 percent difference if it is the difference between 6 points and 3 points.) Unless you have some knowledge of statistics, it is probably best not to assume that findings are statistically significant unless it is clearly stated or implied that they are.

Nevertheless, it may be helpful to you to have some rough idea of when a difference in frequency of effect in the experimental and control groups may be said to be statistically significant at the 0.05 level. Table 12-1 provides some examples.

Suppose there are ten individuals each in the randomly selected experimental and control groups. To be statistically significant at the 0.05 level, the difference between experimental and control group in frequency of the effect must exceed 40 percentage points. If there are twenty-five people in each group, then *d* must exceed 27 points to be statistically significant, and so forth.

TABLE 12-1   Approximate Statistically Significant d's at 0.05 Level

Number in Experimental Group (with Similarly Sized Control Group)	Approximate Figure That d Must Exceed to Be Statistically Significant (in Percentage Points)
10	40
25	27
50	19
100	13
250	8
500	6
1,000	4
1,500	3

Even if it is clear in a controlled experiment that d is significant, there are a few more considerations to keep in mind when reviewing reports of experimental findings. First, the results of controlled experiments are often extended analogically from the target population (e.g., rats) to another population (e.g., humans). Such analogical extensions should be evaluated in accordance with the criteria for analogical arguments discussed in the previous chapter. In particular, before accepting such extensions of the findings, you should consider carefully whether there are important relevant differences between the target population in the experiment and the population to which the results of the experiment are analogically extended.

Second, it is important in controlled experiments that the sample from which the experimental and control groups are formed be representative of the target population, and thus it is essential that the sample be taken at random. Further, because the experimental and control groups should be as similar as possible, it is important that the assignment of subjects to these groups also be a random process. In reputable scientific experiments it is safe to assume that randomization has been so employed, but one must be suspicious of informal "experiments" in which no mention of randomization is made.

And while we're talking about reputable sources, remember that any outfit can call itself the "Cambridge Institute for Psychological Studies" and publish its reports in its own "journal." Organizations with prestigious-sounding place names (Princeton, Berkeley, Palo Alto, Bethesda, and so on), proper names (Fulbright, Columbia, and so on), or concepts (institute, academy, research, advanced studies) *could* consist of little more than a couple of university dropouts with a dubious theory and an axe to grind.

■ *Nonexperimental Cause-to-Effect Studies*

A **nonexperimental cause-to-effect study** (or argument) is another type of study designed to test whether something is a causal factor for a given effect.

Cigarettes, Cancer, and the Genetic-Factors Argument

For years the tobacco industry challenged the data showing that smoking causes lung cancer. The industry argued that certain unknown genetic factors (1) predispose some people to get cancer and also (2) predispose those same people to smoke.

The tobacco people are just doing what critical thinkers should do, looking for a common underlying cause for two phenomena that seem on the face of things to be related directly by cause and effect. However, they have never found any such common cause, and the claim that there *might be* one is not equivalent to the claim that there *is* one. Further, even if the industry theory is correct, that wouldn't diminish the other risks involved in smoking.

We should point out, however, that scientists have recently discovered that a chemical found in cigarette smoke damages a gene, known as p53, that acts to suppress the runaway growth of cells that lead to tumors. Researchers regard the discovery as finding the exact mechanism of causation of cancer by cigarette smoke; the discovery seems to put the whole issue of whether cigarettes cause cancer beyond much doubt.

In this type of study, members of a target population (say, humans) who have not yet shown evidence of the suspected effect E (e.g., cancer of the colon) are divided into two groups that are alike in all respects except one. The difference is that members of one group, the experimental group, have all been exposed to the suspected cause C (fatty diets, for example), whereas the members of the other group, the control group, have not. Such studies differ from controlled experiments in that the members of the experimental group are not exposed to the suspected causal agent *by the investigators*—clearly, one limit of experimental studies is that investigators can't purposely expose human subjects to potentially dangerous agents. Eventually, just as in the controlled experiment, experimental and control groups are both compared with respect to the frequency of E. If the frequency in the experimental group exceeds the frequency in the control group by a statistically significant margin, we may conclude that C is the cause of E in the target population.

In reports of nonexperimental cause-to-effect studies, as in reports of controlled experiments, if it is not stated or clearly implied that the findings are significant, do not assume that they are merely because either (1) the samples are large or (2) the difference in the frequency of the effect in absolute terms or percentages is striking.

Likewise, (3) if a causal relationship found to hold in the target population on the basis of such a study is extended analogically to other populations, you should evaluate this analogical extension very carefully, especially with respect to any relevant differences between the target population and the analogical population.

And, finally, (4) note the following important difference between controlled experiments and nonexperimental cause-to-effect studies: In a *controlled* experiment, the subjects are assigned to experimental and control groups by a random process, after which the experimental subjects are exposed to C. This randomization ensures that experimental and control groups will be alike except for the suspected causal agent that the experimental group is then exposed to. But in the *nonexperimental* study, the experimental group (which is still so called even though no experiment is performed) is composed of randomly selected individuals who have already been exposed to the suspected causal agent or who say they were. And the individuals who have already been exposed to C (or who say they were) may differ from the rest of the target population in some respect in addition to having been exposed to C. For example, there is a positive correlation between having a fatty diet and drinking alcoholic beverages. Thus, an experimental group composed by random means from those in the general population who have fatty diets would include more than its fair share of drinkers. Consequently, the high rate of colon cancer observed in this experimental group might be due in part to the effects of drinking.

It is important, then, that the process by which the individuals in the general population "self-select" themselves (regarding their exposure to C) not be biased in any way related to the effect. In good studies, any factors that might bias the experimental group are controlled by one means or another. Often, for example, the control group is not randomly selected, but rather is selected to match the experimental group for any other relevant factors. Thus, in a study that seeks to relate fatty diets to cancer of the colon, an experimenter will make certain that the same percentage of drinkers is found in the control group as in the experimental group.

Nonexperimental studies of the variety explained here and in the next section are *inherently* weaker than controlled experiments as arguments for causal claims. Because we do not have complete knowledge of what factors are causally related to what other factors, it is impossible to say for certain that all possibly relevant variables in such studies have been controlled. It is good policy to imagine what characteristics those who have been exposed to the suspected causal agent might have and contemplate whether any of these factors may be related to the effect. If you can think of any relevant variables that have not been controlled, you should have doubts about any causal claim that is made on the basis of such studies.

■ *Nonexperimental Effect-to-Cause Studies*

A **nonexperimental effect-to-cause study** is a third type of study designed to test whether something is a causal factor for a given effect. In this type of study, the "experimental group," whose members already display the *effect* being investigated, E (e.g., cancer of the mouth), is compared with a control group none of whose members have E, and the frequency of the suspected cause, C (e.g., using chewing tobacco), is measured. If the frequency of C in

When Is Affirmative Action Not Affirmative Action?

A letter-writer to the "Ask Marilyn" column in *Parade* magazine mentions a case worth your attention:

The writer, Christopher McLaughlin, of Orange Park, Florida, reported a company that opened a factory generating 70 white-collar jobs and 385 blue-collar jobs.

For the 70 white-collar positions, 200 males and 200 females applied; 15 percent of the males were hired, and 20 percent of the females were hired.

For the 385 blue-collar jobs, 400 males applied and 100 females applied; 75 percent of the males were hired, and 85 percent of the females were hired.

In short, the percentage of female applicants hired was greater than the percentage of male applicants hired in both categories. A victory for women, yes?

Nope—at least not according to the Equal Employment Opportunity Commission. The EEOC calculated that a female applying for a job at the factory had a 59 percent chance of being denied employment, whereas a male applicant had only a 45 percent chance of not being hired. So the company actually discriminated against women, the EEOC said.

Here's why: When you consider *total* applications, out of 600 male applicants, 330 were hired, and out of 300 female applicants, 125 were hired. That means that 55 percent of the male applicants—but only 41 percent of the female applicants—were hired.

(This case should remind you of the Saint Simpson's example in Chapter 11—see the box on page 394.)

the experimental group significantly exceeds its frequency in the control group, then C may be said to cause E in the target population.

Cautionary remarks from the discussion of nonexperimental cause-to-effect studies apply equally to nonexperimental effect-to-cause studies. That is, if it isn't clear that the findings are significant, don't assume that they are merely because (1) the samples seem large or (2) the difference in the frequency expressed in absolute terms seems striking; and (3) evaluate carefully analogical extensions of the results to other populations.

Notice further that (4) the subjects in the experimental group may differ in some important way (in addition to showing the effect) from the rest of the target population. Thus, for instance, former smokers are more likely than others to use chewing tobacco and are also more likely to get mouth cancer. If you sample randomly from a group of victims of mouth cancer, therefore, you are likely to produce more ex-smokers in your sample than occur in the general population. The result is that you are likely to discover more chewing-tobacco users in the sample, even if chewing tobacco plays no role whatsoever in causing cancer of the mouth. Any factor that might bias the experimental group in such studies should be controlled. If, in evaluating

Learning Australian, Lesson 42: That's Australian for "Another Round!"

Long term heavy drinkers are not damaging their mental faculties, contrary to previous suggestions, despite consuming the equivalent of eight pints of beer a day, researchers say.

Drinkers scored just as well on psychological and intellectual tests and showed no more signs of brain shrinkage than non-drinkers or those who consumed alcohol only in moderation.

A number of studies have suggested that heavy long-term alcohol use can cause brain damage, including a type of alcohol-induced dementia.

However, researchers from Australia say they can find no evidence that persistent lifelong consumption of alcohol is related to cognitive functioning in men in their 70s.

The researchers, from the Australian National University, Canberra, and the Center for Education and Research on Aging in Sydney, looked at 209 men with an average age of 73 who were veterans of World War II. They were given 18 tests to measure intellectual function, as well as scans for brain atrophy.

The daily alcohol consumption of the men [averaged two and one-half pints of beer and went as high as eight pints].

—CHRIS MIHILL, *Scripps Howard News Service*

We'd look for confirmation of these results before we'd recommend regular trips to the pub. Notice that this study ignores *other* problems caused by alcohol.

such a study, you can think of any factor that has not been controlled, you can regard the study as having failed to demonstrate causation.

Notice, finally, that (5) effect-to-cause studies show only the probable frequency of the cause, not the effect, and thus provide no grounds for estimating the percentage of the target population that would be affected if everyone in it were exposed to the cause.

Appeal to Anecdotal Evidence

In Chapter 11, we discussed the mistake of trying to reach a conclusion by citing one or two examples i.e., by appealing to anecdotes. There is another type of appeal to anecdotal evidence that relates to causal arguments, as distinct from generalizations: trying to either prove or disprove that X is a causal factor for Y by citing an example or two of an X that did (or didn't) cause a Y. Arguing that red wine prevents colds because we know someone

Too Little Sleep as Discoordinating as Too Much Booze

That's what the headline of this Associated Press article asserted. The report went on to claim, "too little sleep can slow you down as much as too many drinks," and then described the research that supported these claims.

Well, the research, which came out of Stanford's Sleep Disorders Clinic and Research Center, did indeed show that people with too little sleep did as poorly on a test of reaction time as people who were too drunk to drive legally in California.

The problem is that, in this case, the people with too little sleep suffered from sleep apnea, a condition in which you stop breathing dozens of times an hour, interrupting your sleep without your knowing about it. It's not at all clear from this that a little or even a great loss of sleep from other causes will slow down your reaction time as much as drinking to the point of legal drunkenness.

You just have to watch those headlines.

(But see the box on page 433, where the headline is okay, but not the story.)

who drinks red wine and never catches cold would be an instance of this type of weak argument. It would be similarly weak to argue that red wine doesn't prevent colds because we've never observed that effect in us. Those who submit that smoking doesn't cause cancer because they know a smoker who lived to ninety-eight and died of old age are guilty of the causal type of anecdotal argument.

To establish that X is a causal factor for Y, we have to show that there would be more cases of Y if everyone did X than if no one did, and you can't really show this—or demonstrate that X isn't a causal factor for Y—by citing an example or two. Isolated incidents can reasonably serve to raise suspicions about causal factors, but that is all.

One of the most common mistakes made in everyday reasoning is to appeal to anecdotal evidence in one or the other of the ways discussed here and in Chapter 11. And now that you know what is involved in saying that something is a causal factor, you know why you can't establish this sort of causal claim by appealing to an anecdote.

Recap

A causal claim asserts that one thing causes another, and a causal argument attempts to support a causal claim. Many causal arguments are about causation among specific events; others are about causation in populations.

When making a causal argument in situations involving specific events, we often look for the relevant difference between two events that are different from one another in some other way. We then conclude that one different feature is the cause of the other. This is called only-relevant-difference reasoning or, for short, relevant-difference reasoning.

Alternatively, we look for the relevant common thread among multiple events that share some other common feature. We then conclude that the one common thread is the cause of the other. This is called only-relevant-common-thread reasoning or, for short, common-thread reasoning.

When we employ either of these patterns of reasoning, we need to eliminate alternative possible causes of the feature in question. Failure to do so can mean that our reasoning commits the mistake known as *post hoc, ergo propter hoc.*

Causal arguments about populations are usually based on one of three types of studies (that is, arguments): (1) controlled cause-to-effect experiments, (2) nonexperimental cause-to-effect studies, and (3) nonexperimental effect-to-cause studies.

Reports of population studies include (or should include) information about whether the results are statistically significant; that is, we are told how confident we can be that the relationship observed is really a causal relationship and not just a matter of chance.

Appeal to anecdotal evidence is a faulty way of trying to prove or disprove a causal argument; it involves citing an isolated example or two as proof.

Having read this chapter and the chapter recap, you should be able to

- ▲ Distinguish reasoning that seeks to establish the cause of specific events from reasoning that seeks to establish causation in populations
- ▲ Describe and identify the two most common patterns of reasoning that seek to establish the causation of specific events
- ▲ Ask the questions that need to be asked when you encounter either pattern of reasoning
- ▲ Explain and identify the types of reasoning used to establish causation in populations
- ▲ Understand statistical significance in relation to these patterns of reasoning

Additional Exercises

Exercise 12-14

Identify each of the following as (a) a claim about causation between specific occurrences, (b) a claim about causal factors in populations, or (c) neither of these.

▲ 1. The hibiscus died while we were away. There must have been a frost.

2. Carlos isn't as fast as he used to be; that's what old age will do.

3. Kent's college education helped him get a high-paying job.

▲ 4. The most frequently stolen utility vehicle is a 2000 Jeep Wrangler.

5. Vitamin C prevents colds.

6. The man who put this town on the map was Dr. Jaime Diaz.

▲ 7. The high reading on the thermometer resulted from two causes: This thermometer was located lower to the ground than at other stations, and its shelter was too small, so the ventilation was inadequate.

8. Oily smoke in the exhaust was caused by worn rings.

9. The initial tests indicate that caffeine has toxic effects in humans.

▲ 10. Neonatal sepsis is usually fatal among newborns.

11. WIN 51,711 halted development of paralysis in mice that had recently been infected with polio-2.

12. A stuck hatch cover on *Spacelab* blocked a French ultraviolet camera from conducting a sky survey of celestial objects.

13. An experimental drug has shown broad antiviral effects on a large number of the picornaviruses against which it has been tested.

▲ 14. Investigation revealed the problem was a short-circuited power supply.

15. Arteriovenous malformations—distortions of the capillaries connecting an arteriole and a small vein in the brain—can bleed, causing severe headaches, seizures, and even death.

16. Because of all the guns that its citizens own, America has never been invaded.

▲ 17. According to two reports in the *New England Journal of Medicine*, oil from fish can prevent heart disease.

18. The most important cause in the growing problem of illiteracy is television.

19. "Raymond the Wolf passed away in his sleep one night from natural causes; his heart stopped beating when the three men who slipped into his bedroom stuck knives in it."

Jimmy Breslin, The Gang That Couldn't Shoot Straight

▲ 20. The dramatic increases in atmospheric CO_2, produced by the burning of fossil fuels, are warming the planet and will eventually alter the climate.

Exercise 12-15

According to the Centers for Disease Control, between 1990 and 1994 there were 427,743 premature deaths from smoking. (In other words, there were 427,743 cases in which smoking was the relevant difference between living and not living.) Critics of the CDC say that 60 percent of those deaths were people 70 or older, 45 percent were people over 75, and

17 percent were people over 85. According to the critics, these people would have died anyway from nonsmoking-related diseases.

What data would you need to determine whether the critics are correct?

Exercise 12-16

Go to Church and Live Longer

According to Bill Scanlon, a reporter for the Scripps Howard News Service, researchers from the University of Colorado, the University of Texas, and Florida State University determined that twenty-year-olds who attend church at least once a week for a lifetime live on the average seven years longer than twenty-year-olds who never attend. The data came from a 1987 National Health Interview Survey that asked 28,000 people their income, age, church-attendance patterns, and other questions. The research focused on 2,000 of those surveyed who subsequently died between 1987 and 1995.

Propose two different causal hypotheses to explain these findings.

Hypothesis One:

What data would you need to have greater confidence in this hypothesis?

Hypothesis Two:

What data would you need to have greater confidence in this hypothesis?

Other Hypotheses:

What data would you need to have greater confidence in these hypotheses?

Exercise 12-17

The Indian chief Tecumseh put a curse on U.S. presidents elected in years ending in 0. Seven such presidents in a row died in office. Ronald Reagan, elected in 1980, survived an assassination attempt, breaking Tecumseh's curse.

The New York Public Library Desk Reference

Propose two different hypotheses to explain these facts:

Hypothesis One:

What data would you need to have greater confidence in this hypothesis?

Hypothesis Two:

What data would you need to have greater confidence in this hypothesis?

Exercise 12-18

There is no single event, activity, decision, law, judgment, in this period of time that I call the 'three strikes' era—other than 'three strikes'—that could explain the tremendous acceleration in the drop in crime.

Dan Lungren, former California Attorney General, who helped draft California's

Three Strikes law.

Under this law, conviction for a third felony carried with it a mandatory sentence of twenty-five years to life. Although the crime rate in California had been falling before the law took effect in 1994, it reportedly fell even faster after the law was enacted, and California's crime rate dropped to levels not seen since the 1960s.

Provide two reasonable alternative hypotheses to explain the acceleration of the drop in crime rate in California. What data would you need to be convinced that Lungren's hypothesis is the best?

Exercise 12-19

1. Suppose we wished to know who are worse drivers, men or women. What data would we need?

   In groups (or individually if the instructor prefers) arrive at a consensus answer. Groups may then compare answers to see which group has the best answer.

   Remember to be clear about what you mean by "worse." Also remember, if your answer involves comparing accident statistics, that such statistics would need to take into account differences between the genders in the number of drivers, number of miles driven, number of hours driven, time of day of driving, conditions of driving, and other variables.

2. Have you ever had the feeling that somebody is watching you? Suppose we wished to know whether people can sense whether they are being watched. How could we find out? In groups (or individually if the instructor prefers) describe an experiment that might be used with students in this class. Groups may then compare proposals to see who has the best idea.

3. Suppose we wished to know whether students who go to bed early have a higher GPA than people who stay up late. In groups (or individually if the instructor prefers), describe the data we would need to find out. Groups may then compare ideas to see who has the best answer.

4. Suppose a university teacher wants to know whether or not requiring attendance improves student learning. How could she find out? In groups (or individually if the instructor prefers) describe an experiment that an instructor might actually use. Groups may then compare proposals to see who has the best idea.

5. Suppose we wanted to find out which does a better job educating children in our county, the public schools or the private schools. What data would we need? Would comparing test scores of the children tell us what we need to know? In groups (or individually if the instructor prefers) arrive at consensus answers and then compare your group's answers with those of other groups.

6. According to research done by Colorado College psychology professor Tomi-Ann Roberts, wearing a swimsuit impairs a woman's ability to do mathematics more than it impairs a man's.

   In groups (or individually if the instructor prefers) decide how you might test to see if this claim is true. Alternatively, assume the claim is true, and propose a hypothesis to explain why it is true; then describe the data you would need to test your hypothesis. Groups may then compare ideas.

Exercise 12-20

Read this passage, which was adapted from the source indicated, and then answer the questions that follow.

> A report in the *New England Journal of Medicine* states that an experimental vaccine against chicken pox has been found effective in tests on nearly 1,000 children.
>
> The new vaccine uses a live but weakened form of the virus developed in Japan. Dr. Robert E. Weibel, of the Children's Hospital of Philadelphia, and others gave it to 468 healthy children, while a control group of 446 received a placebo. During a nine-month follow-up period, not a single case of chicken pox occurred in the vaccinated group, whereas 39 of the control group contracted the disease.
>
> *Christine Russell,* Washington Post, *reprinted in* Reader's Digest

▲ 1. What is the causal claim at issue?

▲ 2. What is the target population?

▲ 3. What type of investigation is described?

▲ 4. Summarize the differences between the experimental and control groups, including size.

▲ 5. What is the frequency of the effect in the experimental and control groups? (In nonexperimental effect-to-cause studies, what is the frequency of the cause in the experimental and control groups?)

▲ 6. Does the report state or imply, or is there otherwise reason to believe, that the findings are (or are not) statistically significant?

▲ 7. Are there any other important aspects of the study that are unreported, or is there any other notable weakness in the investigation?

▲ 8. What causal claim, if any, does the report seem to support?

Exercise 12-21

Research at the University of Pennsylvania and the Children's Hospital of Philadelphia indicates that children who sleep in a dimly lighted room until age two may be up to five times more likely to develop myopia (nearsightedness) when they grow up.

The researchers asked the parents of children who had been patients at the researchers' eye clinic to recall the lighting conditions in the children's bedroom from birth to age two.

Of a total of 172 children who slept in darkness, 10 percent were nearsighted. Of a total of 232 who slept with a night light, 34 percent were nearsighted. Of a total of 75 who slept with a lamp on, 55 percent were nearsighted.

The lead ophthalmologist, Dr. Graham E. Quinn, said that, "just as the body needs to rest, this suggests that the eyes need a period of darkness."

Adapted from an AP report by Joseph B. Verrengia

1. What causal hypothesis is at issue in this report?

2. What type of investigation is being reported?

3. Can you suggest an alternative explanation for the effect?

Exercise 12-22

Does smoking cost the government money? Some people say yes. They say smoking-related illnesses cost the government money. Others say no. They say cigarettes are heavily taxed and that those who die early due to smoking stop paying that tax, and in addition collect no retirement, health care, or nursing home benefits.

What data would you need to have to determine which side is correct?

Exercise 12-23 ———————————————————

Evaluate the following numbered passages by answering each of the lettered questions.

a. What is the causal claim at issue?

b. What is the target population?

c. What type of investigation is described?

d. Summarize the differences between the experimental and control groups, including size.

e. What is the frequency of the effect in the experimental and control groups? (In nonexperimental effect-to-cause studies, what is the frequency of the cause in the experimental and control groups?)

f. Does the report state or imply, or is there otherwise reason to believe, that the findings are (or are not) statistically significant?

g. Are there any other important aspects of the study that are unreported, or is there any other notable weakness in the investigation?

h. What causal claim, if any, does the report seem to support?

▲ 1. You want to find out if the coffee grounds that remain suspended as sediment in French press, espresso, and Turkish and Greek coffee can cause headaches.

You divide fifty volunteers into two groups and feed both groups a pudding at the same time every day. However, one group mixes eight grams of finely pulverized used coffee grounds into the pudding before eating it (that's equivalent to the sediment in about one and a half liters of Turkish coffee). Within three weeks, you find that 50 percent of the group that has eaten grounds have had headaches; only 27 percent of the other group have experienced a headache. You conclude that coffee grounds may indeed cause headaches and try to get a grant for further studies. (This is a fictitious experiment.)

2. Do you enjoy spicy Indian and Asian curries? That bright yellow-orange color is due to curcumin, an ingredient in the spice turmeric. An experiment conducted by Bandaru S. Reddy of the American Health Foundation in Valhall, New York, and reported in *Cancer Research,* suggests that curcumin might suppress the development of colon cancer.

Places where turmeric is widely used have a low incidence of colon cancer, so the research team decided to investigate. They administered a powerful colon carcinogen to sixty-six rats, and then added curcumin at the rate of 2,000 parts per million to the diet of thirty of them. At the end of a year, 81 percent of the rats eating regular rat food had developed cancerous tumors, compared with only 47 percent of those that dined on the curcumin-enhanced diet. In addition, 38 percent of the tumors in rats eating regular food were invasive, and that was almost twice the rate in rodents eating curcumin-treated chow.

Adapted from Science News

▲ 3. Does jogging keep you healthy? Two independent researchers interested in whether exercise prevents colds interviewed twenty volunteers about the frequency with which they caught colds. The volunteers, none of whom exercised regularly, were then divided into two groups of ten, and one group participated in a six-month regimen of jogging three miles every other day. At the end of the six months the frequency of colds among the joggers was compared both with that of the nonjoggers (group A) and with that of the joggers prior to the experiment (group B). It was found that, compared with the nonjoggers, the joggers had 25 percent fewer colds. The record of colds among the joggers also declined in comparison with their own record prior to the exercise program.

4. "A major new study has found that taking an aspirin every other day cuts the risk of having a first heart attack nearly in half. The study, sponsored by the National Heart, Lung and Blood Institute, indicated that aspirin was so effective in reducing the risk of a heart attack that the study was prematurely terminated so that all 22,071 participants, half of whom did not take aspirin, could benefit from the newly gained knowledge. The data will be published this Thursday in the *New England Journal of Medicine*. The editor of the journal called the study 'a milestone in the continuing struggle' against heart attack.

"In the fifty-seven-month study, whose participants were all male physicians, 104 of those who took aspirin had heart attacks, as compared with 189 heart attacks in those who took only a sugar pill. This means ordinary aspirin reduced the heart attack risk for healthy men by 47 percent. At least seven long-term studies of more than 11,000 heart attack victims have shown that one-half or one aspirin per day can reduce the risk of a second attack by up to 20 percent."

Adapted from the Los Angeles Times

5. "Although cigarette ads sometimes suggest that smoking is 'macho,' new studies indicate that smoking can increase the risk of impotence. In a study of 116 men with impotence caused by vascular problems, done at the University of Pretoria, South Africa, 108 were smokers. Two independent studies, one done by the Centre d'Etudes et de Recherches di l'Impuissance in Paris, and reported in the British medical journal *Lancet,* and the other done by Queen's University and Kingston General Hospital in Ontario, found that almost two-thirds of impotent men smoked.

"To test whether smoking has an immediate effect on sexual response, a group of researchers from Southern Illinois and Florida State universities fitted 42 male smokers with a device that measures the speed of arousal. The men were divided into three groups, one group given high-nicotine cigarettes, one group cigarettes low in nicotine, and one group mints. After smoking one cigarette or eating a mint, each man was placed in a private room and shown a two-minute erotic film while his sexual response was monitored. Then he waited ten minutes, smoked two more cigarettes or ate another mint, and watched a different erotic film, again being monitored.

"The results: Men who smoked high-nicotine cigarettes had slower arousal than those who smoked low-nicotine cigarettes or ate mints."

Adapted from Reader's Digest

6. "Scientists at the Lawrence Livermore National Laboratory in California report that they have isolated and cloned two human genes that control and repair defective and damaged cells. A biophysicist and a biologist at the laboratory inserted the cloned normal genes from human DNA into the genetically defective cells of Chinese hamsters. The human repair genes took over the cellular machinery of the hamsters and corrected their defects, the scientists said. Approximately two-thirds of the cells that received the cloned genes returned to normal, while only about one-tenth of 1 percent of similar, untreated cells achieved a normal condition. It is hoped that the research will eventually produce an effective treatment for radiation-damaged tissue in humans, according to a spokesman for the laboratory."

The figures are hypothetical, invented to illustrate studies at Lawrence Livermore Laboratories, as reported by David Perlman in the San Francisco Chronicle

▲ 7. "The Food and Drug Administration recently gave final approval to the use of alpha-interferon, a hormone produced by the human body, for treating genital warts, a contagious viral disease that is spread sexually and affects about 8 million people a year. The FDA said alpha-interferon, injected into the warts, cleared or substantially reduced the lesions in 66 percent of the 192 patients who participated in three studies of the drug. Eighteen percent of patients had a 50 percent to 74 percent reduction in their warts."

From a report by United Press International

8. "Anesthesiologists at Harvard Medical School have challenged the long-standing belief among physicians that newborn infants cannot feel pain. One study cited by the Harvard group showed that almost all circumcised infants exhibit changes in their behavior for more than 22 hours after circumcision.

"Another study compared infants given an anesthetic before circumcision with those who were not. The researchers found that for at least two days after the operation, babies who got the anesthetic were more attentive and less irritable, had better motor responses, and had a greater ability to quiet themselves when disturbed.

"The doctors concluded that, without anesthesia, such painful procedures may have 'prolonged effects on the babies' neurological and social development.'"

"Dr. Dean Edell's Medical Journal," reporting on an article in the New England Journal of Medicine

9. "A study published in the July 27 *Journal of the American Medical Association* indicates that taking androgen (a male sex hormone) in high doses for four weeks can have important effects on the high density lipoproteins (HDLs) in the blood, which are believed to protect against the clogging of

vessels that supply the heart. Ben F. Hurley, an exercise physiologist from the University of Maryland in College Park who conducted the study at Washington University, monitored the levels of HDL in the blood of sixteen healthy, well-conditioned men in their early thirties who were taking androgens as part of their training program with heavy weights. Prior to use of the hormone, all had normal levels of HDLs. After four weeks of self-prescribed and self-administered use of these steroids the levels dropped by about 60 percent.

"Hurley is cautious in interpreting the data. 'You can't say that low HDL levels mean that a specified person is going to have a heart attack at an earlier age. All you can say is that it increases their risk for heart disease.'"

D. Franklin, Science News

▲ 10. "New studies reported in the *Journal of the American Medical Association* indicate that vasectomy is safe. A group headed by Frank Massey of UCLA paired 10,500 vasectomized men with a like number of men who had not had the operation. The average follow-up time was 7.9 years, and 2,300 pairs were followed for more than a decade. The researchers reported that, aside from inflammation in the testes, the incidence of diseases for vasectomized men was similar to that in their paired controls.

"A second study done under federal sponsorship at the Battelle Human Affairs Research Centers in Seattle compared heart disease in 1,400 vasectomized men and 3,600 men who had not had the operation. Over an average follow-up time of fifteen years, the incidence of heart diseases was the same among men in both groups."

Edward Edelson, New York Daily News; *reprinted in* Reader's Digest

▲ 11. "Canadian researchers led by D. G. Perrin of the department of pathology at the Hospital for Sick Children in Toronto have found an important biochemical difference in the bodies of children who died from sudden infant death syndrome (SIDS), compared with infants who died from other causes. According to the scientists, the research suggests that infants at high risk for SIDS may manufacture the brain chemical transmitter dopamine at abnormally high levels. Theoretically, if the results of the investigations are borne out, a child at risk might be treated with dopamine-blocking drugs as a preventive measure, but the scientists caution it is too early to consider doing that. 'Just because [dopamine] is abnormal does not necessarily mean it's a primary cause,' says Perrin. 'It may be a secondary cause [a result of some other abnormality].'

"Perrin and his colleagues examined the carotid bodies of 13 SIDS babies and five infants who died from other causes. All but two of the SIDS babies had dopamine levels far in excess of those in the controls.

"SIDS claims about ten thousand infants between two months and four months of age each year in the United States. All SIDS deaths involve the mysterious cessation of breathing during sleep."

J. Greenberg, Science News

▲ 12. "A new study shows that the incidence of cancer tumors in rats exposed to high doses of X-rays dropped dramatically when the food intake of the rats was cut by more than half. Dr. Ludwik Gross of the Veterans Administration Medical Center noted that this study is the first to demonstrate that radiation-induced tumors can be prevented by restricting diet.

"The experimenters exposed a strain of laboratory rats to a dose of X-rays that produced tumors in 100 percent of the rats allowed to eat their fill—about five or six pellets of rat food a day.

"When the same dose of X-rays was given to rats limited to two pellets of food a day, only nine of 29 females and one of 15 males developed tumors, the researchers reported.

"The weight of the rats on the reduced diet fell by about one-half, but they remained healthy and outlived their counterparts who died of cancer, Gross said. He noted that the restricted diet also reduced the occurrence of benign tumors. There is no evidence that restriction of food intake will slow the growth of tumors that have already formed in animals, he said."

Paul Raeburn, Sacramento Bee

▲ 13. "Encephalitis, or sleeping sickness, has declined greatly in California during the past thirty years because more people are staying inside during prime mosquito-biting hours—7 P.M. to 10 P.M., researchers said. Paul M. Gahlinger of San Jose State University and William C. Reeves of the School of Public Health at UC Berkeley conducted the study. 'People who watch television on warm summer evenings with their air conditioners on are less likely to be exposed during the peak biting period of mosquitoes that carry encephalitis,' Reeves said.

"The researchers found that those counties in California's Central Valley with the highest television ownership had the lowest encephalitis rates for census years. Of 379 Kern County residents interviewed by telephone, 79 percent said they used their air conditioners every evening and 63 percent said they watched television four or more evenings a week during the summer.

"The percentage of residents who spend more time indoors now because of air conditioning than in 1950 more than doubled, from 26 percent to 54 percent, the researchers said."

Associated Press, Enterprise-Record *(Chico, California)*

14. "Tests of a novel self-care program suggest it is possible to handle minor illnesses at home and help cut down on the staggering national medical bill. A 1,625-member health-maintenance organization called the Rhode Island Group Health association took part in the program. Randomly chosen members used selected medical self-care books and brochures, backed up, in some cases, by a telephone hot line and a counseling session with a nurse, to care for their families. A control group of families had no special educational help. The result was a 17 percent drop in visits to a doctor's office by the self-care families—and corresponding savings in medical costs."

William Hines, Reader's Digest

15. "Pap-smear tests are so effective they have cut the incidence of cervical cancer two-thirds among women who had at least one screening in ten

years, according to a Swedish study. The study, which followed 207,455 women for a decade, also found that the incidence of cervical cancer among those women who never had smears taken was two to four times higher than among those who had the tests.

"Study co-author Cecil Fox, of the National Cancer Institute, stated that he thinks 'this study laid to rest, once and for all, the question, "Are Pap smears effective in reducing cancer of the cervix?" '

"Sweden has a population registry that enabled researchers to follow all the women in the study without losing track of any. The women ranged in age from thirty to over seventy. 'It's the first time anyone has studied a population of women across the entire spectrum of a society,' Fox said."

Reader's Digest

▲ 16. "A study released last week indicated that Type A individuals, who are characteristically impatient, competitive, insecure and short-tempered, can halve their chances of having a heart attack by changing their behavior with the help of psychological counseling.

"In 1978, scientists at Mt. Zion Hospital and Medical Center in San Francisco and Stanford University School of Education began their study of 862 predominantly male heart attack victims. Of this number, 592 received group counseling to ease their Type A behavior and improve their self-esteem. After three years, only 7 percent had another heart attack, compared with 13 percent of a matched group of 270 subjects who received only cardiological advice. Among 328 men who continued with the counseling for the full three years, 79 percent reduced their Type A behavior. About half of the comparison group was similarly able to slow down and cope better with stress.

"This is the first evidence 'that a modification program aimed at Type A behavior actually helps to reduce coronary disease,' says Redford Williams of Duke University, an investigator of Type A behavior."

Science News

Exercise 12-24

Here's a news report on the costs of drug abuse that appeared during the administration of George H. W. Bush. See if you can find any flaws in the reasoning by which the figures were reached.

J. Michael Walsh, an officer of the National Institute on Drug Abuse, has testified that the "cost of drug abuse to U.S. industry" was nearly $50 billion a year, according to "conservative estimates." President Bush has rounded this figure upward to "anywhere from $60 billion to $100 billion." This figure would seem to be a difficult one to determine. Here's how Walsh arrived at it. After a survey of 3,700 households, a NIDA contractor analyzed the data and found that the household income of adults who had *ever* smoked marijuana daily for a month [or at least twenty out of thirty days] was 28 percent less than the income of those who hadn't. The analysts called this difference "reduced productivity due to daily marijuana use." They calculated the total "loss," when extrapolated to the general population, at $26 billion. Adding the estimated costs of drug-related crimes, accidents, and medical care produced a grand total of $47 billion for "costs to society of drug abuse."

Writing Exercises

1. Turn to Selection 12A on gun control at the back of the book and draft a rebuttal to it, paying particular attention to any causal arguments and claims made in it.

2. Read the following story carefully and note what conclusions you think would most likely be drawn from it by most readers. Then determine how well those conclusions are actually supported by the evidence as described in the account. Identify any problems of vagueness or any other lack of clarity, missing information, and so forth. We have given an evaluation in the answer section.

Prayer Heals!

A study by Duke University researchers found that angioplasty patients with acute heart ailments who were prayed for by seven religious groups did 50 to 100 percent better while in the hospital than patients who received no prayers.

The researchers divided 150 patients at the Durham Veterans Affairs medical center into five 30-person groups. All groups received traditional medical treatment.

The control group received only the traditional medical treatment. Three groups received nontraditional therapies: stress relaxation, guided imagery, or touch therapy. The names of the remaining group were sent to seven different prayer groups, which prayed for all 30 patients by name.

Neither the patients nor the hospital staff knew the treatment assignment of the control group or the group whose members were prayed for.

The researchers, Dr. Mitch Krucoff, a Duke cardiologist, and nurse Suzanne Crater, developed statistical measures using EEG monitoring, heart rate, blood pressure, and clinical outcomes to examine the effectiveness of the four different treatments.

In addition to the improvements recorded in those who received prayers, the patients who received the other nontraditional treatments did 30 to 50 percent better than the control group.

"If people are seeking to put themselves into the right relationship with God, which is what prayer is, then you would expect it to have some beneficial effects," said Dr. Geoffrey Wainwright, a professor at the Duke University School of Divinity.

—**Adapted from an** *Associated Press* **report written by Scott Mooneyham**

3. Which of the following causal hypotheses do you accept? Select one that you accept and write a one-page essay presenting evidence (giving arguments) for the claim. When you are finished, write down on a separate piece of paper a number between 1 and 10 that indicates how strong you think your overall "proof" of the claim is, with 10 = very strong and 1 = very weak. Take about ten minutes to complete your essay. Write your name on the back of your paper.

Causal hypotheses:

Pot leads to heroin/crack addiction.
The death penalty is a deterrent to murder.

The death penalty is not a deterrent to murder.
Chocolate causes acne.
Welfare makes people lazy.
Spare the rod and spoil the child.
People think better after a few beers.
Pornography contributes to violence against women.
If you want to get someone to like you, play hard to get.
Vitamin C prevents colds.
Rap music (TV, the movies) contributes to the crime problem.

4. When everyone is finished, the instructor will collect the papers and re-distribute them to the class. In groups of four or five, read the papers and assign a number from 1 to 10 to each one (10 = very strong; 1 = very weak). When all groups are finished, return the papers to their authors. When you get your paper back, compare the number you assigned to your work with the number the group assigned to it. The instructor may ask volunteers to defend their own judgment of their work against the judgment of the group. Do you think there is as much evidence for the claim you selected as you did when you argued for it initially?

Chapter 13

Moral, Legal, and Aesthetic Reasoning

by Nina Rosenstand
and Anita Silvers

*I*n preceding chapters we discussed the basic components of critical thinking, including claims, arguments, deductive and inductive reasoning, and logic. We turn now to an overview of some of the broad areas in which critical thinking is commonly used in our lives. Specifically, we consider how to use critical thinking to engage in and evaluate moral reasoning, legal reasoning, and aesthetic reasoning.

Moral Reasoning

Astrid has a problem. Her good friend Gina asked to borrow money. Astrid is aware that Gina needs the money—but at the same time Astrid suspects Gina may find it difficult to repay the loan, and Astrid knows it will trouble their relationship if Gina doesn't. Unfortunately, Astrid is also convinced that refusing to make the loan will strain the relationship, too. So she isn't at all sure what she should do.

Astrid is pondering a moral issue. Moral questions arise all the time—whenever we wonder what we or others ought to do or what is right or proper or fair or appropriate. You may perhaps have the idea that morality is "just a matter of personal opinion" and that there isn't much of a place for reasoning when it comes to moral issues. But you can—and do—reason about moral issues. You consider options, weigh consequences, think about what is right and wrong, and make a decision. When you try to figure out what you should do, you employ moral reasoning.

■ Descriptive and Prescriptive Moral Claims

Fortunately, moral reasoning is basically no different from reasoning about matters of other kinds, except for one thing: Moral arguments all contain conclusions that are value judgments, judgments that evaluate something. "I shouldn't lend Gina money" is a value judgment; it assigns a negative value to a course of action. "I should lend Gina money" assigns a positive value to the action. Moral philosophers often use the term **prescriptive claim** interchangeably with "value judgment," and we'll often use that terminology as well, for reasons that will become clear shortly.

A prescriptive claim (value judgment) like "I shouldn't lend Gina money" is quite different from a claim like "Gina has brown hair." If you say that Gina has brown hair, you're merely stating what you take to be a fact. A claim of that sort, which does not assign a value to things but instead just asserts what you take to be a fact, is said to be a **descriptive claim.**

Here are some descriptive claims:

Gina is twenty-seven.

The steaks are frozen.

Yo-Yo Ma plays the cello.

The president has never been divorced.

Here are some prescriptive claims:

Gina shouldn't ask people for money.

It is wrong to eat meat.

Children should be taught to appreciate music.

The president ought to be able to be divorced if she wants to be.

Moral prescriptive claims characteristically dictate or specify—that is, prescribe—what actions we should take or avoid, what ends each of us should seek to bring about by our actions, or what kind of person each of us should try to be. Thus, moral reasoning is distinguished from other kinds of reasoning by the fact that the conclusions it reaches (or tries to reach) are moral prescriptive claims, or value judgments. All the prescriptive claims in the example above are moral prescriptive claims.

Distinguishing moral prescriptive claims from other prescriptive claims
Not all prescriptive claims assign moral values to things. For example, if we complain that the coffee is bitter or maintain that dogs make better companions than cats, we are making value judgments (prescriptive claims) that have nothing to do with moral issues. To take another kind of example, if we assert that Gina is beautiful, or that Beethoven's Ninth Symphony is stirring, or that Tom Cruise is a better actor than Keanu Reeves, or that the 2001 Lexus is a work of art, then we are making aesthetic evaluations. Later in this chapter we take a look at evaluations (prescriptive claims, value

judgments) of the aesthetic variety, but here we are focusing on moral evaluations.

One general point to keep in mind is that prescriptive claims typically employ key words such as "good," "bad," "ought," "should," "right," "wrong," "proper," and "improper." These particular words often—but not always—signal a moral evaluation. For example, if somebody tells you that you ought to keep your promises, that's a moral judgment. But if he or she says you ought to keep your knees bent when you're skiing, he or she is merely giving you practical advice.

Exercise 13-1

Determine which of the following claims are descriptive and which are prescriptive. (Remember that not all prescriptive claims are moral claims.)

▲ 1. Marina's car runs terribly; she should get it tuned up.

2. Marina chose the most expensive automobile in the dealer's lot.

3. Ms. Beeson ought not to have embezzled money from the bank.

▲ 4. If Ms. Beeson had wanted to avoid being caught, she would not have embezzled so much money from the bank.

5. After the surgery, Nicky's eyesight improved considerably.

▲ 6. Violence is always wrong.

▲ 7. Algernon's answers on his math test are almost always wrong.

8. Matt ought to wear that sweater more often; it looks good on him.

9. Matt doesn't wear his blue sweater very often, because it's scratchy.

10. If Matt won't wear the blue sweater, he ought to give it away to someone who will appreciate it.

Exercise 13-2

Identify which of the following claims express moral values, which express nonmoral values, and which express no values at all.

▲ 1. My computer software is really good; it even corrects my grammar.

2. "Little Lisa has been very good tonight," said the babysitter.

3. The judge in this case is a very well-informed person.

▲ 4. The judge's decision was clearly the right one, since they all got just what they deserved.

5. The editor couldn't use my illustrations; she said they were awful.

▲ 6. Wow. That *was* a tasty meal.

▲ 7. Dr. Lopez's dog is very old.

8. The last set of essays was much better than the first set.

9. Always act in a way that brings about the best consequences for everyone involved.

10. Never do anything you wouldn't allow others to do in a similar situation.

Getting an "ought" from an "is": Descriptive premises and prescriptive claims   It has been said that no claim about plain fact—that is, no description—can imply a claim that attributes a moral value or a moral obligation. In other words, we cannot legitimately infer what *ought (morally) to be* the case from a claim about what *is* the case. Using the terminology from the previous section, we can put it this way: No prescriptive conclusion can follow from a set of purely descriptive premises. For example, consider the following argument:

> 1a. Mr. Jones is the father of a young child. Therefore, Mr. Jones ought to contribute to his child's support.

We hear such claims often in the context of everyday life, and we are often persuaded by such conclusions. But we should beware, for the conclusion doesn't follow from the premise; it is, in other words, a **non sequitur.** Jumping to such conclusions is a common phenomenon that philosophers generally refer to as the **naturalistic fallacy.** Let us take a closer look. The premise of this argument states a (nonmoral) fact, but the conclusion is an "ought" claim that prescribes a moral obligation for Mr. Jones. As the philosopher David Hume pointed out, there is nothing in a purely descriptive statement of fact that implies a moral duty—the concept of duty is added to the statement by our sense of right and wrong.

However, this seems to lead to an unacceptable situation, for shouldn't we, on the basis of facts and statistics, be able to make policies about social and moral issues? If we know that child abuse is likely to create a new generation of adults who will also practice child abuse, shouldn't we then have the right to state that "Child abuse should be prevented by all means" without being accused of committing a non sequitur? The answer is that of course facts and statistics can be used to formulate social and moral policies, but not the facts and statistics *by themselves:* We must add a premise to make the argument valid. In this case the premise is the moral statement that "Child abuse is wrong." Adding this statement may seem trivial, and you may object that this evaluation is already given with the word "abuse," but the fact is that our moral sense, whether it is based on feelings or reasoning or both, is what allows us to proceed from a set of facts to a conclusion about what ought to be done. Let us return to Mr. Jones:

> 1b. Premise: Mr. Jones is the father of a young child.
>
> Premise: Parents ought to contribute to the support of their young children.
>
> Conclusion: Therefore, Mr. Jones ought to contribute to his child's support.

The result is now a valid deductive argument. Now, in a real-life dispute about whether Mr. Jones has an obligation toward his child, an argument like example 1b is not likely to convince anyone that Mr. Jones has this obligation if he or she doesn't agree with the premise that parents should take care of their children. But the fact that the argument is valid does help clarify matters. It may be an undisputed fact that Jones is a parent, but it may not be as undisputed that parents ought to take care of their young children under all circumstances. In other words, if you disagree with the conclusion, you need not start disagreeing with the factual claim of the first premise, but you can enter into a discussion about the truth of the second premise. It is important to be able to enter into such discussions apart from the case of Mr. Jones, for otherwise it would be too easy for us to let our thinking be prejudiced by the facts presented in the first premise.

Let us consider a few additional examples:

2a. Sophie promised to pay Jennifer five dollars today. So Sophie ought to pay Jennifer five dollars today.

It is perfectly natural to want to see this as a convincing argument as it stands. But, in keeping with our strategy, we require that an "ought" claim be explicitly stated in the premises. In this case, what would you say is the missing premise? The most obvious way of putting it is "One ought to keep one's promises." If we add the required premise we get this:

2b. Sophie promised to pay Jennifer five dollars today. One ought to keep one's promises. So Sophie ought to pay Jennifer five dollars today.

If it seems to you that the second premise is not really necessary in order for the conclusion to follow, that is probably because you accept that making a promise involves a moral duty to keep the promise. In that case, the second premise would just be true by definition, but even so, there is no harm in stating it. And suppose it is *not* true by definition? Not all implicit moral evaluations are; and if they are not, then adding the premise is absolutely necessary in order for the argument to be valid. Consider this example:

3a. It is natural for women to have children. Therefore, women ought to have children, and those who try to avoid having children are unnatural.

The trouble with this argument is the concept of "natural," a very ambiguous word. There are several hidden assumptions behind this argument, and one of these—which we'll call the missing premise here—is the following: "What is natural is morally good, and going against nature is evil." We might also say, "What is natural reveals God's intentions with his creation, and if one goes against God's intentions, one is evil (or sinful)." This also explains the concept of "unnatural," for although "natural" in the premise looks completely descriptive, "unnatural" in the conclusion has a judgmental slant. If we add the missing premise, the argument will look like this:

> 3b. It is natural for women to have children. What is natural is morally good, and going against nature is evil. Therefore, women ought to have children, and those who try to avoid having children are unnatural.

Now the argument is valid, but you may not want to agree with the conclusion. If so, although in some sense it is, overall, "natural" for females to have offspring, you may want to dispute the premise that what is natural is always morally good. After all, many "natural" things, such as leaving severely disabled individuals to fend for themselves or scratching oneself in public, are considered unacceptable in our culture.

Whether an "ought" claim can ever follow directly from an "is" claim has been a controversial issue among philosophers; some point out that a statement such as "An open flame can burn you, so stay away from the campfire" makes an unproblematic transition from an "is" to an "ought"; other philosophers point out that there is a hidden premise that is taken for granted: that getting burned is bad because it hurts.

Exercise 13-3

In each of the following passages, a moral principle must be added as an extra premise to make the argument valid. Supply the missing principle.

Example

> Mrs. Montez's new refrigerator was delivered yesterday, and it stopped working altogether. She has followed the directions carefully but still can't make it work. The people she bought it from should either come out and make it work or replace it with another one.

Principle

> People should make certain that the things they sell are in proper working order.

1. After borrowing Morey's car, Leo had an accident and crumpled a fender. So, Leo ought to pay whatever expenses were involved in getting Morey's car fixed.

▲ 2. When Sarah bought the lawn mower from Jean, she promised to pay another fifty dollars on the first of the month. Since it is now the first, Sarah should pay Jean the money.

3. Kevin worked on his sister's car all weekend. The least she could do is let him borrow the car for his job interview next Thursday.

4. Harold is obligated to supply ten cords of firewood to the lodge by the beginning of October, since he signed a contract guaranteeing delivery of the wood by that date.

▲ 5. Since it was revealed yesterday on the 11:00 news that Mayor Ahearn has been taking bribes, he is expected to step down any day now.

6. As a political candidate, Ms. Havenhurst promised to put an end to crime in the inner city. Now that she is in office, we'd like to see some results.

▲ 7. Use a gun, go to jail.

▲ 8. Laura's priest has advised Laura and her husband not to sign up for the in vitro fertilization program at the hospital because such treatments are unnatural.

9. Ali has been working overtime a lot lately, so he should expect to receive a bonus.

10. It is true there are more voters in the northern part of the state. But that shouldn't allow the north to dictate to the south.

■ *Consistency and Fairness*

A common mistake made in moral reasoning is inconsistency—treating cases that are similar as if they weren't that way. For example, suppose Moore announces on the first day of class that the final in the class will be optional "except," he says, pointing at some person at random, "for the young woman there in the third row. For you," he says, "the final is mandatory."

The problem is that Moore is treating a student who is similar to the rest of the class as if she were different. And the student will want to know, of course, why she has been singled out: "What's so different about me?" she will wonder (as she drops the course).

A similar sort of problem occurs if Moore gives two students the same grade despite the fact that one student did far better in the course than the other. Treating dissimilar cases as if they were similar isn't inconsistent; it just involves a failure to make relevant discriminations.

As you have probably foreseen by now, when we treat people inconsistently, the result is often *unfair.* It is unfair to the woman in the third row to require her alone to take the final; alternatively, it would be unfair to the rest of the class to make the final mandatory for them and to make it optional for the woman in the third row. From the perspective of critical thinking, what is so troubling about unfairness is that it is illogical. It is like saying "All Xs are Y" and then adding, "Some Xs are not Y."

This doesn't mean, of course, that if you have been treating people unfairly, you should *continue* to treat them unfairly on the grounds that it would be inconsistent for you to change your policy. There is nothing illogical in saying, in effect, "I treated the Xs I encountered to date wrongly, but now I will not treat the Xs I encounter wrongly." People sometimes adhere to a bad policy simply on the grounds that it would be inconsistent of them to change, but there is no basis in logic for this idea.

Not all cases of inconsistency result in unfairness. For example, let's imagine that Parker approved of the Korean War and opposed the war in Vietnam but is unable to point out any relevant differences between the two cases. This isn't a matter of unfairness, exactly; it's just inconsistency on Parker's part.

When are two or more cases sufficiently similar to warrant our calling somebody inconsistent who treats them as if they were different? The answer is that there is no hard-and-fast rule. The point to keep in mind, however, is that the burden of proof is on the person who appears inconsistent to show that he or she is not treating similar cases dissimilarly. If, when challenged, Parker cannot *tell* us what's different about Vietnam and Korea that justifies his difference in attitude between the two, then we are justified in regarding him as inconsistent.

Imagine that Carol is a salesperson who treats black customers and white customers differently: She is, let us imagine, much more polite to customers of her own racial group (we needn't worry about which group that is). Can Carol explain to us what is so different about black and white customers that would justify her treating them differently? If not, we are justified in regarding her practices as inconsistent.

Suppose, however, that Carol thinks that skin color itself is a difference between blacks and whites relevant to how people should be treated, and she charges us with failing to make relevant discriminations. Here it would be easy for us to point out to Carol that skin color is an immutable characteristic of birth like height or eye color; does Carol adjust her civility to people depending on those characteristics?

It isn't difficult to perceive the inconsistency on the part of a salesperson who is more polite to customers of one group; but other cases are far tougher, and many are such that reasonable people will disagree about their proper assessment. Is a person inconsistent who approves of abortion but not capital punishment? Is a person inconsistent who, on the one hand, believes that the states should be free to reduce spending on welfare but, on the other, does not think that the states should be able to eliminate ceilings on punitive damages in tort cases? No harm is done in asking "What's the difference?" and because much headway can be made in a discussion by doing so, it seems wise to ask.

Exercise 13-4

Answer the question or respond to the statement that concludes each item.

▲ 1. Tory thinks that women should have the same rights as men. However, he also thinks that although a man should have the right to marry a woman, a woman should not have the right to marry a woman. Is Tory being consistent in his views?

▲ 2. At Shelley's university, the minimum GPA requirement for admission is relaxed for 6 percent of the incoming students. About half of those allowed to attend the university under one of its special admissions programs are affirmative action students—women and members of minorities. The other half are athletes, children of alumni, and talented art students. Shelley is opposed to special admissions programs for affirmative action students. She is not opposed to special admissions programs for art students, athletes, and children of alumni. Is Shelley consistent?

▲ 3. Marin does not approve of abortion because the Bible says explicitly, "Thou shalt not kill." "'Thou shalt not kill' means thou shalt not kill," he says. Marin does, however, approve of capital punishment. Is Marin consistent?

4. Koko believes that adults should have the unrestricted right to read whatever material they want to read, but she does not believe that her seventeen-year-old daughter Gina should have the unrestricted right to read whatever she wants to read. Is Koko consistent?

5. Jack maintains that the purpose of marriage is procreation. On these grounds he opposes same-sex marriages. "Gays can't create children," he explains. However, he does not oppose marriages between heterosexual partners who cannot have children due to age or medical reasons. "It's not the same," he says. Is Jack being consistent?

6. Alisha thinks the idea of outlawing cigarettes is ridiculous. "Give me a break," she says. "If you want to screw up your health with cigarettes, that's your own business." However, Alisha does not approve the legalization of marijuana. "Hel-loh-o," she says. "Marijuana is a *drug,* and the last thing we need is more druggies." Is Alisha being consistent?

7. California's Proposition 209 amends the California state constitution to prohibit "discrimination or preferential treatment" in state hiring based on race, gender, or ethnicity. Opponents say that Proposition 209 singles out women and members of racial and ethnic minorities for unequal treatment. Their argument is that Proposition 209 makes it impossible for members of these groups to obtain redress for past discrimination through preferential treatment, whereas members of other groups who may have suffered past discrimination (gays, for example, or members of religious groups) are not similarly restricted from seeking redress. Evaluate this argument.

▲ 8. Harold prides himself on being a liberal. He is delighted when a federal court issues a preliminary ruling that California's Proposition 209 (see previous item) is unconstitutional. "It makes no difference that a majority of California voters approved the measure," Harold argues. "If it is unconstitutional, then it is unconstitutional." However, California voters also recently passed an initiative that permits physicians to prescribe marijuana, and Harold is livid when the U.S. Attorney General says that the federal government will ignore the California statute and will use federal law to prosecute any physician who prescribes marijuana. Is Harold consistent?

9. Graybosch is of the opinion that we should not perform medical experiments on people against their will, but he has no problem with medical experiments being done on dogs. His wife disagrees. She sees no relevant difference between the two cases.

"What, no difference between people and dogs?" Graybosch asks.

"There are differences, but no differences that are relevant to the issue," Graybosch's wife responds. "Dogs feel pain and experience fear just as much as people."

Is Graybosch's wife correct?

10. Mr. Bork is startled when a friend tells him he should contribute to the welfare of others' children as much as to his own.

"Why on earth should I do that?" Mr. Bork asks his friend.

"Because," his friend responds, "there is no relevant difference between the two cases. The fact that your children are yours does not mean that there is something different about them that gives them a greater entitlement to happiness than anyone else's children."

How should Mr. Bork respond?

11. The university wants to raise the requirements for tenure. Professor Peterson, who doesn't have tenure, says that doing so is unfair to her. She argues that those who received tenure before she did weren't required to meet such exacting standards; therefore, neither should she. Is she correct?

12. Reverend Heintz has no objection to same-sex marriages, but is opposed to polygamous marriages. Is there a relevant difference between the two cases, or is Reverend Heintz being inconsistent?

■ *Major Perspectives in Moral Reasoning*

Moral reasoning usually takes place within one or more frameworks or perspectives. Here we present some of the perspectives that have been especially influential in Western moral thought.

Relativism   A popular view of ethics, especially perhaps among undergraduates taking a first course in philosophy, is **moral relativism,** which we'll define as the idea that what is right and wrong depends on and is determined by one's group or culture.

A mistake sometimes made in moral reasoning is to confuse the following two claims:

1. What is believed to be right and wrong may differ from group to group, society to society, or culture to culture.

2. What is right and wrong may differ from group to group, society to society, or culture to culture.

Please reread the two claims. They are so similar it may take a moment to see that they are actually different. The first claim seems incontestable: Who could dispute that different cultures have different ethical *views?* The majority view in the German Third Reich may have been that it was wrong to protect Jews trying to avoid extermination camps; if so, that would certainly be different from the view of contemporary American society. But the second claim is much more controversial: Are we prepared to say, for instance, that those who helped hide Anne Frank's family from the Gestapo *actually were* immoral? Once we see the difference between (1) and (2), we may not be nearly as apt to accept (2).

Another popular moral perspective is an extreme form of relativism known as **subjectivism,** according to which what is right and wrong is just a matter of subjective opinion. The theory often loses its appeal when some of its implications are noticed. For example, what if Parker thinks that it is right for a person to do X, and Moore thinks that it is wrong for a person to do X? Is it right or wrong for a person to do X? Subjectivism seems to place its adherents in a logically untenable situation.

Subjectivists sometimes think they avoid problems by saying something like "Well, it's right for Parker to do X, but wrong for Moore to do it." However, let's suppose that X in this case is torturing a pet. Would we wish to say, "Well, because Parker doesn't think there is anything wrong with torturing a pet, then there isn't anything wrong with *his* doing it"?

Relativism and subjectivism were popular among cultural anthropologists in the 1920s and still have popular appeal. But neither has won widespread acceptance among moral philosophers.

Utilitarianism   The perspective we call **utilitarianism** rests on the idea that if an individual can feel pleasure and pain, then he or she deserves moral consideration. (This broad criterion has led many utilitarians to include animals in their considerations.) The theory is based on one principle, the **principle of utility:** Maximize happiness and minimize unhappiness. This means that the utilitarian is concerned with the *consequences* of actions and decisions. If an act will produce more happiness than will the alternatives, the act is the right one to do; if it will produce less happiness, it would be morally wrong to do it in place of one of its alternatives.

Many of us use a pro-and-con list of consequences as a guideline when considering what course of action to take. Let's assume you have to decide whether to go home for Thanksgiving or to spend the long weekend writing a term paper that is due. Your family is expecting you, and they will be disappointed if you don't come home. However, their disappointment will be lessened by their knowing that your studies are important to you. On the other hand, if you stay to finish the paper, you will miss seeing your friends at home. But if you go home, you will not finish the paper on time, and your final grade may be adversely affected. As a utilitarian, you try to weigh the consequences of the alternatives on everyone's happiness. You also have to factor in how *certain* the outcomes of each alternative are with respect to happiness, assigning relatively more weight to relatively more certain positive outcomes. Because you can generally be more certain of the effect of an act on your own happiness and on the happiness of others you know well, it is often morally proper to favor that act that best promotes your own or their happiness. Of course, you must not use this as an excuse to be entirely self-serving: Your own happiness isn't more important morally than another's. The best course of action morally is not always the one that best promotes your own happiness.

In sum, utilitarians weigh the consequences of the alternatives, pro and con, and then choose the alternative that maximizes happiness. One of the original and most profound intellects behind utilitarianism, Jeremy Bentham (1748–1832), even went so far as to devise a "hedonistic calculus"—a method of assigning actual numerical values to pleasures and pains based on their intensity, certainty, duration, and so forth. Other utilitarians think that some pleasures are of a higher quality (e.g., reading Shakespeare is of a higher quality than watching Daffy Duck). Although there are other important issues in utilitarianism, the basic idea involves weighing the consequences of possible actions in terms of happiness. Utilitarianism has considerable popular appeal, and real-life moral reasoning is often utilitarian to a considerable extent.

Nevertheless, some aspects of the theory are problematic. Typically, when we deliberate whether or not to do something, we don't always take into consideration just the effect of the action on happiness. For example, other people have *rights* that we sometimes take into account. We would not make someone our family slave even if the happiness doing so produced for the family outweighed the unhappiness it created for the slave. We also consider our *duties* and *obligations*. We think it is our duty to return a loan to someone even if we are still short on cash and the other person doesn't need the money and doesn't even remember having loaned it to us. If we make a date and then want to break it because we've met the love of our life, we think twice about standing up our original date, even if we believe that our overall happiness will far outweigh the temporary unhappiness of our date. To many, the moral obligation of a promise cannot be ignored for the sake of the overall happiness that might result from breaking it.

In estimating the moral worth of what people do, utilitarianism also seems to discount people's *intentions*. Suppose a mugger attacks somebody just as a huge flower pot falls from a balcony above. The mugger happens to push the individual the instant before the flower pot lands on the exact spot where the victim had been standing. The mugger has saved the victim's life, as it turns out. But would we say that the mugger did a morally good deed just because his action had a happy result? According to utilitarianism we would, assuming the net result of the action was more happiness than would otherwise have been the case. So utilitarianism doesn't seem to be the complete story in moral reasoning.

Duty theory/deontologism   Immanuel Kant (1724–1804), who witnessed the beginning phases of the utilitarian philosophy, found that philosophy deficient because of its neglect, among other things, of moral duty. Kant's theory is a version of what is called **duty theory,** or **deontologism.**

Kant acknowledged that our lives are full of imperatives based on our own situations and our objectives. If we want to advance at work, then it is imperative that we keep our promises; if we are concerned about our friends' happiness, then it is imperative that we not talk about them behind their backs. But this type of "hypothetical" imperative, which tells us we ought

Acts and Rules

Let's say you are thinking of cheating on a test. It isn't inconceivable that the sum total of happiness in the world would be increased by this single *act* of cheating. But it also isn't inconceivable that if the *principle* involved were adopted widely, the sum total of happiness would be decreased.

This raises an interesting question: When calculating happiness outcomes, should we contemplate happiness outcomes of the particular *act* in question? Or should we contemplate happiness outcomes of adoption of the *principle* involved in the act?

Clearly there are difficult issues here. Accordingly, some philosophers have made a distinction between "act utilitarianism," which evaluates the moral worth of an act on the happiness it would produce, and "rule utilitarianism," which evaluates the moral worth of an act on the happiness that would be produced by adoption of the principle it exemplifies. (A possible middle ground might be to attempt to factor in, as a part of the happiness outcomes of a particular act, the likelihood that doing it will contribute to a general adoption of the principle involved. This is often what we do when we ask, "But what if everyone did this?")

to do (or ought not to do) something in order to achieve such and such a result, is not a *moral* imperative, Kant argued. Keeping a promise so we'll get a solid reputation is neither morally praiseworthy nor morally blameworthy, he said. For our act to be *morally* praiseworthy, it must be done, not for the sake of some objective, but simply because *it is right.* Our action of keeping our promise is morally praiseworthy, he said, only if we do it simply because it is right to keep our promises. A moral imperative is unconditional or "categorical"; it prescribes an action, not for the sake of some result, but simply because that action is our moral duty.

It follows from this philosophy that when it comes to evaluating an action morally, what counts is not the result or consequences of the action, as utilitarianism maintains, but the intention from which it is done. And the morally best intention, indeed in Kant's opinion the *only* truly morally praiseworthy intention, is that according to which you do something just because it is your moral duty.

But what makes something our moral duty? Some deontologists ground duty in human nature; others ground it in reason; in Western culture, of course, many believe moral duty is set by God. How can we tell what our duty is? Some believe our duty is to be found by consulting conscience; others believe that it is just self-evident or is clear to moral intuition. Those who maintain that human moral duties are established by God usually derive their specific understanding of these duties through interpretations of religious texts such as the Bible, though there is disagreement over what the correct interpretation is and even over who should do the interpreting.

Kant answered the question, How can we tell what our moral duty is? as follows: Suppose you are considering some course of action—say, whether to borrow some money you need very badly. But suppose that you know you can't pay back the loan. Is it morally permissible for you to borrow money under such circumstances? Kant said to do this: First, find the *maxim* (principle of action) involved in what you want to do. In the case in question, the maxim is "Every time I'm in need of money, I'll go to my friends and promise I'll pay it back, even if I know I can't." Next, ask yourself, "Could I want this maxim to be a *universal* law or rule, one that everyone should follow?" This process of *universalization* is the feature that lets you judge whether something would work as a moral law, according to Kant. Could you make it a universal law that it is okay for everybody to lie about paying back loans? Hardly: If everyone adopted this principle, then there would be no such thing as loan making. In short, the universalization of your principle undermines the very principle that is universalized. If everyone adopted the principle, then nobody could possibly follow it. The universalization of your principle is illogical, so it is your duty to pay back loans.

As you can see, the results of acting according to Kant's theory can be radically different from the results of acting according to utilitarianism. Utilitarianism would condone borrowing money with no intention of repaying it, assuming that doing so would produce more happiness than would be produced by not doing so. But Kant's theory would not condone it.

Kant also noted that if you were to borrow a friend's money with no intention of repaying it, you would be treating your friend merely as a means to an end. If you examine cases like this, in which you use other people as mere tools for your own objectives, then, Kant said, you will find in each case a transgression of moral duty, a principle of action that cannot be universalized. Thus, he warned us, it is our moral duty never to treat someone else *merely* as a tool, as means to an end. Of course Kant did not mean that Moore cannot ask Parker for help on some project; doing so would not be a case of Moore's using Parker *merely* as a tool.

Kant's theory of the moral necessity of never treating other people as mere tools can be modified to support the ideas that people have rights and that treatment of others must always involve fair play. Regardless of whether you subscribe to Kant's version of duty theory, the chances are that your own moral deliberations are more than just strictly utilitarian and may well involve considerations of what you take to be other moral requirements, including your duties and the rights of others.

Divine command theory Those who believe moral duty is set by an authority of some sort subscribe to "command" duty theory. (Some authorities view Kant's duty theory as a version of command duty theory, with the authority for Kant being *reason*.) In our culture probably the most popular version of command duty theory is that according to which our moral duty is set by God; it thus is known as **divine command theory.** As noted above, those who hold this view generally derive their understanding of God's commandments by interpretation of religious texts like the Bible. How, for example, is "Thou shalt not kill" to be understood? Should it be understood as prohibiting capital punishment, or killing in self-defense, or killing in wartime? Does it cover abortion? There is obviously room for disagreement here; likewise, there is room for disagreement over who is to do the interpreting, whether it is to be oneself, or one's minister, or the head of one's church, or whoever.

A philosophical difficulty in divine command theory lies in the question, Is God *justified* in decreeing an act to be right, or is his decree simply arbitrary? On the one hand, we don't want to say that God hands down rules arbitrarily; yet the first alternative seems to imply that there is some standard of rightness and wrongness *above* or *apart* from God, in terms of which God finds the justification for his edicts.

Virtue ethics   Utilitarianism and duty theory, as well as most other classical approaches to moral theory, focus on the question of what to do. For that reason they are commonly referred to as ethics of conduct. However, another approach was predominant in classical Greek thinking and has regained popularity in recent years. That approach, known as **virtue ethics,** focuses not on *what to do,* but on *how to be;* in other words, the moral issue is not one of single actions or types of actions but of developing a *good character.*

The ancient Greeks believed it was supremely important for a person to achieve psychological and physical balance and to do that, the person needed to develop a consistently good character. A person out of balance will not be able to assess a situation properly and will tend to overreact or not react strongly enough; moreover, such a person will not know his or her proper limits. People who recognize their own qualifications and limitations and who are capable of reacting to the right degree, at the right time, toward the right person, and for the right reason are virtuous persons. They understand the value of the idea of moderation: not too much and not too little, but in each case a response that is just right.

Aristotle (384–322 B.C.E.) regarded virtue as a trait, like wisdom, justice, or courage, that we acquire when we use our capacity to reason to moderate our impulses and appetites. The largest part of Aristotle's major ethical writing, the *Nicomachean Ethics,* is devoted to analysis of specific moral virtues as means between extremes (for example, courage is the mean between fearing everything and fearing nothing). He also emphasized that virtue is a matter of habit; it is a trait, a way of living.

Virtue ethics is not an abstruse ethical theory. Many of us (fortunately) wish to be (or become) persons of good character. And as a practical matter, when we are deliberating a course of action, our approach often is to consider what someone whose character we admire would do in the circumstances.

Still, it is possible that virtue theory alone cannot answer all moral questions. Each of us may face moral dilemmas of such a nature that it simply isn't clear what course of action is required by someone of good character.

Why Moral Problems Seem Unresolvable

Differences of opinion over ethical issues sometimes seem irreconcilable. Yet this fact often strikes thoughtful people as amazing, because ethical opponents often share a great deal of common ground. For example, pro-life and pro-choice adherents agree on the sanctity of human life. So why in the world can't they resolve their differences? Likewise, those who favor affirmative action and those who agree that racism and sexism still exist and are wrong and need to be eradicated—why on earth can't they resolve their differences?

The answer, in some cases, comes down to a difference in moral perspective. Take affirmative action. Those who favor affirmative action often operate within a utilitarian perspective: They assume that whether a policy should be adopted depends on whether adopting the policy will produce more happiness than will not adopting it. From this perspective, if policies of affirmative action produce more happiness over the long run, then they should be adopted—end of discussion. But those who oppose affirmative action (on grounds other than blatant racism) do so because they believe deontologism trumps utilitarianism. From the deontologist perspective, even if affirmative action policies would produce more happiness in the long run, if they involve even temporarily using some people as a means to that objective, then they are wrong—end of discussion.

In other disputes the root difference lies elsewhere. Pro-life and pro-choice adherents often both are deontologists and agree, for example, that in the absence of a powerful justification, it is wrong to take a human life. They may disagree, however, either as to what counts as a human life or as to what counts as a powerful justification. This difference, then, comes down to a difference in basic definitions—which fact, incidentally, illustrates how silly it can be to dismiss a discussion as "mere semantics."

■ Moral Deliberation

Before you began this chapter, you may have assumed that moral discussion is merely an exchange of personal opinion or feeling, one that reserves no place for reason or critical thinking. But moral discussion usually assumes some sort of perspective like those we have mentioned here. Actually, in real life, moral reasoning is often a mixture of perspectives, a blend of utilitarian considerations weighted somewhat toward one's own happiness, modified by ideas about duties, rights, and obligations, and mixed often with a thought, perhaps guilty, about what the ideally virtuous person (a parent, a teacher) would do in similar circumstances. It also sometimes involves mistakes—descriptive and prescriptive claims may be confused, inconsistencies may occur, inductive arguments may be weak or deductive arguments may be invalid, pseudoreasoning may be present, and so forth.

We can make headway in our own thinking about moral issues by trying to get clear on what perspective, if any, we are assuming. For example, suppose we are thinking about the death penalty. Our first thought might be that society is much better off if murderers are executed. Are we then assuming a utilitarian perspective? Asking ourselves this question might lead us to consider whether there are *limits* on what we would do for the common good—for example, would we be willing to risk sacrificing an innocent person? It might also lead us to consider how we might *establish* whether society is better off if murderers are executed—if we are utilitarians, then ultimately we will have to establish this if our reasoning is to be compelling.

Or suppose we have seen a friend cheating on an exam. Should we report it to the teacher? Whatever our inclination, it may be wise to consider our perspective. Are we viewing things from a utilitarian perspective? That is, are we assuming that it would promote the most happiness overall to report our friend? Or do we simply believe that it is our duty to report him or her, come what may? Would a virtuous person report the person? Each of these questions will tend to focus our attention on a particular set of considerations—those that are the most relevant to our way of thinking.

It may occur to you to wonder at this point if there is any reason for choosing among perspectives. The answer to this question is yes: Adherents of these positions, philosophers such as those we mentioned, offer grounding or support for their perspectives in theories about human nature, the natural universe, the nature of morality, and other things. In other words, they have *arguments* to support their views. If you are interested, we recommend a course in ethics.

Exercise 13-5

1. Roy needs to sell his car, but he doesn't have money to spend on repairs. He plans to sell the vehicle to a private party without mentioning that the rear brakes are worn. Evaluate Roy's plan of action from a Kantian perspective—that is, can the maxim of Roy's plan be universalized?

2. Defend affirmative action from a utilitarian perspective.

3. Criticize affirmative action from a Kantian perspective. (Hint: Consider Kant's theory that people must never be treated as means only.)

4. Criticize or defend medical experimentation on animals from a utilitarian perspective.

5. Criticize or defend medical experimentation on animals from a divine command perspective.

6. A company has the policy of not promoting women to be vice presidents. What might be said about this policy from the perspective of virtue ethics?

7. What might be said about the policy mentioned in item 6 from the perspective of utilitarianism?

8. Evaluate bisexuality (in humans) from a divine command perspective.

9. In your opinion, would the virtuous person, the person of the best moral character, condemn, approve, or be indifferent to bisexuality?

10. "We can't condemn the founding fathers for owning slaves; people didn't think there was anything wrong with it at the time." Comment on this remark from the standpoint of duty theory.

11. "Let's have some fun and see how your parrot looks without any feathers." (The example is from philosopher Joseph Grcic.) Which of the following perspectives seems best equipped to condemn this suggestion?
    a. utilitarianism
    b. Kantian duty theory
    c. divine command theory
    d. virtue ethics
    e. relativism

12. "Might makes right." Could a utilitarian accept this? Could a virtue ethicist? Could Kant? Could a relativist? Could someone who subscribes to divine command theory?

Exercise 13-6

> This is Darwin's natural selection at its very best. The highest bidder gets youth and beauty.

These are the words of fashion photographer Ron Harris, who is auctioning the ova of fashion models via the Internet <www.ronsangels.com>. The model gets the full bid price, and the Web site takes a commission of an additional 20 percent. The bid price includes no medical costs, though it lists specialists who might be willing to perform the procedure. Harris, who created the video "The 20 Minute Workout," says the egg auction gives people the chance of reproducing beautiful children who will have an advantage in society. Critics, however, are numerous. "It screams of unethical behavior," one said. "It is acceptable for an infertile couple to choose an egg donor and compensate her for her time, inconvenience and discomfort," he said. "But this is something else entirely. Among other things, what happens to the child if he or she turns out to be unattractive?"

Discuss the (moral) pros and cons of this issue for five or ten minutes in groups. Then take a written stand on the question, "Should human eggs be auctioned to the highest bidder?" When you are finished, discuss which moral perspective seems to be the one in which you are operating.

Exercise 13-7

> Jesus wants to be our best friend. . . . If we let him direct our lives, he will give us the desires of our heart . . . we must yield to God and let him direct our future plans.

Selection 7 in the back of the book concerns a student who was denied permission to deliver a valedictorian speech at his public high school graduation that contained this statement.

The principal held that religious points of view cannot be presented at an event sponsored by a publicly funded agency. If the student had given his speech, the principal said, it would be as if the school had condoned the strong religious message the words contained.

The student, on the other hand, said he should be free to express his opinions and beliefs in a graduation speech. He said:

> I would not object if a Buddhist student gave a graduation speech and thanked Buddha, or a graduation speaker thanked Satan and urged people to follow Satan's example. Our country was founded on godly principles. God is on all of our money. It's pretty absurd that you can't even mention God at a graduation.

Should the student have been denied permission to include the statement we've quoted in his graduation speech? Think about the issue for a few minutes and then discuss it in groups of four or five for another five or ten minutes. After that, take a position on the issue and, on a piece of paper, defend the position with the best argument you can think of. Groups should then decide which moral perspective or combination of moral perspectives your defense seems to adopt.

Legal Reasoning

When we think about arguments and disputes, the first image to come to most minds is probably that of an attorney arguing a case in a court of law. Although it's true that lawyers require a solid understanding of factual matters related to their cases and of psychological considerations as well, especially where juries are involved, it is still safe to say that a lawyer's stock-in-trade is argument. Lawyers are successful—in large part—to the extent that they can produce evidence in support of the conclusion that most benefits their client—in other words, their success depends on how well they can put premises and conclusions together into convincing arguments.

■ Legal Reasoning and Moral Reasoning Compared

There are some obvious similarities between moral and legal claims. For example, they are both often prescriptive—they tell us what we should do. Both play a role in guiding our conduct, but legal prescriptions carry the weight of society behind them in a way that moral prescriptions do not: We can be punished if we fail to follow the former. In terms of specific actions, it's obvious that the class of illegal activities and the class of immoral activities greatly overlap. Indeed, a society whose moral and legal codes were greatly at odds would be very difficult to understand.

In our own society, we use the term "morals offenses" for a certain class of crimes (usually related to sexual practices), but in reality, most of the crimes we list in our penal codes are also offenses against morality: murder, robbery, theft, rape, and so on. There are exceptions both ways. Lying is almost always considered immoral, but it is illegal only in certain circumstances—under oath or in a contract, for example. On the other hand, there are many laws that have little or nothing to do with morality: laws that govern whether two people are married, laws that determine how far back from the street you must build your house, laws that require us to drive on the right side of the road, and so on. (It may be morally wrong to endanger others by driving on the wrong side of the road, but it is of no moral consequence whether the *correct* side is the right or the left. Hence, the actual content of the law is morally neutral.)

■ *Two Types of Legal Studies: Justifying Laws and Interpreting Laws*

Two principal kinds of questions are asked in legal studies. (Such studies, incidentally, are known variously as "jurisprudence" and "philosophy of law.") The first kind of question asks what the law *should be* and what procedures for making law should be adopted; the second kind asks what the law *is* and how it should be applied. Typically, philosophers are more interested in the former type of question and practicing attorneys in the latter.

By and large, reasoning about the first kind of question differs very little from moral reasoning as described in the first part of this chapter. The difference is simply that the focus is on justifying *laws* rather than on justifying moral statements or principles. We are often most interested in the justification of laws when those laws forbid us from doing something we might otherwise want to do or when they require us to do something we might otherwise want not to do. Justifications, as you may remember from Chapter 7, are simply arguments that try to establish the goodness, value, or acceptability of something. Here, they are used to try to answer the question, What should the law be?

Consider whether a law that forbids doing X should be enacted by your state legislature.* Typically, there are four main grounds on which a supporter of a law can base his or her justification. The first is simply that doing X is immoral. The claim that the law should make illegal anything that is immoral is the basis of the position known as **legal moralism.** One might use such a basis for justifying laws forbidding murder, assault, or unorthodox sexual practices. For a legal moralist, the kinds of arguments designed to show that an action is immoral are directly relevant to the question of whether the action should be illegal.

The next ground on which a law can be justified is probably the one that most people think of first. It is very closely associated with John Stuart Mill (1806–1873) and is known as the **harm principle:** The only legitimate basis for forbidding X is that doing X causes harm to others. Notice that the

---

*The example here is of a criminal law—part of a penal code designed to require and forbid certain behaviors and to punish offenders. The situation is a little different in civil law, a main goal of which is to shift the burden of a wrongful harm (a "tort") from the person on whom it falls to another, more suitable person—usually the one who caused the harm.

harm principle states not just that harm to others is a good ground for forbidding an activity, but that it is the *only* ground. (In terms of the way we formulated such claims in Chapter 10, on truth-functional logic, the principle would be stated, "It is legitimate to forbid doing X *if and only if* doing X causes harm to others.") A person who defends this principle and who wants to enact a law forbidding X will present evidence that doing X does indeed cause harm to others. Her arguments could resemble any of the types covered in earlier chapters.

A third ground on which our hypothetical law might be based is legal paternalism. **Legal paternalism** is the view that laws can be justified if they prevent a person from doing harm to him- or herself; that is, they forbid or make it impossible to do X, *for a person's own good.* Examples include laws that require that seat belts be worn while riding in automobiles and that helmets be worn while riding on motorcycles.

The last of the usual bases for justifying criminal laws is that some behavior is generally found offensive. The **offense principle** says that a law forbidding X can be justifiable if X causes great offense to others. Laws forbidding burning of the flag are often justified on this ground.

The second question mentioned earlier—What *is* the law and how should it be applied?—may be more straightforward than the first question, but it can still be very complicated. We needn't go into great detail here about why this is the case, but an example will provide an indication. Back in Chapter 2 we discussed vague concepts, and we found that it is impossible to rid our talk entirely of vagueness. Here's an example from the law. Let's suppose that a city ordinance forbids vehicles on the paths in the city park. Clearly, a person violates the law if he or she drives a truck or a car down the paths. But what about a motorbike? A bicycle? A go-cart? A child's pedal car? Just what counts as a vehicle and what does not? This is the kind of issue that must often be decided in court because—not surprisingly—the governing body writing the law could not foresee all the possible items that might, in somebody's mind, count as a vehicle.

The process of narrowing down when a law applies and when it does not, then, is another kind of reasoning problem that occurs in connection with the law.

■ *The Role of Precedent in Legal Reasoning*

Generally speaking, legal reasoning is like other reasoning insofar as it makes use of the same kinds of arguments: They are deductive or inductive; if the former, they can be valid or invalid; if the latter, they can range from strong to weak. The difference between legal and other types of reasoning is mainly in the subject matter to which the argumentative techniques are applied, a taste of which we have sampled in the preceding paragraphs.

There is one kind of argument that occupies a special place in reasoning about legal matters, however: the **appeal to precedent.** This is the practice in the law of using a case that has already been decided as an authoritative guide in deciding a new case that is similar. The appeal to precedent is a variety of argument by analogy in which the current case is said to be sufficiently like the previous case to warrant deciding it in the same way. The general principle of treating like cases alike, discussed in the previous section on moral reasoning, applies here for exactly the same reasons. It would be illogical—and most would say, in some cases at least, unfair or immoral—to treat similar cases in different ways. The Latin name for the principle of appeal to precedent is **stare decisis** ("don't change settled decisions," more or less). Using terminology that was applied in the Chapter 11 discussion of analogical argument, we'd say that the earlier, already settled case is the sample, the current case is the target, and the property in question is the way in which the first case was decided. If the target case is sufficiently like the sample case, then, according to the principle of *stare decisis*, it should be decided the same way. Arguments in such situations, naturally, tend to focus on whether the current case really is like the precedent in enough relevant respects. Aside from the fact that such disputes sometimes have more significant consequences for the parties involved, they are not importantly different from those over analogies in other subject matters.

Exercise 13-8

For each of the following kinds of laws, pick at least one of the four grounds for justification discussed in the text—legal moralism, the harm principle, legal paternalism, and the offense principle—and construct an argument designed to justify the law. You may not agree either with the law or with the argument; the exercise is to see if you can connect the law to the (allegedly) justifying principle. For many laws, there is more than one kind of justification possible, so there can be more than one good answer for many of these.

▲ 1. Laws against shoplifting

▲ 2. Laws against forgery

   3. Laws against suicide

▲ 4. Laws against spitting on the sidewalk

   5. Laws against driving under the influence of drugs or alcohol

▲ 6. Laws against adultery

   7. Laws against marriage between two people of the same sex

   8. Laws that require people to have licenses before they practice medicine

   9. Laws that require drivers of cars to have driver's licenses

▲ 10. Laws against desecrating a corpse

   11. Laws against trespassing

   12. Laws against torturing your pet (even though it may be legal to kill your pet, if it is done humanely)

Exercise 13-9 _____

This exercise is for class discussion or a short writing assignment. In the text, "Vehicles are prohibited on the paths in the park" was used as an example of a law that might require clarification. Decide whether the law should be interpreted to forbid motorcycles, bicycles, children's pedal cars, and battery-powered remote-control cars. On what grounds are you deciding each of these cases?

Exercise 13-10 _____

The U.S. Supreme Court came to a decision not long ago about the proper application of the word "use." Briefly, the case in point was about a man named John Angus Smith, who traded a handgun for cocaine. The law under which Smith was charged provided for a much more severe penalty—known as an enhanced penalty—if a gun was used in a drug-related crime than if no gun was involved. (In this case, the enhanced penalty was a mandatory thirty-year sentence; the "unenhanced" penalty was five years.) Justice Antonin Scalia argued that Smith's penalty should not be enhanced because he did not use the gun in the way the writers of the law had in mind; he did not use it *as a gun.* Justice Sandra Day O'Connor argued that the law only requires the *use* of a gun, not any particular *kind* of use. If you were a judge, would you vote with Scalia or with O'Connor? Construct an argument in support of your position. (The decision of the court is given in the answer section at the back of the book.)

Aesthetic Reasoning

Like moral and legal thinking, aesthetic thinking relies on a conceptual framework that integrates fact and value. Judgments about beauty and art—even judgments about whether something is a work of art or just an everyday object—appeal to principles that identify sources of aesthetic or artistic value. So when you make such a judgment, you are invoking aesthetic concepts, even if you have not made them explicit to yourself or to others.

■ *Eight Aesthetic Principles*

Here are some of the aesthetic principles that most commonly support or influence artistic creation and critical judgment about art. The first three identify value in art with an object's ability to fulfill certain cultural or social functions.

1. *Objects are aesthetically valuable if they are meaningful or teach us truths.* For example, Aristotle says that tragic plays teach us

general truths about the human condition in a dramatic way that cannot be matched by real-life experience. Many people believe art shows us truths that are usually hidden from us by the practical concerns of daily life.

2. *Objects are aesthetically valuable if they have the capacity to convey values or beliefs that are central to the cultures or traditions in which they originate, or that are important to the artists who made them.* For example, John Milton's poem *Paradise Lost* expresses the seventeenth-century Puritan view of the relationship between human beings and God.

3. *Objects are aesthetically valuable if they have the capacity to help bring about social or political change.* For instance, Abraham Lincoln commented that Harriet Beecher Stowe's *Uncle Tom's Cabin* contributed to the antislavery movement, which resulted in the Civil War.

Another group of principles identifies aesthetic value with objects' capacities to produce certain subjective—that is, psychological—states in persons who experience or appreciate them. Here are some of the most common or influential principles of the second group:

4. *Objects are aesthetically valuable if they have the capacity to produce pleasure in those who experience or appreciate them.* For instance, the nineteenth-century German philosopher Friedrich Nietzsche identifies one kind of aesthetic value with the capacity to create a feeling of ecstatic bonding in audiences.

5. *Objects are aesthetically valuable if they have the capacity to produce certain emotions we value, at least when the emotion is brought about by art rather than life.* In the *Poetics*, Aristotle observes that we welcome the feelings of fear created in us by frightening dramas, whereas in everyday life fear is an experience we would rather avoid. The psychoanalyst Sigmund Freud offers another version of this principle: While we enjoy art, we permit ourselves to have feelings so subversive that we have to repress them to function in everyday life.

6. *Objects are aesthetically valuable if they have the capacity to produce special nonemotional experiences, such as a feeling of autonomy or the willing suspension of disbelief.* This principle is the proposal of the nineteenth-century English poet Samuel Taylor Coleridge. One of art's values, he believes, is its ability to stimulate our power to exercise our imaginations and consequently to free ourselves from thinking that is too narrowly practical.

Notice that principles 4 through 6 resemble the first three in that they identify aesthetic value with the capacity to fulfill a function. According to these last three, the specified function is to create some kind of subjective or inner state in audiences; according to the first three, however, art's function is to achieve such objective outcomes as conveying information or knowledge or preserving or changing culture or society. But there are yet other influential aesthetic principles that do not characterize art in terms of capacities for performing functions. According to one commonly held principle, art objects attain aesthetic value by virtue of their possessing a certain special aesthetic property or certain special formal configurations:

> 7. *Objects are aesthetically valuable if they possess a special aesthetic property or exhibit a special aesthetic form.* Sometimes this aesthetic property is called "beauty," and sometimes it is given another name. For instance, the early-twentieth-century art critic Clive Bell insists that good art is valuable for its own sake, not because it fulfills any function. To know whether a work is good aesthetically, he urges, one need only look at it or listen to it to see or hear whether it has "significant form." "Significant form" is valuable for itself, not for any function it performs.

Finally, one familiar principle insists that no reasons can be given to support judgments about art. Properly speaking, those who adhere to this principle think that to approve or disapprove of art is to express an unreasoned preference rather than to render judgment. This principle may be stated as follows:

> 8. *No reasoned argument can conclude that objects are aesthetically valuable or valueless.* This principle is expressed in the Latin saying *"De gustibus non est disputandum,"* or "Tastes can't be disputed."

The principles summarized here by no means exhaust the important views about aesthetic value, nor are they complete expositions of the views they represent. Historically, views about the nature of art have proven relatively fluid, for they must be responsive to the dynamics of technological and cultural change. Moreover, even though the number of familiar conceptions of aesthetic value is limited, there are many alternative ways of stating these that combine the thoughts behind them in somewhat different ways.

Consequently, to attempt to label each principle with a name invites confusion. For example, let's consider whether any of the principles might be designated *formalism,* which is an important school or style of art. Although the seventh principle explicitly ascribes aesthetic value to a work's form as opposed to its function, the formal properties of artworks also figure as valuable, although only as means to more valuable ends, in certain formulations of the first six principles. For instance, some scholars, critics, and artists think certain formal patterns in works of art can evoke corresponding emotions, social patterns, or pleasures in audiences—for example, slow music full of minor chords is commonly said to make people feel sad.

You should understand that all of the principles presented here merely serve as a basic framework within which you can explore critical thinking about art. If you are interested in the arts, you will very likely want to

The story is told of the American tourist in Paris who told Pablo Picasso that he didn't like modern paintings because they weren't realistic. Picasso made no immediate reply. A few minutes later the tourist showed him a snapshot of his house.

"My goodness," said Picasso, "is it really as small as that?"

—Jacob Braude

develop a more complex and sophisticated conceptual framework to enrich your thinking about this subject.

■ *Using Aesthetic Principles to Judge Aesthetic Value*

The first thing to notice about the aesthetic principles we've just discussed is that some are compatible with each other. Thus, a reasonable thinker can appeal to more than one in reaching a verdict about the aesthetic value of an object. For instance, a consistent thinker can use both the first and the fifth principle in evaluating a tragic drama. Aristotle does just this in his *Poetics*. He tells us that tragedies are good art when they both convey general truths about the human condition and help their audiences purge themselves of the pity and fear they feel when they face the truth about human limitations. A play that presents a general truth without eliciting the proper catharsis (release of emotion) in the audience, or a play that provokes tragic emotions unaccompanied by recognition of a general truth, is not as valuable as a play that does both.

However, some of these principles cannot be used together consistently to judge aesthetic value. These bear the same relationship to each other as do contrary claims (recall the square of opposition in Chapter 9). They cannot both be true, although both might be false. For instance, the principle that art is valuable in itself, by virtue of its form or formal configuration (not because it serves some function), and the principle that art is valuable because it serves a social or political function cannot be used consistently together. You might have noticed also that the eighth principle contradicts the others; that is, the first seven principles all specify kinds of reasons for guiding and supporting our appreciation of art, but the last principle denies that there can be any such good reasons.

Finally, it is important to understand that the same principle can generate both positive and negative evaluations, depending on whether the work in question meets or fails to meet the standard expressed in the principle. For example, the fourth principle, which we might call aesthetic hedonism, generates positive evaluations of works that produce pleasure but negative evaluations of works that leave their audiences in pain or displeased.

Exercise 13-11

Suppose that the two statements in each of the following pairs both appear in a review of the same work of art. Identify which of the eight aesthetic principles each statement in the pair appeals to. Then state whether the principles are compatible (that is, they do not contradict each other) and thus form the basis for a consistent critical review, or whether they contradict each other and cannot both be used in a consistent review.

▲ 1. a. Last weekend's performance of the Wagnerian operatic cycle was superb; the music surged through the audience, forging a joyous communal bond.

    b. Smith's forceful singing and acting in the role of Siegfried left no doubt why Wagner's vision of heroic morality was attractive to his Teutonic contemporaries.

2. a. Leni Riefenstahl's film *Triumph of the Will* proved to be effective art because it convinced its audiences that the Nazi party would improve the German way of life.

    b. Despite its overtly racist message, *Triumph of the Will* is great art, for films should be judged on the basis of their visual coherence and not in terms of their moral impact.

3. a. All lovers of art should condemn Jackson Pollock's meaningless abstract expressionist splatter paintings.

    b. These paintings create neither sadness nor joy; those who view them feel nothing, neither love nor hate nor any of the other passions that great art evokes.

▲ 4. a. Laurence Olivier's film production of *Hamlet* has merit because he allows us to experience the impact of the incestuous love that a son can feel for his mother.

    b. Nevertheless, Olivier's *Hamlet* is flawed because it introduces a dimension inconceivable to an Elizabethan playwright.

5. a. There is no point arguing about or giving reasons for verdicts about art, because each person's tastes or responses are so personal.

    b. Those who condemn sexually explicit performance art do not recognize that art is valuable to the extent it permits us to feel liberated and free of convention.

■ *Evaluating Aesthetic Criticism: Relevance and Truth*

Is any evaluation of a work of art as good as any other in creating a critical treatment of that work? The answer is no, for two reasons: (1) the principles of art one adopts function as a conceptual framework that distinguishes relevant from irrelevant reasons; (2) even a relevant reason is useless if it is not true of the work to which it is applied.

Let's consider the first reason. What would convince you of the value of a work if you accepted principles 4 through 6—all of which maintain that aesthetic value resides in the subjective responses art evokes in its audiences? In this case, you are likely to be drawn to see Picasso's *Guernica* if you are told that it has the power to make its viewers experience the horrors of war; but you would not be attracted by learning, instead, that *Guernica* explores the relationship of two- and three-dimensional spatial concepts. Suppose you reject principles 1 through 3, which conceive of aesthetic value in terms of the work's capacity to perform an objective, cognitive, moral, social, or political function. The fact that Picasso was a Communist will strike you as irrelevant to appreciating *Guernica* unless you accept one or more of the first three principles.

To illustrate the second reason, look at the nearby reproduction of *Guernica*. Suppose a critic writes, "By giving his figures fishlike appearances

▲　*Pablo Picasso,* Guernica

and showing them serenely floating through a watery environment, Picasso makes us feel that humans will survive under any conditions." But no figures in *Guernica* look anything like fish; moreover, they are surrounded by fire, not water, and they are twisted with anguish rather than serene. So, this critic's reasons are no good. Because they are not true of the work, they cannot guide us in perceiving features that enhance our appreciation. A similar problem occurs if reasons are implausible. For instance, an interpretation of *Guernica* as a depiction of the Last Supper is implausible, because we cannot recognize the usual signs of this theme, the twelve disciples and Christ at a table (or at least at a meal), in the far fewer figures of the painting.

The aim of art is to represent not the outward appearance of things, but their inward significance.

—ARISTOTLE

Exercise 13-12

State whether each of the reasons below is relevant according to any one of the aesthetic principles. If the reason is relevant, identify the principle that makes it so. If no principle makes the reason relevant, state that it is irrelevant.

▲ 1. Raphael's carefully balanced pyramidal compositions give his paintings of the Madonna such beautiful form that they have aesthetic value for Christian and atheist alike.

2. By grouping his figures so that they compose a triangle or pyramid, Raphael directs the viewer's eye upward to heaven and thereby teaches us about the close connection between motherhood and God.

3. The melody from the chorus "For unto Us a Child Is Born" in Handel's *Messiah* was originally composed by Handel for an erotic love song. Consequently, it evokes erotic responses which distract and detract from the devotional feeling audiences are supposed to experience when they hear *Messiah* performed.

▲ 4. Vincent van Gogh tells us that he uses clashing reds and greens in *The Night Café* to help us see his vision of "the terrible passions of humanity"; it is the intensity with which he conveys his views of the ugliness of human life that makes his work so illuminating.

5. The critics who ignored van Gogh's painting during his lifetime were seriously mistaken; by damaging his self-esteem, they drove him to suicide.

6. Moreover, these critics misjudged the aesthetic value of his art, as evidenced by the fact that his paintings now sell for as much as $80 million.

▲ 7. By showing a naked woman picnicking with fully clothed men in *Déjeuner sur l'herbe*, Édouard Manet treats women as objects and impedes their efforts to throw off patriarchal domination.

Exercise 13-13

June the chimp has been very sad and lonely, so the zoo director gives her some paper, paints, and brushes to keep her busy. Look at the photograph of the chimpanzee painting and at the photograph of the chimpanzee's painting. Does June's work have aesthetic value? Use each of the eight principles to formulate one reason for or against attributing aesthetic value to June's work. You should end up with eight reasons, one appealing to each principle.

▲ *June the chimpanzee.*

▲ *June's painting*

■ Why Reason Aesthetically?

The various aesthetic principles we've introduced are among those most commonly found, either explicitly or implicitly, in discussions about art.

Moreover, they have influenced both the creation of art and the selection of art for both private and public enjoyment. But where do these principles come from? There is much debate about this; to understand it, we can draw on notions about definition (introduced in Chapter 2) as well as the discussion of generalizations (Chapter 11).

Some people think that aesthetic principles are simply elaborate definitions of our concepts of art or aesthetic value. Let's explain this point. We use definitions to identify things; for example, by definition we look for three sides and three angles to identify a geometric figure as a triangle. Similarly, we can say that aesthetic principles are definitions; that is, these principles provide an aesthetic vocabulary to direct us in recognizing an object's aesthetic value.

If aesthetic principles are true by definition, then learning to judge art is learning the language of art. But because artists strive for originality, we are constantly faced with talking about innovative objects to which the critic's familiar vocabulary does not quite do justice. This aspect of art challenges even the most sophisticated critic to continually extend the aesthetic vocabulary.

Others think that aesthetic principles are generalizations that summarize what is true of objects treated as valuable art. Here, the argument is by analogy from a sample class to a target population. Thus, someone might hold that all or most of the tragic plays we know that are aesthetically valuable have had something important to say about the human condition; for this reason, we can expect this to be true of any member of the class of tragic plays we have not yet evaluated. Or, also by inductive analogy, musical compositions that are valued so highly that they continue to be performed throughout the centuries all make us feel some specific emotion, such as joy or sadness; so we can predict that a newly composed piece will be similarly highly valued if it also evokes a strong, clear emotion. Of course, such arguments are weakened to the extent that the target object differs from the objects in the sample class. Because there is a drive for originality in art, newly created works may diverge so sharply from previous samples that arguments by analogy sometimes prove too weak.

It is sometimes suggested that these two accounts of the source of aesthetic principles really reinforce each other: Our definitions reflect to some extent our past experience of the properties or capacities typical of valuable art, and our past experience is constrained to some extent by our definitions. But if art changes, of what use are principles, whether analytic or inductive, in guiding us to make aesthetic judgments and—even more difficult—in fostering agreement about these judgments?

At the very least, these principles have an emotive force that guides us in perceiving art. You will remember that emotive force (discussed briefly in Chapter 2) is a dimension of language that permits the words we use to do something more than convey information. In discussion about art, the words that constitute reasons can have an emotive force directing our attention to particular aspects of a work. If the critic can describe these aspects accurately and persuasively, it is thought, the audience will focus on these aspects and experience a favorable (or unfavorable) response similar to the critic's. If a critic's reasons are too vague or are not true of the work to which they are applied, they are unlikely to bring the audience into agreement with the critic.

The principles of art, then, serve as guides for identifying appropriate categories of favorable or unfavorable response, but the reasons falling into these categories are what bring about agreement. They are useful both in developing our own appreciation of a work of art and in persuading others. The reasons must be accurately and informatively descriptive of the objects to which they are applied. The reasons enable us (1) to select a particular way of viewing, listening, reading, or otherwise perceiving the object and (2) to recommend, guide, or prescribe that the object be viewed, heard, or read in this way.

So, aesthetic reasons contain descriptions that prompt ways of perceiving aspects of an object. These prescribed ways of seeing evoke favorable (or unfavorable) responses or experiences. For instance, suppose a critic states that van Gogh's brush strokes in *Starry Night* are dynamic and his colors intense. This positive critical reason prescribes that people focus on these features when they look at the painting. The expectation is that persons whose vision is swept into the movement of van Gogh's painted sky and pierced by the presence of his painted stars will, by virtue of focusing on these formal properties, enjoy a positive response to the painting.

To learn to give reasons and form assessments about art, practice applying these principles as you look, listen, or read. Consider what aspects of a painting, musical performance, poem, or other work each principle directs you to contemplate. It is also important to expand your aesthetic vocabulary so that you have words to describe what you see, hear, or otherwise sense in a work. As you do so, you will be developing your own aesthetic expertise. And, because your reasons will be structured by aesthetic principles others also accept, you will find that rational reflection on art tends to expand both the scope and volume of your agreement with others about aesthetic judgments.

Recap

Reasoning about morality is distinguished from reasoning about matters of fact only in that the former always involves claims that express moral values. Such claims are called *prescriptive* because they prescribe what a person ought to do. Claims about matters of fact, by contrast, are called *descriptive* because they describe what is believed to be the case. Certain words— especially "ought," "should," "right," and "wrong"—are used in prescriptive claims in a moral sense, although these terms can also be used in a nonmoral sense.

A prescriptive conclusion can't be reached solely from premises that are purely descriptive; in other words, you can't get an "ought" from an "is."

To be valid, an argument that has a value-expressing conclusion—that is, a moral argument—must also have a value-expressing premise. Although such premises often remain unstated, we need to state them deliberately to avoid assuming that the value somehow can be derived from a factual premise. Then, in case we disagree with the moral conclusion but can't dispute the factual premise, we can point to the value-expressing premise as the point with which we disagree.

People are sometimes inconsistent in their moral views: They treat similar cases as if the cases were different even when they cannot tell us what is importantly different about them. When two or more cases that are being treated differently seem similar, the burden of proof is on the person who is treating them differently to explain what is different about them.

Moral reasoning is usually conducted within a perspective or framework. In this chapter we considered relativism, subjectivism, utilitarianism, Kantian duty theory, divine command theory, and virtue ethics. Often, different perspectives converge to produce similar solutions to a moral issue; on other occasions they diverge. Keeping in mind our own perspective can help focus our own moral deliberations on relevant considerations.

There are similarities between the subjects of moral reasoning and legal reasoning, especially in that they both make important use of prescriptive claims. Legal studies are devoted to problems like that of justifying laws that prescribe conduct; we looked at legal moralism, the harm principle, legal paternalism, and the offense principle as grounds for such justification. Problems in determining just when and where a law applies often require making vague claims specific.

Precedent is a kind of analogical argument by means of which current cases are settled in accordance with guidelines set by cases decided previously. Whether a precedent governs in a given case is decided on grounds similar to those of any other analogical argument.

To reason aesthetically is to make judgments within a conceptual framework that integrates facts and values. Aesthetic value is often identified as the capacity to fulfill a function, such as to create pleasure or promote social change. Alternatively, aesthetic value is defined in terms of a special aesthetic property or form found in works of art. Still another view treats aesthetic judgments as expressions of tastes. Reasoned argument about aesthetic value helps us to see, hear, or otherwise perceive art in changed or expanded ways and to enhance our appreciation of art. A critic who gives reasons in support of an aesthetic verdict forges agreement by getting others to share perceptions of the work. The greater the extent to which we share such aesthetic perceptions, the more we can reach agreement about aesthetic value.

Having read this chapter and the chapter recap, you should be able to

▲ Distinguish between descriptive and prescriptive moral claims, show how to get from a descriptive to a prescriptive moral claim, and explain the role of consistency in moral reasoning

▲ Describe the major perspectives in moral reasoning outlined in the chapter and explain how these perspectives might be used in everyday reasoning

▲ Explain the differences between the two principal types of legal reasoning and discuss the grounds on which a law might be justified

▲ Explain the principle of precedent in legal reasoning

▲ Describe the eight aesthetic principles listed in the chapter and show how to use them in aesthetic reasoning

▲ Explain the importance of relevance and truth in aesthetic criticism

▲ Discuss the importance of aesthetic reasoning

Additional Exercises

Exercise 13-14

State whether the following reasons are (a) helpful in focusing perception to elicit a favorable response, (b) helpful in focusing perception to elicit an unfavorable response, (c) too vague to focus perception, (d) false or implausible and therefore unable to focus perception, or (e) irrelevant to focusing perception. The information you need is contained in the reasons, so try to visualize or imagine what the work is like from what is said. All of these are paraphrases of testimony given at a hearing in 1985 about a proposal to remove *Tilted Arc*, an immense abstract sculpture, from a plaza in front of a federal office building.

▲ 1. Richard Serra's *Tilted Arc* is a curved slab of welded steel 12 feet high, 120 feet long, weighing over 73 tons, covered completely with a natural oxide coating. The sculpture arcs through the plaza. By coming to terms with its harshly intrusive disruption of space, we can learn much about how the nature of the spaces we inhabit affects our social relations.

2. Richard Serra is one of our leading artists, and his work commands very high prices. The government has a responsibility to the financial community. It is bad business to destroy this work because you would be destroying property.

3. *Tilted Arc*'s very tilt and rust remind us that the gleaming and heartless steel and glass structures of the state apparatus can one day pass away. It therefore creates an unconscious sense of freedom and hope.

▲ 4. *Tilted Arc* looks like a discarded piece of crooked or bent metal; there's no more meaning in having it in the middle of the plaza than in putting an old bicycle that got run over by a car there.

5. *Tilted Arc* launches through space in a thrilling and powerful acutely arched curve.

6. *Tilted Arc* is big and rusty.

▲ *Richard Serra*, Tilted Arc

▲ 7. Because of its size, thrusting shape, and implacably uniform rusting surface, *Tilted Arc* makes us feel hopeless, trapped, and sad. This sculpture would be interesting if we could visit it when we had time to explore these feelings, but it is too depressing to face every day on our way to work.

8. Serra's erotically realistic, precise rendering of the female figure in *Tilted Arc* exhibits how appealingly he can portray the soft circularity of a woman's breast.

9. *Tilted Arc* is sort of red; it probably isn't blue.

Exercise 13-15

Artemisia Gentileschi was a painter who was very successful in her own time. Success came despite the trauma of her early life, when she figured as the victim in a notorious rape trial. But after she died, her work fell into obscurity; it was neither shown in major museums nor written about in art-history books. Recently, feminist scholars have revived interest in her work by connecting the style and/or theme of such paintings as her *Judith* with her rape and with feelings or issues of importance to women. But other scholars have pointed out that both her subject matter and her treatment of it are conventionally found as well in the work of male painters of the Caravaggist school, with which she is identified. Based on this information, and using one or more of the aesthetic principles described in this chapter, write an essay arguing either that the painting

▲ *Artemisia Gentileschi,* Judith

Judith has aesthetic value worthy of our attention or that it should continue to be ignored.

Writing Exercises

1. In the movie *Priest,* the father of a young girl admits to the local priest—in the confessional—that he has molested his daughter. However, the man lacks remorse and gives every indication that he will continue to abuse the girl. For the priest to inform the girl's mother or the authorities would be for him to violate the sanctity of the confessional, but to not inform anyone would subject the girl to further abuse. What should the priest do? Take about fifteen minutes to do the following:

     a. List the probable consequences of the courses of action available to the priest.

     b. List any duties or rights or other considerations that bear on the issue.

When fifteen minutes are up, share your ideas with the class.

     Now take about twenty minutes to write an essay in which you do the following:

     a. State the issue.

     b. Take a stand on the issue.

     c. Defend your stand.

     d. Rebut counterarguments to your position.

When you are finished, write down on a separate piece of paper a number between 1 and 10 that indicates how strong you think your argument is (10 = very strong; 1 = very weak). Write your name on the back of your paper.

     When everyone is finished, the instructor will collect the papers and redistribute them to the class. In groups of four or five, read the papers and assign a number from 1 to 10 to each one (10 = very strong; 1 = very weak). When all groups are finished, return the papers to their authors. When you get your paper back, compare the number you assigned to your work with the number the group assigned it. The instructor may ask volunteers to defend their own judgment of their work against the judgment of the group. Do you think there is as much evidence for your position as you did at the beginning of the period?

2. Follow the same procedure as above to address one of the following issues:

     a. A friend cheats in the classes he has with you. You know he'd just laugh if you voiced any concern. Should you mention it to your instructor?

     b. You see a friend stealing something valuable. Even though you tell your friend that you don't approve, she keeps the item. What should you do?

     c. Your best friend's fiancé has just propositioned you for sex. Should you tell your friend?

     d. Your parents think you should major in marketing or some other practical field. You want to major in literature. Your parents pay the bills. What should you do?

Appendix 1

Conflicting Claims

In our discussion of the square of opposition (Chapter 9), there is an account of claims that conflict with one another—that are contraries or contradictories. But the discussion there is limited to corresponding standard-form categorical claims. Such a limited discussion cannot do justice to the full range of examples of contradiction and contrariety, so we've included this appendix to fill in the gaps. You do not have to have read the material in Chapter 9 to follow this discussion.

When we say that two claims are **conflicting claims** we mean simply that they cannot both be true. So, if we know one to be true, we can infer that the other is false. We make use of this feature of claims whenever we reject one that conflicts with what we already believe to be true. We often do this almost automatically—with very little conscious thought about it.

But conflict between claims is a little more complicated than we might think. In particular, we should notice that claims can conflict in more than one way. The most thorough kind of conflict occurs when claims are **contradictory claims,** or exact opposites: They cannot both be true at the same time, and they cannot both be false at the same time. The claims that follow are each the contradictory of the other member of the pair:

1. a. Sydney is the capital of Australia.
   b. Sydney is not the capital of Australia.

2. a. Baltimore orioles migrate over a thousand miles each year.
   b. It is not the case that Baltimore orioles migrate over a thousand miles each year.

3. a. All members of the faculty took a cut in pay.
   b. At least one member of the faculty did not take a cut in pay.

4. a. There is no alternative to nuclear power for the production of electricity in the twenty-first century.

      b. There is at least one alternative to nuclear power for the production of electricity in the twenty-first century.

Each of these claims must have a different truth value from the other one in the pair. Therefore, if we know that one of them is false, we can infer that the other member of the pair is true.

    Notice that the claims in the following pairs, although they do conflict and they may at first appear to be contradictories, are not really exact opposites in the way that contradictories are:

1. a. Sydney is the capital of Australia.
   b. Canberra is the capital of Australia.

2. a. Baltimore orioles migrate to Africa in the winter.
   b. Baltimore orioles migrate to South America in the winter.

3. a. All members of the faculty took a cut in pay.
   b. Faculty in the English Department did not take a cut in pay.

4. a. Solar energy is an alternative to nuclear power for the production of electricity in the twenty-first century.
   b. There is no alternative to nuclear power for the production of electricity in the twenty-first century.

The claims in each of these pairs cannot both be true, but they are *not* exact opposites: For each pair, it is possible for *both* claims to be false. For example, if Melbourne were the capital of Australia, then both (a) and (b) of the first pair would be false. Similarly, if the members of the English Department faculty did take a cut in pay but the members of the Sociology Department faculty did not take a cut, then both (a) and (b) of the third pair would be false. For a little practice, think of a situation that would make both claims of the second pair false and one that would make both of the fourth pair false.

    By inventing these situations we are showing that the claims in these pairs are **contrary claims,** which means simply that they cannot both be true but they can both be false. Because there are at least some circumstances under which both of a pair of contraries can be false, knowing that one is false is not enough to infer that the other is true.

    The contrary/contradiction difference makes trouble when someone takes a pair of claims to be contradictories when in fact they are contraries. For example, creationism is often taken to be contradictory to evolution. Thus, someone may believe that by producing an argument *against* one of them, he or she is arguing *for* the other view. But the two views are contrary, not contradictory—they could both be false. Therefore, even if somebody succeeded in proving one of them false, this would not prove that the other is true.

    Some claims may appear to conflict without actually doing so. For example:

Conflicting Claims? You Decide

It means that there is not a sexual relationship, an improper sexual relationship, or any other kind of improper relationship.

—BILL CLINTON, January 1998

Indeed, I did have a relationship with Ms. Lewinsky that was not appropriate. In fact, it was wrong.

—BILL CLINTON, January 1999

1. a. Silas Marner hot dogs are at least 30 percent pork.
   b. Silas Marner hot dogs are at most 30 percent pork.

2. a. Silas Marner hot dogs are at least 20 percent pork.
   b. Silas Marner hot dogs are at least 30 percent pork.

The claims in the first pair can both be true, provided that the hot dogs are *exactly* 30 percent pork. The claims in the second pair are both true if the hot dogs are 30 percent pork or more. It pays to look carefully at a claim before deciding that it conflicts with another.

The following exercises will give you some practice in identifying claims that are contrary to one another and claims that are contradictory.

Exercise A1-1 _____

Determine whether the claims in the following pairs are contraries, are contradictories, or do not conflict.

▲ 1. a. A drink or two a day won't hurt anyone's health.
   b. Heart patients absolutely should not drink at all.

2. a. None of the legal staff showed up for work today.
   b. Some of the legal staff showed up for work today.

3. a. The temperature was over 90 degrees by three o'clock.
   b. The temperature was over 85 degrees by three o'clock.

▲ 4. a. It's unpleasantly cool today.
   b. It's over 90 degrees today.

5. a. Duluth is bigger than Terre Haute.
   b. Terre Haute is at least as big as Duluth.

6. a. Eisenhower was the president who first remarked that "the future lies ahead."
   b. Hoover was the president who first remarked that "the future lies ahead."

▲ 7. a. There were no games in the 1994 World Series in which more than twelve runs were scored.

   b. There were two games in the 1994 World Series in which more than twelve runs were scored.

   8. a. The rate of inflation in 1991 was 5 percent or more.

   b. The inflation rate in 1991 was less than 5 percent.

   9. a. All digital communications will require fiber optics by the year 2010.

   b. Fiber optics will not be necessary for all digital communications by the year 2010.

▲ 10. a. Winthrop, South Carolina, is the only town in the country that has a law against carrying an ice cream cone in one's pocket.

   b. Monfort, Florida, has a law against carrying an ice cream cone in one's pocket.

Exercise A1-2

Determine whether these pairs are contradictories, are contraries, or do not conflict. Some of these are a little less clear than those in the previous exercise. Whether they are contradictories or contraries may depend on whether certain assumptions are made. For example, in (1) we'll get one answer if we make the reasonable assumption that there is no more than one payday per week. But if we allow the possibility of two paydays per week, we'll get another answer. Identify any assumptions, problems of vagueness, or other considerations that have to be kept in mind when producing your answers.

▲ 1. a. Friday is payday.

   b. No, I'm sorry; Monday is payday.

   2. a. Helgren is going to fail his logic course.

   b. Helgren is going to pass his logic course.

   3. a. Everybody in Helgren's class passed the exam.

   b. George is in Helgren's class, and he did not pass the exam.

▲ 4. a. Everybody in Helgren's class passed the exam.

   b. No, at least one person in Helgren's class did not pass the exam.

   5. a. Since the stock market crash, investors have not had as much confidence in stocks.

   b. Some investors have regained as much confidence in stocks as they had before the crash.

   6. a. All good paper has at least 40 percent rag content.

   b. No good paper has at least 40 percent rag content.

▲ 7. a. All good paper has at least 40 percent rag content.

   b. Some good paper has no more than 30 percent rag content.

   8. a. All good paper has at least 40 percent rag content.

   b. Some good paper has at least 50 percent rag content.

9. a. The odds against you in roulette are so bad that nobody can win in the long run.
   b. Harry played roulette in Atlantic City and won a huge amount of money.

▲ 10. a. The sentence after this one is true.
   b. The sentence before this one is false.

Exercise A1-3

Although you now have a precise understanding of the terms "conflicting," "contradictory," and "contrary," a lot of other people have vague or even mistaken ideas about these concepts. Read the following, and determine whether the italicized words are being used correctly. Do the claims in each set really conflict? If they do, are they contrary or contradictory?

▲ 1. "In Visalia (Tulare County) yesterday, Oscar-winner Kevin Costner's assertion that he wasn't a high-achieving student in high school was *contradicted* by a former classmate. 'He was above average,' said Leo Costa."

San Francisco Chronicle

2. "Dr. Marcus Conant, a physician at the University of California, San Francisco, pointed out that Marinol, a drug that contains the active ingredient in marijuana, does not always work as well for AIDS and cancer patients as smoking marijuana. 'Even though insurance will pay for Marinol,' Conant said recently, '. . . some patients spend their own money, and risk breaking the law, for the more effective marijuana. That's fairly good evidence that smoking the drug is superior to taking it orally.'

   "But, according to Clinton Administration drug czar Barry McCaffrey, Conant's view is *contradicted* by the conclusion of a National Institutes of Health study, which said, 'There is no scientifically sound evidence that smoked marijuana is medically superior to currently available therapies.'"

Adapted from Newsweek

3. "Some believe that older drivers should have to pass vision and reaction-time tests in order to keep their driving licenses past the age of seventy-five. (Statistics tell us that the average seventy-five-year-old driver is as dangerous per mile as a newly-licensed, lead-footed seventeen-year-old.) But a *contrary* view is offered by the AARP, the powerful senior citizens' lobbying group. They oppose the licensing tests as discriminatory against the elderly."

New Times

4. "Blockbuster Entertainment Corp. said it won't sell information about its customers' video rentals, *contradicting* earlier statements about such a plan by a top company executive. Last week, the *Wall Street Journal* reported descriptions by Blockbuster Vice President Allan Caplan of a project to collect computerized records about individual customers' rentals and sell them to direct mailers. . . . But in an interview Monday, Scott Beck, Blockbuster's vice chairman and chief operating officer, said the giant video chain never had

any plan to sell data about customers' rentals. He said that Mr. Caplan 'misspoke,' and said that he may have been describing an unapproved proposal."

5. "General Norman Schwarzkopf said yesterday that *contrary* to his comments on a TV interview, he agreed '100 percent' with President Bush's decision to halt the Persian Gulf war. . . . In the interview, which aired on U.S. public television Wednesday, Schwarzkopf said allied forces could have wiped out Iraq's retreating army if the ground offensive had not been halted. 'Frankly, my recommendation had been . . . [to] continue the march. I mean, we had them in a rout, and we could have continued to heap great destruction on them. We could have made it a battle of annihilation,' he said. On Thursday, Bush and Secretary of Defense Dick Cheney disputed Schwarzkopf and said all had been in total agreement. And yesterday, it was the general who did the retreating: 'If I could do the whole thing all over again, I know I would change the word "recommend" to say "we initially planned." Because that's what it was. We initially planned to do one thing. But let me, just for the record . . . make it very clear . . . that I was consulted on the decision, I agreed 100 percent with the decision, and I think it was the correct decision,' he said."

▲ 6. [Refer to the previous item for background.] "President Bush took some of the sting out of his *contradiction* of General Norman Schwarzkopf's comments about ending the Persian Gulf War, telling the four-star commander yesterday that the uproar is 'much ado about nothing.' "

Appendix 2

Analytic Claims

A way of classifying claims into two kinds has received considerable attention from a number of eminent philosophers.* The two kinds of claims are **analytic claims** and **synthetic claims.** There are more and less technical ways of distinguishing these two types of claims, and we'll settle for a relatively straightforward way of doing it: An analytic claim is one whose truth value can be determined purely on the basis of the claim's meaning. A synthetic claim, by contrast, is one whose truth value can be determined only on the basis of observations beyond the meaning of the claim. We realize that these definitions are not self-evident and hasten to explain them.

Once you know exactly what an analytic claim means, you already know enough to determine whether it's true or false. For example,

> A vixen is a female fox.

If you know the meanings of all the words in this claim and if you understand exactly what it says, then you know that it is true. Analytic claims are like that: Once you understand them, you know whether they are true or false, because they don't depend on any "outside" circumstance or situation for their truth. Compare such claims with a claim like this:

> At midnight, December 31, 1997, the main entrance to the Smithsonian Institution was locked.

We cannot determine the truth or falsity of a claim like this simply on the basis of knowing what it says. To find out whether it is true or false, we

---

*We make whatever apologies are appropriate here to Leibniz, Hume, and Kant, who wrote the book on this subject. Their book, however, was not an introductory-level critical-thinking book.

would have to know what the situation was at the main entrance to the Smithsonian at the particular moment in question. This business of having to know something *beyond* the meaning of the claim—some fact about the world, if you like—is characteristic of synthetic claims.

The names "analytic" and "synthetic" result from the following: If we analyze the subject of an analytic claim, we find the rest of the claim hiding in there, in a manner of speaking. For example, if we analyze the concept of "vixen," we find that the word simply *means* the same as "female fox." So *of course* the claim "All vixens are female foxes" has to be true. It's "true by definition," if you like. The claim "Either it is Thursday, or it is not" is true no matter what day it is, because of the logical operations signified by the words "or" and "not." (You'll find an account of how such operations work in Chapter 10.)

A synthetic claim is a "synthesis" of concepts—it brings together two or more concepts that are not linked by definition. The main entrance to the Smithsonian, for example, may be locked or unlocked, but whichever it is, it is not so *by definition*. We require some further data beyond the meaning of the claim itself to determine whether the claim is true or false. Were we observing the Smithsonian's entrance at the appointed moment, we might determine the claim's truth value. But the crucial fact is that simply understanding the claim is not enough to determine its truth or falsity. This is the mark of a synthetic claim.

Analytic claims can tell us what words mean and how one concept is connected with another. But such claims can tell us nothing about the (nonlinguistic) world. An analytic claim can tell us that no bachelors have spouses (because part of the meaning of "bachelor" is that it refers to someone with no spouse), but the claim does not tell us anything else about bachelors, including whether there are any. Similarly, what if your local channel's weather forecaster were to come on the evening news and tell you, "Either it will rain on Saturday, or it won't"? That forecast would be true, but notice that *it doesn't tell you anything at all about the weather.* Analytic claims are like that: They never tell you anything about what's going on in the world; they can only tell you how words and concepts relate to one another.

The differences between analytic and synthetic claims hold interest for some philosophers, logicians, and linguists, but why, you might well ask, would the rest of us care about such differences? There are occasions, as it turns out, when the key to understanding a puzzle depends on knowing the difference between analytic and synthetic claims. Here's an example that receives considerable attention from time to time and often goes unexplained (or, worse, *wrongly* explained) because most people do not understand the difference between analytic and synthetic claims:

Every person always acts purely selfishly.

This looks like a pretty remarkable claim—certainly it looks more interesting than "All vixens are female foxes" or "Either it will rain on Saturday, or it won't." At first, the claim looks interesting and informative in the way of a synthetic claim; it seems to say something about human nature. But if you try to argue against the claim, you may find that it's invulnerable to attack. For example, let's say you point to Mother Theresa, who received a Nobel Prize for her work on behalf of India's poor, as an exception to the claim. But the claim's defender then points out that Mother Theresa must have worked for the poor because it made her feel good, which is a selfish motive, or because she would have felt guilty if she had not worked for the poor, which is another kind of selfish motive. Every example is handled this way: Did you contribute some of your paycheck to charity? Well, doing so must have made you feel pleased or happy, because otherwise you wouldn't have done it. Or it prevented you from feeling guilty, which also means you did it for your own benefit and hence you did it out of selfishness.

It's time now to notice that something suspicious has happened. In general, enjoying what you're doing does not automatically make what you're doing an act of selfishness. *That* isn't what the word "selfish" means in everyday English. However, if we expand the meaning of "selfish" to include every action that a person might want to perform for any reason—in other words, if we *redefine* the term—then of course it turns out that every human action is a selfish one by this new definition. Then, the claim we started out with, "Every person always acts purely selfishly," is true simply by virtue of the expanded definition of "selfish." Thus, we have changed it from a synthetic claim to an analytic one. However, by making the claim analytic, we have made it much less interesting than it originally appeared—it is certainly not the profound statement about human nature it originally seemed to be. In fact, it is about as interesting a comment as the claim "Either it will rain Saturday, or it won't." The former tells us exactly as much about human behavior as the latter tells us about the weather—namely, nothing at all.

If you'd like another example, consider this: Let's say that somebody decides to redefine the word "elderly" to make it refer to everybody over the age of twelve, and the person then goes on to claim that "All teenagers are elderly." This claim is now true, given the new definition of "elderly," but it's also boring. It may *sound* interesting or important, but in fact it's neither.

Exercise A2-1 ————————————————————————

Determine whether the following claims express analytic truths. Explain why or why not. (Problems like this can get pretty complicated—some of the later ones in this exercise are sneaky and may require careful discussion. You'll find some tips in the answer section that, we hope, are helpful.)

Example

Squares have four sides.

Answer

This is an analytic truth, because it's true by definition of the word "square."

▲ 1. All thieves are criminals.

2. It is fun to be rich.

3. It is uncomfortable to live in a hot climate without air conditioning.

▲ 4. If you've written a book, then you're an author.

5. Adultery is a sin.

6. Eighteen is a smaller number than twenty.

▲ 7. All citizens of the United States are Americans.

8. If nobody can get into the concert without a ticket, then anybody without a ticket can't get in.

9. Matter occupies space.

▲ 10. Normal people act like the majority of people.

11. You can't see what doesn't exist.

12. You can't hate and love a person at the same time.

▲ 13. Nobody could ever build a machine that would take a person back in time.

14. Everyone is getting older.

15. I exist.

Some Common Patterns of Deductive Arguments

Some types of valid and invalid arguments are encountered so often that it makes sense to remember their patterns. In the three sections of this appendix are some of the most common valid **argument patterns.** Chapters 9 and 10 go into deductive logic in much more detail.

First, here are three valid patterns for you to remember.

1. Modus ponens (affirming the antecedent):

If P then Q.*

P.

Therefore, Q.

Example:

If Jones bought tickets, then she is in the audience.

She bought tickets.

Therefore, she is in the audience.

2. Modus tollens (denying the consequent):

If P then Q.

Not-Q.

Therefore, not-P.

Example:

If Jones bought tickets, then she is here.

She is not here.

Therefore, she didn't buy tickets.

3. Chain argument:

Example:

---

*As you can tell from the example, P and Q stand for any claims you want them to. Note also that the order in which the premises of an argument appear does not affect their validity.

Indirect Proof

One common strategy for establishing the truth of a claim is showing that its contradictory implies something false, absurd, or contradictory. This strategy, called **indirect proof,** is based on the same idea as remarks like this: "If Phillips is a conservative, then I'm the King of England." Obviously, this is just a way of saying that Phillips is not a conservative—because it is clearly not the case that the speaker is the King of England.

If we want to argue that a claim is *true* by using indirect proof, we begin with its contradictory. To argue either for P or for not-P, we begin with the other one and try to show that it implies a false claim.

An example: Say we want to establish the claim that Moore and Parker *cannot* afford to buy a big yacht. We begin with the assumption that they *can* afford to buy a big yacht. This can then be shown to imply that they can afford large payments, expensive berthing fees, regular maintenance fees, insurance, and so forth. Because it's obviously false that Moore and Parker can afford such expenses (as would be clear if you knew us better), that shows the assumption that leads to these consequences is false. Therefore, the contradictory of that assumption—Moore and Parker cannot afford a big yacht—is true.

This pattern of reasoning is sometimes called **reductio ad absurdum** (reducing to an absurdity, or RAA, for short), because it involves showing that a claim implies a false, absurd, or contradictory result. Once again, the strategy is this:

To prove P,

Assume not-P.

Show that a false, absurd, or contradictory result follows from not-P.

Conclude that not-P must be false.

Conclude that P must be true.

If P then Q.	If Jones bought tickets, then she is here.
If Q then R.	If she is here, then we will see her.
Therefore, if P then R.	Therefore, if Jones bought tickets, then we will see her.

And now here are two common invalid patterns:

1. Affirming the consequent: *Example:*

If P then Q.	If Jones bought tickets, then she is here.
Q.	She is here.
Therefore, P.	Therefore, she bought tickets.

2. Denying the antecedent:
If P then Q.

Not-P.
Therefore, not-Q.

Example:
If Jones bought tickets, then she is here.
Jones didn't buy tickets.
Therefore, she is not here.

Exercise A3-1

In order to determine whether an argument fits certain of the patterns described, it's necessary to be able to put claims in the "if . . . then" form. This exercise will provide some practice. (Your instructor may refer you to some items in Chapter 10.) Which of the following claims is equivalent to the numbered claim?

▲ 1. Only if you are an athlete are you a 49er.
   a. If you are an athlete, then you are a 49er.
   b. If you are a 49er, then you are an athlete.

2. Only if you are a Republican are you a conservative.
   a. If you are a Republican, then you are a conservative.
   b. If you are a conservative, then you are a Republican.

3. You cannot speak French without an accent unless you were born in France.
   a. If you were born in France, then you can speak French without an accent.
   b. If you cannot speak French without an accent, then you were not born in France.
   c. If you can speak French without an accent, then you were born in France.

▲ 4. You can eat mushrooms every day—but not if you mind spending a lot of money.
   a. If you do not mind spending a lot of money, then you can eat mushrooms every day.
   b. If you can eat mushrooms every day, then you do not mind spending a lot of money.
   c. If you cannot eat mushrooms every day, then you mind spending a lot of money.
   d. More than one of the above is correct.

5. If I did not make over $100,000, I owe no money on my taxes.
   a. If I made over $100,000, then I owe some money on my taxes.
   b. If I owe no money on my taxes, then I did not make over $100,000.

Exercise A3-2

Now let's see if you can recognize the valid and invalid argument patterns. Mark (a) if valid, (b) if invalid, or (c) if not an argument.

▲ 1. If you attend classes and maintain at least a 2.0 GPA, you will graduate. Samantha, however, did not graduate. This means either she did not attend classes, or she did not maintain at least a 2.0 GPA.

2. If cat fur is a problem in Marco's house, obviously he owns a cat. From this it may be deduced that, since Marco hates cats and doesn't own one, cat fur isn't a problem in his house.

3. Parker slept in if he didn't have a great deal of work to do, or if he was up late the night before. However, he wasn't up late the night before. Furthermore, he didn't have a great deal of work to do. We can conclude, therefore, that Parker did not sleep in.

▲ 4. If the orbit of the meteor cloud brings the cloud within 30 million miles of the earth, telecommunications will be disrupted for the next several days. But apparently scientific estimates were wrong about the orbit of the cloud. It is known now that it won't fall within those parameters. Therefore, tele-communications won't suffer disruption for the next seven days.

5. According to the U.S. tax code, if you made $10,000 or more from income generated by rental property you own and manage, you must itemize depre-ciable business expenses on your tax form. Now, you did not make $10,000 or more from rental property that you own and manage. Therefore, you do not have to itemize your depreciable business expenses.

6. Let this rule be true: "If a card has an even number on one side, then it has an odd number on the other side." Now suppose you are handed a card that has an odd number on it. Again, assume the stated rule is true. It follows that the card has an even number on the other side.

▲ 7. If the day I am thinking of is the day before the day after tomorrow, then I am thinking of tomorrow. Therefore, the day I am thinking of is not tomorrow, since the day I am thinking of is not the day before the day after tomorrow.

8. If Jesus is God, then there is nothing Jesus cannot do. If there is nothing Jesus cannot do, then Jesus can make a rock heavier than he can lift. If Jesus can make a rock heavier than he can lift, then he cannot lift it. If he cannot lift it, then, since he is God, there is something God cannot do. If there is something God cannot do, then God is not all powerful. Therefore, if Jesus is God, then God is not all powerful.

9. The world is horribly flawed. Pain and suffering exist. Selfishness, cruelty, inhumanity, rape, torture, and incest are real. So are cancer, leprosy, cholera, famine, and pestilence. If God were good and all-powerful, then pain and suf-fering would not exist, since if he were good he would hate pain and suffering, and if he were all-powerful he could get rid of them. Yet, pain and suffering do exist. Therefore, either God is not all good or he is not all powerful.

Set 2

Here is another group of commonly encountered valid and invalid argument patterns:*

---

*In this group, X and Y stand for classes of things.

Valid conversion 1:
No Xs are Ys.
Therefore, no Ys are Xs.

Example:
No ticket takers are members.
Therefore, no members are ticket
    takers.

Valid conversion 2:
Some Xs are Ys.
Therefore, some Ys are Xs.

Example:
Some ticket takers are members.
Therefore, some members are
    ticket takers.

Here are some similar patterns that are invalid:

Invalid conversion 1:
All Xs are Ys.
Therefore, all Ys are Xs.

Example:
All ticket takers are members.
Therefore, all members are ticket
    takers.

Invalid conversion 2:
Some Xs are not Ys.

Therefore, some Ys are not Xs.

Example:
Some ticket takers are not
    members.
Therefore, some members are not
    ticket takers.

One other form deserves special emphasis because it is so common:

Unnamed invalid inference:
Some Xs are Ys.
Therefore, some Xs are not Ys.

Example:
Some ticket takers are members.
Therefore, some ticket takers are
    not members.

It is also invalid to run the last argument in reverse:

Some Xs are not Ys.

Therefore, some Xs are Ys.

Some ticket takers are not
    members.
Therefore, some ticket takers are
    members.

Set 3

Here is one more group of commonly encountered valid and invalid argument patterns:*

---

*In this group, X, Y, and Z stand for classes of things.

Valid syllogism 1:
All Xs are Ys.
All Ys are Zs.

Therefore, all Xs are Zs.

Example:
All ticket takers are employees.
All employees are responsible
  individuals.
Therefore, all ticket takers are
  responsible individuals.

Valid syllogism 2:
All Xs are Ys.
No Ys are Zs.
Therefore, no Xs are Zs.

Example:
All ticket takers are employees.
No employees are members.
Therefore, no ticket takers are
  members.

And here are some common invalid syllogisms:

Invalid syllogism 1:
All Xs are Ys.
All Zs are Ys.
Therefore, all Xs are Zs.

Example:
All ticket takers are employees.
All members are employees.
Therefore, all ticket takers are
  members.

Invalid syllogism 2:
All Xs are Ys.
No Zs are Xs.
Therefore, no Ys are Zs.

Example:
All ticket takers are employees.
No members are ticket takers.
Therefore, no employees are
  members.

There are a lot of patterns to remember, but you were probably already familiar with many of them. Usually people don't take valid argument patterns as invalid, except modus tollens (denying the consequent), which, for some reason, people sometimes have difficulty recognizing as valid. The more common mistake is to take invalid patterns as valid. So we especially recommend that you study the invalid patterns in each of the preceding three sets so that you won't make this mistake.

Exercise A3-3

Identify the valid or invalid pattern of each of the following.

Example

Jan's dog must be at least thirteen years old; and if it's that old, Jan should take it to the veterinarian at least twice a year. So, Jan should take her dog to the vet at least twice a year.

Answer

P = Jan's dog is at least thirteen years old.
Q = Jan should take the dog to the vet at least twice a year.

Argument pattern:
P.
If P then Q.
Therefore, Q.
Name of pattern: Modus ponens (affirming the antecedent)—valid

▲ 1. If Baffin Island is larger than Sumatra, then two of the five largest islands in the world are in the Arctic Ocean. And Baffin Island, as it turns out, is about 2 percent larger than Sumatra. Therefore, the Arctic Ocean contains two of the world's five largest islands.

2. If the danger of range fires is greater this year than last, then state and federal officials will hire a greater number of fire fighters to cope with the danger. Since more fire fighters are already being hired this year than were hired all last year, we can be sure that the danger of fires has increased this year.

3. If Jack Davis robbed the Central Pacific Express in 1870, then the authorities imprisoned the right person. But the authorities did not imprison the right person. Therefore, it must not have been Jack Davis who robbed the Central Pacific Express in 1870.

▲ 4. If the recent tax cuts had been self-financing, then there would have been no substantial increase in the federal deficit. But they turned out not to be self-financing. Therefore, there will be a substantial increase in the federal deficit.

5. The public did not react favorably to the majority of policies recommended by President Ronald Reagan during his second term. But if his electoral landslide in 1984 had been a mandate for more conservative policies, the public would have reacted favorably to most of those he recommended after the election. Therefore the 1984 vote was not considered a mandate for more conservative policies.

6. If Paul attends the ceremony, then so will Charles. And if Charles attends, he will take Susan. Therefore, if Paul attends the ceremony, Charles will take Susan.

▲ 7. Alexander will finish his book by tomorrow afternoon only if he is an accomplished speed reader. Fortunately for him, he is quite accomplished at speed reading. Therefore, he will get his book finished by tomorrow afternoon.

8. If higher education were living up to its responsibilities, the five best-selling magazines on American campuses would not be *Cosmopolitan, People, Playboy, Glamour,* and *Vogue.* But those are exactly the magazines that sell best in the nation's college bookstores. Higher education, we can conclude, is failing in at least some of its responsibilities.

9. Broc Glover was considered sure to win if he had no bad luck in the early part of the race. But we've learned that he has had the bad luck to be involved in a crash right after the start, so we're expecting another driver to be the winner.

▲ 10. If the right amount of heat is applied to water at 212°F in a sealed container, then the pressure in the container will increase without any increase in the temperature. This follows from the facts that if the proper amount of heat is applied to water at 212°, then steam at 212° is produced; and if steam at 212° is produced from water at the same temperature, the pressure in the container will increase without any increase in temperature.

11. If Boris is really a spy for the KGB, then he has been lying through his teeth about his business in this country. But we can expose his true occupation if he's been lying like that. So, I'm confident that if we can expose his true occupation, we can show that he's really a KGB spy.

12. The commission will extend the bow-hunting season only if it cuts back the rest of the primitive-arms season. Furthermore, if the commission is fair, then it will simply *have* to extend the bow-hunting season at least a few days. Consequently, the commission can be fair only if it cuts back the rest of the primitive-arms season.

▲ 13. The alternator is not working properly if the ammeter shows a negative reading. The current reading of the ammeter is negative. So, the alternator is not working properly.

14. Fewer than 2 percent of the employees of New York City's Transit Authority are accountable to management. If such a small number of employees are accountable to the management of the organization, no improvement in the system's efficiency can be expected in the near future. So, we cannot expect any such improvements any time soon.

15. If Charles did not pay his taxes, then he did not receive a refund. Thus, he did not pay his taxes, since he did not receive a refund.

16. If they wanted to go to the party, then they would have called by now. But they haven't, so they didn't.

▲ 17. If drugs are legalized, then quality will be monitored by the government. If quality is monitored by the government, then there will be fewer drug-caused deaths. Therefore, if drugs are legalized, then there will be fewer drug-caused deaths.

18. "You'll get an A in the class," she predicted.
"What makes you say that?" he asked.
"Because," she said, "if you get an A, then you're smart, and you *are* smart."

19. If Florin arrived home by eight, she received the call from her attorney. But she did not get home by eight, so she must have missed her attorney's call.

20. The acid rain problem will be solved, but only if the administration stops talking and starts acting. So far, however, all we've had from the president is words. Words are cheap. Action is what counts. The problem will not be remedied, at least not while this administration is in office.

Exercise A3-4

Identify the valid or invalid pattern of each of the following.

Example

> Everybody who is out after the curfew will be arrested. So, since nobody who gets arrested will be able to leave the country next week, nobody who is able to leave the country next week will be out after the curfew.

Answer

> All people out after the curfew are people who will be arrested.
> No people who are arrested are people able to leave the country next week.
> Therefore, no people able to leave the country next week are people out after the curfew.

Pattern

> All Xs are Ys.
> No Ys are Zs.
> Therefore, no Zs are Xs.

This is a version of valid syllogism 2, as you can see if you convert the conclusion via valid conversion 1.

▲ 1. All creationists are religious, and all fundamentalists are religious, so all creationists are fundamentalists.

2. Every sportscaster is an athlete, and no athlete is a college professor. Therefore, no sportscasters are college professors.

3. Anyone who voted for the Democrats favors expansion of medical services for the needy. So, the people who voted for the Democrats all favor higher taxes, since anyone who wants to expand medical services must favor higher taxes.

▲ 4. All cave dwellers lived before the invention of the radio, and no one alive today is a cave dweller. Thus, no person who lived before the invention of the radio is alive today.

5. Conservationists don't vote for Republicans, and all environmentalists are conservationists. Thus, environmentalists don't vote for Republicans. (Hint: Remember, the order of the premises can be reversed.)

6. Nobody who subscribes to *National Geographic* owns an all-terrain vehicle. So, none of the owners of all-terrain vehicles subscribe to *National Geographic*.

7. Some students are not radicals; it follows, therefore, that there are some radicals who are not students.

▲ 8. Since all philosophers are skeptics, it follows that no theologian is a skeptic, since no philosophers are theologians. (Hint: Don't forget to convert, if necessary—and if permissible!)

9. Each philosopher is a skeptic, and no philosopher is a theologian. Therefore, no skeptic is a theologian. (Hint: Remember, you can convert some claims about classes.)

▲ 10. Peddlers are salesmen, and confidence men are, too. So, peddlers are confidence men.

11. Should drug addicts be treated as criminals? Well, addicts are all excluded from the class of decent people, yet all criminals belong to that class. Accordingly, no addicts are criminals.

12. Critical thinkers recognize invalid syllogisms; therefore, critical thinkers are logicians, since logicians can spot invalid syllogisms, too.

▲ 13. Look, some people don't find this course particularly useful, so there must be those who do.

14. All environmentalists are gun-control nuts, so all gun-control nuts are environmentalists.

15. Some nail polishes contain enamels. This is surely the case, since some things that contain enamels are nail polishes.

16. We shouldn't worry so much. Some critics weren't impressed with our first edition, right? It follows that some *were* impressed, no?

▲ 17. The Mohawk Indians are Algonquin, and so are the Cheyenne. So, the Mohawks are really just Cheyenne.

18. Idiots would support the measure, but no one else would. Whatever else you may think of the school board, you can't say they are idiots. [Therefore . . .]

19. Most mechanics aren't particularly dishonest, so at least some are. You just have to know how to spot them.

▲ 20. Cases of "aesthetic surgery," which are all designed to make a patient look better, are classified in a category different from cases of reconstructive surgery. It must be, then, that reconstructive surgery is never designed to make a patient look better.

Glossary

ad hominem A form of pseudoreasoning in which a claim or an argument is rejected because of some fact about the author or source of the claim or argument.

affirmative claim A claim that includes one class or part of one class within another: A- and I-claims.

affirming the antecedent *See* modus ponens.

affirming the consequent An argument consisting of a conditional claim as one premise, a claim that affirms the consequent of the conditional as a second premise, and a claim that affirms the antecedent of the conditional as the conclusion.

ambiguous claim A claim that could be interpreted in more than one way and whose meaning is not made clear by the context.

analogical argument (argument from analogy) An argument in which something that is said to hold true of a sample of a certain class is claimed also to hold true of another member of the class.

analogy A comparison of two or more objects, events, or other phenomena.

analytic claim A claim that is true or false by virtue of the meanings of the words that compose it. *Contrast with* synthetic claim.

analytical definition A definition that specifies (1) the type of thing the defined term applies to and (2) the difference between that thing and other things of the same type.

antecedent *See* conditional claim.

appeal to anecdotal evidence, fallacy of A form of hasty generalization presented in the form of an anecdote or story. Also the fallacy of trying to prove (or disprove) that x is a causal factor for y by citing an example or two of an x that did (or didn't) cause y.

appeal to ignorance The view that an absence of evidence *against* a claim counts as evidence *for* that claim.

appeal to indignation (or anger) A pattern of pseudoreasoning in which someone tries to induce acceptance of a claim by arousing indignation or anger.

appeal to pity A pattern of pseudoreasoning in which someone tries to induce acceptance of a claim by eliciting compassion or pity.

appeal to popularity A pattern of pseudoreasoning: "X is true because everyone (lots of people, most societies, others, I, etc.) thinks that X is true."

appeal to precedent The claim (in law) that a current case is sufficiently similar to a previous case that it should be settled in the same way.

apple polishing A pattern of pseudoreasoning in which flattery is disguised as a reason for accepting a claim.

argument A set of claims, one of which, known as the conclusion, is supposed to be supported by the rest, known as the reasons or premises.

argument from analogy *See* analogical argument.

argument pattern The structure of an argument. This structure is independent of the argument's content. Several arguments can have the same pattern (e.g., modus ponens) yet be about quite different subjects. Variables are used to stand for classes or claims in the display of an argument's pattern.

background information The body of true and justified beliefs that consists of facts we learn from our own direct observations and facts we learn from others.

bandwagon *See* peer pressure.

begging the question *See* question-begging argument.

behavioral explanation An explanation that attempts to clarify the causes of behavior in terms of psychology, political science, sociology, history, economics, and other behavioral and social sciences.

Also included are explanations of behavior in terms of "commonsense psychology"—that is, in terms of someone's reasons or motives.

biased generalization, fallacy of A generalization about an entire class based on a biased sample.

biased sample A sample that is not representative.

burden of proof A form of pseudoreasoning in which the burden of proving a point is placed on the wrong side. One version occurs when a lack of evidence on one side is taken as evidence for the other side, in cases where the burden of proving the point rests on the latter side.

categorical claim Any standard-form categorical claim or any claim that means the same as some standard-form categorical claim. *See* standard-form categorical claim.

categorical imperative Kant's term for an absolute moral rule that is justified because of its logic: If you can wish that your maxim were a universal law, your maxim qualifies as a categorical imperative.

categorical logic A system of logic based on the relations of inclusion and exclusion among classes ("categories"). This branch of logic specifies the logical relationships among claims that can be expressed in the forms "All Xs are Ys," "No Xs are Ys," "Some Xs are Ys," and "Some Xs are not Ys." Developed by Aristotle in the fourth century B.C., categorical logic is also known as Aristotelian or traditional logic.

categorical syllogism A two-premise deductive argument in which every claim is categorical and each of three terms appears in two of the claims—for example, all soldiers are martinets and no martinets are diplomats, so no soldiers are diplomats.

causal claim A statement that says or implies that one thing caused or causes another.

causal factor A causal factor for some specific effect is something that contributes to the effect. More precisely, in a given population, a thing is a causal factor for some specified effect if there would be more occurrences of the effect if every member of the population were exposed to the thing than if none were exposed to the thing. To say that C is a causal factor for E in population P, then, is to say that there would be more cases of E in population P if every member of P were exposed to C than if no member of P were exposed to C.

causal hypothesis A statement put forth to explain the cause or effect of something, when the cause or effect has not been conclusively established.

chain argument An argument consisting of three conditional claims, in which the antecedents of one premise and the conclusion are the same, the consequents of the other premise and the conclusion are the same, and the consequent of the first premise and the antecedent of the second premise are the same.

circumstantial ad hominem Attempting to discredit a person's claim by referring to the person's circumstances.

claim A statement that is either true or false.

claim variable A letter that stands for a claim.

common practice A form of pseudoreasoning in which an action is defended by calling attention to the fact that the action is a common one (not to be confused with appeals for fair play).

common thread in question In only-relevant-common-thread reasoning, multiple occurrences of a feature are said to be united by a single relevant common thread. This common thread is the "common thread in question."

complementary term A term is complementary to another term if and only if it refers to everything that the first term does not refer to.

composition, fallacy of To think that what holds true of a group of things taken individually necessarily holds true of the same things taken collectively.

conclusion In an argument, the claim that is argued for.

conditional claim A claim that state-of-affairs A cannot hold without state-of-affairs B holding as well—e.g., "If A then B." The A-part of the claim is called the *antecedent*; the B-part is called the *consequent*.

conditional proof A deduction for a conditional claim "If P then Q" that proceeds by assuming that P is true and then proving that, on that assumption, Q must also be true.

confidence level *See* statistical significance.

conflicting claims Two claims that cannot both be correct.

conjunction A compound claim made from two simpler claims. A conjunction is true if and only if both of the simpler claims that compose it are true.

consequent *See* conditional claim.

contradictory claims Two claims that are exact opposites—that is, they could not both be true at the same time and could not both be false at the same time.

contrapositive The claim that results from switching the places of the subject and predicate terms in a claim and replacing both terms with complementary terms.

contrary claims Two claims that could not both be true at the same time but could both be false at the same time.

control group *See* controlled cause-to-effect experiment.

controlled cause-to-effect experiment An experiment designed to test whether something is a causal factor for a given effect. Basically, in such an experiment two groups are essentially alike, except that the members of one group, the *experimental group*, are exposed to the suspected causal factor, and the members of the other group, the *control group*, are not. If the effect is then found to occur with significantly more frequency in the experimental group, the suspected causal agent is considered a causal factor for the effect.

converse   The converse of a categorical claim is the claim that results from switching the places of the subject and predicate terms.

critical thinking   The careful and deliberate determination of whether to accept, reject, or suspend judgment about a claim.

deduction (proof)   A numbered sequence of truth-functional symbolizations, each member of which validly follows from earlier members by one of the truth-functional rules.

deductive argument   An argument that is either valid or intended by its author to be so.

definition by example   Defining a term by pointing to, naming, or describing one or more examples of something to which the term applies.

definition by synonym   Defining a term by giving a word or phrase that means the same thing.

denying the antecedent   An argument consisting of a conditional claim as one premise, a claim that denies the antecedent of the conditional as a second premise, and a claim that denies the consequent of the conditional as the conclusion.

denying the consequent   *See* modus tollens.

deontologism   *See* "duty theory."

dependent premises   Premises that depend on one another as support for their conclusion. If the assumption that a premise is false cancels the support another provides for a conclusion, the premises are dependent.

descriptive claim   A claim that states facts or alleged facts. Descriptive claims tell how things are, or how they were, or how they might be. Contrast with prescriptive claims.

difference in question   In only-relevant-difference reasoning, one item is said to have a feature ("the feature in question") that other similar items lack, and there is said to be only one other relevant difference ("the difference in question") between the item that has the feature in question and the other items that don't have the feature in question.

disjunction   A compound claim made up of two simpler claims. A disjunction is false only if both of the simpler claims that make it up are false.

divine command theory   The view that our moral duty (what's right and wrong) is dictated by God.

division, fallacy of   To think that what holds true of a group of things taken collectively necessarily holds true of the same things taken individually.

downplayer   An expression used to play down or diminish the importance of a claim.

duty theory   The view that a person should perform an action because it is his or her moral duty to perform it, not because of any consequences that might follow from it.

dysphemism   A word or phrase used to produce a negative effect on a reader's or listener's attitude about something or to tone down the positive associations the thing may have.

emotive force   The feelings, attitudes, or emotions a word or an expression expresses or elicits.

equivalent claims   Two claims are equivalent if and only if they would be true in all and exactly the same circumstances.

error margin   A range of possibilities; specifically, a range of percentage points within which the conclusion of a statistical inductive generalization falls, usually given as "plus or minus" a certain number of points.

euphemism   An agreeable or inoffensive expression that is substituted for an expression that may offend the hearer or suggest something unpleasant.

experimental group   *See* controlled cause-to-effect experiment.

expert   A person who, through training, education, or experience, has special knowledge or ability in a subject.

explanation   A claim or set of claims intended to make another claim, object, event, or state of affairs intelligible.

explanatory comparison   A comparison that is used to explain.

explanatory definition   A definition used to explain, illustrate, or disclose important aspects of a difficult concept.

extension   The set of things to which a term applies.

fact   A claim that is either true or for which there is excellent evidence or justification. Sometimes "fact" is used for the circumstances asserted by such a claim, as when we say that a claim "states a fact." This means only that the claim is true or that there is excellent evidence or justification for it.

factual matter   An issue that there are generally accepted means of settling, whether or not it has actually been settled.

fallacy   An argument in which the reasons advanced for a claim fail to warrant acceptance of that claim.

false dilemma   This pattern of pseudoreasoning: "X is true because either X is true or Y is true, and Y isn't," said when X and Y could both be false.

feature in question   *See* difference in question.

functional explanation   An explanation of an object or occurrence in terms of its function or purpose.

gambler's fallacy   The belief that recent past events in a series can influence the outcome of the next event in the series. This reasoning is fallacious when the events have a predictable ratio of results, as is the case in flipping a coin, where the predictable ratio of heads to tails is 50–50.

generalization   An argument offered in support of a general claim.

genetic fallacy The belief that a perceived defect or deficiency in the origin of a thing discredits the thing itself.

good argument An argument that provides grounds for accepting its conclusion.

grouping ambiguity A kind of semantical ambiguity in which it is unclear whether a claim refers to a group of things taken individually or collectively.

harm principle The claim that the only way to justify a restriction on a person's freedom is to show that the restriction prevents harm to other people.

hasty generalization, fallacy of A generalization based on a sample too small to be representative.

hedonistic calculus The utilitarian method of calculating the consequences of an intended act in terms of pleasure and pain for everyone involved. Also known as the "happiness calculus" and the "hedonic calculus."

horse laugh A pattern of pseudoreasoning in which ridicule is disguised as a reason for rejecting a claim.

hyperbole Extravagant overstatement.

hypothetical imperative Kant's term for a command that is binding only if one is interested in a certain result; an "if-then" situation.

implied target class In an analogical argument, the class to which the sample items and the target item belong.

independent premises Premises that do not depend on one another as support for the conclusion. If the assumption that a premise is false does not cancel the support another premise provides for a conclusion, the premises are independent.

indirect proof Proof of a claim by demonstrating that its negation is false, absurd, or self-contradictory.

inductive analogical argument See analogical argument.

inductive argument An invalid argument whose premises are intended to provide some support, but less than conclusive support, for the conclusion.

inductive generalization See generalization.

innuendo An insinuation of something deprecatory.

intension The set of characteristics a thing must have for a term correctly to apply to it.

invalid argument An argument whose conclusion does not necessarily follow from the premises.

issue A point that is or might be disputed, debated, or wondered about. Issues are often introduced by the word "whether," as in the example "whether this train goes to Chattanooga."

law of large numbers A rule stating that the larger the number of chance-determined, repetitious events considered, the closer the alternatives will approach predictable ratios. Example: The more times you flip a coin, the closer the results will approach 50 percent heads and 50 percent tails.

legal moralism The theory that, if an activity is immoral, it should also be illegal.

legal paternalism The theory that a restriction on a person's freedom can sometimes be justified by showing that it is for that person's own benefit.

line-drawing fallacy The fallacy of insisting that a line must be drawn at some precise point when in fact it is not necessary that such a line be drawn.

loaded question A question that rests on one or more unwarranted or unjustified assumptions.

logic The branch of philosophy concerned with whether the reasons presented for a claim, if those reasons were true, would justify accepting the claim.

matter of fact See factual matter.

matter of pure opinion An issue that there are no generally accepted means of settling.

mean A type of average. The arithmetic mean of a group of numbers is the number that results when their sum is divided by the number of members in the group.

median A type of average. In a group of numbers, as many numbers of the group are larger than the median as are smaller.

mode A type of average. In a group of numbers, the mode is the number occurring most frequently.

modus ponens An argument consisting of a conditional claim as one premise, a claim that affirms the antecedent of the conditional as a second premise, and a claim that affirms the consequent of the conditional as the conclusion.

modus tollens An argument consisting of a conditional claim as one premise, a claim that denies the consequent of the conditional as a second premise, and a claim that denies the antecedent of the conditional as the conclusion.

moral relativism The view that what is morally right and wrong depends on and is determined by one's group or culture.

naturalistic fallacy The assumption that one can conclude directly from a fact (what "is") what a rule or a policy should be (an "ought") without a value-premise.

negation The contradictory of a particular claim.

negative claim A claim that excludes one class or part of one class from another: E- and O-claims.

nonexperimental cause-to-effect study A study designed to test whether something is a causal factor for a given effect. Such studies are similar to controlled cause-to-effect experiments, except that the members of the experimental group are not exposed to the suspected causal agent by the investigators; instead, exposure has resulted from the actions or circumstances of the individuals themselves.

nonexperimental effect-to-cause study A study designed to test whether something is a causal factor for a given effect. Such studies are similar to nonexperimental cause-to-effect studies, except that the members of the experimental group display *the effect*, as compared with a control group whose members do not display the effect. Finding that the suspected cause is significantly more frequent in the experimental group is reason for saying that the suspected causal agent is a causal factor in the population involved.

non sequitur The fallacy of irrelevant conclusion; an inference that does not follow from the premises.

obverse The obverse of a categorical claim is that claim that is directly across from it in the square of opposition, with the predicate term changed to its complementary term.

objective claim A claim about a factual matter. Objective claims are true or false regardless of our personal experiences, tastes, biases, and so on.

offense principle The claim that an action or activity can justifiably be made illegal if it is sufficiently offensive.

opinion A claim that somebody believes to be true.

peer pressure A pattern of pseudoreasoning in which you are in effect threatened with rejection by your friends, relatives, etc., if you don't accept a certain claim.

perfectionist fallacy Concluding that a policy or proposal is bad simply because it does not accomplish its goal to perfection.

personal attack A pattern of pseudoreasoning in which we refuse to accept another's argument because there is something about the person we don't like or of which we disapprove. A form of ad hominem.

persuasive comparison A comparison used to express or influence attitudes or affect behavior.

persuasive definition A definition used to convey or evoke an attitude about the defined term and its denotation.

persuasive explanation An explanation intended to influence attitudes or affect behavior.

physical explanation An explanation that tells us how or why something happens in terms of the physical background of the event.

poisoning the well Attempting to discredit in advance what a person might claim by relating unfavorable information about the person.

***post hoc, ergo propter hoc,* fallacy of** Reasoning that X caused Y simply because Y occurred after X.

precising definition A definition that limits the applicability of a term whose usual meaning is too vague for the use in question.

predicate term The noun or noun phrase that refers to the second class mentioned in a standard-form categorical claim.

predictable ratio The ratio that results of a series of events can be expected to have given the antecedent conditions of the series. Examples: The predictable ratio of a fair coin flip is 50 percent heads and 50 percent tails; the predictable ratio of sevens coming up when a pair of dice is rolled is 1 in 6, or just under 17 percent.

premise The claim or claims in an argument that provide the reasons for believing the conclusion.

prescriptive claim A claim that states how things ought to be. Prescriptive claims impute values to actions, things, or situations. Contrast with descriptive claims.

principle of utility The basic principle of utilitarianism, to create as much overall happiness and/or to limit unhappiness for as many as possible.

proof surrogate An expression used to suggest that there is evidence or authority for a claim without actually saying that there is.

property in question In inductive generalizations and analogical arguments, the members of a sample are said to have a property. This property is the "property in question."

pseudoreason A consideration offered in support of a position that is not relevant to the truth or falsity of the issue in question.

pseudorefutation This pattern of pseudoreasoning: "I reject your claim because you act as if you think it is false," or "You can't make the claim now because you have in the past rejected it." A form of ad hominem.

question-begging argument An argument whose conclusion restates a point made in the premises or clearly assumed by the premises. Although such an argument is technically valid, anyone who doubts the conclusion of a question-begging argument would have to doubt the premises, too.

random sample A sample drawn from a target population in such a way that each member of the target population has an equal chance of being selected.

red herring *See* smokescreen.

reductio ad absurdum An attempt to show that a claim is false by demonstrating that it has false or absurd logical consequences; literally, "reducing to an absurdity."

refutation via hasty generalization When we ask someone to reject a general claim on the basis of an example or two that run counter to the claim, we commit a fallacy known as "refutation via hasty generalization."

relevant/relevance A consideration is relevant to an issue if it is not unreasonable to suppose that its truth has some bearing on the truth or falsity of the issue. *See also* relevant difference

relevant difference A relevant difference is one that is not unreasonable to suppose caused the feature in question.

representative sample A sample that possesses all relevant features of a target population and possesses them in proportions that are similar to those of the target population.

rhetoric In our usage, "rhetoric" is language used primarily to persuade or influence beliefs or attitudes rather than to prove logically.

rhetorical devices Rhetorical devices are used to influence beliefs or attitudes through the associations, connotations, and implications of words, sentences, or more extended passages. Rhetorical devices include slanters and pseudoreasoning. While rhetorical devices may be used to enhance the persuasive force of arguments, they do not add to the logical force of arguments.

rhetorical force *See* emotive force.

sample That part of a class referred to in the premises of a generalizing argument.

sample size One of the variables that can affect the size of the error margin or the confidence level of certain inductive arguments.

scare tactics A pattern of pseudoreasoning in which someone says, in effect, "X is so because Y [where Y is a fact that, it is hoped, induces fear in the listener]."

self-contradictory claim A claim that is analytically false.

semantically ambiguous claim An ambiguous claim whose ambiguity is due to the ambiguity of a word or phrase in the claim.

slanter A linguistic device used to affect opinions, attitudes, or behavior without argumentation. Slanters rely heavily on the suggestive power of words and phrases to convey and evoke favorable and unfavorable images.

slippery slope A form of pseudoreasoning in which it is assumed that some event must inevitably follow from some other, but in which no argument is made for the inevitability.

smokescreen An irrelevant topic or consideration introduced into a discussion to divert attention from the original issue.

social utility A focus on what is good for society (usually in terms of overall happiness) when deciding on a course of action. *See also* principle of utility.

sound argument A valid argument whose premises are true.

spin A type of rhetorical device, often in the form of a red herring or complicated euphemism to disguise a politician's statement or action that might otherwise be perceived in an unfavorable light.

square of opposition A table of the logical relationships between two categorical claims that have the same subject and predicate terms.

standard-form categorical claim Any claim that results from putting words or phrases that name classes in the blanks of one of the following structures: "All _____ are _____"; "No _____ are _____"; "Some _____ are _____"; and "Some _____ are not _____."

stare decisis "Letting the decision stand." Going by precedent.

statistical significance To say that some finding is statistically significant at a given *confidence level*—

say, .05—is essentially to say that the finding could have arisen by chance in only about five cases out of one hundred.

stereotype An oversimplified generalization about the members of a class.

stipulative definition A definition used to introduce an unfamiliar term (that's what this definition does) or to assign a new meaning to a familiar term.

straw man A type of pseudoreasoning in which someone ignores an opponent's actual position and presents in its place a distorted, exaggerated, or misrepresented version of that position.

strong argument An argument that has this characteristic: On the assumption that the premises are true, the conclusion is unlikely to be false.

subcontrary claims Two claims that can both be true at the same time but cannot both be false at the same time.

subject term The noun or noun phrase that refers to the first class mentioned in a standard-form categorical claim.

subjective claim A claim about a matter of pure opinion for which no commonly accepted method exists for establishing truth or falsity.

subjectivism The view that what is morally right and wrong is just a matter of subjective opinion.

subjectivist fallacy This pattern of pseudoreasoning: "Well, X may be true for you, but it isn't true for me," said with the intent of dismissing or rejecting X.

syllogism A deductive argument with two premises.

syntactically ambiguous claim An ambiguous claim whose ambiguity is due to the structure of the claim.

synthetic claim A claim whose truth value cannot be determined simply by understanding the claim—an observation of some sort is also required. *Contrast with* analytic claim.

target In the conclusion of an inductive generalization, the members of an entire class of things is said to have a property or feature. This class is the "target" or "target class." In the conclusion of an analogical argument one or more individual things is said to have a property or feature. The thing or things is the "target" or "target item."

target class The population, or class, referred to in the conclusion of a generalizing argument.

target item *See* target.

term A word or an expression that refers to or denotes something.

truth-functional equivalence Two claims are truth-functionally equivalent if and only if they have exactly the same truth table.

truth-functional logic A system of logic that specifies the logical relationships among truth-functional claims—claims whose truth values depend solely upon the truth values of their simplest component parts. In particular, truth-functional logic deals with the logical functions of the terms "not," "and," "or," "if . . . then," and so on.

truth table A table that lists all possible combinations of truth values for the claim variables in a symbolized claim or argument and then specifies the truth value of the claim or claims for each of those possible combinations.

two wrongs make a right This pattern of pseudo-reasoning: "It's acceptable for A to do X to B because B would do X to A," said where A's doing X to B is not necessary to prevent B's doing X to A.

utilitarianism The moral position unified around the basic idea that we should promote happiness as much as possible and weigh actions or derivative principles in terms of their utility in achieving this goal.

vague claim A claim that lacks sufficient precision to convey the information appropriate to its use.

valid argument An argument that has this characteristic: On the assumption that the premises are true, it is impossible for the conclusion to be false.

Venn diagram A graphic means of representing a categorical claim or categorical syllogism by assigning classes to overlapping circles. Invented by English mathematician John Venn (1834–1923).

virtue ethics The moral position unified around the basic idea that each of us should try to perfect a virtuous character that we exhibit in all actions.

weaseler An expression used to protect a claim from criticism by weakening it.

wishful thinking This pattern of pseudoreasoning: believing that something is true because you want it to be true (or believing that it is false because you don't want it to be true).

Answers, Suggestions, and Tips for Triangle Exercises

Chapter 1: What Is Critical Thinking?

Exercise 1-1

1. A claim is a statement that is either true or false.

4. Critical thinking is the careful, deliberate determination of whether we should accept, reject, or suspend judgment about a claim—and of the degree of confidence with which we accept or reject it.

7. An argument is a set of claims, one of which is supposed to be supported by the others. The claim supposed to be supported is the conclusion; the claims providing the support are premises. In short: *Premises* are supposed to give reasons for believing *conclusions*.

10. If asked a question about an embarrassing issue or one to which he or she has no answer, a person may shift to another issue, one that furnishes no embarrassment or that he or she knows more about.

13. No.

16. . . . it addresses a matter of pure opinion. There are no generally accepted means for settling disputes about such matters.

19. False. Many issues are important to how we live our lives—for example, issues like whether God exists, whether this or that action is immoral—but it is controversial whether these issues are factual in the same way as the issue of whether Moore and Parker exist or whether lead is heavier than gold.

22. This is false. There are objective claims which, as a matter of current practical fact, it is not possible for us to confirm or refute. For example, "There are 590 quadrillion gallons of water in the Mediterranean Sea, give or take a couple of gallons." We know exactly what it would take to determine the truth or falsity of this claim—a measurement of the water in the Mediterranean—but we do not have the means to carry out such a measurement.

25. We would be justified in saying we know the paper is flammable if we believe it to be flammable and have evidence that makes it beyond any reasonable doubt that it is flammable—for example, if we are currently observing the paper burn.

Exercise 1-2

1. a. The other three claims in the paragraph are offered as *reasons* for the claim that Hank ought not to take the math course.

3. d. The other two claims are given as reasons for believing claim d; they are premises of an argument and claim d is the conclusion.

4. c. The remainder of the passage provides examples of what is claimed in c. The claims in which these examples appear function as premises for c.

13. b. There is a lot of information in this passage, but answer (b) is certainly the *main* issue of the se-

A-1

lection. The easiest way to see this is to notice that almost all of the claims made in the passage support this one. We'd put answer (c) in second place.

14. c. Answers (a) and (b) don't capture the futility of the prison policy expressed in the passage; answer (d) goes beyond what is expressed in the passage.

15. c. Answer (b) is in the running, but it is clear from the passage that the author isn't interested so much in whether the permit holders are individuals or corporations as in whether they are big-time operators or small-time operators.

Exercise 1-6

1. Factual matter

2. Matter of opinion. Whether most people—or even everybody—*think* that diet soda tastes bland is a matter of fact. We have ways of finding an answer to this question: We ask people. But if two people disagree about whether diet soda tastes bland, there isn't any straightforward way to settle the matter.

4. Factual matter

7. Factual matter

10. Matter of opinion, when understood in the most obvious way—that is, that the lake is unpleasantly cold. But, if we interpret this to mean, for example, that swimmers could not *survive* in such water, then it would be a factual matter.

13. This can be either a factual matter or a matter of opinion, depending on what one means by "smarter." There are standards sometimes used to measure how smart a person is—I.Q. tests and such—and it is a factual matter whether one or the other would have scored higher. But "smarter" could refer to vague notions (such as cunning) that are difficult or impossible to quantify. On such an interpretation, we'd say the item is a matter of opinion. We'll learn more about how vague terms operate in the next chapter.

Exercise 1-7

1. b

3. a

6. c

Exercise 1-8

1. c. Both items are arguments.

4. d. Both items offer advice as to how to achieve a given objective.

7. c. Both items seek to say something unpleasant without giving offense.

10. d. Both items cite some fact as a reason for doing something.

Exercise 1-9

1. No argument

4. Argument

7. Argument

10. No argument

13. No argument (Warren says that there are reasons for her conclusion, but she doesn't tell us what they are.)

16. No argument

19. No argument

Exercise 1-10

1. Whether police brutality happens very often

4. Whether there exists a world that is essentially independent of our minds

7. Whether a person who buys a computer should take some instruction lessons

10. Whether Native Americans, as true conservationists, have something to teach readers about our relationship to the earth. There are other points made in the passage, but they are subsidiary to this one.

Exercise 1-11

1. There are two issues: whether they're going on Standard Time the next weekend and whether they'll need to set the clocks forward or back. Both speakers address both issues.

4. The issue is whether complaints about American intervention abroad are good or bad. Both speakers address this issue.

Exercise 1-12

1. Suburbanite misses Urbanite's point. Urbanite addresses the effects of the requirement; Suburbanite addresses the issue of whether he and his neighbors can afford to comply with it.

3. On the surface, it may seem that both Hands address the issue of whether a person such as One Hand can feel safe in her own home. But it's clear that One Hand's real issue is whether the large number of handguns on the streets makes one unsafe in one's own home. Other Hand ignores this issue completely.

5. The issue for both parties is whether Fed-Up will be happier if he retires to Arkansas.

Exercise 1-13

1. Neutral statement of fact

4. Neutral statement of fact

7. Subjective opinion ("vigorous" and "sharp")

10. Neutral statement of fact (although the quoted phrase is a subjective opinion of Bennett's)

13. Subjective opinion ("seamlessly" and "appropriate")

Chapter 2: Critical Thinking and Clear Writing

Exercise 2-2

7, 6, 4, 1, 3, 2, 5

Exercise 2-3

1. "Piano" is defined analytically.

4. "Red planet" is defined by synonym. (This one is tricky because it looks like a definition by example. But there is only *one* red planet, so the phrase refers to exactly the same object as the word "Mars.")

8. "Chiaroscuro" is defined by synonym.

11. "Significant other" is defined by example—several of them.

Exercise 2-4

1. The Raider tackle blocked the Giants linebacker.

4. How Therapy Can Help Victims of Torture

7. Intentional ambiguity. (One's fingers are *digits*, remember. Even critical thinkers sometimes make bad jokes!)

10. 6 Coyotes That Maul Girl Are Killed by Police

13. Second sentence: More than one disease can be carried and passed along to humans by a single tick.

16. We give to life good things.

19. Dunkelbrau—for those who crave the best-tasting real German beer

22. Jordan could write additional profound essays.

25. When she lay down to nap, she was disturbed by a noisy cow.

28. When Queen Elizabeth appeared before her troops, they all shouted "harrah."

32. AT&T, for as long as your business lasts.

33. This class might have had a member of the opposite sex for a teacher.

34. Married 10 times before, woman gets 9 years in prison for killing her husband.

Exercise 2-5

1. As a group

4. As a group

7. It's more likely that the claim refers to the Giants as a group, but it's possible that it refers to the play of individuals.

10. As individuals

12. Probably as individuals

15. Ambiguous. If the claim means that people are living longer than they used to, the reference is to people as individuals. If the claim means that the human race is getting older, then the reference is to people as a group. If the claim expresses the truism that to live is to age, then the reference is to people as individuals.

Exercise 2-6

In order of decreasing vagueness:
1. (d), (e), (b), (c), (f), and (a). Compare (e) and (b). If Eli and Sarah made plans for the future, then they certainly discussed it. But just discussing it is more vague—they could do that with or without making plans.

4. (c), (d), (e), (a), (b)

Exercise 2-7

1. a

4. b

7. a. But it's close

10. b

15. a

Exercise 2-8

1. Too vague. Sure, you can't say exactly how much longer you want it cooked, but you can provide guidelines; for example, "Cook it until it isn't pink."

4. Not too vague.

7. Not too vague.

10. If this is the first time you are making frosting or if you are an inexperienced cook, this phrase is too vague.

Exercise 2-10

"Feeding" simply means "fertilizing" and is not too vague. "Frequently" is too vague. "No more than half" is not too vague. "Label-recommended amounts" is not too vague. "New year's growth begins" and "each bloom period ends" are pretty vague for a novice gardener, but because pinpoint timing apparently isn't crucial, the vagueness here is acceptable. "Similar" is too vague for a novice gardener. "Immediately after bloom" suggests that precise timing is important here, and we find the phrase too vague, at least for novices. "When the nights begin cooling off" is too vague even if precision in timing isn't terribly important.

Exercise 2-11

1. Twenty percent more than what? (You might wonder what "real dairy butter" is, but it's probably safe to assume that it's just plain old butter.)

4. This is not too bad, but the word "desert" covers a lot of territory—not all deserts are like the Sahara.

7. The comparison is okay, but don't jump to the conclusion that today's seniors are better students. Maybe the teachers are easier graders.

10. In the absence of absolute figures, this claim does not provide any information about how good attendance was (or about how brilliant the season was).

Exercise 2-12

1. Superior? In what way? More realistic character portrayal? Better expression of emotion? Probably

the claim means only "I like Paltrow more than I like Blanchett."

4. Fine, but don't infer that they both grade the same. Maybe Smith gives 10 percent A's and 10 percent F's, 20 percent B's and 20 percent D's, and 40 percent C's, whereas Jones gives everyone a C. Who do you think is the more discriminating grader, given this breakdown?

7. Well, first of all, what is "long-distance"? Second, and more important, how is endurance measured? People do debate such issues, but the best way to begin a debate on this point would be by spelling out what you mean by "requires more endurance."

10. This is like a comparison of apples and oranges. How can the popularity of a movie be compared with the popularity of a song?

Exercise 2-13

1. The price-earnings ratio is a traditional (and reasonable) measure of a stock, and the figure is precise enough. Whether this is good enough reason to worry about the stock market is another matter; such a conclusion may not be supported by the price-earnings figure.

4. "Attend church regularly" is a bit vague; a person who goes to church each and every Christmas and Easter is a regular, although infrequent, attender. We don't find "majority" to vague in this usage.

7. "Contained more insights" is much too vague. The student needs to know more specifically what was the matter with his or her paper, or at least what was better about the roommate's paper.

10. These two sorts of things are much too different to be compared in this way. If you're starving, the chicken looks better; if you need to get from here to there, it's the Volkswagen. (This is the kind of question Moore likes to ask people. Nobody can figure out why.)

Exercise 2-15

1. Students should choose majors with considerable care.

4. If a nurse can find nothing wrong with you in a preliminary examination, a physician will be recommended to you. However, in this city physicians wish to protect themselves by having you sign a waiver.

7. Soldiers should be prepared to sacrifice their lives for their comrades.

10. Petitioners over sixty should have completed form E-7. ["He(she)" is awkward and retains sexist implications.]

13. Language is nature's greatest gift to humanity.

16. The proof must be acceptable to the rational individual.

17. The country's founders believed in the equality of all.

20. Athletes who want to play for the National Football League should have a good work ethic.

24. Most U.S. senators are men.

27. Mr. Macleod doesn't know it, but Ms. Macleod is a feminist.

30. To be a good politician, you have to be a good salesperson.

Exercise 2-16

In case you couldn't figure it out, the friend is a woman.

Chapter 3: Evaluating Informative Claims

Exercise 3-8

1. In terms of expertise, we'd list (d), (c), and (b) first. Given what we've got to go on, we wouldn't assign expert status to either (a) or (e). We'd list all entries as likely to be fairly unbiased except for (a), which we would expect to be very biased.

3. Expertise: (b) first, then (a), then (c) and (d) about equal, and (e) last. We'd figure that (b) is most likely to be unbiased, with (c), (d), and (e) close behind; Choker would be a distant last on this scale. Her bad showing on the bias scale more than makes up for her high showing on the expertise scale.

Exercise 3-9

1. The most credible choices are either the FDA or *Consumer Reports,* both of which investigate health claims of the sort in question with reasonable objectivity. The company that makes the product is the least credible source because it is the most likely to be biased. The owner of the health food store would not qualify in the area of drugs, even if she is very knowledgeable regarding nutrition. Your local pharmacist can reasonably be regarded as credible, but he or she may not have access to as much information as the FDA or *CR.*

2. It would probably be a mistake to consider any of the individuals on this list more expert than the others, although different kinds and different levels of bias are fairly predictable on the parts of the victim's father, the NRA representative, and possibly the police chief. The senator might be expected to have access to more data that are relevant to the issue, but that would not in itself make his or her credibility much greater than that of the others. The problem here is that we are dealing with a value judgment that depends very heavily upon an individual's point of view rather than his or her expertise. What is important to this question is less the credibility of the person who gives us an answer than the strength of the supporting argument, if any, that he or she provides.

3. Although problem 2 hinges on a value judgment, this one calls for an interpretation of the original intent of a constitutional amendment. Here our choices would be either the Supreme Court justice or the constitutional historian, with a slight preference for the latter because Supreme Court justices are concerned more with constitutional issues as they have been interpreted by other courts than with original intent. The NRA representative is paid to speak for a certain point of view and would be the least credible in our view. The senator and the U.S. President would fall somewhere in between: Both might reasonably be expected to be knowledgeable about constitutional issues, but much less so than our first two choices.

Exercise 3-10

1. Professor Hilgert would possess the greatest degree of credibility and authority on (d), (f), and (h), and, compared with someone who had not lived in both places, on (i).

Exercise 3-15

1. We'd accept this as probably true—but probably only *approximately* true. It's difficult to be precise about such matters; Campbell will most likely lay off *about* 650 workers, including *about* 175 at its headquarters.

8. We'd accept this as likely.

12. No doubt cats that live indoors do tend to live longer than cats that are subject to the perils of

outdoor life. If statistics on how much longer indoor cats live on the average were available, we'd expect the manufacturer to know them. But we suspect that such statistics would be difficult to establish (and probably not worth the effort), and

we therefore have little confidence in the statistic cited here.

20. We'd reject this.

Chapter 4: Persuasion Through Rhetoric

Exercise 4-1

1. d
4. d
7. a
10. c
13. T
16. d
19. c
22. T

Exercise 4-2

(1) hyperbole (in Chapter 6 we'll call this "straw man"), (2) dysphemism, (3) not a rhetorical device, (4) dysphemism, (5) not a rhetorical device, (6) dysphemism

Exercise 4-3

(1) dysphemism, (2) dysphemism, (3) hyperbole, (4) weaseler, (5) proof surrogate, (6) not a downplayer in this context, (7) loaded question

Exercise 4-6

1. "It may well be" and "some sort" are both weaselers. "Nevertheless" is a downplayer (of the preceding remark). And "it is clearly true" is a proof surrogate.

4. The word "adjusted" is a euphemism.

Exercise 4-7

1. The quotation marks downplay the quality of the school.

4. Persuasive definition

6. No rhetorical device present

8. "Gaming" is a euphemism for "gambling."

Exercise 4-8

1. "Japan, Inc." is a dysphemism.

4. "Getting access" is a euphemism, and, in this context, so is "constituents." We'll bet it isn't just *any* old constituent who gets the same kind of "access" as big campaign contributors.

7. The last sentence is hyperbolic.

10. (We really like this one.) "Even," in the first sentence, is innuendo, insinuating that members of Congress are more difficult to embarrass than others. The remainder is another case of innuendo with a dash of downplaying. Although it's a first-class example, it's different from the usual ones. Mellinkoff makes you think that Congress *merely* passes a law in response to the situation. But stop and think for a moment: Aside from the odd impeachment trial or congressional hearing, *all that Congress can do is pass laws!* So Mellinkoff's charge really should not be seen as belittling Congress at all.

13. "As you know" is a variety of proof surrogate. The remainder is a persuasive comparison.

16. This looks like a persuasive something-or-other (identification), but it is probably most easily seen as hyperbole. The writer may have had some ridicule in mind as well.

19. Lots of them here! To begin, "orgy" is a dysphemism; "self-appointed" is a downplayer. The references to yurts and teepees is ridicule, and "grant-maintained" is a downplayer. The rest of it employs a heavy dose of sarcasm.

Exercise 4-12

The main difference is that the author who weasels may want to bring attention to a claim but hold open a way out if the claim is challenged; the author who downplays wants to call attention away from a claim in the first place. The latter may even *hope* for a successful challenge to the downplayed claim.

Exercise 4-13

This one is easy: Persuasive definitions define or appear to define, persuasive explanations explain or appear to explain, and persuasive comparisons compare two things. All are phrased in emotive language, and all may make use of hyperbole.

Chapter 5: More Rhetorical Devices

Exercise 5-2

1. Appeal to popularity
4. Appeal to pity
7. Subjectivist fallacy
10. Appeal to indignation. There is also an example of straw man in the last sentence—we'll meet straw man in Chapter 6.

Exercise 5-3

1. No
3. Yes. A popular automobile may have continued support from its maker, and this can be advantageous to the owner of such a car.
7. No. Notice, though, that our likes and dislikes seem to be influenced by the opinions of others, whether we want them to be or not.
10. It can be. Advertising a product as best-selling may create a feeling on the part of consumers that they will be out of step with the rest of society if they don't purchase the advertised product. (But within limits almost any product can be *said* to be popular or a best-seller, so the fact that such a claim is made is no reason for one to feel out of step by not purchasing the product.) Usually, however, the "best-seller" tag is intended to make us think that the product must be good because so many people cannot be wrong. In other words, such ads in effect are appeals to the "authority of the masses" or the "wisdom of society." However, unless you have some reason to believe (a) that the claims made in the ad about *unusual* popularity are *true*, and either (b) that the buyers of the product have themselves bought the product for some reason that applies in your case as well or (c) that you could indirectly benefit from the popularity of the item (popular cars, for instance, hold their resale value), then to buy a product on the basis of such advertising would be pseudoreasoning.

Exercise 5-5

1. Scare tactics

4. Apple polishing, with a touch of peer pressure
7. No pseudoreasoning
10. Smokescreen/red herring

Exercise 5-6

1. *Issue:* Whether one should vote no on 11
   Feeling or sentiment: Fear of sanitation problems and chemical sprays
   Relevant? Yes. These problems are relevant to the issue. The problem is therefore one of evaluating the likelihood that Proposition 11 will lead to these problems.

4. *Issue:* Whether George ought to accompany his friends to the river
   Feeling or sentiment: Embarrassment about studying instead of horsing around
   Relevant? No
   Name: Peer pressure

7. *Issue:* Whether the speaker's suggestion is worthwhile
   Feeling or sentiment: Vanity
   Relevant? No
   Name: Apple polishing

10. *Issue:* Whether college students should be allowed to vote locally
    Feeling or sentiment: Anger
    Relevant? No
    Name: Appeal to indignation

Exercise 5-7

1. *Issue:* Whether Mary Smith is the best candidate
   Feeling or sentiment: Fear of getting a poor schedule
   Relevant? No
   Name: Scare tactics

4. *Issue:* Whether one should purchase this company's mortgage insurance
   Feeling or sentiment: Fear of one's family losing its home on one's death
   Relevant? No, although it is relevant to the issue of whether to purchase *some* mortgage insurance

7. *Issue:* Whether covenants excluding blacks are a denial of equal protection of the law
Feeling or sentiment: A sense of fair play
Relevant? No. The fact that state courts were willing to allow blacks to discriminate against whites in buying property does not justify allowing whites to discriminate against blacks. (This case reminds us of Anatole France's famous remark about the law against sleeping under the bridge; it was said to be fair because it applied to rich and poor alike.)
Name: Two wrongs make a right

10. We can't do this one quite so neatly as the others because we don't know what issue is before the two speakers (they differed on almost everything). But it is ridicule that is being employed—however cleverly—and it is not relevant to any substantive issue. Remember, the cleverest speaker, the one with all the good lines, is not necessarily the one with the best arguments.

14. *Issue:* Whether to defraud the automobile insurance company
Feeling or sentiment: Greed, although the pseudo-reasoning is not tied directly to the sentiment in this case
Relevant? No
Name: Common practice

17. *Issue:* Whether the EPA has any business investigating showers
We find ridicule in the first paragraph, a red herring in the second, and a loaded question in the third.

Chapter 6: More Pseudoreasoning and Other Rhetorical Ploys

Exercise 6-2

1. Pseudorefutation

4. Genetic fallacy

7. Circumstantial ad hominem

10. This is probably best seen as a circumstantial ad hominem, although the charge of being in Washington or associated with an "ivory tower think tank" does not automatically predispose a person to a certain position on the issue at hand. It would also not be out of the question to think of Wilson's characterizations (as long-time Washingtonians, ivory tower types, and such) as personal attacks.

Exercise 6-3

1. d

4. b

7. a

10. b

Exercise 6-4

1. c

4. c

7. b

10. c

Exercise 6-5

1. b

4. b

7. e

10. a

Exercise 6-6

1. Straw man, smokescreen/red herring

4. No pseudoreasoning. Notice that the passage is designed to attack the company, not the company's product. The wages it pays are relevant to the point at issue.

7. No pseudoreasoning

10. False dilemma

13. Genetic fallacy

16. Line-drawing fallacy (false dilemma)

19. Ad hominem ("tu quoque")

Exercise 6-7

1. Circumstantial ad hominem

4. Straw man (Jeanne responds as if Carlos wanted to sleep until noon). Can also be analyzed as false dilemma ("Either we get up right now, at 4:00 A.M., or we sleep until noon.")

7. This begs the question. The conclusion merely restates the premise.

10. False dilemma

13. Burden of proof

Exercise 6-8

1. This is an example of burden of proof. Yes, it is indeed slightly different from the varieties explained in the text, and here's what's going on. The speaker is requiring proof of a sort that *cannot be obtained*—actually *seeing* smoke cause a cancer. So he or she is guilty of one type of "inappropriate burden of proof."

4. This is false dilemma because Sugarman's alternatives are certainly not the only ones. Notice that he is giving *no argument* against the Chicago study; he is simply using the false dilemma to deny the study's conclusion.

7. Pseudorefutation

10. This is a case of illegitimate burden of proof. The speaker maintains that the government is violating the law. The burden of proof therefore falls on the speaker to justify his or her opinion. Instead of doing that, he or she acts as if the fact that officials haven't disproved the claim is proof that the claim is true.

Exercise 6-10

1. Assuming that the sheriff's department has more than two officers, the speaker is misrepresenting her opponent's position. Straw man.

4. Inappropriate burden of proof

7. Perfectionist fallacy

10. This is an ad hominem. It rides the border between personal attack and the circumstantial variety.

Exercise 6-11

1. Ad hominem: pseudorefutation. You hear this kind of thing a lot.

4. Ad hominem: personal attack

7. Slippery slope

10. Ad hominem: personal attack

Exercise 6-13

1. Begging the question

4. Straw man

7. Straw man

10. Line-drawing fallacy (false dilemma)

Exercise 6-16

1. Perfectionist fallacy (false dilemma)

5. Apple polishing

9. Appeal to pity and appeal to indignation

13. Two wrongs; a case can easily be made for common practice as well.

16. Straw man, technically, but this is also ridicule.

Exercise 6-17

1. This is an example of burden of proof. The fact that the airplane builders *might* be cutting corners is not evidence that they are *in fact* cutting corners. The speaker's contention that the manufacturers may be tempted to cut corners may be good grounds for scrutinizing their operations, but it's not good grounds for the conclusion that they really are cutting corners.

4. Yes—this is clearly pseudoreasoning. Bush's remark is irrelevant to the Democrats' claim. This case does not fit one of our regular categories. It's a smokescreen.

5. The quoted remark from Harris is not relevant to the conclusion drawn in this passage. This passage doesn't fit neatly into any of our categories, although ad hominem would not be a bad choice. Notice a possible ambiguity that may come into play: "Having an impact" might mean simply that Harris wants his work to be noticed by "movers and shakers"—or it could mean that he wishes to sway people toward a certain political view. It's likely that he intended his remark the first way, but it's being taken in the second way in this passage.

9. This is a borderline circumstantial ad hominem. It certainly does not follow that Seltzer and Sterling are making false claims from the fact that they are being paid by an interested party. But remember the cautions from Chapter 3: Expertise can be bought, and we should be very cautious about accepting claims made by experts who are paid by someone who has a vested interest in the outcome of a controversy.

Chapter 7: Explanations

Exercise 7-1

1. Explanation
4. Explanation
7. Explanation
10. Explanation

Exercise 7-4

1. a. This passage functions both as an explanation and an argument. The speaker wants the listener to agree that a person will choose 7, and the explanation about subtracting 5 from 12 provides a reason for thinking that the person might do so.

4. a

7. b

Exercise 7-5

1. This is just an explanation of how the garage got this cluttered.

4. This is an argument that Parker is giving a test today.

8. Host gives an explanation of why he can't shave. The explanation is intended to serve as a justification.

10. The speaker is explaining why this is a great movie, and in doing so is arguing that it is a great movie.

12. This is an explanation of why the contamination is getting worse and worse.

15. This is an explanation of why you are unable to sleep.

18. The speaker explains how touching the pins can fry the logic circuits and in doing so argues that if you touch the pins, you can expect this to be the result.

21. The author is explaining why women are worse off than men economically and in doing so is arguing that women are worse off. Don't be discouraged by the subtlety of real-life specimens.

25. The writer is explaining what the purpose of the Humane Society is and by doing so is arguing that the Humane Society is not an animal rights organization.

26. This is an explanation used as a justification.

Exercise 7-6

1. b

4. b

7. a. The last part of the passage is designed to explain why the Republicans called for the release, but it also functions as a reason for rejecting the claim that they are seeking to embarrass the president as much as they can.

10. a

Exercise 7-7

1. This is a behavioral explanation: It gives Francis's reasons for using an artificial sweetener. Remember that it is not inaccurate to think of a reasons/motives explanation as a functional explanation of an instance of behavior.

4. Behavioral explanation

7. Physical explanation

10. Behavioral explanation of the reasons/motives variety

14. Physical explanation

16. A physical explanation is given for how the youngster contracted polio. Also, there is an implicit behavioral explanation of why the Supreme Court let the family sue the government.

Exercise 7-8

1. Yes

5. We generally hold that physical theories and laws admit of fewer exceptions and are better confirmed than psychological theories and generalities.

9. Pick another item, Y, with which the listener is familiar and which has as much in common with X as possible. Then list the important differences between X and Y for the listener.

10. The point of such a comparison is to produce as good a general conception of the unfamiliar item as possible. Sometimes this is accomplished more easily if the comparison is general rather than precise and elaborately detailed. The detailed comparison may be more accurate but less effective in conveying the general idea.

14. Less likely. Natural regularities have fewer exceptions than do behavioral generalities.

Exercise 7-9

Let's begin with a precise statement of what needs to be explained: the *apparent* disappearance of milk when it is offered to the statues. The two explanations offered are (1) it's a miracle and (2) the milk is pulled from containers by the surface of the statues, which affects the surface tension of the fluid; it then spreads into a thin film, coating the entire surface of the statue.

Explanation (1) is not much of an explanation. Notice that it fails on several of our criteria for the evaluation of explanations, including unnecessary assumptions and conflict with well-established theory; depending on what meaning is given to the word "miracle," it can also be seen as circular. In fact, saying that the phenomenon is a miracle is hardly to explain it at all. How is this claim different from saying that we don't have any idea of what's happening?

Notice Mr. Soti's remark that "the gods have come down to earth to solve our problems." Unexplained phenomena are often given interpretations that are completely unsupported by any evidence whatsoever. Even if the event *were* entirely unexplainable—if it were an abridgement of physical laws—it would still lend no credibility to any particular interpretation. What one person makes of it ("This guarantees the world will end in the year 2000!") would be as legitimate as what someone else makes of it ("This guarantees the world will last another thousand years!").

Explanation (2) is almost certainly correct. The test of its reliability was given when colored milk was used, and the idol wound up coated in the colored milk, indicating that this "natural" explanation was correct.

The extent to which people believe in supernatural, inexplicable, miraculous explanations is often the effect of how much they *want* to believe in them, not of what the evidence actually indicates.

Exercise 7-11

1. This explanation is full of problems. It is untestable; its relevance is questionable (we couldn't have predicted blue eyes from a previous incarnation unless we knew more about the incarnation, but the explanation is too vague to enable us to do that); it contains unnecessary assumptions; and it conflicts with well-established theory about how we get our eye color.

4. Reasonable explanation

7. Poor explanation; circular

10. Poor explanation; untestable (given the fact that subconscious desires are allowed); excessively vague; questionable relevance; conflicts with well-established theory

13. Reasonable explanation

17. Before we accepted this explanation of violence we'd want to consider alternatives: poverty, hopelessness, and discrimination, to name a few. Rap music and TV/movie violence may be reflections of violence rather than causes.

19. This is a psychological explanation of why academic writing is sometimes unintelligible. It is, of course, intended to be humorous, so we wouldn't hold it to the same standards of rigor as we would serious explanations. As a serious explanation it would be a poor one, principally because it ignores the obvious alternative explanation that much academic writing deals with technical problems and issues that require special training to understand.

21. This poor explanation is untestable, unreliable, and extremely vague. The nondevout might add that it requires unnecessary assumptions.

Exercise 7-13

1. On the information supplied alone, explanation B could be taken as slightly more likely because it would explain both the extinctions and the wobbly orbits of the other two planets.

2. It would very nearly eliminate explanation A. A feasible explanation must account for the regular timing of the extinctions.

3. It would detract from explanation B (see answer 1).

4. Both would be considerably less likely.

5. Both would be somewhat less likely, although explanation A might not be as greatly affected as explanation B: Nemesis might have a somewhat unstable orbit itself, accounting for some variations in the cycle of extinctions.

Exercise 7-14

1. At least three: poltergeists, RSPK, and trickery on Tina's part. The RSPK explanation has two versions: purposeful (Tina is controlling the "force") and nonpurposeful (Tina generates but does not consciously control the "force").

2. The writer seems to give the RSPK explanation and the natural explanation about equal weight. Notice that if all supernatural explanations are discounted, this becomes a much less interesting story. The writer knows, of course, that stories about people who do not exhibit strange or supernatural powers are a dime a dozen, even if they describe teenagers under stress.

4. Hint: Does one require more unusual assumptions than the other?

Chapter 8: Understanding and Evaluating Arguments

Exercise 8-1

1. a. Premise
   b. Premise
   c. Conclusion

2. a. Premise
   b. Premise
   c. Conclusion

3. a. Conclusion
   b. Premise

4. a. Premise
   b. Premise
   c. Conclusion

5. a. Premise
   b. Conclusion
   c. Premise
   d. Premise

Exercise 8-2

1. Premise: All Communists are Marxists.
   Conclusion: All Marxists are Communists.

4. Premise: That cat is used to dogs.
   Conclusion: Probably she won't be upset if you bring home a new dog for a pet.

7. Premise: Presbyterians are not fundamentalists.
   Premise: All born-again Christians are fundamentalists.
   Conclusion: No born-again Christians are Presbyterians.

10. Premise: If we've got juice at the distributor, the coil isn't defective.
    Premise: If the coil isn't defective, then the problem is in the ignition switch.
    [Unstated premise: We've got juice at the distributor.]
    Conclusion: The problem is in the ignition switch.

Exercise 8-3

1. Conclusion: There is a difference in the octane ratings between the two grades of gasoline.

4. Conclusion: Scrub jays can be expected to be aggressive when they're breeding.

7. Conclusion: Dogs are smarter than cats.

10. Unstated conclusion: She is not still interested in me.

Exercise 8-4

1. Dependent

3. Independent

6. Independent

9. Independent

12. Independent

15. Dependent

Exercise 8-5

1. Dependent

4. Dependent; one premise is unstated: What's true for rats is probably true for humans.

8. Independent

10. Independent

Exercise 8-6

3. Valid; true

6. False

9. False

Exercise 8-7

(Refer to Exercise 8-2)

1. Invalid

4. Invalid

7. Valid

10. Valid

(Refer to Exercise 8-3)

1. Invalid

4. Invalid

7. The unstated premise "Being more easily trained is a *sure* sign of greater intelligence" would make the argument valid. An unstated premise such as "Being more easily trained is a *good* sign of greater intelligence" would make the argument fairly strong but invalid.

10. Valid

Exercise 8-8

1. Probably true; had "out of order" been written in pencil on the meter, we'd have a different opinion, since most of the meters in our town have those words scrawled on them.

5. Probably true; a restaurant that does a good job on these three different kinds of entrees will probably do a good job on the rest.

9. Probably true; it's possible that the killer cleaned up very thoroughly, but it's more likely that the body was brought from somewhere else.

12. True beyond a reasonable doubt; it may be that consumption will drop in the future or that discovery of new reserves will increase, but as long as consumption at some level continues, *eventually* all the oil will be used up.

Exercise 8-9

1. Assumed premise: All well-mannered people had a good upbringing.

4. Assumed conclusion: He will not drive recklessly.

7. Assumed premise: All dogs that scratch a lot have fleas or dry skin.

10. Assumed premise: Every poet whose work appears in many Sierra Club publications is one of America's outstanding poets.

Exercise 8-10

1. Assumed premise: Most people who are well-mannered had a good upbringing.

4. Assumed conclusion: He will drive safely.

7. Assumed premise: Most dogs that scratch a lot have fleas or dry skin. (Or: When this dog scratches a lot, he usually has either fleas or dry skin.)

10. Assumed premise: Most poets whose work appears in many Sierra Club publications are among America's outstanding poets.

Exercise 8-11

1. Assumed premise: All stores that sell only genuine leather goods have high prices.

4. Assumed premise: No ornamental fruit trees bear edible fruit.

7. Assumed premise: Nobody convicted of cocaine use could be a very effective mayor.

10. Assumed premise: If population studies show that smoking causes lung cancer, then all smokers will get lung cancer.

Exercise 8-12

1. Assumed premise: Most stores that sell only genuine leather goods have high prices.

4. Assumed premise: Few ornamental fruit trees bear edible fruit.

7. Assumed premise: Few people convicted of cocaine use could be very effective mayors.

10. Assumed premise: If population studies show that smoking causes lung cancer, then most smokers will get lung cancer.

Exercise 8-13

1. ② + ③
   ↓
   ①

4.
   ①
   ↙ ↘
   ②   ③
   ↘ ↙
   ④
   ↓
   ⑤
   ↓
   ⑥

Exercise 8-14

(See Exercise 8-2)

1. ① All Communists are Marxists.
   ② All Marxists are Communists.

4. ① That cat is used to dogs.
   ② She won't be upset if you bring home a new dog for a pet.

7. ①Presbyterians are not fundamentalists.
②All born-again Christians are fundamentalists.
③No born-again Christians are Presbyterians.

10. ①If we've got juice at the distributor, the coil isn't defective.
②If the coil isn't defective, then the problem is in the ignition switch.
③The problem is in the ignition switch.

(See Exercise 8-3)

1. ①The engine pings every time we use the regular unleaded gasoline.
②The engine doesn't ping when we use super.
③There is a difference in octane ratings between the two.

4. ①When blue jays are breeding they become very aggressive.
②Scrub jays are very similar to blue jays.
③Scrub jays can be expected to be aggressive when breeding.

7. ①It's easier to train dogs than cats.
②Dogs are smarter than cats.

10. ①If she were still interested in me, she would have called.
②She didn't call.
③[Unstated] She's not still interested in me.

(See Exercise 8-4)

6. ①You're overwatering your lawn.
②There are mushrooms growing around the base of the tree.
③Mushrooms are a sure sign of overwatering.
④There are worms on the ground.
⑤Worms come up when the earth is oversaturated.

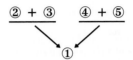

9. ①If you drive too fast, you're more likely to get a ticket.
②(If you drive too fast,) you're also more likely to get into an accident.
③You shouldn't drive too fast.

12. ①You should consider installing a solarium.
②Installing a solarium can get you a tax credit.
③Installing a solarium can reduce your heating bill.
④Installing a solarium correctly can help you cool your house in the summer.

15. ①We must paint the house now.
②If we don't, we'll have to paint it next summer.
③If we have to paint it next summer, we'll have to cancel our trip.
④It's too late to cancel our trip.

(See Exercise 8-5)

1. ①All mammals are warm-blooded creatures.
②All whales are mammals.
③All whales are warm-blooded creatures.

4. ① Rats that have been raised . . . have brains that weigh more. . . .
② The brains of humans will weigh more if humans are placed in intellectually stimulating environments.

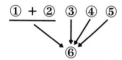

8. ① The mayor now supports the initiative for the Glen Royale subdivision.
② Last year the mayor proclaimed strong opposition to further development in the river basin.
③ Glen Royale will add to congestion.
④ Glen Royale will add to pollution.
⑤ Glen Royale will make the lines longer at the grocery.
⑥ [Unstated] The mayor should not support the Glen Royale subdivision.

10. ① Jesse Brown is a good person for your opening in Accounting.
② He's as sharp as they come.
③ He has a solid background in bookkeeping.
④ He's good with computers.
⑤ He's reliable.
⑥ He'll project the right image.
⑦ He's a terrific golfer.
⑧ I know him personally.

Exercise 8-15

1. ① Your distributor is the problem.
② There's no current at the spark plugs.
③ If there's no current at the plugs, then either your alternator is shot or your distributor is defective.
④ [Unstated] Either your alternator is shot or your distributor is defective.
⑤ If the problem were in the alternator, then your dash warning light would be on.

⑥ The light isn't on.

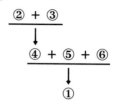

4. ① They really ought to build a new airport.
② It [a new airport] would attract more business to the area.
③ The old airport is overcrowded and dangerous.

Note: Claim number ③ could be divided into two separate claims, one about overcrowding and one about danger. This would be important if the overcrowding were clearly offered as a reason for the danger.

Exercise 8-16

1. ① Cottage cheese will help you to be slender.
② Cottage cheese will help you to be youthful.
③ Cottage cheese will help you to be more beautiful.
④ Enjoy cottage cheese often.

4. ① The idea of a free press in America is a joke.
② The nation's advertisers control the media.
③ Advertisers, through fear of boycott, can dictate programming.
④ Politicians and editors shiver at the thought of a boycott.
⑤ The situation is intolerable.
⑥ I suggest we all listen to NPR and public television.

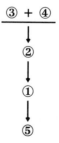

Note: The writer may see claim ① as the final conclusion and claim ⑤ as his comment upon it. Claim ⑥ is probably a comment on the results of the argument, although it too could be listed as a further conclusion.

7. ①Consumers ought to be concerned about the FTC's dropping the rule requiring markets to stock advertised items.
②Shoppers don't like being lured to stores and not finding advertised products.
③The rule costs at least $200 million and produces no more than $125 million in benefits.
④The figures boil down to a few cents per shopper over time.
⑤The rule requires advertised sale items to be on hand in reasonable numbers.

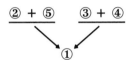

10. ①Well-located, sound real estate is the safest investment in the world.
②Real estate is not going to disappear as can dollars in savings accounts.
③Real estate values are not lost because of inflation.
④Property values tend to increase at a pace at least equal to the rate of inflation.
⑤Most homes have appreciated at a rate greater than the inflation rate. . . .

13. ①About 100 million Americans are producing data on the Internet. . . .
②Each user is tracked so private information is available in electronic form.
③One Web site . . . promises, for seven dollars, to scan . . . etc.
④The combination of capitalism and technology pose a threat to our privacy.

16. ①Measure A is consistent with the City's General Plan and city policies. . . .
②A "yes" vote will affirm the wisdom of well-planned, orderly growth. . . .
③Measure A substantially reduces the amount of housing previously approved for Rancho Arroyo.
④Measure A increases the number of parks and amount of open space.
⑤Measure A significantly enlarges and enhances Bidwell Park.
⑥Approval of Measure A will require dedication of 130.8 acres to Bidwell Park.
⑦Approval of Measure A will require the developer to dedicate seven park sites.
⑧Approval of Measure A will create 53 acres of landscaped corridors and greenways.
⑨Approval of Measure A will preserve existing arroyos and protect sensitive plant habitats. . . .
⑩ Approval of Measure A will create junior high school and church sites.
⑪ Approval of Measure A will plan villages with 2,927 dwellings.
⑫ Approval of Measure A will provide onsite job opportunities and retail services.
⑬ [Unstated conclusion:] You should vote for Measure A.

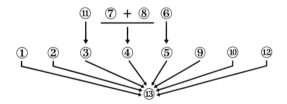

19. ①In regard to your editorial, "Crime bill wastes billions," let me set you straight. [Your position is mistaken.]
②Your paper opposes mandatory life sentences for criminals convicted of three violent crimes, and you whine about how criminals' rights might be violated.
③Yet you also want to infringe on a citizen's rights to keep and bear arms.
④You say you oppose life sentences for three-time losers because judges couldn't show any

leniency toward the criminals no matter how trivial the crime.

⑤What is your definition of trivial, busting an innocent child's skull with a hammer?

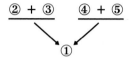

20. ①Freedom means choice.

②This is a truth antiporn activists always forget when they argue for censorship.

③In their fervor to impose their morality, groups like Enough Is Enough cite extreme examples of pornography, such as child porn, suggesting that they are available in video stores.

④This is not the way it is.

⑤Most of this material portrays, not actions such as this, but consensual sex between adults.

⑥The logic used by Enough Is Enough is that if something can somehow hurt someone, it must be banned.

⑦They don't apply this logic to more harmful substances, such as alcohol or tobacco.

⑧Women and children are more adversely affected by drunken driving and secondhand smoke than by pornography.

⑨Few Americans would want to ban alcohol or tobacco even though they kill hundreds of thousands of people each year.

⑩[Unstated conclusion] Enough Is Enough is inconsistent.

⑪[Unstated conclusion] Enough Is Enough's antiporn position is incorrect.

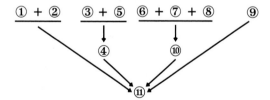

Box: Beer Makes You Smarter

1 = A herd of buffalo can only move as fast as the slowest buffalo.

2 = When the herd is hunted, it is the slowest and weakest ones at the back that are killed first.

3 = This natural selection is good for the herd as a whole.

4 = The general speed and health of the whole group keeps improving by the regular attrition of the weakest members.

5 = The human brain can only operate as fast as the slowest brain cells.

6 = Excessive intake of alcohol kills brain cells.

7 = Alcohol attacks the slowest and weakest brain cells first.

8 = Regular consumption of beer eliminates the weaker brain cells.

9 = The brain is made a faster and more efficient machine.

10 = You always are smarter after a few beers.

Note: 1–4 are offered as an analogy, not as an argument that 10 is true.

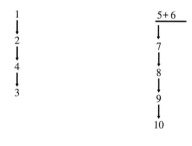

Chapter 9: Deductive Arguments I: Categorical Logic

Exercise 9-1

1. All salamanders are lizards.

4. All members of the suborder Ophidia are snakes.

7. All alligators are reptiles.

10. All places there are snakes are places there are frogs.

13. All people who got raises are vice presidents.

16. All people identical with Socrates are Greeks.

19. All examples of salt are things that preserve meat.

Exercise 9-2

1. No students who wrote poor exams are students who were admitted to the program.

4. Some first basemen are right-handed people.

7. All passers are people who made at least 50 percent.

10. Some prior days are days like this day.

13. Some holidays are holidays that fall on Saturday.

16. All people who pass the course are people who pass this test. Or: No people who fail this test are people who pass the course.

19. All times they will let you enroll are times when you've paid the fee.

Exercise 9-3

1. Translation: Some anniversaries are not happy occasions. (True)
Corresponding A-claim: All anniversaries are happy occasions. (False)
Corresponding E-claim: No anniversaries are happy occasions.
(Undetermined)
Corresponding I-claim: Some anniversaries are happy occasions.
(Undetermined)

4. Translation: Some allergies are things that can kill you. (True)
Corresponding A-claim: All allergies are things that can kill you. (Undetermined)
Corresponding E-claim: No allergies are things that can kill you. (False)
Corresponding O-claim: Some allergies are not things that can kill you. (Undetermined)

Exercise 9-4

1. No non-Christians are non-Sunnis. (Not equivalent)

4. Some Christians are not Kurds. (Not equivalent)

7. All Muslims are Shiites. (Not equivalent)

10. All Muslims are non-Christians. (Equivalent)

Exercise 9-5

1. Some students who scored well on the exam are not students who didn't write poor essays. (Equivalent)

4. No students who were not admitted to the program are students who scored well on the exam. (Not equivalent)

7. All people whose automobile ownership is not restricted are people who don't live in the dorms. (Equivalent)

10. All first basemen are people who aren't right-handed. (Equivalent)

Exercise 9-6

2. All encyclopedias are nondefinitive works.

4. No sailboats are sloops.

Exercise 9-7

Translations of lettered claims:

a. Some people who have been tested are not people who can give blood.

b. Some people who can give blood are not people who have been tested.

c. All people who can give blood are people who have been tested.

d. Some people who have been tested are not people who can give blood.

e. No people who have been tested are people who can give blood.

2. Equivalent to (c).

4. Equivalent to (c).

Exercise 9-8

1. Obvert (a) to get "Some Slavs are not Europeans."

4. Obvert the conversion of (b) to get "Some members of the club are not people who took the exam."

7. Contrapose (a) to get "All people who will not be allowed to perform are people who did not arrive late." Convert (b) to get "Some people who will not be allowed to perform are people who did not arrive late."

10. Convert the obverse of (b) to get "No decks that will play digital tape are devices that are equipped for radical oversampling."

Exercise 9-9

1. Invalid (this would require the conversion of an A-claim).

4. Valid (this requires the conversion of an I-claim, which is valid).

7. Valid (the premise is the obverse of the conclusion).

10. Invalid (this conclusion does not follow, although it's subcontrary, "Some people not allowed to play are people in uniform," does follow).

Exercise 9-10 _____

1. The converse of (a) is the contradictory of (b), so (b) is false.

3. The contrapositive of (a) is a true O-claim that corresponds to (b); and that means that (b), its contradictory, is false.

5. Contrapose (a) to get "Some unproductive factories are not plants not for automobiles." Then obvert (b) to get "No unproductive factories are plants not for automobiles." Because (a) is true, (b) is undetermined.

9. The translation of (a) is "Some people enrolled in the class are not people who will get a grade." The obverse of the converse of (b) is "Some people enrolled in the class are not people who will get a grade." Wow! They're identical! So (b), too, is true.

Exercise 9-11 _____

1. Valid:
   All P are G
   No G are S
   ‾No S are P‾

4. Invalid:
   All T are E.   (T = times Louis is tired, etc.)
   All T-T are E. (T-T = times identical with today)
   ‾All T-T are T.‾

7. Valid:
   All H are S.
   No P are S.
   ‾No P are H.‾

10. Invalid:
    All C are R.
    All V are C.
    ‾No R are V.‾

   (Note: There is more than one way to turn this into standard form. Instead of turning nonresidents into residents, you can do the opposite.)

Exercise 9-12 _____

1. No blank disks are disks that contain data.
   Some blank disks are formatted disks.
   ‾Some formatted disks are not disks that contain data.‾
   Valid:

4. All tobacco products are substances damaging to people's health.
   Some tobacco products are addictive substances.
   ‾Some addictive substances are substances damaging to people's health.‾

   Valid:

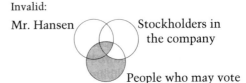

7. All people who may vote are stockholders in the company.
   ·Mr. Hansen is not a person who may vote.
   ‾Mr. Hansen is not a stockholder in the company.‾

   Invalid:

   Mr. Hansen   Stockholders in
                   the company

                  People who may vote

Note: Remember that claims with individuals as subject terms are treated as A- or E-claims.

10. After converting, then obverting the conclusion:
    No arguments with false premises are sound arguments.
    Some arguments with false premises are valid arguments.
    ‾Some valid arguments are not sound arguments.‾

Valid:

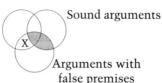

Valid
arguments

Valid
arguments

X

Sound arguments

Arguments with
false premises

Exercise 9-13

1. A

4. B

Exercise 9-14

1. a

4. b

Exercise 9-15

1. 0

4. 1

Exercise 9-16

1. c

4. c

7. b

10. e

Exercise 9-17

1. All T are F
    Some F are Z
    Some Z are T

    Invalid; breaks rule 2

4. There are two versions of this item, depending
    on whether you take the first premise to say *no*
    weightlifters use motor skills or only some don't.
    We'll do it both ways:

    All A are M
    No W are M
    No W are A

    Valid

    All A are M
    Some W are not M
    No W are A

    Invalid; breaks rule 3

7. Using I = people who lift papers from the Internet
    C = people who are cheating themselves
    L = people who lose in the long run

    All I are C
    All C are L
    All I are C

    Valid

10. D = people who dance the whole night
    W = people who waste time
    G = people whose grades will suffer

    All D are W
    All W are G
    All D are G

    Valid

Exercise 9-18

(Refer to Exercise 9-11 for these first four items.)

2. (Given in standard form in the text)
    Invalid: breaks rule 2

5. All voters are citizens.
    Some citizens are not residents.
    Some voters are not residents.
    Invalid: breaks rule 2

7. All halyards are lines that attach to sails.
    No painters are lines that attach to sails.
    No painters are halyards.
    Valid

8. All systems that can give unlimited storage . . . are
    systems with removable disks.
    No standard hard disks are systems with removable
    disks.
    No standard hard disks are systems that can give
    unlimited storage. . . .
    Valid

(Refer to Exercise 9-12 for the next four items.)

2. After obverting both premises, we get:
    No ears with white tassels are ripe ears.
    Some ripe ears are not ears with full-sized kernels.
    Some ears with full-sized kernels are not ears with
    white tassels.
    Invalid: breaks rule 1

5. After obverting the second premise:
    Some compact disc players are machines with 24x
    sampling.
    All machines with 24x sampling are machines that
    cost at least $100.
    Some compact disc players are machines that cost
    at least $100.
    Valid

7. All people who may vote are people with stock.

No [people identical with Mr. Hansen] are people who may vote.
No [people identical with Mr. Hansen] are people with stock.
Invalid: breaks rule 3 (major term)

8. No off-road vehicles are vehicles allowed in the unimproved portion of the park.
Some off-road vehicles are not four-wheel-drive vehicles.
Some four-wheel-drive vehicles are allowed in the unimproved portion of the park.
Invalid: breaks rule 1

Exercise 9-20

1. A = athletes; B = baseball players; C = basketball players
Some A are not B.
Some B are not C.
Some A are not C.
Invalid: breaks rule 1

3. T = worlds identical to this one; B = the best of all possible worlds; M = mosquito-containing worlds
No B are M.
All T are M.
No T are B.
Valid

6. P = plastic furniture; C = cheap furniture; L = their new lawn furniture
All L are P.
All P are C.
All L are C.
Valid

9. D = people on the district tax roll; C = citizens; E = eligible voters
All D are C.
All E are C.
All D are E.
Invalid: breaks rule 2

12. C = people identical to Cobweb; L = liberals; T = officials who like to raise taxes
All C are L.
All L are T.
All C are T.
Valid

17. P = poll results; U = unnewsworthy items; I = items receiving considerable attention from the networks
All P are I.
Some P are U.
Some I are U.
Valid

18. E = people who understand that the Earth goes around the Sun; W = people who understand what causes winter and summer; A = American adults

All W are E.
Some A are not E.
Some A are not W.
Valid

20. N = the pornographic novels of "Madame Toulouse"; W = works with sexual depictions patently offensive to community standards and with no serious literary, artistic, political, or scientific value; O = works that can be banned as obscene since 1973
All O are W.
All N are W.
All N are O.
Invalid: breaks rule 2

Exercise 9-21

1. True. A syllogism with neither an A- nor an E-premise would have (I) two I-premises, which would violate rule 2; or (II) two O-premises, which would violate rule 1; or (III) an I-premise and an O-premise. Alternative (III) would require a negative conclusion by rule 1, and a negative conclusion would require premises that distribute at least two terms, the middle term and (by rule 3) at least one other. Because an I-premise and an O-premise collectively distribute only one term, alternative (III) won't work either.

4. True. An AIE syllogism whose middle term is the subject of the A-premise breaks exactly two rules. If the middle term is the predicate of the A-premise, this syllogism breaks three rules.

Exercise 9-24

1. L = ladybugs; A = aphid-eaters; G = good things to have in your garden

All L are A
[All A are G]
All L are G

Valid

4. S = self-tapping screws; B = boons to the construction industry; P = things that allow screws to be inserted without pilot holes

All S are P
[All P are B]
All S are B

Valid

Chapter 10: Deductive Arguments II: Truth-Functional Logic

Exercise 10-1

1. $Q \to P$
2. $Q \to P$
3. $P \to Q$
4. $Q \to P$
5. $(P \to Q) \& (Q \to P)$

Exercise 10-2

1. $(P \to Q) \& R$
2. $P \to (Q \& R)$

Notice that the only difference between (1) and (2) is the location of the comma. But the symbolizations have two different truth tables, so moving the comma actually changes the meaning of the claim. And we'll bet you thought that commas were there only to tell you when to breathe when you read aloud.

5. $P \to (Q \to R)$. Compare (5) with (3).

11. $\sim C \to S$

12. $\sim(C \to S)$

16. $S \to \sim C$. Ordinarily, the word *but* indicates a conjunction, but in this case it is present only for emphasis—*only if* is the crucial truth-functional phrase.

20. $\sim(F \vee S)$ or $(\sim F \& \sim S)$. Notice that when you "move the negation sign in," you have to change the wedge to an ampersand (or vice versa). Don't treat the negation sign as you would treat a minus sign in algebra class, or you'll wind up in trouble.

Exercise 10-3

1.

P	Q	R	$(P \to Q)$	$(P \to Q) \& R$
T	T	T	T	T
T	T	F	T	F
T	F	T	F	F
T	F	F	F	F
F	T	T	T	T
F	T	F	T	F
F	F	T	T	T
F	F	F	T	F

5.

P	Q	R	$Q \to R$	$P \to (Q \to R)$
T	T	T	T	T
T	T	F	F	F
T	F	T	T	T
T	F	F	T	T
F	T	T	T	T
F	T	F	F	T
F	F	T	T	T
F	F	F	T	T

12.

C	S	$C \to S$	$\sim(C \to S)$
T	T	T	F
T	F	F	T
F	T	T	F
F	F	T	F

Exercise 10-4

1. Invalid:

		(Premise)	(Premise)	(Conclusion)
P	Q	$\sim Q$	$P \vee \sim Q$	$\sim P$
T	T	F	T	F
T	F	T	T	F
F	T	F	F	T
F	F	T	T	T

(Row 2)

4. Invalid:

			(Conclusion)		(Premise)		(Premise)
P	Q	R	$(P \to Q)$	$\sim(P \to Q)$	$(Q \to R)$	$P \to (Q \to R)$
T	T	T	T	F	T	T
T	T	F	T	F	F	F
T	F	T	F	T	T	T
T	F	F	F	T	T	T
F	T	T	T	F	T	T
F	T	F	T	F	F	T
F	F	T	T	F	T	T
F	F	F	T	F	T	T

(Row 4)

7. Invalid:

			(Premise)	(Premise)	(Conclusion)	
P	Q	R	~Q	P & R	(P & R) → Q	~P
T	T	T	F	T	T	F
T	T	F	F	F	T	F
T	F	T	T	T	F	F
T	F	F	T	F	T	F
F	T	T	F	F	T	T
F	T	F	F	F	T	T
F	F	T	T	F	T	T
F	F	F	T	F	T	T

(Row 4)

Exercise 10-5

We've used the short truth-table method to demonstrate invalidity.

1. Valid. There is no row in the argument's table that makes the premises all T and the conclusion F.

2. Invalid. There are two rows that make the premises T and the conclusion F. (Such rows are sometimes called "counterexamples" to the argument.) Here they are:

L	W	S	P
T	F	F	F
T	T	F	F

(Remember: You need to come up with only *one* of these rows to prove the argument invalid.)

3. Invalid. There are two rows that make the premises T and the conclusion F.

M	P	R	F	G
T	T	F	F	T
T	T	F	T	F

4. Invalid. There are three rows that make the premises true and the conclusion F:

D	G	H	P	M
F	T	T	T	T
F	T	F	T	T
F	T	F	F	T

5. Invalid. There are two rows that make the premises T and the conclusion F:

R	S	B	T	E
T	T	F	F	F
F	F	T	F	F

Exercise 10-6

1. Chain argument

2. Disjunctive argument

3. Constructive dilemma

4. Modus tollens

5. Destructive dilemma

Exercise 10-7

1. 1. R → P   (Premise)
   2. Q → R   (Premise) / ∴ Q → P
   3. Q → P   1,2, CA

4. 1. P → Q   (Premise)
   2. ~P → S   (Premise)
   3. ~Q   (Premise) / ∴ S
   4. ~P   1,3, MT
   5. S   2,4, MP

7. 1. ~S   (Premise)
   2. (P & Q) → R   (Premise)
   3. R → S   (Premise) / ∴ ~(P & Q)
   4. ~R   1,3, MT
   5. ~(P & Q)   4,2, MT

10. 1. (T v M) → ~Q   (Premise)
    2. (P → Q) & (R → S)   (Premise)
    3. T   (Premise) / ∴ ~P
    4. T v M   3, ADD
    5. ~Q   1,4, MP
    6. P → Q   2, SIM
    7. ~P   5,6, MT

Exercise 10-8

1. 4. 1,3, CA
   5. 2, CONTR
   6. 4,5, CA

4. 4. 3, CONTR
   5. 2,4, MP
   6. 2,5, CONJ
   7. 1,6, MP

Exercise 10-9

There is usually more than one way to do these.

1. 1. P & Q   (Premise)
   2. P → R   (Premise) / ∴ R
   3. P   1, SIM
   4. R   2,3, MP

2. 1. R → S   (Premise)
   2. ~P v R   (Premise) / ∴ P → S
   3. P → R   2, IMPL
   4. P → S   1,3, CA

4. 1. ~P v (~Q v R)   (Premise)

2. P (Premise) /∴ Q → R
3. P → (~Q v R) 1, IMPL
4. ~Q v R 2,3, MP
5. Q → R 4, IMPL

8.1. ~Q & (~S & ~T) (Premise)
2. P → (Q v S) (Premise) /∴ ~P
3. (~Q & ~S) & ~T 1, ASSOC
4. ~Q & ~S 3, SIM
5. ~(Q v S) 4, DEM
6. ~P 2,5, MT

Exercise 10-10

1. 1. P → R (Premise)
2. R → Q (Premise) /∴ ~P v Q
3. P → Q 1,2, CA
4. ~P v Q 3, IMPL

4. 1. P v (Q & R) (Premise)
2. (P v Q) → S (Premise) /∴ S
3. (P v Q) & (P v R) 1, DIST
4. P v Q 3, SIM
5. S 2,4, MP

7. 1. (M v R) & P (Premise)
2. ~S → ~P (Premise)
3. S → ~M (Premise) /∴ R
4. P → S 2, CONTR
5. P 1, SIM
6. S 4,5, MP
7. ~M 3,6, MP
8. M v R 1, SIM
9. R 7,8, DA

10. 1. P v (R & Q) (Premise)
2. R → ~P (Premise)
3. Q → T (Premise) /∴ R → T
4. (P v R) & (P v Q) 1, DIST
5. P v Q 4, SIM
6. ~P → Q 5, DN/IMPL
7. R → Q 2,6, CA
8. R → T 3,7, CA

Exercise 10-11

1. D → ~B
4. B → ~D
7. C → (B & ~D)

Exercise 10-12

1. Equivalent to (b)
4. Equivalent to (c)
7. Equivalent to (c)

Exercise 10-13

1. 1. P (Premise)
2. Q & R (Premise)
3. (Q & P) → S (Premise) /∴ S
4. Q 2, SIM
5. Q & P 1,4, CONJ
6. S 3,5, MP

4. 1. P v Q (Premise)
2. (Q v U) → (P → T) (Premise)
3. ~P (Premise)
4. (~P v R) → (Q → S) (Premise) /∴ T v S
5. Q 1,3, DA
6. Q v U 5, ADD
7. P → T 2,6, MP
8. ~P v R 3, ADD
9. Q → S 4,8, MP
10. T v S 1,7,9, CD

7. 1. P → Q (Premise) /∴ P → (Q v R)
2. ~P v Q 1, IMPL
3. (~P v Q) v R 2, ADD
4. ~P v (Q v R) 3, ASSOC
5. P → (Q v R) 4, IMPL

10. 1. (S → Q) → ~R (Premise)
2. (P → Q) → R (Premise) /∴ ~Q
3. ~R → ~(P → Q) 2, CONTR
4. (S → Q) → ~(P → Q) 1,3, CA
5. ~(S → Q) v ~(P → Q) 4, IMPL
6. ~(~S v Q) v ~(~P v Q) 5, IMPL (twice)
7. (S & ~Q) v (P & ~Q) 6, DEM/DN (twice)
8. ((S & ~Q) v P) & ((S & ~Q) v ~Q) 7, DIST
9. (S & ~Q) v ~Q 8, SIM
10. ~Q v (S & ~Q) 9, COM
11. (~Q v S) & (~Q v ~Q) 10, DIST
12. ~Q v ~Q 11, SIM
13. ~Q 12, TAUT

Exercise 10-14

1. 1. P → Q (Premise)
2. P → R (Premise) /∴ P → (Q & R)
3. P CP Premise
4. Q 1,3, MP
5. R 2,3, MP
6. Q & R 4,5, CONJ
7. P → (Q & R) 3–6, CP

4. 1. P → (Q v R) (Premise)
2. T → (S & ~R) (Premise) /∴ (P & T) → Q
3. P & T CP Premise
4. P 3, SIM
5. T 3, SIM
6. Q v R 1,4, MP
7. S & ~R 2,5, MP
8. ~R 7, SIM
9. Q 6,8, DA

10. (P & T) → Q   3–9, CP

7. 1. P v (Q & R)   (Premise)
    2. T → ~(P v U)   (Premise)
    3. S → (Q → ~R)   (Premise) /∴ ~S v ~T
    ④. S   CP Premise
    5. Q → ~R   3,4, MP
    6. ~Q v ~R   5,   IMPL
    7. ~(Q & R)   6,   DEM
    8. P   1,7, DA
    9. P v U   8,   ADD
    10. ~~(P v U)   9,   DN
    11. ~T   2,10, MT
    12. S → ~T   4–11, CP
    13. ~S v ~T   12,   IMPL

10. 1. (P & Q) v R   (Premise)
    2. ~R v Q   (Premise) /∴ P → Q
    ③ P   CP Premise
    ④ ~Q   CP Premise
    5. ~R   2,4, DA
    6. P & Q   1,5, DA
    7. Q   6,   SIM
    8. ~Q → Q   4–7, CP
    9. Q v Q   8,   IMPL
    10. Q   9,   TAUT
    11. P → Q   3–10, CP

Exercise 10-15

1. C → ~S
    ~L → S
    ———
    C → L
    Valid

4. ~M v C
    ~M → ~K
    C v H
    T → ~H
    ———
    T → K
    Invalid

7. C v S
    S → E
    C → R
    ———
    R v E
    Valid

10. C → ~L
    (E → (~C → ~T)) & E
    ———
    L → ~T
    Valid

13. S → ~F
    ~S → ~T
    T
    ———
    ~F
    Valid

Chapter 11: Inductive Arguments

Exercise 11-1

1. a
4. a
7. a
10. b

7. a
10. b
13. b
16. b
19. a

Exercise 11-2

1. a
4. a
7. a
10. a

Exercise 11-5

1. "Tests in this class" is perfectly clear.

4. "Women" is clear.

7. Weather in Iowa is pretty vague.

10. "Artsy people" is way too vague.

13. "Suspicious people" is pretty vague.

Exercise 11-4

1. a
4. b

Exercise 11-6

1. "Hard" is not too vague for these circumstances, we think.

4. Tolerating stress needs to be quantified; as it stands, it's too vague.

7. We've never heard a meteorologist use "sucks" to categorize weather. We think this is too vague.

10. Once again, way too vague.

13. "Tend to be quite unhappy" may be all right in some circumstances, but we think this is too vague to be very useful.

Exercise 11-7

1. a

4. a

7. b

10. d

13. c

Exercise 11-8

1. In order of increasing guardedness, we'd say d, f, b, e, a

Exercise 11-9

1. Too unguarded

4. Too guarded

Exercise 11-10

1. We think this conclusion is about right for the evidence given.

2. The conclusion could be less guarded, since these circumstances would rule out the possibility of the previous rides being in bad weather and the next ride in good weather.

5. More guarded; we have a significant difference here between the sample rides and the target ride.

Exercise 11-11

1. More guarded

4. More guarded

7. Neither more nor less guarded; the fact of the eclipse is not significant to the property in question.

10. More guarded

Exercise 11-12

2. (1) Aha! An unstated sample! Beatrice is reasoning from her experience of people in the past who have been polite, well informed, and kind, to a new case.
   (2) The target is the Tri-State representative.
   (3) The target class is all people who have the features mentioned above.
   (4) The property in question is that of not being misleading.

5. (1) As with item 2, the reasoning is mainly from past experience with hit records: In the past, follow-ups to hit records that imitate the hit's sound tend to sell well, so the same will be the case with this hit record. The sample is previous hits and their follow-ups.
   (2) The target item is the new hit's follow-up.
   (3) The target is follow-ups to hits in general.
   (4) The property in question is selling well.

8. (1) Sample: cyclamates, saccharin
   (2) The new artificial sweetener
   (3) All artificial sweeteners
   (4) Being carcinogenic

Exercise 11-13

1. More guarded

4. Less guarded

Exercise 11-18

1. No. If he bet that *exactly* 60 percent held the belief, he would be allowing for no error margin whatsoever. If he makes that bet, take him up on it.

4. 66 percent.

7. With a sample of 100, he can safely bet that no more than 70 percent share the belief, because the error margin is now ± 10 percent.

Exercise 11-19

1. The six students who turned in written evaluations

4. Generalization

7. No

9. It's not very strong. The sample is small, given that it's not random, and it's very likely to be unrepresentative: The students who bothered to write have relatively strong feelings about Ludlum one way or the other, and there is no reason to think that the spread of their opinions reflects the spread among Ludlum's students in general.

Exercise 11-20

1. Biased generalization

4. Hasty generalization; quite likely biased, too

10. Hasty generalization; biased, too

12. Biased generalization

15. Refutation by hasty generalization

Chapter 12: Causal Arguments

Exercise 12-1

1. c

3. a

Exercise 12-2

1. a

4. b

7. a

10. b

13. a

16. b

19. a

Exercise 12-3

1. c

4. a

7. a

10. a, b

13. c

Exercise 12-4

1. a; b is okay if you didn't know that unusually wet weather could cause both

4. d

7. a

10. d (the fall may have broken the rope)

13. d

16. b (coincidence) or d (a long life may make him happy)

Exercise 12-5

1. Cause: the bad call by the officials; effect: Houston's 21-point scoring streak

4. Cause: hot weather; effect: the singing of the birds

7. Cause: Democrats winning second terms in the White House; effect: lower hemlines on women's skirts

10. Cause: taking vitamins; effect: having more energy

13. Cause: child abuse; effect: eating disorders

14. Cause: Caroline's new high-pressure job; effect: her face breaking out

17. Cause: playing on the home field; effect: winning

Exercise 12-6

In 14, Caroline might feel pressure because of her complexion, although the wording suggests the complexion problem arose after she started the job. In 17, which looks tempting as a possible case of reversed causation, the problem is actually one of ignoring a common cause: being a good team is the common cause both of the winning record that results in home-field advantage and of victory in the Superbowl.

Exercise 12-9

1. Cause: too much sleep; effect: lack of stamina required to jog up the entire hill

4. Cause: lifting weights; effect: backache

7. Cause: actions of the Mustang's occupants; effect: the burglaries

8. Cause: being cooped up in a car with other people; effect: catching cold

13. Cause: Violette's watching a Dallas game; effect: Dallas losing

14. Cause: earthquakes around the Pacific Rim; effect: volcanic eruptions in Hawaii.

16. If there is a causal claim presumed here, then most likely it has Mr. O'Toole's catching cold as a cause and Mrs. O'Toole and the daughter catching cold later as effects.

17. Cause: listening to rap music; effect: sexual assaults

Exercise 12-10

Of the marked items in Exercise 12-9, the ones that attempt to use only-relevant-common-thread reasoning are 7, 8, 14, 16, and 17.

Exercise 12-11

Of the items mentioned in Exercise 12-10, we think it is probably not reasonable to suspect a common cause for number 17—at least not a common cause of the sort identified.

Exercise 12-14

1. a

4. c

7. a

10. b, but the claim is vague

14. a

17. b

20. a

Exercise 12-20

1. An experimental vaccine prevents chicken pox.

2. Target population: children.

3. Type of investigation: controlled cause-to-effect experiment.

4. The 468 children in the experimental group received the vaccine; the 446 in the control group did not.

5. One hundred percent of the experimental group had the effect (i.e., no chicken pox); 91 percent of the control group had the effect (407/446).

6. Yes. Given the credibility of the investigation, the claim "an experimental vaccine has been found effective" implies that the finding is statistically significant. Also, given the size of the samples and the difference in frequencies, you could conclude from what you have read in this chapter that the difference was statistically significant at 0.05.

7. Yes. Efforts taken to ensure that there were no important differences between control and experimental groups were not reported. But we'd assume, given the nature of the study and the credentials of the investigators, that the groups did not differ in any important way.

8. The experimental vaccine tested has been shown in this study to be effective in preventing chicken pox for at least nine months.

Exercise 12-23

1. a. Coffee grounds suspended as sediment in coffee cause headaches.
   b. People in general.
   c. Controlled cause-to-effect experiment.
   d. No indication of differences between the two groups is given. Because it is said that the experimenter divided the volunteers into two groups, we might assume that the grouping was done competently—i.e., at random.
   e. The frequency of the effect in the experimental group is 50 percent; in the control group, it is 27 percent.
   f. The indication is that the difference in frequency of effect, 23 percentage points, is significant. According to Table 12-1, the difference should exceed 27 points to be significant. This study's results are not too far from the minimum difference needed, and this may be enough to warrant further study (with a larger sample). But we cannot conclude that the causal claim is true based on this experiment.
   g. It appears that the experimenter treated the two groups alike—i.e., that he or she controlled for extraneous variables that might have interfered with the result. However, a possible problem is that the subjects in the experimental group knew they were mixing coffee grounds into their pudding. The thought of doing this gives *us* a headache.
   h. This gives only very weak support—see (f), above—to the claim that suspended grounds in coffee cause headaches.

3. a. Exercise prevents colds.
   b. Target population: humans.
   c. Type of investigation: controlled cause-to-effect experiment.
   d. The experimental group consisted of ten. There are two control groups, each with ten. The first, group A, consisted of the other ten nonexercising volunteers. The second, group B, consisted of the experimental group prior to the jogging program.
   e. The experimental group had 25 percent fewer colds than control group A. Members of the experimental group also had fewer colds than the members of group B.
   f. There were no reasons to assume that these findings are statistically significant. We know nothing about the researchers or their affiliations, and we know nothing about the publication in which their research was reported. Hence, we cannot take it on faith that the results are statistically significant.
   g. We don't know anything about the gender or age or health or anything else about the volunteers. We also don't know anything about the process

by which the volunteers were divided into two groups, so we don't know whether group B and control group A were alike in all relevant respects. Given no information about the researchers, we cannot assume selection in the two groups was random.

h. Jogging may reduce the frequency of colds; then again, it may not. This study wouldn't induce us to take up jogging.

7. a. Injection of alpha-interferon into genital warts reduces or eliminates them.
   b. Target population: the eight million individuals who suffer from the warts.
   c. This is a controlled cause-to-effect experiment, although the report does not identify a specific control group.
   d. The experimental group consisted of 192 patients. The control group, we must presume, consisted of other, unidentified individuals who have been diagnosed as suffering from the warts. The size of the latter group cannot be determined from the information given.
   e. Sixty-six percent of the experimental group showed clearing or reduction of the warts. We can probably assume that the warts do not ordinarily clear or reduce without treatment (a good report would have mentioned whether this is the case). If this is true, then the difference in frequency is very substantial indeed: 66 percent versus 0 percent.
   f. Yes. Even if there is a modest amount of spontaneous clearing or reduction of genital warts among untreated patients, 66 percent is surely a significantly greater improvement among the treated patients.
   g. Had the reporter not omitted the usual rate of spontaneous reduction of the warts—as indicated in (e), above—we could determine the value of the treatment with greater confidence.
   h. The claim at issue seems to be supported by the study.

10. *First Study*
    a. Vasectomies don't cause disease.
    b. Target population: adult male humans.
    c. Type of investigation: nonexperimental cause-to-effect study.
    d. The matched control and experimental groups consisted of 10,500 men; members of the experimental group were all vasectomized.
    e. The frequency of the effect in the groups was "similar."
    f. The report claims that the frequency of effect (disease) in the groups was "similar," so it is safe to assume, given the sources, that no statistically significant difference in frequency was found.
    g. The characteristics for which the pairs were matched are unreported.

h. The study strongly supports the claim that vasectomies don't cause disease, at least during the first ten years after the procedure.

Second Study
a. Vasectomies don't cause heart disease.
b. Target population: adult male humans.
c. Type of investigation: nonexperimental cause-to-effect study.
d. The experimental group consisted of 1,400 vasectomized men. The control consisted of 3,600 men who had not had the operation.
e. The frequency of heart disease was "the same."
f. Yes, for the same reasons given for the first study.
g. Yes. Steps taken to ensure the similarity of the control and experimental groups were not mentioned. This is probably only a failure in the report, however.
h. Vasectomies probably do not cause heart disease in the first fifteen years after the operation.

11. a. An abnormally high level of dopamine is a causal factor in SIDS.
    b. Target population: human infants.
    c. Type of investigation: nonexperimental effect-to-cause study.
    d. The experimental group consisted of thirteen infants deceased from SIDS. The control group consisted of five infants who died from other causes.
    e. Eleven out of thirteen (85 percent) of the experimental group had dopamine levels "far in excess" of those of the controls.
    f. Not really. It's not clear how the dopamine levels were quantified. Certainly the words of the investigator suggest caution.
    g. Yes, the report does not state what steps were taken, if any, to match the subjects in the experimental group for other factors that might be relevant. The investigator's claim that dopamine could be a secondary cause indicates he thinks that there may be other important medical factors involved that cause both SIDS and the high dopamine levels.
    h. What you should accept is the cautious claim of the investigator that a high dopamine level *may* be a cause of SIDS but may also be a secondary cause—that is, it and SIDS may both be the effect of some other cause.

12. a. Radiation-induced tumors are prevented by dietary restrictions in rats exposed to high doses of X-rays.
    b. Target population: rats.
    c. Type of investigation: controlled cause-to-effect experiment.
    d. The control group contained an unspecified number of rats that had been subjected to X-rays sufficient to produce tumors in all of them.

The experimental group consisted of forty-four rats given the same dose of X-rays. The experimental rats were limited to two pellets of food a day; the control-group rats were allowed to eat their fill.

e. None of the control-group rats had the effect (i.e., all the rats had tumors). Thirty-five out of forty-four experimental-group rats had the effect (i.e., no tumors). Thus, the frequency of the effect in the experimental group (35/44 = 80 percent) exceeded the frequency in the control group (0.00) by 80 percentage points.

f. The investigator is reported as saying that the study "demonstrates" that radiation-induced tumors can be prevented by restricting diet. The clear implication is, thus, that the results are statistically significant.

g. Yes. Neither the size of the control group nor attempts to randomize selection are mentioned. But this is clearly a reputable scientific investigation, so we'd assume that there are no breakdowns in the experimental design at these points.

h. The study strongly supports claim (a).

13. a. Encephalitis has declined in California during the past thirty years because more people are staying inside from 7 P.M. to 10 P.M. with their air conditioners on, watching television.

b. Target population: residents of California's Central Valley.

c.–f. By the time you reach this question, you should spot some confusion either in the investigation or in the report of the investigation. To establish a causal relationship between staying indoors and not getting encephalitis, you would have to show that there would be fewer cases of the disease if everyone stayed indoors than if no one did. But you could establish a *correlation* between staying indoors and not getting encephalitis merely by showing that the encephalitis rate was lower among those who stayed inside than among those who didn't, and this is apparently what the investigation attempted to do. However, that even this simple correlation was shown by the investigation is not clear from the report, because, according to the report, television *ownership* was compared with the encephalitis rate, not television viewing. Further, the statistics quoted—that 79 percent of the interviewed Kern County residents said they used their air conditioners every evening and that 63 percent said they watched television four or more evenings a week during the summer—are entirely unhelpful to the question of whether the encephalitis rate is related to either television ownership or television use. Finally, the last sentence of the report is totally incoherent. It makes no sense to talk of comparing the percentage of residents who spent more time indoors now with the percentage who spent more time indoors in 1950. (More time indoors than when?)

g. Yes. No information is provided about actual encephalitis rates or about earlier use of air conditioning and television. Further, staying at home, watching TV, and using the air conditioner—three different activities—seem to be treated interchangeably and confusingly here. We don't really know what is being measured or against what. Given the investigators, who are associated with reputable institutions, our suspicion is that the report may be more to blame for the various confusions than the study.

h. As reported, the study supports only the statistic about television and air conditioner use among those who have a telephone in Kern County.

16. a. A behavior modification program aimed at Type A individuals prevents heart attacks.

b. Target population: Type A individuals.

c. Type of investigation: controlled cause-to-effect experiment.

d. The experimental group consisted of 592 out of 862 predominantly male victims of heart attack. Members of the group were given group counseling to ease Type A behavior. (Evidently all 592 were deemed Type A persons.) The matched control groups consisted of 270 subjects who received only cardiological advice.

e. After three years, 7 percent of the experimental group had another heart attack, compared with 13 percent of the control group.

f. The material in this chapter suggests that the finding is probably statistically significant (at 0.05 level), given the size of the groups and the percentages involved.

g. The report doesn't explicitly state that all subjects were of Type A, though perhaps this may be assumed, and the report also fails to clarify what variables were matched. But, more important, details about how long counseling lasted are missing, and these details could be important because the report implies that continuation of the program was voluntary. Also, there seems to be confusion about what the investigators were researching—the relationship between the program and heart attack rate, between an actual behavioral modification and heart attack rate, between counseling and behavioral modification, or some combination or interplay of these.

h. The conclusion the study supports (as reported here) is that Type A individuals who have had one heart attack can significantly reduce their chances of a second heart attack by participating (for some unspecified amount of time) in whatever kind of counseling program was conducted in the experiment.

Writing Exercises

2. The implication most people would be likely to draw from the story is that the nontraditional treatments, especially having people pray for patients, produced significant improvements in the patients' conditions. We think there are serious problems that must be overcome before such conclusions can be reached.

   One difficulty is that, if the prayer groups were given only names and not descriptions of those they were to pray for, their prayers would not have been directed at individuals—unless, which is highly unlikely, these names were unique to just those individuals in the whole world. It is possible, however, that more information was given to the prayer groups than was disclosed in the article.

   A more serious problem is that it is *very* unclear what it means to say that the patients in the prayed-for group did "50 to 100 percent better." This is a huge spread. If the statistic is a range for the group as a whole, it is too broad to be meaningful. If it reports a range of improvement among the members of the group taken individually, then it has no meaning for a population study such as this. In short, the study (or at least the report) gives no intelligible information about *d*.

   Some other problems:

   What about E? What does "did better" mean, and how was it quantified? The patients' EEGs, heart rate, blood pressure and other "clinical outcomes" evidently were measured, but what would count as a significant difference in such data from group to group?

   Neither the patients nor the hospital staff knew the assignments of the control or experimental group—but did the researchers know? We aren't told.

   One would expect patients who receive extra attention in the form of stress-relaxation or touch therapy to have lower blood pressure, heart rate, and so forth.

Chapter 13: Moral, Legal, and Aesthetic Reasoning

Exercise 13-1

1. Prescriptive
4. Descriptive
6. Prescriptive
7. Descriptive

Exercise 13-2

1. Nonmoral value
4. Moral value
6. Nonmoral value
7. No value

Exercise 13-3

2. People ought to keep their promises.
5. A mayor who takes bribes should resign.
7. Using a gun is illegal (unless certain circumstances apply) and should be punished.
8. Whatever is unnatural is wrong and should be avoided.

Exercise 13-4

1. Tory is being consistent in that what he is proposing for *both* sexes is that members of both should have the right to marry members of the *other* sex.

2. To avoid inconsistency, Shelley must be able to identify characteristics of art students, athletes, and children of alumni—for whom she believes special admissions programs are acceptable—and show that, unless they are also in one of the listed categories, these characteristics are not true of affirmative action students: women and members of minorities. Furthermore, the characteristics she identifies must be relevant to the issue of whether an individual should be admitted into the university. It may well be possible to identify the characteristics called for. (Remember that consistency is a necessary condition for a correct position, but it is not a sufficient one.)

3. Marin could be consistent only if he could show that the process of abortion involves killing and capital punishment does not. Because this is impossible—capital punishment clearly does involve killing—he is inconsistent. However, Marin's inconsistency is the result of his blanket claim that *all* killing is wrong. He could make a consistent case if he were to maintain only that the killing of

innocent people is wrong, and that abortion involves killing innocent people but capital punishment does not. (Each of these last claims would require strong arguments.)

8. To avoid inconsistency, Harold would have to identify a relevant difference between the discrimination law and the marijuana law. In fact, there is one fairly obvious one to which he can appeal: The former has been declared contrary to the state constitution; the latter has not been alleged to be contrary to any constitution. So Harold may object to the failure to implement the latter on grounds that it, unlike the discrimination law, is unconstitutional. (It is a separate matter, of course, whether he can build a strong argument in the case of the marijuana law.)

Exercise 13-8

1. The harm principle: Shoplifting harms those from whom one steals.

2. The harm principle: Forgery tends to harm others.

4. We think the offense principle is the most relevant, because the practice in question is found highly offensive by most people (at least we believe—and hope—so). But one might also include the harm principle, because spitting in public can spread disease-causing organisms.

6. Legal moralism, because many people find adultery immoral; and, to a lesser extent, both the harm principle and legal paternalism, because adultery can increase the spread of sexually transmitted diseases.

10. The offense principle.

Exercise 13-11

1. a. Principle 4
   b. Principle 2
   Compatible

4. a. Principle 5
   b. Principle 2
   Compatible

Exercise 13-12

1. Relevant on Principle 7

4. Relevant on Principle 1

7. Relevant on Principle 3

Exercise 13-13

Principle 1: June's picture does not teach us anything, for no chimp can distinguish between truth and falsity; it is a curiosity rather than a work of art.

Principle 2: By looking at June's very symbolic paintings, we are compelled to accept her vision of a world in which discourse is by sight rather than by sound.

Principle 3: Perhaps the most far-reaching impact of June's art is its revelation of the horrors of encaging chimps; surely beings who can reach these heights of sublimely abstract expression should not see the world through iron bars.

Principle 4: Dear Zookeeper: Please encourage June to keep painting, as the vibrant colors and intense brushstrokes of her canvases fill all of us with delight.

Principle 5: I never thought I would wish to feel like a monkey, but June's art made me appreciate how chimps enjoy perceiving us humans as chumps.

Principle 6: This is not art, for no monkey's product can convey the highest, most valuable, human states of mind.

Principle 7: Whether by the hand of monkey or man, that the canvases attributed to June show lovely shapes and colors is indisputable.

Principle 8: What is art is simply what pleases a person's taste, and June obviously finds painting tasty, as she tends to eat the paint.

Exercise 13-14

1. a

4. b

7. b

Appendix 1: Conflicting Claims

Exercise A1-1

1. Contraries

4. These do not conflict.

7. Contraries

10. Contraries

Exercise A1-2

1. Contraries, because some other day may be payday. That would make both of these false. Notice that this answer rests on the assumption that there are not two paydays each week; if that assumption is not true, then both Friday and Monday could be payday, and hence both claims could be true—that is, not in conflict.

4. Contradictories

7. Contraries

10. We meant to puzzle you with this one. The two claims make a paradox. Look at either one. If it were true, it would have to be false; but if it were false, it would have to be true. The strangeness comes from the fact that the claims are "self-referential"—that is, they refer back to themselves. Such references can (obviously) cause trouble (or amusement).

Exercise A1-3

1. We don't think there's even a conflict here. Kostner could be above average, at least a *little* above average, and still not qualify for what most people would call "high achiever."

6. Under the most obvious interpretation, we see this as a real contradiction. If we take it to mean that Schwarzkopf said originally that he thought the war should *not* have been halted, and if Bush is saying that Schwarzkopf agreed with him that the war *should* have been halted, this is a clear-cut contradiction.

Appendix 2: Analytic Claims

Exercise A2-1

1. Analytic truth. "Theft" is by definition a criminal activity.

4. Analytic truth

7. Analytic truth

10. Analytic, in one sense of the word "normal," meaning "usual," "standard," or "ordinary." If "normal" were taken to mean something like "perfectly average," or "paradigmatic," then this would not be analytic. In that case, it wouldn't even be true, because few people are perfectly average, if indeed anybody is.

13. In spite of recent speculation by some physicists that travel back into time may be possible, we believe that it isn't and hence that the claim is analytically true.

Appendix 3: Some Common Patterns of Deductive Arguments

Exercise A3-1

1. b

4. b

Exercise A3-2

1. Valid

4. Invalid

7. Invalid

Exercise A3-3

1. P = Baffin Island is larger than Sumatra.
Q = Two of the largest islands in the world are in the Arctic Ocean.
Argument pattern:
  If P then Q.
  P.
  Therefore, Q.
Modus ponens; valid

4. P = The recent tax cuts are self-financing.
Q = There is no substantial increase in the federal deficit.
Pattern:
  If P then Q.
  Not-P.
  Therefore, not-Q.
Denying the antecedent; invalid

7. P = Alexander will finish his book by tomorrow afternoon.
    Q = He is an accomplished speed reader.
    Pattern:
        If P then Q.
        Q.
        Therefore, P.
    Affirming the consequent; invalid

10. P = The proper amount of heat is applied to water at 212°F in a sealed container.
    Q = Steam at 212° is produced from water at the same temperature.
    R = The pressure in the container will increase without any increase in the temperature.
    Pattern:
        If P then Q.
        If Q then R.
        Therefore, if P then R.
    Chain argument; valid

13. P = The ammeter shows a negative reading.
    Q = The alternator is not working properly.
    Pattern:
        If P then Q.
        P.
        Therefore, Q.
    Modus ponens; valid

17. P = Drugs are legalized.
    Q = Quality will be monitored by the government.
    R = There will be fewer drug-caused deaths.
    Pattern:
        If P then Q.
        If Q then R.
        Therefore, if P then R.
    Chain argument; valid

Exercise A3-4

1. All Xs are Ys.
    All Zs are Ys.
    Therefore, all Xs are Zs.
    Valid syllogism 1

4. All Xs are Ys.
    No Zs are Xs.
    Therefore, no Ys are Zs.
    Invalid syllogism 2

8. All Xs are Ys.
    No Xs are Zs.
    Therefore, no Zs are Ys.
    This becomes invalid syllogism 2 after the second premise and the conclusion are each converted.

10. All Xs are Ys.
    All Zs are Ys.
    Therefore, all Xs are Zs.
    Invalid syllogism 1

13. Xs = people
    Ys = people who find this course particularly useful
    Some Xs are not Ys.
    Therefore, some Xs are Ys.
    Unnamed invalid inference

17. All Xs are Ys.
    All Zs are Ys.
    Therefore, all Xs are Zs.
    Invalid syllogism 1

20. All Xs are Ys.
    No Xs are Zs.
    Therefore, no Zs are Ys.
    This becomes invalid syllogism 2 when the second premise and conclusion are each converted.

Essays for Analysis

▲ The following selections may all be used for the purposes of identifying, summarizing, and evaluating arguments.

▲ Selection 4 is useful for evaluating credibility and potential bias.

▲ The following are ideal for picking out rhetorical devices, including slanters and pseudoreasoning: 5A, 5B, 6A, 6B, 7, 9A, 9B, 10A, 10B, 11A, 11B, 12A, 12B, 13A, 13B, 14, 15, and 16.

▲ Selections 1, 2, 9A, 9B, 10A, 10B, and 11A, 11B are useful for picking out syllogisms in real life. These items work especially well as group exercises, because they are difficult until you get the hang of it.

Other assignment ideas are given at the beginning of selections. Your instructor may have other uses for some of the selections.

Selection 1

Instructions: Fill in the blanks in the following essay appropriately:

The main issue in this essay is whether _____ . Cynthia Tucker's position on this issue is _____ .

Ms. Tucker thinks many Americans will approve the decision of the Jasper, Texas, jury to execute John William King. King was accused of _____ . Tucker thinks many people will favor the death penalty for King because _____ .

Tucker, however, believes _____ . She gives _____ main arguments for her position.

First, she argues _____ .

Second, she argues _____ .

[Third, fourth, etc., however many arguments Tucker uses.]
I agree [or disagree, your call] with Tucker. Here's why: _____ .

Alternative Assignment: Find as many categorical syllogisms (Chapter 9 and Appendix 3) or common deductive argument patterns (Chapter 10 and Appendix 3) as you can. Here is one example, from the last paragraph of the essay (see below):

> ". . . the system did not catch all of its errors and some of those who were wrongly convicted have already been sent to their deaths. How many? There is no way to know, but even one is too many. The execution of even one innocent man puts us law-abiding citizens uncomfortably close to the level of a John King."

When we paraphrase, we get something like this:

> Capital punishment has resulted in the execution of at least one innocent person.
>
> If capital punishment has done this, then capital punishment puts us close to the level of a John King.
>
> [Therefore, capital punishment puts us close to the level of a John King.] [unstated conclusion.]

This is an example of modus ponens (Appendix 3).
    Notice that you could also treat this as a categorical syllogism (Chapter 9):

C = capital punishment
E = policies that have resulted in the execution of at least one innocent person
L = policies that put us close to the level of a John King

All C are E
All E are L
Therefore, all C are L.

DEATH PENALTY HAS NO PLACE IN U.S.

Cynthia Tucker

Many Americans will applaud the decision of a Jasper, Texas, jury to condemn John William King to die. They will argue that the death penalty is exactly what King deserves for chaining James Byrd Jr. to the back of a pickup truck and dragging him until his body was torn apart—his head and right arm here, his torso there.   1

    If there is to be capital punishment in this country, isn't this just the sort   2
of case that demands it? King is the epitome of cold-blooded evil, a man who bragged about his noxious racism and attempted to win converts to his

views. He believed he would be a hero after Byrd's death. He has proved himself capable of the sort of stomach-churning cruelty that most of us would like to believe is outside the realm of human behavior.

Besides, there is the matter of balancing the books. King is a white man who (with the help of accomplices, apparently) killed a black man. For centuries, the criminal justice system saw black lives as so slight, so insignificant, that those who took a black life rarely got the death penalty. Isn't it a matter of fairness, of equity, of progress, that King should be put to death?   3

No. Even though King is evil. Even though he is utterly without remorse. Even though he is clearly guilty. (After the prosecution mounted a case for five days, King's lawyers mounted a defense of only one hour. The jury of 11 whites and one black then deliberated only two and half hours to determine King's guilt.)   4

This is no brief for King, who would probably chain me to the back of a pickup truck as quickly as he did Byrd. This is a plea for America, which is strong enough, just enough and merciful enough to have put aside, by now, the thirst for vengeance.   5

The question is not, Does John William King deserve the death penalty? The question is, Does America deserve the death penalty?   6

Capital punishment serves no good purpose. It does not deter crime. If it did, this country would be blessedly crime-free. It does not apply equally to all. King notwithstanding, the denizens of death row are disproportionately blacks and Latinos who have killed whites. It remains true that the lives of blacks and Latinos count for less, that their killers are less likely to be sentenced to die.   7

Death row also counts among its inmates a high quotient of those who are poor, dumb and marginalized. Those criminals blessed with education, status and connections can usually escape capital punishment: 8

Last Tuesday, William Lumpkin, an attorney in Augusta, Ga., was found guilty of capital murder in the death of real estate agent Stan White, who owned the title to Lumpkin's home and was about to evict him. Lumpkin beat White to death with a sandbag and dumped the body in the Savannah River. But Lumpkin descends from Georgia gentry; one ancestor was a state Supreme Court justice. He was sentenced to life in prison.   9

Worse than those inequities, capital punishment is sometimes visited upon the innocent. Lawrence C. Marshall, a law professor at Northwestern University, is director of the National Conference on Wrongful Convictions and the Death Penalty. Since 1972, he says, 78 innocent people have been released from death row.   10

It does not strain the imagination to think that maybe, just maybe, the system did not catch all of its errors and some of those who were wrongly convicted have already been sent to their deaths. How many? There is no way to know, but even one is too many. The execution of even one innocent man puts us law-abiding citizens uncomfortably close to the level of a John William King.   11

Instructions: Identify the main issue in this essay and the author's position on this issue. Then state in your own words three arguments given by the author in support of his position.

      As an additional exercise, show how at least two of these arguments can be treated either as categorical syllogisms (Chapter 9), truth-functional arguments (Chapter 10), or common deductive argument patterns (Appendix 3).

HETERO BY CHOICE?

Richard Parker

For a while there, everybody who could get near a microphone was claiming that only he or she and his or her group, party, faction, religion, or militia stood for real American family values.   1

    Now, it was seldom made clear just what those values were supposed to be. I have a notion that if [my son] Alex and I were to go out and knock over a few gas stations and convenience stores, the mere fact that we did it together would make it count as somebody's family values.   2

    For some, the phrase "family values" never amounted to more than a euphemism for gay-bashing. I remember a [few] years ago, during the loudest squawking about values, when a reporter asked Dan Quayle whether he believed that a gay person's homosexuality was a matter of his or her psychological makeup or whether it was a matter of choice. He answered that he believed it was mainly a matter of choice. Two weeks later, Barbara Bush was quoted as saying that sexual orientation is mainly a matter of choice. Since then, it's turned up frequently.   3

    It seems to me that people who make such a remark are either being remarkably cynical (if they don't really believe it themselves) or remarkably fatuous (if they do believe it).   4

    If it were *true* that a person's sexual preference were a matter of choice, then it must have happened that each of us, somewhere back along the way, *decided* what our sexual preference would be. Now, if we'd made such decisions, you'd think that somebody would remember doing it, but nobody does.   5

    In my case, I just woke up one morning when I was a kid and discovered that girls were important to me in a way that boys were not. I certainly didn't sit down and *decide* that it was girls who were going to make me anxious, excited, terror-struck, panicky, and inclined to act like an idiot.   6

    Now, if the people who claim to hold the "choice" view were right, it must mean that gay people have always chosen—they've *decided*—to have the sexual orientation they have. Can you imagine a person, back in the '50s, say, who would *choose* to have to put up with all the stuff gay people had to put up with back then? It's bad enough now, but only the mad or the criminally uninformed would have *chosen* such a life back then.   7

(Actually, it seems clear to me that the whole idea of a preference rules   8
out the notion of choice. I choose to eat chocolate rather than vanilla, but I
don't choose to *prefer* chocolate to vanilla. One simply discovers what one
prefers.)

If it's clear that people don't consciously choose their sexual preferences,   9
why would anybody make such claims? I can think of a cynical reason: It
only makes sense to condemn someone for something they choose, not for
things they can't do anything about.

Is it just a coincidence that people who claim we choose our sexual   10
preferences are often the same people who demonize homosexuals? No, of
course not. In fact, their cart comes before their horse: They are damned sure
going to condemn gay people, and so, since you can only condemn someone
for voluntary actions, it *must* be that one's sexuality is a voluntary choice.
Bingo! Consistent logic. Mean, vicious, and mistaken. But consistent.

Selection 3

In a brief essay, argue for whether Bonnie and Clyde should receive the same
or different punishment.

BONNIE AND CLYDE

Bonnie and Clyde are both driving on roads near a mountain community in   1
northern California. Both are driving recklessly—much faster than the
posted speed limit. Each of them has a passenger in the car.

At a sharp and very dangerous curve, Bonnie loses control of her car and   2
crashes into some nearby trees; only moments later, on another dangerous
section of road, Clyde's car goes into a skid, leaving the road and rolling over
several times down an embankment.

As a result of their accidents, Bonnie and Clyde are bruised and shaken,   3
but not seriously hurt. However, both of their passengers are hurt badly and
require medical attention. Passersby call an ambulance from the next town,
and soon it arrives, taking the injured passengers to the only medical facility
in the area.

A neurosurgeon who is on duty examines both passengers when they   4
arrive at the medical center. She determines that both have suffered serious
head injuries and require immediate cranial surgery if they are to survive.
However, she is the only person available who is competent to perform the
surgery, and she cannot operate on both patients at once. Not knowing what
to do, she tries to find someone to call for advice. But she can reach nobody.
So she flips a coin.

As a result of the coin flip, the surgeon operates on Bonnie's passenger   5
and leaves Clyde's passenger in the care of two medical technicians. The
latter do the best they can, but Clyde's passenger dies. Because of the atten-

tion of the physician, Bonnie's passenger survives and, in time, makes a complete recovery.

Identify rhetorical devices, including slanters and pseudoreasoning, and evaluate the credibility and potential bias of the author.

WILL OZONE BLOB DEVOUR THE EARTH?

Edward C. Krug

At the time this essay was first published, Edward C. Krug was director of environmental projects for CFACT, Committee For A Constructive Tomorrow, a group based in Washington, D.C., that promotes free-market solutions to current environmental concerns.

The great and good protectors of the environment are hailing the latest bit of science-by-press-release. 1

Simultaneously staged with the announcement that the National Aeronautics and Space Administration (NASA) and the National Oceanic and Atmospheric Administration have begun studying the possible development of an ozone hole over the Northern Hemisphere, the Bush administration, Greenpeace, Sen. Al Gore (D-Tenn.), and others proclaimed that this "discovery" justifies the banning of all human-made substances that contain chlorine and bromine. Chlorine and bromine, by the way, are common elements also found in seawater, in plants, and in you and me. 2

I've been asked why I, a scientist, would dare question all this concern for the environment. The answer: Real science operates quite differently from what passes for environmental "science" these days. 3

Take physics, for example. Cold-fusion scientists were vilified by the scientific community a few years ago for their violation of scientific ethics when they went to the media with their supposed findings before their articles had been peer-reviewed. 4

The release of such unproven scientific findings is materially and sociologically devastating. It is highly misleading and causes the misallocation of limited social resources. It also undermines the very process of science and the public's faith in the objectivity of science. 5

The science of physics, which stones to death false prophets and therefore produces new miracles every day, operates in a way exactly the opposite of the new environmental "science," which stones to death the real prophets and therefore produces new scandals every day. 6

The Feb. 3 NASA press release on the new ozone hole over the Northern Hemisphere is being widely lauded. But there has been no peer review of the data. Indeed, peer review cannot even begin until after the end of March, because all the data have not yet been collected. 7

Even so, the details of the press release give pause. It states that according   8
to ozone hole theory, we could have been losing 1 percent to 2 percent of our
ozone per day in mid-January. But this appears not to have happened. Furthermore, it notes that we have information on only about half of the theoretically relevant chemical processes in the atmosphere, and only about 30
percent of the theoretically relevant range of altitude.

Why couldn't NASA obey the time-honored ethics of science and wait   9
until sometime after March to make its findings known?

For the same reason that biologist Paul Ehrlich in 1968 dared anybody to   10
prove wrong his theory that the world would run out of food in 1977. And
for the same reason that the Environmental Protection Agency Administra-
tor William Reilly announced last April that unpublished NASA satellite
data would show ozone depletion had speeded up to twice its previous rate.
By the time 1977 rolled around and people were still eating food, and by the
time NASA finally published its satellite data showing that ozone is increasing (not decreasing), nobody cared anymore.

Environmentalists also abuse the scientific method. In real science, one   11
must prove the positive, not the negative. If a hypothesis cannot explain all
the data, it gets thrown out. In the new environmental "science," by contrast, utterances of doom are automatically assumed to be correct. And it is
assumed that society must act on them, unless someone can prove the environmental fantasy has absolutely no possibility of ever coming true.

Since it is logically impossible to prove the negative, environmentalists   12
have a sweet racket going: We must subordinate ourselves to their will lest
their horrible predictions come to pass.

These are also the rules for the "space invaders" game. In this game, the   13
leader says we face dreadful danger from hostile invaders from space. Since
it is impossible to prove there is no alien life in the universe, we are forced
to make the leader emperor of Earth so that he or she can save us all from
this potential horror.

One might wish that NASA played "space invaders" instead of issuing   14
"ozone-blob-that-may-swallow-Earth" press releases into the real world.

Selections 5A and 5B

Evaluate the arguments on both sides. Who has the stronger arguments, and
why? Make certain your response does not rest too heavily on rhetorical
devices. As an alternative assignment, determine which author relies more
heavily on rhetorical devices to persuade the audience.

EQUAL TREATMENT IS REAL ISSUE—NOT MARRIAGE

USA Today

Our view: The fact is that marriage is already a messy entanglement of
church and state.

With shouting about "gay marriage" headed for a new decibel level . . .   1
chances for an amicable resolution seem bleak.

Traditionalists see the issue in private, religious terms, and with legisla-   2
tors in many states mobilizing around their cause, they're in no mood to
compromise. They say marriage, by common definition, involves a man and
a woman. And for most people, it's just that. In polls, two-thirds of the public
supports the status quo.

But looking through the lenses of history and law, as judges must, mar-   3
riage is far from a private religious matter. So much so that short of a constitutional amendment, compromise is inevitable.

Not only does the state issue marriage licenses and authorize its officers   4
to perform a civil version of the rite, it gives married couples privileged
treatment under law.

For example, when one spouse dies the house and other property held   5
jointly transfer easily for the other's continued use and enjoyment. The sur-
vivor gets a share of continuing Social Security and other benefits. Joint
health and property insurance continues automatically.

If there's no will, the law protects the bereaved's right to inherit. There's   6
no question of who gets to make funeral arrangements and provide for the
corpse.

It's the normal order of things, even for households that may have existed   7
for only the briefest time, or for couples who may be long estranged though
not divorced.

But some couples next door—even devoted couples of 20 or 30 years'   8
standing—don't have those rights and can't get them because of their sex.

Support for marriage is justified as important to community stability,   9
and it undoubtedly is. But when it translates into economic and legal discrimination against couples who may be similarly committed to each other,
that should be disturbing.

The U.S. Constitution says every person is entitled to equal protection   10
under law. Some state constitutions go farther, specifically prohibiting sexual discrimination. . . .

Ironically, people who oppose gay marriages on religious grounds would   11
have their way but for the fact that marriage has evolved as a messy entanglement of church and state. To millions, marriage is a sacrament, and the
notion that the state would license or regulate a sacrament ought to be an
outrage. Imagine the uproar if a state legislature tried to license baptisms or
communions, and wrote into law who could be baptized or who could receive bread and wine. Or worse yet gave tax breaks to those who followed
those practices.

Short of getting out of the marriage business altogether, which isn't   12
likely to happen, the state must figure a way to avoid discrimination. The
hundreds of employers now extending workplace benefits to unmarried but
committed couples and the handful of municipalities offering informal
"domestic partner" status may be pointing in the right direction.

The need is not necessarily to redefine marriage but to assure equal treat-   13
ment under the law.

GAY MARRIAGE "UNNATURAL"

The Rev. Louis P. Sheldon

The Rev. Louis P. Sheldon is chairman of the Traditional Values Coalition, a California-based organization of some 32,000 churches.

Opposing view: Opinion polls show that nearly 80% of Americans don't accept "homosexual marriage."

1   In everything which has been written and said about . . . homosexual marriage . . . , the most fundamental but important point has been overlooked. Marriage is both culturally and physiologically compatible but so-called homosexual marriage is neither culturally nor physiologically possible.

2   Homosexuality is not generational. The family tree that starts with a homosexual union never grows beyond a sapling. Without the cooperation of a third party, the homosexual marriage is a dead-end street. In cyber language, the marriage is not programmed properly and there are hardware problems as well.

3   . . . Across America, "rights" are being created and bestowed routinely by judges indifferent to the wishes and values of their communities. This new wave of judicial tyranny confers special rights upon whichever group can cry the shrillest claim of victimhood.

4   At the core of the effort of homosexuals to legitimize their behavior is the debate over whether or not homosexuality is some genetic or inherited trait or whether it is a chosen behavior. The activists argue that they are a minority and homosexuality is an immutable characteristic.

5   But no school of medicine, medical journal or professional organization such as the American Psychological Association or the American Psychiatric Association has ever recognized the claim that homosexuality is genetic, hormonal or biological.

6   While homosexuals are few in number, activists claim they represent about 10% of the population. More reliable estimates suggest about 1% of Americans are homosexual. They also are the wealthiest, most educated and most traveled demographic group measured today. Per capita income for the average homosexual is nearly twice that for the average American. They are the most advantaged group in America.

7   Homosexuality is a behavior-based life-style. No other group of Americans have ever claimed special rights and privileges based solely on their choice of sexual behavior, and the 1986 Supreme Court decision of Bowers vs. Hardwick said sodomy is not a constitutionally protected right.

8   When the state enacts a new policy, it must be reflected in its public school curriculum. Textbook committees and boards of education will ensure that all of that flows into the classroom. American families do not want the "normalcy" of homosexual marriage taught to their children.

9   Churches may not be forced to perform homosexual weddings but individual churches that resist may be subjected to civil suit for sexual discrimination. Resistance may be used as a basis for denying them access to

federal, state or local government programs. In the Archdiocese of New York, Catholic churches were singled out by the city and denied reimbursement given to every other church for providing emergency shelter to the city's homeless. The reason cited was Catholic opposition to homosexual "rights" ordinances.

Whatever the pronouncements of the . . . nation's highest court, Americans know that "homosexual marriage" is an oxymoron. Calling a homosexual relationship a marriage won't make it so. There is no use of rhetoric that can sanitize it beyond what it is: unnatural and against our country's most basic standards. Every reputable public opinion poll demonstrates that nearly 8 of every 10 Americans don't accept the pretense of "homosexual marriage."   10

Selections 6A and 6B

Evaluate the arguments on both sides. Who has the stronger arguments, and why? Make certain your response does not rest too heavily on rhetorical devices.

Alternative assignment: Determine which author relies more heavily on rhetorical devices to persuade his or her audience.

LATEST RULING IS GOOD SCOUT MODEL

USA Today

Groups that take in public funds can't shut out minorities.

The Boy Scouts still don't get it. They want all the perquisites and support   1 due a welcoming, public-service organization—while retaining a '50s-style right to discriminate against minorities.

Fortunately, most similar organizations understand by now that it's   2 wrong to invite the public in, use taxpayer-financed facilities and then claim the right to act like a small and sectarian private club.

The Scouts, virtually alone, still want it both ways. And they're vowing   3 to go to the U.S. Supreme Court in defense of their hypocrisy.

The national Scout bureaucracy professes shock at the New Jersey Supreme Court's decision this week in favor of a highly honored Scout who was   4 expelled by the organization for being gay.

The reason ought to be obvious: The Scouts solicit and get generous   5 public support in troop sponsorship, free space for their activities and cash contributions. And they attempt, nonselectively, to bring in almost every pre-teen in pants. Therefore they are subject to New Jersey's law barring discrimination on the basis of race, religion or sexual orientation.

Their claim to "freedom of association" smacks of what the Jaycees argued in the Supreme Court in 1984 in defense of barring women—and lost.   6

It's what Rotary clubs argued in 1987—and lost. It's what businessmen's clubs argued in 1988—and lost.

The argument is embarrassingly similar to that used by the white- 7
supremacist defenders of racial segregation as a way of life in the 1950s and '60s.

Civil rights watchdogs say the Scouts are about the last national organi- 8
zation to make such a claim. Others, including Jaycees and Rotary, say they are stronger for having abandoned their former discriminatory practices.

Unfortunately, the Scouts' arguments have worked in states with weaker 9
anti-discrimination laws or more pliable courts. California's Supreme Court even found a tortuous distinction between the Boys Clubs, covered by that state's law, and the Scouts, who aren't. The ayatollahs of California Scouting were permitted to kick out otherwise model Scouts who made the mistake of being honest about their religious uncertainties or sexual makeup.

The reaction has been a backlash: In California, Illinois, Maine and else- 10
where, some governments, local charities and corporations are unwilling to fund and sponsor Scout programs because the Scouts insist on discriminat-ing. And more lawsuits are soaking up Scout funds.

The Scouts' lofty objectives and 80-year record of success with nearly 11
100 million boys are commendable. The Scout Law soundly directs a Scout to "seek to understand others," to "treat others as he wants to be treated."

The bosses of Scouting—and their apologists—ought to reread that good 12
advice.

DECISION ASSAULTS FREEDOM

Larry P. Arnn

Larry P. Arnn is president of the Claremont Institute in California.

Opposing view: The organization has the right to select its associates.

Since 1911, Boy Scouts have been required to swear: "On my honor I will do 1
my best to do my duty to God and country and to obey the Scout Law; To help other people at all times; To keep myself physically strong, mentally awake, and morally straight." This oath has shaped the character and habits of generations of young men.

In New Jersey, the Boy Scout oath and the principles behind it are effec- 2
tively voided. The state's Supreme Court ruled that the Scouts must readmit James Dale, a scoutmaster who revealed his homosexuality in 1990.

The court said that the Scouts' decision to expel Dale was "based on 3
little more than prejudice" and was "not justified by the need to preserve the organization's expressive rights."

Nonsense. The court's decision [tramples] on the rights of privacy, free 4
association, and religious liberty to promote homosexuality as a civil right. The implications go far beyond the Boy Scouts.

Under American civil rights law, once a group becomes a protected 5
minority, a myriad of constitutional forces is called to its defense. If

homosexuality is granted this special status, it will affect every family in the land.

Furthermore, the court said that the Scouts are a "place of public accom-   6
modation" because they have a broad-based membership and work closely with other public service groups. But the Boy Scouts do not hang a sign that says all may enter. As the name implies, they are looking first of all for boys. More specifically, boys who will promise to follow the creed that makes scouting what it is. We can change that only by destroying scouting.

The rights of the Boy Scouts, not James Dale, are being violated. Each of   7
us has under the Constitution the right to associate with whom we please. That means necessarily the right not to associate, too. If that right cannot be protected here, it cannot be protected anywhere. Indeed, churches will be next.

This case likely will go to the U.S. Supreme Court. But maybe the next   8
president will sign a Defense of the Boy Scouts Act. We must hope for that, and also for a good decision from the U.S. Supreme Court.

Selection 7

Determine whether this essay contains an argument, and if it does, what it is.

Alternative assignment: Identify rhetorical devices, including slanters and pseudoreasoning.

IS GOD PART OF INTEGRITY?

Editorial from *Enterprise Record*, Chico, California

What Oroville High School was trying to do last Friday night, said Superin-   1
tendent Barry Kayrell, was "maintain the integrity of the ceremony."

The ceremony was graduation for approximately 200 graduates.   2

The way to maintain "integrity," as it turned out, was to ban the words   3
"God" and "Jesus Christ."

The result was a perfect example of out-of-control interpretation of the   4
separation of church and state.

The high school's action in the name of "integrity" needlessly disrupted   5
the entire proceeding as almost the entire graduating class streamed out of their seats in support of Chris Niemeyer, an exemplary student who had been selected co-valedictorian but was barred from speaking because he wanted to acknowledge his belief in God and Jesus Christ.

The speech, said Kayrell, "was more of a testimonial."   6

It was preaching, added OHS principal Larry Payne.   7

"I truly believe in the separation (of church and state)," explained   8
Kayrell.

It was a complicated story that led to last Friday night.   9

Niemeyer and fellow senior Ferin Cole had prepared their speeches   10
ahead of time and presented them to school officials. Cole, who plans to
attend Moody Bible College, had been asked to deliver the invocation.

Both mentioned God and Jesus Christ. Both were told that was   11
unacceptable.

Both filed a last-minute action in federal court, challenging the school's   12
censorship. At a hearing Friday, just hours before graduation, a judge refused
to overrule the school on such short notice. The suit, however, continues,
and the judge acknowledged it will involve sorting out complex constitutional questions.

Defeated in court, Niemeyer and Cole met with school officials to see   13
what could be salvaged.

Both agreed to remove references to the deity, but Cole wanted to men-   14
tion why, in an invocation—by definition a prayer—he was not allowed to
refer to God. That was nixed, and Cole simply bowed out.

Niemeyer was supposed to deliver his revised draft to Payne by 5 P.M.   15

He missed the deadline, but brought the draft with him to the ceremony.   16

When it was his turn to speak, Niemeyer came forward, but Payne in-   17
stead skipped over the program listing for the valedictory address and announced a song. The two debated the question on stage as the audience and
graduates-to-be looked on.

Finally turned away, Niemeyer left the stage, tears of frustration on his   18
cheeks, and his classmates ran to his side in a dramatic show of support.

You might say they were inspired by integrity.   19

The object of the First Amendment to the U.S. Constitution is to bar   20
government-enforced religion. It was not designed to obliterate belief in God.

To stretch that command to denying a student the right to acknowledge   21
what has spurred him on to the honor he has won is a bitter perversion.

That would apply whether the student was Islamic, Buddhist or any   22
belief—atheist included. There is room, it would seem, for diversity in valedictory speeches, too.

Not at Oroville High School. There God and integrity don't mix.   23

It's spectacles like that played out last Friday night that have prompted   24
Congress to consider a constitutional amendment aimed at curbing such
misguided excess.

Earlier in the week it drew a majority vote in House, but fell short of the   25
two-thirds margin needed.

Maybe such actions as witnessed locally can push it over the top.   26

Selection 8

Identify the conclusion of the article. How many arguments are given
for it?

SHORTEN FEDERAL JAIL TIME

From the *Washington Post*

Don Edwards

U.S. Rep. Don Edwards, D-Calif., was chairman of the House Judiciary Subcommittee on Civil and Constitutional Rights.

1 A debate is raging in the federal judiciary about whether the number of federal judges should be increased. This question should not be decided by Congress until it straightens out the mess it has made of the courts' jurisdiction.

2 Beginning in 1981, with the highly publicized "War on Crime," Congress has swamped the federal courts with thousands of criminal cases, many unsuited for the federal judiciary. The result is that civil cases are neglected and our federal prisons are bulging with prisoners, many of whom should not be there at all.

3 In its effort to be tough on drug offenders and other criminals, Congress enacted mandatory minimum laws that require judges to impose a certain sentence on the offender regardless of the person's background and the nature of the crime. The statutes now number over 100, with many more proposed. Not only must we not enact new ones, but Congress should repeal the ones now on the books for the following reasons:

- The federal prison population has tripled since 1980 and is projected to quintuple by the year 2000. Three-quarters of new arrivals are drug offenders; by 1996, these offenders will comprise two-thirds of the prison population. Ninety-one percent of mandatory minimum sentences are imposed on nonviolent first-time offenders.

- To accommodate this influx of new prisoners, we opened 29 new federal prisons between 1979 and 1990. They cost $1.7 billion to maintain, and each new cell cost $50,000. With the continued precipitous increase in population, by 2002 we will be spending $2.8 billion annually.

  If we had instead sentenced these inmates to an alternative to prison, such as probation or a halfway house, we could have saved $384 million in 1992 and, projections show, an astounding $438 million in 1993. The Bureau of Prisons says that the recidivism rate for offenders sentenced to alternatives is extremely low—only 14 percent.

- Because of mandatory sentencing laws, federal district judges have no discretion in sentencing. They must send offenders to prison for long terms. Between 1984, when mandatory minimums were first enacted, and 1991, the sentence length for a nonviolent offender increased an average of 48 months. Ironically, mandatory sentencing laws often mean that nonviolent offenders receive longer sentences than violent offenders.

- We are filling our prisons with nonviolent, first-time offenders while dangerous and violent criminals often avoid mandatory minimum sentences.

- Morale in the federal judiciary is often low. The Judicial Conference, representing all federal judges, has come out against mandatory minimum sentences, and two senior judges recently announced publicly that they would no longer preside over drug trials because of these inequities. . . .

We must reverse the congressional policies that have created this mindless mandatory minimum sentencing, which overcrowds our federal prisons. At $30,000 per year to maintain these inmates, we not only cannot afford to implement these senseless policies, but we are creating a criminal training ground for first-time nonviolent offenders who might otherwise be turned into law-abiding citizens.   4

Selections 9A and 9B

Evaluate the arguments on both sides. Who has the stronger arguments, and why?

Alternative assignment: Identify rhetorical devices and determine which author relies more heavily on such devices.

Second alternative assignment: In each of the two essays, find four arguments that can be treated as categorical syllogisms. Set up a key, letting a letter stand for a relevant category. Be sure you identify the category in plain English. Then circle all and only the distributed terms. Then state whether each syllogism is valid, identifying rules broken by any syllogisms that are not.

CLEAN NEEDLES BENEFIT SOCIETY

USA Today

Our view: Needle exchanges prove effective as AIDS counterattack. They warrant wider use and federal backing.

Nothing gets knees jerking and fingers wagging like free needle-exchange programs. But strong evidence is emerging that they're working.   1

The 37 cities trying needle exchanges are accumulating impressive data that they are an effective tool against spread of an epidemic now in its 13th year.   2

- In Hartford, Conn., demand for needles has quadrupled expectations—32,000 in nine months. And free needles hit a targeted population: 55% of used needles show traces of AIDS virus.

- In San Francisco, almost half the addicts opt for clean needles.
- In New Haven, new HIV infections are down 33% for addicts in exchanges.

Promising evidence. And what of fears that needle exchanges increase 3
addiction? The National Commission on AIDS found no evidence. Neither
do new studies in the *Journal of the American Medical Association.*

Logic and research tell us no one's saying, "Hey, they're giving away free, 4
clean hypodermic needles! I think I'll become a drug addict!"

Get real. Needle exchange is a soundly based counterattack against 5
an epidemic. As the federal Centers for Disease Control puts it, "Removing contaminated syringes from circulation is analogous to removing
mosquitoes."

Addicts know shared needles are HIV transmitters. Evidence shows 6
drug users will seek out clean needles to cut chances of almost certain death
from AIDS.

Needle exchanges neither cure addiction nor cave in to the drug scourge. 7
They're a sound, effective line of defense in a population at high risk. (Some
28% of AIDS cases are IV drug users.) And AIDS treatment costs taxpayers
far more than the price of a few needles.

It's time for policymakers to disperse the fog of rhetoric, hyperbole and 8
scare tactics and widen the program to attract more of the nation's 1.2 million IV drug users.

We're a pragmatic society. We like things that work. Needle exchanges 9
have proven their benefit. They should be encouraged and expanded.

PROGRAMS DON'T MAKE SENSE

Peter B. Gemma Jr.

Opposing view: It's just plain stupid for government to sponsor dangerous, illegal behavior.

If the Clinton administration initiated a program that offered free tires to 1
drivers who habitually and dangerously broke speed limits—to help them
avoid fatal accidents from blowouts—taxpayers would be furious. Spending
government money to distribute free needles to junkies, in an attempt to
help them avoid HIV infections, is an equally volatile and stupid policy.

It's wrong to attempt to ease one crisis by reinforcing another. 2

It's wrong to tolerate a contradictory policy that spends people's hard- 3
earned money to facilitate deviant behavior.

And it's wrong to try to save drug abusers from HIV infection by perpet- 4
uating their pain and suffering.

Taxpayers expect higher health-care standards from President Clinton's 5
public-policy "experts."

Inconclusive data on experimental needle-distribution programs is no 6
excuse to weaken federal substance-abuse laws. No government bureaucrat

can refute the fact that fresh, free needles make it easier to inject illegal drugs because their use results in less pain and scarring.

Underwriting dangerous, criminal behavior is illogical: If you subsidize something, you'll get more of it. In a Hartford, Conn., needle-distribution program, for example, drug addicts are demanding taxpayer-funded needles at four times the expected rate. Although there may not yet be evidence of increased substance abuse, there is obviously no incentive in such schemes to help drug-addiction victims get cured.   7

Inconsistency and incompetence will undermine the public's confidence in government health-care initiatives regarding drug abuse and the AIDS epidemic. The Clinton administration proposal of giving away needles hurts far more people than [it is] intended to help.   8

Selections 10A and 10B

Evaluate the arguments on both sides. Who has the stronger arguments, and why?

Alternative assignment: Identify rhetorical devices and determine which author relies more heavily on them.

Second alternative assignment: In the first essay, find as many arguments as you can that can be treated as categorical syllogisms. Set up a key, letting a letter stand for a relevant category. Be sure you identify the category in plain English. Then circle all and only the distributed terms. Then state whether each syllogism is valid, identifying rules broken by any syllogisms that are not.

MAKE FAST FOOD SMOKE-FREE

USA Today

Our view: The only thing smoking in fast-food restaurants should be the speed of the service.

Starting in June, if you go to Arby's, you may get more than a break from burgers. You could get a break from tobacco smoke, too.   1

The roast-beef-sandwich chain on Tuesday moved to the head of a stampede by fast-food restaurants to limit smoking.   2

Last year, McDonald's began experimenting with 40 smokeless restaurants. Wendy's and other fast-food chains also have restaurants that bar smoking.   3

But Arby's is the first major chain to heed a call from an 18-member state attorneys general task force for a comprehensive smoking ban in fast-food restaurants. It will bar smoking in all its 257 corporate-owned restaurants and urge its 500 franchisees to do the same in their 2,000 restaurants.   4

Other restaurants, and not just the fast-food places, should fall in line.   5

The reason is simple: Smoke in restaurants is twice as bad as in a   6
smoker's home or most other workplaces, a recent report to the *Journal of the American Medical Association* found.

Fast-food restaurants have an even greater need to clear the air. A quarter   7
of their customers and 40% of their workers are under 18.

Secondhand smoke is a class A carcinogen. It is blamed for killing an   8
estimated 44,000 people a year. And its toxins especially threaten youngsters' health.

The Environmental Protection Agency estimates that secondhand   9
smoke causes up to 1 million asthma attacks and 300,000 respiratory infections that lead to 15,000 hospitalizations among children each year.

All restaurants should protect their workers and customers. If they   10
won't, then local and state governments should do so by banning smoking in them, as Los Angeles has.

A person's right to a quick cigarette ends when it threatens the health of   11
innocent bystanders, and even more so when many of them are youngsters.

They deserve a real break—a meal in a smoke-free environment that   12
doesn't threaten their health.

DON'T OVERREACT TO SMOKE

Brennan M. Dawson

Opposing view: With non-smoking sections available, and visits brief, what's the problem?

If the attorneys general from a handful of states—those charged with uphold-   1
ing the law—were to hold a forum in Washington, you might expect them to be tackling what polls say is the No. 1 public issue: crime.

Not these folks. They're worried someone might be smoking in the   2
smoking section of a fast-food restaurant. And, there might be children in the non-smoking section. Thus, they say, fast-food chains should ban all smoking.

Some would argue that this raises serious questions about priorities. But   3
it may be worth debating, since this is supposed to be about protecting children. Everyone is (and should be) concerned with children's health and well-being.

But what are we protecting them from—the potential that a whiff of   4
smoke may drift from the smoking section to the non-smoking section during the average 20-minute visit for a quick burger?

Anyone knowledgeable would tell you that none of the available studies   5
can reasonably be interpreted to suggest that incidental exposure of a child to smoking in public places such as restaurants is a problem. After all, with the almost universal availability of non-smoking sections, parents have the option of keeping their kids out of the smoking section.

A recent study published in the *American Journal of Public Health* re-   6
ported that the separate smoking sections in restaurants do a good job of minimizing exposure to tobacco smoke. According to the figures cited,

customers would have to spend about 800 consecutive hours in the restaurants to be exposed to the nicotine equivalent of one cigarette.

That would represent about 2,400 fast-food meals. Under those conditions, most parents would worry about something other than smoking.   7

Selections 11A and 11B

Evaluate the arguments on both sides. Who has the stronger arguments, and why?

Alternative assignment: Identify rhetorical devices and determine which author relies more heavily on them.

Second alternative assignment: In each of the two essays, find as many arguments as you can that can be treated as categorical syllogisms. Set up a key, letting a letter stand for a relevant category. Be sure you identify the category in plain English. Then circle all and only the distributed terms. Then state whether each syllogism is valid, identifying rules broken by any syllogisms that are not.

BUYING NOTES MAKES SENSE AT LOST-IN-CROWD CAMPUSES

USA Today

Our view: Monster universities and phantom professors have only themselves to blame for note-selling.

Higher education got a message last week from a jury in Gainesville, Fla.: Its customers, the students across the nation, deserve better service.   1

The jury found entrepreneurs are free to sell notes from college professors' lectures. And Ken Brickman is an example of good, old free enterprise, even if his services encourage students to skip class.   2

Brickman is a businessman who pays students to take notes in classes at the University of Florida. From a storefront a block off campus, he resells the notes to other students with a markup.   3

Professors and deans bemoan Brickman's lack of morals. They even use the word "cheating." They'd be more credible if their complaints—and the university's legal resources—were directed equally at Brickman's competitor in the note-selling business a few blocks away.   4

The difference: The competition pays professors for their notes; Brickman pays students. Morals are absent, it seems, only when professors aren't getting their cut.   5

The deeper issue is why Brickman has found a lucrative market. It's easy to say that uninspired students would rather read someone else's notes than spend time in class, but that's not the point.   6

Why are students uninspired? Why are they required to learn in auditorium-size classes where personal attention is non-existent, taking   7 attendance impossible, and students can "cut" an entire semester with no one noticing?

Why are students increasingly subjected to teaching assistants— 8
graduate students who know little more than they—who control classes while professors are off writing articles for esoteric journals that not even their peers will read?

Why are there not more professors—every former student can remember 9
one—who transmit knowledge of and enthusiasm for a subject with a fluency and flair that make students eager to show up? No one would prefer to stay away and buy that professor's notes.

The debate over professorial priorities—students vs. research—is old. 10
But so long as students come in second, they'll have good reasons to go to Ken Brickman for their notes.

BUYING OR SELLING NOTES IS WRONG

Opposing view: Note-buyers may think they're winners, but they lose out on what learning is all about.*

It's tough being a college student. Tuition costs and fees are skyrocketing. 1
Classes are too large. Many professors rarely even see their students, let alone know their names or recognize their faces. The pressure for grades is intense. Competition for a job after graduation is keen.

But that's no excuse for buying the notes to a teacher's course. What goes 2
around comes around. Students who buy someone else's notes are only cheating themselves—by not engaging in the learning process to the fullest extent. They aren't learning how to take notes. Or how to listen. Or how to put what someone is saying into their own words.

What happens if the notes are inaccurate? Will a commercial note-taker 3
guarantee the notes? Would you want to take a test using someone else's notes?

Besides, what the professor says is her own property. It is the result of 4
hard work on her part. A professor's lectures are often her principal means of livelihood. Nobody but the professor herself has the right to sell her property. Buying the notes to her lectures without her permission is just like selling a book that she wrote and keeping the money for yourself.

And buying the notes from someone who is selling them without the 5
teacher's permission is the same as receiving stolen goods.

And that's assuming that there will be anyone out there to buy the notes 6
in the first place. After all, most students will want to take notes for themselves, because they know that is their only guarantee of accuracy. People who think they can get rich selling the notes to someone's lectures should take a course in critical thinking.

*The author of the companion piece to the *USA Today* editorial on this subject would not give us permission to reproduce her essay in a critical thinking text, so we wrote this item ourselves.

The pressure for good grades doesn't justify buying or selling the notes to 7
a professor's lectures without her permission. If you can't go to class, you
shouldn't even be in college in the first place. Why come to school if you
don't want to learn?

Selections 12A and 12B

Evaluate the arguments on both sides. Who has the stronger arguments,
and why?

Alternative assignment: Identify rhetorical devices and determine
which author relies more heavily on them.

NEXT, COMPREHENSIVE REFORM OF GUN LAWS

USA Today

Our view: Waiting periods and weapon bans are welcome controls, but
they're just the start of what's needed.

The gun lobby got sucker-punched by the U.S. Senate last weekend. It 1
couldn't happen to a more deserving bunch.

For seven years, gun advocates have thwarted the supersensible Brady 2
bill, which calls for a national waiting period on handgun purchases.
Through a mix of political intimidation, political contributions and perverse
constitutional reasoning, gun lobbyists were able to convince Congress to
ignore the nine out of 10 Americans who support that idea.

But suddenly, after two days of filibuster, the Senate abruptly adopted 3
the Brady bill. The House has already acted, so all that remains is to do some
slight tinkering in a House-Senate conference, and then it's off to the White
House for President Clinton's signature.

That's not the end of welcome gun control news, though. As part of the 4
anti-crime bill adopted last week, the Senate agreed to ban the manufacture
and sale of 19 types of assault-style semiautomatic weapons. Although these
weapons constitute fewer than 1% of all guns in private hands, they figure in
nearly 10% of all crime. The bill also bans some types of ammunition and
restricts gun sales to, and ownership by, juveniles.

These ideas are worthy, but they can't do the whole job. Waiting pe- 5
riods and background checks keep criminals from buying guns from legal
dealers. Banning certain types of anti-personnel weapons and ammunition
will keep those guns and bullets from growing more common and commonly
lethal.

Yet the wash of guns and gun violence demands much, much more. The 6
judicial ability to process firearm-related crimes with certainty and speed is
part of the solution. But even more so is the adoption of laws that permit
gun licensing, gun registration and firearm training and education.

After years of denying the popular mood, Congress appears ready to honor it. That merits applause. But its new laws are just a start. Without truly comprehensive controls, the nationwide slick of gun carnage is bound to continue its bloody, inexorable creep.   7

GUN LAWS ARE NO ANSWER

Alan M. Gottlieb

Opposing view: Disarming the law-abiding populace won't stop crime. Restore gun owners' rights.

Every time another gun control law is passed, violent crime goes up, not down, and the gun-ban crowd starts to yelp for more anti-gun laws.   1

So it's no surprise that the gun-banners are already snapping at the heels of our Bill of Rights.   2

They turn a blind eye to the fact that California, with a 15-day waiting period, experienced a 19% increase in violent crime and a 20% increase in homicide between 1987 and 1991. And that a 1989 ban on "assault weapons" in that state has also resulted in increased violent crime.   3

In Illinois, after a 30-day waiting period was installed, that state experienced a 31% increase in violent crime and a 36% increase in the homicide rate.   4

And, a handgun ban in Washington, D.C., has made it the murder capital of the world!   5

The results are in. Gun control makes the streets safe for violent criminals. It disarms their victims—you and me. The people's right to protect themselves should be restored, not restricted.   6

Case in point: Bonnie Elmasri of Wisconsin, who was being stalked by her estranged husband despite a court restraining order, was killed along with her two children while she waited for the handgun she purchased under that state's gun-waiting-period law.   7

Bonnie and her children are dead because of gun control laws, as are thousands of other victims each year.   8

Anybody who believes that disarming the law-abiding populace will help reduce crime has rocks in the head.   9

The next time a violent criminal attacks you, you can roll up your copy of USA TODAY and defend yourself with it. It may be all you'll have left for self-protection.   10

Selections 13A and 13B

Evaluate the arguments on both sides. Who has the stronger arguments, and why?

Alternative assignment: Identify rhetorical devices and determine which author relies more heavily on them.

HOW CAN SCHOOL PRAYER POSSIBLY HURT? HERE'S HOW

USA Today

> Our view: Mississippi case shows how people's rights can be trampled by so-called "voluntary prayer."

What harm is there in voluntary prayer in school?   1

That's the question . . . House Speaker Newt Gingrich and others pose in their crusade to restore prayer to the classroom. They argue that a constitutional amendment to "protect" so-called voluntary school prayer could improve morals and at worst do no harm.   2

Well, a mother's lawsuit filed Monday against Pontotoc County, Miss., schools says otherwise. It shows government-sponsored voluntary prayer in school threatens religious liberty.   3

All the mother, Lisa Herdahl, wants is that her six children get their religious instruction at home and at their Pentecostal church, not at school.   4

But their school hasn't made that easy. Prayers by students go out over the public address system every day. And a Bible study class is taught at every grade.   5

School officials argue that since no one is ordered to recite a prayer or attend the class, everything is voluntary.   6

But to Herdahl's 7-year-old son, it doesn't seem that way. She says he was nicknamed "football head" by other students after a teacher told him to wear headphones so he wouldn't have to listen to the "voluntary" prayers.   7

And she says her 11-year-old son was branded a "devil worshiper" after a teacher told students he could leave a Bible class because he didn't believe in God.   8

Indeed, Herdahl's children have suffered exactly the kind of coercion to conform that the Supreme Court found intolerable when it banned state-written prayers in 1962 and outlawed Alabama's moment of silence for meditation or voluntary prayer in 1985.   9

As the court noted in those cases, when government—including schools—strays from neutrality in religious matters, it pits one religion against another. And youngsters especially can feel pressured to submit to a majority's views.   10

That's why a constitutional amendment to protect "voluntary prayer" in school is so dangerous.   11

Students don't need an amendment to pray in school now. They have that right. And they can share their religious beliefs. They've formed more than 12,000 Bible clubs nationwide that meet in schools now, only not during class time.   12

For the Herdahls, who refused to conform to others' beliefs, state-sponsored voluntary prayer and religious studies have made school a nightmare.   13

For the nation, a constitutional amendment endorsing such ugly activities could make religious freedom a joke.   14

WE NEED MORE PRAYER

Armstrong Williams

Armstrong Williams is a Washington, D.C.–based business executive, talk-show host, and author of The Conscience of a Black Conservative.

Opposing view: The tyranny of the minority was never envisioned by the nation's Founding Fathers.

1   The furor aroused by . . . Newt Gingrich's remarks about renewing school prayer illustrates how deep cultural divisions in American society really are.

2   A few moments of prayer in schools seems a small thing—harmless enough, almost to the point of insignificance. Yet it has provoked an impassioned firestorm of debate about the dangers of imposing viewpoints and the potential for emotionally distressing non-religious children.

3   The Constitution's framers were wary of a "tyranny of the majority," and so they imposed restraints on the legislature. They never foresaw, nor would they have believed, the tyranny of the minority made possible through an activist judiciary changing legal precedents by reinterpreting the Constitution.

4   The American ideal of tolerance has been betrayed by its use in directly attacking the deeply held convictions of millions of Americans.

5   The fact that this country was once unashamedly Christian did not mean that it was necessarily intolerant of other views—at least not nearly so intolerant of them as our rigid secular orthodoxy is toward all religious expression. Through the agency of the courts, a few disgruntled malcontents have managed to impose their secular/humanist minority views on the majority.

6   But it has not always been so.

7   The confidence with which some maintain that school prayer is manifestly unconstitutional belies an ignorance of our nation's history. America was founded by religious men and women who brought their religious beliefs and expressions with them into public life.

8   It was in 1962 that an activist Supreme Court ruled that denominationally neutral school prayer was judged to violate the establishment clause of the First Amendment. Since then, the "wall of separation" between church and state has rapidly become a prison wall for religious practice.

9   The drive to protect the delicate sensibilities of American children from the ravages of prayer is particularly ironic when our public schools have become condom clearinghouses that teach explicit sex.

10   The real heart of the school prayer issue is the role of religion in our public life.

Selection 14

Summarize the author's argument or arguments, if any.
    Alternative assignment: Identify rhetorical devices, if any.

PLANET OF THE WHITE GUYS
Barbara Ehrenreich

On the planet inhabited by the anti–affirmative action activists, the only   1
form of discrimination left is the kind that operates against white males.
There, in the name of redressing ancient wrongs, white men are routinely
shoved aside to make room for less qualified women and minorities. These
favored ones have no problems at all—except for that niggling worry that
their colleagues see them as underqualified "affirmative-action babies."
Maybe there was once an evil called racism in this charmed place—30 or
300 years ago, that is—but it's been replaced by affirmative action.

Now I agree that discrimination is an ugly thing no matter who's at the   2
receiving end, and that it may be worth reviewing affirmative action . . . to
see whether it's been fairly applied. People should not be made to suffer for
the wicked things perpetrated by their ancestors or by those who merely
looked like them. Competent white men should be hired over less competent women and minorities; otherwise, sooner or later, the trains won't run
on time and the planes will fall down from the sky.

But it would be a shame to sidestep the undeniable persistence of racism   3
in the workplace and just about everywhere else. Consider the recent lesson
from Rutgers University. Here we have a perfectly nice liberal fellow, a
college president with a record of responsiveness to minority concerns.
He opens his mouth to talk about minority test scores, and then—like a
Tourette's syndrome victim in the grip of a seizure—he comes out with
the words "genetic hereditary background." Translated from the academese:
minorities are dumb, and they're dumb because they're born that way.

Can we be honest here? I've been around white folks most of my life—   4
from left-wingers to right-wingers, from crude-mouthed louts to prissy-
minded élitists—and I've heard enough to know that *The Bell Curve* is just
a long-winded version of what an awful lot of white people actually believe.
Take a look, for example, at a survey reported by the National Opinion Research Center in 1991, which found a majority of whites asserting that
minorities are lazier, more violence-prone and less intelligent than whites.
Even among the politically correct, the standard praise word for a minority
person is "articulate," as if to say, "Isn't it amazing how well he can speak!"

Prejudice of the quiet, subliminal kind doesn't flow from the same   5
place as hate. All you have to do to be infected is look around: at the top of
the power hierarchy—filling more than 90% of top corporate-leadership
slots and a grossly disproportionate share of managerial and professional
positions—you see white men. Meanwhile, you tend to find minorities clus-
tered in the kind of menial roles—busing dishes, unloading trucks—that our
parents warned were waiting for us too if we didn't get our homework done.

So what is the brain to make of this data? It does what brains are designed   6
to do: it simplifies and serves up the quickie generalizations that are meant
to guide us through a complex world. Thus when we see a black colleague,
who may be an engineer or a judge, the brain, in its innocence, announces
helpfully, "Janitor-type approaching, wearing a suit."

Maybe it's easier for a woman to acknowledge this because subliminal 7
prejudice hurts women too. Studies have shown, for example, that people are
more likely to find an article convincing if it is signed by "Bob Someone"
instead of, say, "Barbara Someone." It's just the brain's little habit of parceling
reality into tidy equations, such as female=probable fluffhead. The truth is
that each of us carries around an image of competence in our mind, and its
face is neither female nor black. Hence our readiness to believe, whenever
we hear of a white male losing out to a minority or a woman, that the white
guy was actually more qualified. In Jesse Helms' winning 1990 campaign
commercial, a white man crumples up a rejection letter, while the voice-
over reminds him that he was "the best-qualified." But was he? Is he always?
And why don't we ever hear a white guy worry out loud that his colleagues
suspect he got the job—as white men have for centuries—in part because
he's male and white?

It's a measure of the ambient racism that we find it so hard to believe 8
that affirmative action may actually be doing something right: ensuring that
the best guy gets the job, regardless of that guy's race or sex. Eventually, when
the occupational hierarchy is so thoroughly integrated that it no longer
makes sense for our subconscious minds to invest the notion of competence
with a particular skin color or type of genitalia, affirmative action can indeed
be cast aside like training wheels.

Meanwhile, aggrieved white men can console themselves with the gains 9
their wives have made. Numerically speaking, white women are the biggest
beneficiaries of affirmative action, and because white women tend to marry
white men, it follows that white men are, numerically speaking, among the
top beneficiaries too. On this planet, Bob Dole and Pat Buchanan may not
have been able to figure that out yet, but most white guys, I like to think, are
plenty smart enough.

Selection 15

Summarize the author's argument or arguments, if any.
    Alternative assignment: Identify rhetorical devices, if any.

DO WOMEN REALLY NEED AFFIRMATIVE ACTION?

Joanne Jacobs

Joanne Jacobs is a columnist for the *San Jose Mercury News*.

I was an affirmative action hire, back in 1978. As a result, I became the first 1
woman on my newspaper's editorial board. Was I qualified? I certainly didn't
have much experience. My boss took a chance on me. I like to think it paid
off for him, as well as for me.

At any rate, I made the editorial board safe for women, who now make 2
up half the editorial pages staff.

Defenders of affirmative action have a new strategy: Consider the ladies.   3
Recently, a liberal coalition kicked off a campaign to cast affirmative action
as a gender issue rather than a racial issue. Affirmative action is essential for
women's advancement, argued feminist leaders. "Women will not quietly
accept a rollback of our rights that have been part of the American scene for
over a generation," said Katherine Spillar of the Feminist Majority.

It's a smart, though doomed, strategy.   4

The smart part is that women (if not feminists) are a majority of the   5
population. If women were persuaded that affirmative action guarantees
not only our benefits but also our "rights," public thinking would shift
dramatically.

Poll data suggest that the majority of Americans accept preferences for   6
women in jobs and college admissions; most are deeply hostile to preferences
for minority group members.

The doomed part is that most white women don't think they'd lose their   7
rights or their jobs if affirmative action ceased to exist; some are concerned
about the job prospects of their white male husbands.

Affirmative action used to mean reaching out to people excluded from   8
opportunities by overt discrimination or old-boy networks, giving everyone
a chance to compete fairly. Now it means judging members of previously
excluded groups by different, generally lower, standards than others.

Are women less able to compete [today] because of past discrimination?   9
Certainly not women under the age of 45.

In the past, affirmative action helped women—especially educated,   10
middle-class women—enter occupations previously reserved for men. Some
argue that affirmative action primarily benefited white women who were
most prepared to take advantage of opportunities, and most likely to have
connections to powerful men.

Certainly, it appears that affirmative action has done most for those who   11
needed it least. It has opened doors; it has not built ladders.

While women haven't achieved parity in income or in top executive   12
ranks or in all careers, affirmative action can provide little help in achieving
those goals in the future.

In education, affirmative action already is passé. Women don't need to be   13
judged by different standards to get into college, and they're not. Females earn
higher high school grades than males, and are more likely to attend college.

Women are underrepresented in the mathematical sciences and in en-   14
gineering studies. An affirmative action program that admitted calculus-
deficient women to physics class would do them no favor. The solution is
not changing the standards; it's persuading more girls to take more math in
high school.

Women do worry about workplace equity, but here too affirmative action   15
isn't likely to play much of a role. The much-discussed "glass ceiling" for
women in business is related to two factors: family and calculus.

Women are more likely than men to put family needs ahead of career   16
advancement. These choices have consequences. Women who work more at
home don't get to be CEO.

Marcia Clark, chief prosecutor in the O.J. Simpson case, illustrates the   17
trade-offs. Because of her professional success, she [risked losing] custody of
her kids to her ex-husband, who works less demanding hours.

The other factor that keeps businesswomen under the glass ceiling is   18
insufficient math training. Studies show that women who break through
the glass took calculus in college; women with less math don't make it to
the top.

Women can prepare themselves to compete on an equal basis by getting   19
the same academic training as their male colleagues.

Corporations are talking "diversity" these days, mostly for reasons of   20
self-interest. Executives know it's impossible to build a viable all-white, all-
male work force; they want people who can sell to increasingly diverse
markets and understand increasingly diverse customers.

Certainly, women are now an integral part of the work force, essential to   21
the success of virtually every company. Women's gains are not going to be
rolled back. We're in too far.

The line now being drawn between the successful and the unsuccessful   22
has nothing to do with gender or race or ethnicity or citizenship. It is a line
between the well educated and the poorly educated. Women can move to
the right side of the line without asking for preferences based on gender, or
accepting the affirmative action stigma.

Selection 16

Identify claims, arguments, positions, and rhetorical devices. Attempt to
support or rebut arguments.

IN DEFENSE OF A LITTLE VIRGINITY:

A Message from Focus on the Family

The federal government has spent billions of our tax dollars since 1970 to   1
promote contraceptives and "safe sex" among our teenagers.[1] Isn't it time we
asked, **What have we gotten for our money?** These are the facts:

- The federal Centers for Disease Control estimate that there are now 1
  million cases of HIV infection nationwide.[2]
- 1 in 100 students coming to the University of Texas health center now
  carries the deadly virus.[3]
- The rate of heterosexual HIV transmission has increased 44% since
  September 1989.[4]
- Sexually transmitted diseases (STDs) infect 3 million teenagers
  annually.[5]
- 63% of all STD cases occur among persons under 25 years of age.[6]

- 1 million new cases of pelvic inflammatory disease occur annually.[7]
- 1.3 million new cases of gonorrhea occur annually;[8] strains of gonorrhea have developed that are resistant to penicillin.
- Syphilis is at a 40-year high, with 134,000 new infections per year.[9]
- 500,000 new cases of herpes occur annually;[10] it is estimated that 16.4% of the U.S. population ages 15–74 is infected, totaling more than 25 million Americans—among certain groups the infection rate is as high as 60%.[11]
- 4 million cases of chlamydia occur annually;[12] 10–30% of 15-to-19-year-olds are infected.[13]
- There are now 24 million cases of human papilloma virus (HPV), with a higher prevalence among teens.[14]

To date, over 20 different and dangerous sexually transmitted diseases are rampant among the young. Add to that the problems associated with promiscuous behavior: infertility, abortions and infected newborns. The cost of this epidemic is staggering, both in human suffering and in expense to society; yet epidemiologists tell us we've only seen the beginning. 2

Incredibly, the "safe-sex" gurus and condom promoters who got us into this mess are still determining our policy regarding adolescent sexuality. Their ideas have failed, and it is time to rethink their bankrupt policies. 3

How long has it been since you've heard anyone tell teenagers why it is to *their* advantage to remain virgins until married? The facts are being withheld from them, with tragic consequences. Unless we come to terms with the sickness that stalks a generation of Americans, teen promiscuity will continue, and millions of kids . . . thinking they are protected . . . will suffer for the rest of their lives. Many will die of AIDS. 4

There is only one safe way to remain healthy in the midst of a sexual revolution. It is to abstain from intercourse until marriage, and then wed and be faithful to an uninfected partner. It is a concept that was widely endorsed in society until the 1960s. Since then, a "better idea" has come along . . . one that now threatens the entire human family. 5

Inevitable questions are raised whenever abstinence is proposed. It's time we gave some clear answers: 6

Why, apart from moral considerations, do you think teenagers should be taught to abstain from sex until marriage? 7

No other approach to the epidemic of sexually transmitted diseases will work. The so-called "safe-sex" solution is a disaster in the making. Condoms can fail at least 15.7 percent of the time annually in preventing pregnancy.[15] They fail 36.3 percent of the time annually in preventing pregnancy among young, unmarried, minority women.[16] In a study of homosexual men, the *British Medical Journal* reported the failure rate due to slippage and breakage to be 26 percent.[17] Given these findings, it is obvious why we have a word for people who rely on condoms as a means of birth control. We call them . . . "parents." 8

Remembering that a woman can conceive only one or two days per month, we know the failure rate for condoms must be much higher when it comes to preventing disease, which can be transmitted 365 days per year! If the devices are not used properly, or if they slip just once, viruses and bacteria are exchanged and the disease process begins. One mistake after 500 "protected" episodes is all it takes to contract a sexually transmitted disease. The damage is done in a single moment when rational thought is overridden by passion.

Those who would depend on so insecure a method must use it properly on *every* occasion, and even then a high failure rate is brought about by factors beyond their control. The young victim who is told by his elders that this little latex device is "safe" may not know he is risking lifelong pain and even death for so brief a window of pleasure. What a burden to place on an immature mind and body!

In fact, the University of Texas Medical Branch recently found that condoms are only 69 percent effective in preventing the transmission of the human immunodeficiency virus (HIV) in heterosexual couples. Dr. Susan Weller of UTMB conducted a meta-analysis of 11 independent HIV transmission studies. Her conclusion: "When it comes to the sexual transmission of HIV, the only real prevention is not to have sex with someone who has or might have HIV."[18]

This surely explains why not one of 800 sexologists at a conference a few years ago raised a hand when asked if they would trust a thin rubber sheath to protect them during intercourse with a known HIV-infected person.[19] Who could blame them? They're not crazy, after all. And yet they're perfectly willing to tell our kids that "safe sex" is within reach and that they can sleep around with impunity.

There is only one way to protect ourselves from the deadly diseases that lie in wait. It is abstinence before marriage, then marriage and mutual fidelity for life to an uninfected partner. Anything less is potentially suicidal.

That position is simply NOT realistic today. It's an unworkable solution: Kids will NOT implement it.

Some will. Some won't. It's still the only answer. But let's talk about an "unworkable solution" of the first order. Since 1970, the federal government has spent billions of our tax dollars to promote contraception and "safe sex." This year alone, hundreds of millions of your tax dollars will go down that drain! (Compared with less than $8 million for abstinence programs, which Sen. Teddy Kennedy and company have sought repeatedly to eliminate altogether.) Isn't it time we ask what we've gotten for our money? After 22 years and billions of dollars, some 58 percent of teenage girls under 18 still did not use contraception during their first intercourse.[20] Furthermore, teenagers tend to keep having unprotected intercourse for a full year, on average, before starting any kind of contraception.[21] That is the success ratio of the experts who call abstinence "unrealistic" and "unworkable."

Even if we spent another $50 billion to promote condom usage, most teenagers would still not use them consistently and properly. The nature of human beings and the passion of the act simply do not lend themselves to a disciplined response in young romantics.

But if you knew a teenager was going to have intercourse, wouldn't you   17
teach him or her about proper condom usage?

No, because that approach has an unintended consequence. The pro-   18
cess of recommending condom usage to teenagers inevitably conveys five dangerous ideas: (1) that "safe sex" is achievable; (2) that everybody is doing it; (3) that responsible adults expect them to do it; (4) that it's a good thing; and (5) that their peers know they know these things, breeding promiscuity. Those are very destructive messages to give our kids.

Furthermore, Planned Parenthood's own data show that the number one   19
reason teenagers engage in intercourse is peer pressure![22] Therefore, anything we do to imply that "everybody is doing it" results in more . . . not fewer . . . people who give the game a try. Condom distribution programs do not reduce the number of kids exposed to disease . . . they radically increase it!

Since the federal government began its major contraception program in   20
1970, unwed pregnancies have increased 87 percent among 15-to-19-year-olds.[23] Likewise, abortions among teens rose 67 percent;[24] unwed births went up 83.8 percent.[25] And venereal disease has infected a generation of young people. Nice job, sex counselors. Good thinking, senators and congressmen. Nice nap, America.

Having made a blunder that now threatens the human family, one would   21
think the designers would be backtracking and apologizing for their miscalculations. Instead, they continue to lobby Congress and corporate America for more money. Given the misinformation extant on this subject, they'll probably get it.

But if you were a parent and knew that your son or daughter was having   22
sex, wouldn't you rather he or she used a condom?

How much risk is acceptable when you're talking about your teenager's   23
life? One study of married couples in which one partner was infected with HIV found that 17% of the partners using condoms for protection still caught the virus within a year and a half.[26] Telling our teens to "reduce their risk" to one in six (17%) is not much better than advocating Russian roulette. Both are fatal, eventually. The difference is that with a gun, death is quicker. Suppose your son or daughter were joining an 18-month skydiving club of six members. If you knew that one of their parachutes would definitely fail, would you recommend that they simply buckle the chutes tighter? Certainly not. You would say, "Please don't jump. Your life is at stake!" How could a loving parent do less?

Kids won't listen to the abstinence message. You're just wasting your   24
breath to try to sell them a notion like that.

It is a popular myth that teenagers are incapable of understanding that it   25
is in their best interest to save themselves until marriage. Almost 65 percent of all high school females under 18 are virgins.[27]

A few years ago in Lexington, Kentucky, a youth event was held that   26
featured no sports contest, no rock groups—just an ex-convict named Harold Morris talking about abstinence, among other subjects. The coliseum seated

18,000 people, but 26,000 teenagers showed up! Eventually more than 2,000 stood outside the packed auditorium and listened over a hastily prepared public address system. Who says kids won't listen to this time-honored message?

Even teens who have been sexually active can choose to stop. This is often called "secondary virginity," a good concept that conveys the idea that kids can start over. One young girl recently wrote Ann Landers to say she wished she had kept her virginity, signing the letter, "Sorry I didn't and wish I could take it back." As responsible adults we need to tell her that even though she can't go back, she can go forward. She can regain her self-respect and protect her health, because it's never too late to start saying "no" to premarital sex. **27**

Even though the safe-sex advocates predominate in educational circles, are there no positive examples of abstinence-based programs for kids? **28**

Thankfully, some excellent programs have been developed. Spokane-based *Teen-Aid* and Chicago's *Southwest Parents Committee* are good examples. So are *Next Generation* in Maryland, *Choices* in California and *Respect Inc.* in Illinois. Other curricula such as *Facing Reality; Sex Respect; Me, My World, My Future; Reasonable Reasons to Wait; Sex, Love & Choices; F.A.C.T.S.,* etc., are all abstinence-themed programs to help kids make good sexual decisions. **29**

A good curriculum for inner-city youth is Elayne Bennett's *Best Friends Program*. This successful "mentoring" project helps adolescents in Washington, D.C., graduate from high school and remain abstinent. In five years, not one female has become pregnant while in the *Best Friends Program!* **30**

Establishing and nurturing abstinence ideas with kids, however, can be like spitting into the wind. Not because they won't listen, because most will. But pro-abstinence lessons are drowned out in a sea of toxic teen-sex-is-inevitable-use-a-condom propaganda from "safe sex" professionals. **31**

You place major responsibility on those who have told adolescents that sexual expression is their right as long as they do it "properly." Who else has contributed to the epidemic? **32**

The entertainment industry must certainly share the blame, including television producers. It is interesting in this context that all four networks and the cable television entities are wringing their hands about this terrible epidemic of AIDS. They profess to be very concerned about those who are infected with sexually transmitted diseases, and perhaps they are sincere. However, TV executives and movie moguls have contributed mightily to the existence of this plague. For decades, they have depicted teens and young adults climbing in and out of each other's beds like so many sexual robots. Only the nerds were shown to be chaste, and they were too stupid or ugly to find partners. **33**

Of course, the beautiful young actors in those steamy dramas never faced any consequences for their sexual indulgence. No one ever came down with herpes, or syphilis, or chlamydia, or pelvic inflammatory disease, or infertility, or AIDS, or genital warts, or cervical cancer. No patients were ever told by a physician that there was no cure for their disease or that they would **34** have to deal with the pain for the rest of their lives. No one ever heard that genital cancers associated with the human papilloma virus (HPV) kill more women than AIDS,[28] or that strains of gonorrhea are now resistant to penicillin.[29]

No, there was no downside. It all looked like so much fun. But what a price we are paying now for the lies we have been told.   35

The government has also contributed to this crisis and continues to exacerbate the problem. For example, a current brochure from the federal Centers for Disease Control and the City of New York is entitled, "Teens Have the Right," and is apparently intended to free adolescents from adult authority. Inside are the six declarations that make up a "Teenager's Bill of Rights," as follows: 36

- I have the right to think for myself.
- I have the right to decide whether to have sex and whom to have it with.
- I have the right to use protection when I have sex.
- I have the right to buy and use condoms.
- I have the right to express myself.
- I have the right to ask for help if I need it.

Under this final item (the right to ask for help) is a list of organizations and phone numbers that readers are encouraged to call. The philosophy that governs several of the organizations includes presenting homosexuality as an acceptable lifestyle and vigorous promotion of a teen's right to sexual expression.   37

Your tax dollars at work!   38

Surely there are other Americans who recognize the danger now threatening a generation of our best and brightest. It is time to speak up for an old-fashioned value called virginity. *Now, more than ever, virtue is a necessity.*   39

If you agree with Focus on the Family that it is time for a new approach to adolescent sexuality, tear out this ad and save it. Take it to your next school board meeting. Send it to your congressman or senator. Distribute copies to the PTA. And by all means, share it with your teenagers. Begin to promote abstinence before marriage as the *only* healthy way to survive this worldwide epidemic.   40

Data Sources: 1. Adolescent enrollment in only one federal program—Title X—from 1970–1992 totals more than $1 billion. 2. Pamela McDonnell, Sexually Transmitted Diseases Division, Centers for Disease Control, U.S. Dept. of Health & Human Services, t.i., March 16, 1992. 3. Scott W. Wright, "1 in 100 tested at UT has AIDS virus," *Austin American Statesman,* July 14, 1991, p. A14; the federally funded study was based on a non-random sample. 4. "Heterosexual HIV Transmission Up in the United States," *American Medical News* (Feb. 3, 1992): 35. 5. U.S. Dept. of Health & Human Services, Public Health Service, Centers for Disease Control, *1991 Division of STD/HIV Prevention,* Annual Report, p. 13. 6. Ibid. 7. McDonnell, CDC, HHS, t.i., March 18, 1992. 8. *STD/HIV Prevention,* CDC, p. 13. 9. Ibid. 10. Ibid. 11. Robert E. Johnson et al., "A Seroepidemiologic Survey of the Prevalence of Herpes

Simplex Virus Type 2 Infection in the United States," *New England Journal of Medicine* 321 (July 6, 1989) 7–12. 12. *STD/HIV Prevention*, CDC, p. 13. 13. C. Kuehn and F. Judson, "How common are sexually transmitted infections in adolescents?" *Clinical Practice Sexuality* 5 (1989) 19–25; as cited by Sandra D. Gottwald et al., "Profile: Adolescent Ob/Gyn Patients at the University of Michigan, 1989," *The American Journal of Gynecological Health* 5 (May–June 1991), 23. 14. Kay Stone, Sexually Transmitted Diseases Division, Centers for Disease Control, U.S. Dept. of Health & Human Services, t.i., March 20, 1992. 15. Elise F. Jones and Jacqueline Darroch Forrest, "Contraceptive Failure in the United States: Revised Estimates from the 1982 National Survey of Family Growth," *Family Planning Perspectives* 21 (May/June 1989): 103. 16. Ibid., p. 105. 17. Lode Wigersma and Ron Oud, "Safety and Acceptability of Condoms for Use by Homosexual Men as a Prophylactic Against Transmission of HIV During Anogenital Sexual Intercourse," *British Medical Journal* 295 (July 11, 1987): 94. 18. Susan C. Weller, "A Meta-Analysis of Condom Effectiveness in Reducing Sexually Transmitted HIV," *Social Science & Medicine* (June 1993): 1635–1644. 19. Theresa Crenshaw, from remarks made at the National Conference on HIV, Washington, D.C., Nov. 15–18, 1991. 20. William D. Mosher and James W. McNally, "Contraceptive Use at First Premarital Intercourse, United States, 1965–1988," *Family Planning Perspectives* 23 (May–June 1991): 111. 21. Cheryl D. Hayes, ed., *Risking the Future: Adolescent Sexuality, Pregnancy, and Childbearing* (Washington, National Academy Press, 1987), pp. 46–49. 22. Planned Parenthood poll, "American Teens Speak: Sex, Myths, TV and Birth Control" (New York: Louis Harris & Associates, Inc., 1986), p. 24. 23. "Condom Roulette," *In Focus* 25 (Washington: Family Research Council, Feb. 1992), p. 2. 24. Gilbert L. Crouse, Office of Planning and Evaluation, U.S. Dept. of Health & Human Services, t.i., March 12, 1992, based on data from Planned Parenthood's Alan Guttmacher Institute. Increase calculated from 1973, first year of legal abortion. 25. *Monthly Vital Statistics Report*, National Center for Health Statistics, Vol. 41, No. 9, supplement, February 25, 1993. 26. Margaret A. Fischl et al., "Heterosexual Transmission of Human Immunodeficiency Virus (HIV): Relationship of Sexual Practices to Seroconversion," III International Conference on AIDS, June 1–5, 1987, *Abstracts Volume*, p. 178. 27. U.S. Dept. of Health & Human Services, National Centers for Health Statistics, Centers for Disease Control, "Percent of Women 15–19 Years of Age Who Are Sexually Experienced, by Race, Age, and Marital Status: United States, 1988," *National Survey of Family Growth.* 28. Joseph S. McIlhaney, Jr., M.D., *Sexuality and Sexually Transmitted Diseases* (Grand Rapids, Baker Publ., 1990), p. 137. 29. A. M. B. Goldstein and Susan M. Garabedian-Ruffalo, "A Treatment Update to Resistant Gonorrhea," *Medical Aspects of Human Sexuality* (August 1991): 39.

Credits

from *USA Today*, 11/22/93. Reprinted by permission. **585** "Gun Laws Are No Answer" by Alan M. Gottlieb, *USA Today*. Reprinted with permission of Alan M. Gottlieb. **586** "How Can School Prayer Possibly Hurt? Here's How," *USA Today*, 12/22/94. Reprinted by permission. **587** "We Need More Prayer" by Armstrong Williams, *USA Today*. Reprinted with permission of Armstrong Williams. **588** "Planet of the White Guys" by Barbara Ehrenreich, *Time*, March 13, 1995. Copyright © 1995 Time Inc. Reprinted by permission. **589** "The Glass Ceiling Can Be Broken with Academic Training, Do Women Need Affirmative Action?" by Joanne Jacobs, *San Jose Mercury News*, March 6, 1995, p. 7B. Copyright © 1995 San Jose Mercury News. All rights reserved. Reproduced with permission. Use of this material does not imply endorsement of the San Jose Mercury News. **591** "In Defense of a Little Virginity: A Message from Focus on the Family." Copyright © 1993 Focus on the Family. Reprinted with permission of Focus on the Family.

PHOTOS AND ILLUSTRATIONS

2 © Associated Press AP. **7** © Associated Press AP. **100** © Rick Owens. **101** © David O'Keefe. **146** © Associated Press AP. **151** © Associated Press AP. **160** © 1998 California Department of Health Services/Asher & Partners. **162** © AP/Wide World Photos. **178** © Jason Trigg/Archive Photos. **184** © Reuters/Rick Wilking/Archive Photos **245** © William Saul. **349** © Marilyn vos Savant/Parade Magazine. **352** © Reuters/Brian Snyder/Archive Photos. **430** © AP/Wide World Photos. **494** © 2000 Estate of Pablo Picasso/Artists Rights Society (ARS), New York/Giraudon/Art Resource, New York. **495** (left) Courtesy of Discover Magazine. **495** (right) Courtesy of Discover Magazine. **500** © 2000 Richard Serra/Artists Rights Society (ARS), New York. *The Deconstruction of "Tilted Arc": Documents*, edited by Clara Weyergraf-Serra and Martha Buskirk. Copyright 1991 MIT Press. **501** © Scala/Art Resource, New York.

Index